LEONARDO

CARLO PEDRETTI

LEONARDO

ARCHITECT

Translated by Sue Brill

Rizzoli

NEW YORK

Design by Diego Birelli

Edited by I. Grafe

Published in the United States of America in 1985 by
RIZZOLI INTERNATIONAL PUBLICATIONS, INC.
597 Fifth Avenue, New York, NY 10017

Copyright © 1981 by Electa Editrice, Milan, Italy

Library of Congress Cataloging in Publication Data

Pedretti, Carlo.
    Leonardo, architect.

    Translation of: Leonardo architetto.
    Bibliography: p.
    Includes index.
    1. Leonardo, da Vinci, 1452-1519 – Criticism and
interpretation. 2. Architecture, Renaissance –
Italy. I. Title.
NA1123.L4P41513   1985   720'.92'4   85-42954
ISBN 0-8478-0646-4

Printed and bound in Italy

Contents

For Rossana
twenty years later

Foreword

In the pages that follow, I approach the subject of Leonardo as architect in the same way as I approached the subject of Leonardo as painter in my book Leonardo: A Study in Chronology and Style *(1973), namely with an almost dogmatic brevity and without footnotes.*

Moreover, I have tried to produce, in Leonardo's words, "opera e materia nuova, non più detta," (a new work and materials, never spoken of before), even when returning to materials handled earlier. It should not be difficult to understand the plan I had in mind in the work as a whole, and which is also clarified by the comment, Decline or Apotheosis, *dealing with the last years of Leonardo's architectural work.*

Finally, this book would be a personal expression of its author's ideas, save that the wealth of illustrative material it contains also makes it a corpus *of Leonardo's architectural studies.*

C.P.

1. *Studies of underwater attack devices,* c. 1485-87, Codex Atlanticus, f. 333 v-a.

2. *Devices for raising water,* c. 1482. Codex Atlanticus, f. 386 r-b, detail.

1. Brunelleschian Technology

The Codex Atlanticus page, opposite, familiar to Leonardo scholars for its studies of underwater warfare devices, is still generally thought to relate to his Venetian visit in 1500, although, in fact, it dates from the 1480's. Its drawings have the rough and impulsive character of Leonardo's earliest technological essays and the notes are written in the lively, exuberant tone of a youth whose imagination is fired by an idea of the heroic, but also by that of an unusual financial gain. His phrase "Do not teach and you alone will excel," which one might be tempted to interpret in an abstract, theoretical sense, must instead be seen as directly relating to the practical aims Leonardo proposed to himself: "But first make an agreement by deed," that is by an actual notarized document, "that half the reward is to be yours, free, without any exception, that the deposit of the prisoners be with Manetto and that the payment be made into the hand of Manetto, that is of the said reward." Lacking the protection of a patent, Leonardo took refuge in the "secret." The plan of attack, which was to be preceded by an ultimatum, consisted of a series of instructions for setting up a commando raid using divers and, it seems, an explosive vessel. The hulls of the enemy ships were to be shattered by machines using screws, on the principle of the bottle screw or the corkscrew. Leonardo noted: "An impression must be taken of one of the three iron screws of the Workshop of Santa Liberata, the form in plaster and the cast in wax." This phrase alone establishes a direct relationship between Leonardo and the already legendary figure of Brunelleschi. The screw from which he wanted to take an impression and obtain a duplicate is one of the devices that Brunelleschi invented when he was building the dome of Florence Cathedral, probably to hold cables in tension. It may be one of those still preserved at the Cathedral Workshop (Santa Reparata, or Liberata as it was known in Leonardo's day).

Leonardo's early sheets showing devices that use the Archimedes screw for raising water are well known. The traditional forms of Tuscan architecture also often appear in them: the same towers and arcades that we see in the background of paintings by artists ranging from Masaccio to Benozzo Gozzoli. The spiral, or "snail's shell" form as Leonardo called it, soon dominated his thought as a symbol of motion and power. Even the idea of a helicopter would manifest itself in a machine which "makes itself a screw in the air," and the ascending air currents themselves would later be visualized as powerful whirlpools, enormous screws of energy which find a parallel in the form of a rope or a spiralling column. And river currents, in overcoming obstacles or dykes, twist themselves into spirals which carry away the land and demolish the banks like drills, according to a principle which Alberti had already thought might be turned to practical ends:

"The rotation of the waters or a whirlpool is like a liquid drill, and there is nothing hard enough to withstand it for any length of time" (*De re aedif.* X, x). "Solid rock of the Mugnone," Leonardo was later to write, "strongly carved out by the water into vase shapes: you would think it

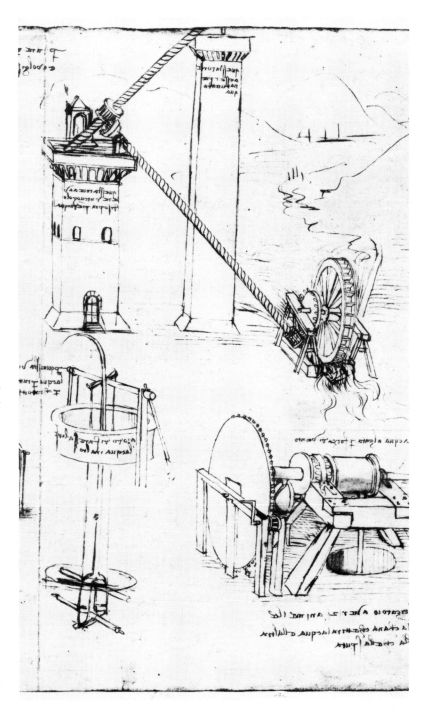

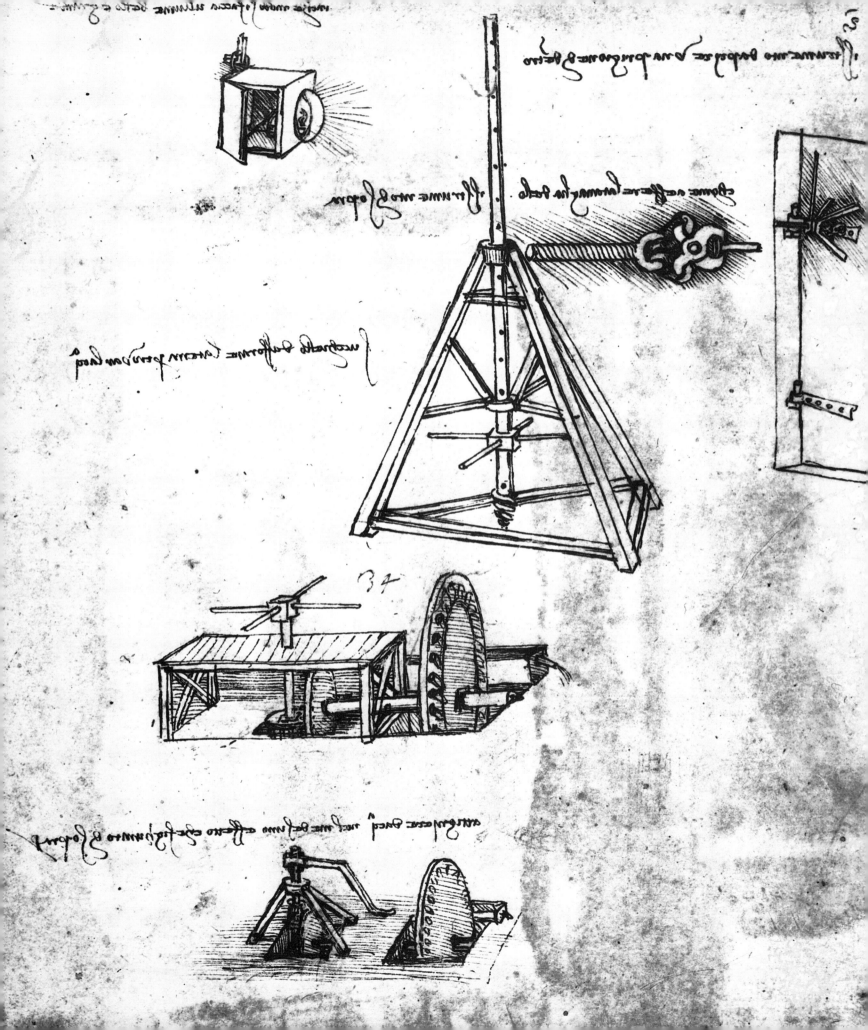

3. Studies of hydraulic machines, a lamp and a device "for opening a prison from within," c. 1482, Codex Atlanticus, f. 9 v-b.

4. Device for prising loose the bars of a window, c. 1480. Codex Atlanticus, f. 394 r-b, detail.

had been done by man, it is so accurate" (Arund. f. 29 v).

Architects, even in antiquity, had known of the power produced and multiplied by the screw and used it to lift and transport enormous weights. Brunelleschi made use of this power, too, as we learn from the memoirs of his follower Jacopo Mariano Il Taccola, whose treatise *De ingeniis* is illustrated with drawings in an archaic style that stand as testimony to a tradition which goes back to antiquity. This style persisted all through the fifteenth century and can still be detected in early drawings of Leonardo, and in those of his contemporaries Buonaccorso Ghiberti, Francesco di Giorgio and Giuliano da Sangallo. Only later, following his study of the human mechanism, did Leonardo develop his technological drawing into a visual language which could explain the parts and function of a machine and which, in architecture, could substitute for the model.

A curious use of the screw is the one illustrated in an early Codex Atlanticus sheet, f. 9 v-b, dating from about 1482. It is a device for removing a prison door from its hinges, from the inside: "instrument for opening a prison from within," with a sketch which explains "how the pincers of the above instrument should be." Another early sheet in the same Codex, f. 394 r-b, contains the design for a similar device, actually shown in the process of prising loose the bars from a window. In these notes we have perhaps the echo of an unknown episode in Leonardo's life – "When I made our Lord as a child, you put me in prison; now if I make him grown-up you will do even worse to me." Or perhaps we could relate them to the episode recounted by Vasari in the Life of Il Caparra, the Florentine blacksmith (IV, 446), in which mention is made of the design of some "young citizens," one of whom might conceivably have been Leonardo: "Some young citizens brought him a design so that he might make them an iron for prising open and breaking other irons by means of a screw; but he would not assist them, saying: I do not wish to help you in any way in such a thing, for these are nothing but the tools of thieves, either for stealing or for dishonouring young girls. You look like respectable young men and I tell you this is no business for you, or for me. When they saw that Il Caparra would not help them, they asked him who else there was in Florence who might, but he had grown very angry, and insulting them furiously, turned his back on them."

As in the screw, so also in weight (and in percussion) Leonardo recognized another of the great forces of nature. The motive force produced by weight had constituted an extensive field of study in the Middle Ages, which the Scholastics had developed from their antique texts into a corpus of theoretical knowledge called the Science of Weights, *De ponderibus*. This had been applied in a practical way to architecture at the time of the great cathedrals and these same conceptions were still valid at the dawn of the fifteenth century when Brunelleschi, although certainly turning back to antique models, also took into consideration the great mediaeval tradition which had come down to him, still alive and functioning, through the teachings of Biagio da Parma (Il Pelacane, whose *De ponderibus* Leonardo knew and often

discussed) and Paolo dal Pozzo Toscanelli. In Brunelleschi that keenness for solving problems right on the building-site was intensified. There theories could immediately be put to the test and ideas worked out while construction was in progress. This practise came to dominate the whole of the fifteenth century, despite the influential theoretical preoccupations of Alberti (for whom the architect's work began and ended on the drawing-board) and despite the growing practise and indeed, necessity, of presenting the patron with written reports which expanded into treatises. Even Bramante, who brought architecture to a degree of imperial majesty through his study of Vitruvius and the antique, followed Brunelleschi's practical example and codified ideas by means of models and actual buildings. It is not without significance that his notes, now lost, were entitled *Pratica di Bramante.*

2. *The Lantern and the Dome*

The story of Leonardo's apprenticeship in Verrocchio's workshop originates with Vasari (1550), but attempts have been made, even quite recently, to discredit it by stating that no document exists to provide confirmation. However, such a document does exist. Pomponio Gaurico, in his *De sculptura*, published in Florence in 1504 – when Leonardo was working on the *Battle of Anghiari* – records Leonardo as a pupil of Verrocchio, specifying – almost as if to underline the nature of the training received – that Leonardo was also renowned for his Archimedean genius. Other references which help to confirm Vasari's story include Albertini's record of 1510 regarding the angel painted by Leonardo in Verrocchio's *Baptism* and the famous accusation of sodomy of 1476 from which we learn that Leonardo "is with Andrea de Verrocchio" (which however could be taken as an indication of domicile, and not necessarily of profession, in the sense of service or apprenticeship). And above all, we have the clue offered by Leonardo himself much later, in about 1515, when he was working in Rome on a project for the industrial utilization of parabolic mirrors made of sections soldered together. "Remember," writes Leonardo, "the method of soldering used for the ball of Santa Maria del Fiore." This is a reference to the copper sphere commissioned from Verrocchio in 1469 and placed on the lantern of the Cathedral in 1471, a commission which constituted the final touch to a programme begun by Brunelleschi in 1420, and which as such could be considered as a part of the largest architectural undertaking of the fifteenth century in Florence. Leonardo speaks of it with the clarity of someone who, many years later, can still remember every detail because he took part in it. This interpretation can be corroborated, even though only indirectly, by a series of early drawings in the Codex Atlanticus, all datable to around 1478-80, in which he illustrates the apparatus set up by Brunelleschi for the construction of the lantern ("how the lantern of the dome of Santa Liparata was built" can be read in a similar drawing by Giuliano da Sangallo), the same type of apparatus as was required for the raising and placing of Verrocchio's sphere. In fact, a view of Florence in the

12

6, 7. *Rotating crane on circular tracks:*
Leonardo *(Codex Atlanticus, f. 295 r-b) and*
Buonaccorso Ghiberti *(Zibaldone, MS. BR*
228, *f. 105 r).*

10. *View of Florence in 1470. Detail from*
The Three Archangels and Tobias *by*
Giovanni Battista Utili. Florence, Bartolini
Salimbeni Collection.

8, 9. Leonardo *(Codex Atlanticus, f. 349 r-a)*
and Buonaccorso Ghiberti *(Zibaldone, MS.*
BR 228, *f. 106 r).*

11. *Study of a tempietto, c. 1504.* Codex
Atlanticus, *f. 202 v-a, detail.*

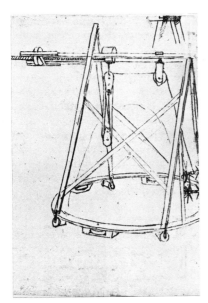
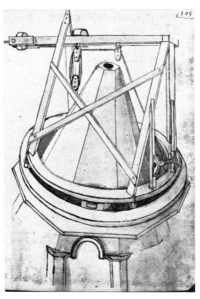
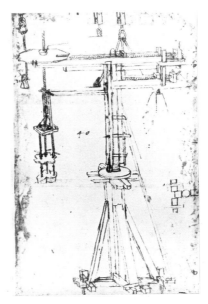
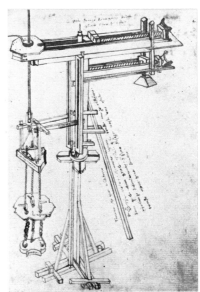

background of the painting of the *Three Archangels and Tobias* by "Utili" in the Bartolini Salimbene collection in Florence shows the dome with just such an apparatus erected and the sphere not yet in place. Brunelleschi's machinery, which was certainly still available at that time, and which is known from the drawings of Buonaccorso Ghiberti, Giuliano da Sangallo and the young Leonardo, reveals once more the importance of the screw as the multiplier of power in the raising of great weights.

It would be difficult to believe that Leonardo never climbed to the top of Brunelleschi's dome, and, indeed, there is reason to think that he went there often at the time when Verrocchio's sphere was being placed in position. He would certainly have realized that the lantern could be understood as a building in its own right, a tempietto linked to the dome by buttresses which seem to rise out of its rib structure and form an airy passageway as if through "chapels" opening into space. He would also have grasped the thematic relationship which Brunelleschi himself had intended to establish between it and the *Tempio degli Angioli*, a building in fact situated exactly on the central axis of a visual cone the angle of which is determined by the walls of one of the "chapels" of the lantern and the corresponding ribs of the dome. One is even tempted to think that the *Tempio degli Angioli* may have first been visualized in relation to a view from the top of the Cathedral, with a lively and vigorous crowning-piece which from that viewpoint would have the same plastic effect as a model placed on a table. This would explain the plan, revealed by documents, to clear the space around the building in the direction of the Cathedral. Perhaps it is not wholly by chance that Leonardo introduced into architectural drawing the type of perspective representation which is obtained from the same viewpoint – from above and threequarters – as used in looking at a model.

A study of Leonardo's thoughts on the theme of ecclesiastical architecture leads time and again to Brunelleschi's dome, from the structural elements to the decorative panelings, and most of all to the sense of form which emerges from the articulation of the walls of the exedrae and from the interplay of mass and void in the lantern.

3. The Baptistry Steps

We know very little about Leonardo's apprenticeship in Verrocchio's workshop, but the short account provided by Vasari confirms that it included architectural and technological design, according to a concept that was being revived on the model of Vitruvius, as reproposed by Alberti. (It is not just by chance that Poleni, in 1739, in his bibliographical analysis of the 1521 Como Vitruvius mentions Leonardo's drawings of mills when speaking of Cesariano's illustrations to the tenth book on machines). Vasari, in fact, even seems to suggest in what order the stages of his apprenticeship took place, dominated by geometry in the sense of volume and surface, and thus moving from sculpture to architecture and finally to painting: "He did not practise one profession alone, but all those in which design has a part. Possessed of a divine and

14. Anonymous sixteenth-century artist,
Copies of youthful drawings by Leonardo.
Florence, Uffizi, Gabinetto dei Disegni e
delle Stampe.

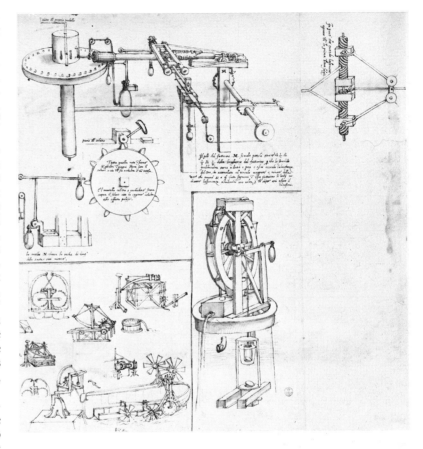

marvellous intellect, and being an excellent geometrician, he not only worked in sculpture, creating in his youth some terra-cotta heads of smiling women, of which plaster casts are still being made, and children's heads also, executed as though by a master, but he also prepared many architectural ground-plans and elevations, and he was the first, though so young, to propose to canalize the Arno from Pisa to Florence. He made designs for mills, fulling machines, and other devices to be powered by water, but his profession he wished to be that of painting."

Naturally enough, the reference to the project of canalizing the Arno leads back to Brunelleschi, whose attempt to flood Lucca was still a vivid memory. Cavalcanti, Machiavelli and Ammirato all recorded this as a failure which had damaged the architect's reputation. This must certainly have presented a challenge to a young man busy exercising his mind in a spirit of emulation on projects which had so far proved impracticable. Listed among those projects is also the great river-boat, the famous "Badalone," which Brunelleschi had invented and even patented, to transport marble from Pisa to Florence along the Arno. Leonardo would undoubtedly have heard of this as a boy, and he might even have seen the wreck aground in the basin of the Arno at Empoli, which was as far as it had been able to manoeuvre. "Your 'Badalone' which flies over the waters," as Aquettini da Prato remembered it in a cruel sonnet, must have been a huge barge, probably with a paddle system which gave it the look of an ungainly water-bird. We may have another record of it in one of the drawings which an anonymous sixteenth-century architect copied from some of Leonardo's early pages, now in part lost.

Thus it is in the years of apprenticeship with Verrocchio that Leonardo's exuberant inventiveness originates, and which he sums up, with the emphasis on aspects of military engineering, in the famous letter to Lodovico il Moro with which his first Florentine period ends and his Milanese one begins. Vasari's account, once we have looked beyond the anecdotal, is actually an indispensable introduction to a commentary on that letter, which goes back, as a document in the history of Renaissance architecture, to workshop teachings based on the principle of the model and of demonstration and in which we see the beginnings of Leonardo's technological language, both in design and rhetoric. In fact many designs for war machines in the Codex Atlanticus can be related to the paragraphs of that letter. (Nor must we forget the final statement: "and in times of peace I believe I may be most favourably compared to any other in the field of architecture, in the designing of public and private buildings, and in conducting water from one place to another.") Here then is Vasari: "And there was infused in that genius so much grace from God and a power of expression so formidable that, matched by his intellect and memory and the talent in his hands, he could express his ideas so well that his arguments and reasonings confounded his boldest opponents. Every day he made models and designs for the removal of mountains with ease, and to bore through them so as to pass from one

15. *Technological and architectural studies,*
c. 1495. Codex Atlanticus, f. 298 r-b.

16. *Architecture and geometry on a sheet*
of studies for The Last Supper, *c. 1495.*
Windsor, RL 12542 r.

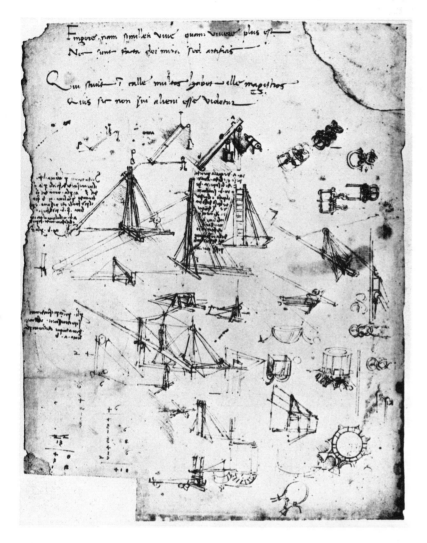

plane to another, and by means of levers, cranes and winches, to raise and draw heavy weights; he devised a method for cleansing harbours, and pumps to raise water from great depths, schemes which his mind never ceased to evolve."

Vasari follows this, by way of digression, with a reference to the designs of knots for the *cartelle*, or ornamental name-plates of the Accademia Vinciana, almost as if to suggest that even those fanciful patterns belong to architectural design, and he concludes: "Among these models and designs there was one which he showed several times to many of those discerning citizens who were then governing Florence, of a method for raising the temple of San Giovanni in Florence and putting steps under it without it falling down. He argued with such persuasion that it was not until after his departure that they recognized the inherent impossibility of such an enterprise."

Nothing is left of this early project (but the fact that it was proposed "several times" might suggest that Leonardo returned to it, even at a later date), and no other historical source speaks of it. Vasari's account preserves for us an oral tradition which probably no-one took too seriously, even though the actual moving of a tower in Bologna by Aristotile Fioravanti in 1455 was certainly still remembered. Once again we must consider Vasari's story beyond the level of anecdote. It is easy to visualize the new relationship that that project would have established between the Baptistry and the Cathedral. The entrances of both, aligned as they are on the same longitudinal axis, would have been brought to the same level. Moreover, it is probable that the theatrical effect produced by such an arrangement would have been accentuated by a temporary platform serving as a bridge between the two buildings during religious ceremonies. This would have allowed ecclesiastical processions to pass above the spectator's eye-level, so that they could be seen from every part of the piazza. Furthermore, the Baptistry would have acquired the visual autonomy proper to a centrally-planned building, since the steps, while linking the vertical building to the horizontal piazza, would also, almost paradoxically, separate its volume from the surrounding space by forming an abstract element above which the building would seem to be "lifted." The concept of the steps as an inclined zone of transit has an inherent dynamism which would add visual impetus to the suggestion that the building could be "lifted up," just as a model could be.

There is perhaps little point in pondering over what solution Leonardo might have devised for raising the Baptistry "without it falling down." Doubtless the first stage of the operation would have been the exposure of the building's foundations, excavating the piazza for a wide space all around it. It would then have been necessary to place a number of beams under the floor to ensure its stability, and to provide a platform beneath which to exert the pressure of the lifting machinery. It is probable, in fact, that Leonardo would have envisaged the use of gigantic perpetual screws, placed perpendicularly under the platform and operated simultaneously. The operation would have been carried

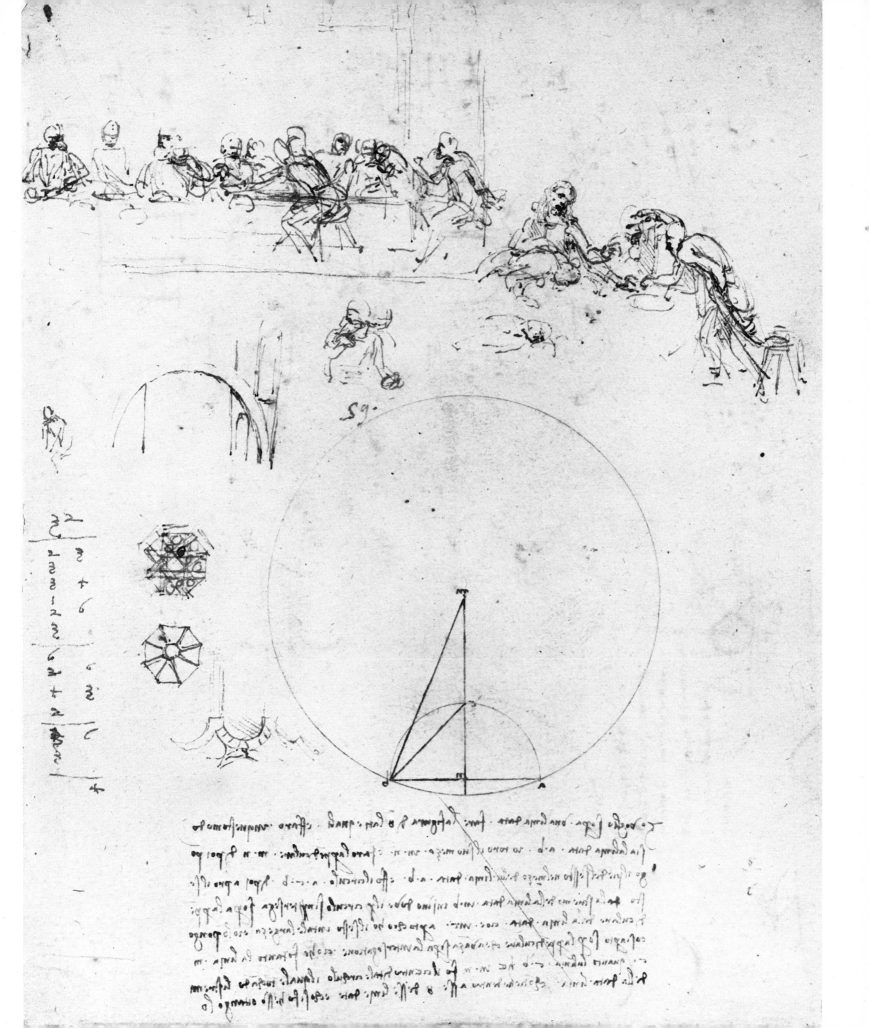

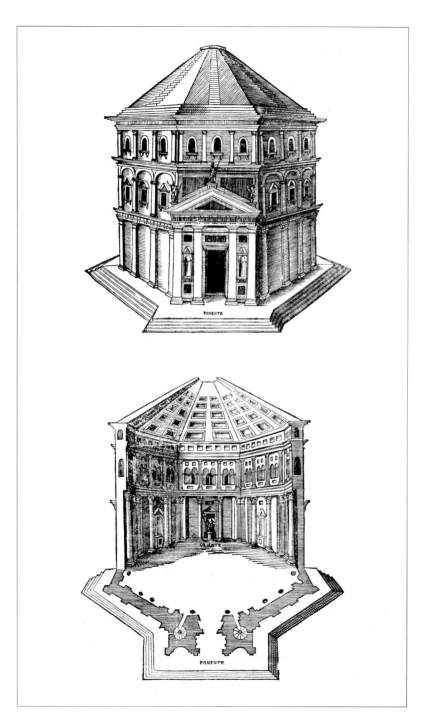

out slowly to avoid shocks and dangerous shifts of level, and would certainly have taken several days. In the meantime, the new pillars to hold the structure in the desired position would have been built, after which the screws would have been removed, the area of excavation filled in and the steps constructed.

There is a page in the Codex Atlanticus (f. 298 r-b) in which a centrally-planned building is studied in relation to a system of foundations of inverted and inclined arches which would have been suitable for this kind of operation. Richter once suggested that these drawings refer to the Baptistry project, but the page is datable to about 1495, the same time as a Windsor sheet with studies for the *Last Supper*, in which references to the same structure appear, this time with an octagonal plan. These drawings probably have to do with the project for a mausoleum with a crypt, perhaps related to the studies for the Sforza Sepulchre, but the supporting structure, which brings to mind the studies for the tiburio of Milan Cathedral, could go back to the early idea of raising the "Tempio di San Giovanni" to place steps under it. Later on, in the sixteenth century, the Baptistry was the subject of an erudite archaeological analysis by Vincenzo Borghini, Vasari's friend and adviser, who proposed to present "il Bel San Giovanni" as an antique temple, majestically placed on a platform of steps. Let us read Vasari again: "Among these models and designs there was one which he showed several times to many citizens... of a method for raising the temple of San Giovanni." These models and designs have been lost, like so much of Leonardo's work. Or could they possibly have been preserved for us, although without their paternity, in the two prints published in Borghini's *Discorsi* of 1584?

Architectural Studies under Ultraviolet Light: New Documentation on Leonardo's Work at Pavia

The most substantial documentation for the start of Leonardo's architectural activity dates from the first decade of his stay in Lombardy, from 1482 onwards. This is the well-known series of studies of civil and military architecture in Manuscript B in the Institut de France, the earliest Leonardo manuscript known as a codex, that is, compiled in the form of a book and not composed of sheets which were originally separate. The contents of MS. B were studied in depth, especially from the chronological point of view and therefore in relation to other Leonardo folios, by Gerolamo Calvi in 1925; while the architectural studies contained in it have been the subject of extensive analysis, from the work by Geymüller in Richter's anthology of 1883 to Heydenreich's fundamental and still very important study of 1929. To these have recently been added the contributions of Firpo, Garin, Maltese and others, and as a result the question of the theoretical premises for Leonardo's so-called "ideal city" can be regarded as settled. In addition, S. Lang has suggested that the series of studies of centrally-planned temples in MS. B should be related to the project for a Sforza mausoleum, long cherished by Francesco Sforza and taken up again by Lodovico il Moro with the new tribune of Santa Maria delle Grazie. Three facsimile editions exist of MS. B, which is perhaps the most fascinating of all the Leonardo manuscripts that have come down to us, and yet we still lack a critical edition with a commentary, to show what we know and what we do not yet know of its origin and character.

According to an early theory of Solmi's, long set aside, Leonardo compiled almost all of MS. B during his stay in Pavia in 1490, when he was called there with Francesco di Giorgio and Amadeo for a consultation on work then being carried out on that cathedral. According to Solmi, that visit may have lasted several months – not just a few days, as has since become more probable – and during that time Leonardo would have produced the designs from which the project for Pavia Cathedral was developed. Anna Maria Brizio, in reconsidering the documents relating to that visit, has rightly noted that they presuppose a previous contact between Leonardo and the ecclesiastical authorities of Pavia, and that such a contact could go back precisely to the time when the first plans for the new cathedral were being made in 1488. Thus we might look again at Solmi's thesis, or at least some aspects of it, especially since MS. B has now been proved to be datable between 1487 and 1490. This is the same period which saw the beginning of Leonardo's anatomical studies, and in fact a few pages of anatomy drawings at Windsor contain architectural sketches which directly relate to the contents of MS. B, while the first pages of MS. B itself contain notes on the proportions of the limbs which reflect those in a whole series of anatomical sheets at Windsor. The Windsor anatomical pages which also contain architectural studies are reproduced here from photographs recently taken under ultraviolet light. The unsuspected wealth of details traced by Leonardo in metal-point and hence invisible to the naked eye constitutes entirely new evidence, on the basis of which we can take a fresh look at Leonardo's activity as an architect in Pavia. Moreover, this

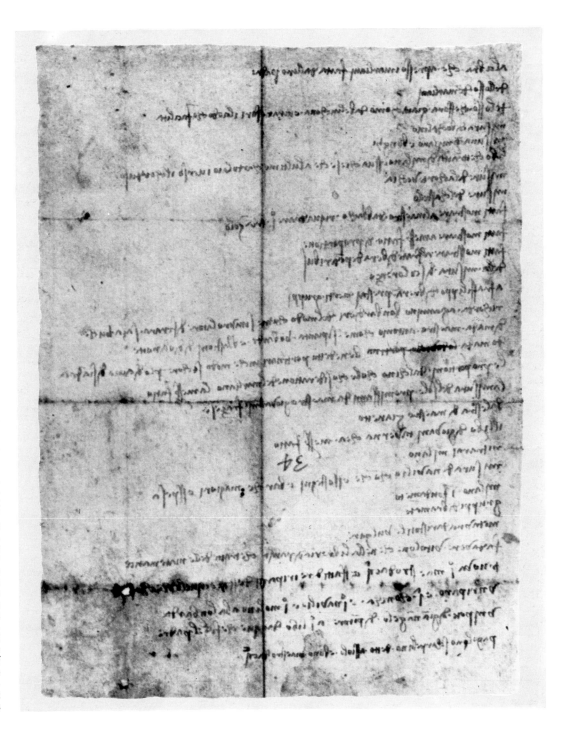

particular opportunity for reconsideration gives just a hint of what we can still expect from a study of MS. B, the well known and much studied codex with which Leonardo's Lombard period begins.

From the notes which I contributed to an article by Jane Roberts on new Leonardo material at Windsor (*Burlington Magazine*, June 1977) I present here those which refer to architecture, amplifying them with further comparisons and observations. The drawings are all in metal-point, partly gone over in pen, on blue prepared paper, and are all datable about 1487-88 or perhaps even a little earlier, about 1485. The measurements are given in centimetres (height before width) and the reproductions are in actual size whenever possible. The order of presentation follows that of the inventory numbers.

I have appended to these notes a facsimile, with an annotated transcription, of the memorandum in the Codex Atlanticus, f. 225 r-b, a small sheet similar in size and script to those dated 1489 in the series of the so-called "Anatomical Manuscript B" at Windsor (compare RL 19059 v, dated on the recto 2 April 1489). This is a document of great interest for the start of Leonardo's activity in Lombardy in the fields of anatomy and physiology as well as of architecture, and I shall often have occasion to refer to it in the course of the present work. It was published for the first time by Richter in 1883 and was later discussed by Solmi and others (cf. my Richter *Commentary*, note to § 1448). It will be reconsidered here in particular for what may be seen in it as a reflection of Leonardo's movements between Milan and Pavia at a time when he occupied himself with canalization, civil and military architecture, anatomy, physiology, and other things; a synthesis, therefore, of the context of MS. B in Paris. It is in this memorandum, incidentally, that Leonardo mentions Bramante for the first time.

RL 12560. 18.3 x 13.7

Ultraviolet light has made many of the metal-point drawings on this sheet visible for the first time particularly the architectural and technological sketches in the lower part. What had already been visible to the naked eye, and even in the better reproductions such as the facsimile produced by the Commissione Vinciana (II. 42), was very difficult to decipher. It has now become clear that the architectural studies belong to the project for a church, with particular regard to the relationship between bell-tower and apse. What had seemed to be a round-headed window, similar to those represented in MS. B, f. 68 r, and in the Codex Atlanticus, f. 295 v-a, turns out to be the front view of an elaborate apse with double niches and an architrave surmounted by a large shell which finishes in volutes and is flanked by some kind of finials, similar to candelabra. The shell motif is repeated in the vaults of the two niches, anticipating the use of Lombard and Venetian forms that characterizes the work of Alvise Lamberti in Russia. The vertical panels within the niches and the partitions of the high socle seem to suggest the use of polychrome marble veneer with an effect reminiscent of the exuberant ornamentation of the Certosa of Pavia, or even that of S. Maria

20, 21. *Studies of architecture and hydraulics relating to Pavia*, c. 1488. *Codex Atlanticus, f. 341 v-b and f. 7 v-b.*

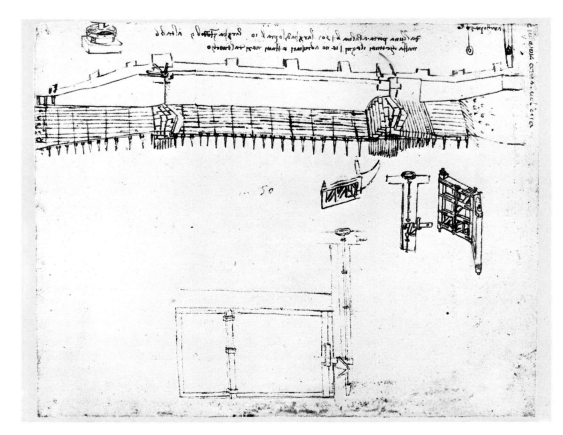

dei Miracoli in Venice. The latter is evoked even more clearly in the drawing next to this, above all by the way in which the bell-tower is attached to the side of the apse. This drawing is now clearly recognizable as a study of one part of a much larger ecclesiastical complex. One can, in fact, interpret it in two ways, either as a perspective view from the rear of a church with one nave, or as the side view of a church showing how a chapel or an arm of the transept is to incorporate a square bell-tower. Two separate studies show the alternative of an octagonal bell-tower as at San Gottardo, yet retain a square plan for the height of the socle that runs all around the building. On the right one can make out a faint sketch of a façade, this too evoking Lombard or Venetian forms, vividly articulated with pilasters, cornices, double windows and roundels so arranged as to imply the future use of polychrome marble facing. Lower down, near the bottom edge of the page, one can make out the fragments of two sketches of ornamental motifs, which suggests that the page was originally larger and has been cut down.

For the technological sketches and the study for a Nativity see the notes in Clark's catalogue of Leonardo's drawings at Windsor. However, I might add that similar sketches of drills are found on a sheet of the same period in the Codex Atlanticus, f. 7 v-b, where there are also some architectural sketches that have already been interpreted as possible ideas for Pavia Cathedral. The sheet also relates directly to another in the Codex Atlanticus, f. 341 v-b, where there is a study of a system of palisading which can be related to a project of work on the city walls at Pavia as mentioned by Leonardo in MS. B, f. 66 r. See, further on, the note to Windsor RL 12668.

RL 12608. 30 x 21.4

The drawing of the two superimposed columns of composite order is in metal-point, partially gone over in pen, so that the reading of the capital which forms the base for the second column has always been uncertain. The tracing offered by Firpo (p. 9) and taken from the Commissione Vinciana facsimile (V. 182) contains lines which are neither in the original nor in the facsimile published in the edition of the *Quaderni di Anatomia* (V. 17). The ultraviolet light reveals the drawing of the capital in all the accuracy of its details, so that it can easily be recognized as being of the same type as the one sketched in the Codex Atlanticus, f. 266 v, datable about 1495. An almost identical capital, originally in a late Quattrocento house at 20 Via Broletto in Milan and now in the courtyard of the Castello Sforzesco, has been reproduced by Baroni (*Atti del primo Congresso Nazionale di Storia dell'Architettura*, 1936, p. 70, tav. XIII). We find the same type of capital again in two other buildings in Milan: Palazzo Carmagnola, which Lodovico Sforza had given to Cecilia Gallerani in 1491, when it was enlarged according to a project that probably involved Leonardo and his friend Jacomo Andrea da Ferrara, and also the Villa Gualtiero, suburban residence of Gualtiero Bascapè, Lodovico Sforza's secretary. This building was later incorporated into the better known Villa Simonetta. The Bramantesque character of these columns is more apparent than real and in any case

22. *Architectural and anatomical studies*, c. 1488. Windsor, RL 12608 r.

23. *Study of the apse of a church*, c. 1488. Windsor, RL 12609 v.

24. *Studies of ecclesiastical architecture*, c. 1488. Codex Atlanticus, f. 42 v-c.

25, 26. *Milan, Church of S. Sepolcro, interior looking towards the apse and detail of the crypt.*

does not prove that the relationship between Leonardo and Bramante went back to 1485-87, even though this is probable. They can be compared to those of Bramante's Nicchione at Abbiategrasso, but this is from a later date: 1497 (and not 1477 as given in the two editions of Clark's catalogue). Pacioli, in Chapter XX of the treatise on architecture appended to his *Divina Proportione*, says that the theme "Of columns placed above other columns on buildings" had not been considered theoretically since Vitruvius had dealt with it in Chapter I of the fifth book of his treatise. Leonardo's drawing could therefore be considered the first Renaissance illustration of a Vitruvian theory, but the changes made to the proportional system prescribed by Vitruvius ("columne superiora quarta parte minores quam inferiores sunt constituende") suggest a practical destination for the drawing, which might be the one shown in perspective in RL 12609 v below, to which see note. The delicate classicism which appears in these first architectural studies made by Leonardo in Milan points more towards the Po Valley than to Tuscany and could be explained as a reflection of his friendship with Jacomo Andrea da Ferrara, an architect active in Milan in the last twenty years of the Quattrocento and known above all through the praises of Pacioli, who calls him a very great friend of Leonardo and a most accurate commentator on Vitruvius. He is also recorded in connection with the work carried out towards the end of the fifteenth century in the cloisters and the new sacristy of S. Maria delle Grazie.

RL 12609. 19.8 x 28.6

In the previous reproductions of this sheet very little could be seen beyond the pen tracings with which Leonardo had begun to go over a very elaborate design in metal-point representing the perspective view of the apse of a church. Ultraviolet light shows an almost scenographic character in the manner of presenting the interior of the church, as if it were the section of a wooden model. The plan is delineated with bold foreshortening as if to give prominence to the central element of the apse with its shell-vaulted niche, aedicula and ambulatory. It is now clear that the identical design was envisaged for the side apses, even though this is only hinted at in the one on the right, with no details being specified beyond a vertical line drawn with a ruler corresponding with the right edge of the central apse. This line is perpendicular to a ground line, also drawn with a ruler, which defines the ends of the side aisles. The arches which lead into the apses are coffered while the semicircular wall of the central apse is panelled in rectangles (probably marble facings) lined up with the pairs of arches above, which serve as a base for the shell. The resulting effect of plasticity is intensified by a delicate shading, which gives body to the volumes by taking into account the diffused light which falls from the upper left. The cupola is lightly indicated as a hemisphere resting directly on the pendentives (as in Haghia Sophia) in each one of which there is a medallion. These and other details invisible under normal light confirm the suspected correspondence with the two pen sketches of the interior elevation of a church in the Codex Atlanticus, f. 42 v-c, which in turn correspond precisely with the plans in MS. B, f. 57 r, identified by

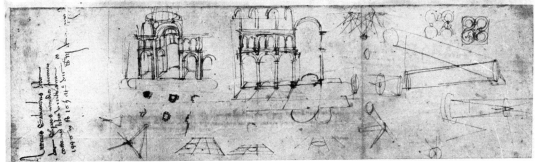

Leonardo himself as those of the Romanesque church of S. Sepolcro in Milan and of its crypt. Heydenreich, who had already perceived these correlations in 1929, stresses the importance of Leonardo's record of such an early church, which was later drastically altered by Baroque transformations. Moreover, he rightly pointed out that the handwriting on the Codex Atlanticus sheet, which is a fragment of a page from an account book discarded by the administration of Milan Cathedral, can stylistically be associated with writings of Leonardo's datable about 1485. This could suggest a chronological relationship to the series of anatomical studies at Windsor to which 12609 belongs.

All these elevation sketches, at times interpreted as records of S. Lorenzo in Milan (for example by Firpo), could be Leonardo's own suggestions of modifications to existing structures. The present drawing in particular seems to reflect a restoration program possibly inspired by Bramante. This could explain the drawing of the superimposed columns on the preceding sheet, RL 12608, as a study for the arch-supporting columns at the entrance to the apses. A sketch in metal-point revealed by ultraviolet light on the left of the main drawing on 12609 may indicate the existing structure which Leonardo intended to modify by introducing this system of superimposed columns. It is also possible that the structures of the Milanese church of S. Sepolcro, whether or not they needed restoration, were being considered by Leonardo, in all these drawings, in relation to the first projects for the Cathedral of Pavia. The little sectional drawing in Codex Atlanticus, f. 7 v-b, a page datable *c.* 1487 and containing sketches of devices for regulating rivers that relate to Pavia (see note to RL 12560 above) bears a direct relation to the drawing on the present sheet and could reflect a first idea for the Cathedral in Pavia, as Pozzi and Solmi had suspected.

RL 12626. 21.9 x 30.5
Ultraviolet light reveals a greater definition of details and a stronger modelling in the anatomical drawings on this sheet and the sketch of a sanctuary, already visible under ordinary light although drawn in metal-point, acquires greater clarity and legibility. The building is shown beside a lake with the summary indication of a small bay. A straight bridge seems to join the sanctuary to a promontory on the opposite bank where there is an open space or platform with some sort of central element encircled by arches or trees. Columns or trees are indicated on the shoreline near the promontory, but it may be that all of the landscape was added later. In fact the lines of the bridge have been drawn over a ground plan of the sanctuary. Similar quick sketches can be made out near the edge of another sheet at Windsor, RL 12295, of a somewhat earlier date. A similar centrally-planned building is sketched in metal-point, and so invisible in reproduction, on the verso of a sheet at Turin of studies for the horses of the Sforza monument. See my catalogue of Leonardo's drawings at Turin (Florence 1975), no. 11.

The sketch of the sanctuary on the present sheet is reminiscent of the church of S. Maria della Croce in Crema by Battagio, datable *c.* 1493. According to the original project indicated by Valeria Mariani (*Studi Bramanteschi,*

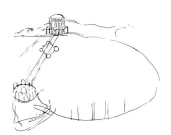

1974, pp. 239-44), Battagio's building at Crema was to have had a hemispherical dome like the one shown in Leonardo's sketch. For the relationship between Leonardo and Battagio at the time of MS. C, *c.* 1490, see Beltrami in *Raccolta Vinciana*, IV, 1908, p. 75. See also my *Commentary*, II. 290, and the note to RL 12668, which follows.

RL 12668. 22.4 x 16.8

This small sheet does not belong to the series of anatomical studies considered in the preceding notes, but its technique, style and date are the same. Like them it is on blue prepared paper, and almost all the sketches it contains were first drawn in metal-point and then gone over with pen and ink. The ultraviolet light, in revealing the preliminary drawing, helps to clarify Leonardo's intentions. Not only do we now have a better definition of the pose and modelling of the figure of the workman, but the machine for preparing mortar which he operates now clearly seems to be placed near a river. The outline of a barge can be made out behind him, and we can now also see that the hanging sieve on the right lets the sand fall not into the rectangular tank but onto the ground beside it. The indirect relationship of this small sheet to those of the anatomical series of the same date may be shown, apart from the identity of technique and style, in the character of the human figure, drawn as if it were an anatomical model intended to show the musculature.

But the rapport is not just one of stylistic and conceptual affinities, since we know that at that time Leonardo was simultaneously occupied with both architecture and anatomy, and it would not be surprising if the first impetus to study anatomy came to him through contacts with professors at the *studio* in Pavia, in particular with Fazio Cardano, whose name appears several times in the Codex Atlanticus memorandum, f. 225 r-b, the small sheet of 1489 reproduced, with commentary, on the following pages. In their turn, these Windsor sheets in which Leonardo's architectural and anatomical interests seem to come together, can be related to the contents of MS. B. In fact, the studies of basic architectural tools (levels, plumb-lines, rakes and picks) shown in this sheet help to substantiate the suspicion that Leonardo had been in Pavia even before his visit there with Francesco di Giorgio in June 1490. First of all, the Codex Atlanticus, f. 341 v-b, cited in note to RL 12560 above, besides containing the drawing of a palisade identifiable as a reference to the foundations of part of the walls of Pavia, also includes a sketch of a plumb-line. Although this has been partly cut away along the upper edge of the sheet, it clearly relates, even in its style of drawing, to the tools and levels on the present sheet. Moreover, all these notes, like those in the Codex Atlanticus f. 295 v-a and f. 346 v-b, are developed, or simply transcribed, in a section of MS. B between f. 63 v and f. 68 r, in which Leonardo discusses various types of levels, tools for excavating and collecting gravel, ways of demolishing walls and removing foundations, and finally a way of reinforcing the earth through the use of a palisade. In a note on f. 66 r of MS. B, developed from notes in the Codex Atlanticus, f. 346 v-b, Leonardo, in describing how to plant stakes, adds the observation: "I have watched the

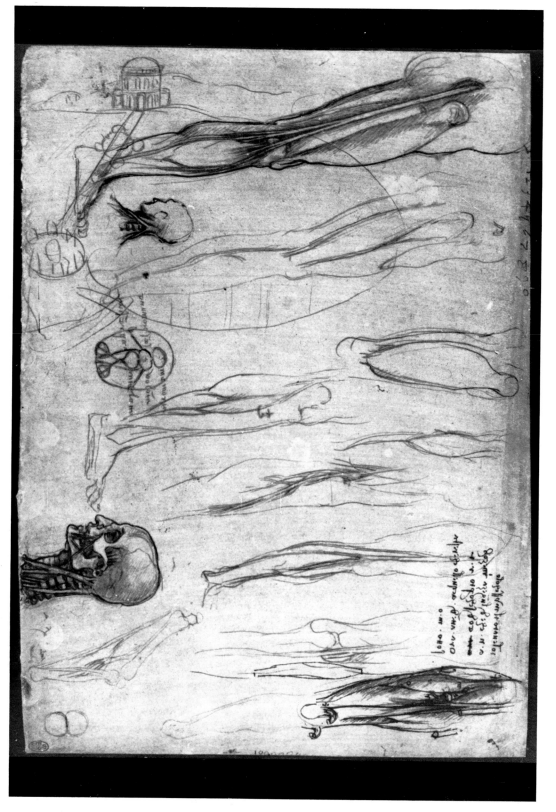

rebuilding of parts of the old walls of Pavia, which are founded on the banks of the Ticino river." This very operation is illustrated on f. 69 v and f. 70 r of MS. B, with figures of workmen drawn in the same style as the one on the present sheet. Besides all this, the note referring to the walls of Pavia on f. 66 r of MS. B is followed by a note on the use of mortar to complete the work of building the palisade "... and then throw on enough of the fresh mortar to reach the top of the stakes." Here then is the explanation of the machine for mixing mortar illustrated on the present sheet.

Another point of contact between this Windsor sheet and f. 64 v of MS. B leads back again to Pavia. On the Paris page are two drawings of levels ("level for buttresses" and "level for placing perpendicular lines") which can be compared to those on the Windsor sheet while the sketch of "boots for water" (indication of a program of work carried out near a river) is taken up from f. 346 v-b of the Codex Atlanticus. Next to this last sketch is the diagrammatic on which shows how "the piles are put half way down the wall underneath." And the drawing below it is none other than a perspective view of a part of the walls of Pavia, like the one in Codex Atlanticus, f. 341 v-b, already mentioned. Moreover, on this same sheet of MS. B Leonardo had begun to sketch – and then crossed out – the plan of a wall with windows, which is then taken up again a few pages later, on f. 68 r, together with a mullioned window which Calvi (*Manoscritti*, p. 110) had already related to one on f. 295 v-a of the Codex Atlanticus, mentioned above as containing studies connected with work on the walls of Pavia. That work is not documented. The only reference, in a document of 1493 (Magenta, II, 454-55), does not preclude the possibility that it had been carried out some time before, and in fact the handwriting of Leonardo's notes, including those in MS. B, assigns them to a period no later than 1487-88. If Leonardo did visit Pavia at that time it is possible that he participated in some way in the first phase of the project for the new cathedral. Could he not be, in fact, that "expert architect" alluded to in the documents as the author of the first designs sent to Cardinal Ascanio Sforza in Rome? That would explain the surprising affinity which Solmi detected between certain drawings of churches in MS. B and the architectural design then taking shape in the model by Rocchi, and would also explain why, when Leonardo was called to Pavia in 1490 as a consultant on the cathedral building work, he was considered (and the merit of having discovered this goes to Anna Maria Brizio) the equal of Francesco di Giorgio and Amadeo. It is therefore quite probable that Leonardo was in Pavia on the 29th of June, 1488, when the first stone of the new cathedral was laid, or on the 22nd of August of the same year, when a committee of experts with Bramante at its head met to examine "certain designs and certain models" prepared by Rocchi and Amadeo. The members of that committee were Rocchi, Amadeo, Bartolomeo da Castelnuovo, Giacomo da Candia and Martino Fugazza. Perhaps Leonardo was only there as an auditor, alongside Bramante. It is true that in 1487-90 he was occupied with the studies for the tiburio of Milan Cathedral, but the *Annali della Fabbrica* do not

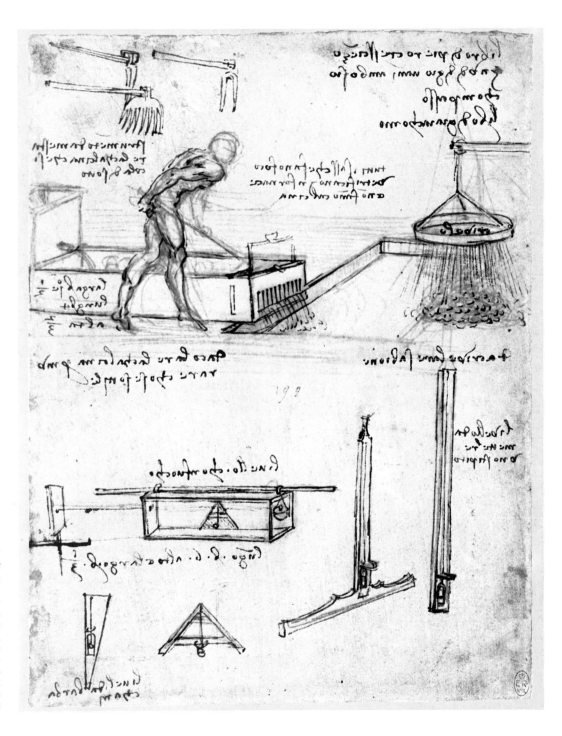

record any meetings in 1488 and 1489, so that Leonardo could have gone off to Pavia with Bramante and Amadeo. The drawings of churches in MS. B which could be assigned to the first projects or ideas for the new Pavia Cathedral, and which derive from the Milanese models of San Sepolcro and San Lorenzo, are in particular – as Solmi had already suggested – those on f. 24 r, f. 52 r (a sheet with sketches of workmen) and f. 55 r (a sheet which contains also a graphic record of the church of Santa Maria della Pertica in Pavia). These drawings are often cited as anticipating Bramante's project for the new St. Peter's. The Windsor sheet contains a memorandum published for the first time by Richter in 1883 (§ 1435). This includes a reference to the treatise *De agricoltura* by Pietro Crescenzio, which among other things contains the first Renaissance treatise on rural architecture; following this a reference to the *ignudi* of Giovanni Ambrogio (probably his associate De Predis), and to a *compasso* (see the compasses in MS. B, f. 57 v, which faces the page containing a note on the *camini* of the Castle of Pavia). The reference to a "book of gia iachomo" with which the list ends, probably alludes to a book compiled by or belonging to Gian Giacomo Dolcebuono, the architect who collaborated with Amadeo on works including Milan Cathedral and who, in 1489-92, completed the construction of Santa Maria Incoronata at Lodi, begun by Battagio in 1488.

The Memorandum of 1489
Codex Atlanticus, f. 225 r-b. 17.6 x 13.2

(1) An algebra, which the Marliani have, written by their father.
(2) On the bone, by the Marliani.
(3) On the bone which pierces Gian Giacomo da Bellinzona, and draws the nail out easily.
(4) The measurement of Bocalino.
(5) The measurement of Milan and suburbs.
(6) A book that treats of Milan and its churches which is to be had at the last stationer's on the way to Cordusio.
(7) The measurement of the Corte Vecchia.
(8) The measurement of the Castello.
(9) Get the master of arithmetic to show you how to square a triangle.
(10) Get Messer Fazio to show you about proportion.
(11) Get the Brera friar to show you *de Ponderibus*.
(12) On the measurement of Santo Lorenzo.
(13) I lent certain groups to Fra Filippo di Brera.
(14) Remind Giannino the bombardier about how the tower of Ferrara was walled without holes.
(15) Ask Maestro Antonio how bombards and bastions are planted by day or by night.
(16) Ask (*Lodovico Portina...*) Benedetto Portinari how the people go on the ice in Flanders.
(17) The Proportions of Alchino, with notes by Marliano that Messer Fazio has.
(18) The measurement of the sun, promised me by Maestro Giovanni Francese.
(19) The crossbow of Maestro Gianetto.

(20) The book by Giovanni Taverna that Messer Fazio has.
(21) Draw Milan.
(22) The measurement of the canal, locks and supports, and large boats; and the expense.
(23) Milan in foundation.
(24) Groups by Bramante.
(25) *Metaura* by Aristotle in Italian.
(26) Try to get Vitolone, which is in the library at Pavia, and which treats of mathematics.
(27) Find a master of waterworks, and get him to explain their repairs and what it costs.
(28) A dam and a lock and a canal and a Lombard mill.
(29) A grandson of Gian Angelo the painter has a book on water which was his father's.
(30) Pagolino Scarpellino, called Assiolo, has great knowledge of waterworks.

Notes
The lines of the memorandum are numbered from 1 to 30, referring to the notes which follow. The anthology of A.M. Brizio (Turin 1952), the *Studi Vinciani* by Marcolongo (Naples 1938) and the work by Solmi on the sources of the Leonardo manuscripts (Turin 1908) are cited in abbreviated form.

[1] Brizio, p. 659, note 8, observes that the name of Giuliano de' Marliani, and generically that of the Marliani recurs several times in the Leonardo manuscripts of the Sforza period. Giuliano is recorded in the Forster Codex III, f. 37 v for a *bello erbolaro*, which Solmi thinks may refer to a *Herbarius* published in Pavia in 1485-86. According to Marcolongo, p. 36, note 17, the Marliani mentioned here would be Girolamo and Pier Andrea, sons of Giovanni, the doctor and mathematician who taught in Milan and Pavia, and who died in 1483. He was the master of Giorgio Valla and Pietro Pomponazzi, author of a great number of works not all published. Among those which could have interested Leonardo, Marcolongo cites: (a) *De proportione motuum in velocitate questio subtilissima* (still existing in a codex at San Marco in Florence), Pavia, 1482, and reproduced in the undated edition of all the works of Marliani; (b) *Probatio cujusdam consequentie Calculatoris in De motu locali*; (c) *Algebra*, which Solmi believes unpublished, for all that Marliani in (a) may speak of it (c. 48) as a *libellus quem edidi alcibra subtilissimus*. Leonardo mentions Marliani again in the Codex Atlanticus, f. 204 r-a, c. 1487-90: "How certain dense bodies can be made that will not cast shadows... hence Marliani's theory is false."

[2] See the preceding note. Here and in no. 3 it is impossible to say what bone Leonardo may refer to.

[3] Gian Giacomo da Bellinzona could be the same person recorded in Windsor RL 12668 (see the relevant comments, above), that is, Dolcebuono, whose birthplace, however, we do not know. Cf. C. Baroni, *L'architettura lombarda da Bramante al Richini*, Milan 1941, pp. 112-41.

[4] Bocalino may be a place-name, possibly the plain of Bocellina near Bormio, an area in Valtellina which must have been known to Leonardo.

[5] Perhaps a plan to scale of Milan and suburbs to be found or to be made.

[6] Cordusio, even today, is the central zone of Milan, half way between the Cathedral and the Castello.

[7] The palace of the Corte Vecchia stood where the Palazzo Reale is today, between the Cathedral and the church of San Gottardo. Isabella of Aragon resided there from 1494 when she was left a widow by Gian Galeazzo Sforza. Leonardo himself lived and had his studio there. It was here that he modelled the horse for the Sforza monument. See my *Commentary* II, 186 and 221.

[8] The Castello Sforzesco. See my *Commentary* II, 54-6 and 184-85.

[9] Probably a Lombard accountant. For the squaring of the triangle see Codex Atlanticus, f. 29 v-a, which however is rather later, c. 1510.

[10] This is Fazio Cardano, less famous than his son Gerolamo, but equally learned in the physical and mathematical sciences, a devotee of occult sciences and professor of jurisprudence and medicine at Pavia. We owe to him, among other things, the first edition of the *Prospettiva* of John Peckham (Milan, c. 1480), known to Leonardo. See also nos. 17 and 20 below.

[11] Friar of the Brera, that is of the monastery of the Umiliati of the Benedictine Order at Santa Maria in Brera, afterwards converted into the palace of the same name. Perhaps he is identical with the Fra Filippo di Brera recorded in no. 13 below.

[12] The basilica of San Lorenzo in Milan.

[13] Cf. no. 11 above. The "certain groups" are probably designs of decorative interlacings like those attributed to Bramante in no. 24, below.

[14] Giannino Alberghetti of Ferrara, bombardier and metal founder, recorded by Bellincioni. Cf. Solmi. The tower of Ferrara is the unfinished bell-tower of the cathedral, the design for which was attributed to Alberti by A. Venturi (*L'Arte*, XVII, 1914, pp. 153-56, and XX, 1917, pp. 351-54). A method of building a wall "without holes" is mentioned by Alberti, *De re aedificatoria*, III, xii.

[15] A system of planting bombards and bastions "by night" is described in MS. B, f. 70 r, beside notes on pile driving which refer to works at Pavia.

[16] On the Portinari, celebrated Florentine family of bankers and merchants, and in particular on Benedetto, see Solmi. Cf. the note on skating in the Forster Codex III, f. 46 r, c. 1493.

[17] Alchino or Alkendi or Kendi (died in 874), one of the most famous Arab scientists, whose work on optics, in particular, had a great influence on that of Alhazen, Vitellio and Bacon. With the "proportions of Alchino" Leonardo means the *Libellum sex quantitatum*, greatly praised by Gerolamo Cardano in *De subtilitate*, XVI. Cf. Marcolongo, pp. 38-9. Messer Fazio, Gerolamo's father, is the one also recorded in nos. 10 and 20.

[18] The same Giovanni Francese is recorded on a sheet of 1489 in Anatomical Manuscript B at Windsor, f. 2 r (RL 19019). Calvi, *Manoscritti*, p. 138, thinks it improb-

able that the person meant here is Jean Perréal, as Dorez and others have suggested. It is more likely to refer to Jean Pelerin Viator, who mentions in the third edition of his *De artificiali perspectiva*, Toul 1521, f. 1 r, a certain "leonard" as one of his Italian friends and colleagues.

He might have been in Pavia in about 1490, in order to consult the codex of "Vitolone" referred to by Leonardo in no. 26 of the present list. Cf. Liliane Brion-Guerry, *Jean Pélerin Viator*, Paris, 1962, pp. 436-37, and the same author's "Qui était 'Maestro Giovanni Francese?,'" in *Jean Alazard: Souvenirs et Mélanges*, (1962), pp. 149-55

[19] Perhaps the same as the Giannino recorded in no. 14.

[20] Giovanni Taverna, teacher at Pavia in 1470, is identified by Solmi as the father of the better-known jurist Francesco. Messer Fazio is the Fazio Cardano noted above in nos. 10 and 17.

[21] That is, make a plan (or perspective view) of Milan. Compare no. 23 below.

[22] Numerous notes on canalization and systems of locks are found on sheets from the first decade of Leonardo's stay in Lombardy. See in particular f. 7 v-b and f. 341 v-b of the Codex Atlanticus, reproduced above for the indirect references to Pavia. It is probable that at that time Leonardo was occupied with the Binasco canal. Probably his notes 27 and 28 refer to the same circumstance.

[23] That is, a plan of Milan. Cf. no. 21 above.

[24] Decorative interlacings, like the "certain groups" recorded in no. 13 above. Frequent traces of them are found on sheets of the 1480's, for example in MS. B, f. 73 r, and those, perhaps a little earlier, in the Codex Atlanticus, f. 385 v-b. See also the one revealed by ultraviolet light on the anatomical sheet at Windsor, RL 12627 r (*Burlington Magazine*, June 1977).

[25] The *Meteora* by Aristotle, that is the books on meteorology.

[26] The same recorded in MS. B, f. 58 r: "In Vitolone are 805 conclusions of perspective." In the so-called "Ligny Memorandum" in the Codex Atlanticus, f. 247 r-a, just before returning to Florence in 1499, Leonardo notes: "take the book of Vitolone and the measurements of the public buildings." Cf. also Codex Arundel, f. 79 v.

[27 & 28] See notes to nos. 22 and 30. The "Lombard mill" is probably of the same type as the "Pavian mill" mentioned in the Codex Atlanticus, f. 24 v-b, a small sheet of blue prepared paper with notes in metal-point, like the series of anatomical studies at Windsor datable about 1487.

[29] Andrea Gian Angelo is recorded as "ducalis ingeniarius et pinctor" in the *Annali della Fabbrica* of Milan Cathedral, at the time of Lodovico Sforza. We have no other mention of him.

[30] An unknown master of waterworks, perhaps the same one who would have been able to satisfy the needs shown in no. 27.

29. Naval architecture: the submarine. The so-called "submarine of Leonardo" is often mentioned in connection with the supposed project for an attack on the Turkish fleet proposed to the Venetians by Leonardo in 1500. But it has been shown that the few notes relating to it are all assignable to the first years of his stay in Lombardy, about 1483-85, except for the project for a device for skin-diving, which is datable about 1507-8. Leonardo himself, in a late note in the Codex Hammer (Leicester), alludes to the invention of a new way of going underwater, that is without the float for the breathing tube – an invention which he said he had destroyed so that "the evil nature of men" would not make use of it to attack ships by surprise and sink them. This particular aspect of naval architecture had interested others, too, in Leonardo's time. Besides Alberti's well-known attempts to raise the Roman ships sunk in the Lake of Nemi (and we know that Alberti wrote a treatise De navis, now lost but known to Leonardo), we have a reference, as exact as it is neglected, of a real submarine designed and built by Cesariano, a pupil of Bramante. The information is contained in a note written, by Cesariano himself in his copy of Vitruvius (Como 1521), f. 178 r, as a comment on chapter 13, of Book X on siege machines. Taking as his starting point Vitruvius's reference to the protective covering of the "battering-ram" in the form of a testudo, he states that he had used the same form for an underwater boat which he built and put into operation in the moat of the Castello in Milan and on Lake Como. The idea for the shape of the hull and the glass oculi for underwater observation seems to have come from a type of covering used by strolling peddlers. In fact Cesariano says, "Just as the hawkers of peddlers use to set up over themselves in the piazzas in many cities in Italy, and also outside Italy." And he adds: "But these are also used on some waterways with glass oculi on the back made the same way that I, Cesare, already made the prototype of a boat which

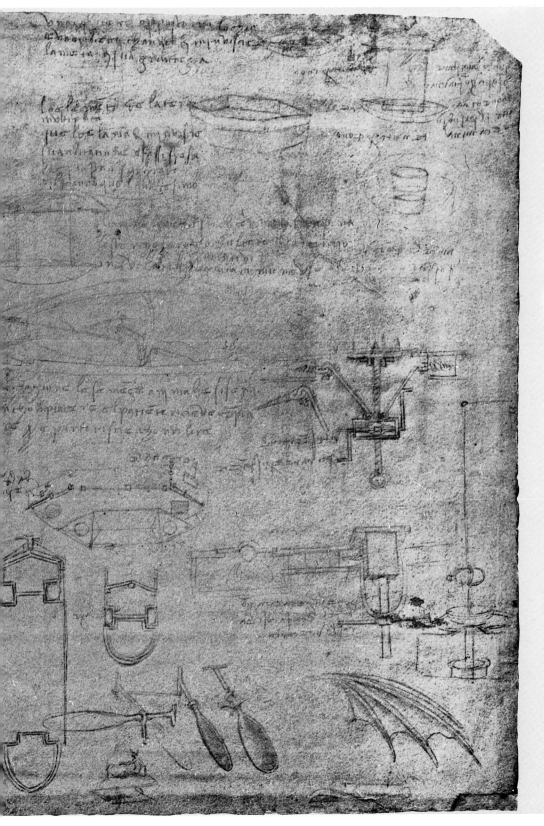

was able to go underwater and go into the great Castello of Milan and to the site of the mighty Castello di Musso on Lake Como." Leonardo's drawings of naval architecture which probably have something to do with Cesariano's underwater boat are those on f. 320 v-b of the Codex Atlanticus, done in silverpoint on blue prepared paper. This is a double-page sheet datable to the time of the first anatomical studies at Windsor, c. 1485-87, which are on paper of the same type and size. In fact there are on this sheet hints of anatomical studies in the margins, together with sketches of ground-plans of buildings. One sketch in the margin shows a boat for only one person, and in fact the reduced dimensions of the craft are confirmed by the drawing in the centre where a human leg is shown in relation to the motor mechanism. It seems that the hull consisted of two parts that could be separated. The bottom part could be lowered by means of ropes and ballast, while the level of the upper part could be regulated by the amount of air blown into inflatable skins placed in suitable spaces in the keel. It seems that surface navigation was to be effected by means of a sail, and underwater propulsion by oars or fins.

These studies precede by a little the compilation of MS. B, the codex filled in great part with studies of civil and military architecture, and indeed we find there (f. 11 r) another reference to a similar craft – a boat with a conning-tower, and a note made cryptic by a word abbreviated into shorthand: "Remember before you enter and lock up, to let out the lt. and to recover a great amount of the empty space." This, as another note explains, is a "boat to be used to sink ships with the instrument that you know of." The allusion to an underwater craft is quite clear, and the word in shorthand may stand for alito, that is, air. We have no other indications as to how Leonardo meant to construct this submarine, but it was probably the same boat as that recorded by Cesariano.

30, 31. *A friend of Leonardo's. A sheet of architectural
sketches in the Codex Atlanticus (f. 362 r-b, v-b), with notes
on centrally-planned churches elaborated on various pages of
MS. B and therefore probably related to the studies for the
Cathedral of Pavia. It contains a note in another hand which
until now has been left unexplained:*
benedictus de benedictis de pisis
amicus Leonardj deuincis de florentie
*With all probability this is the person that is also recorded
in the annals of the Studio Fiorentino recently published by
Armando Verde (Pistoia 1977, vol. III, t. I, pp. 167-69).
Benedetti was a scolaro in law at Pisa, where he received his
degree in 1491, after a protracted student life. In 1499 he
was Orator at Venice and died there in 1500. That is all we
know of him. It is probable that about 1487-90 he was in*

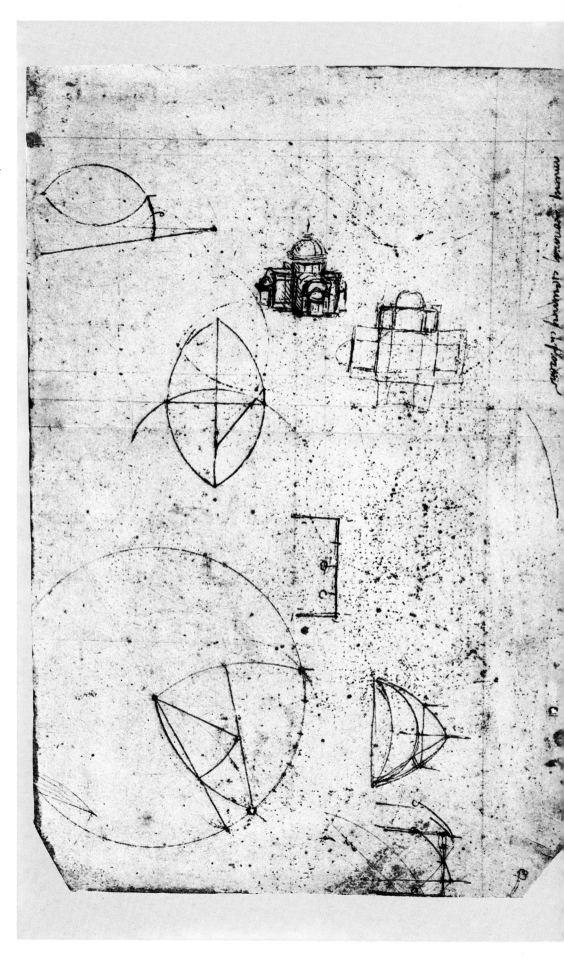

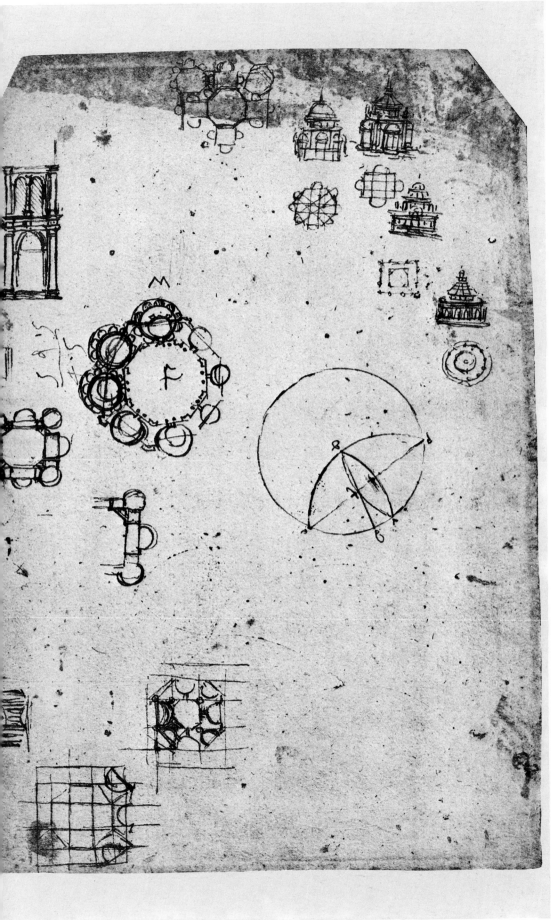

Pavia or in Milan, where he professed himself a friend of Leonardo's. It is not known how or whether he occupied himself with architecture or geometry. The geometrical problems Leonardo hints at are taken up again in MS. B, in particular on f. 40 r. The sheet itself is a fragment, probably only half of a piece of paper which Leonardo or someone else had prepared with a network of squares, which would seem to indicate the intention of laying out a detailed ground-plan to scale. Benedetti's note may not be extraneous to that preparation as it corresponds exactly to the limits produced by two of those parallel lines. Not being used for its original purpose, the sheet was utilized by Leonardo for geometrical and architectural sketches. These last show an awareness of models and ideas that go back to Brunelleschi, Sangallo and Francesco di Giorgio, and which are in fact the components of a pictorially volumetric sense of form.

32. Sketches of underwater attack devices on a sheet from a ledger of Milan Cathedral, c. 1485 (?). Codex Atlanticus, f. 346 r-a, detail.

33. Sketches of architecture, c. 1482. Codex Atlanticus, f. 324 r, detail.

4. The Tiburio of the Cathedral

Leonardo's connections with the Workshop of Milan Cathedral, which on the basis of documents are assigned to the period 1487-90, probably date back to about 1483, to the first years he spent in Lombardy and the time when he was commissioned to paint the *Virgin of the Rocks*. This is suggested by clues provided by his manuscripts. Folio 333 v of the Codex Atlanticus, with the studies of underwater warfare mentioned at the beginning of the first chapter in reference to Brunelleschi's screws (a sheet which still has the calligraphy and drawing style characteristic of his first Florentine period), is closely connected in content and style with another sheet of the same codex, f. 346 r-a, v-a, which is of the identical format and type of paper. In fact, both sheets come from a discarded ledger of the Administration of Milan Cathedral. Leonardo used those pages which were blank or had very little writing on them. Some lines of fifteenth-century writing can be noted on f. 346 r-a while f. 333 v contains, upside-down in the bottom left-hand corner, the number 467, which is the page number the sheet had in that ledger. Another sheet of the same time or a little earlier, f. 324 r, contains a list of materials and works of art that Leonardo was taking with him to Milan or that he had left in Florence. (Note, besides this, the sketches of ground-plans of a large palace like the one that Giuliano da Sangallo was to plan for King Ferrante of Naples in 1488). The list mainly has to do with drawings or paintings, but it is not surprising to find there also "certain instruments for ships," which probably refers to the Brunelleschian screw adapted as a keel-breaker, just as the preceding item, "certain bodies of perspective," can lead back to Paolo Uccello and the fifteenth-century perspective tradition represented by drawings of *mazzocchi* and other geometrical bodies.

The proof that these studies of underwater warfare belong to the same period as those for the tiburio of Milan Cathedral lies in a note, very faded and therefore until now undeciphered, in Codex Atlanticus, f. 148 r-a, a sheet belonging to the series of studies for the tiburio: "bianchetto / il martello / refe / Manetto" (white lead / hammer / string / Manetto). The same words as in this memorandum recur in the notes relating to underwater warfare on f. 333 v, which therefore places the underwater project in the first years of Leonardo's activity in Milan. Calvi had already suggested that it could be connected with a Sforza project to face the problem of the piratical vessels that were infesting the Tyrrhenian coast at the time of the annexation of Liguria to the Duchy of Milan, around 1487. Thus we must dismiss Solmi's theory that the "Manetto" mentioned by Leonardo was the Venetian Lodovico or Alvise Manetti who, in 1500, took part in the attempts to free Lepanto and the Venetians held prisoner by the Turks, after the naval battle of Zonchio. Considering the close alliance existing between Milan and Florence in 1480, it would not be surprising if the Manetti mentioned by Leonardo were the Florentine humanist and architect Antonio di Tuccio Manetti (1423-97). He is well known, among other things, for the *Dialogo circa el sito forma et misure dello Inferno di Dante Alighieri*,

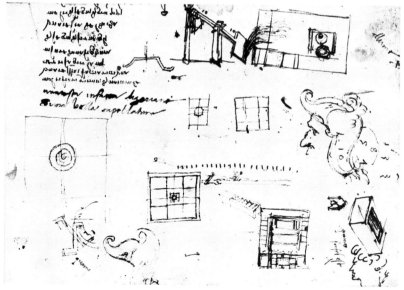

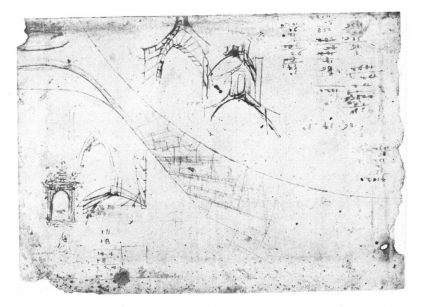

published in 1506, which should be reconsidered in relation to the interest shown by Brunelleschi, Bramante, Michelangelo – and, I believe, Leonardo – in the architecture of Dante's poem. Undoubtedly, then, Florentine mercantile interests were affected by the same problem that Milan had to face. This could explain the note "per a Lucca" (on the way to Lucca) in MS. B, accompanying the drawing of a river barrier which it is thought could refer to a system devised by Brunelleschi in 1430.

Relationships of this sort between Milan and Florence had been maintained for years. One only has to recall Filarete's and Michelozzo's activity in Milan from 1450 onwards, and it has recently been ascertained that Brunelleschi himself visited Milan in the 1430's. Furthermore, the other Antonio Manetti (*c.* 1400-60), Brunelleschi's assistant and biographer, was sent to Milan by the Florentines in 1460 to show Duke Francesco Sforza the project for Pisa's citadel and discuss its plan with him. From 1452 he was in charge of the works connected with the dome of Florence Cathedral, taking over the coveted position that had been left vacant at Brunelleschi's death in 1446. It was in those years and under Manetti's supervision that the lantern was completed, and it was in 1460 that the rotunda at the Santissima Annunziata was begun on his design. Leonardo could have received information about him, as well as the other Manetti, from Luca Fancelli, Alberti's assistant in Mantua, who was called to Milan in 1487. He stayed there for about nine months, serving as a consultant at the Cathedral Workshop with the specific task of studying the problem of the tiburio and judging the competitors' models, among them those of Bramante and Leonardo. As if to underline the stimulus which Leonardo continued to receive from the teachings of Tuscan tradition, we could recall that the letter of 12 August 1487, in which Luca Fancelli in Milan informed Lorenzo de' Medici in Florence about the Cathedral's problems (and Lorenzo was well known as an expert judge of architecture), also contains a plan for the canalization of the Arno which recalls very closely those by Leonardo. Since Leonardo, according to Vasari, had already occupied himself with this as a young man in Florence it would seem logical to think that he might have discussed it again with Fancelli in 1487, and in fact a series of notes for the Arno project in the Codex Atlanticus can be dated in the early nineties, when Leonardo was in Milan and when he went so far as to outline a financing scheme to be submitted to the wool merchants guild, the powerful Florentine corporation with which Brunelleschi had been closely connected.

"By the German at the Cathedral," Leonardo wrote near one of the eight diagrams showing in plan the way to raise a dome over a square space, on f. 10 v of MS. B, the codex in which he was gathering notes of a primarily architectural character at the time of his studies for the tiburio, around 1487. It has been suggested, and with good reason, that the "German at the Cathedral" might be the Dominican friar Johannes Mayer, a member of the team which the master Johannes Nexemperger had brought with him from Strasbourg in 1483, when he was officially

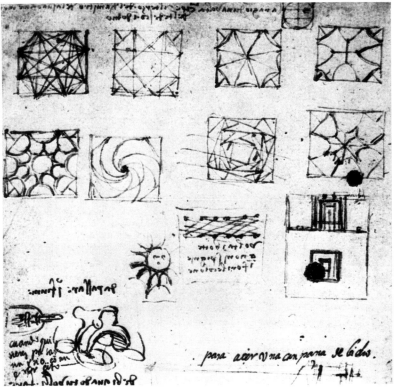

appointed to deal with the problem of the tiburio, left pending at the time of the death of Guiniforte Solari in 1481. To the difficulties of the tiburio problem itself were soon added those of his relations with the Italian technicians, and in 1486 Nexemperger abandoned the undertaking, while Mayer stayed on in Milan to take part independently in the competition announced in 1487. The Workshop Overseers in 1488 paid him for his model, which had been rejected, and in 1490 let him know that their connections with him were terminated. A long note in his handwriting, the rough draft of a petition relating to an ecclesiastical appointment, is found in Leonardo's MS. A, a codex dated 1492 but which could go back to 1490, particularly as regards the studies of arches. This is an important indication of the familiarity Leonardo could have with persons who were occupying themselves with the same architectural problem as he was himself. It is therefore probable that the other seven sketches of vaults on the MS. B sheet refer to as many solutions put forward for the tiburio and are not merely theoretical exercises. It is curious how one of these, perhaps the most daring of all inasmuch as it seems to anticipate Guarini's cupola designs, is crossed out with pen lines. In another we can see a spiral composition which suggests the use of Brunelleschi's herring-bone system. The one on the right of the "German's" shows the umbrella vault which Bramante would later use in the choir of S. Maria delle Grazie and which Amadeo, too, was to adopt for the tiburio. None of these, however, seems to reproduce the one proposed by Leonardo.

The first notice we have that Leonardo took part in the project is dated 30 July 1487, when a sum of money was paid in advance to, the carpenter Bernardino in Abbiate for the construction of Leonardo's model. Subsequent documents show that the carpenter was helped by a partner, Bernardino de Madiis, and that completion of the work, final payment for which was made on 28 September, involved 34 working days and a cost of 34 imperial lire. Leonardo was paid a total of 16 imperial lire in two instalments, the first on 8 August and the second on 30 September. Over three months later, on 11 January 1488, Leonardo received 40 imperial lire for work carried out on his model and as the payment was made to him and not to the carpenters, we can assume that he himself had carried out finishing touches and alterations, possibly even in consultation with Fancelli, who is known to have remained in Milan until 22 December 1487.

Fancelli's letter to Lorenzo de' Medici, written on 12 August 1487, while Leonardo's model was being constructed, contains a revealing sentence. Having informed Lorenzo that he had already been in Milan for six months, he stated: "the main reason is that the cathedral's cupola here seems to have been about to collapse. It has therefore been pulled down and enquiries are being made into the rebuilding of it and as this structure lacks bones and proportions, planning it will not be easy." This indicates that the problem which Leonardo and the other architects had to face was to make up for the lack of an adequate building skeleton or framework to support the projected dome and heavy main spire. It was, above all, a problem of statics which had to be solved structurally, so it is likely that Leonardo's model, at least as far as it had progressed after only 34 days of carpentry work, consisted mainly of a framework to which he had added such suitable elaborations as might demonstrate the validity of a solution based on a precise knowledge of the problem. There is reason to believe, in fact, that his studies for the tiburio were carried out at the same time both on paper and on the model, which would explain the schematic character of many of his plan-drawings and the absence of comprehensive axonometric views. The famous vertical sections which show the interconnection of the hewn stones in the arches give no idea of the volume or of the direction in depth of the arches. A few sketches in the Trivulzio codex hint at three-dimensional views which leave in doubt whether Leonardo intended to adopt a square or an octagonal plan and which translate into elevations the plan diagrams in the same codex that illustrate a method of distributing the weight of the tiburio onto the adjacent piers as well as onto the four main ones.

At the beginning of 1488 the model was ready. The rough draft of a letter of Leonardo's, preserved in the Codex Atlanticus, f. 270 r-c, confirms the procedure which was adopted. It shows, in fact, how Leonardo started from the prerequisite of a knowledge of what ailed the "sick cathedral" in order to find remedies to propose, in the same way as a doctor must understand the nature of an illness before finding a cure for it. Moreover, Leonardo reveals a theoretical knowledge that shows an understanding of Vitruvius ("authority of the ancient architects") no less than of the principles of mechanics which go back to the mediaeval teachings of the science *de ponderibus* and which, from the initial stimulus of a pratical application, he developed into extended treatments throughout the whole of the 1490's, beginning with the compilation of MS. A.

The conception of a building as an organism (and Fancelli had spoken of a structure lacking "bones and proportions,") which revives an ancient anthropomorphic and proportional concept, may have been what stimulated Leonardo to take up his anatomical studies once again: not only those done in 1489, possibly while waiting for a decision from the Cathedral Workshop Overseers, which concentrated on the human head, "the home of the intellect," analyzed in vertical section like an architectural model, but also those slightly earlier ones on the structure of the limbs which were still drawn with Florentine grace. These include an arm and hand which resemble those of the *Virgin of the Rocks* of 1483, and legs seen from behind which remind one of the melodically poised young men in the studies for the *Adoration of the Magi*. The architecture on these sheets, and in the studies of proportions which lead to the famous drawing of the Vitruvian man in Venice, already presents Lombard forms: sketches of centrally-planned buildings reminiscent of Battagio's sanctuaries, others which remind one of San Lorenzo, and details of columns which seem to bespeak a first contact with Bramante. This is all material which shares in the formation of that great reportoire of architectural forms and ideas which is MS. B, datable exactly between 1487-90, at the beginning of which there is, almost like a symbolic introduction, a page of notes on the proportions of human limbs. With this in mind we can now read again his letter to the Overseers of the Workshop of Milan Cathedral:

"Sirs, Father Deputies, Just as it is necessary for physicians, guardians and healers of the sick to know what man is, what life is, what health is and how a balance and agreement of elements maintains it while a discordance of them ruins and undoes it; and he who has a good knowledge of all the above-mentioned elements will be better able to repair than one who lacks it...

You know that medicines, when properly used, give health to the sick, and he who knows them well will use them properly when he also knows what man is, what life and constitution are, what health is; knowing these well, he will also know their opposites and this being so, he will be nearer a cure than anyone else. This same thing is needed by the sick cathedral, that is a physician architect who understands what building is, and from what rules correct building derives; and where the said rules come from, and in how many parts they are divided, and what the causes are that hold a building together and make it last, and what the nature of weight is, and that of energy in force and how they should be interwoven and linked, and once combined what effect they might produce. He who has real knowledge of these things will leave you satisfied with his planning and his work.

Therefore with this I shall do my best, neither belittling nor discrediting anyone, to satisfy, partly by reasoning and partly by works, sometimes demonstrating the effects by their causes, sometimes proving the reasoning by experiment, making use of the authority of ancient architects and the proofs offered by buildings that have been erected and for what reasons they have been ruined or have survived, etc. And in addition I shall demonstrate the nature of the first cause of the load, and what and how many are the causes of damage to buildings, and the way they can be made stable and permanent.

But, so as not to be verbose, I will first of all speak to your Excellencies of the invention of the Cathedral's first architect, and I shall clearly demonstrate what his intentions were, proving it by looking at the way the building was begun, and once you have understood this, you will be able to recognize clearly that the model which I have made contains that same symmetry, correspondence and conformity as the original building.

What is a building, and from where do the rules for correct building derive, and what and how many are the parts which belong to them; either I, or another who may demonstrate it better than I, choose him, and put aside all passions."

The end of the letter, with the noble phrase "either I, or another who may demonstrate it better than I," alludes to the animated discussions which the different proposals had provoked and in which the competitors must have taken part, each in defense of his own model. In the Workshop's Annals for 1488 and 1489 we find no mention of any meetings, and the tiburio is recorded only in 1488 when payments for two models were recorded: on 14 May the one by Johannes Mayer (the "German at the Cathedral") and on 31 May the one by Pietro da Gorgonzola, which had had to be remade because the preceding one had been destroyed "in ejus absentia." Leonardo's letter, which may not have ever been sent, should thus be assigned to the time of the deliberations, between April and June, 1490. We do know that on 10 May he had taken back his model in order to add to it the "shoulders" which had been damaged, or, as the document says, "areptas seu devastatas," pledging himself to return it whenever they should request it. Seven days later, on 17 May, Leonardo received twelve lire for work on the model.

On 27 June 1490 the commission for the tiburio was given to Francesco di Giorgio, Amadeo and Dolcebuono, and four years later Leonardo still owed the sum given him on 17 May of that year, so we must conclude that he kept the model and that the cathedral authorities had not asked for it back.

At this point it is necessary to reconsider the events which took place in rapid succession in the first six months of 1490, between the dates of the two deliberations:

13 April: It is decided that the building of the tiburio should be entrusted to Giovanni Antonio Amadeo and Gian Giacomo Dolcebuono. They are to prepare a model which takes into account the ones already existing in the Workshop and which must be approved by two architects, Francesco di Giorgio and Luca Fancelli.

19 April: Caradosso is sent to Siena to escort Francesco di Giorgio to Milan.

10 May: Leonardo collects the model in order to repair it.

17 May: Payment of 12 lire to Leonardo for repairs to the model.

31 May: Francesco di Giorgio is in Milan. He has a meeting in the Archbishop's Palace with Amadeo, Dolcebuono and some other engineers (Bramante? Leonardo?), with whom he discusses the problem of the tiburio at length. No decision is taken.

8 June: Lodovico Sforza requests from Pavia that "that Sienese engineer" be sent there for consultation on the works in that cathedral. In a postscript he requests that Amadeo and Leonardo should also be sent.

10 June: From Milan a letter is written to Lodovico Sforza to inform him that Francesco di Giorgio is working on the model and that in eight days time he could leave to go to Pavia. Leonardo states that he is quite prepared to accompany Francesco di Giorgio, but Amadeo is absent.

21 June: Francesco di Giorgio and Leonardo are in Pavia.

27 June: Meeting of those in charge of the Workshop and the contestants at the Sforza Castle in the presence of the Archbishop of Milan and Lodovico Sforza, for the final decision. Models being discussed: one by Francesco di Giorgio, one by Amadeo and Dolcebuono, one by Simone Sirtori and another by Battagio. It is decided that Francesco di Giorgio, Amadeo and Dolcebuono be elected engineers of

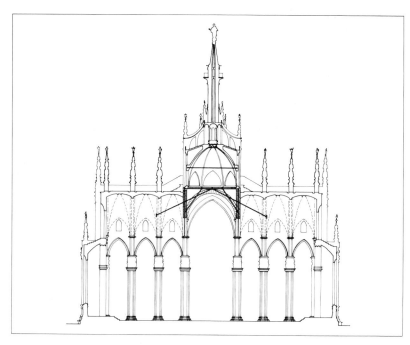

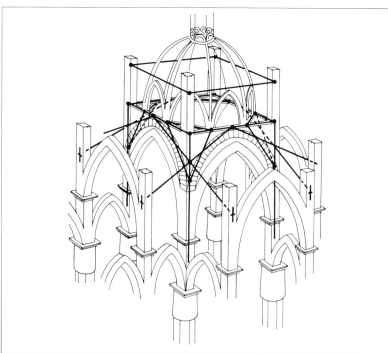

the Workshop with the task of building the tiburio according to a new model which the three would prepare in common agreement and following the specifications presented by Francesco di Giorgio in an accompanying report.

In this last document Leonardo and Bramante are not named, but one may presume that they were among the "many Master engineers" present at the meeting. It was probably on that occasion that Bramante wrote his opinion on the various models (including those not brought to the last meeting, for example Pietro da Gorgonzola's, but excluding those by Leonardo and Francesco di Giorgio, although as we shall see, he does seem to allude to them). The *Bramanti opinio* is placed in the Annals after Francesco di Giorgio's report, but it is not dated. The model which Leonardo had taken back the month before (10 May) for repair disappears from the scene.

There is something puzzling here. Why on earth should Leonardo have wanted to keep to himself a model which belonged to the Workshop (and to whom he should have paid for it) *after* the Workshop had approved someone else's model, i.e. Francesco di Giorgio's? This fact has always been taken as proof that Leonardo had withdrawn from the competition (which he could have done without losing any money over it), but no one has ever asked how Francesco di Giorgio, who had arrived in Milan at the end of May, was able to have a model ready in a few days when, on top of it all, he had to leave Milan and go to Pavia – accompanied by Leonardo – for a consultation on the works of that cathedral.

On 23 April of that same year Leonardo had started working again on the horse for the equestrian Sforza statue, and it has been thought, perhaps rightly, that the renewed zeal put into that project distracted him more and more from the problem of the tiburio. It is also possible, however, that the meeting with Francesco di Giorgio and a profitable exchange of ideas with him (it was probably then that Leonardo came into possession of a manuscript by his Sienese colleague) led him to give his own model to Francesco di Giorgio, who could then have modified it within a few days and presented it as his own. After all, Bramante himself had stated that one could arrive at a satisfactory solution "in less than an hour," by making use of the various models prepared, "taking one thing off this one, and another off that one, as I have said before, we could make one which will be suitable." (And that the models were tampered with during the discussions is proved by the shoulder torn out of Leonardo's and the total demolition of Pietro da Gorgonzola's). One should even consider the possibility that Leonardo's model may not have been greatly different from the solution suggested in Francesco di Giorgio's report, which Roberto Papini has skilfully paraphrased and translated into graphic images. This is the document of 27 June, solemnly approved and signed by the chosen architects (with the exception of Amadeo) which explains how the weight of the tiburio should be directed perpendicularly onto the four central piers according to the following specifications:

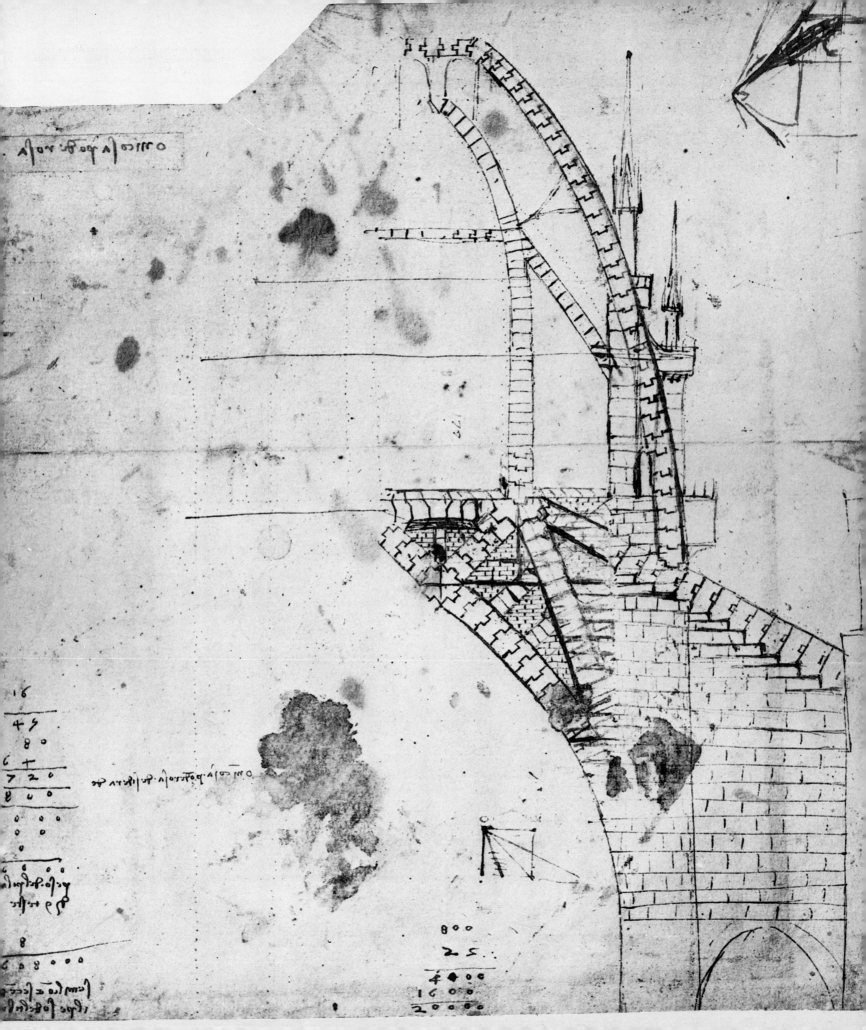

(1) Build over every pointed arch a round-headed one in marble of the same thickness as the pointed one; externally to the four round arches build four identical arches connected to them which will support the corridors.

(2) In the corners of the central square make the pendentives with hewn stones connected with one another through dovetailing and curved in such a way that their load should go onto the piers and not onto the sides.

(3) For the perfection of the work place four tie-irons, which fortify the sides of the square space, above the four round arches, and connect these with four other vertical tie-irons on the axis of the piers.

(4) Place four transverse tie-irons so that they connect the points where the octagon separates from the square and two other tie-irons on each face of the square so that they go from the corners of the octagon to the vertical tie-irons, and connect with them.

(5) Put two tie-irons, one on the right and one on the left of every arch, which start from the middle of the tie-iron at the top of each arch, connect to the vertical tie-iron, and go on as far as the piers of the aisles, with care that they tighten very well.

(6) Raise the wall above the arches enclosing the tie-irons in the masonry both along the square and along the octagon, so as to reach the top of the roof of the central nave.

(7) Above this wall build the eight-sided cupola and the vertical wall-faces twelve braccia (*c.* 7.20 m) high in which the windows will open: above the straight part of the wall where the cornices go, link a further number of tie-irons and buttress the lot so that the load may concentrate on the vertical of the piers together with the load of the lantern, pinnacles, floral decorations and other ornaments.

(8) In the said cupola make a circle of the ribs from the impost to the top for a vertical height of 28 braccia (*c.* 17 m).

(9) At the top of the ribs build arches from one rib to another on which to place the base of the lantern.

(10) Build the lantern, the floral decorations and ornaments according to the style of the rest of the church.

(11) From the floor to the top of the dome there must be 112 braccia (*c.* 66.50 m)

(12) In the pendentives replace the marble busts of the Doctors of the Church with others in bas-relief in copper gilt, so as not to jeopardize the solidity of the wall structure; and also the other decorative details should be in embossed copper.

Let us now see how certain aspects of Francesco di Giorgio's proposal can be related to Leonardo's drawings. Perhaps there has been a little too much stress placed on the idea that Leonardo's proposal aimed at a solution "that could be called dynamic" (Beltrami). In fact the intention of channelling the weight of the tiburio onto the piers next to the central ones (as seems to be the case above all in the famous drawings in vertical section) is more apparent than real. The pier which extends upward and becomes a turret (as Francesco di Giorgio calls it), next to the cupola, is

emphatically defined as an element absorbing the thrusts directed to it by the "ribs" of dovetailed ashlar which transform the pointed arch into a bearing arch, an arrangement which Francesco di Giorgio simplifies with the use of a round arch above the pointed one; only a minimal part of those thrusts is directed sideways towards the masonry buttress, whose function is mainly to act as a shoulder to the pier. Like Francesco di Giorgio, Leonardo also assigns great importance to the tie-irons, which in these drawings can be glimpsed in the wall section and between the two levels of turrets of the cupola. The various plan sketches in the Trivulzio Codex which show the central piers linked to the lateral ones must be understood as studies for the placing of the tie-irons and not of masonry buttressing. This detail is quite sufficient to allow us to connect Leonardo's idea with that of Francesco di Giorgio. Some elevation sketches on a page of the Trivulzio Codex (f. 8 r) clearly show the linking together of the four central piers by means of tie-irons, even those at the very top of the turrets (No. 7 in Francesco di Giorgio's report). Leonardo adds abutments like reversed arches which remind one of those planned by Brunelleschi for Santa Maria degli Angioli. They lock the four piers to the fabric of the building, while the load of the tiburio is perpendicularly directed to those piers. In another sheet of the Trivulzio Codex (f. 22 v) the pier is transformed from a circular to a cruciform section at the point which corresponds to the crossing of the tie-irons and to the beginning of the vault ribs, which are also cruciform in section. In the sketch of the whole on the same sheet Leonardo studies the relationship between spire and cupola and considers the problem of relieving the cupola of the weight of the spire by unloading it laterally onto the turrets and therefore onto the piers below. It is only as an alternative that Leonardo considers the possibility of prolonging the thrust to the pier's buttress. The idea of shifting the weight of the spire onto the piers and not onto the cupola is made clear in the small sketch on the upper left of this sheet which, in fact, illustrates the use of rampant arches, elegantly tapering, through which the weight of the spire is directed only towards the piers. They form a bearing structure which is placed above the tiburio and would be covered by a second cupola. The presence of the two shells (as in Brunelleschi's dome, but farther apart from each other) is seen in the larger drawing as well, where the rampant arches have become even more elongated in order to fit between the two shells. A detailed study of one of these rampant arches, probably in the same dimensions as those in the model, is on f. 148 r-a of the Codex Atlanticus. As Firpo has pointed out, this involves the same principle as the "very strong and light arches" illustrated in MS. B, f. 78 v; and we shall see that the identical idea reappears in the project for the Sforza Sepulchre in 1497.

The facts and clues thus far gathered together, and interpreted in terms of a tacit association between Leonardo and Francesco di Giorgio on the project for the tiburio, must now be looked at from the viewpoint of Bramante's *opinio*, the document which Anna Maria Brizio is the first to have understood correctly. Bramante's statement consists of a declara-

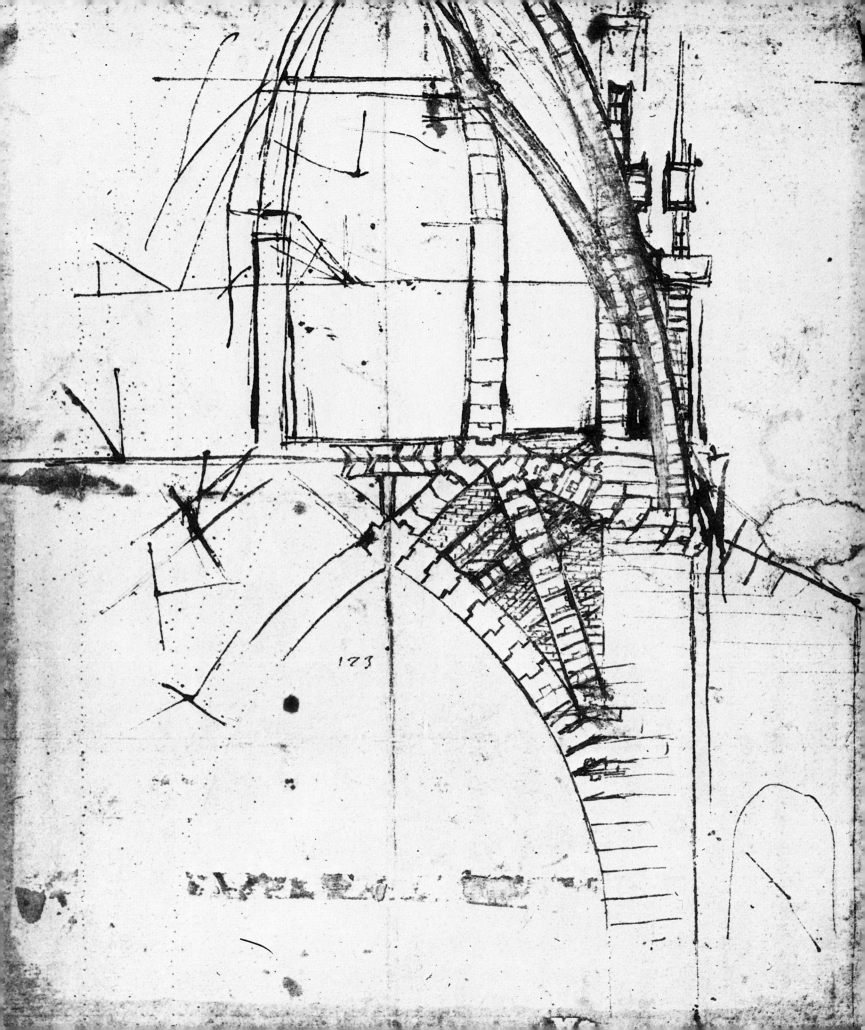

40-47. Studies of architecture in the Codex Trivulzianus, ff. 27 v, 3 v-4 r, 2 v-3 r, 7 v-8 r, 11 v-12 r, 8 v-9 r, 20 v-21 r, 22 v-23 r. The Codex Trivulzianus, which is of the same time as MS. B and is filled in great part with lists of words, contains architectural studies relating to the tiburio of Milan Cathedral and to a project for stables more fully developed in MS. B (see Excursus 5). *This is the time of Leonardo's first anatomical studies, c. 1487-90, and in fact two of the sheets in the Trivulzianus (f. 3 r and 4 r) contain drawings of legs like those at Windsor reproduced on p. 54, but invisible in reproduction because they were drawn in metal-point but not gone over in pen. On the same pages Leonardo adds notes of an architectural character: on f. 3 r we see a room without windows drawn in perspective like a stage setting. The ceiling is slightly curved and contains a skylight, whose opening is probably adjustable. On the left wall small vaults are sketched out. It is not clear for what purpose such a room could have been intended, but the way of controlling the light could suggest an artist's studio. On the other hand, if it is true that Bramante's frescoes at Casa Panigarola were in a room originally without windows, it may be that the illusionistic effect of the painted architecture was "dramatized" by a diffused light, with variable intensity, coming from above. On the next sheet is the drawing of a vault with a complex system of radial trusses holding up a wooden ceiling. Sketches added later illustrate a "way of raising and lowering the curtains of the Signore's silver," that is a device for manoeuvring the curtains in front of the show-cases in which were kept the objects of silver belonging to the "signore," probably Lodovico Sforza. At the top of the page, as a kind of memorandum, he writes: "to heal is to restore the balance of unequal elements; illness is the discordance of the elements infused in the vital body." This is the concept Leonardo develops in the third paragraph of his letter to the Overseers of the Workshop of Milan Cathedral (Codex Atlanticus, f. 270 r-c), where he reproposes the relationship between medicine and architecture in considering the "sick cathedral."*

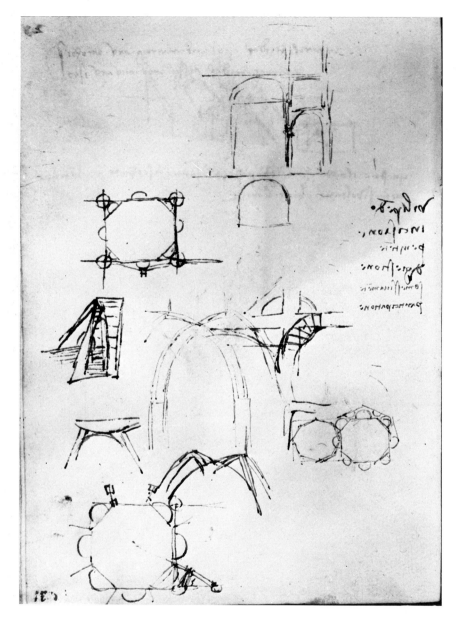

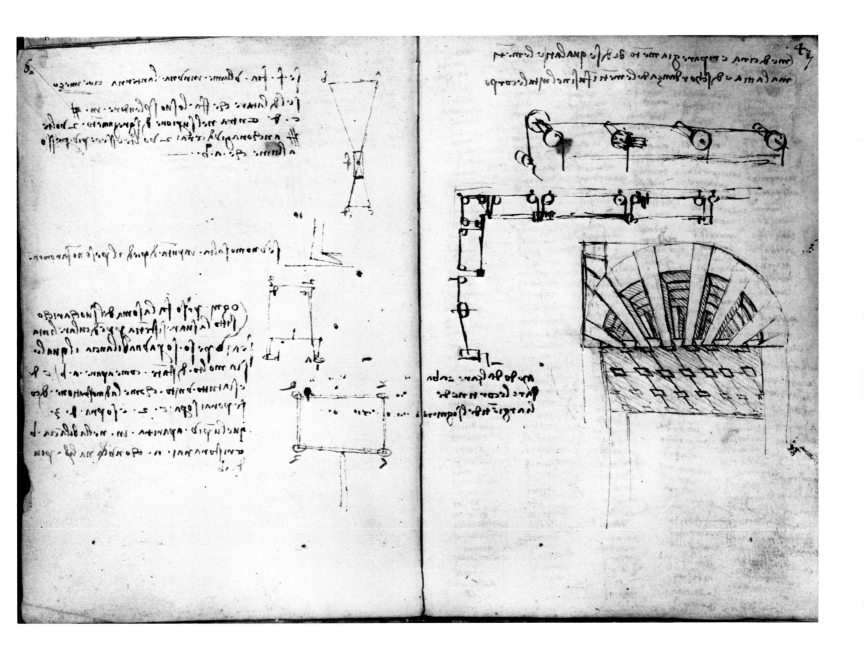

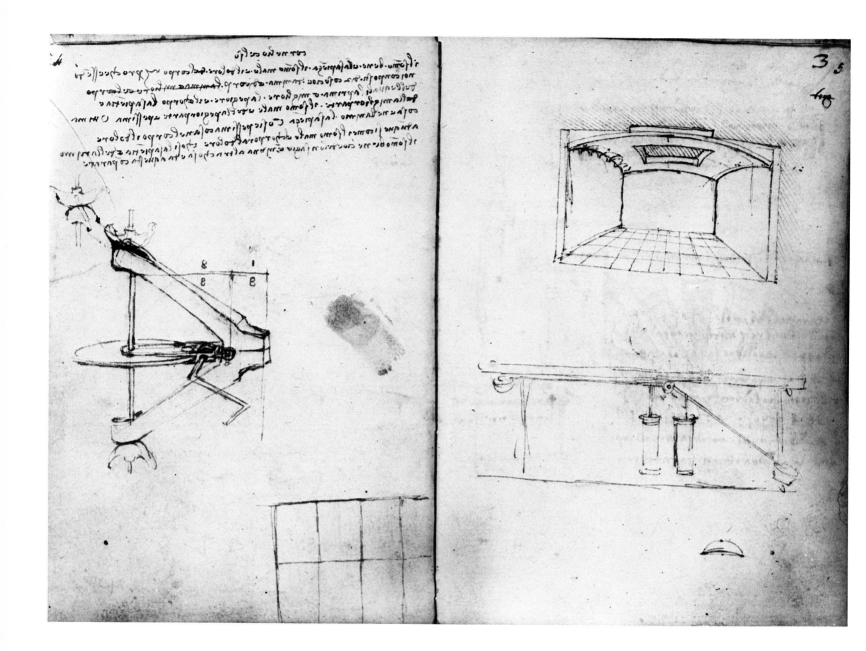

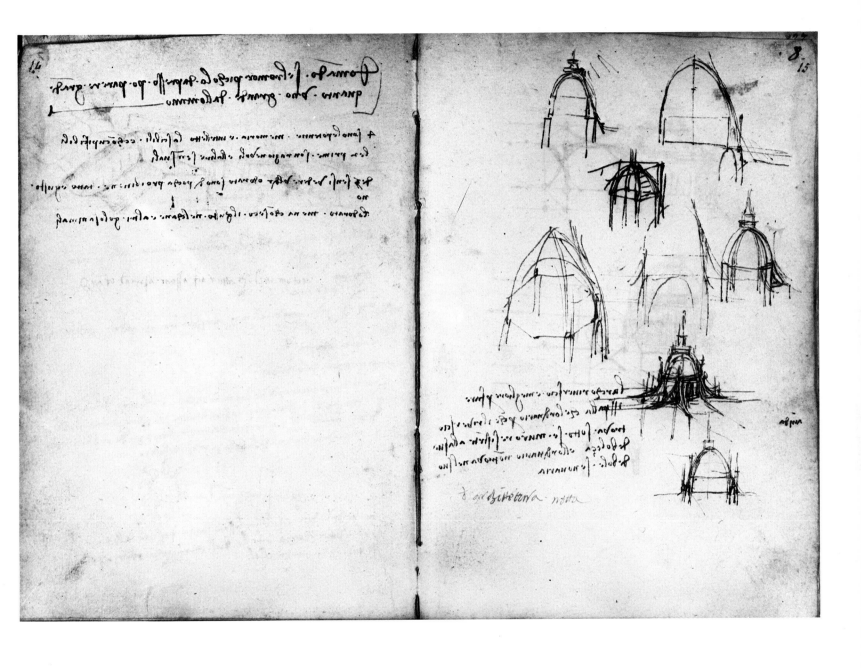

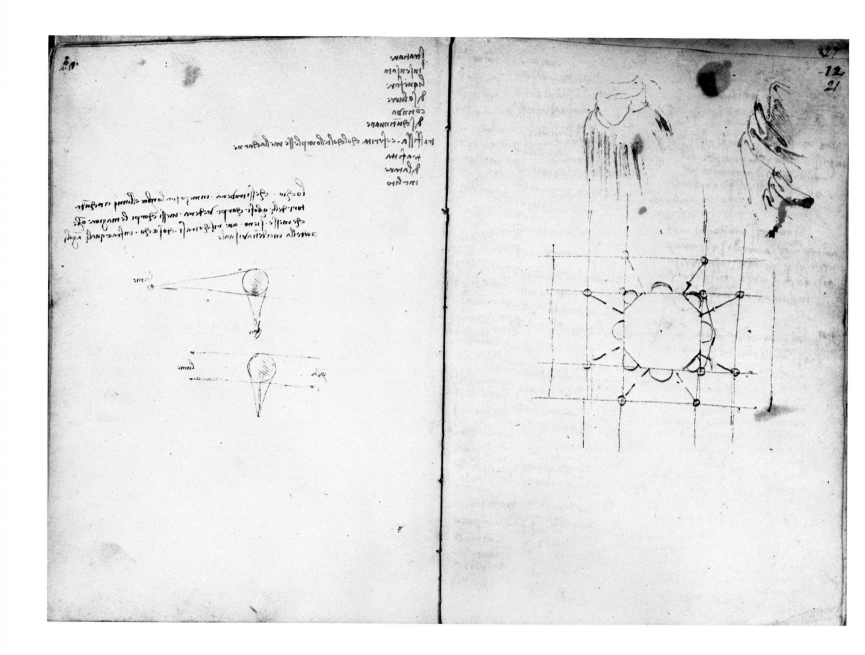

44

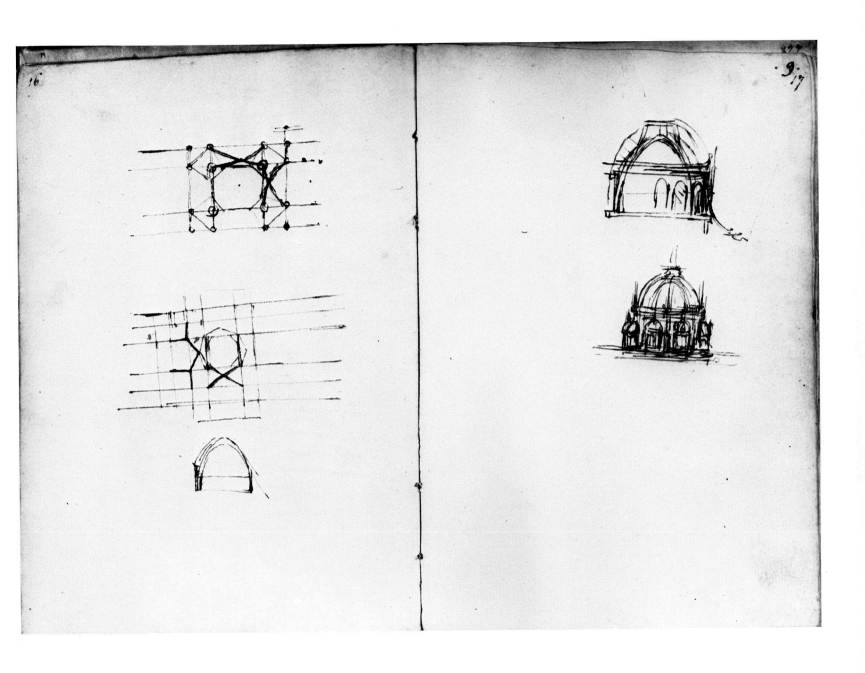

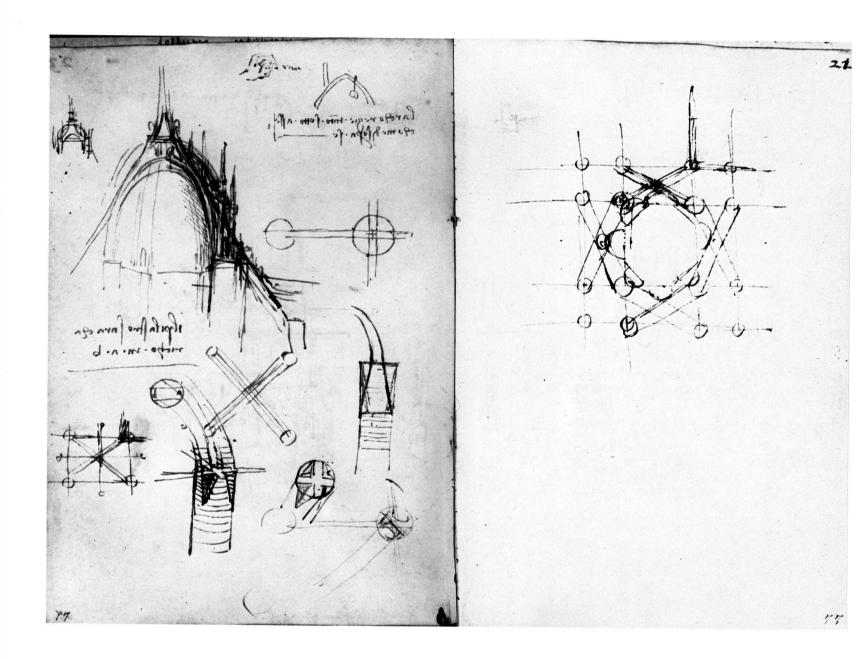

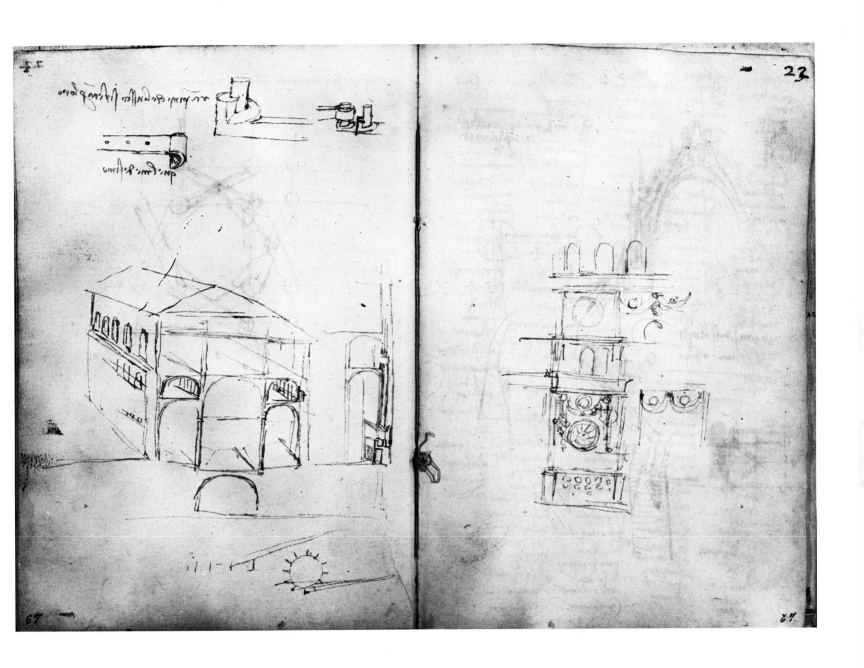

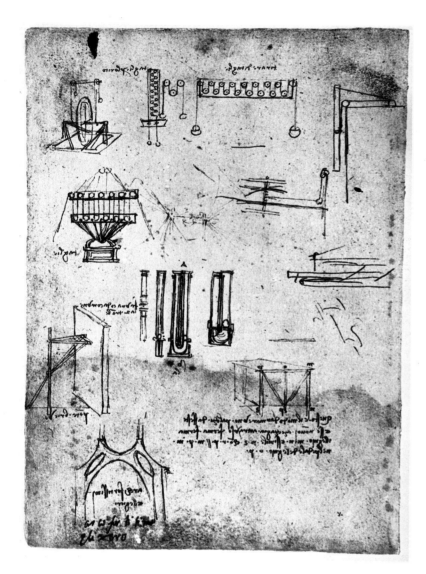

tion of principle, based on Vitruvian classification, of the requirements which the model must satisfy: "strength," "conformity with the rest of the building," in the sense not of stylistic, but of structural and proportional accord, "lightness," and finally "beauty." "As to the first point," states Bramante, "viz. strength, I say that the square is much stronger and better than the octagon, since it accords better with the rest of the building." It is exctly this accord that Bramante, and Leonardo too, call "conformity with the rest of the building," and there is no doubt that "strength" and "accord" are the two principal elements on which Leonardo's and Francesco di Giorgio's projects are based. The linking together of the four piers by means of tie-irons, explained by Francesco di Giorgio and illustrated by Leonardo, suggests that shape which Bramante chooses as best – the square – inasmuch as it provides the largest base for bearing the weight and distributes it equally to each one of the four piers. In his consideration, immediately afterward, of the octagonal tiburio Bramante seems to allude to Leonardo's and Francesco di Giorgio's proposal, which starts from the square (the linkage of the piers) in order to become an octagon (insertion of the pendentives of dovetailed ashlar): "Not for this do I believe the octagon can stay up; I think that it can, but with more effort from itself, and from the ingenuity of the person who will have to build it, since it springs directly from the straight, where there should be more strength, I mean from the piers down below, and for this reason we must provide them with lightness above and good foundations and buttressing below."

At this point Bramante begins to mentally construct the ideal model, made up of parts taken from the various models presented: thus the one by Pietro da Gorgonzola becomes the "seed" of a "better manner" by means of "certain relieving arches which spring from the top of the master arch to the one on the side," which seems to allude to a similar system to the one of "ribs" of dovetailed stones in Leonardo's drawings or better still to the one represented in detail on one of Leonardo's anatomical sheets dating from that time (RL 19134 v). It does as a matter of fact seem implicit that the "seed" of the "better manner" consisted in replacing this system with a round arch such as Francesco di Giorgio was to adopt, this being the shape which Bramante approves: "As for the master arch, I say it is better round than pointed for many reasons." And the reasons, naturally, are above all of a technical nature. The buttressing, still in Bramante's opinion, is best understood by Amadeo "because from the eight piers which are adjacent to the four main ones, he makes eight arches spring which correspond to the eight corners of the tiburio." These same arches are shown in the vertical section drawings by Leonardo. "And this is good for two reasons: first for the strength of the tiburio; second for conformity with the rest of the building, as we shall see below." Then follows the explanation of what is to be understood by conformity, that is how the new element of the tiburio fits into the proportional articulation, in plan and elevation, of the existing structure, with the result that the shape of tiburio most suitable to the space where it is to fit is the square, and consequently the cube. Here Bramante reveals how the Workshop Overseers had already indicated their preference for the octagonal shape, which is probably the one Solari had wanted: "But since you break up the order of the fabric in your desire to have an octagon, it is advisable to break up the straight quality of the buttressing so that it should be appropriate to the tiburio." This "order" he speaks of is then clarified in the next sentence: "And even if this does deviate from the original order of things, it would deviate still further should the tiburio be made round and without any buttressing because he who builds on the square cannot stray from the straight," and he concludes: "from the square to the octagon the difference is this, that two thirds rest on the upright and the other one does not."

After these structural considerations of strength and conformity, Bramante acknowledges that the third requirement, "lightness," had been properly understood by everyone and particularly by Amadeo, who, however, had put the principle of lightness before that of proportionality, so that "he erred in the height by being overly concerned with making it light."

Here is where the element of "beauty" emerges, which is sought above all through relationships – proportional, perspectival, even urban. "... and whoever will build the said structure differently, will not be able to see it either from within or from without, since in order to glimpse it above the roof of the church one must go a mile outside of Milan." And so, the soaring verticality of the tiburio recommended by Bramante harks back to the concept propounded by the "first architect of the cathedral," as Leonardo calls him. There is, then, after all, also an aspect of "stylistic conformity," which Bramante indeed underlines in the case of the decoration, which was to be based on the example of the decorative partitions of the sacristy, "and it can be even better understood from some drawings in the Workshop which were made at the time that this cathedral was built." The conclusion, as we have seen, is that in "less than an hour" an ideal model can be put together with parts taken from various other models.

None of Leonardo's drawings indicates the presence of the round arch which Francesco di Giorgio suggested should be constructed over the pointed one and which Bramante calls "the master arch." On the other hand such an arch had already been envisaged by Solari following the very similar arrangement adopted by him in the Certosa of Pavia. Beltrami already pointed out how Francesco di Giorgio's suggestion followed essentially the building concept introduced by Solari, in that the large marble arches he proposed would have been built next to those in flint stone which Solari had incorporated into the walls. This has been confirmed by investigations of the wall structure during recent restoration work. The large flint stone arches, in projection, appear to have wide shoulders as in a bridge. Beltrami therefore was right in suspecting that Francesco di Giorgio's proposal was nothing but the simple amplification of a concept already adopted by Solari. And so, the

moment Francesco di Giorgio had left, Amadeo went back to Solari's arrangements and discarded the proposal for large supplementary marble arches, in order to preserve the original arrangement of the pendentives and of the sculptures which had already been placed there. On 11 September 1490 the Archbishop laid the first stone of the tiburio. Ten years later, on 24 September 1500, the work was completed. The story told by the structure itself, according to the recent report by Carlo Ferrari da Passano and Ernesto Brivio (1967) often contradicts the historical testimonies and even the documents. Luca Fancelli had spoken of a building which lacked "bones and proportions" and of a cupola so unsafe that "it has been pulled down and enquiries are being made into the rebuilding of it." Leonardo spoke of the "sick cathedral," and Francesco di Giorgio Martini suggested a remedy that was approved in the solemn form of a document which only Amadeo did not sign, probably because as Solari's true successor he was capable of evaluating the efficacy of the arrangement that master had desired, and he reverted to it as soon as he had rid himself of Martini. It is possible that Leonardo, too, realized the effectiveness of the original project and therefore no longer insisted on an idea which Martini had made his own. Leonardo mentioned the tiburio once more, about 1497, in notes relating to some aviation experiments that he was conducting on the roof of his residence in the nearby Corte Vecchia: "and if you are on the roof, by the side of the tower, you will not be seen by those of the tiburio." In sheets dating from his final days in France we find hints of rampant arches similar to those with which he had thought to support the spire of the tiburio, and there is even a sketch in cross section of a Gothic church which could be a recollection of the model he had put forward.

After Amadeo's death, in 1521, two years after Leonardo had died, Cesariano, Bramante's pupil, brought out his edition of Vitruvius in which he prophesied the collapse of the tiburio: "It will be a matter of great wisdom to pull down such work, and reduce it to its most natural form." He sees the only hope in rebuilding the tiburio much lighter ("in pumice-stone") – that tiburio which after five hundred years is still standing.

5. Sforza Town-planning: a / Pavia and the New City

On 20 June 1490, Leonardo and Francesco di Giorgio were in Pavia together for a consultation on the building of the city's cathedral. A few days later, on 24 June, Francesco di Giorgio was in Milan where he took part in the meeting on the tiburio. Quite probably Leonardo attended that meeting too, but he because increasingly involved with the horse for the monument to Francesco Sforza, and he was also busy compiling notes on mechanics, hydraulics and painting. MS. C, f. 15 v, gives us the date of his taking up work on the horse again: "On the 23rd day of April 1490 I began this book and I began again on the horse." (The date which follows, 22 July, refers to the arrival of Salai and shows that Leonardo was in Milan). On 7 May 1491, the colossus was finished and

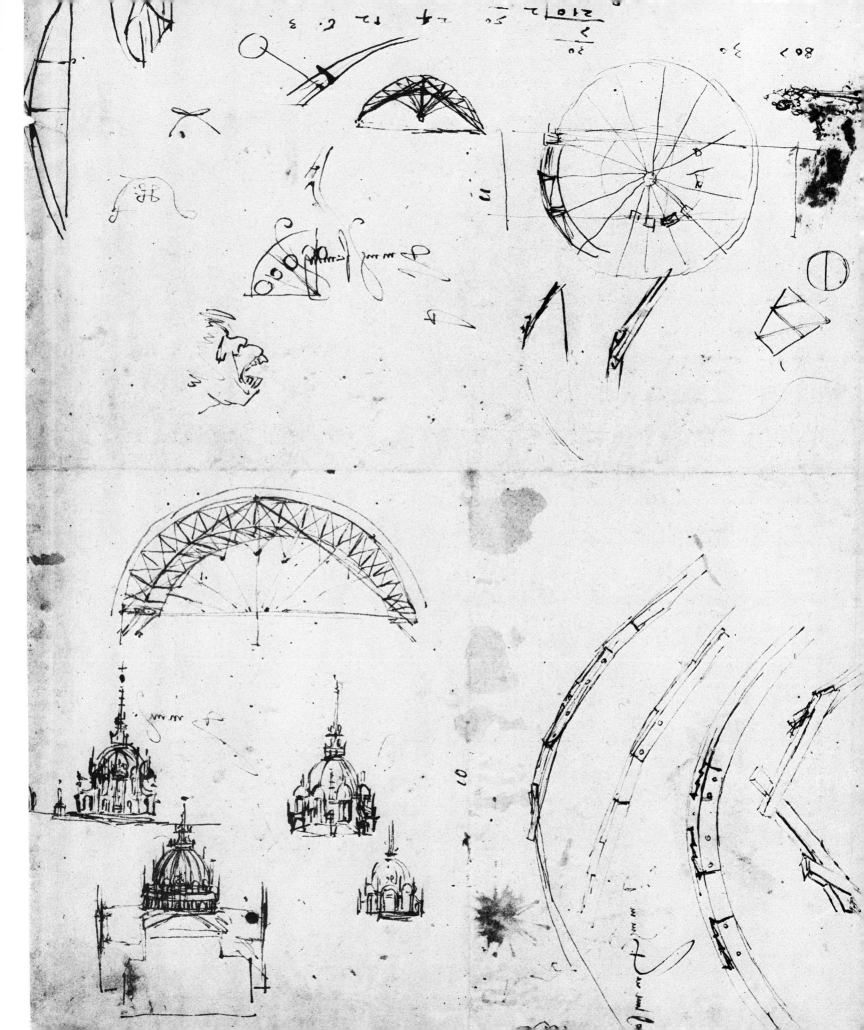

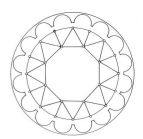

for the next two years, right through December 1493, he was absorbed in the preparations for its casting. On 13 October 1492, Giuliano da Sangallo came to Milan in order to present the model of a palace to Lodovico Sforza; Vasari (IV. 276) says that on that occasion he gave Leonardo advice on the subject of bronze casting.

A reflection of Sangallo's visit appears in his Barberino Codex, which contains among other things a plan of S. Lorenzo in Milan, while besides the drawing of the so-called "tower of Boethius" in Pavia is the ground plan of an enormous palace which, it has been suggested, may represent the one planned for Sforza. Leonardo too was probably interested in the celebrated octagonal tower in Pavia, an ancient building which collapsed towards the end of the sixteenth century and which was characterized by figures of prisoners or of Marsyas placed like caryatids in the spaces between the windows. It would be strange, in fact, if he had ignored it when, in addition to the statue of the "Regisole," he noted with attention a building like S. Maria alla Pertica, the castle chimneys, the foundations of the old town walls, and even the arrangement of the rooms in a brothel (MS. B, f. 58 r). One is tempted to think, looking at Sangallo's drawing, that Leonardo may have actually climbed up that tower to look at the human figures close at hand. By leaning out of the little chamfered windows he would only have been able to get a good view of the legs up to the thighs. Certain anatomical studies of legs at Windsor (RL 12632 and 12634) on paper which came originally from an account book of the Milan Cathedral Workshop seem to record just such an observation. And since these drawings are datable about 1487-88, they would offer a further clue, in addition to those collected in the first document section, for suspecting that Leonardo went to Pavia even before June 1490, when he was called there with Francesco di Giorgio to discuss the work on the city's cathedral.

It has been suggested that Leonardo may have drawn the ground plans of S. Spirito and the Tempio degli Angioli in MS. B, f. 11 v, on the basis of information obtained from Giuliano da Sangallo, in whose Barberino Codex there are also found drawings of those plans. But the date of MS. B cannot be stretched to 1492, and furthermore the two plans had already been drawn when Leonardo filled the remaining empty spaces on the page with notes that have the same characteristics as those of the anatomical studies of 1489 at Windsor. It is more probable that Leonardo obtained information on the two Brunelleschian buildings from Luca Fancelli at the time of his work on the model for the tiburio in 1487. But Sangallo's trip to Milan in 1492 to present the model of a palace to Lodovico Sforza is an indication of a building and town-planning program which would certainly have been known to Leonardo as the projected monument to Francesco Sforza was to be a part of it. The celebrated notes in MS. B relating to a city on two levels, with its buildings planned in relation to streets, squares and canals, are datable about 1487 and probably reflect the first proposals for an urban renewal of Milan following the plague which shortly before, in 1484-85, had struck down a third of the population. These notes have the sense of

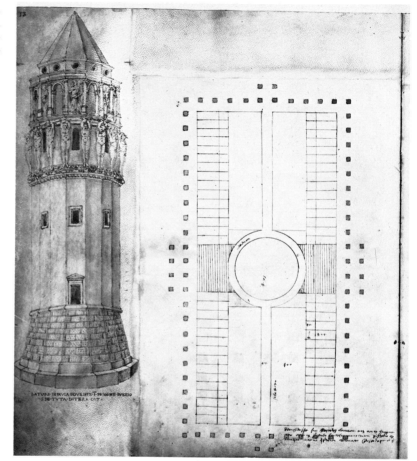

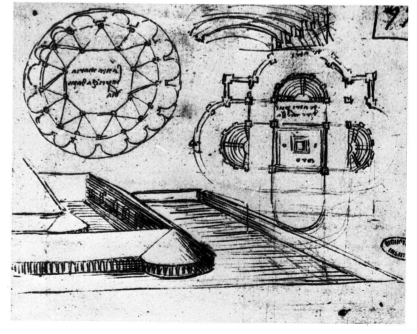

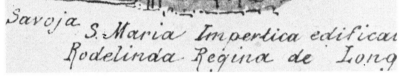

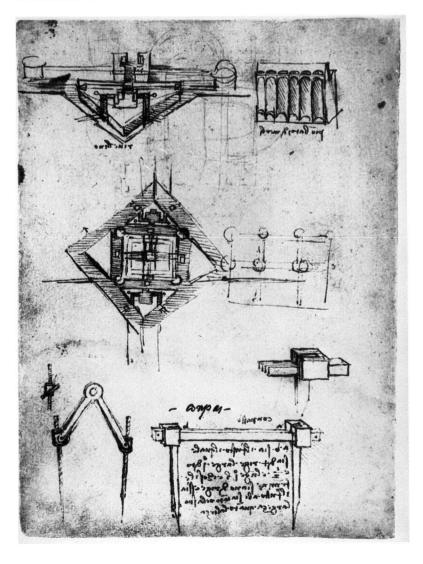

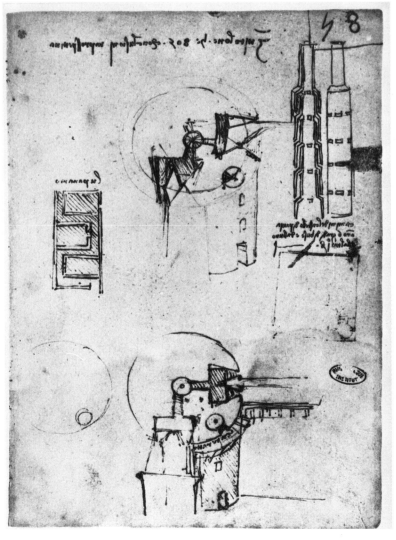

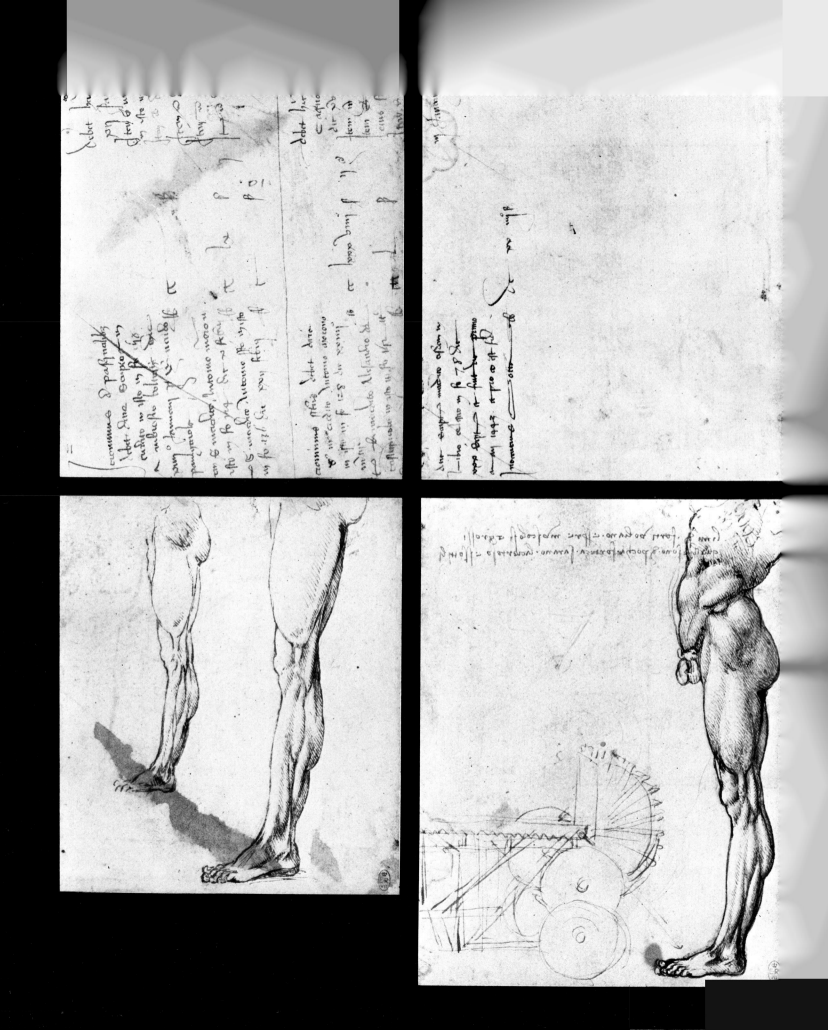

immediacy of a practical proposal and yet Leonardo gives them the character of a treatise in the tradition of Vitruvius, Alberti and Filarete in proposing the features of an ideal city. It seems in fact that he realized the need for a radical solution to the problem of overcrowding in the city center: not only decentralization by increasing building activity in suburban areas, but also by actually founding a new city in the duchy, which would be geometrically laid out around a system of canals fed by a great river, the Ticino (MS. B, f. 38 r). This was envisaged as a city on a square plan like a Roman military camp, or else spindle-shaped to make the downflow of the waters more efficient, as in his projects for Romorantin in France thirty years later. Only in this way would it have been possible to proceed to a clearance and reorganization of the overcrowded city, whose population had grown densest around the cathedral and the Castello and in the area between the two known as the Foro dei Mercanti. The idea of opening a large piazza in front of the cathedral had been in the air for some time, but it only entered the phase of execution about 1490 when it was decreed that the Castello, too, should have its own piazza. An arterial road would have obviously united the two centres, in the same way that the cathedral in Florence had been connected to the Palazzo Pubblico by a road in line with Giotto's campanile and directed to the Loggia dei Lanzi. Such a program is indicated in a late sketch of Leonardo's in the Codex Atlanticus, f. 95 r-a, datable about 1515, in which the Castello is shown in plan while the longitudinal axis of the piazza is continued in a straight road toward the cathedral. On the right the ground-plans of large buildings are sketched out within a system of streets, arcaded squares, and what may be canals, while lower down, where the straight road to the cathedral begins, is the outline of an enigmatic building on a square plan which could be a temporary construction of a triumphal arch, although its dimensions are the same as those of the Castello. The plan of the same or a very similar building appears in the Codex Atlanticus, f. 293 r-a, datable towards the end of the Quattrocento. These important details are undoubtedly part of the sketch of the plan of the Castello and its piazza, although this is always reproduced, from a tracing made by Beltrami, without them.

b/ The Expansion of Milan

The problems posed by a state of emergency such as the epidemic of 1484-85 were rapidly turning into a planning problem of political and social dimensions. An occasion was thus presented to reinforce the Sforza state by means of an efficient development of the city according to a proper town-plan and with suitable administrative regulations. With shrewd intuition Leonardo grasped the situation and, in about 1493, proposed a town-plan that was no longer Utopian in the Quattrocento sense of an ideal city, but was based on practical considerations following a procedure which, starting from Vitruvian premises, aimed realistically at a planned objective – a procedure that epitomized Brunelleschi's attitude in architecture and Machiavelli's in

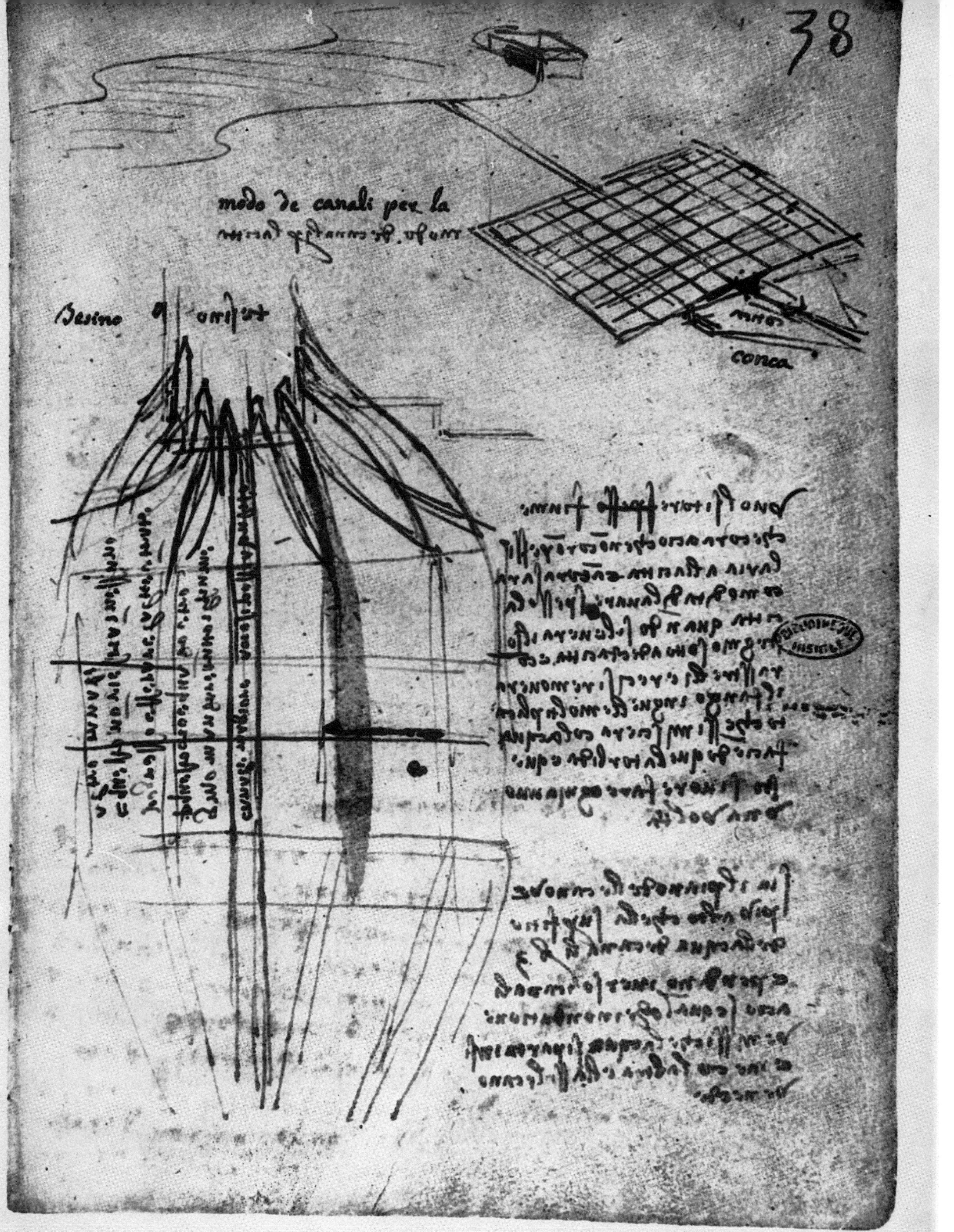

modo de canali per la

Basino a

conca

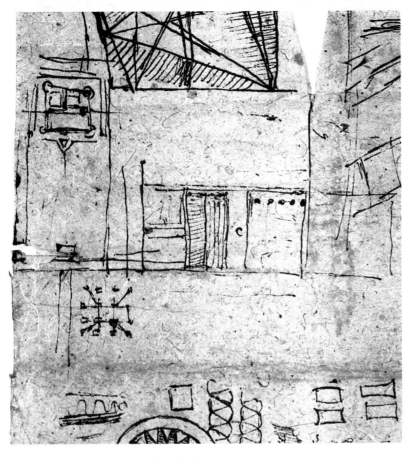

61. Town-planning study relating to the Castello Sforzesco, c. 1513-15. Codex Atlanticus, f. 95 r-a, detail.
62. Technological studies and plan of a building based on a Greek cross, c. 1500. Codex Atlanticus, f. 293 r-a.

politics. Leonardo proposed in fact that the realization of the plan for a vast urban enlargement of Milan – taking the form of a wide peripheral belt bounded by streets and canals – should begin with an experimental section equivalent to one tenth of that belt. It seems therefore to have been an authentic "pilot project," a new quarter with the autonomy of a town nucleus, which would develop from its initial function as a "model" into a satellite city.

The indispensable prerequisite to working out such a scheme was a precise knowledge of the existing urban complex. This could be obtained not only by examining existing plans, and we know that Leonardo tried to procure these, but above all by making a direct topographical study, and this too he intended to undertake. A memorandum in the Codex Atlanticus, f. 225 r-b, datable 1489, reveals that he certainly had these intentions at that time:

> ...
> The measurement of Milan and suburbs
> A book that treats of Milan and its churches which is to be had at the last stationer's on the way to Cordusio.
> Measurement of the Corte Vecchia.
> Measurement of the Castello.
>
> ...
> On the measurement of San Lorenzo

and, further on,

> Draw Milan.
> The measurement of the canal, locks and supports, and large boats; and the expense.
> Milan in foundation.

There seems to be no doubt that Leonardo had drawn a map of Milan ("Milan in foundation") on a large scale, or at least of the same dimensions as the map of Imola, but the well-known sketches in the Codex Atlanticus and at Windsor which one is tempted to see as referring to that map were done later, about 1510, and refer to the system of canals. The only sketch that could be ascribed to a map of Milan planned by Leonardo in the early 1490's is on the last page of MS. A, f. 114 v, which carries the date 10 July 1492. This sketch is too summary to allow us to propose an identification, but the layout of the streets is fairly typical of certain districts of Milan such as those near the Ospedale Maggiore or in the area towards Porta Vercellina. Lower down on the same page a detail of the plan of a building is sketched with the hint of staircases and rooms laid out on each side of a central entrance hall. This could be, Firpo seems to suggest, the same public building as shown in plan in MS. B, f. 16 v, which is characterized by a wide entrance loggia with paired columns. The same geometric articulation of rooms, loggias and porticoes is found sketched out in a detail of a plan in the Codex Atlanticus, f. 65 v-b, the same page which contains the outline of the project for the expansion of Milan.

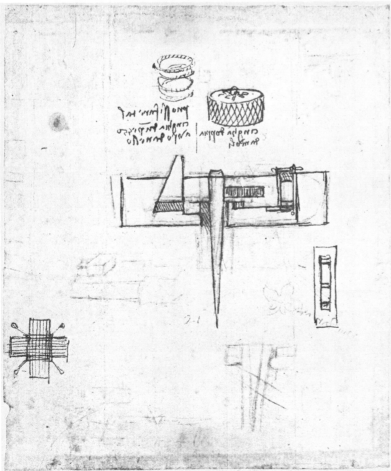

63. Sketch of an urban district and plan of a building. MS. A, f. 114 v.

64. Technological and architectural studies MS. B, f. 16 v.

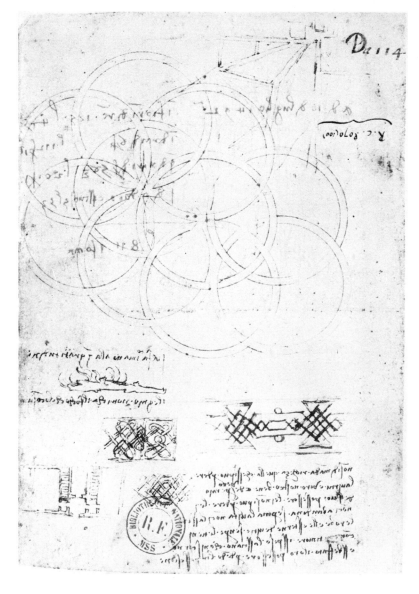

Here, as on the last sheet of MS. A, Leonardo used red chalk and ink. The sketch-plan of Milan and three lines of writing at the top of the page are in red, while the rest of the notes are in ink, and a detail of the plan has also been gone over in ink. On the basis of the handwriting alone one can assign these notes to about 1492-93, but there is more evidence: a preliminary note relating to a paragraph of the text is found in the Codex Forster III, f. 23 v, i.e. in a notebook of 1493.

The schematic plan of Milan consists of two concentric circles marking the boundaries of the peripheral belt. The belt itself appears to be subdivided into sections by the streets which radiate out from the town's main gates.

The detail reinforced in pen can be recognized as the experimental sector, which Leonardo places in the zone between Porta Tosa (now Vittoria) and Porta Romana, a location confirmed by the presence of the monastery of S. Pietro in Gessate, which Leonardo notes half-way along the street coming from Porta Tosa. This shows plots of land, streets and canals disposed symmetrically around the central space of a great piazza flanked by porticoes and at the centre of which Leonardo wrote "spesa" to show where the market was to be. On the right of this sketch of the whole zone is a detail in pen showing a complex of houses which in the "pilot scheme" area occupies a sector next to the city along the Naviglio, as is indicated by the note written there in the space corresponding to the North side: "Have the Navilio drained and the canals cleaned." And it was the Naviglio which was to feed the canals planned by Leonardo in the new suburban zone both for irrigation and for the carrying away of refuse, an aspect to which he attributed great importance in the new urban planning, as we can deduce from the sketch in the middle of the page, with the notation "navilio," and "fish-pond," which illustrates the note: "The bottom level of the waters which are behind the gardens should be as high as the ground level of the gardens, and by means of discharge-pipes they can bring water to the gardens every evening, every time that it rises, raising the joint half a braccio; and the old people are to see to this." And further down: "And nothing is to be thrown into the canals, and every barge is to be made to carry away so much mud from the Navilio and this is afterwards to be thrown on the bank." We find this last phrase again, in more rudimentary form, together with the schematic sketch of the same projected urban zone, in the Codex Forster III, f. 23 v, of 1493: "that nothing is to be thrown into the canals and that these canals go behind the houses."

The other notes on the page of the Codex Atlanticus illustrate the political, social and economic advantages of the project, with arguments which sound like the draft of a memorandum intended for the Duke. The note in red chalk at the top of the page is almost like a slogan, the sort of thing one might expect at the beginning of a letter: "Give me authority whereby without any expense to you it may come to pass that all the lands obey their rulers, who then..." Another slogan-sentence, in pen, appears further down: "The first fame will be eternal together with the inhabitants of the city he has built or enlarged." This makes clear

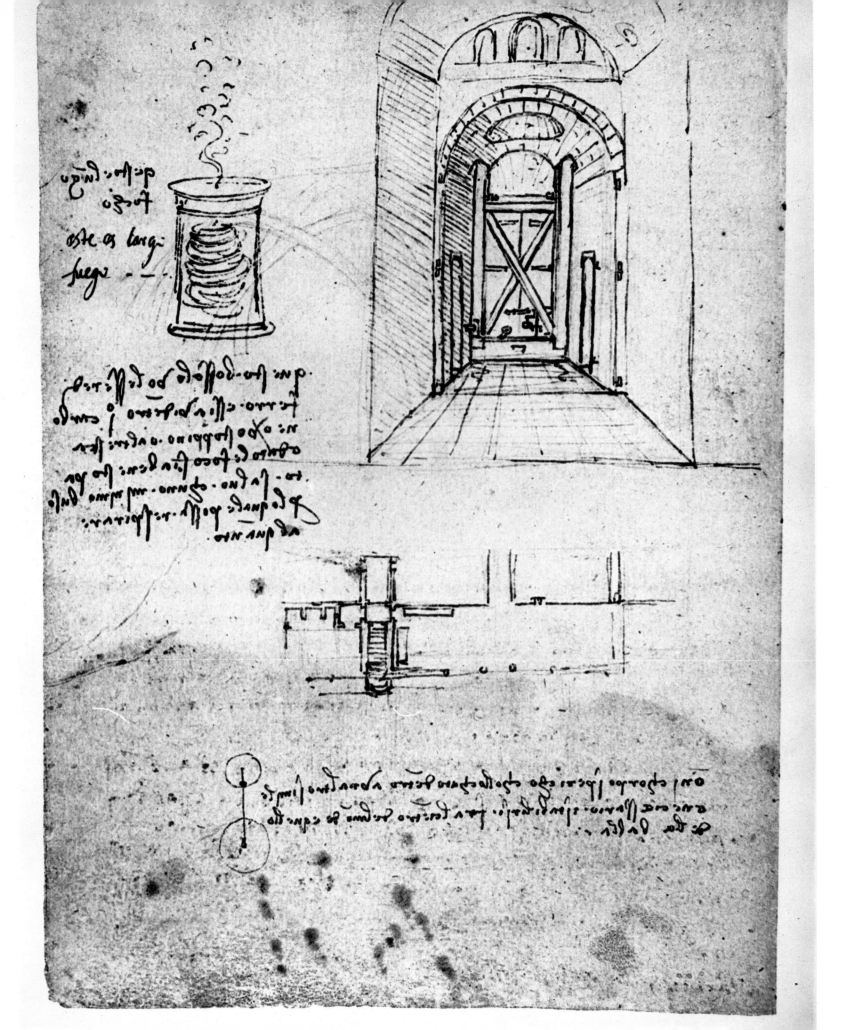

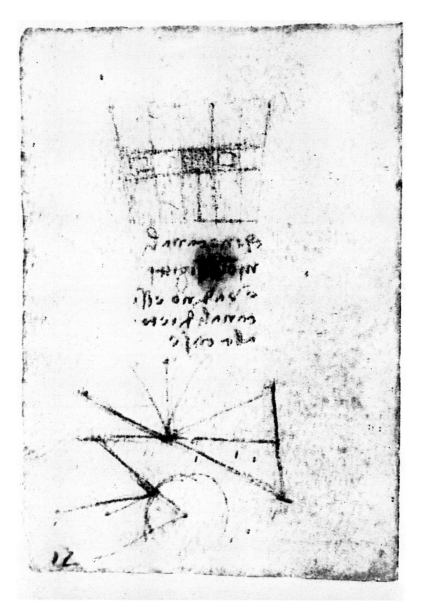

Leonardo's intentions in putting forward the idea that the ruler will gain fame not only as "builder" of the city (the program of town-planning involving the zone within the walls), but also as its "enlarger" (the program of decentralization involving the peripheral zone). The notes which follow, at the foot of the page and in a column on the left, represent perhaps the only document that has come down to us of the political thought of Leonardo: "All people obey and are swayed by their magnates, and these magnates ally themselves with and are constrained by their rulers in two ways, either by blood-relationship or by the tie of property; blood-relationship when their sons, like hostages, are a surety and a pledge against any suspicion of their good faith; the tie of property when you let each of them build one or two houses within your city, from which he may draw some revenue; and (in addition to this) he will draw from ten cities of five thousand houses with thirty thousand inhabitants, and you will disperse so great a concourse of people, who, herding together like goats one upon the back of another filling every part with their stench, sow the seeds of pestilence and death.

And the city will be of a beauty equal to its name, and useful to you for its revenues and the perpetual fame of its growth.

The municipality of Lodi will bear the expense, and keep the revenue which once a year it pays to the Duke.

To the stranger who has a house in Milan it will often befall that in order to be in a more imposing place he will go and live in his own house; and whoever is in a position to build must have some store of wealth, and in this way the poor people will become separated by such settlers, and when these and the assessments will increase the fame of its greatness; and even if he should not wish to reside in Milan he will still remain faithful, in order not to lose the profit of his house at the same time as the capital."

The notebook of 1493, with the note relating to the organization of the canals, contains other references that can be related to the memorandum in the Codex Atlanticus. Above all the notes in red chalk and in normal, not mirror, writing with which Leonardo, or someone who seems to have been helping him, formulated the appropriate mode of address (MS. Forster III, f. 62 v):

> Most Illustrious and Excellent
> To my Most Illustrious Lord Lodovico
>   Duke of Bari
> Leonardo Da Vinci
>   Florentine, etc.
> Leonardo

This would indirectly confirm the suggested date since Lodovico is addressed as the Duke of Bari, not of Milan which was a title that he did not officially assume until 1494.

On folio 15 r of the same notebook, below the chalk diagram of a machine for excavating canals, is a note in ink: "There are here, my

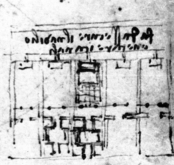

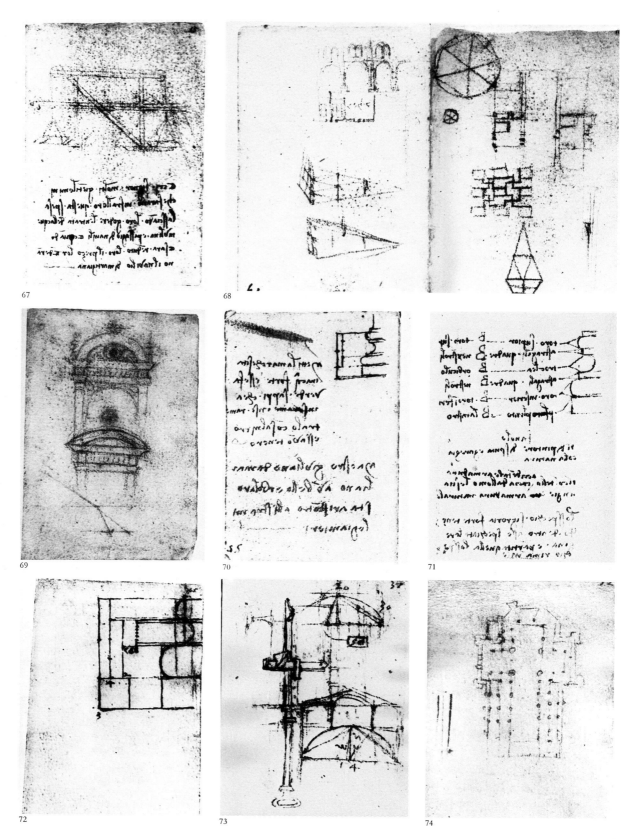

67-74. *Architectural and town-planning notes in the Codex Forster III of 1493.*

67. *f. 15 r, Rough draft of the report on the financing of the programme of building development in Milan.*

68. *ff. 15 v-16 r, Elevation of a Milanese building and diagrams of the urban layout.*

69. *f. 22 r, Sketches of portals or cymae.*

70-72. *ff. 37 v, 44 v, 45 r, analyses of the bases of columns.*

73. *f. 54 v, Diagrams of vaults.*

74. *f. 55 v, Plan of Milan Cathedral.*

67

68

69

70

71

72

73

74

Lord, many gentlemen who will undertake this expense among them, if they are allowed to enjoy the use of admission to the waters, the mills and the passage of vessels, and when it is sold to them the price will be repaid to them by the canal of Martesana."

This, probably, is another reference to the plan of financement. And then, on f. 68 r, again in ink: "May it please you to see a model, which will prove useful to you and to me, also it will be of use to those who will be the cause of your usefulness." This note seems to put forward the idea of the "pilot project," here described by the word "model," a term which in Leonardo's time could very well be applied not just to a topographical drawing but actually to the experimental phase of the proposed town plan.

The Forster Codex III can be studied for other possible mentions of Leonardo's project for the planned expansion of Milan. In particular, the two facing pages 15 v and 16 r should be considered . The first of these, on the left, contains a sketch of the elevation of a building whose façade is reminiscent of Filarete's Ospedale Maggiore, and the other, on the right, lines of streets and canals laid out in a way that closely recalls the sketches in the Codex Atlanticus, with a linking pattern in the shape of a swastika. There are similar drawings on f. 63 r. Then on f. 22 r are the stupendous sketches of portals or cymae which are by now very well known, and other architectural sketches appear on f. 37 v, f. 44 v and f. 45 r (analyses of the bases of columns), f. 54 v (vertical section of a vaulted building, perhaps relating to S. Maria delle Grazie), f. 55 v (plan of Milan Cathedral).

No other traces have remained of Leonardo's grandiose plan for the urban expansion of Milan in 1493. Firpo places it in conceptual relationship to the noted fable (Codex Atlanticus, f. 175 v-a) of the stone which leaves its solitary hill to join its companions in the valley only to find itself upside-down in the mud and filth and tormented by the passage of carts and wayfarers. The fable, which translates Alberti's *Lapides*, and which can be dated precisely to the time of the Milanese project, *c.* 1494, puts the accent on the evils of the city: "It happens thus to those who want to leave the solitary and contemplative life to live in the cities among crowds of people full of infinite ills."

The radical remedy proposed by Leonardo to cope with the "infinite ills" which assailed Milan represents a decisive turning-point in Renaissance town-planning ideas, and what is more, the subsequent growth and development of Milan was realized exactly according to Leonardo's scheme. Firpo writes: "The walls disappear together with the very concept of the fortress-city, of the menacing rock which protects the sovereign and safeguards his dominion: beyond the curtains of stone once built to resist sieges, peaceful urban life finally spreads out, as if foreseeing a more wide-ranging political security and the transition from the domination of petty tyrants to the modern State."

c/ Vigevano

In the first months of 1494 Leonardo was in Vigevano. A note of 2 February of that year, in MS. H, f. 65 v, records a system of stepped irrigation observed at La Sforzesca, the farmstead villa which the Sforza were transforming into a summer residence. The next date, 20 March, in the same notebook (f. 38 r) shows that Leonardo was still at Vigevano, where he observed the method of protecting the vines during the winter by burying them. There are also references, undated, to a "wooden pavilion at Vigevano," apparently a construction which could be taken apart and transported. Leonardo furnishes minute particulars of its construction and measurements, without however mentioning what it might have been intended for.

It has often been noted that Leonardo's stay at Vigevano coincided with Bramante's visit there when the work on the new piazza, decreed by Lodovico Sforza in 1492, was nearing completion. The same can be said of the work being done on the Castello, already underway from 1490 – at least as far as the new stables were concerned, which some have thought may relate to the celebrated "polita stalla" project in Leonardo's MS. B. It is true that Leonardo could have already had some connection with Vigevano at the time of his visit to Pavia in 1490, and it is probable that he was consulted, along with Bramante, over the work on the new piazza. But it is improbable that in 1494 he could have still contributed to any aspect of the architectural and planning problems offered by the urban development program in general and by the ducal palace in particular. At the most his participation could have been in the concluding phase of the pictorial decoration (and the same MS. H which contains the records made at Vigevano also contains estimates of expenditure for wall decorations), but even here decisive proof is lacking. What is indisputable, however, is Leonardo's presence at La Sforzesca, the huge farm building which Lodovico Sforza wanted transformed into the sumptuous suburban villa extolled by Ermolao Barbaro in couplets preserved for us by Bellincioni. In 1499 Lodovico gave it to the convent of S. Maria delle Grazie as a final tribute to the memory of his wife Beatrice.

And so hardly a year after having formulated the grandiose town-plan for Milan, Leonardo was reduced to studying water conduits at Vigevano, and to planning the construction of a wooden pavilion no bigger than a sacristy wardrobe. However, it is worth looking more closely at the details of that construction and trying to put in focus its character and above all, its purpose. The pavilion as central point of interest in park or garden, and therefore as a place of recreation often associated with outdoor bathing, was a very widespread element in Renaissance architecture, especially in northern Italy, but this was certainly not the result of some external influence, such as a northern tradition of the mediaeval courts or the even more elusive one of the Moslem world. Its direct ancestor is the Roman military tent, and the tents used in the field by kings and princes in Leonardo's time were still works of mobile architecture of notable complexity. Indeed, there are studies of such tents in MS. H, near those of the wooden pavilion. This explains, incidentally, where Leonardo got the idea of the para-

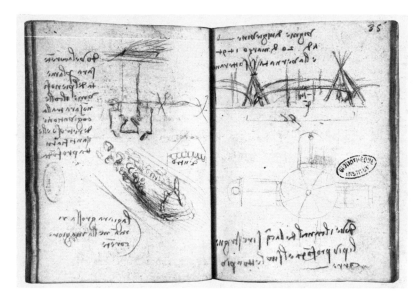

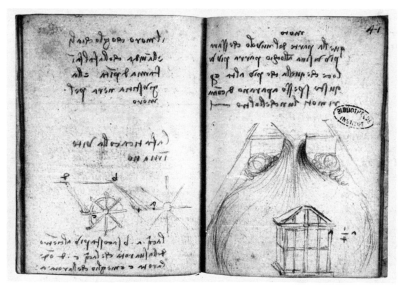

chute. "If a man has a pavilion of reinforced cloth," he wrote on f. 381 v-a of the Codex Atlanticus in about 1487, "that is twelve braccia across and twelve high, he will be able to throw himself from any great height without injuring himself."

Like a military tent, the garden pavilion could be quite complex and assume the aspect of a miniature building. This is the case in the well-known drawings in MS. B, f. 12 r, which show the plan and perspective section of what Leonardo calls a "pavilion of the garden of the Duchess of Milan." There has been a good deal of discussion as to whether this note refers to a construction that was carried out (or only planned) by Leonardo and whether the garden he mentions was that of the Castello in Milan or in Pavia. Yet he was clearly speaking of a structure which already existed in the park of the Castello in Milan, as recorded in 1480 by the Florentine humanist Giovanni Ridolfi in one of his travel commentaries contained in the Codex Magliabechianus, II. IV. 195, f. 223 r: "1480. Travel from Milan to Venice, and from Venice to Florence... and besides this, in Milan, a castle where the court is, beautiful and very strong, placed by the ditches on the land between Porta Vercellina and Porta Comasina, which is half a mile or more in size, with three miles of walled garden surrounding it, within which there is a house they call *la cascina* that has a drawbridge and is enclosed by a wall, where the Duke sometimes goes to dine, and there is a pavilion there on a brick floor with streams all round it and hedges forming a maze."

The reference to the maze makes the proposed identification certain, as Leonardo himself wrote under the plan he had drawn: "foundation of the pavilion which is in the middle of the Duke of Milan's maze."

It is surprising that a building of such dimensions and grandeur existed in Milan before the arrival of Leonardo, and perhaps even before Bramante. The internal space is indicted as 20 braccia, equal to about 12 metres, which is little less than the rotunda of S. Maria degli Angioli by Brunelleschi. It is likely, but not certain, that the construction was of wood. In Leonardo's sketch, which shows it in section, it looks like a wooden model, and Ridolfi would certainly not have limited himself to mentioning the brickwork below if the whole building had been constructed that way. The cupola, however, would probably have been covered with sheet metal tiles. We get the impression of a sacred building, a tempietto or an oratory, of undoubtedly Brunelleschian character. And, interestingly enough, on the facing page Leonardo has drawn in the same pen and ink (the other notes on the two sheets are from different times), the plans of S. Maria degli Angioli and of Santo Spirito. Brunelleschi's presence in Milan about 1430 has recently been ascertained, and it is quite possible that he could have furnished the design for such a construction. A precedent like that would explain the care with which Leonardo devoted himself to a similar project for Vigevano, even if it was a less complex work and of a much more modest size.

We have a precise idea of the wooden building for Vigevano from

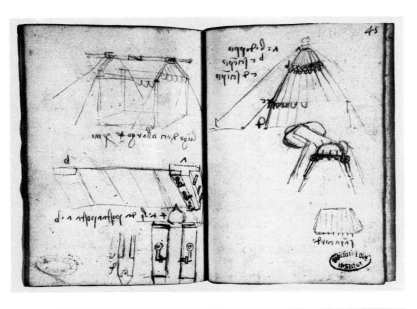

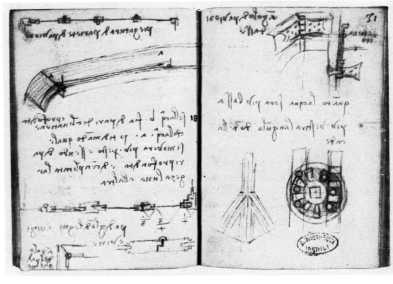

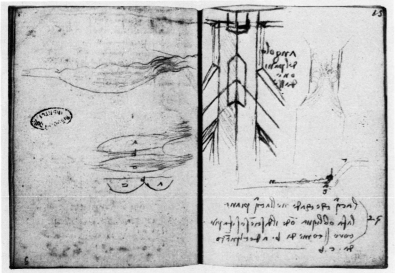

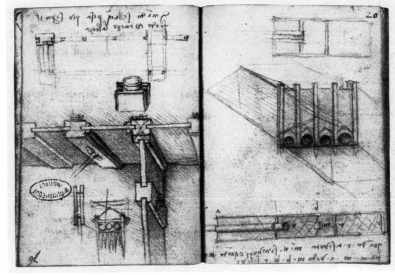

a sketch in MS. H, f. 89 r, which offers a perspective view of the framework of the construction. The external post, on the right, is marked with the letter "a" to which the note beside it makes reference: "a ¼" that is the width of the post is a quarter of a braccio, a measurement which is found again in other notes relating to the same construction, including those on the two pages of the Codex Atlanticus. In the plan diagram in MS. H, f. 78 v, which shows one side of the pavilion with panels inserted between the posts, the measurements of the corner post are indicated (¼), as are those of the span of the panel (¾) and of the adjacent half-post (⅛). The same measurements are met again in the drawing in the Codex Atlanticus, f. 283 r-b (which, like the others in the same codex, f. 34 v-b and f. 283 v-c, dates from the same time, 1494), where one of the sections is shown as a door: "a b from head to foot may be the doorway, 4 ⅓ braccia high." Keeping in mind the half-post which on each side acts as a frame to the door, we obtain an opening of one braccio (¾ + ⅛ + ⅛), i.e. about 60 centimetres. The whole side can therefore be calculated at 4 ½ braccia, equal to about 2.70 m; and since we have seen that the door is 4 ⅓ braccia high, we can deduce that the building was envisioned as a cube surmounted by a tent-like roof. We have, therefore, a construction of small dimensions whose main feature was that it could be dismantled into many small pieces, as is suggested by the removable pins of the hinges: "little bolts for detaching and connecting" (Codex Atlanticus, f. 283 v-c).

In the drawing on f. 34 v-b of the Codex Atlanticus the two central panels are divided into halves and the upper part can be opened like a window, as Leonardo himself points out. On the margin is the statement "all the iron-work goes inside" so from the outside the building really could assume the appearance of a piece of furniture, as it does in fact appear in a view of the whole thing on f. 283 v-c of the Codex Atlanticus.

What purpose could such a building serve? As a hunting pavilion or cover for bathing it is too small. The bath in the garden of the Castello at Pavia consisted of a pavilion on a square plan like this, but of a good 18 paces each side. Here, however, there is just the space necessary to contain a bed, a little table and one or two chairs. Easily transportable from one place to another, it could even have been erected inside a building, set up like a marionette theatre within a large room. A detail in Codex Atlanticus, f. 34 v-b, shows a hinge placed on the corner of a wall – and the fact that it is a wall is made plain not only by Leonardo himself who names it as such (*muro*) but also by the metallic piece projecting from the hinge which is only needed when fixing some element solidly to a wall structure, as we can see in the drawings of door hinges in Madrid MS. I, f. 66 v and f. 99 v.

It seems probable therefore that the wooden building was to be hinged to the corner of a house or wall in such a way that its position could be changed, as would be necessary for instance if it were to pivot to follow the course of the sun. It seems, in fact, that Leonardo took pains to avoid any changes in the way that the light was brought to the interior:

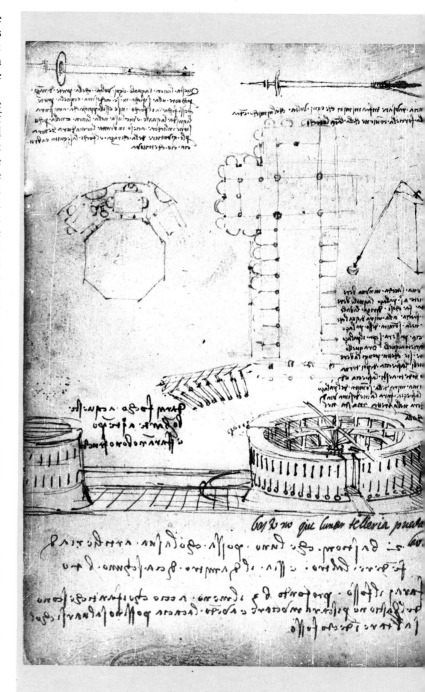

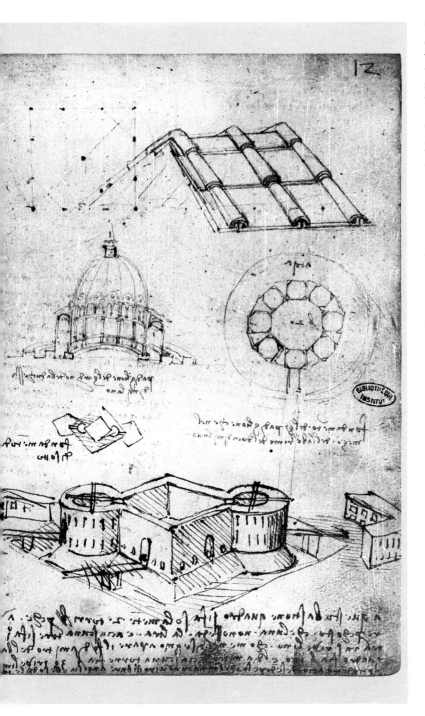

"every axle must be hidden within the surface of the wood as far as the centre of the pole; and this rule will mean that on opening the doors and windows they will not let in any gleam of light." Finally, on f. 283 r-b of the Codex Atlanticus we read the note: "boards for the bottom of the studio" written beside a diagram that looks like a metallic structure of the same type as that which in Madrid MS. I, f. 96 r, is indicated as "manner of releasing or of blocking a pressure." On the same sheet there is also a detail of a "double window" that can be understood as a device for regulating the intensity of light.

We might wonder, therefore, if these drawings of a pavilion for Vigevano, by now so well known, could not represent the project for a mobile studio, planned by Leonardo in the expectation of moving from one centre to another of the duchy. On the same sheet on which Leonardo notes the output of a "mill at Vigevano" (MS. H, f. 94 r-v) we find notes and memoranda relating to his work as a painter: "Ferando" is mentioned, the Spanish painter who was to assist him when he worked on the *Battle of Anghiari*, and also "Iacopo Andrea," probably the Ferrarese architect whom we will find with him at S. Maria delle Grazie; and finally the note: "the duke's panel," which would indicate a commission Leonardo was attending to in 1494 and about which nothing is known. This, however, could be a further indication that he went to Vigevano primarily as a painter and that, as such, he thought of building himself a portable studio. This is of course only a hypothesis which, however, seems worthy of consideration since we lack any more satisfactory interpretation of the little movable building.

d/ Patrician Residences

In Milan, the last decade of the fifteenth century was characterized by a fervour of building activity, which Lodovico Sforza enthusiastically supervised in person, discussing projects with his architects and engineers approving plans, and visiting the sites where building was in progress. It is probable that his desire to renew the city was inspired by the example of Duke Federigo da Montefeltro, who had turned his residence at Urbino into a city-palace. One could say that Lodovico, working on a much vaster territorial scale, wanted to transform Milan into a palace-city; and indeed something similar was taking place during the same years at Ferrara, with the plan of urban renewal that Ercole d'Este had entrusted to Biagio Rossetti, while the Pallavicino had already created a model Vitruvian town at Cortemaggiore in 1480. "Messer Attaviano Pallavisino pel suo Vitruvio," we read in a later note by Leonardo.

Lodovico Sforza's program was dominated by unifying principles. The directions he issued in 1493 which decreed the demolition of the porticoes (the characteristic *coperti* which had been there since the Middle Ages), the loggias and *baldresche* fronting the city streets, were not only intended to give the houses some breathing-space and to thin out the traffic, but were also aimed at reshaping the façades of the buildings to the greater dignity of the city. It was a cause for reproof, for

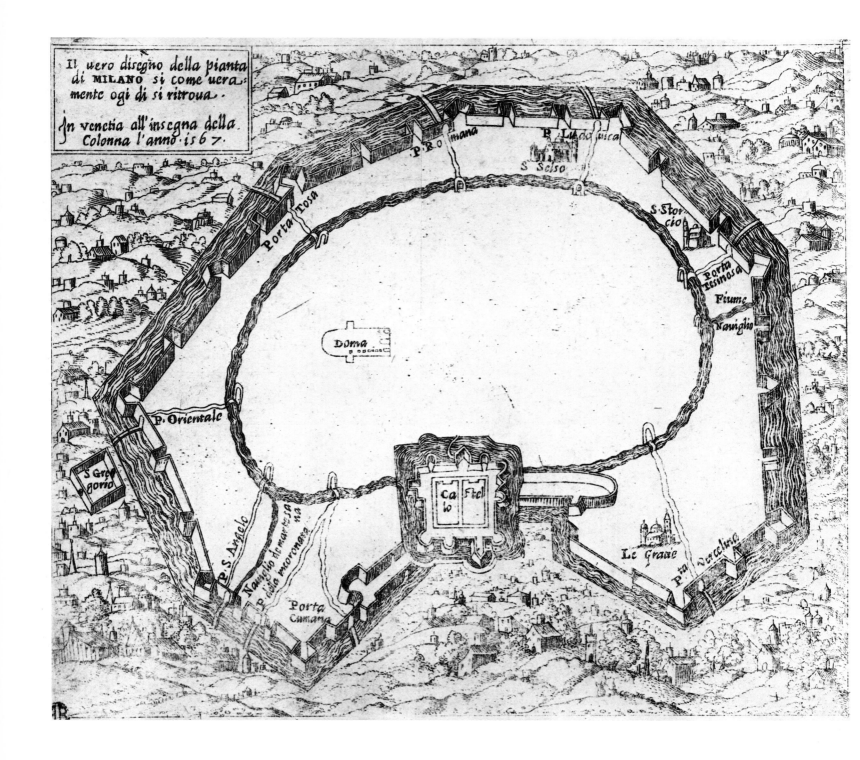

83, 84. *Studies for the wooden pavilion at*
Vigevano. Codex Atlanticus, ff. 283 v-c,
283 r-b.

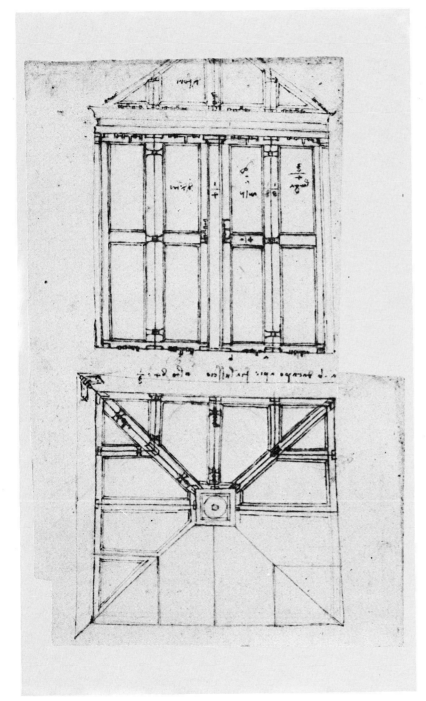

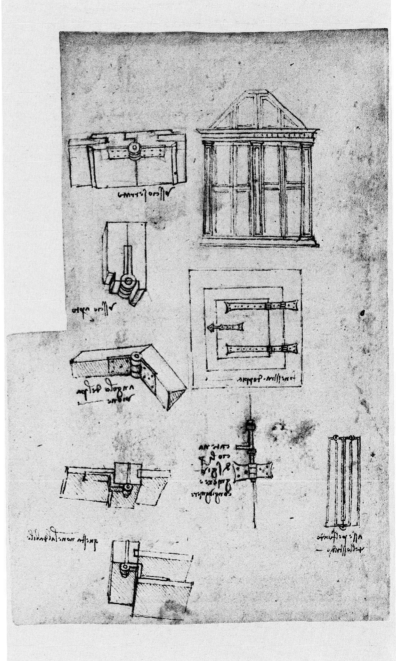

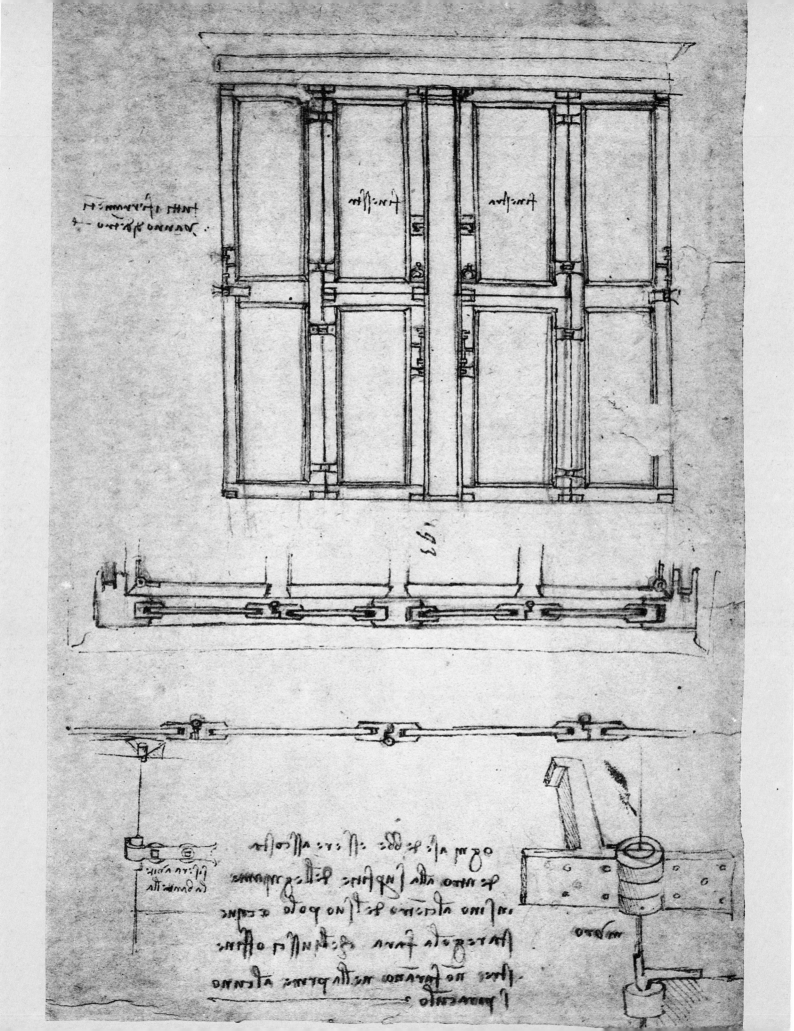

example, that "in the friezes... the houses are not equal, one being tall and another low, and it is our intention that the eaves should be level." Il Moro himself, addressing the Collector of excise taxes in 1495, recorded how he had already striven for two years "ut civitas hec nostra tota moeniorum errectione illustretur et ad esplendorem reducatur." A very detailed report on the building renewal undertaken by Il Moro is found in the *Storia di Milano* by Bernardino Arluno, published in Basel in 1530, the original manuscript of which is in the Ambrosiana. There we find a reference to the way the buildings were being arranged and embellished, even to the monochrome decorations on the façades: "Aedificiis admodum delectatus peropacam urbem impeditamque porticibus ac pro tectis inaequalem, dimotis umbraculis, ad unumque rigorem perductis omnibus, tum superiecto fuco pigmentatis insignius illustravit."

This program, beginning in 1493, at the time of Leonardo's town-plan, was carried forward with sustained intensity and with the active participation of the citizens, who were spurred to voluntary efforts of "sumptuous building" by favourable provisions for expropriation. Old buildings were therefore remodeled and with them the urban fabric of which they formed a part and by which they were often suffocated. Often the construction of new buildings was planned in advance through a radical work of demolition that drastically modified neighbourhoods or districts that had still maintained a mediaeval character. We need only mention the celebrated example of Tommaso Marini, who prepared the setting for the palace built by Alessi sixty years later by marking out its boundaries within a thickly populated area, and by proposing the opening of a monumental arterial road to connect his planned palace with the entrance to the piazza in front of the Cathedral. And with the development of the residential area around the Castello and outside Porta Vercellina the prominent citizens who held high positions in the Sforza court competed in the fervour of building activity which was transforming the appearance of the city. Perhaps this is the origin of those models of urban perspectives which bear Bramante's name and which are associated with the patronage of Cardinal Ascanio Sforza, Lodovico il Moro's brother, who built Pavia Cathedral, the new cloisters of Sant'Ambrogio and many other buildings in Lombardy. The vision of a renewed city inspired the court poet Baldassare Taccone, spokesman of civic pride:

> See how Milan rises beautiful,
> And renews her worn clothes:
> Look what a piazza the Castello has,
> How delightful and pleasing to see it today;
> Look at this house and that ornamented,
> Everything strives for perfection.

The town-planning adventure started with modifications to two nerve points: the Cathedral square and the rebuilding of the church of S.

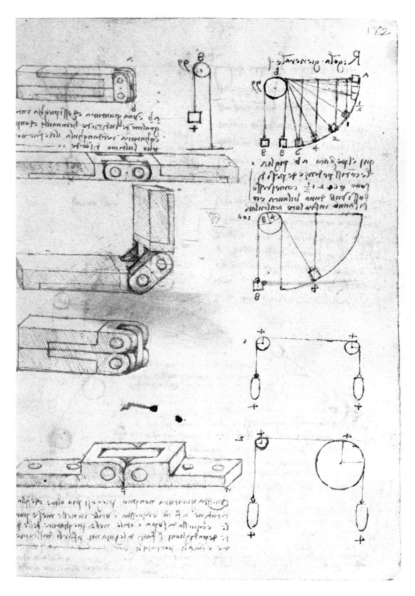

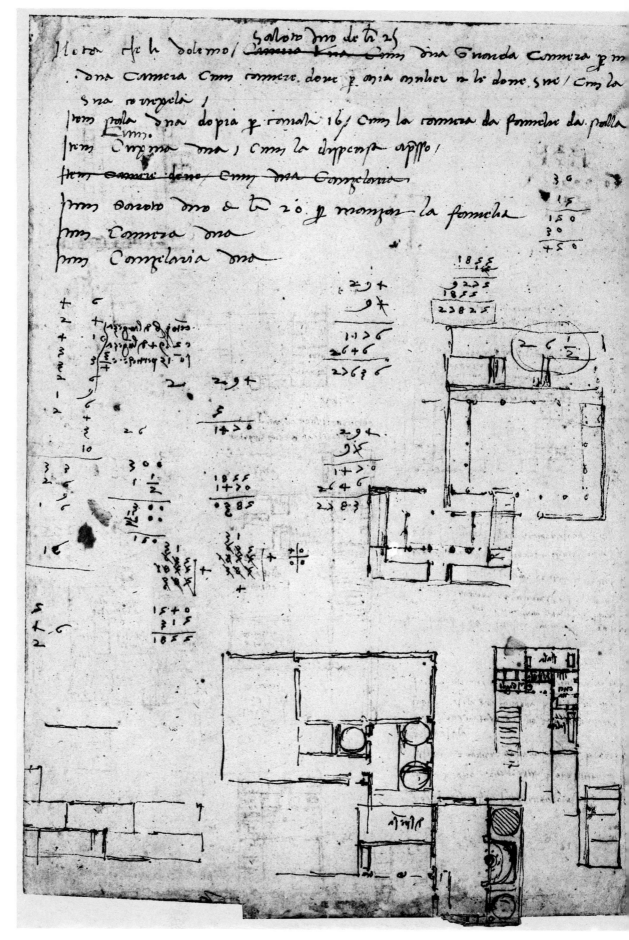

87, 88. *Casa Guiscardi. An example of an architectural project by Leonardo, Codex Atlanticus, f. 158 r-a, v-a, c. 1497. An unknown patron (Mariolo de' Guiscardi?) writes and specifies how he wants his house to be built, and Leonardo uses the same sheet to work out the plans according to the orders received. We can therefore follow the development of his ideas, not only through the sketches of ground-plans in which he was studying the layout of the rooms requested, considering them individually as well as in their relationship to each other, but also, even more, through his comments (possibly a rough draft of a report to be presented to the patron). These notes can be read in their own right as a theoretical essay on the subject of domestic architecture. Leonardo spends some time over the planning of the owner's quarters and those of his servants, which occupy the left wing of the palace close to the domestic offices (kitchen, larder, wood store, etc.). The right wing, shown in a cursory sketch in the centre of the sheet (verso), seems to be laid out symmetrically in the same way, probably for the "wife" and her servants, plus stables for sixteen horses and the groom's lodgings. The plan on the left (third from the top) shows the rooms identified by letters corresponding with those in the list beside it: "a Sitting-room of the Master, d bedroom, b kitchen, c larder, n Guard room, o Servants' hall." Immediately above the plan we read: "The servants' hall beyond the kitchen, so that the Master does not hear their noise, and that the kitchen is convenient to them so that the pewter needing to be washed should not be seen being carried through the house." The larger plan, in the centre (fourth from the top) is preceded by the note: "The famiglia (that is, the servants) are not to use in the kitchen the wood that is stored nearby." The rooms are labelled from top to bottom as follows: "Drawing-room; larder; kitchen; scullery;*

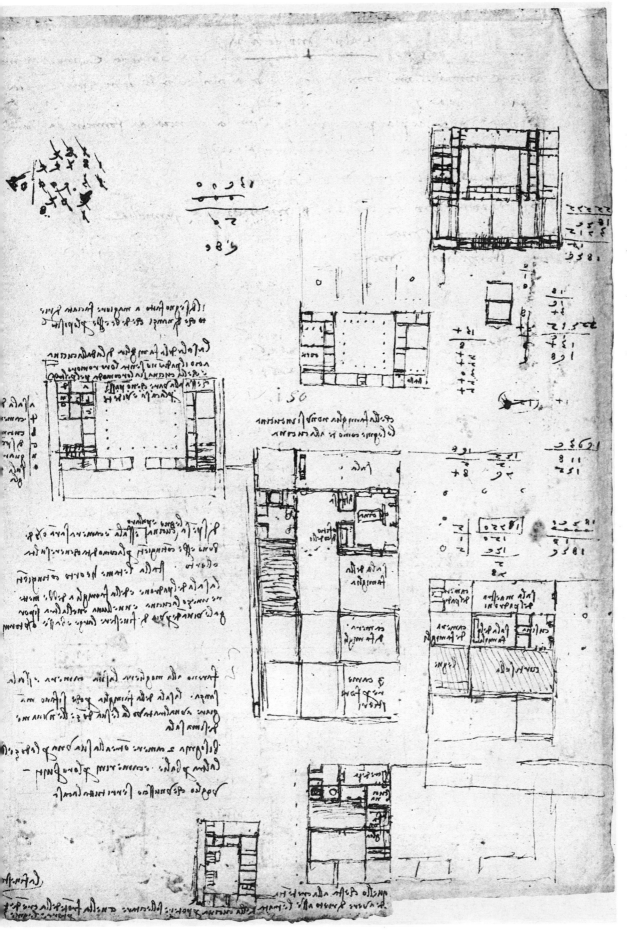

servants' hall; servants' bedroom; 3 bedrooms for visitors." To the left we read the following notes: "Larder, wood store, and hen-coop and hall and bedroom will, or should be, close together for the sake of convenience, and the orchard, stable, manure-heap and kitchen-garden close to each other and the kitchen must be put in between the sitting-room of the Master and that of the servants and in both of these the food may be served by means of low, wide windows or turnstiles," and then after a short gap, "we will make for the wife her bedroom and sitting-room, without the hall for the servants because her attendants will take their meals at another table in the same hall; two bedrooms will be necessary besides hers, one for the attendants, the other for nurses and maids to serve them." And finally: "I want one door to lock the whole house."

The other inscriptions are as follows: (plan on the right, third from the bottom) "Main room of the master; master's bedroom; kitchen; servants' hall; servants bedroom; small courtyard; wood store."
(Plan below this) "pantry; kitchen; servants."
Finally, at the bottom of the sheet: "Whoever works in the pantry must have the entrance to the kitchen behind him so as to be able to be quick, and the front of the pantry the kitchen window for taking wood."
The reference to the entrance that "locks the whole house" can be related to a note in MS. B, f. 12 v, which accompanies the perspective view of a noble apartment in vertical section: "if you keep servants in the house, arrange their living quarters in such a way that at night neither they nor the strangers whom you may lodge may be masters of the door of the house, and that they cannot enter the quarters where you live and sleep; lock the door m and the whole house is locked."

Tecla, decreed on 10 August 1491 – and the opening up of the vast square in front of the castle, decreed on 22 August 1492, with a plan that involved expropriations and demolitions. And it was right at the edge of the area thus defined that the wealthy courtiers were encouraged to construct or rebuild their splendid mansions. Among these was the house that the Countess of Melzo had received as a gift from Galeazzo Maria Sforza in 1475, and the one belonging to Marchesino Stanga, ducal secretary, who in 1493 was able to incorporate the house given him by the duke into a new construction, making of it a vast suite of rooms with stables for twenty horses. This whole complex, because of its proximity to the castle, could fulfill various functions, housing ambassadors or welcoming great numbers of people when ceremonies and performances were organized in the piazza.

Marchesino Stanga's property extended in the direction of Porta Vercellina and adjoined the property belonging to another prominent figure in the Sforza government, Galeazzo da Sanseverino, Count of Caiazzo, Captain of the Sforza army and son-in-law of Lodovico Sforza. He was famous not only for his horses, which he kept in sumptuous stables and which Leonardo himself admired, but also as a patron of the arts. It was he, for example, who welcomed Luca Pacioli into his home when he moved from Venice to Milan as a teacher of mathematics in 1496. The original manuscript of the *Divina Proportione* in the Ambrosiana is dedicated to him, and Pacioli made for him a series of geometrical bodies, the same ones that Leonardo represented in perspective in the illustrations he prepared for that book. Pacioli himself numbered Sanseverino among the illustrious personages and scholars who in 1498 attended his lessons on Vitruvian principles as applied to problems relating to the Cathedral of Milan. The great palace and the stables were devastated in 1499 at the entrance of the French. Ruins of the stables could still be seen in Vasari's time, and he recorded them in describing the paintings of Bramantino: "And outside Porta Vercellina, near the castle, he painted certain stables now in ruins, and some servants who were currying the horses; among whom there was one so lively and well painted that another horse, thinking he was real, aimed a good number of kicks at him" (II. 493).

There is no documentary proof for the theory often put forward that Leonardo was the architect of Galeazzo's stables; but from the well-known notes relating to the misdeeds of Salai we learn that on 26 January 1491 Leonardo was in the middle of organizing a costume entertainment in that gentleman's house. Later Leonardo's connections with the owners of the patrician residences built near the castle became even closer. Il Moro, generous in his donations in support of his closest and most faithful followers (in 1495 he had given Galeazzo's brother, Antonio Maria Sanseverino, the house which had been Piero de' Medici's, the famous *Banco dei Medici*, evicting the Florentine Ambassador to do so) finally remembered Leonardo. In 1498, a year after the *Last Supper* was completed, he gave him, with a very elaborate and solemn notarial act, sixteen pertiche of land, cultivated as a vineyard in

the desirable residential area outside Porta Vercellina, near S. Maria delle Grazie where the prestigious dwellings of the Atellani, of Mariolo de' Guiscardi, Bergonzo Botta and Bartolomeo Calchi had already been built. Numerous notes of Leonardo's datable precisely to that time show that he was busy with architectural projects which he himself indicates were related to some of those properties.

The notes I refer to are in MS. I, datable from 1497 to 1499; Calvi has already illustrated them and related them to a sheet in the Codex Atlanticus, f. 158 r-a, v-a, on which an unknown person told Leonardo how his house should be constructed:

"Note that we want there (*one bedroom with*) ∧ one drawing-room of 24 braccia ∧∨ a Guard Room* for me.
One bedroom with two bedrooms for my wife and her ladies, with her small courtyard.
Item a double stable for 16 horses, with the bedroom of the stable servants.
Item a kitchen, with the pantry nearby.
(*Item two bedrooms with a chancellory*)
Item one dining-hall of 20 braccia for the servants.
Item one bedroom.
Item a chancellory."

The rest of the sheet is filled with calculations, plans and notes through which Leonardo developed the architectural project according to the instructions he had received. For a detailed examination of this document and those related to it the reader is referred to a chapter in my book on the Palace of Romorantin, where I present the various reasons for an identification of the unknown patron as Mariolo de' Guiscardi, Lodovico il Moro's chamberlain, whose property was very near Leonardo's vineyard. In 1499 Mariolo's palace, not yet finished, fell to the same fate as so many other residences in the area, and in fact the report that Corio offers of the devastation perpetrated by the French troops refers specifically to Mariolo's house as the one which was "newly built and not yet roofed." And the property, by then abandoned in ruins, was recorded again in 1540 in a document of the sale of land "super quibus alias aderat pallatium seu domus que nunc sunt directe, salvis muris circumdantibus dicta bona."

Leonardo's notes on the Codex Atlanticus sheet represent an interesting aspect of architectural planning. They could even be read as a sketch of a treatise on domestic architecture, in which are listed propositions to be submitted to the patron together with the proposed solution. (These are transcribed in the caption to the reproduction of the sheet.) These notes go back to an early project which has not come down to us, in

---

* Calvi reads "*Grande* camera," but what is written is "*Guarda* camera" (vestibule or reception), and Leonardo writes this too at the letter "n" of the plan upper left on the reverse of the sheet.

which Leonardo had exchanged the dimensions of the front façade with those of the rear: "the drawing has made the rear façade larger than the front, which must be reversed."

We can gain quite a reliable idea of the dimensions of the building from the plan sketches themselves. The space on the plan marked by the letter "o," on the upper left of the reverse of the sheet, is indicated as "hall of the *famiglia*" (that is, of the servants), which the patron himself had said should be of 20 braccia, about 12 metres. From this we can work out, in proportion, an extent of about 200 braccia for the front (*c.* 120 metres) and 120 braccia for the side (*c.* 72 metres), without counting the area of the park or garden hinted at in one of the plans. We are dealing therefore with a building of considerable dimensions.

A note on the recto of the sheet informs us that "one hundred braccia of width and 294 of length are 15 pertiche and ¾," but there is no way of ascertaining if Leonardo is speaking here of the measurements of the lot to be built on, which would be almost identical to that of his own property (16 pertiche). Similar measurements recur in MS. I, for example on f. 50 v: "If I take 95 braccia of width and 294 of length I have 15 pertiche. If I take 100 braccia of width and 294 of length I have ¾ of a pertica more than I need, which remains behind." The shape of the lot Leonardo repeatedly refers to does not seem to allow for the building of a structure which in the plans appears to be wider than it is long; besides we know that the property acquired by Mariolo de' Guiscardi included several houses which had to be demolished to make room for the new palace, and it could be that Leonardo took note of other plots of land which Mariolo intended to acquire. Another sheet in the Codex Atlanticus, f. 393 r-a, belonging to the same series of studies, contains the notation "90 in front and 330 long" with two rather summary plans which seem to show a way of arranging a park or garden along the sides of an avenue or a straight water-course. The same type of plan is found on f. 377 v-a of the same codex, which also contains a note relating to a building project: "the boundary is 18 braccia of empty space or 19 overall. The entrance 6 braccia and the study 11½. A hall 18 braccia long and 12 wide and 8 high. And the height of the study 7½ braccia. The hall and bedrooms, a granary 4 braccia high." And finally, in one corner of the sheet is a little topographical sketch of the whole area outside Porta Vercellina with the monastic complex of S. Maria delle Grazie in the centre. The material relating to the Guiscardi project is reduced to a few sketches, which are subject to being interpreted in various ways and often only identifiable as such on the basis of circumstantial evidence. The final plans are unfortunately lost, as are the topographical reliefs which Leonardo would certainly have made to present the project in its appropriate urban context, and there are no studies of the elevation of the building. It is therefore only as a working hypothesis that one can consider other notes in the same MS. I, which contains the direct references to the problem in question. The plan of a palace drawn in red chalk on f. 18 v recalls those on f. 158 of the Codex Atlanticus, but the dimensions indicated in ink on the four sides suggest that it may be a pre-existing building and not so regular as Leonardo makes it appear in the drawing: the façade is 75 braccia, the rear 55, the right side 136 and ⅓ and the left 133 and ⅓. We have not met any of these measurements among the notes so far considered, with the exception of the "75," which could relate to the note on f. 118 v of MS. I: "the street of Messer Mariolo is 13 and ¼ braccia. The house of Vangelista is 75 braccia." Here is a reference to another building – the house of Vangelista – of which we know nothing.

Thus we do not seem to be able to directly connect even the well-known sketch on f. 56 r of MS. I, the plan and elevation of a vast suburban villa, with the Guiscardi project. The central loggia, accentuated by the Serlian motif which underlines the presence of a longitudinal axis, vaguely anticipates the façade of the courtyard of the Palazzo del Te at Mantua, but here the building has two storeys and a tower at the center which gives it a monumental character. It seems to blend Tuscan and Lombard elements, if not styles – Brunelleschian and Bramantesque, in a type of architecture that perhaps was realized in Milan but of which no example has remained to take its stand stylistically, chronologically or even topographically beside the cloisters of Sant'Ambrogio and the apse of S. Maria delle Grazie.

In truth, none of the patrician dwellings which were features of the Sforza programme of urban renewal has come down to us intact. The fragments of palace façades transferred into the first courtyard of the Castello give us an approximate image of a type of architecture still intimately associated with the local building tradition. There seems nothing in it that could be associated with the style of the cloisters of Sant'Ambrogio, which derived from Urbino, or with the sense of monumentality already present in Bramante's urban perspectives of about 1495 and in Leonardo's sketches of that time (for example MS. I, f. 56 v and f. 52 v), in which columns and pilasters lend plasticity to the walls. I believe that the marvellous detail of a palace façade with double orders, pilaster strips adorned with figures, very elegant cornices and timpani ornamented with statues, in a Windsor drawing (RL 12579 v) which is assigned to the same time as the studies for the Villa Melzi at Vaprio in 1513, preserves for us an image of the type of patrician residence which was already being built in Milan in the last years of the fifteenth century.

The loss of these buildings cannot be attributed exclusively to the disaster of 1499; we need only recall that the Casa Panigarola was still in existence in 1900, when Bramante's frescoes were detached and transferred to the Brera Gallery, and that in 1920 Leonardo's vineyard was to all intents and purposes still intact. Another celebrated building, the Palazzo Carmagnola, also known as *Broletto Nuovissimo*, underwent drastic modifications only at the end of the last century. Fragments of that part of the courtyard which was demolished to widen the Via del Broletto were transferred to the Castello Sforzesco together with those of other houses in the same street, but no record was kept of their original locations.

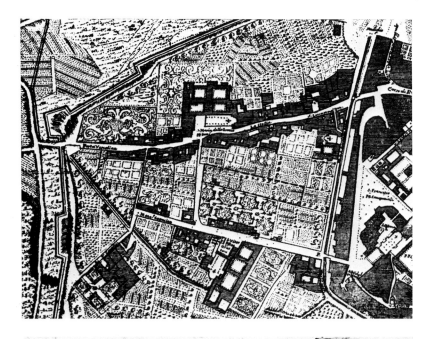

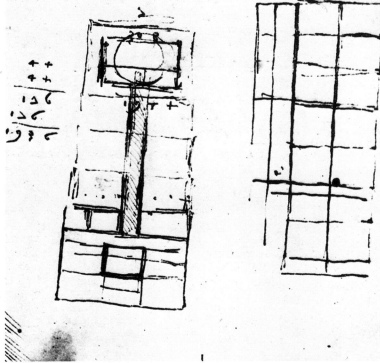

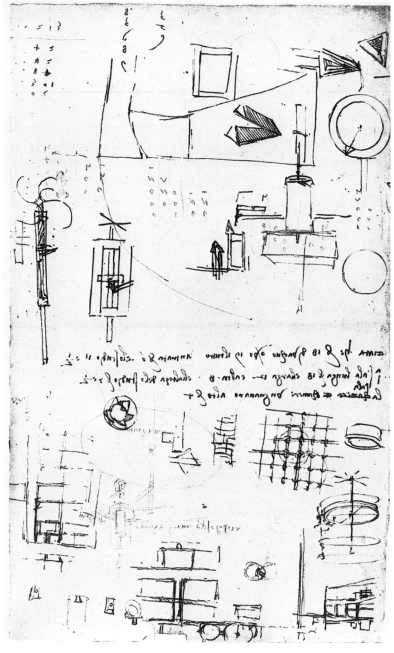

93. *Plan of a palazzo, c. 1497-98. MS. I,*
f. 18 v.

94-96. *Studies of a suburban villa,*
c. 1497-98. MS. I, ff. 56 r, 56 v, detail,
and 52 v, detail.

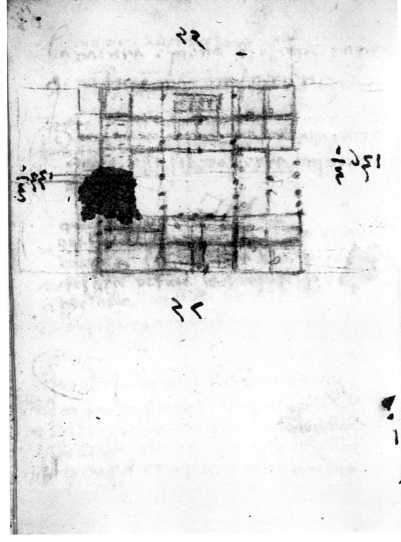

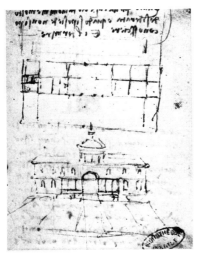

In a late sheet of the Codex Atlanticus, f. 371 r-a, datable to just before his move to Rome in 1513, Leonardo reminds himself to "go in *istrada solata*" which is the ancient name for Via Broletto. The district, where Michelozzo's Banco dei Medici also stood, must have been well known to Leonardo even before 1500. It seems, for example, that he had reason to go to the nearby convent of S. Maria del Carmine, for about 1498 he recorded a mechanism for window curtains there, perhaps of his own invention: "How the Carmine device works" we read in Madrid, MS. I, f. 133 r.

For a comparison such as Baroni had made between a drawing by Leonardo in Codex Atlanticus, f. 266 v (which is datable to the time of the *Last Supper, c.* 1495) and a capital from a house at No. 20 Via Broletto, it would be useful to know something more about the context to which the capital belonged. I think an even more telling comparison can be made between the same drawing and a capital from Palazzo Carmagnola in the same district, a palace that Leonardo had particular reason to visit even before the French confiscated it to lodge count Louis de Ligny there, with whom we know that Leonardo was in touch. A plan in the Bianconi collection shows us the palace before the changes made in the last century, a rectangular complex constituting two main parts, each one placed around a square courtyard, and thus with two entrances: one from Via S. Nazaro, today Via Rovello, which is the original entrance, and the other in Via Solata, which belongs to the part built later. We know, in fact, that the original part of the building, Carmagnola's part, which faces S. Nazaro, goes back to the beginning of the fifteenth century while the rest was still a garden. It was inherited in this form by the Dal Verme and when that family died out in 1485 with the death of Count Pietro, Lodovico Sforza took it over, confiscating it as the entitlement of the sovereign. The Dal Verme residence, dominated by towers and by their annexes, was on the Via Solata side and faced onto a courtyard garden.

This layout was profoundly altered a little later by the decision of Lodovico Sforza in 1491 to enlarge the palace and turn it into a sumptuous patrician dwelling for his mistress Cecilia Gallerani. On 7 April of that year, the Duke of Ferrara's orator recorded a visit he made with Lodovico to look round the palace: "the third day of Easter he took me with him to the house that used to belong to Count Pietro Dal Verme, where he had several engineers come in order to reconstruct it and remake it for Cecilia, his woman..."

It would not be surprising if Leonardo had been included among the "several engineers," or that in any case he might have been called for consultation during the course of the work which went on until at least 1497, when Sanuto mentioned that palace as occupied by Cecilia Gallerani and "not yet completely finished." Cecilia herself, if not Lodovico, would have wanted the advice of Leonardo, "of the master who in truth," as she wrote in 1498 to Isabella d'Este, "I believe has no equal." At that time – the last decade of the fifteenth century – Leonardo was recognized not only as an illustrious painter, just as

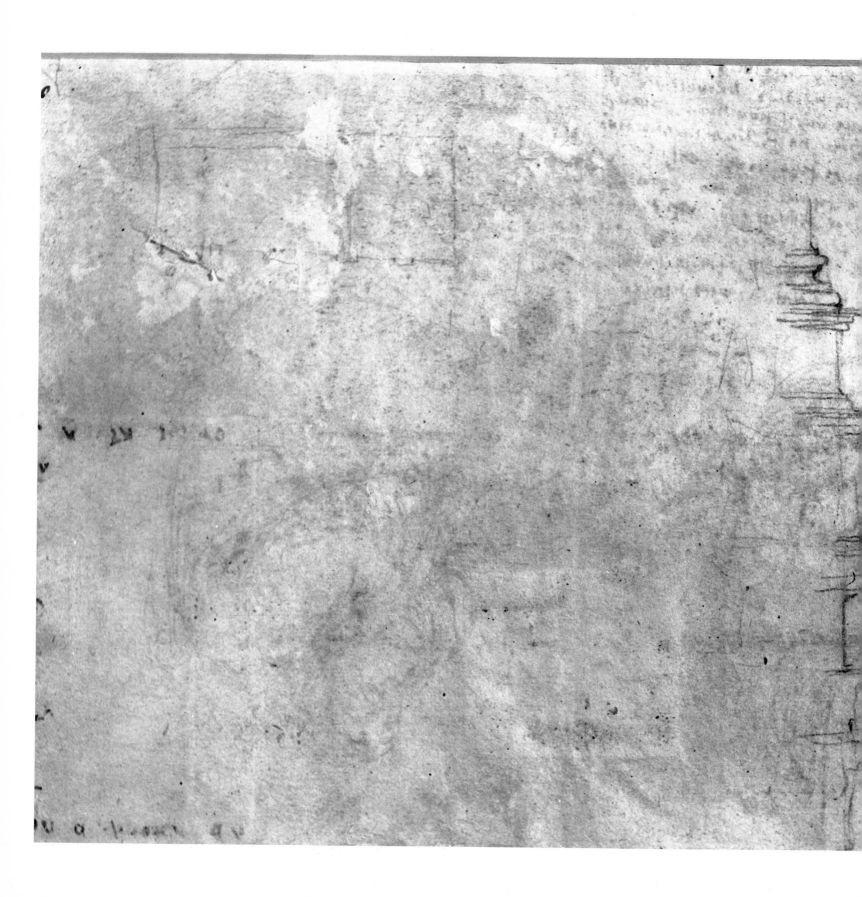

97. *Studies of a palace façade*, c. 1513.
Windsor, RL 12579 v.

98. *Façade of a fifteenth-century house.*
Milan, Courtyard of the Castello Sforzesco.

99. *Drawing of a capital*, c. 1495. *Codex Atlanticus, f. 266 v-a, detail.*
100. *Capital from 20 Via Broletto, Milan.*

101. *Plan of the Palazzo Carmagnola. Milan, Biblioteca Trivulziana, Bianconi Collection.*

102. *1925 photograph of the fifteenth-century portico of the Villa Gualtieri which the Gonzaga absorbed into their Villa Simonetta.*

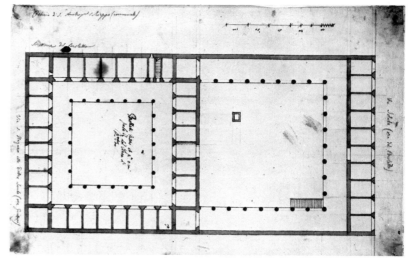

famous for his portrait of Cecilia, celebrated by Bellincioni in 1493, as for the *Last Supper*, completed about 1497; but also as an architect. Sabba da Castiglione wrote, referring to those very years, "whenever he should have attended to his painting, at which without doubt he was to become a new Apelles, he devoted himself completely to geometry, architecture and anatomy."

Unfortunately there is no hint in Leonardo's manuscripts to suggest his possible participation in the adaptation and decoration of Cecilia Gallerani's house. The design of the capital mentioned above is not sufficient proof of such a participation. A contract exists, dated 3 November 1495, which names the masters to whom the work was entrusted: Antonio de Bodis, Pietro de Castoldi and Battista Alberti. Alberti issued a deposition in 1506 in which he refers to the time when he was working on the new sacristy of S. Maria delle Grazie, around 1498-99, stating that he had had connections with Leonardo and with the architect Andrea da Ferrara, whom Pacioli called a brotherly friend of Leonardo's. It is not surprising, therefore, that the capitals in the Gallerani house should recall those of the same period used in the new sacristy of S. Maria delle Grazie. It has also been noted that similar capitals are found in the four arches of the southern portico in the Villa Simonetta, that is in the original late fifteenth-century nucleus of the Villa Gualtiera, the suburban home of Gualtiero Bascapè, another prominent personage of the Sforza court, who was also in touch with Leonardo.

A document concerning Cecilia Gallerani's house, originally belonging to the Administration of Milan Cathedral, and now known only through a copy published by Amoretti in 1804, mentions a quantity of marble which was placed at the disposal of the ducal engineer Giovanni de Busti in 1493, "pro ponendo in opere in domo domine Cecillie Pergamine." Another document, from the same source and also now lost, tells us that Cristoforo Solari, called Il Gobbo, was unable to take on further commissions because the duke had employed him to work on the palace of Cecilia Gallerani. Here is another artist who has connections with Leonardo, and who later will work on the Sforza tomb in S. Maria delle Grazie.

If we were to conjecture on a relationship between some of Leonardo's drawings and the work carried out on the Gallerani house, we could perhaps consider certain studies of decorative motifs in notebooks datable from 1493 to 1495, especially geometric motifs suitable for wall decorations. We know that during alteration work in 1891 a few traces of painted decorations were discovered, but they were immediately covered again, and no visual record was kept. They were described as "a fragment of fifteenth-century polychrome decoration with a row of alternating black and white rhombi, a frieze of flowers on a black background, and a wall with panels of various geometric motifs." This description unfortunately allows no direct comparison with Leonardo's drawings, but it seems to me that this aspect of his possible participation is worth further consideration, inasmuch as the very dress which Cecilia

103. *Knot designs for architectural decoration on a sheet of studies for the casting of the Sforza horse, 1493. Windsor, RL 12351 v.* ▶

104. *Study of an apostle for* The Last Supper *and architectural sketches, c. 1495. Windsor, RL 12552.* ▶

wears in his famous portrait of her is unusually richly ornamented with motifs of knots, surely a reflection of the taste and predilections of the owner of the house. I might add, incidentally, that when he began the portrait Leonardo had intended to represent the lady within her house. In fact, a door or arched window appears in ultraviolet photographs in the background just above her left shoulder. Studies of knots are found in various places in Leonardo's notebooks much earlier than he would have had reason to use them in the decoration of the Sala delle Asse in 1498. I have seen several, undoubtedly studies for wall decorations, which were never published and unfortunately have recently been destroyed. (Photographic records do exist, but regrettably I have not yet been permitted to reproduce them. I shall say only that one of the knots is the cross once adopted as the editorial emblem of the Commissione Vinciana!) These drawings are all datable about 1493-95. This helps to explain the presence of such knots as ideas for wall decorations in other sheets, such as those at Windsor (for example RL 12351 v) in the series of studies for the casting of the horse for the Sforza Monument.

We may also recall that the walls under the arcade of the new courtyard were decorated with *istorie* exalting the Sforza dynasty through reference to heroes of antiquity. Those estimates for wall paintings in MS. H that are variously attributed to Vigevano or the Castello Sforzesco come to mind.

Finally we might also consider those towers, or *tiburi*, which flanked the Dal Verme residence and which were probably eliminated with the new building for Cecilia. In a completely hypothetical way we could think of the architectural sketches in the celebrated study for the apostle St. James the Greater at Windsor (RL 12552): three views of the corner tower of a castle transformed into a building with a cupola of an exquisitely refined character, and a ground-plan. These sketches are usually thought to refer to the Castello Sforzesco although they contrast greatly with the character and military functions of that building. Imaginative cupolas and soaring pinnacles more adapted to a French castle, a *tiburio* which has more the look of a garden pavilion than the crown of a fortress tower, especially when observed in the round from a viewpoint that almost gives it the separate character of a *tempietto*. What if it were an idea, never realized, for Cecilia's palace?

I might add that these architectural pen sketches in the Windsor drawing are probably much later than the study for the apostle, and that we find the same profile of the corner of a building again in MS. I, f. 24 r, next to studies of heraldic shields datable about 1498-99. In the adjacent sheet in that notebook we find details of battlements and fortified walls that have a more distinctly military character, although they are found again on f. 19 r, which is placed facing the palace plan already mentioned for its reference to a façade of 75 braccia.

It is certainly dangerous to try to reconstruct in imagination what was or could have been Cecilia's house. Lodovico himself wanted to transform it into a patrician residence whose exterior would add dignity to the city and whose interior would be appropriate to those intellectual activities that were stimulated by Cecilia's presence. Better than imagination or hypothesis is the portrait of that ambience left to us by Bandello: "Here military men discuss the soldier's art, musicians sing, architects and painters draw, natural philosophers pose questions, and the poets recite their own and other compositions, in such a way that everyone who delights in excellence or in talking or listening to discussion finds food met for his appetite, since in the presence of this heroine, pleasant, virtuous and gentle things are always spoken of."

6. Santa Maria delle Grazie

A letter from Lodovico Sforza to his secretary Marchesino Stanga, dated 29 June 1497, is a well-known document in Leonardo and Bramante studies. It shows that both the *Last Supper* and the new tribune of S. Maria delle Grazie had just been completed, and that thought was being given to the project of rebuilding the whole church, including the façade. Instructions were in fact given "to have a meeting of all the best architectural experts in order to examine the problem of S. Maria delle Grazie, and have a model made for its façade, taking into account the height to which the whole church ought to be brought in proportion to the tribune."

The fact that Leonardo and Bramante were to be found together in Milan for over ten years has led to the suggestion that their relationship was not only one of work but also of friendship, and an attempt has been made to establish the extent of a reciprocal exchange of ideas through an examination of Leonardo's drawings and Bramante's buildings. It is certainly not wise to overemphasize considerations which are not founded on one piece of documentary evidence, even though an anonymous seventeenth century writer (probably Father Sebastiano Resta) called Leonardo "the architect of the dome of the Grazie in Milan." I propose therefore to start with a question – whether or not Leonardo could have been considered one of the "best architectural experts" mentioned in the letter of 1497. The affirmative answer comes to us from notes in MS. I, the notebook which, as we have seen, Leonardo used in precisely that period, 1497-99. It consists of three parts, dated by Leonardo himself or datable with accuracy on the basis of internal elements already illustrated with great acumen by Calvi in 1925: the first part, up to folio 48, dated about 1498-99, the other two dated 1497-98. Calvi had also identified in the 1497-98 section, a series of notes referring to an urban systematization of the land outside Porta Vercellina, and had established a relationship between these notes and the gift made to Leonardo by Lodovico Sforza in 1498 of a vineyard in that area, exactly between the church of S. Maria delle Grazie and San Vittore, and with architectural projects being undertaken at that time by such prominent members of the Sforza court as Sanseverino, Guiscardi, Botta, Curzio and others. It has been seen, in fact, how Leonardo may have taken part in the vast project of urban reorganization of the area of S. Maria delle Grazie, where the construction of a large palace planned by Leonardo for Mariolo de' Guiscardi was begun. Corio speaks of the

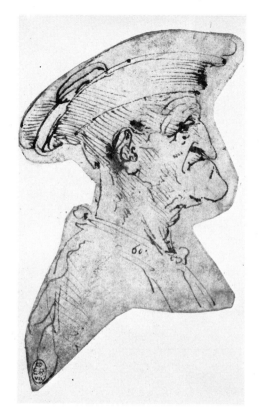

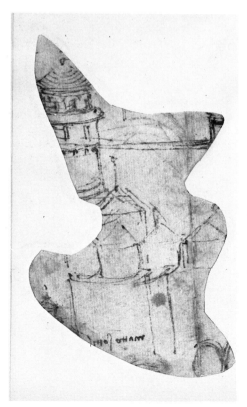

105, 106. Fragment containing architectural studies on the verso of the drawing of an old man in profile, c. 1495-97. Windsor, RL 12475 r-v.

107, 108. Studies of architecture and decoration, c. 1497. MS. I, ff. 23 v-24 r and 24 v-25 r.

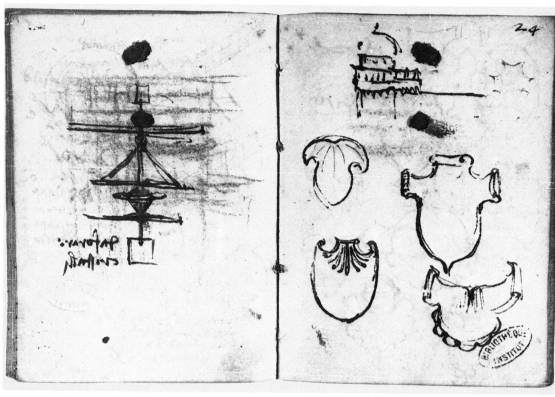

destruction in 1499 and 1500, following the French invasion, of all that the ducal ambition had realized in the space of a few years in the area outside Porta Vercellina, and he mentions the supporters of that building renewal, that is, the prominent citizens who were closest to the Sforza, through family ties, friendship or governmental positions. S. Maria delle Grazie had become the center (indeed not very far from the new ducal residence, the Castello Sforzesco), of an area selected for residence by Lodovico Sforza's faithful collaborators. The duke's program was clearly set forth by a contemporary, Bernardino Arluno, who listed the names of those who contributed to its realization: Leonardo, "pictorem mollissimum, cuius in hunc diem picturae vivunt," Bramante, "architecturae magistrum," Caradosso and Iacopo Antiquario.

Leonardo's association with Bramante at that time is also documented by a note in MS. M (f. 53 v), a notebook of 1499 in which is found the sketch of a drawbridge "which Donnino showed me." The identical mechanism is found again in greater detail in Codex Atlanticus, f. 284 r-a, a sheet of notes and calculations typical of someone about to take a trip, and which in fact, contains the note: "On 1 April 1499 I find myself with 218 lire." We are therefore at the end of the first period of the association between the two artists and at the end of the Sforza dynasty, when Leonardo, in MS. L was to record the "buildings of Bramante" among the works for Lodovico Sforza that could not be finished.

The circumstances which I have pointed out help to explain the Bramantesque character of the architectural sketches in Leonardo's MS. I, including the famous drawing for a suburban villa, on f. 56 r. In this drawing attempts have been made to discern anticipations of late sixteenth-century forms and motifs, such as those used by Giulio Romano at Mantua, but it has also quite rightly been shown that those forms and motifs derive from Tuscan elements of the Brunelleschian tradition, if not directly (bearing in mind that the portico of the Pazzi Chapel was added after Brunelleschi's death), then at least conveyed through Giuliano da Sangallo who was in Milan in 1492. This point seems particularly important to me as the indication of a unifying principle in the architectural and urban program which in those years occupied both Leonardo and Bramante. It also serves to explain the Brunelleschian component which Bruschi has so perceptively detected in the plan of the tribune of S. Maria delle Grazie. On the other hand, we know of a visit by Bramante to Florence precisely during those years. We may therefore ask whether Leonardo participated in or contributed to that plan for the tribune, within the programme to rebuild the whole church. He must have followed Bramante's work on S. Maria delle Grazie from the start, in 1492. In a notebook of 1493, MS. H³, f. 123 r, there is a red chalk sketch for a church on the Greek cross plan with angle towers. This may be linked to a famous series of studies of churches in the preceding MS. B, *c.* 1487-90, which has recently been interpreted as pertaining to the idea for a Sforza mausoleum, a project said to have been replaced by that of reconstructing S. Maria delle Grazie so as to have the same function as a family tomb. This sketch, therefore, suggests a continuity between the first series of studies by Leonardo and the work undertaken by Bramante. Alongside the notes relating to the attitudes and gestures of the Apostles in the *Last Supper* (MS. Forster II, f. 63 r and f. 62 v, *c.* 1495), Leonardo also made a sketch on the adjoining page (f. 63 v) of the profiles of the second and third socles of the apses of Bramante's tribune. This shows how far the work had progressed when Leonardo was about to start his painting in the refectory. In another sketch in the same notebook (f. 53 r) we now recognize the profile of the full elevation of one of those apses, and this time the proposed identification leaves no doubt because Leonardo gives the measurements of each individual element of the apse which amount to a total of 28 ¾ braccia (*c.* 17 metres), that is almost exactly the height of the apse as realized, which is 16.10 metres. This type of annotation allows us to assume that Leonardo did not limit himself merely to recording what Bramante was doing, but that he was himself contributing to Bramante's plan.

Added to these clues is yet another, which has recently come to light. This is a note in Madrid MS. I, f. 113 v, datable to around 1497, which accompanies two diagrammatic sketches of a dome vault identified by Leonardo himself as "arches of the Grazie." Leonardo discusses a principle of mechanics which is in fact applied in the dome of S. Maria delle Grazie: "The part of the distributed weight which exerts most pressure is that closest to the centre of its burden. It is clear that the inner part of an arch or tiburium exerts greater pressure at points b and c than outside at a and d.

The perpendicular $g\,p$ is more resistant than the curve $f\,g$ [sic – $f\,h$] by five ninths."

The gallery at the base of the dome of S. Maria delle Grazie appears in section as in Leonardo's first sketch: thus the observation on "distributed weight" which alludes to the system of the double shell used by Brunelleschi in the dome of Florence Cathedral. The other sketch illustrates the case of the half arch and could refer to the vault of the apse extension, the *scarsella*, which leans on the adjacent arch of the apse, or to the large arch by which, as a temporary measure (later becoming permanent), the tribune was joined to Solari's nave. From here we can go on to consider Leonardo's method of dealing with the problems which presented themselves at the time of the 1497 document, when the apse was already complete and the addition of a new nave to thus complete the program was being considered, with a façade appropriate to the new structure.

A reference to these problems is found in MS. I, right next to the pages which contain the survey of the plots of land outside Porta Vercellina. These are two pages (f. 69 v and f. 70 r) filled with notes in ink on the movement of water, but those of f. 70 r on the right cover the very faint image of a quick sketch in red chalk. Between the pen-and-ink lines a number, 58, can also be discerned and two isolated words which the editor of the Codex, Ravaisson-Mollien, failed to transcribe.

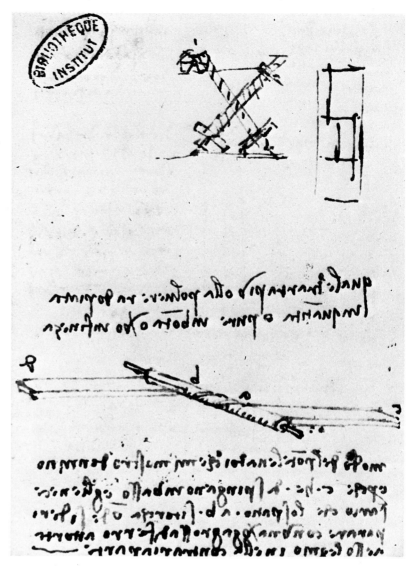

109, 110. *Sketches of Bramante's drawbridge, 1499. MS. M, f. 53 v, and Codex Atlanticus, f. 284 r-a (dated 1 April 1499).*

These words are *monaci* (monks), and further down, *iacometto*. An examination of the original sheet and a good photograph of it reveals the plan of a building which very closely recalls the ground plan of the tribune of S. Maria delle Grazie. The word *monaci* is written within the space of one of the large semicircular apses. The number 58, if taken as a dimension calculated in braccia, could refer to the length of the complex, which is in fact about 58 braccia – that is, about 34 metres. However, the proof that it actually is S. Maria delle Grazie comes from the apparently isolated name at the bottom, *iacometto*. In fact this name identifies one of the noble citizens faithful to the Sforzas, Giacomo Atellani, whose house, famous for Luini's decorations of Sforza portraits and of interlaced motifs (the *gruppi di Bramante* as Leonardo called them), was located exactly beside the tribune of the Grazie, on the other side of the street, as indicated by Leonardo. Beltrami, in his book on Luini, quotes a document in which the "sepulchrum d. Jacobeti Athellani et heredum ejus" is mentioned.

In Leonardo's sketch, separated by a tracing from the superimposed writing, there clearly appears an element of the greatest importance, the system by which the tribune is attached to what must be the nave of the Solari church. This nave appears to be in line with the square of the tribune just as Brusci had guessed. Furthermore, the junction point forms two recesses in the alignment of the outer walls, producing an interval which suggests that the tribune could be taken as a centralized and autonomous structure, well in keeping with that sense of ambiguity which is characteristic of both Bramante and Leonardo. The theme originated fifty years before in Florence with the Annunziata is resumed in full, and we may ask again whether Leonardo, "architetto et pictore" (as he was recorded in the Codex Magliabechianus in 1500), confined himself simply to recording one of Bramante's ideas.

An unpublished sketch on the back of a well-known drawing of 1490 in the Louvre represents the plan of a centralized building reminiscent of the plan of Pavia Cathedral (and Leonardo, as we have seen, was in Pavia with Francesco di Giorgio in 1490), which shows an analogous system of opening one side to a passage which might lead to another building. Thus we have a clue to what must have been the program for the transformation of the Solari church. When it is compared to the ground plan of the actual church, we cannot fail to detect the ingenuity of the conception, also from the technical point of view. The demolition would have consisted of eliminating the external area of the chapels, but the foundations of the central nave and the side aisles would have been utilized in such a way that the central nave would have been elongated to form a connecting passage to the tribune for a space corresponding to that of the two chapels. The interval provided by this connecting zone which would have provided a shaded architectural pause almost like a vestibule, would have thus corresponded to the length of the choir opposite in a way which brings to mind the atrium of the Portinari Chapel in Sant'Eustorgio. The result of this would have been an emphatic longitudinal axis leading the visitor to the culminating

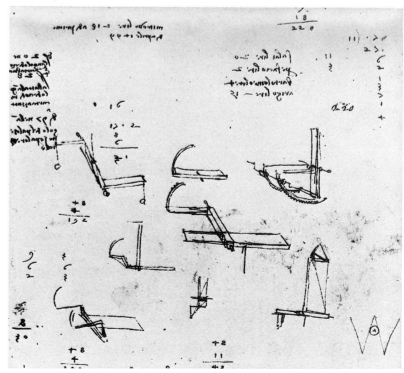

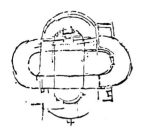

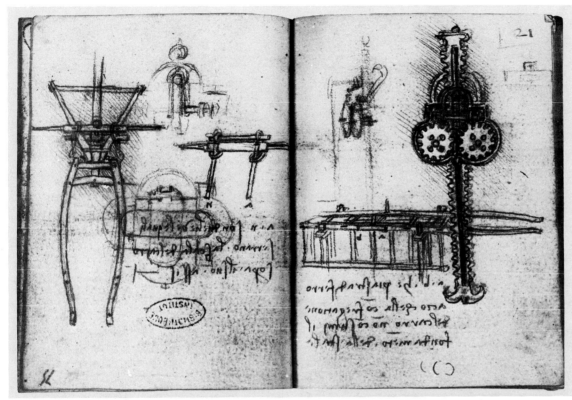

111. MS. H., *ff. 123 r-122 v, and tracing of the centrally-planned church.*

112, 113. *Sketches of the apse profiles of S. Maria delle Grazie, c. 1495. Codex Forster II, ff. 53 r and 63 v.*

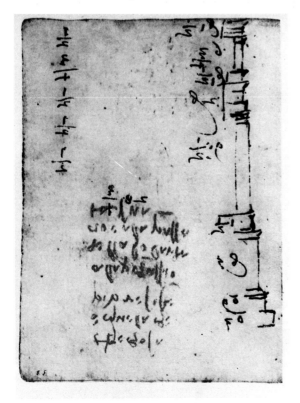

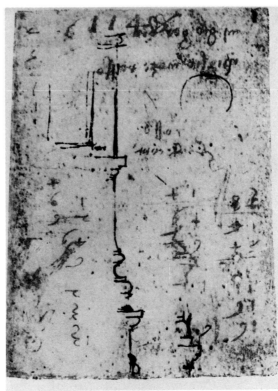

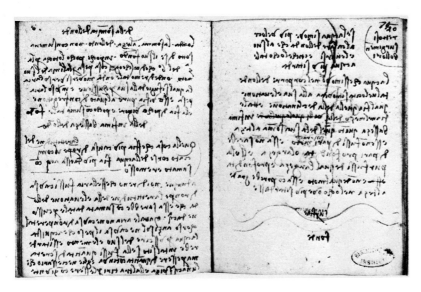

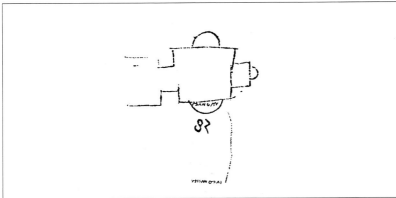

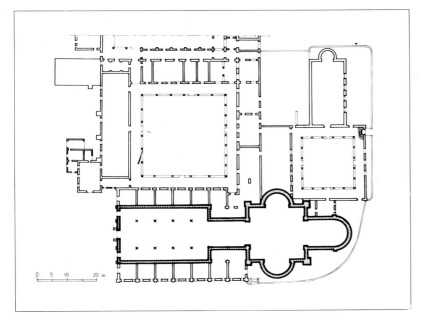

experience of the centrally-planned building, that is to that tribune which, at the death of Beatrice in 1497, had assumed the funerary and celebratory function of a Sforza mausoleum, following a model of *martirium* already taken up again in the fifteenth century, and subsequently adopted by Michelangelo.

Something of the kind had already been done in San Lorenzo in Florence, whose longitudinal axis leads to the tombstone placed at the crossing to indicate the crypt below, where Cosimo de' Medici was buried. It is no surprise that the geometric motif on that stone, designed by Verrocchio, evokes the plan of a centrally-planned church of a type frequently drawn by Leonardo around 1490, and later applied by Bramante in the reconstruction of St Peter's. This model is substantially the same as the one offered by San Lorenzo in Milan, the building well known to both Leonardo and Bramante not only for the plasticity of its centrally-planned form, but also for the presence of a longitudinal axis determined by the open space in front of it, which had the function of a pronaos. It may even be that a solution of this kind was considered for the Tempio Malatestiano at Rimini: the frontal view of Alberti's model on Matteo de' Pasti's medal shows the huge cupola resting on a low drum which is in line with the outer walls of the church.

A side view of the model would appear awkward without a caesura between nave and tribune, and in fact an early seventeenth-century interpretation of Alberti's plan shows the addition of a transept as a visual device to single out the bulky tribune from the nave. This is indeed an arbitrary interpretation which does not take into account the precedent of the SS. Annunziata, in which the attachment of the tribune to the church, externally, has the function of caesura. A drawing attributed to Fra Giocondo in the Uffizi (No. 1697 A) presents the same theme solved in a way which by then was codified in treatises on architecture (for example in the one by Francesco di Giorgio). With the Loreto project, immediately after S. Maria delle Grazie, Bramante conceived of a whole apostolic palace, framing a vast piazza, as a longitudinal element directed towards the focal point of the architectural complex, the Santa Casa situated at the centre of the crossing of the church, after an intermediate zone – the caesura constituted by the nave.

In the context of these ideas, Alberti may again be mentioned for San Sebastiano in Mantua. This is a centrally-planned building, like the tribune of S. Maria delle Grazie, in the form of a Greek cross, one arm of which becomes the atrium which serves as a transition zone from the vestibule to the central hall. The vestibule is the same width as this hall, but this is not true of the atrium, on each side of which space for a bell-tower has been left. The same principle was applied to S. Maria delle Grazie, the difference being that the vestibule is elongated to become a nave. We might even speculate, in fact, whether the two recesses produced in the area where tribune and nave join were planned to house bell-towers, which could have been incorporated there as in S. Maria dei Miracoli in Venice, or left slightly detached as at San Biagio in

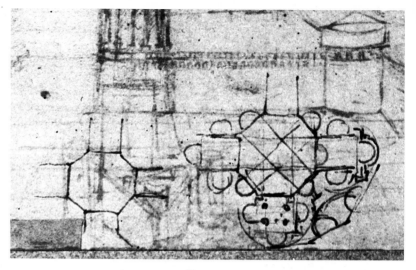

Montepulciano. Responding to the theme suggested by Alberti, Leonardo strove for volumetric effects of a degree of plasticity only actually realized much later, with Palladio's Redentore. This is shown in the sketches in the Codex Atlanticus, f. 37 r-a of 1507-8, some of which look like clay models placed on a circular platform. These may be studies for S. Maria alla Fontana in Milan, construction of which was begun in 1507, and as such are certainly reconsideration of a theme which had already occupied Leonardo in about 1490, perhaps with the project for a Sforza Mausoleum in mind. Two of the sketches represent the plan and elevation of the same building: it is clear that the plan is derived from Alberti's San Sebastiano, with a vestibule just slightly separate from the central area, formed by the elongation of one arm of the Greek cross, so that in elevation the result is a triumphal arch reminiscent of Alberti's façade of S. Andrea.

In the plastic realization of the interior of S. Maria delle Grazie, light would have come exercise to a unifying function in the atmospheric sense understood by Leonardo: the shady atrium as a transition from the worldly splendour of the nave to the diffused and mystical light of the tribune, almost an architectural paradigm inspired by Dante.

At this point it would be easy rhetoric to recall the *Last Supper*, which Leonardo had just completed in the adjoining refectory; but I do so for another reason, that is, to call attention to an architectural background of disconcerting simplicity, almost a tacit tribute to Brunelleschian tradition, which the sumptuous overlay of official Medici taste had not succeeded in erasing from the Florentine consciousness. It seems to me important that such an affirmation, towards the end of the fifteenth century, should be formulated by a Florentine who was far away from Florence and right beside a work by Bramante. And it even seems to me justifiable to think that it may have been just this archaic Brunelleschian method of creating depth of space as in a theatrical scene that showed Bramante the course to follow for the completion of S. Maria delle Grazie. (And who is not reminded, too, of the perspective panels at Urbino, the first symptoms of a purifying phase leading to the classic monumentality of the sixteenth century?) Undoubtedly, the new church had to be given some vertical stress (remember the document of 1497 in which "the height to which the whole church ought to be brought in proportion to the tribune" is mentioned). This vertical seems to be missing in the *Last Supper*. On the other hand, our familiarity with the painting, which countless reproductions have rendered monotonous and even tedious, prevents us from noting this at once, for it is shown in a subtle disguise as an element of ambiguity which is common to Leonardo and to Bramante. Leonardo himself instructs us to look into a mirror to see the things which we do not ordinarily notice. However even if the mirror trick can be used to make us see the distorted smile of *Mona Lisa*, it cannot do anything with the perfectly symmetrical *Last Supper*.

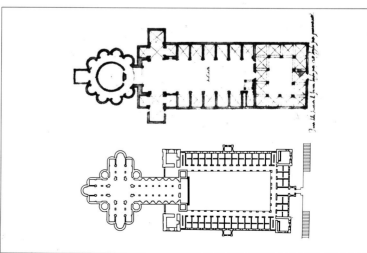

The *Last Supper* has been studied and admired by generations of critics and art historians, by novelists, writers and poets and philosophers, but

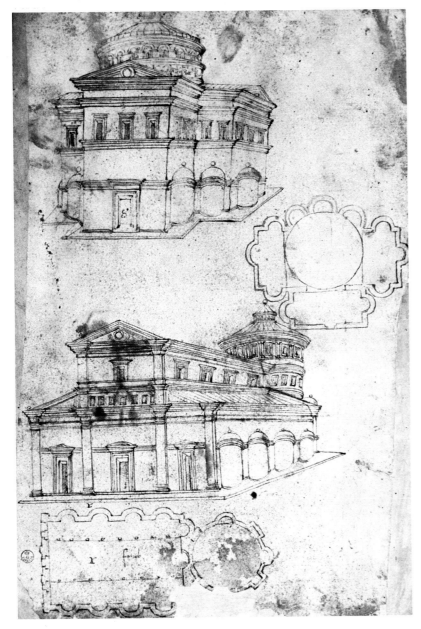

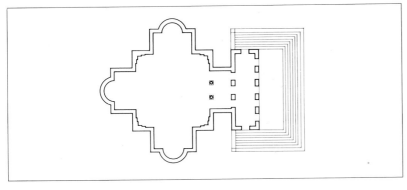

not by architects. An analysis similar to that made by Bruschi of the Prevedari print could well reveal much more to us than we can actually see.

Yet there is one way of seeing the *Last Supper* as it has never been seen before: by turning it upside-down. In fact, in so doing we see only the architecture, with the ceiling, which becomes a pavement, rapidly brought towards our feet and carried underneath what used to be the area of the three lunettes above.

In this way the *Last Supper* acquires an unexpected verticality, contradicting the horizontality of a table which for centuries has polarized the attention of the spectators as the main element of a stage set.

This somewhat irreverent upturning of a masterpiece at least has the virtue of leading to a final hypothesis. Once again the things we see lead to a question. What type of façade would have completed Bramante's backward enterprise? In 1498 Luca Pacioli speaks of Leonardo's *Last Supper* and says it was carried out "in the holy temple of the Grazie." Here is a key word: "temple." And here is Bramante's famous drawing of the façade of a "temple" published by Beltrami in 1901 as a study for San Satiro. Both Forster and Bruschi have shown that the interpretation is questionable for technical reasons, and Bruschi concludes that the façade would have been suitable for a building much taller than San Satiro. What if this were a study for the façade of S. Maria delle Grazie? I shall leave the examination of these theories to others and confine myself to observing the articulation of this surface, which well reflects the interfor structure which was to replace the Solari church. (The lateral projections could have been simple decorative elements to bring it into line with the great semicircular apses of the tribune.) As the façade of a "temple" it could recall the Albertian precedent of S. Maria Novella (another Dominican building), and find seducing reflections in drawings by Leonardo, from the early sketch in the background of the *Saint Jerome* to the late drawing of a church, now in Venice, which echoes the volumetric articulations of the cathedral of Pavia and anticipates the vertical thrust of Il Gesù. (Note that the side of the church is divided into partitions corresponding to five chapels, just as the new nave of S. Maria delle Grazie would be.) Bramante's drawing in the Louvre has been illustrated in celebrated studies, such as Wittkower's, so I shall confine myself to indicating in it what I would call an "elective affinity" with the architecture of the *Last Supper*, an affinity which goes beyond relationship of style or of architectural principles, and which expands melodically from the central motif of the three windows.

At this point one may argue that the tablets placed on the lateral extensions do not bear the names of Lodovico and Beatrice Sforza, but are inscribed with those of Lodovico and Lodovica Fogliani, whose marriage took place at a time (1479) sufficiently near to the construction of San Satiro to justify Beltrami's hypothesis that they wanted to celebrate their union with a gesture of patronage of the arts. Little is known of Foglaini, son of a friend and captain of Francesco Sforza and

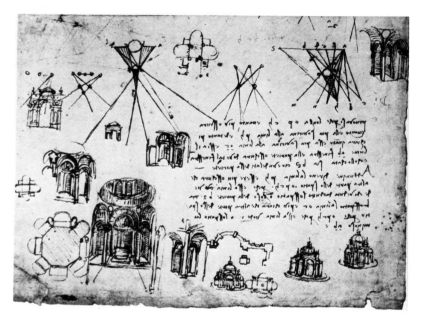

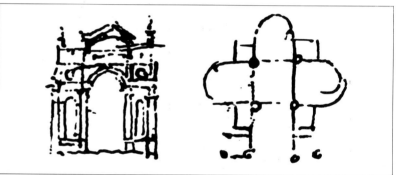

descendant of the celebrated Guidoriccio da Fogliano, depicted by Simone Martini in the famous fresco in Siena. The few clues offered by Litta are, however, promising: in 1492, when the construction of S. Maria delle Grazie was undertaken and when the architectural transformation of the area outside Porta Vercellina had already begun, Lodovico Fogliani was appointed ducal councillor. He thus became a peer of the persons closest to the Sforzas, the same ones who had chosen the area around S. Maria delle Grazie for their residences. It is thus legitimate to suspect that he could have taken on the role of patron in regard to the "temple" which the Sforzas had chosen as a family mausoleum. It would be worth investigating this possibility in greater depth, and I hope that others will wish to do so. Remaining also to be considered is the pagan symbol of the cornucopia which figures so prominently on the pediment (as it does in another Bramante drawing in the Ambrosiana), and which Bruschi placed in relation to the humanistic interpretation of the function of the Vitruvian basilica. I go no further than to recall that the motif of cornucopia can be seen again in association with the Sforza emblem of the caduceus in the decoration of the sacristy of S. Maria delle Grazie and also appears in one of Leonardo's drawings in that same MS. I (f. 97 r) which contains the references to S. Maria delle Grazie. Finally, let us remember what Litta says of Fogliani: "He died, probably in 1510, in Castelnovo de' Terzi, where he had founded the Benedictine monastery called *Beata Vergine delle Grazie*, which was suppressed in 1815." Fogliani, therefore, closed his existence with a work of devotion dedicated to that same Virgin in whose honour the "sacred temple of the Grazie" had been erected in Milan.

7. The Sforza Sepulchre

"Cordial, dear, delightful associate." Thus the author of the *Antiquarie prospetiche romane*, now recognized as Bramante (see *Excursus 2*) addresses Leonardo in about 1500. Evidence of such an association points, as we have seen, to a time just before the publication of the poem on Roman antiquities dedicated to Leonardo. In 1497, the year in which the tribune of the Grazie was completed and the rebuilding of the rest of the church was being prepared, Lodovico Sforza ordered that a start should be made on the building of a family tomb to be placed in the centre of that tribune. With that official act S. Maria delle Grazie assumed the role of a Sforza Mausoleum. Lodovico's daughter Bianca, who died in 1496, had already been interred in the tribune, and shortly after, in 1497, the body of the Duchess Beatrice was laid there, awaiting the final placing in the projected sepulchre.

The idea of a Sforza mausoleum stems from a project of Filarete's, known through a medal by Sperandio. This seems to have been taken up again by Leonardo and developed in a series of studies of centrally-planned temples in MS. B in about 1487-90, that is, at the time of his participation in the project for the tiburio of Milan Cathedral. It is possible that at that time he already had a friendly working relationship

128. Bramante: Temple façade. Paris, Louvre.
129. The temple in the background of Leonardo's St. Jerome. Vatican, Pinacoteca.
130. Study of a basilica. Venice, Accademia.

with Bramante. The earliest reference to Bramante in Leonardo's manuscripts in the one in the Codex Atlanticus, f. 225 r-b, the sheet of *c.* 1490 which has already been cited for the memoranda relating to the topography and buildings of Milan. The reference is to *Gruppi di Bramante* or "Bramante's knots," that is, the type of interwoven plant decoration which Lomazzo records as an invention of Leonardo himself: "As for trees, a beautiful motif has been invented by Leonardo, that of making their branches interlace in bizarre groups; this weaving together of branches was also used by Bramante." If this, as it appears, is a reference to the *Sala delle Asse*, we may recall that when Leonardo was working there, in about 1498, Bramante, as an architect, was busy on the adjoining rooms, including the *ponticella*. As regards the illusionistic element present in Leonardo's decoration as an example of "architectural perspective," we must not forget that from Mantegna's similar premises, albeit with a strong Urbino component, Bramante had already arrived at the same result with the feigned choir of San Satiro, which dates from the early 1480's, when Leonardo was just arriving in Milan. The difference is that the *Sala delle Asse*, almost paradoxically, has more of "architecture" than the choir of San Satiro, inasmuch as it can be observed by the moving eye, while the San Satiro choir requires the eye to be held static at a pre-established viewpoint, as in looking at a painting. And in Milan Bramante called himself first and foremost a painter; so much so that, in 1500, having just arrived in Rome, his qualification as "Prospectivo Melanese dipintore" could show itself not only in the poetry of the *Antiquarie prospetiche romane*, but also in the symbolic fresco in the Lateran, in which an arcade in perspective frames the allegorical papal tent in a way which was to inspire Borromini when he came to design the central motif of his sepulchres in the same basilica.

As a background to a consideration of the evolution of Milanese funerary architecture in the late fifteenth century, it may be useful to go back to the time of Bramante's frescoes in the Casa Panigarola, a building close to Sant'Ambrogio and so only a few steps from the monastery of San Francesco Grande, where Leonardo, with the contract of 1483, had been employed to paint a large altarpiece which was to include the *Virgin of the Rocks*. In 1482 the Confraternity of the Immaculate Conception had already had an elaborate wooden frame prepared which, on the basis of the few descriptive details provided by the 1483 contract, must have resembled that type of wall sepulchre which was coming into use outside Milan as well, above all in the work of the Lombardo, such as the Vendramin monument in Venice. We must keep in mind that the church of San Francesco Grande had assumed the role of "cimitero di santi," where the Milanese nobility sought to erect their own funeral monuments. We need only remember the tombs of the Borromeo and Birago families. Particularly interesting is the record of an underground passage, indicated as a *grotta*, which led to the buried ruins of the Polyandrium of Caio, thus suggesting a possible connection with the iconography of Leonardo's *Virgin of the*

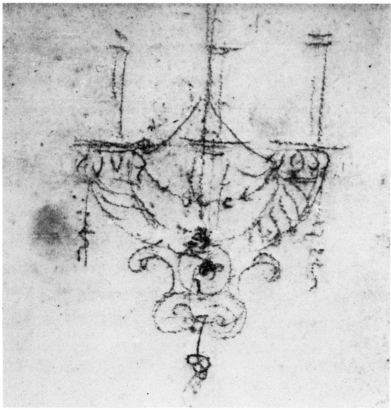

Rocks. A revision of the reading of the 1483 contract reveals that the altarpiece actually included a symbolic sarcophagus, "archa . in forma . di . caxamento" (ark in the form of an edifice), that is, with partitions in the forms of arcades after a fairly common Early Christian model, and thus offering spaces which Leonardo and his associates were to decorate with the figures of Sibyls, like the Sibyls which appear in the Sistine Chapel, which was also dedicated to the Immaculate Conception. Unfortunately we do not know how much of the pictorial work specified in the contract was carried out by Leonardo and his helpers, the De Predis brothers. All that remains of the altarpiece, which was destroyed at the end of the eighteenth century, is the central panel – the London *Virgin of the Rocks*, and the two side-panels, each representing a musician angel standing in a niche.

It is precisely the motif of a figure standing in a niche which Bramante had made the principal feature of his decoration of the room of the Men at Arms in the nearby Casa Panigarola. No documentation proves that Leonardo was in contact with Bramante at the time, but one aspect of those frescoes seems to point to the fact. I am referring to the famous fresco of *Heraclitus and Democritus*, which represents the two philosophical attitudes of crying and laughing at human wretchedness, and which was situated above the entrance door, not inside the room as is generally thought, but outside it, as attested by an eighteenth-century visitor. The subject is exactly the one that Ficino wanted in the meeting room of his academy. But aside from reflecting philosophical attitudes derived form the intellectual circles of Urbino and Florence, Bramante's fresco can be taken as a paradigm of the type of *istoria* postulated by Alberti and Leonardo, with the accent on the depiction of those *moti mentali* which Leonardo discusses in his *Treatise on Painting*. Like Alberti, Leonardo realized that the depiction of laughter can easily be mistaken for that of weeping, and advised the painter to pay this due attention. In fact he set himself to study the subtle variations in the expression of sorrow and joy, as if he had Bramante's fresco in mind. Actually, the figures of Heraclitus and Democritus, placed against an architectural background different from that of the figures of the Men at Arms, seem not fully to harmonize with those elements of Bramante's style which are usually attributed to the influence of Piero, Melozzo and Mantegna. They seem to show, in fact, an awareness of that sense of form which led Leonardo to employ chiaroscuro to enhance colour and expression. Democritus's raised hand is worthy of Leonardo himself, and could be placed between that of the Virgin in the Uffizi *Annunciation* and the foreshortened one of the *Virgin of the Rocks*. The same may be said of the globe, in which the configuration of the mountainous regions is depicted with the same naturalism as is found in Leonardo's maps.

There was an eighteenth-century theory, to which perhaps we ought not to give too much weight, that attributed this fresco to Leonardo on the basis of a rather forced interpretation of the monogram XL at the centre of the classical frieze, but there is another element in this painting which seems to have passed unnoticed and which could have something to do with Leonardo: the books open in front of Democritus show what could be defined as a synthesis of Leonardo's mirror-writing, in the same way as the open book in the background of Botticelli's *Saint Augustine* gives the impression of a fifteenth-century manuscript of Pythagoras. A close examination shows that even if the marks do not reproduce legible words, they do give the impression, not by chance, of the ductus of Leonardo's handwriting, certain letters being clearly recognizable, such as the *e*, the *l*, and the *r*, and even the ligature *ch* typical of Leonardo's mirror-writing. Besides, these marks are without doubt the work of a left-handed person because of the way in which the brush has been held in making them, and only someone left-handed would have begun to write on the right-hand page of an open book, and with an initial placed on the outer margin. The book in the foreground has the right-hand page completely covered with writing, whereas the left-hand page contains only a few lines. In the other book the situation is reversed, but this may have been done deliberately because of the large area of shadow across the right-hand page.

If, as seems probable, the two philosophers are portraits of actual persons, as we know is the case with the Men at Arms in the niches, it would be tempting to recognize Leonardo himself in the melancholy Heraclitus, whose face recalls that of the Vitruvian man in Leonardo's famous drawing in Venice, and to recognize Bramante in the cheerful Democritus, whose thin hair seems to be a sign of incipient baldness. One wonders whether it is pure coincidence that the Heraclitus in a painting of the same subject attributed to a later follower of Leonardo, probably Lomazzo, is without doubt a portrait of Leonardo with a beard.

Of course, this type of speculation cannot be taken too seriously even when one considers that in Leonardo's estimates for mural painting in MS. H, already mentioned, there is a reference to scenes depicting philosophers of antiquity and other classical subjects. In any case, the Casa Panigarola frescoes cannot be excluded from a consideration of the relationship between Leonardo and Bramante, if only for their proximity to the place where Leonardo was working at that time, which, in about 1485-90, was the church of San Francesco Grande, "cimitero di santi." Shortly thereafter, in about 1492, both Leonardo's and Bramante's field of action moved to the nearby Dominican monastery of S. Maria delle Grazie, which Lodovico Sforza intended to transform into a family mausoleum and make it thus a "cimitero di duchi."

The document of 1497 which seems to imply that the tribune as well as the *Last Supper* were already finished, lists a number of works that Lodovico Sforza wished to have promptly carried out. Among these is the *sepultura,*" that is the Sforza Sepulchre, and the high altar: "*Item* to see whether Il Gobbo, besides the sepulchre, could make part of the altar during the present year; find out whether he has all the necessary marble for it, and if more is needed send to Venice or Carrara for it. *Item* in order that the sepulchre be finished all at once see that Il Gobbo

134. Detail of the Sala delle Asse in the Castello Sforzesco, Milan.

135. Funerary monument of Andrea Vendramin. Venice, Church of Santi Giovanni e Paolo.

136. Details of the contract relating to the commission for The Virgin of the Rocks, 1483. Milan, Archivio di Stato.

be urged to work at the lid and to look after all the other parts of it, so that when the *navello* is finished the rest of the sepulchre will be ready." Cristoforo Solari Il Gobbo, a Milanese, was a sculptor and architect of considerable reputation in his time. We need only recall that Michelangelo's 1498 *Pietà* was taken for his work, which led Michelangelo to add his signature to it. It seems that Solari was given the task of supervising the construction of the sepulchre, even if the architectural work was assigned to others. The work was actually completed, but was dismantled in 1564 in compliance with the decrees of the Council of Trent. Only the lid of the sarcophagus with the effigies of Lodovico and Beatrice was saved. It was acquired in 1564 by one Oldrado Lampugnano, and is now in the Certosa of Pavia. Any information which could be discovered on the overall appearance and the siting of that funerary monument would be an invaluable contribution to our knowledge of the architectural program on which the rebuilding of S. Maria delle Grazie was based. In fact, there is no reason to doubt that this monument was intended to be the visual and symbolic focus of the new church.

Lodovico Sforza's instructions to Il Gobbo are dated 31 June 1497. On 3 December 1498, when Lodovico was drawing up his will, the sepulchre had been completed, for he stipulated that his body, with the ducal robes and insignia, should be placed to the right of that of the Duchess Beatrice in the tomb which he had had erected in the tribune of the Grazie – "sepulcro autem locum assignavimus in Capella maiori ipsius templi quod cum capella et sepulcro nos construximus."

We do not know precisely where either the tomb or the high altar was located. Pasquier Le Moine's account of 1515 refers to Beatrice's tomb without indicating its position in the church, merely noting that it was somewhat elevated from the ground and that lower down there was a representation of Christ in the tomb. Later information shows that the monument was to be found under the dome. Leandro Alberti, in his *Descrittione di tutta Italia* of 1550, refers to "that sumptuous cupola, or rather dome (as they say), built by Lodovico Sforza," and adds "beneath which he wished to be buried with his wife, having had a beautiful marble tomb built on which he and his wife Beatrice were sculpted, but this was not granted him, as he died in France. Thus the said tomb remained incomplete, as I have seen." In 1565 Vasari seems to have seen only the figures carved by Il Gobbo: "... which were to have been placed on a marble sepulchre by Giovan Iacomo della Porta, sculptor and architect of the Cathedral of Milan, who in his youth made many works under the aforesaid Gobbo, and the above mentioned, which were to have gone onto the said tomb, were carried out with great skill" (VII. 544).

According to Alberti's account of 1550 it would seem that "the beautiful marble sepulchre" had remained incomplete, in the sense that the original project had only been realized in part. This brings to mind Leonardo's famous reflection: "the duke lost his state and his possessions and his freedom, and not one of his works was completed for him."

137. Bramante: Heraclitus and Democritus.
Milan, Pinacoteca di Brera.

138. Bramante: Heraclitus and Democritus,
detail. Milan, Pinacoteca di Brera.
139. Cristoforo Solari: Sepulchre of
Lodovico and Beatrice Sforza. Church
of the Certosa at Pavia.

Leonardo's MS. L, at the beginning of which we find the notes which include this reflection, is a notebook that he began to use in 1497, although the greater part of the notes deal with the period of his employment as military architect in the service of Cesare Borgia in 1502. On f. 14 r is the rough sketch of a rectangle subdivided into rhombi, in which the monograms LV and BE alternate, standing for Lodovico and Beatrice. This may be interpreted as an idea for a wall or ceiling decoration, dating from the time of Leonardo's work at the Sforza Castle in 1498, but it could also suggest a motif suitable to be sculpted on the ceiling of a funerary monument – what Leonardo himself would call "soffitta alla sepoltura," as he does in the estimate for the Trivulzio Monument. This conjecture seems to find support in the proportions of the sketch, which are in fact the same as those of the lid of the sarcophagus now at Pavia. Leonardo's other notebooks which have already provided indications of his activity at S. Maria delle Grazie do not contain anything which could be connected with the project for the sepulchre, but a sheet in the Codex Atlanticus, f. 10 r-a, contains red chalk sketches, almost invisible in the old facsimile, which in all probability are the initial ideas for the Sforza sepulchre.

The sheet can be dated to 1497, not only on the basis of the handwriting, but even more on the basis of its technological content, which is closely related to that in Leonardo's notebooks of that time and in Madrid MS. I.

Besides this we must consider f. 372 r-b of the same Codex, which was originally joined to f. 10 r-a and from which a fragment now at Windsor, RL 12722, was extracted. (Apart from the correspondence of contents, an early collector had numbered them consecutively, 19 and 20). On the twin page are studies for a printing press and for an elegant lady's purse. It is probable that the standing human figure in the Windsor fragment is connected with the studies for the sepulchre. In fact it looks like a clay model with a framework of iron wires. A figure in a similar pose and represented in the process of being cast is shown in Codex Atlanticus, f. 68 v-a, a sheet dated by Leonardo himself both 1497 and 1498. It is a pose which would be suitable for a personification of Fame, like the one placed above Bambaia's tomb of Lancinus Curtius. The allegory of Fame which appears on the title-page of Curtius's *Epigrammata Libri* could aptly illustrate Leonardo's idea, drawn from Virgil, that "the figure of Fame should be depicted covered all over with tongues in place of feathers, and in the form of a she-bird." The theme of Fame contrasted by Infamy is examined by Leonardo in studies for political allegories inspired by Lodovico Sforza. And it is therefore probable that an allegory of Fame was envisaged for the Sforza Sepulchre, in the same way as Fame and Victory appear on the tomb of Galeazzo Visconti in Pavia.

A drawing of a human figure which, however, can unquestionably be assigned to an architectural work is to be found in a fragment at the Ambrosiana datable on the basis of style to around 1497. It shows a putto bent in the act of raising a curtain, while pushing with his feet on

the outer edge of a cornice and half sitting on a rosette which can only
be understood as the terminal element of a tympanum or a volute. We
can thus imagine the whole drawing as showing the top of an altarpiece,
of a ciborium or even of a funerary monument, to which the motif of the
curtain better lends itself.

With this in mind one comes to realize that the studies on f. 10 r-a of the
Codex Atlanticus refer to a sepulchre in the form of a ciborium. The
structure is deliberately left open, as in a baldachino, and in fact the lid
consists of a hemispherical dome, the ribs of which are turned into four
flying buttresses to direct the weight of the lantern onto the four
columns, a system immediately recognizable as the one proposed by
Leonardo for the Milan Cathedral tiburio some ten years before. Inside
the structure, at the centre of the platform, we recognize the characteristic boat-shaped outline of the tomb – the *navello* mentioned in the
document of 1497. The drawing directly below shows the same
structure, modified by transforming the platform into a socle and by
introducing hanging curtains, open as in the canopy of a bed, or as in
funerary monuments – for example those of the Borromeo family at
Isola Bella (originally in San Francesco) or that of the Malatesta at
Rimini. This second drawing shows that the covering, too, is modified: it
now has the shape of the roof of the Basilica at Vicenza or the Pavillon
de l'Horloge at the Louvre, but there is no way of ascertaining whether
it is a "transparent" roof, consisting only of ribs, or is covered in metal
or some other light material. After passing a sketch that is too slight to
contribute to an interpretation, we come to the last image, in which the
sepulchre takes the form of an octagonal tempietto with a socle and
columns. The dome-shaped space suggested by the ribs which shift the
weight of the lantern onto the eight columns encloses a bell-shaped roof.
A few touches of the chalk suggest a roof laid in fish-scale pattern.
At this point we could also perhaps recall the architectural sketches on a
famous sheet of studies for the *Last Supper* at Windsor, RL 12542 r,
which have not yet received an adequate interpretation. Here we have
an idea for a building on an octagonal plan. Leonardo even indicates the
design for the floor, which consists of bands corresponding to the axes
of the octagonal surface, with circles placed in the resulting triangular
spaces. Studies for the same building are to be found in the Codex
Atlanticus, f. 298 r-b, in which we can see how the pillars of a massive
circular or octagonal (or even cubic) construction come to rest on
reversed arches which are placed immediately below ground level and
which rest on inclined arches placed in a circle around the space of a
crypt, like the one at Pavia Cathedral. Firpo suggests a relationship
between this system of reversed arches and the studies for the tiburio.
But in the context of studies which point to the time of the construction
of the tribune of S. Maria delle Grazie they might better be assigned to
an idea for the Sforza Sepulchre or for its setting. It is certain, at any
rate, that at the time of the studies for the *Last Supper* Leonardo was
thinking of a centrally-planned building characterized by a spacious
crypt and by a geometric motif in the decoration of the floor. The

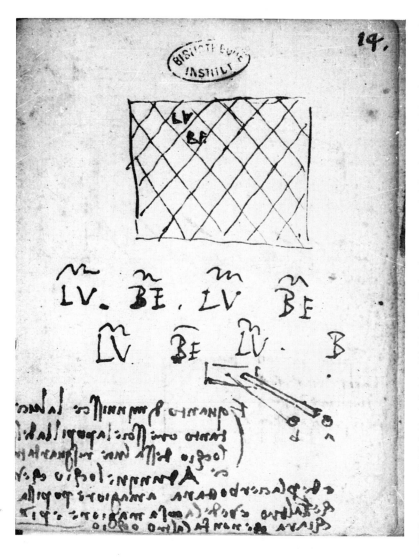

tribune of S. Maria delle Grazie has no crypt, and in fact the lack of adequate foundations made the structure unstable enough to cause apprehension towards the end of the sixteenth century and to require drastic repairs even recently.

A mysterious octagonal building appears once again, much later, in the context of the studies for the royal palace at Romorantin, and again it has the tent-like covering as shown on the sheet of *Last Supper* sketches. Perhaps Leonardo had thought of a chapel or temple as a part of the royal residence, with a covering made of interlocking bricks inserted in "rachetribs" – a system reminiscent of the herring-bone one introduced by Brunelleschi, which Leonardo knew well, as we see in a sketch in the Codex Atlanticus, f. 341 v-a, datable around 1495.

Reflections of what may have been ideas for the Sforza Sepulchre are detectable in the later studies for the Trivulzio monument which is also a sepulchre and which was also initially envisaged as a free-standing structure in the centre of a chapel. The studies on Windsor RL 12353 show how such a structure could even assume the form of a tempietto, but it is in the final project (Windsor RL 12356), which comes closest to the description made by Leonardo himself in the estimate of costs in Codex Atlanticus, f. 179 v-a, that the architectural basis of the equestrian group takes on a shape which conforms completely with the central program of the Sforza Sepulchre: the sarcophagus with the recumbent effigy of the deceased on its lid is set up on a platform and framed by a ciborium-like structure, a simple aedicula which could have been placed at the centre of a hall or against a wall, as shown in Windsor RL 12356. Leonardo obviously intended to keep the sarcophagus completely exposed, limiting to four the columns supporting the base of the equestrian group and creating with them a slender framing element for the space occupied by the sarcophagus. However, such a solution would not have been visually satisfying, and Leonardo himself seems to have realized this, for he experimented with reducing the space above the sarcophagus by introducing an arch, as shown in Windsor RL 12355. Furthermore we know from the estimate of costs that in the end he had decided to double the number of columns. There seems to be no doubt, therefore, that the light, open structure of the Sforza Sepulchre could not have been applied to the Trivulzio Monument because of the bulk and weight of the bronze statue. And yet the quantity of marble specified in Leonardo's estimate for the Trivulzio Monument is roughly the same as that which Cristoforo Solari received in 1497 and 1498 for the Sforza Sepulchre.

One of the most famous studies for the Trivulzio Monument, Windsor RL 12353, shows how Leonardo may have thought of an architectural base in the form of an antique aedicula with four façades crowned by pediments and a door which also has a pediment. And as a variation on the theme, Leonardo broke through the façades to make them into triumphal arches, thus forming an *arcus quadrifrons* beneath which to place the sarcophagus. Each of the four corners of the trabeation, level with the pediments, is occupied by the figure of a prisoner in a lively

142. *Studies for the Sforza Sepulchre,*
c. 1497-98. *Codex Atlanticus, f. 10 r-a,*
detail.

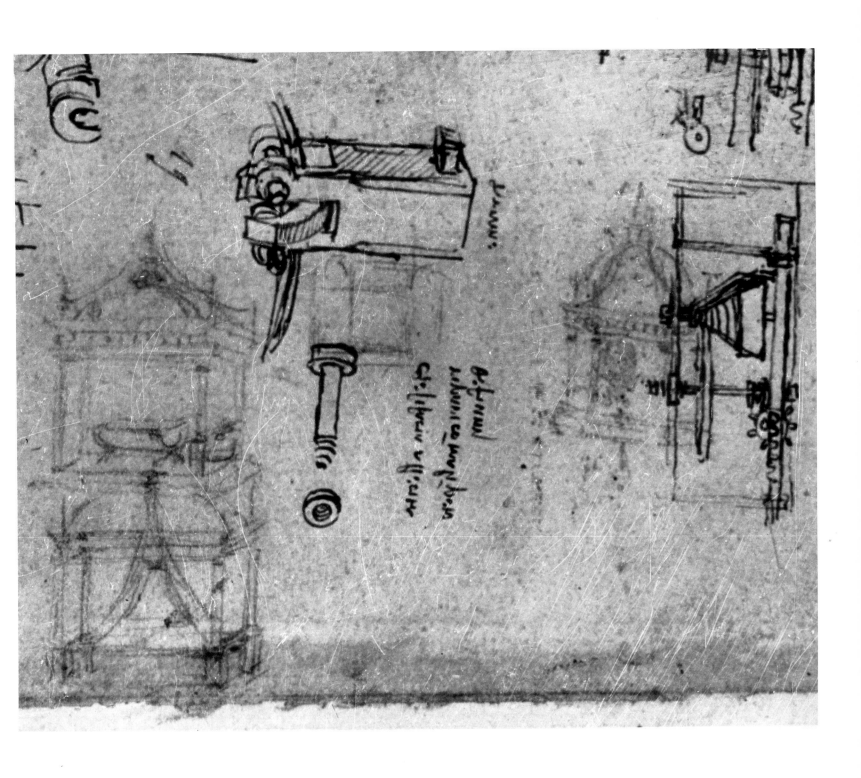

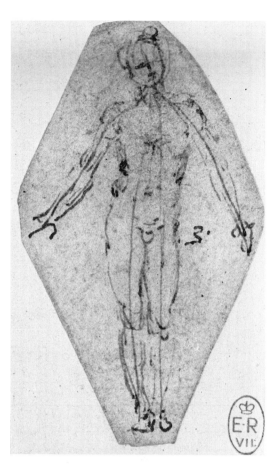

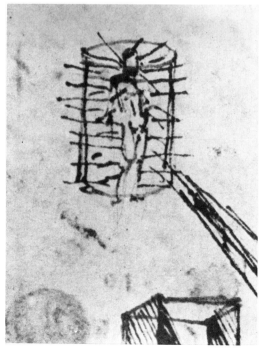

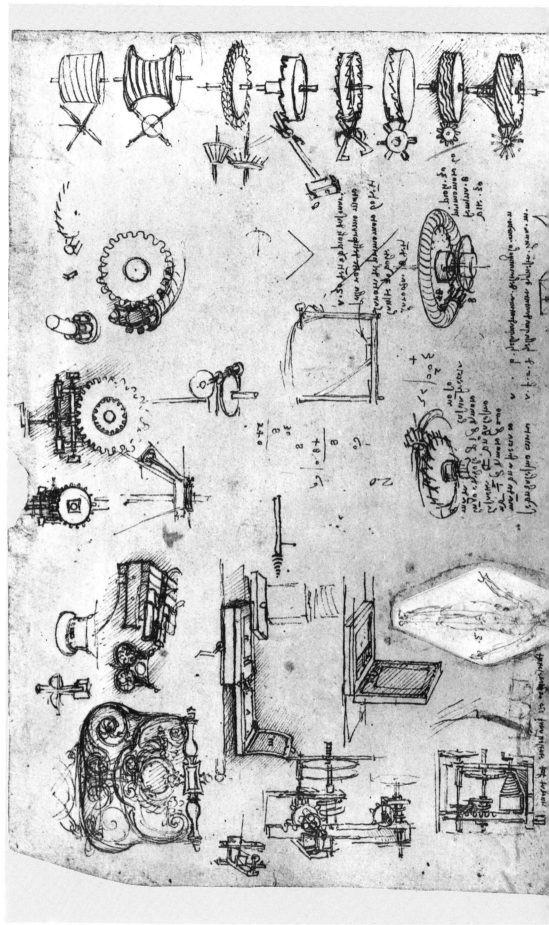

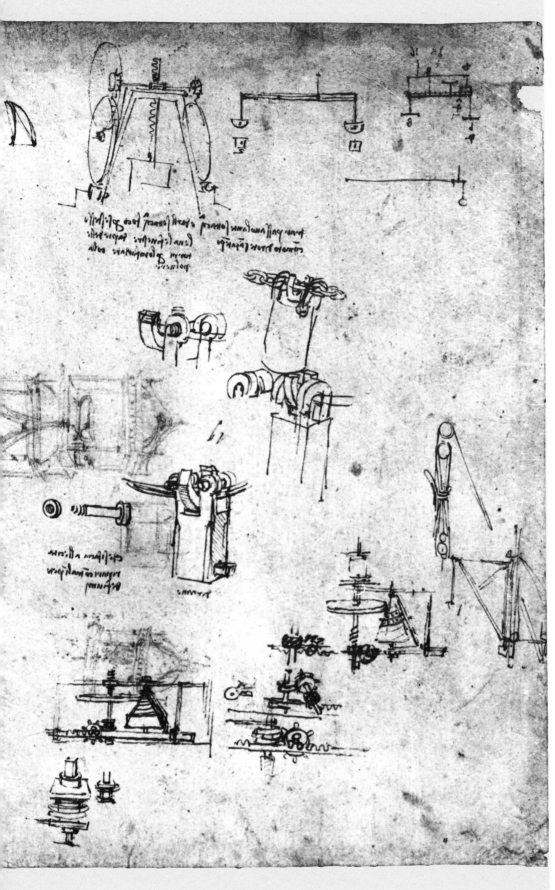

146. *Frontispiece of Lancinus Curtius's* Epigrammata Libri, *Milan 1521.*

147. *Il Bambaia: Sepulchre of Lancinus Curtius. Milan, Museo Archeologico.*

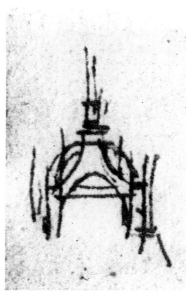

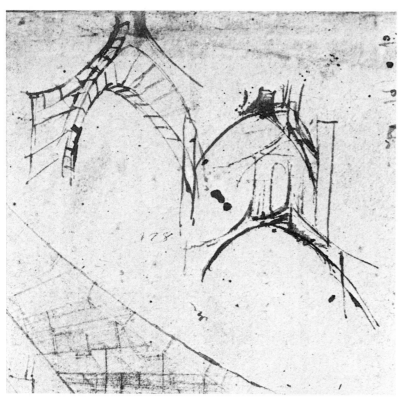

pose. Similar figures appear in a sketch made twenty years before, in Codex Atlanticus f. 148 r-a, one of the sheets of studies for the tiburio. Here too he drew an aedicula (Firpo interprets it as a portal), that might be seen as an anticipation of the base of the Trivulzio Monument, but we do not know its purpose and the vase (urn? fountain?) at the top may simply be a decorative element.

One of the sheets of the Codex Atlanticus, f. 346 r-b, with technological studies which undoubtedly belong to the time of the Sforza Sepulchre, *c.* 1497, contains a minute architectural sketch of what looks like a ciborium. If this also refers to the Sforza Sepulchre, it seems that Leonardo meant to give it a vertical emphasis, which would have been appropriate for a funerary monument intended for the centre of the tribune, in front of the high altar. Its notably Gothic character makes one wonder if Leonardo did not have in mind the tomb of Emperor Henry VII by Tino da Camaino, of 1315, which throughout the fifteenth century had remained in its original location in front of the high altar at the centre of the apse of Pisa Cathedral.

Cosimo de' Medici's tomb in San Lorenzo in Florence could represent a precedent in the placing of a funerary monument in the most prestigious point of a church, that is, at the place where the longitudinal axis leading to the high altar crosses the axis of the transept. After all, San Lorenzo was for the Medici what S. Maria delle Grazie would have been for the Sforza, a family mausoleum. But Cosimo's tomb slab, as has been seen, rests on the ground, with small holes along the sides communicating with the crypt beneath, in which the sarcophagus lies. The tribune of S. Maria delle Grazie affords a greater space from its centre to the altar at the entrance of the choir than the space from Cosimo's tomb to the high altar in San Lorenzo, but even considering this, a funerary monument situated at the centre of the tribune would have blocked the view of the altar. On the other hand, a light and open structure such as appears in Leonardo's sketches would have served the dual purpose of a tomb and a ciborium, and would visually have framed the high altar along the longitudinal axis of the church in the same way that Bernini's baldacchino frames the Cathedra Petri.

These observations lead us to consider once again the monastic complex of S. Maria delle Grazie to seek out a possible unifying principle in the reconstruction program envisaged by Lodovico Sforza. We know from Le Moine's report of 1515 that Beatrice's tomb was "esleuee en haut bein richement" and that beneath it, at ground level, was "nostre Seigneur au tombeau," probably an Entombment with the half-figure of Christ with open arms, supported by two angels. If such a group was found, as seems likely, on the axis which leads to the liturgical focal point of the church, that is, the altar, the accent in the iconographic program would have been emphatically placed upon the idea of the Resurrection. (A phrase comes to mind from Lodovico Sforza's will: "... et nos, cum Deo placuerit, usque ad Resurrectionis tempus requiescere cupimus.") Furthermore, it would have marked the meeting point of another axis, the one which began from the centre of Leonardo's *Last*

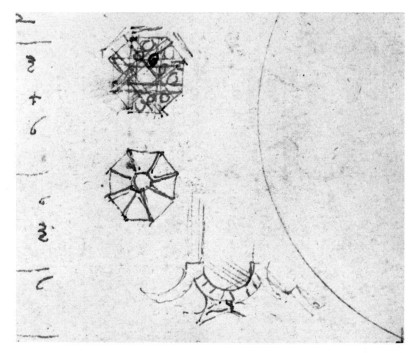

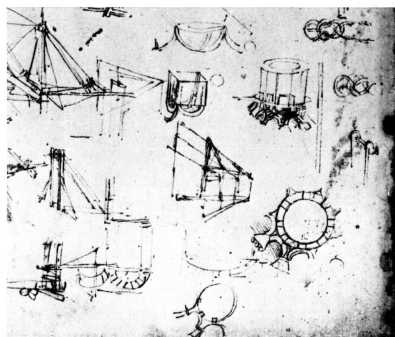

Supper. Leo Steinberg has shown that the central point of the tribune lies on the same axis that touches the entrance to the refectory and the mid-point of Leonardo's *Last Supper*; an axis, therefore, which crosses the Cloister of the Dead diagonally and which connects the tribune and the refectory in a direct line. We are told that every Tuesday and Saturday Lodovico Sforza would visit his wife's tomb and stay to dine with the prior in the refectory. How appropriate that the hand of Leonardo's Christ, opened in a gesture defining the radius of the church dome, extends the promise of everlasting life to those buried within the cloister, while the same gesture is returned by the open hand of "nostre Seigneur au tombeau."

The existence of an overall plan for the coordination of the rebuilding and rearranging of the monastery is clearly discernible from numerous clues and it is reasonable to believe that it should be attributed to Lodovico Sforza himself, guided by his theological and artistic advisers. The sheet of instructions to his secretary Marchesino Stanga of 29 June 1497 gives us hints of his intentions. For example, directly after ordering that the work on the sepulchre be brought to completion he asks that Leonardo be urged to finish "the work begun in the refectory of the Grazie," that is, the *Last Supper*, in order to attend to the other wall of the same refectory. This has been taken as proof of Vasari's statement that the figures of the donors added to either side of Montorfano's fresco are by Leonardo, but there are reasons to believe that Lodovico had something else in mind, for he sees the necessity for a detailed contract – "se facino con luy li capitoli sottoscritti de mano sua che lo oblicano ad finirlo in quello tempo se conuera in luy."

The theme of the Crucifixion is traditionally associated with that of the *Last Supper* in refectory decoration, hence Montorfano's fresco of 1495 is an appropriate counterpart to the one which Leonardo was to complete on the opposite wall two years later. If Lodovico had merely wanted the donor figures to be added he could have asked Montorfano himself or any other painter, and in fact there is nothing in those figures which could be ascribed to Leonardo. It seems more likely that Lodovico wanted to substitute for Montorfano's fresco a mural painting by Leonardo representing the same subject or some other scene from the Passion. Montorfano's fresco may have been judged too inferior to Leonardo's *Last Supper* (as Pasquier Le Moine judged it in 1515), but it is also possible that its iconography with regard to the figures in the foreground was no longer satisfactory, and hence the decision to add, at least, the kneeling figures of the donors. Behind them stand various Dominican saints who appear as retinue of the two saints kneeling on either side of the central cross, their eyes turned to heaven (the one on the left closely resembles the Saint Dominic of Nicolò dell'Arca's portrait in Bologna), and on the ground in front of each of them there is the model of an aedicula or shrine. These are probably two views of the same model, which the two saints present as the offering of the kneeling donors. The more visible of the two is the one represented by Saint Dominic. It consists of a small square building with a canopy roof

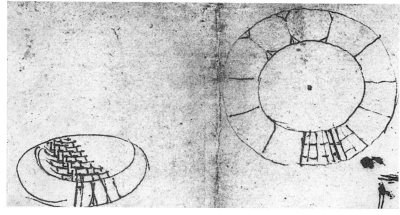

placed on a concave attic, which has a central oculus on each side. The resulting pagoda-like top rests on four pilasters with the spaces between them filled by masonry walls. A high socle is interrupted at the centre by the opening for the door, which is flanked by pilasters and topped by a round pediment. On one side we can see that this is turned into a window with a central column. The model on the right appears to be almost identical, except that the roof rests directly on the entablature. In the context of a Crucifixion these votive chapels may be interpreted as sepulchres, symbolizing the Holy Sepulchre at Jerusalem as does the Rucellai Sepulchre in San Pancrazio. If so, it would be tempting to think of them as first ideas for the Sforza Sepulchre, which at an early stage may have been planned to stand outside the church (note the similarity between roof and lantern and the buildings on the left in the view of Jerusalem in the background), probably at the centre of one of the cloisters – and a chapel of which nothing else is known is mentioned by Arluno. On the other hand, the temporary *tegurio* which Bramante was to build at the crossing of the unfinished new St. Peter's had all the characteristics of an outdoor building like the Casa Santa at Loreto. Indeed, a building of this type could easily be transformed into an indoor structure by simply eliminating its walls and thus bringing it closer to the structure shown by Leonardo in the Codex Atlanticus. It is possible, then, that it was precisely this detail in the Montorfano fresco that prompted Lodovico Sforza to issue new orders in June 1497. After the death of Beatrice in January of that year, a change took place in the iconographic program at S. Maria delle Grazie: the new tribune was destined to hold the Sforza Sepulchre, and was to be linked to a new nave in such a way as to accentuate its purpose as a family mausoleum, almost as if it were a separate building in its own right. It is likely, in fact, that Lodovico himself had conceived the overall plan during the many hours spent with such a theologian as Vincenzo Bandello, the prior of the convent. It has been ascertained that Bramante's name never appears in the earliest accounts of the building activities at S. Maria delle Grazie. It is doubtless significant that the master builder Battista Alberti da Abbiate, who was working in 1498 and 1499 on the new sacristy "and in certain other building works in the same monastery," should recall just a few years later, in 1506, of all the persons he had met there, only Leonardo da Vinci and Andrea da Ferrara.

Nothing is known of Andrea da Ferrara as an architect. According to Luca Pacioli, writing in 1498, he was one of Leonardo's closest friends, "just like a brother to him," and a most knowledgeable commentator of Vitruvius. Faithful to the Sforza, he went into the service of the French, only to favour by treason Lodovico's brief return to Milan in 1500. On 12 May of that year he was executed, his body quartered, and his remains displayed at four different places in the city. In a memorandum of Leonardo's a few years later, we read: "Messer Vincenzo Aliprando who is staying at the osteria dell'Orso has the Vitruvius of Iacomo Andrea" (K. 109 v, c. 1507).

As one recalls Lodovico's instructions to bring together "all the most

157. Detail of architectural studies for the
Trivulzio Monument, c. 1508-10. Windsor,
RL 12355.

158. Study of an aedicule with seated
figures, c. 1487-88. Codex Atlanticus, f. 148
r-a, detail.

159, 160. Study of an aedicule or ciborium,
c. 1497-98. Codex Atlanticus, f. 346 r-b, and
detail.

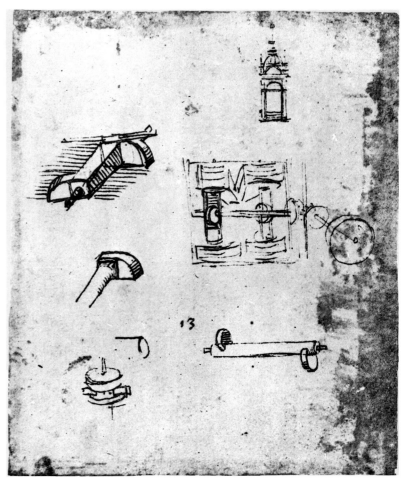

expert to be found in the field of architecture," to study the problem of the new façade planned for S. Maria delle Grazie, one may realize how the architectural project would have proceeded: each of the architects called for consultation, such as Bramante, Leonardo, Andrea da Ferrara and others, would offer ideas to a general coordinator, Lodovico himself. This was not an unusual procedure, since Bramante himself had proposed it in the case of the projects for the tiburio. It is even more likely that this could have been the case with the project for the Sforza Sepulchre. As for Leonardo's possible participation in the scheme, we need only look for clues in the documents.

There is no reason for doubting the attribution to Solari of the effigies of Lodovico and Beatrice now at Pavia. The 1497 document is quite explicit, and yet it has been suggested that Solari had to have helpers in order to meet Lodovico's pressing demands. It has thus been suggested that he may have entrusted the execution of the two effigies to Gian Cristoforo Romano after a design by Boltraffio, Leonardo's well-known pupil. This idea, which, indeed, is not contradicted by the style, is based on a composition by the contemporary poet Gerolamo Casio, entitled *Sonetto per Madonna Giustizia* – Sonnet to Lady Justice:

> The marble which conceals the holy bones
> Of Justice, formerly a living person among us,
> Was found by Boltraffio, and Romano is the sculptor
> Who endeavoured to sculpt her with skill and drive.
> ...

This is important as further proof of the fairly widespread custom of having painters to assist sculptors, but I do not know of any historical account in which Beatrice is referred to as "Lady Justice" or as a personification of Justice – she who is mysteriously called "la Giustizia nera pel Moro," (the black Justice for the Moor) in one of Leonardo's allegories (H. 88 v). On the other hand, Casio's book of epitaphs, which records many members of the Sforza court, including Leonardo himself, never mentions Beatrice by name; and then, a *Sonetto al Duca Lodovico* on f. 121 r is followed by a *Sonetto alla Giustizia*, but unfortunately their contents do not reveal a direct connection, and the juxtaposition may be fortuitous. All that can be drawn with certainty from Casio's poem is that a pupil of Leonardo's, Boltraffio, had provided the design for the "sepulchre of Lady Justice," a monument otherwise unknown to us. All this seems to complicate the problem of the attribution of the Sforza Sepulchre, but at least it has the merit of calling attention to the important aspect of the relationship of Gian Cristoforo Romano with Boltraffio, and thus even with Leonardo himself; a relationship which acquires a special significance when we consider that Gian Cristoforo was to end his career as Bramante's assistant at Loreto, in 1512.

The earliest record of Gian Cristoforo Romano's activity in Lombardy comes from his association with the sculptors employed on the decoration of the façade of the Certosa of Pavia in 1491. Soon afterwards he was commissioned to do the funerary monument of Gian Galeazzo Visconti, also at the Certosa, on which he worked from 1494 to 1497, with the help of Benedetto Briosco, whom Leonardo later recalled as "my friend Benedetto the sculptor" (MS. G, f. 1 v, *c.* 1511). In fact Leonardo must have known Gian Cristoforo well, for he had hoped to employ him as an actor in the part of King Acrisius in Baldassare Taccone's *Danae*, which he produced on 31 January 1496. The stage set studies for *Danae* on one of Leonardo's folios in New York indicate an architectural structure which is remarkably reminiscent of Bramante's feigned choir in San Satiro. A page of the Codex Atlanticus belonging to the same series of notes, f. 358 v-b, contains a sketch which can be taken as an anticipation of Peruzzi's Vitruvian scene, although the source may more probably be found in those urban scenes prepared by Bramante in about 1495. It may also be remembered that in 1495 Gian Cristoforo Romano was working in Vigevano, where Leonardo had been the previous year, and that between 1499 and 1502 he was in Mantua in the service of Isabella d'Este, so Leonardo would certainly have met him when staying in that city during his journey to Venice in 1500. At that time Boltraffio was in Bologna painting an altarpiece for Gerolamo Casio, whom Gian Cristoforo records as his friend and patron in a letter to Isabella d'Este of 29 October 1505. In the same letter he speaks of a project for Isabella that had occupied him a few months before in Milan: the design for a sepulchre for the Blessed Osanna to be erected in the church of San Domenico at Mantua. Detailed information on this project is found in a letter from Gian Cristoforo to Isabella, written from Milan on 17 September 1505. This, and a later reproduction of the monument, which is the only record left of it, suggest that the sculptor had the Sforza Sepulchre in mind. And perhaps we can read something more between the lines of the letter, when the sculptor states that if he had to make another sepulchre of this kind, it would not be enough to ask for 50 ducats more, for he had been able to obtain almost as a gift two columns of the finest marble "which I found in a place among those that were dug for il Moro, and which I got as a gift." We also learn from the same correspondence that Marchesino Stanga, Lodovico Sforza's former secretary, was instrumental in procuring the marble for the sepulchre of the Blessed Osanna. This was probably material which had not yet been used for the Sforza Sepulchre, or which had been destined for the chapel of San Teodoro in San Satiro, another Sforza work planned by Bramante in 1497, and of which we know practically nothing. It is possible, however, that the building had been begun, as in 1515 Le Moine stated that Lodovico had been buried near a pilaster in San Satiro.)

I do not know of any attempt at identifying the funerary monument mentioned by Casio as a work of collaboration between Boltraffio and Gian Cristoforo Romano. As a working hypothesis, I would suggest that this was the sepulchre of the Blessed Osanna even though there is no way as yet to explain why Casio should refer to Osanna Andreati da Mantova, who died in June 1505, as *Madonna Giustizia*. (It is interest-

ing, though, that when Osanna was in Milan as a guest of the Sforza during the 1490s she had a vision of the Temple of Solomon, which she described as a building that had no equal in Milan.) At least it is clear that he is referring to someone who had lived in his own time: "The holy bones of Justice / formerly a living person among us." Maria Reggiani Rajna has suggested that Boltraffio designed the sepulchre of Lady Justice while he was in Bologna, between 1500 and 1502 (in the autumn of 1502 he returned to Milan, where he was painting the *Saint Barbara* for San Satiro), but since Gian Cristoforo Romano was in Bologna again in 1505, Casio could have learned from him of his recent association with Boltraffio on the project of a tomb monument. Of course, it is also possible that Casio had mistaken one Cristoforo for another, namely Cristoforo Solari for Gian Cristoforo Romano. The close association between the two scultptors at Pavia in the early 1490s is well known, as is Boltraffio's participation in the sculptural decoration of Milan Cathedral; in fact it has even been suggested that some of Fusina's and Solari's classicizing statues were inspired by him. This brings to mind a passage in Cesariano's commentary on Vitruvius. Having mentioned Michelangelo, Gian Cristoforo Romano, Cristoforo Solari il Gobbo, Agostino Busti il Bambaia, Tullio Lombardo and others for their achievements in reviving the ideals of antiquity, Bramante's pupil goes on to record the painters: "Non mancho molti pictori Mediolanensi. compagni nostri : come fu la singularità del pingere le Idee de qualcuni uiuendo Ioanne Antonio Boltraphio."

According to Vasari, the Sforza Sepulchre was the work of Giovan Giacomo della Porta, an architect at Milan Cathedral, whose sculptural apprenticeship was spent under Cristoforo Solari. He was the uncle and teacher of Guglielmo della Porta, with whom in 1531 he was to build the ciborium and altar in the Chapel of S. Giovanni at Genoa Cathedral; a ciborium that may in fact retain a memory of the Sforza Sepulchre. When speaking of Guglielmo's apprenticeship under Giovan Iacomo, Vasari records that "in Milan in about 1530 he spent a good deal of time studying how to reproduce the work of Leonardo da Vinci, which was of very great benefit to him." And we know that Guglielmo owned the Leonardo manuscript formerly in the Library of Lord Leicester at Holkham Hall. Finally, through a letter from Guglielmo to Ammannati, we learn of Leonardo's opinion on the study of antiquity: "Leonardo da Vinci used to say, when he was in Milan, that the true teacher of the art which comes under design is Rome."

When he was in Milan! On 24 April 1500 Leonardo was already in Florence, after a short visit to Venice. One of his first works in Florence was the design for the high altar of SS. Annunziata, conceived in the form of a triumphal arch, a kind of Porta Magna as at Preneste and like the *Ianua Coeli* that is implicit in Bramante's program for the *nicchione* at Abbiategrasso of 1497. The setting was, once again, a vast tribune and once again it was another architect, Baccio d'Agnolo, who carried out Leonardo's design.

Meanwhile, the *Antiquarie prospetiche romane* which his friend Bra-

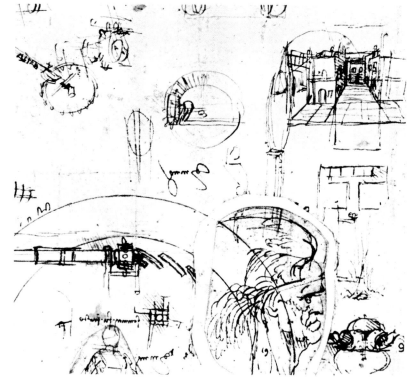

mante dedicated to him as an invitation to join him in Rome were published. "In ancient Tivoli, Hadrian's villa," Leonardo wrote on a folio dated 10 March 1500, which, according to the Florentine calendar, would refer to 1501. Nothing is known of Leonardo's first visit to Rome. Bramante was then about to take up the theme of the architectural setting for a funerary monument on a colossal scale – St. Peter's was being rebuilt to house Michelangelo's tomb of Julius II. And the new apse of S. Maria del Popolo was to be made ready to receive the wall tomb of Cardinal Ascanio Sforza, Lodovico's brother and Bramante's patron in Milan and Pavia.

By 1506, at the time of Bramante's major undertakings in Rome, Leonardo was back in Milan, in the service of the French governor, planning a sepulchre for Marshal Trivulzio, the condottiere who was instrumental in bringing about the fall of the Sforza dynasty. Lodovico was to die, a prisoner in France, far away from the sepulchre which he had built for himself and Beatrice.

And so, once again, there comes to mind Leonardo's notebook, MS. L, in which, on f. 14 r, is the decorative scheme of rhombi with the monograms LV BE, Lodovico and Beatrice. Inside the front cover are the famous observations on the events which followed the fall of the Sforza; observations which begin with the phrase: "Bramante's buildings." And on the inside of the back cover Leonardo transcribed the epigraph written on the sarcophagus of Bishop Serafino di Squillace in the cathedral of Otranto, and which sums up for him an already tragic vision of life: "We are deceived by our vows and deluded by time, and death derides our cares; the anxious life is nothing" (Richter, § 1198).

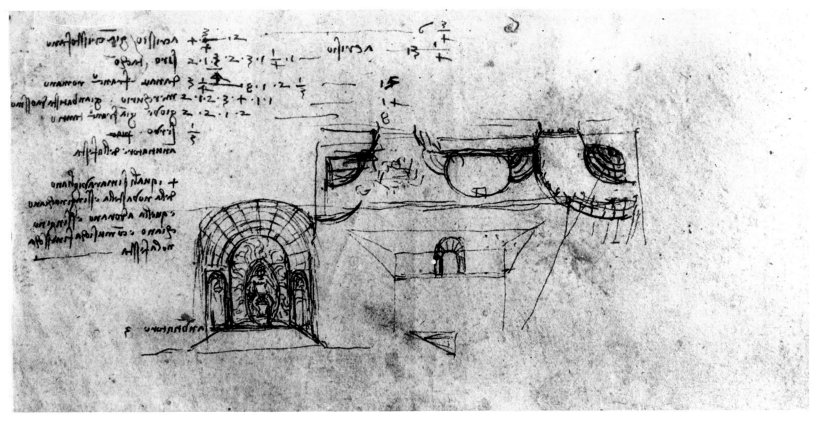

166. Gian Cristoforo Romano (and Boltraffio?), Sepulchre of the Blessed Osanna, formerly in the Church of S. Domenico, Mantua. (Eighteenth-century engraving).

MONUMENTUM B OSANNÆ ORD. PRÆDICAT. MANTUÆ

167. Giacomo and Guglielmo della Porta,
Ciborium and altar in the chapel
of S. Giovanni, Genoa Cathedral.

The "Antiquarie Prospetiche Romane." A Poem by Bramante Dedicated to Leonardo

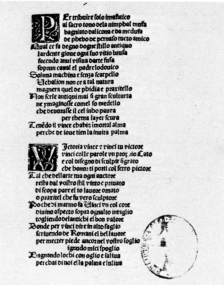

The small work entitled *Antiquarie prospetiche romane*, which is reproduced here in facsimile from the only known copy in the Biblioteca Casanatense in Rome, was made known for the first time by Gilberto Govi in 1875. The author, under the pseudonym of "Prospettivo Milanese Dipintore," declares himself a friend and colleague of Leonardo da Vinci, and dedicates the publication to him with an invitation to join him in Rome. Certain characteristics of the text and of the typeface lead to the conclusion that it was published in Rome about 1500. However, the authorship remained unknown, despite attempts by Govi, Suida and others to attribute it to Bregno or Bramantino, until, in 1966, Guglielmo de Angelis d'Ossat persuasively identified the author as Bramante. Both Bruschi and Fienga have recently further strengthened this hypothesis and now we can add to it a document, which is the key to the enigmatic woodcut on the frontispiece and which shows that the extraordinary nude figure kneeling among the ruins of ancient buildings and vibrant with reflections of Leonardo should be understood as a symbolic self-portrait of Bramante. This document is found in a note-book of Guglielmo della Porta, now in Düsseldorf. It is the rough draft of a letter which Guglielmo himself, at an undetermined date (around 1560) wrote to Ammannati to convince him of the importance, and indeed necessity, of studying in Rome. The arguments he puts forward consist of a review of the opinions of illustrious predecessors on the study of antiquity, starting with Leonardo, who is quoted as having stated, while resident in Milan, "that Rome is the real teacher of the art which comes under *disegno*." After quoting Leonardo's opinion, Della Porta adds Bramante's: "The architect Bramante used to say that all those who come to Rome as masters in this profession must shed, as snakes do, everything that they had learned elsewhere, and he proved this himself with his own example, saying that before he saw this city he used to think himself an excellent painter and architect, but that after practising for many years he became aware of his error, and this was the reason that, after having drawn a great number of the buildings of ancient Rome, of Tivoli, of Praeneste, and many other places, studying, noting and learning something new every day, he opened the way to the good and regulated architecture of antiquity." Here we have a programmatic statement, something that could be called "Bramante's Manifesto" of 1500 when, having left Milan for Rome, he does *shed* all that he has learned up to now to start again at the beginning with the study of antiquity. The same statement is to be found at the conclusion of the sonnets addressed to Leonardo as a dedication at the beginning of the *Antiquarie*:

> Donde per Vinci dire in alto saglio
> Scrivendo de Romani el bel lavore
> per mecter piede ancor nel vostro soglio
> ignudo mi ci spoglio
> (As I mention Vinci I step high up
> writing of the beautiful work of the Romans
> and in order to put my foot upon your threshold
> I strip myself nude.)

It could well be said that the rebus is presented in a Vitruvian key, particularly because the measuring and calculating instruments allude to geometry and perspective. In fact the author defines himself as "prospettivo" in the sense that he has recourse to a scientific system of measuring and representing space which had been a prerogative of the architect since the days of Brunelleschi. The resultant image is an appropriate complement to Raphael's portrait of Bramante in the *School of Athens*. Furthermore Bramante's reputation as "prospettivo" had already been established in Milan, for example in the Prevedari print and in the feigned choir of San Satiro; so much so that he could pass as Milanese, as indeed he is considered by Gerolamo Casio. Lomazzo (*Rime*, 1587) tells of the perspective which Bramante taught to Raphael and he to Peruzzi:

> Egli ha mostrato l'alta prospettiua
> che da Bramante trapassò [a] il Petrucci
> con somma gratia posta al suo vedere.
> (He has shown the fine perspective
> which from Bramante he passed on to Petrucci
> and placed it before him with highest grace.)

Simonetta Valtieri's recent observations on the architecture in Raphael's *School of Athens* have shown how Bramante may have suggested a new method for constructing a harmonious architecture in perspective. This is an important aspect, still largely unexplored, of Renaissance architecture and could be placed in relation to a statement by Anton Francesco Doni on the contents of an architectural treatise, now lost, in which Bramante had dealt with the proportion of buildings. "Whoever reads this," said Doni, "as soon as he has seen a building, may recognize immediately whether it is well-proportioned or not: and he will be able to say whether the individual parts go well together as a whole."

This then is the reason why the author of the *Antiquarie* only needs a single woodcut image to be instantly recognized by name. But the rebus is in fact concluded by the initials PM in the frame of the woodcut. They stand not only for the pseudonym "Prospettiuo Melanese," but also for Bramante's own name, as "Pramante Magister." This is how his name appears, in association with that of Leonardo, in the *Historiarum ab origine Urbis mediolanensis ad nostra usque tempora* by Bernardino Arluno (Basel, 1530). This could also explain the rebus which Bramante had devised for the Belvedere and which would have concealed both the name of the pope and the name of the architect. Vasari's explanation of it only account for the name of the pope, JULIUS II, but nevertheless the PM added to it, which would normally stand for PONTIFEX MAXIMUS, could also be taken as standing for PRAMANTE MAGISTER.

To find this rebus rather childish is to agree with Julius II, who rejected Bramante's suggestion as being comparable to the "Viterbo nonsense," a rebus which a contemporary architect had had carved in the way of a signature on the architrave of the door of a house in Viterbo and which has recently been rediscovered. On the other hand, these games of memory-jogging – hieroglyphics – through which

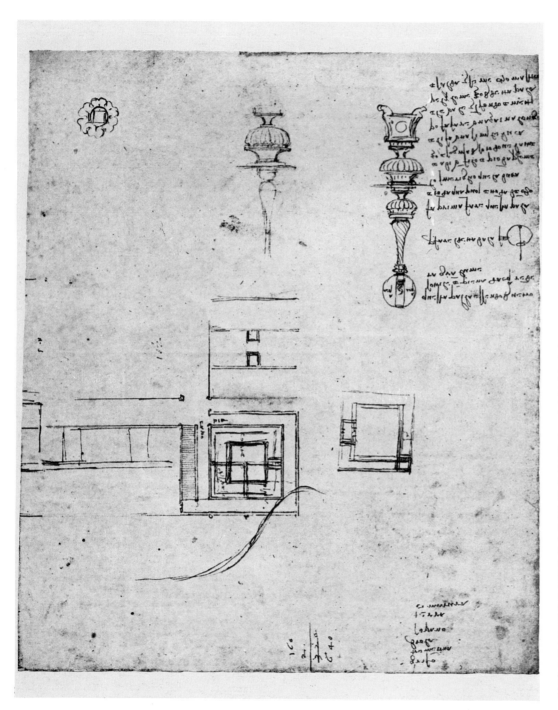

the image of an object becomes associated to an idea, are nothing but one aspect of "artificial memory," a most ancient science, which in turn is a form of "perspective of memory," a means of manipulating the mental construction (just as Brunelleschi had done with the mind of the fat carpenter), and therefore a useful tool in the service of study. In this way one may also explain Leonardo's "nonsense," the rebus on a sheet at Windsor (RL 12692) which covers the plan of a large palace. This same plan is repeated in identical scale on a sheet of the Codex Atlanticus, f. 80 r-a, which is of the same time *c.* 1487-90. We therefore must not exclude the possibility that Leonardo may have considered using rebuses as inscriptions for buildings. The phrase "Up to now I have not carried out any work, but I know that what I have done now will make me triumph," which is the solution to one of his rebuses is not necessarily introspective, and could be expressing the intentions of a patron.

"Tell me, tell me if anything was ever built in Rome," writes Leonardo, trying out his pen, on f. 216 v-b of the Codex Atlanticus, a page of technological studies (transmission of motive power and pulleys for an automaton) which may be assigned to the last years of the fifteenth century because of their relationship to the contents of Madrid MS. I.

Apart from clues like this, which seem to reach us from Leonardo's subconscious, we now have more concrete proof of a first visit of Leonardo to Rome at the beginning of the sixteenth century, and Kenneth Clark took account of these in his brilliant study of "Leonardo and the Antique" of 1969. We can now add that the incentive to go to Rome could have come to Leonardo not only from Bramante, but also from Attalante Migliorotti, his musician friend, who had gone with him to Milan in 1482 and who inexplicably reappeared in Rome between 1513 and 1516, and what is more, was one of the superintendents of the Vatican workshops. That Atalante was at the Vatican even before this we learn from the episode recounted by Michelangelo in a letter of 1524 to Francesco Fattucci: "... On returning to Rome I set myself to making cartoons for the said work, that is, for the heads and faces around the said Chapel of Sixtus, hoping for money to finish the work. I could never obtain any: and complaining one day to Bernardo da Bibbiena and Attalante that I could no longer stay in Rome and would have to leave: Messer Bernardo said to Attalante to remind him that he wanted to have money given to me at all costs. And he saw to it that I was given two thousand *ducati di Camera*, to be added to the first thousand for the marble which they put at my disposal for the tomb; and I estimated that I should have more for the time lost and the work completed. And from this money, as Bernardo and Attalante had helped me, I gave to the one a hundred ducats, and to the other fifty."

Indirect and even documentary evidence of a first visit to Rome by Leonardo at the beginning of the sixteenth century is not, however, enough to give substance to the suspicion that he may have played a part in the designing of Bramante's Tempietto, or for that matter of the new St. Peter's.

Yet the sketches of tempietti in Codex Atlanticus, f. 205

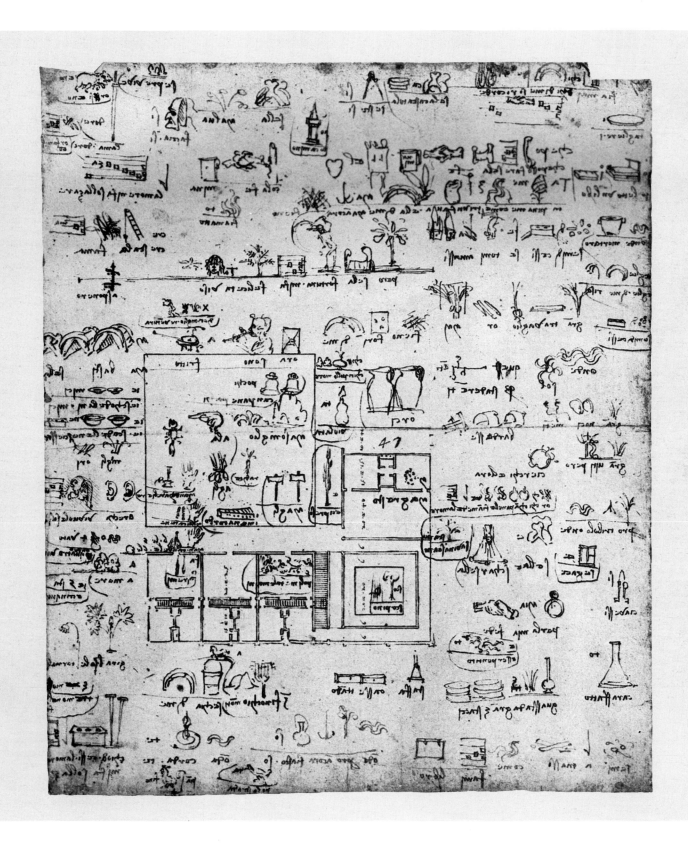

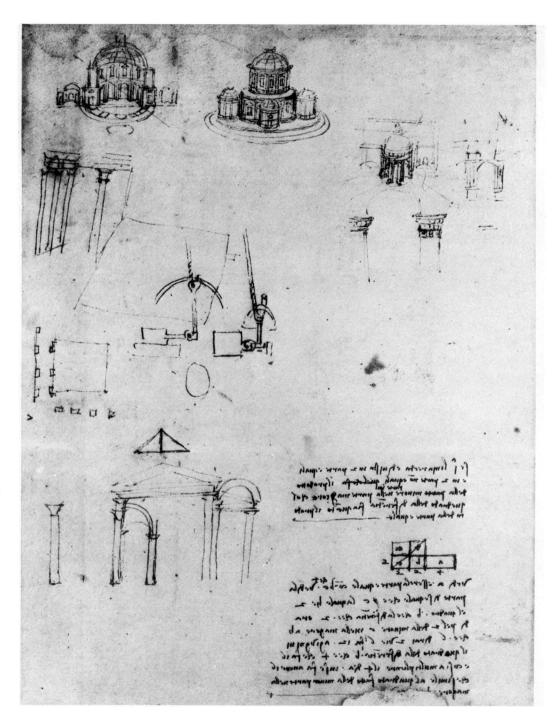

v-a, datable to about 1505-6, one of which is shown as the central feature of a courtyard; the design for a round pedestal for the Trivulzio Monument (Windsor RL 12353) of 1508; and the design in the Louvre for a mausoleum of 1507-8 reflect ideas which could have preceded the construction, if not the conception, of the Tempietto in S. Pietro in Montorio. The Tempietto does not appear in Albertini's guide-book of 1510, which records Bramante's other Roman buildings; and the Anonimo Magliabechiano, who lists Bramante's buildings in chronological order, puts it last. In fact, de Angelis d'Ossat and Bruschi have furnished convincing reasons for suggesting that the building belongs to a more mature phase of Bramante's style, after 1510.

Bramante's Lost Books

It is mainly through the testimony of his contemporaries that Bramante is known as a poet and writer, but apart from about twenty sonnets and the poem on the *Antiquarie prospetiche romane*, which has only recently been recognized as his work, nothing is left of his treatises on architecture, which still existed in manuscript form in the mid-sixteenth century.

On the other hand, something that does not yet seem to have been noticed is that the contents of those books, according to a summary given by Doni, correspond exactly to the section on architecture in the Introduction to Vasari's *Lives* of 1550 and 1568. In fact, Vasari's chapters have titles which reproduce almost the same words Doni used, including the reference to the "German work," and they are in the same sequence as the headings in Bramante's text.

Doni published the second part of his *Libraria* at Venice in 1551, when he could have already seen Vasari's first edition and it may seem, therefore, that he had "invented" the existence of Bramante's books by summarizing Vasari's text. But it is more probable that those books really did exist and that it was Vasari who did the plagiarizing. In 1549 Doni was still in Florence and on very good terms with Vasari, to the point of being involved in the project of the *Lives*, which he himself, rather than Torrentino, was supposed to publish.

Moreover, Vasari refers to an illustration (the façade of a building) which, however, he did not reproduce, not even in the second edition, and this could suggest that he was copying someone else's text. Doni hoped that "he who is keeping this treasure of Bramante's hidden away would bring it out." Perhaps this was the same person he alluded to further on in speaking of Adimari's book on antique scaffolding which had been written "partly by the hand of messer Filippo Brunelleschi," and in which was "drawn a great part of the scaffolding that he made for vaulting the dome of Florence," a book which, "had I been able to read it (since its owner merely allowed me to glance at it), truly I would tell of many beautiful things."

It may be worth considering Doni's statement in his introductory letter "To those who do not read," about the handwritten books he had seen: "I believe few of the

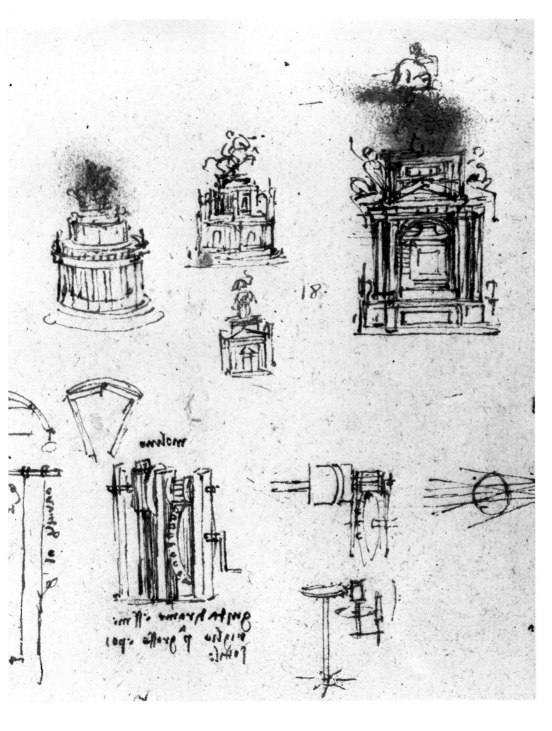

179. Studies for the Trivulzio Monument, c. 1508-10. Windsor, RL 12353.

above books are to be printed since they are rare books and in the hands of persons who do not want to part with them, and would rather have them burnt." To which he adds: "If some gallant person would like to know where these works are, I am happy to let him know on condition of my only revealing those who have given me full license to do so."

180-184. The Etruscan tomb. In the corpus of Leonardo's architectural studies there is still some hesitation in including a drawing at the Louvre which came from Vallardi (no. 2386). This is the well-known representation in plan and elevation of a grandiose sepulchral monument at the summit of a conical tumulus in the midst of a landscape that extends into the distance in a succession of undulating hills, punctuated here and there by cottages. This is a bird's-eye view of unmistakably Leonardesque character, reminiscent of those of the Pisan hills, touched with colour, in MS. II in Madrid of 1503-4, and anticipating the even more caligraphic and lively ones of the Adda in drawings at Windsor of ten years later. And yet the attribution to Leonardo has been contested by Venturi and others exactly on the basis of the style, in which they thought to recognize that of Francesco di Giorgio. It is true that the precision and incisiveness of the architectural drawing can lead back generically to the character of the drawings of the Sienese architect, with whom Leonardo is known to have been in close rapport. On the other hand, it is a character not alien to at least some of Leonardo's own drawings. Remaining examples of this type are scarce, but there is, for instance, the large drawing of a fortress in the Codex Atlanticus, f. 41 v-b, with notes in which Leonardo mentions an event which took place at the Castello in Milan in 1507, thus confirming the late period for this type of drawing by him. Such confirmation has also recently come for the drawing of the

mausoleum at the Louvre. The date 1507, already proposed on stylistic grounds, was that of an archaeological discovery which in January of that year aroused great interest in Tuscany: the Etruscan tombs on the tumulus of Montecalvario at Castellina in Chianti, which Marina Martelli has suggested as the model for Leonardo's drawing. "In 1507 on the 29th day of January, near Castellina, in uprooting a vineyard, a completely subterranean room was discovered, 20 braccia long, 5 high and 3 wide with a few

side projections where statues, ashes, ornaments and Etruscan letters were found." This description of the discovery appears in a little work by Pier Francesco Giambullari published in 1546. Later notes gathered by Marina Martelli confirm the importance attributed to the find in Florentine humanist circles at the beginning of the sixteenth century. It is not surprising therefore that Leonardo himself, on his return from Milan in 1507, should have hastened to carry out an inspection of the Etruscan

tomb, drawing inspiration from it for a project for a mausoleum based on an ideal restoration of the monument. Leonardo's archaelogical imagination" therefore shows itself in the scenic character of an artificial hill enveloping the monument itself, restored to its original function as a burying place, with a round tempietto on top as if to present a symbolic compendium of the humanist vision of the ancient world.

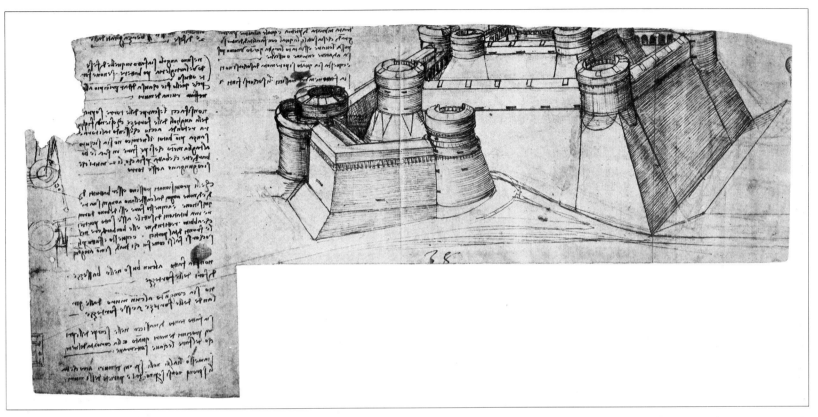

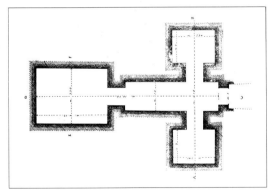

123

8. Venice

"And there is in Venice Leonardo da Vinci, who has shown me a portrait of your Ladyship which is a very good likeness. It is so well done, it could not possibly be better." Thus wrote Lorenzo Gusnasco da Pavia, the lute-maker, to Isabella d'Este on 13 March 1500.

We know that at the fall of the Sforza dynasty in 1499 Leonardo left Milan to return to Florence, making a long detour by way of Mantua and Venice. Although there must have been some other stops in places like Padua, Ferrara and Bologna we have no knowledge of them. In fact, we know very little of Leonardo's activities during the three or four months it took him to return to Florence from Milan, a period which falls exactly between the two manuscripts recently found in Madrid. The first of these bears the dates 1493 and 1497 and the second, 1503 and 1505. This last has an appendix of seventeen sheets which in effect forms a third manuscript, dated by Leonardo himself 1491 and 1493. It is entirely concerned with the project of casting the horse for the Sforza Monument.

Let us examine two pages of the first manuscript, f. 44 v and f. 45 r. They are by now famous both for the ingenuity of the machines represented, and for the clarity and precision of the drawing. The drum-like mechanism within which a spring is wound is made up of a toothed spiral decreasing towards the top, which operates on a conical sprocket by raising it, so that the cogged wheel is lifted upwards to engage with an elongated spool. This apparatus, which could be applied to clocks, clearly illustrates the mechanical principle of compensation, even though Leonardo does not explain this in the note. In unwinding, the spring gradually loses power, but the movement which results from it is kept constant by means of the bevel-gear drive. It is difficult, however, to imagine a practical application for the gadget illustrated on the facing page – a bunch of six rods opening outwards like an umbrella upside-down.

What is most interesting is the manner in which he has represented this, with architectural clarity, both in plan and in elevation. Although the time lapse between the two pages may be brief, perhaps even just a few months, there is enough of a difference between them to allow us to distinguish two stylistic moments and therefore two phases of the compilation. The drawings and notes on the left, that is on f. 44 v, with the exception of the two lines at the top of the page, still resemble Leonardo's first scientific illustrations, such as the 1489 anatomical drawings at Windsor, in which we recognize the same precise, geometric definition of details and the same atmospheric sense of the image in the round. Even the handwriting seems to share this. He lingers with pleasure over the decorative qualities of the initial letter and of the ascending and descending strokes, so that the line takes on an archaic flavour, almost like embroidery. Typographically conceived, the page has the quality of an extremely delicate copper engraving. The adjoining page, f. 45 r, adds to this quality a new graphic idea brought about by the very shape being represented. Of course the cylinder and the spiral

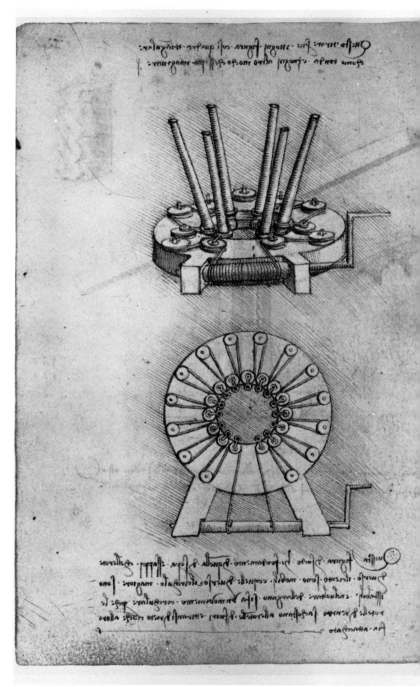

are forms which we already think of as volumetric and dynamic entities, and here the hatching which curves round to follow their forms – as does the line of writing on the cylinder – gives the object a vigorous sense of three-dimensionality, while the parallel diagonal hatching behind it creates an atmospheric background against which it can stand out. This technique can be compared to that used in the representation of the superb female nude of *Leda*, which Leonardo conceived a few years later and which seems to embody the vital forces in Nature. Finally, we note that the writing on this later page is thicker, as if the letters had to express the same sense of immediacy as the drawing, and it is well known that Leonardo's handwriting, delicate and ornate in his youth, took on a resolute fluency in his maturity. Madrid MS. I, therefore, regarded as a document of Leonardo's development as a draughtsman, shows the same stylistic elements that characterize his work as painter and architect at the beginning of the sixteenth century. In fact, at the end of 1499 when he left for Venice, the manuscript must still have had many blank pages and spaces which he did not use until much later. We can see this, for example, on f. 171 v and f. 172 r. The notes on mechanics on f. 171 v are arranged in columns on one side, so as to leave ample free space beside them. This was the style of layout Leonardo used around the year 1499, and the drawings themselves can be compared with pages in other manuscripts of that year. Looking now at the next page, f. 172 r, we recognize the same mechanical studies laid out in the same way so as to leave the same amount of clear space. But in this case Leonardo has taken the book up again and used that space to add five drawings of dismountable joints which, he explains, are suitable for field pavilions, therefore alluding to some military use for them, as in the case of the "camp bed" in MS. L, f. 70 r-v. Great importance has been attached to these drawings, interpreting them as belonging to the well-known project for a wooden pavilion at Vigevano, the date of which, as we have seen, was 1494. The similarity however is only superficial and, in fact, close comparison allows us to dismiss it.

A real similarity exists however in a series of preliminary sketches in the Codex Arundel, f. 150 r, a page containing the memorandum: "Marcantonio Colonna in Sancto Apostolo." This is undoubtedly a reference to the famous military commander who served the Florentine Republic in the war against Pisa, and aside from this, the other part of the sheet contains elements indicating a date about 1505. We can therefore conclude that in the Madrid page Leonardo made a "fair copy" of the Arundel sketches, adding explanations in handwriting with post-1500 characteristics, e.g. the reversed hook on some of the ascenders, as in the *h*, and the "*ecc*" placed at the end.

The last evidence of Leonardo's presence in Milan in 1499, before leaving for Venice, is found in two sheets of the Codex Atlanticus. The first, f. 284 r, is full of the sort of money accounts that one usually makes in preparing for a long journey. The note is dated and records that on 1 April 1499 Leonardo had found himself with 218 lire. As we have seen some of the sketches on this sheet relate to a drawbridge which

186. Notes on mechanics, c. 1499 and studies of dismountable hinges, c. 1503-4. Madrid MS. I, ff. 171 v-172 r.

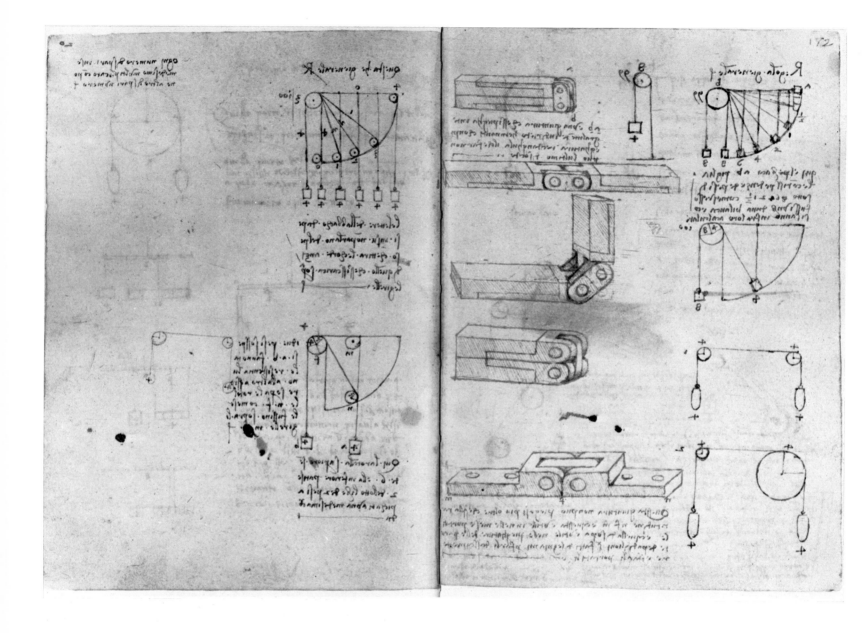

*187, 188. Studies of dismountable hinges for
a camp-bed, c. 1502. MS. L, ff. 70 v-71 r and
70 r-69 v.*

*189. Studies of dismountable hinges,
c. 1504. Codex Arundel, f. 150 r.*

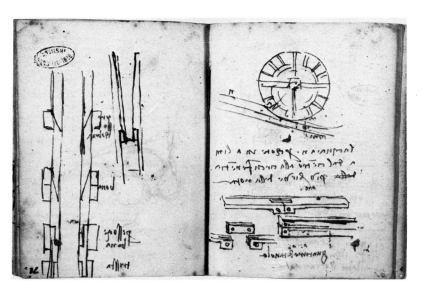

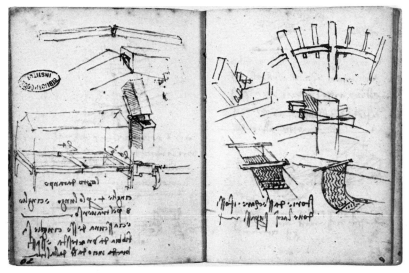

Bramante showed him, as Leonardo himself wrote in MS. M, a notebook of 1499. The sheet also contains a few mechanical studies of the sort found in many pages of Madrid MS. I (for example on f. 158 r). This connection with the Madrid manuscript is even more obvious in the other Codex Atlanticus sheet, f. 104 r-b, which carries the note: "On the 1st day of August 1499 I wrote here about motion and weight." The handwriting too is of the type we have already seen in the Madrid Codex. The evidence may be scant, but it is important for a knowledge of what Leonardo was doing in 1499. This last sheet appears to indicate, moreover, that he was still in Milan, because at the bottom there is a sketch of an appliance for the bath of Duchess Isabella of Aragon. Two documents in the Florentine State Archives show that two installments of three hundred florins each had been sent from Milan, through banking agents, to be held for Leonardo at the Hospital of Santa Maria Nuova, on 7 and 17 January 1500. This proves that he was not yet in Florence, but it does not prove that he had already left Milan, although this is highly probable. When Pacioli recalls the period he spent with Leonardo in Milan between 1496 and 1499 he adds: "Then we departed together from there, because of various events in those parts, and in Florence we took up residence again together," letting us know indirectly that he had accompanied Leonardo to Venice at the close of the century.

We know, moreover, that Pacioli had important contacts in Venice. His connection with the Scuola di Rialto, recently illustrated by Bruno Nardi, should be considered in the light of his association with Leonardo. It was in Venice that he published the *Summa*, a book dated 1494, which Leonardo procured for himself even before meeting the author; and it was again in Venice, in 1509, that two more of his works were to appear: the famous *Divina Proportione* and the edition of Euclid. Leonardo participated in both of these, supplying him with the wonderful series of perspective drawings of the regular bodies and, among other things, according to a statement made by Tory in 1529, the drawings of the Attic lettering with which the geometrical principles governing the construction of the letters of ancient inscriptions are codified according to ideas put forward by Alberti. Looking at the historical, social and cultural aspects of Leonardo's and Pacioli's journey to Venice, one should consider the role which Ermolao Barbaro, the humanist and Venetian Ambassador at the Sforza court, may have played in their decision to go to Venice after the fall of the Sforza.

Were it not for the letter which Gusnasco wrote to Isabella d'Este on 13 March 1500, we would not know exactly when Leonardo was in Venice; at the same time we learn that he had already been in Mantua. This information is confirmed by documents from a later period, including Isabella's own letters to Leonardo when he had returned to Florence.

The chronological picture is therefore as follows: by January 1500 Leonardo had left Milan (probably already before the French invasion

of 1499); on 13 March he was in Venice, where he could have arrived quite some time before, coming from Mantua. A document of 24 April records that he had personally deposited 50 gold florins in his bank account in Florence. If he had stopped in the Veneto even for a couple of months he could still have produced a great deal in that time, whether in writing, drawings or other projects. I am deliberately leaving aside the old question, which stems from Vasari, of Leonardo's influence on Giorgione's style. This is a question which has aroused varying reactions from Boschini's lively and amusing one to the all too repetitious observations of art historians on the conflict between form and colour, which has even been attributed to the different philosophical tendencies of Florence and Venice. It is a problem, in brief, which cannot be tackled without first having an answer to the question: Why did Leonardo go to Venice?

According to a legend which originated no more than seventy years ago and which has met with much appeal, Leonardo went to Venice in 1500 to propose a project to the Venetian Republic for submarine assault devices with which to face the threat of the Turkish fleet. But already in 1925, as we have seen, Calvi proved that all those sketches by Leonardo which are still thought by many to relate to his stay in Venice in 1500 belong in fact to the period 1485-87 and probably refer to a project for freeing the Ligurian waters from the raids of pirates. It would certainly be ironic if one could establish that during that stay Leonardo was not thinking of sinking ships, but rather of raising those already sunk, as was to be done two centuries later, with spectacular methods that Leonardo seems to have prefigured.

Let us linger a moment on the subject of ships, which played such an important part in the traditions and history of Venice. We have a good deal of evidence that Leonardo's nautical studies began to intensify about 1500 and in fact there is a complete section in the second Madrid manuscript which refers to his stay in Piombino in 1504 and contains the outline of an extended treatise on how to handle sailing-boats. An account of Leonardo's studies on naval architecture has still to be done. It is a topic which might be linked with Alberti's *De navis*, a lost treatise which Leonardo owned. Alberti had in fact proposed raising the famous ships lying at the bottom of Lake Nemi. A page on which Leonardo gives something like a summary of the contents of Madrid MS. I has the following reference: "On how to push air under water, and pull up out of it very great weights, that is fill leather sacks with wind which are then tied up under water together with the weights; and to fill ships with sand and tie the weights to such boats as are under water and then empty such boats of their sand." This last operation corresponds exactly to the one described by Alberti in his *De re aedificatoria*, X. xii. Unfortunately the Madrid manuscript has a few pages missing. They could have contained such a treatise, which Leonardo might have thought out in Venice. We find instead, at the bottom of f. 154 r, one of those notes added to the texts on mechanics and thus datable to about 1500 or later in which a system of raising boats in order to repair them in the dockyard is illustrated. The preliminary sketches are found in the Codex Atlanticus, f. 176 v-d, a sheet with notes on mechanics from about 1500. Finally, on the first sheet of Madrid MS. I we read: "I recall having seen many people, and from various countries, who because of their childish credulity, having gone to Venice with great hopes of gain, had made a mill in still waters and not being able, after much expense, to move such a machine were compelled to move themselves out of such a fix with great haste."

The next reference to Venice in Leonardo's manuscripts in a memorandum of 8 April 1503 in the Codex Arundel, f. 229 v, which confirms the trip to Venice and tells us that Leonardo was accompanied on that occasion by his apprentice Salai. (Boltraffio too, who in 1500 painted the Casio altarpiece in Bologna, was probably with him, as seems to be suggested in a poem by Marcello Filosseno published in Venice in 1507.) Leonardo recalls having loaned 20 ducats to the young Salai, specifying "that is, 17 loaned in Milan and 3 in Venice."

Only a few other tesserae are left from this highly complex mosaic: the only other two references to Leonardo's sojourn in the Veneto in 1500 are found in two manuscripts of a later period. They are very important however, because at long last they can give us a more precise idea of the purpose of his visit. f. 79 r-c of the Codex Atlanticus is filled with notes on the movements of wind and water, which Leonardo had dictated to his pupil Francesco Melzi. He himself added comments and sketches which can be directly linked with the series of Deluge drawings at Windsor. They were made at the end of Leonardo's stay in Italy, around 1515-16. Two hardly visible black chalk lines in Leonardo's hand read as follows: "Bombards from Lyon to Venice in the way that I ordered in Gradisca in Friuli and in ovinhio [Avignon?]." These allusions to the time of Francis I's expedition to Italy in 1515 may offer us an indication of the reasons which brought Leonardo into contact with the new French monarch. Contemporary chronicles describe step by step the march of the Most Christian liberator, beginning precisely in Lyons, and mention the ingenious devices adopted for transporting pieces of artillery across the Alps, as a feat of military engineering, the only precedent of which was Hannibal's exploit. Venetian diplomacy of the time, rich in documents and the subject of much study, may still hold surprises when reconsidered in the context of what Leonardo's two lines now seem to suggest. But there is more: he alludes to a system of transport for artillery which he himself had already employed at Gradisca in Friuli. Here we are then, shifting our field of research towards the eastern borders of the Serenissima, and again it is Leonardo himself who enlightens us retrospectively on what his tasks were in that area. The information comes to us in fact from a sheet from his French period concerning the project for a new royal residence at Romorantin. He was studying the systemization of the rivers of the region and suggested lock-mechanisms and mills. The sheet (Codex Arundel, f. 270 v) offers a summary of the various projects and the notes finish with a remark on the necessity of letting the water out all at once through the

191. *Draft copy of a report to the Venetian Senate*
concerning river defense projects, c. 1500. Codex Atlanticus,
f. 234 v-c.

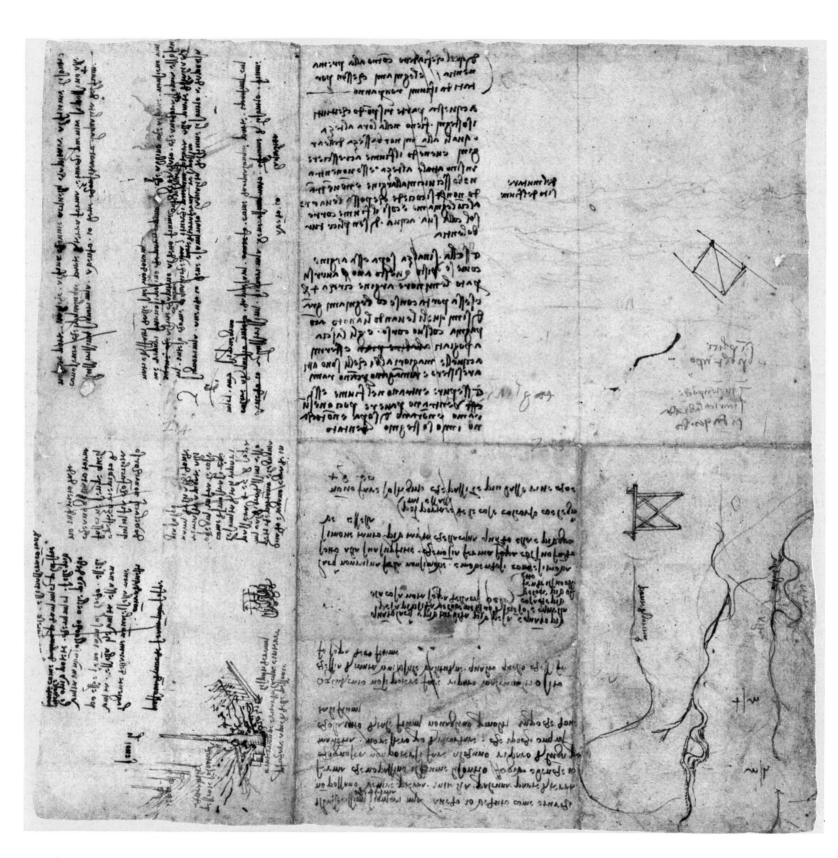

locks so as to clean the canals: "And make the movable barrier such as I ordered in Friuli, where the water coming out of the flood-gate cleared the bottom."

We have here a categorical statement by Leonardo himself which proves that he went to Venice with a specific task and that he had "ordered," that is carried out, a program of military engineering works. It is time therefore that we consider another document which to date has not been given all the importance it deserves – the draft of a report by Leonardo to the Venetian Senate on f. 234 v-c of the Codex Atlanticus. Unfortunately it is only a draft with frequent crossings-out and with one portion missing, as shown by the folds in the sheet. (I would like to suggest, at least in parenthesis, that the missing part could correspond to certain drawings of Alpine ranges at Windsor, but this correspondence could only be ascertained by a simultaneous examination of the originals.)

We have here a detailed defense project devised to face the threatened Turkish invasion, and we notice Leonardo's characteristic way of submitting the proposal almost in the form of a treatise, even to the point of adding beside one paragraph what could have been a chapter heading: "On how to change the river course."

From these fragmentary texts we can draw the conclusion that Leonardo was inspecting sites far and wide, speaking with the locals; and we can also glean some information on that system of river-locks to which he would refer later as work carried out: "the movable barrier such as I ordered in Friuli."

The sheet also includes some notes of a topographical character in which we can recognize the course of the Isonzo by virtue of a reference to "Vilpagho" and to the "Gorizia bridge," while just above we note a light sketch of mountain ranges with some indications of dwellings and a few isolated words such as "Tagliamento" and "senplice / per tenpo / Jn quel tenpo che si carica la bōbarda / si da questo..." (simple / in time / while the bombard is being loaded / this is given...)

The hint of an Alpine landscape which is presented here in a context of military operations cannot fail to remind us of those in the Madrid MS. II – the very beautiful drawings of the Pisan hills, also conceived in the context of military operations and datable a few years later, to 1503. It is but a short step from here to the notes on painting in the same manuscript, which show a keen interest in landscape, aerial perspective and colour. Here we could ponder on the importance that a visit to Venice and the Julian Alps, a few years before, might have had for Leonardo as a painter. But for the moment we must leave aside these tempting aspects of research and remain on solid ground. It is time, in fact, to formulate concrete proposals.

Could it not be that the Archives of the Venetian Republic conserve some trace of Leonardo's plan? Might not old maps of the region be found – old plans of places in which one could recognize elements that may relate to architectural and military engineering drawings by Leonardo which still await interpretation? Could it be that so many

architects, master-builders, hydraulic engineers, Venetian as well as foreign, who in later times were concerned with the same problems did not keep a record of mechanisms and devices that could go back to Leonardo's ideas of 1500?

In the Touring Club Italiano guide to Venezia Giulia, on the page describing Gradisca, we read the following: "From the Church of the Addolorata the campiello Giovanni Emo leads to the Castle, erected in the fifteenth century by Contrin, in collaboration with Leonardo da Vinci, by order of the Venetian Senate." This information has never appeared in any study of Leonardo that I know of. One gets the impression that so categorical a statement comes directly from archival records or from a local tradition which would certainly be worthy of investigation. Such research has just begun and there is hope that it may lead to an explanation of certain studies of military architecture in Leonardo's manuscripts dating shortly before the pages on the fortifications at Piombino in Madrid MS. II.

Only recently have we begun to see in Leonardo's fortification designs of a new element which is made up of forms both receding and aggressively defensive, moulded as they seem to be by the trajectories of the shots fired by besieging artillery – a dynamic element which was later to affect even the civilian architecture of the sixteenth century from Bramante, Peruzzi and from the Sangallos to Michelangelo. These are ideas which have been thought to date back to the time of Leonardo's activity in the service of Cesare Borgia in 1502 and in the service of Jacopo Appiani in Piombino in 1504. But it now appears possible that they could have already emerged in 1500, for this is what a proof of Leonardo's participation in the defensive system at Gradisca could imply. It is a question which should be considered within the whole historical and technological context of Venetian military architecture, leading finally to the famous project of Palmanova – the fortified city that towards the end of the sixteenth century was to take the place of Gradisca on the new borders of the Republic.

Sketches and notes on artillery and military architecture recur constantly in Leonardo's notebooks of 1499 and 1500, and in these same notebooks those curious literary productions known as Leonardo's "profezie" begin to appear. They reappear on a Codex Atlanticus sheet of 1500 next to the outline of an account of an imaginary trip to the Near East. This too is a whole problem which ought to be considered from a chronological standpoint, and in fact it might take on a completely different aspect if we were able to establish, as seems possible, that it actually was in Venice, at the time of the *Hypnerotomachia Poliphili*, that Leonardo first had the idea of such a literary project.

On some of Leonardo's sheets containing outlines of the description of the imaginary journey there are topographical sketches which seem to derive from the maps of one of Ptolemy's atlases. There is a whole series of sheets which can be grouped around that theme, giving us precious pieces of information on various aspects of Leonardo's studies and

192-194. Gradisca. The first phase in the construction of the fortified wall encircling Gradisca goes back to 1479 and the work of the architect E. Gallo. He was succeeded by Giacomo Contrino, who in 1498 (see inscription) concluded the defensive work by building the Torrione della Campana to the north of the city. On the basis of archival research, expressly undertaken by Professor Ennio Concina of the University of Venice, it has been established that this architect and engineer was the same Coltrino or Coltrin who is recorded as the father-in-law of Antonio Vecellio, Titian's uncle, in documents which have still not all been published. However, we have no proof of his hypothetical association with Leonardo. In fact, at the time of Leonardo's visit in 1500, documented by the artist himself, Contrino was elsewhere in Venetian territory and the fortifications of Gradisca, including the castello, were already complete. The fortress, located at the southern end of the citadel and overlooking the Isonzo, is protected by the city wall, which follows an almost rectilinear course to converge on the Torrione della Marcella, making it a nerve point of the defensive system. A drawing in the Codex Atlanticus, f. 47 v-d, which combines with an upside-down sketch on the same sheet, recently revealed by restoration, deals with just such a tower adapted to protect the entrance of a citadel. Leonardo adopts the Vitruvian principle of side-passages which guarantee the maximum control of access. The sketches on the two faces of the sheet are in red chalk, without any notes, and on the basis of style could be assigned to the beginning of the sixteenth century. Reproduced here is a "reconstruction" of the drawing on the recto (shown by the outline of the sheet) made complete on the basis of the information offered by the sketch on the verso. The imposing bastion thus produced, which goes back to ideas already considered by Francesco di Giorgio, seems to foreshadow the type of bastion with casemates which began to appear in France about 1520, and was to be taken up again with complex elaborations by Francesco de' Marchi and Vauban.

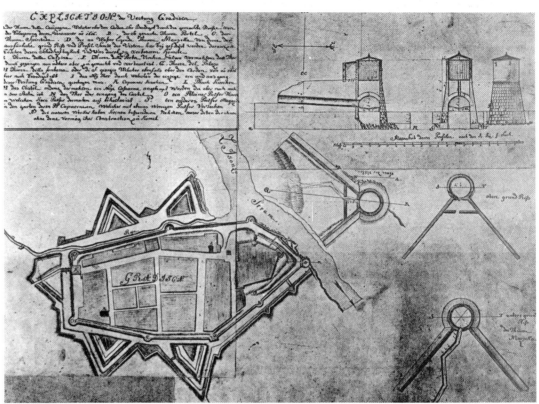

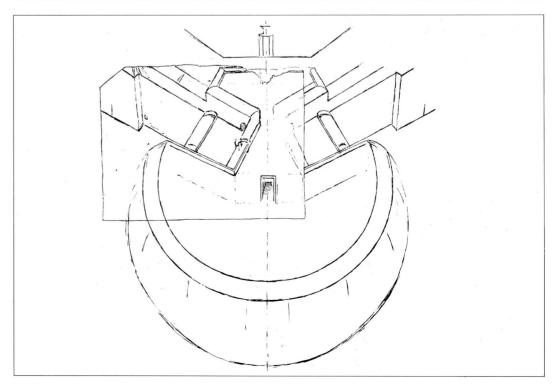

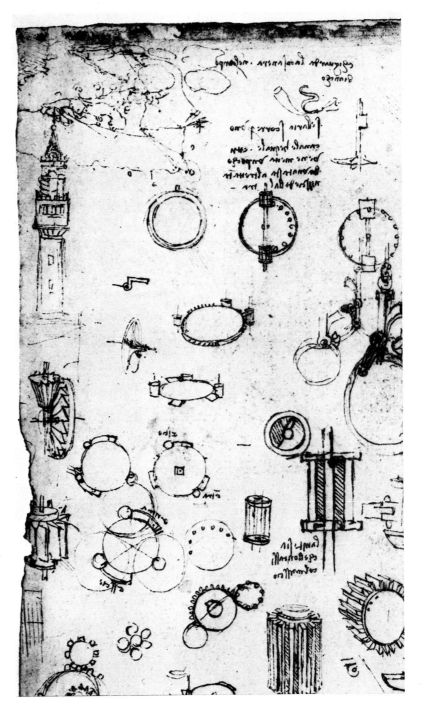

activities from 1499 to 1500. We need only, for the moment, consider one which contains many sketches of mechanical devices that Leonardo elaborated into finished drawings in Madrid MS. I. Passing over these technological elements, however, let us look more closely at the upper left-hand corner of the sheet. We have here a topographical sketch of the regions of the eastern Mediterranean with the indication of a route which, starting from Venice, sweeps down across Greece, touches on Candia (Crete) and goes on toward Palestine, while inland we can just see hints of caravan routes which lead to the Caucasian regions, also touching on the Bosphorus at the entrance to the Black Sea.

This is probably a graphic meditation on the theme of the imaginary journey to the near East. Over the geographical notation, which describes Venice's relationship to the East, is partly superimposed the sketch of a soaring bell-tower. This has almost the exotic character of a minaret, but is still easily recognizable as a recollection of the imposing and elegant tower of the Palazzo Vecchio. There could be no better image to embody the architectural and monumental tradition of Florence, the city to which Leonardo was about to return.

9. Florence

As soon as he had returned to Florence in 1500, Leonardo was consulted, as an architect, on the construction of the bell-tower of San Miniato, which was being started just at that time to Baccio d'Agnolo's design. (Might it have been because of this that Leonardo was thinking about the bell-tower of the Palazzo Vecchio?) At the same time he was also asked to consider the problem of the nearby church of San Salvatore, the foundations of which were threatened because the ground had been made unstable by excavations carried out by a brick factory down below near the Arno. Others who took part in the consultations included Jacopo Pollaiuolo Il Cronaca and Giuliano da Sangallo. It is not surprising therefore that in the Anonimo Magliabechiano's lists Leonardo's name appears under the year 1500 with the title of "architect and painter."

Leonardo's advice regarding S. Salvatore is summarized in a document which we know only through a copy, but it was certainly quite a long report accompanied by drawings, of which not even an outline has come down to us.

"Leonardo spoke of S. Salvatore," we read in the document, "showing with drawings how to prevent the damage caused to it by the sinking of the structure as well as by the waters that seep through the layers of the rock formation all the way to the place where these layers are cut; and thus the building would no longer move by cutting these layers all the way through where they had already been cut. And the sewers should be kept clean."

The problem dragged on until 1506, probably with further consultations taking place. It was then that Leonardo began a treatise on the causes of cracks in walls, many preliminary pages of which are preserved in the Codex Arundel and are complemented by geological observations

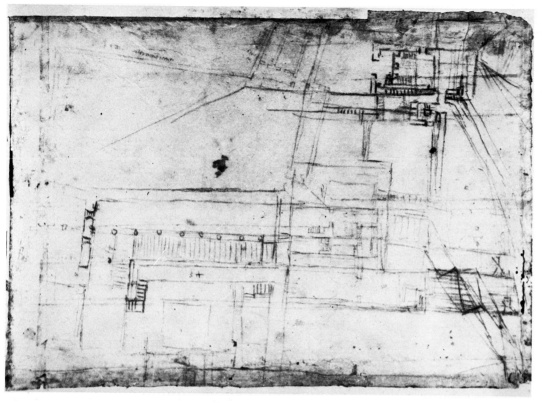

196-198. The "phantom" building. The architectural studies on f. 44 r-b and v-b of the Codex Atlanticus are the only ones which still await an interpretation. As such they are presented here next to an attempt at a scale restoration of the building shown on the recto. This is the plan of a "phantom" building of some considerable size (one of the three parallel walls is shown as being 225 braccia long towards the south, which is equal to about 135 metres.) Leonardo, obviously, is making notes on existing structures, measuring their dimensions and orientation with the surveyor's graduated table and compass which he used in preparing the map of Imola, and which Raphael describes in detail in his celebrated letter to Leo X.

Aside from the few notes to do with measurements and orientations, the drawing offers no clues that would allow us to relate it to notes in other sheets or manuscripts of Leonardo's. The size and quality of the paper suggest a possible relationship with the studies of the port of Civitavecchia, of 1514-15, when Leonardo was staying in the Vatican and making his on-the-spot investigations of the Pontine Marshes and the neighbouring archaeological sites from Circeo to Terracina – the same ones that Bramante had visited in 1497. The hand-writing and his way of using red chalk as an outline to be gone over in pen seem to favour the hypothesis of a fairly late date, certainly after 1500, and probably between 1503-5 and 1515. However, he also used red chalk and pen in 1500 for the draft of a report on the project of river defenses in Friuli on f. 234 r-c of the Codex Atlanticus, and so the "phantom" building could go back to the period immediately following the one spent with the Sforzas. Consequently we may extend the radius of possible explanations to include a possible reference to buildings or structures in the Veneto. The suggestion of thick walls with openings in the characteristic shape of double-splayed

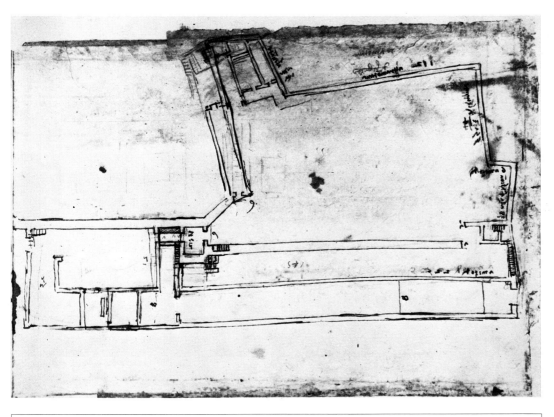

embrasures, among the notes on the verso, confirms that we are dealing with a building used as a fort; a purpose also suggested by the course of the boundary wall shown in the plan on the recto.

Ductus and style could also accord with Leonardo's notes on military architecture made in the Romagna in the service of Cesare Borgia in 1502-3, and at Piombino for the Florentine Republic in 1504. And we must not forget that the time span from c. 1505 to 1515 includes Leonardo's architectural activity in Lombardy for Charles d'Amboise and the King of France from 1506 to 1513, and besides this we know that in 1514 Leonardo was attached to the papal troops of Giuliano de' Medici at Parma and Piacenza, and in 1515-16 he was working on the reorganization of the Medici quarter in Florence.

In order to make a real examination of the structures drawn by Leonardo it will be necessary to keep in mind a peculiarity of the drawing on the recto. Leonardo obviously began by drawing the long walls running south, and then followed the course of the outer wall as it turns east, then for a short distance south, then east again before running back north and finally east. Here, when Leonardo reached the upper edge of the sheet he had to abandon the approximately proportional relationship between the dimensions of the various stretches of wall and even distort their orientation in order to squeeze in the projecting spur. Thus the stretch of wall running north is not parallel to the three walls running south, as it ought to be, while the external wall of the spur running east should be perpendicular to the wall running north. The aim of the attempt at a scale reconstruction is therefore to clarify the outline of the mysterious building and in so doing it becomes, in fact, rather different from the outline drawn by Leonardo. The notes, moving from left to right and then towards the top, can be read as follows: 23 / 8 / 21 [or 12] / within... / of it 12 / 9 [or 6] / 8 / to the south 225 / 7 (?) / 38 to the 4ª of east / 6 to south / 55 to ¾ of east / 112 north / 53 to east / 9 [or 6]).

The number "145" was added by an early collector. The sketches on the reverse, whose relationship to those on the recto cannot be established, are all in red chalk and contain only the number "34" written by Leonardo next to the ramp of a staircase flanked by a loggia or colonnade.

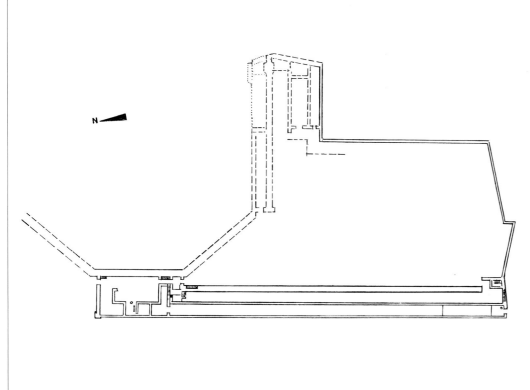

in the Codex Hammer. In this case too, therefore, we see Leonardo's characteristic tendency of moving away from the initial practical assignment towards research of a theoretical nature.

Something of the kind also happened in the case of the Villa Tovaglia, near Florence, which had been built towards the end of the fifteenth century by Lorenzo da Monteacuto, a little-known architect in the service of the Medici. Leonardo was given the task of providing the design for a replica of it to be built for the Marquis of Mantua. Francesco Gonzaga, who had been a guest of Agnolo del Tovaglia in Florence, had had a chance of admiring his villa in Val d'Ema, which still exists, some two kilometres from San Miniato. He expressed his intention of building a replica of it near Mantua, which thus would have anticipated the program of the Palazzo del Te and which has perhaps something to do with Marmirolo. Leonardo sent his drawing to the Marquis and declared himself ready to prepare one of the whole, in colour, or even a model – adding that the replica would be fully satisfactory only if one could transport the surrounding countryside to Mantua as well. This reveals the architect's perception of the intimate relationship between a building and its surroundings, but it is also indicative of a practice which must have been quite widespread at the time, that of planning buildings on drawings prepared by non-local architects, as happened for instance with Alberti's Tempio Malatestiano in Rimini.

Nothing has remained of Leonardo's drawings for the replica of Villa Tovaglia. And yet an idea of this type of drawing may be given by the large drawing on a sheet at Windsor, RL 12689, which represents a villa of rusticated Tuscan type, and which until now, in agreement with Clark, I did not believe to be by Leonardo. There is no doubt that it came from the Leoni volume, together with the other Leonardo drawings at Windsor, and now, looking at the original again, I am convinced that it is by Leonardo. Not only can one see lines drawn with the left hand (all along the plinth course which unites the main building with the loggia), but the trees along the garden wall on the right are utterly characteristic of Leonardo. At first glance one hesitates to admit that he could have produced a work of such naive diligence, especially at such a late period, applying himself, for example, to representing the rusticated wall with such meticulous precision. On the other hand, we find the same character, and I would say the same style and even the same technique, in the famous drawing in Codex Atlanticus, f. 395 r-a, representing the outlets of the San Cristoforo canal in Milan, in a perspective view that shows the same hesitant passages as seen in the Windsor drawing. Yet the canal drawing bears an inscription dated 3 May 1509, which in itself demonstrates Leonardo's aptitude for controlling his hand with careful discipline, even restraint. Were it not for this autograph annotation, the drawing would easily be judged unworthy of Leonardo.

The problem of building a country house on a slope had interested Leonardo around 1503-5, at the time of his frequent visits to Vinci, as

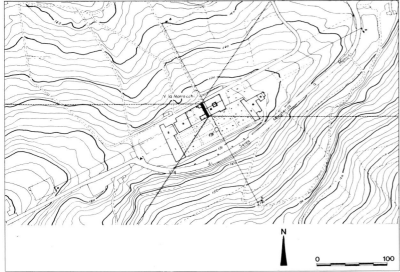

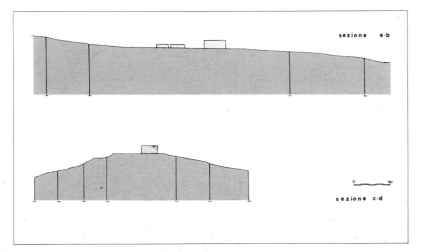

203. Today the villa of the Counts Morrocchi is all that is left of a building constructed between 1480 and 1490 by Lorenzo da Montaguto for Agnolo di Lapo del Tovaglia. In 1507 the villa was inherited by Jacopo di Piero Guicciardini and it remained in his family until 1634. Throughout the seventeenth century, following various changes of ownership, the building underwent changes and alterations and adaptations that might have culminated in an almost complete rebuilding in 1719. Its new proprietors, the Nerli, conceived the idea of a grandiose construction that would have incorporated the old building. But the project was never brought to completion and the new parts, including an imposing façade, were left to appear in strident contrast to the old, thus giving rise to the popular nickname of "La Bugia" (The Fraud), by which it is still called. Notwithstanding this and later modifications, which also included road connections, the fifteenth-century structures have not completely disappeared. Their evidence still remains not only in the clear and simple layout of the rooms, in the character of the perimeter walls which often follow an irregular course, and in the relationship between the ground floor and the basement, but above all in the nucleus of great hall and library, fronted by a loggia with five arches. The great hall (13.20 x 7.10 m) has a coffered barrel-vault ceiling as at Poggio a Caiano, and panels carved in high relief containing the Tovaglia emblems. The central arch of the loggia seems to determine what must have been the longitudinal axis of the original building and it may be that a close investigation of the wall structures would allow us to work out the fifteenth-century ground-plan, above all as regards the original arrangement of the staircases, which are no longer the same. If we could be sure that the "replica" which the Gonzaga wanted in Mantua had actually been carried out on the basis of Leonardo's design and that, as such, it still exists at least in old plans, we would perhaps have a more precise idea of the fifteenth-century prototype, which Leonardo considered inseparable from its surroundings.

204, 205. Views of the countryside near Val d'Ema from the terraces of the Villa Tovaglia. Francesco Gonzaga, Marquis of Mantua, stayed in Florence at the end of the fifteenth century as a guest of Agnolo Tovaglia, a rich merchant who had had a villa built for himself about 1480 on the hills south of Florence near S. Margherita a Montici. The building was altered completely over the last two centuries, and very little can be recognized of the original structure designed by Lorenzo da Montaguto, an architect in the service of the Medici. What does remain unaltered, however, is the fascination of the countryside which frames the villa. Gonzaga found it so much to his liking that he wanted to have a replica of it built near Mantua. Perhaps this idea of his gave rise to the villa of Marmirolo, now vanished, whose fabulous gardens were described by Leandro Alberti in 1550; or perhaps to the Villa Andina, celebrated by Battista Fiera in 1508, or even, later, to the Palazzo del Te. The responsibility for preparing the plans for the replica of the

Villa Tovaglia was given to Leonardo, who had recently returned to Florence after a visit to Mantua and Venice. His drawing, now lost, was sent to Mantua on 11 August 1500, and in the accompanying letter written by Francesco Malatesta to the Marquis he reports an important observation by Leonardo on the relation of architecture to its surroundings: "I am sending Your Most Illustrious Lordship the drawing of Agnolo Tovaglia's house made by the hand of Leonardo Vinci himself, who commends himself to you and to Her Ladyship as your servant. My Lord Agnolo says that he will then wish to come to Mantua in order to judge who will have been the better architect, Your Lordship or himself [that is, Agnolo], although he is certain that he will be surpassed by you, partly because it is easy to add to what has already been invented and partly because his wisdom cannot be compared to Your Lordship's. The aforesaid Leonardo says that to make the thing perfect one would have to transport this site here to the place where Your Lordship wants to build and then you would be truly contented. I have not had the drawing coloured nor had added embellishments of greenery, ivy, box, cypress and laurel trees such as are here, as it did not seem to me to be necessary, but if Your Lordship wishes, the aforesaid Leonardo offers to do this so that the picture can serve as a model, as Your Lordship may wish."

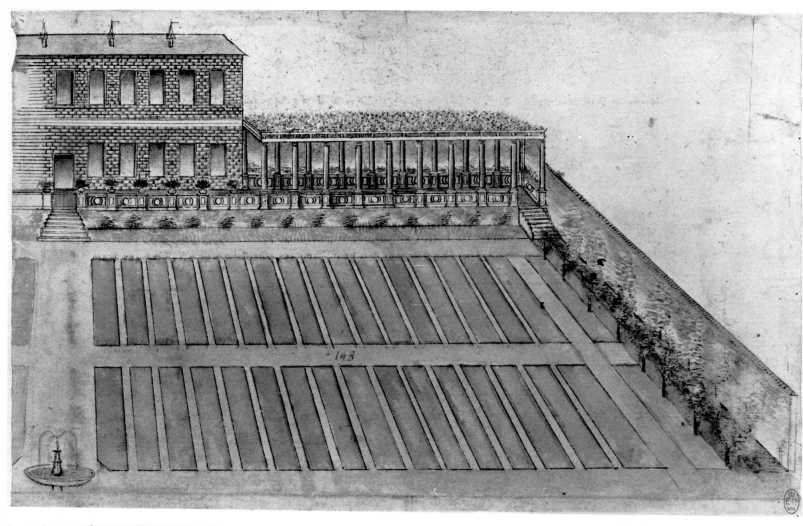

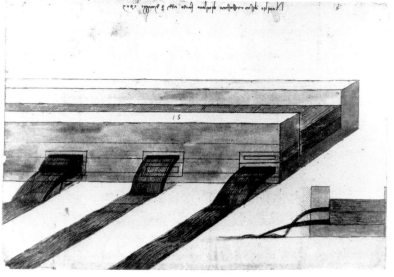

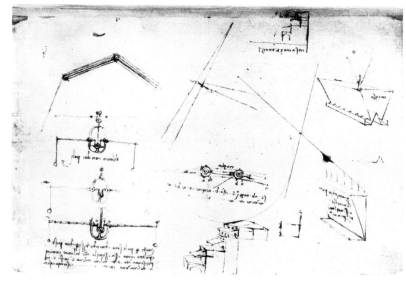

209. *Details of rural buildings,* c. 1503-5.
Codex Atlanticus, f. 215 r-a.
210. *Studies of three-ramp staircases,*
c. 1503-4 (or 1506-7?). *Codex Atlanticus,*
f. 220 v-b.

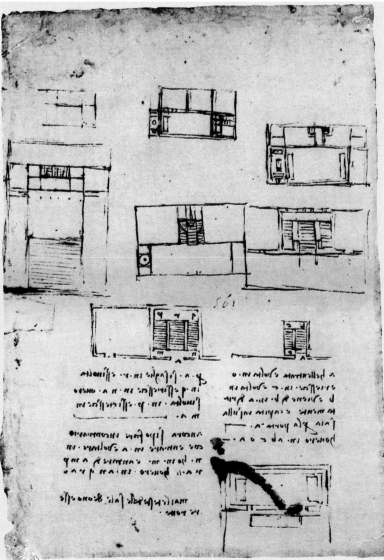

his well-known studies of a "house with three terraces" in the Codex Arundel, f. 126 r, show. On a sheet of the Codex Atlanticus of the same time, f. 215 r-a, there are sketches of a three-storey building with, on top, a loggia with four arches, and wooden scaffolding that extends over an area indicated as "garden," while above is the isolated note: "to Gian Martelli," a Florentine name. Another sheet, also in the Codex Atlanticus, f. 220 r-c and v-b, datable to the very beginning of the sixteenth century, has sketches of a building on a hill which one could, hypothetically, relate to Villa Tovaglia. The villa as it exists today is so much the result of eighteenth and nineteenth century enlargements and alterations that it is nearly impossible to make out its original structure. The building in Leonardo's drawing consists of a square central block inserted between two wings only summarily indicated in the plan (and merely as platforms in the elevation drawing) which extend so as to enclose an open space probably planned to have the same dimensions as the central part of the building. In this last drawing the ground floor rooms are arranged according to a symmetrical plan: an entrance hall with a wide triple-ramped staircase placed on the longitudinal axis, which crosses a great hall and a loggia to continue, as indicated in the elevation drawing, into steps which descend straight down the slope. The five arches of the loggia are reduced to four in a sketch to one side, but this was probably an oversight in proposing the alternative of a loggia no longer covered by a terrace but by a storey with windows and roof. The five arches, in the plan as well, are in fact necessary in order to provide a central passage corresponding with the entrance and thus in line with the stairs on the opposite side. As for the relationship in the great hall to the rooms next to the stairs, it would appear that the intermediate wall was opened up with a colonnade, but this is somewhat uncertain, in the same way as it is difficult to interpret the layout of the rooms on the left of the great hall with indications of some kind of equipment to which the plans on the back of the sheet also seem to refer. The sketch of a water-wheel recalls the water-metre devised by Leonardo for Bernardo Rucellai, a project however of a later date, around 1510. It is true that the elevation drawing seems to hint at it, beyond the extreme left of the loggia, but it would be difficult to justify the presence of a water-metre for irrigation in a building undoubtedly designed as a residence.

A plan even more schematic than those indicated on the back of the sheet is in the Codex Atlanticus, f. 282 r-b, originally a single sheet with f. 282 v-c. It is most probable that it is of the same building, or at least a similar one based on the same idea, in which the rural character is accentuated by an arcade and open spaces in front. The mechanical contrivances drawn on the sheet thus reassembled relate to a "mill at the Doccia in Vinci" and a system for grinding colours by means of a *ritrecine,* that is a water-wheel with horizontal blades. On the verso of this reassembled sheet there is a sketchy outline of a landscape of the Arno Valley with the suggestion of a village which, it has been thought, could be recognized as Leonardo's birthplace. Besides this there are

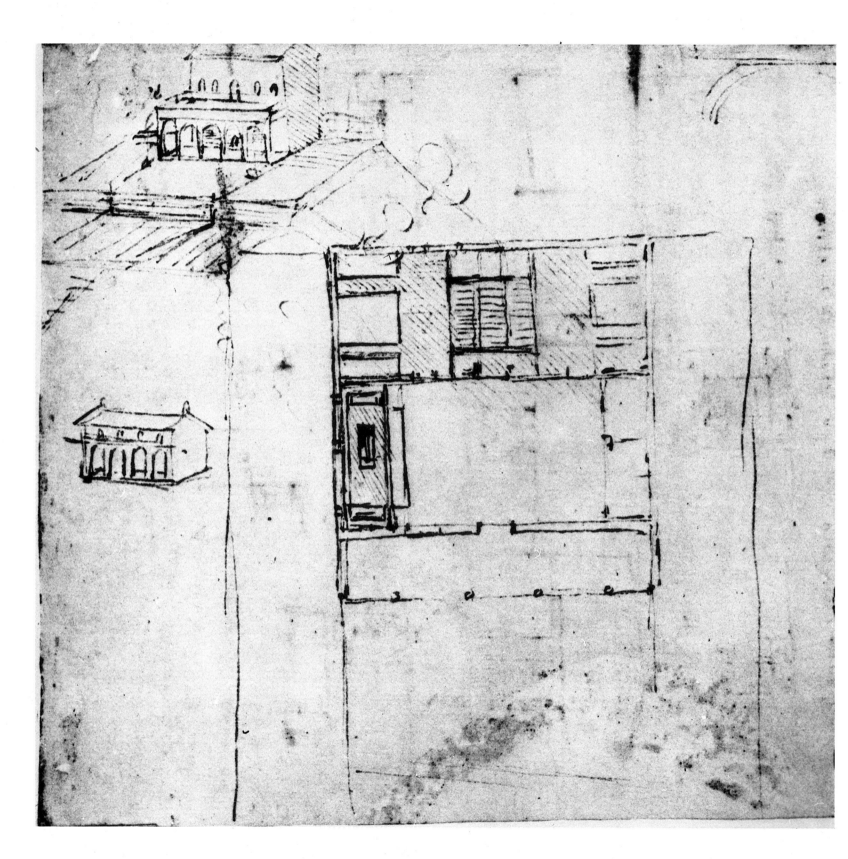

211. *Plan and elevations of a country house on a hillside,*
c. 1503-4 (or 1506-7?). *Codex Atlanticus, f. 220 r-c.*
212. *Architectural and mechanical studies with reference
to the "mill at the Doccia in Vinci,"* c. 1503-4 (or 1506-7?).
Codex Atlanticus, ff. 282 r-b and v-c.

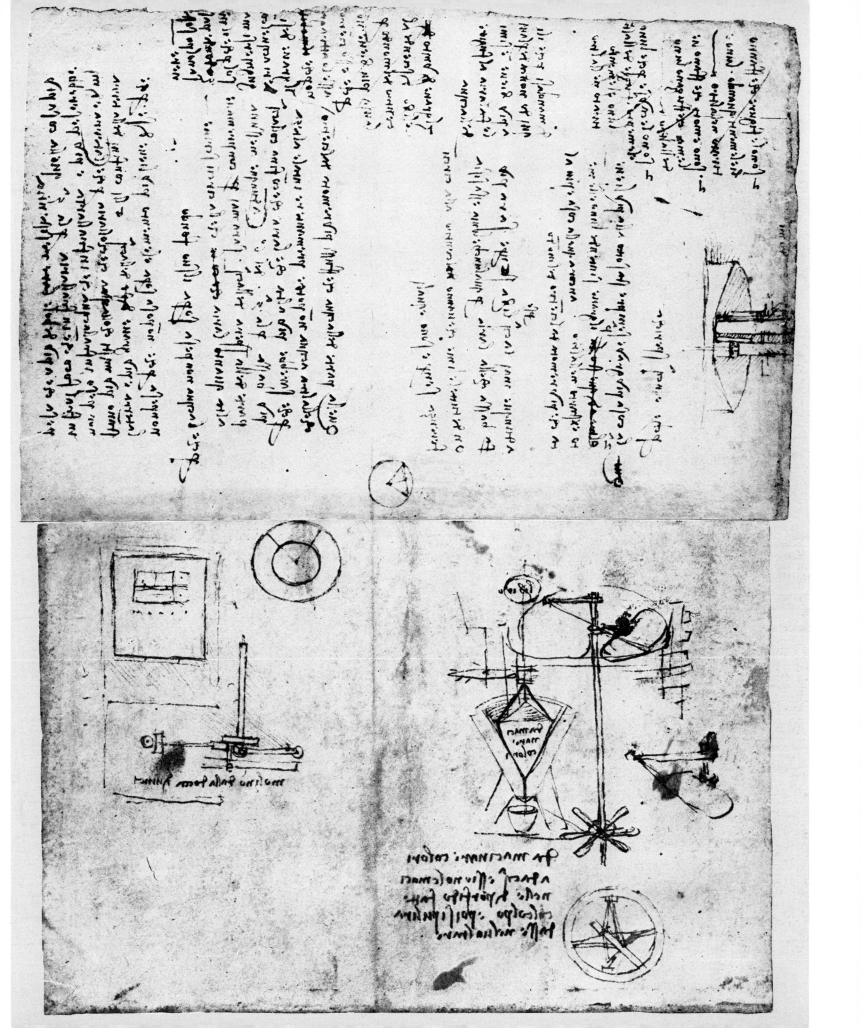

other notes relating to water-wheels. With this sheet we have moved away from the time of the Villa Tovaglia studies to about the year 1505 or even later. On the other hand the writing has the same ductus as that of the notes on the triple-ramped staircase on the reverse of the study for a country house which made us think of the Villa Tovaglia. They are notes which have taken on by this stage a theoretical character, better suited to a treatise than to a project. The triple-ramped staircase system shown here, apart from the occasional examples Leonardo might have seen in Venice or elsewhere, only became established much later, with theatrical emphasis, in buildings of an already Baroque grandiosity. "Choir in the guise of a theatre," "triumphal arch" – these seem terms appropriate to the description of Baroque architecture. However, they are found in a passage of the *Vite de sette Beati Fiorentini* by Michele Pocianti (Florence 1589) which records an unknown work by Leonardo dating from the beginning of 1500: "But no less did the Most Illustrious and Most Excellent Lodovico, second Marquis of Mantua, enlarge it (the SS. Annunziata) in 1477. He had the magnificent dome built, surrounded by nine chapels with squared columns, architraves and cornices made of exposed stone, in the middle of which there is a choir in the guise of a theatre and a most noble altar in the shape of a triumphal arch (Leonardo da Vinci's design) all covered in gold, where there is an extremely rich ciborium for the Most Holy Sacrament together with two doors of variegated polychrome marbles and marble statues..."

The architecture here described is that of a wooden altarpiece commissioned from Baccio d'Agnolo on 15 September 1500, probably of the same type as the one containing the *Virgin of the Rocks* in Milan, but even more monumental and complex, intended to include paintings on both the front and back. Placed at the entrance of the choir, it would thus have had the double purpose of creating a focal point at the end of the church's longitudinal axis and of serving as a partition wall to give an autonomous character to the tribune – taking up again the idea of the tribune at S. Maria delle Grazie.

Leonardo's participation in this project is only known through Pocianti's statement of 1589. Vasari recounts how on his return to Florence in 1500 Leonardo was given hospitality by the Convent of the SS. Annunziata and received the commission for a painting for its high altar. It is said that Filippino Lippi, to whom the commission had originally been given, gave it up willingly in Leonardo's favour. And in his "Life" of Perugino, Vasari tells us that when Leonardo left (not to go to France, but probably to enter into the service of Cesare Borgia), the Servite monks gave the commission once again to Filippino, who in fact began one of the larger paintings of the two sides of the altar, a *Deposition from the Cross* which was left unfinished at his death in 1504; and that eventually Perugino was allocated the decoration of the whole altarpiece in 1505. Perugino completed Lippi's *Deposition,* which was to be placed on the choir side, and prepared an *Assumption of the Virgin* for the side facing the church as well as six other paintings of Saints

standing in front of niches for the side panels of the altarpiece. We know that Perugino's work was so sharply criticized that the *Assumption* panel destined for the front of the altar was put on the back and the *Deposition* designed by Filippino was given pride of place. These two paintings still exist (at the Accademia and at the Annunziata), together with some of the side panels, so that it is possible to get an idea of the size of the altarpiece: the central space was planned to hold the two panels which measure 3.33 x 2.18 m, while the side spaces were, it seems, to take eight panels (four on each side) measuring 1.60 x 0.67 m. This would have formed a truly imposing ensemble, providing for a painting of considerable size in the central part, while we know that the *St. Anne* cartoon which Leonardo prepared in 1501 was small in size with life-size figures (and the Louvre painting as well, which measures 1.68 x 1.12 m, would have been too small for that altarpiece.) Another peculiar fact is that Isabella d'Este's correspondent, in describing Leonardo's cartoon, does not mention that it was for the Annunziata, a church actually patronised by the Gonzaga since the time of the building of the tribune. The only certain fact, therefore, among so much puzzle surrounding the genesis of the *St. Anne*, is that Leonardo provided the design for the architecture of the main altar of the Annunziata. An anonymous drawing at Windsor (RL 0208) possibly reflects this project. In it one can recognize the iconographic program of an altar in the shape of a "triumphal arch" dedicated to Our Lady of the Annunciation, as is shown by the double niche for the figures of the angel Gabriel and the Virgin in the cymatium. We have no clues which would allow us to identify the patron, but the character and the style of the drawing can certainly justify an attribution to Filippino Lippi himself or to Baccio d'Agnolo immediately after Leonardo's return to Florence in 1500.

Through a consideration of Leonardo's connection with Baccio d'Agnolo, a new field of investigation opens on the beginnings of sixteenth-century architecture in Florence. Baccio came to architecture through an apprenticeship as a carpenter, and wood-carving always remained a speciality of his. It may suffice to recall his wooden decorations in the *Sala del Gran Consiglio* – designed by Filippino Lippi at the same time Leonardo was painting the *Battle of Anghiari* there –, and the model of Michelangelo's design for the façade of San Lorenzo. He was, therefore, an artist who carried out other people's designs. One could mention in this context the gallery that Baccio began to build at the base of Brunelleschi's dome in 1515. Work was stopped when only one side had been completed, because of criticisms by Michelangelo, who called it a "cricket cage," and I think that Michelangelo's reaction could be better explained if it could be established that Leonardo had provided the idea, or even the actual design, for that gallery. I know that documents existed relating to Leonardo's connections with Florence Cathedral, which Poggi had put aside for future publication, but they are no longer traceable. Quite apart from this fact which, in any case, it is time to make known, the gallery itself – especially seen from close by – cannot

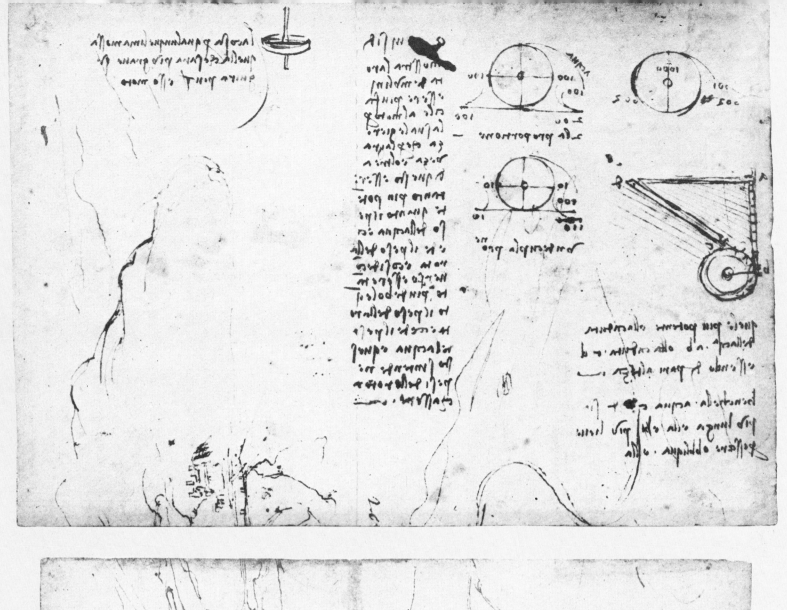

214. *Anonymous drawing (c. 1500) of an altar in the shape of a triumphal arch. Windsor, RL 0208.*
215. *Reconstruction of the altar of the Annunziata.*
216. *Studies of galleries and elevations, c. 1515. Codex Atlanticus, f. 114 r-b, detail.*
217. *The altar of the Annunziata. Detail from the* Miracle of the Blessed Manetto *by Allori. Florence, SS. Annunziata.*

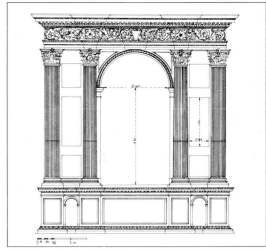

214. *Anonymous drawing (c. 1500) of an altar in the shape of a triumphal arch. Windsor, RL 0208.*
215. *Reconstruction of the altar of the Annunziata.*

216. *Studies of galleries and elevations, c. 1515. Codex Atlanticus, f. 114 r-b, detail.*
217. *The altar of the Annunziata. Detail from the* Miracle of the Blessed Manetto *by Allori. Florence, SS. Annunziata.*

fail to evoke strong analogies with a type of classicism that pervaded Leonardo's architectural drawings after 1500. We need only compare it to the drawing on f. 114 r-b of the Codex Atlanticus, of exactly 1515-16, in which there are also elements reminiscent of the wooden altar of the Annunziata. And when we look at the detail of that altar in the background of Allori's painting of the *Miracle of the Blessed Manetto*, we instantly recognize the same decorative partitionings as those in the Cathedral gallery. A recurrent theme among Leonardo's earliest drawings is that of a religious building surmounted by a dome, in which he more or less directly alludes to the dome of Florence Cathedral as a model of inspiration. Sometimes he uses the model as an excuse for imagining new ways of integrating Arnolfo's and Brunelleschi's work, as in a small sketch on f. 17 v-a of the Codex Atlanticus, a page of studies of wooden bridges dateable *c.* 1485, where Florence Cathedral appears with Giotto's campanile ideally duplicated. In this and in similar sketches from the time of MS. B the motif of a crowning for the drum at the base of the dome appears repeatedly and that crowning is a gallery of the type begun by Baccio d'Agnolo in 1515.

All the more reason then to lament the loss of the main altar of SS. Annunziata, even if we now have the consolation of knowing exactly when it was destroyed. This fact comes from an unpublished document in the library of the University of California in Los Angeles, Stefano Rosselli's manuscript of the history of the *Chiese di Firenze*: "In the year 1477 Lodovico Gonzaga, second Marquis of Mantua, added to it the tribune or dome, below which is the main altar, the choir and the chapels which encircle it, designed and built by Leon Battista Alberti, and the main altar with that extremely beautiful ornament in the form of a triumphal arch, Leonardo da Vinci's invention, which this present year 1655 on the 7th of September has been removed in order to put in its place a very rich Ciborium commissioned by Monsignor Antonio Medici, Most Excellent Physician, at the cost of about eight thousand scudi."

Leonardo's connection with master woodworkers at the beginning of the sixteenth century manifests itself not only through works connected with his service as a military architect, as in the case of temporary bridges, canal excavators and pile-drivers for reinforcing river banks but also in projects of civil architecture.

In a page of the Codex Atlanticus, f. 286 r-a, datable about 1500, there are sketches of an amphitheatre with seats, which can be unmistakably recognized as a timber construction. On the same page is the sketch of an apse together with a detail of the entrance arch, majestic and lofty, with a double order of paired columns as in Bramante's *nicchione* at Abbiategrasso, and perhaps this too should be read in the same way. It may well be an idea for the choir stalls for S. Maria delle Grazie in Milan or for SS. Annunziata in Florence or even for an anatomy theatre – the first theatre of this type was being built just at that time by Alessandro Benedetti in Padua, where Leonardo surely might have stopped on his way to Venice with Pacioli. And Leonardo does record Benedetti's treatise on anatomy in a note of 1508.

Madrid MS. II, of 1503-5 gives us the details of an ingenious windmill with vertical blades erected on top of an elegant building like a small antique temple. For this mill Leonardo planned to use the "abetelli alla Giustizia," that is, the trees from the area near the Porta alla Giustizia in Florence. And we can also recall that, besides the record of payments to Leonardo for painting the *Battle of Anghiari* under the date of 30 August 1504, is one detailing the compensation made to Luca Pacioli for the construction of a series of geometrical bodies for the Signoria as decorative objects and as Platonic symbols of good government. Leonardo had devised a way of making one of these bodies transparent, by means of a wooden framework, a method used everywhere nowadays in similar abstract constructions, and this can be seen in the Codex Atlanticus, f. 190 r-a, on the verso of which he sketched the head of one of the warriors from the *Battle of Anghiari*. The framework idea reappears in a most ingenious dismountable system of "geodesic" roofing for vast areas of land, which can be seen in a later sheet from the Codex Atlanticus, f. 328 v-a of *c.* 1508-10, anticipating the daring constructions of Buckminster Fuller!

The devising of wooden constructions is therefore far from being a secondary facet in the history of Renaissance architecture, although unfortunately it is as yet neglected. We need only recall that Michelangelo wanted the entrance straircase to the Biblioteca Laurenziana to be "in beautiful walnut" and that when the Council Hall was dismantled in 1512, on the return of the Medici, the chronicler Luca Landucci wrote: "And at this time it pleased the new government to ruin the Greater Council Hall, that is the woodwork and many beautiful things which had been made at great expense, and many beautiful seat backs; and they built some small rooms for soldiers and created an entrance way from the great rooms. All this saddened the whole of Florence, not the change of government, but that beautiful woodwork which had cost so much. It had brought great reputation and honour to the city... whenever an Embassy came to visit the Signoria, it amazed those who saw it, when they entered such a great residence..."

Here at least we get some idea of what the architectural framework would have been for Leonardo's and Michelangelo's pictorial decorations! And we need only skim through Landucci's diary to find frequent mentions of the building of decorative wooden sets for celebrations and tournaments. Thus the sets for Leo X's visit in 1515 engaged two thousand workmen, including woodworkers, masons and painters, for over a month and at a cost of more than seven thousand florins "in these things," as Landucci says, "that passed like shadows, when they could have built some very beautiful temple to honour God and to the glory of the city." But it was not only a host of artisans that took part in the projects which for a few days changed the face of the city. The major artists of the day also participated, such as Andrea del Sarto, Jacopo Sansovino, Granacci and the Sangallos, for this presented an opportunity to produce, so to speak, life-size models applied directly to the urban

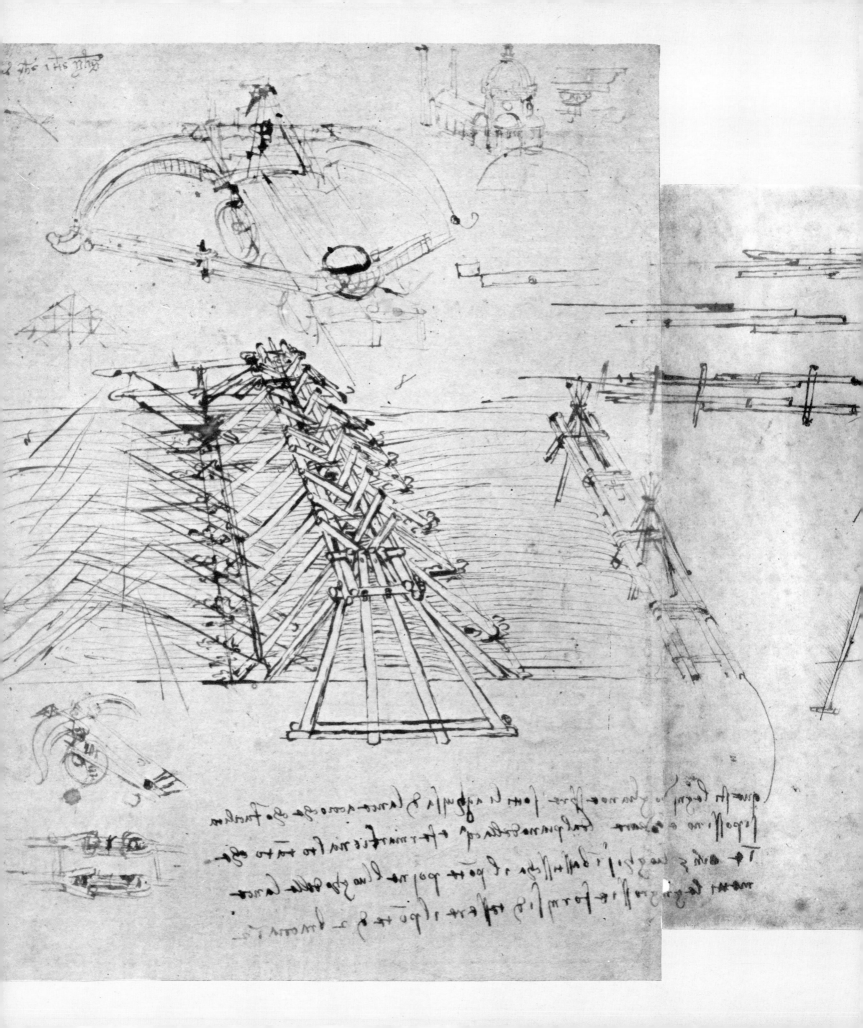

218. Architectural and military engineering studies and sketch of a church inspired by the Cathedral of Florence, c. 1487-88. Codex Atlanticus, ff. 17 v-a and 22 r-a.

219. The gallery by Baccio d'Agnolo at the base of the dome of Florence Cathedral.

On the following pages:
220, 221. Technological studies and studies of wooden architecture (anatomy theatre?), c. 1499-1500. Codex Atlanticus, f. 286 r-a and details.

222. Studies of a windmill, c. 1503-4. Madrid MS. II, f. 55 v.

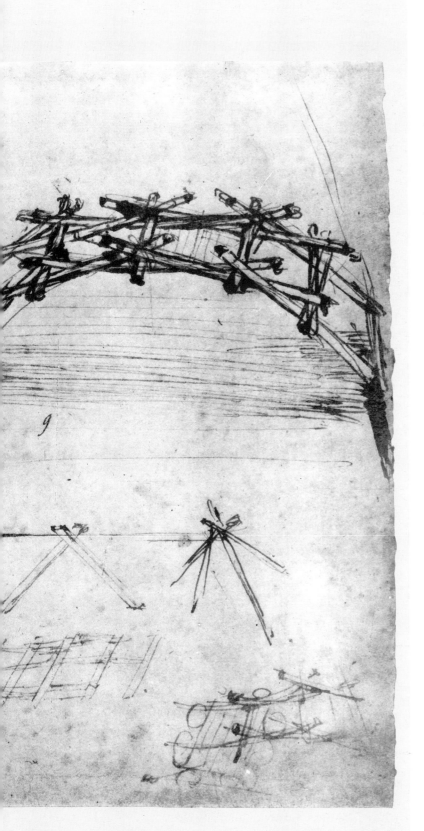

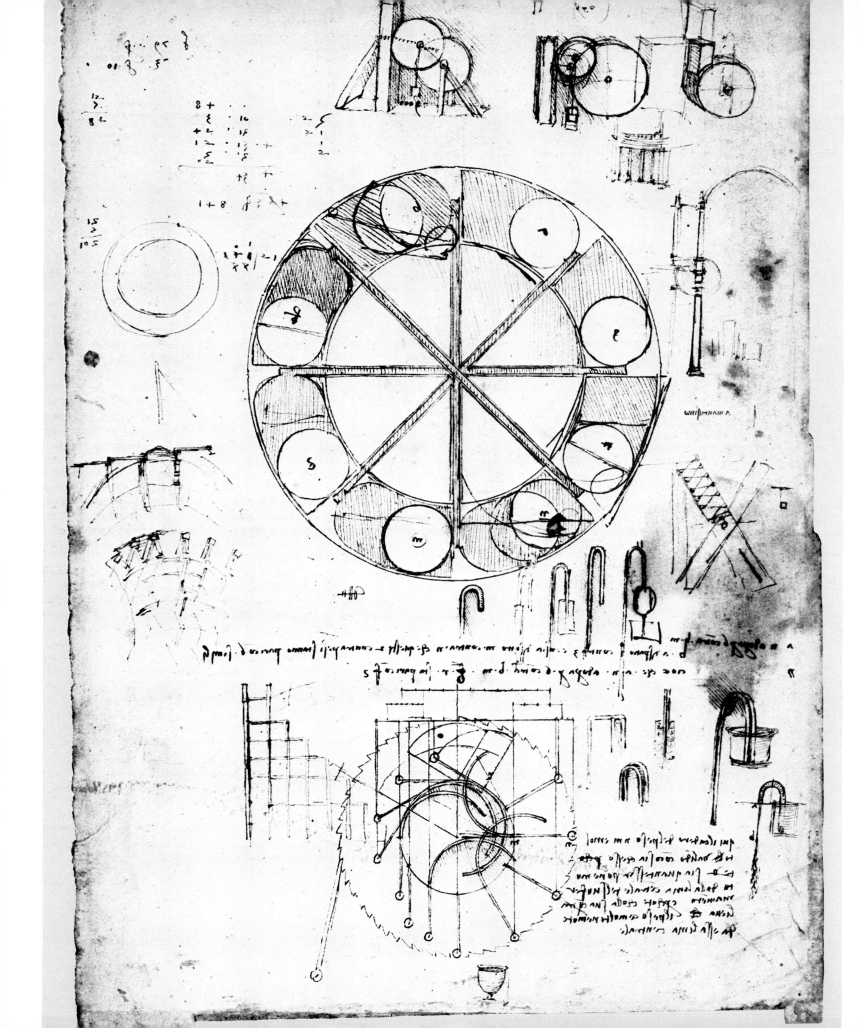

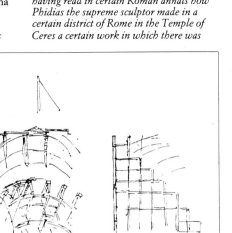

environment. This was certainly the case with the temporary façades for the Cathedral and for San Lorenzo (from which, in fact, the Pope's idea of launching a competition to complete Brunelleschi's church was born) and with the majestic *arcus quadrifrons* which Antonio da Sangallo the Elder built in Piazza della Signoria, on the spot later to be occupied by Ammannati's fountain. This *arcus quadrifrons* may be recognized in some of Leonardo's sketches in the Codex Atlanticus, f. 3 r-b and v-b – and Clemente VII seems to have called it to mind when he suggested to Michelangelo a first idea for the Medici tombs in San Lorenzo. These experiments with wooden constructions can be seen then as the starting point for that ferment of urban renewal, in a mood of festivity and splendour, later carried out in Venice by Sansovino and in Rome by Michelangelo. Their prototype was the planning project for the Medici quarter in Florence suggested by Leonardo precisely at the time of Leo X's visit.

The Council Hall itself, which had been built behind the Palazzo Vecchio between 1495 and 1498, had employed such architects as the Sangallos, Cronaca, Baccio d'Agnolo and the young Michelangelo. According to Vasari, Leonardo too was consulted on this project, but since he was still in Milan in 1495 it may be that his contribution consisted in giving advice, at a later date, to Filippino Lippi and Baccio d'Agnolo who, at the beginning of the sixteenth century, were entrusted with the wooden decoration of the hall. We have no indication of this in any of Leonardo's notes from the time of the *Battle of Anghiari*, except perhaps for the hint of a plan of rooms on a sheet of sketches of horses at Windsor (RL 12326 r), while on another sheet of the same series (Windsor, RL 12328 r-v) are found schematic allusions to excavating machines which reflect the studies for the Arno projects.

On the other hand, the painting itself, being enormous in size, had to rely on one branch of architecture, in that it required the help of carpenters to construct a system of scaffolding that would allow Leonardo freedom of movement. Vasari called this an "extremely artful construction which rises upwards when pressed together and lowers itself when expanded." The construction of that *edificio* is documented: it is mentioned for the first time on 30 August 1504, when a rope-maker was paid for supplying "a number of ropes and cables for Leonardo da Vinci's scaffolding" and an ironmonger was paid for the hardware (*biette*) for "Leonardo's cart." And that "cart, or rather scaffolding" was still being worked upon on 28 February 1505, when four wheels and other hardware were supplied. There is no trace of this *edificio* in Leonardo's manuscripts, not even in the one at Madrid which covers exactly the period to which it must be assigned, 1503-5. In MS. L, f. 65 v and f. 67 r, there are sketches for scaffolding with wheels, cables and supports which seem to be arranged so that it can be raised and lowered. But the mechanical principle which Vasari alludes to can be understood as a reference to a contrivance already known in Leonardo's time and perhaps dating back to Brunelleschi. This Leonardo could have learned about from that manuscript of Francesco di Giorgio which

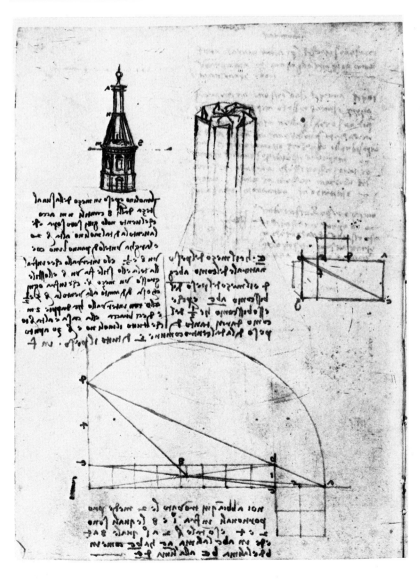

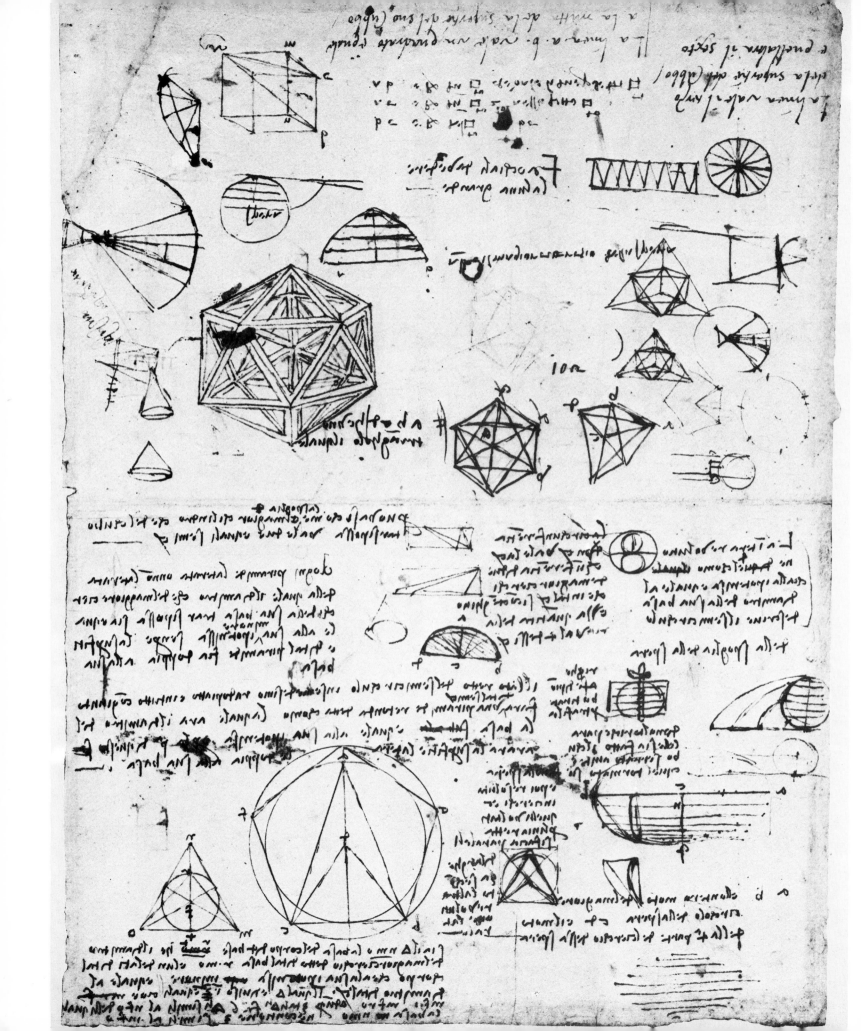

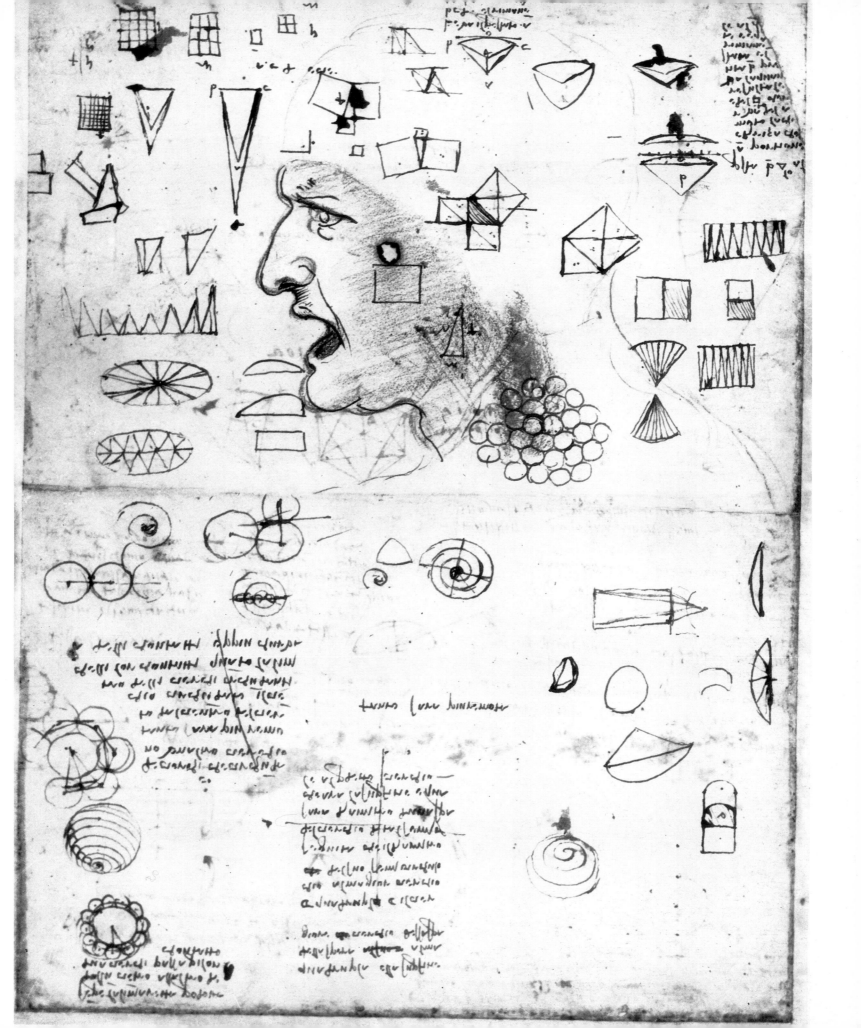

importance may be attached to Vasari's statement that Michelangelo, after having raised the dome of the New Sacristy in S. Lorenzo, "he had Piloto the goldsmith make a ball with seventy-two faces, which is very beautiful" (VII. 192).

225. *Studies of wooden roofing made up of parts that fit together, c. 1508-10. Codex Atlanticus, f. 328 v-a.*

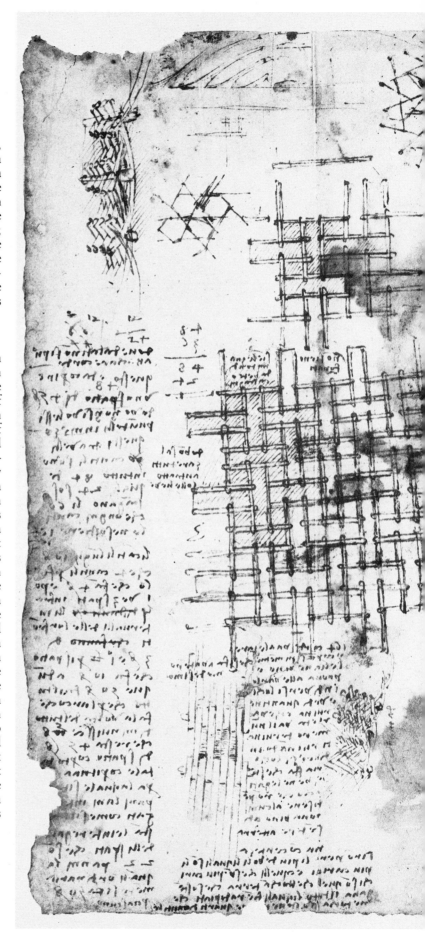

he owned (or had on loan) and was annotating at precisely that time, today's Laurentian Codex Ashburnham 361, on f. 46 r of which we can read: "When one needs to construct a building, first one has to build a wooden framework fitted with wheels, and in it one should dispose carefully centred wooden blocks on either side with a hole in each having a screw-thread into which a screw can be inserted to enable the framework to be made wider or narrower and hence raised or lowered; and on top of it must be placed the screw of the crank that enables the framework to be moved back and forth; and the screw with the screw-threaded hole should be placed on top of the cart. The perpendicular screw can be raised and lowered. Hence the crane is able to raise and set in the desired place the stones hanging from the hook, by means of the screw."

10. Imola

"There cannot be both beauty and usefulness, as is apparent in fortresses and in men." Thus wrote Leonardo in 1490 when he was in Pavia with Francesco di Giorgio, the builder of many fortresses in the Montefeltro duchy and the first to write a treatise on the subject of military architecture in the Renaissance. Leonardo's statement may seem perplexing, yet it serves to explain a turning-point in the history of military and civil architecture in Italy. He was expressing a still mediaeval concept: a fortress in order to be useful cannot be beautiful – not so much in the sense that the building inhabited by soldiers may assume the sinister look of the dwelling of a tyrant, as in the sense that a fortress in order to be of use, by conforming to the nature of the terrain according to considerations of strategic character, often, in plan, lacks geometrical regularity. One thinks, in fact, of a stronghold placed on a height which is usually the position that makes a fortress more efficient and therefore useful. For a Renaissance architect a building acquires beauty by the rigorous application of geometrical rules which establish its proportions in plan and elevation. The ideal form results from the organization of its parts in terms of a central nucleus, according to a scheme which is governed by the use of the circle and the square: the ideal, that is, of the centrally-planned building with which the classical modules of the round temple of antiquity are revived. But why, in Leonardo's comparison, cannot beauty and usefulness coexist even in men? At a time when civic virtues were being glorified, in the sense proclaimed by Matteo Palmieri who had revived in Florence the teachings of Cicero and Quintilian, and when the man of action symbolized by the figure of the condottiere was being identified with heroes of antiquity and reproposed in Herculean proportions, Leonardo was expressing a concept of man which is at the same time classical and mediaeval in an exquisitely pictorial sense. Almost by way of a paradox (as if to say, that is, that only a useless man is beautiful) he asserts that man's beauty lies in the gravity of his gestures, in that sense of measure in his actions which allows, so to speak, a frontal view of the human body, as in a Greek statue. A master of gesture, who thus shuns

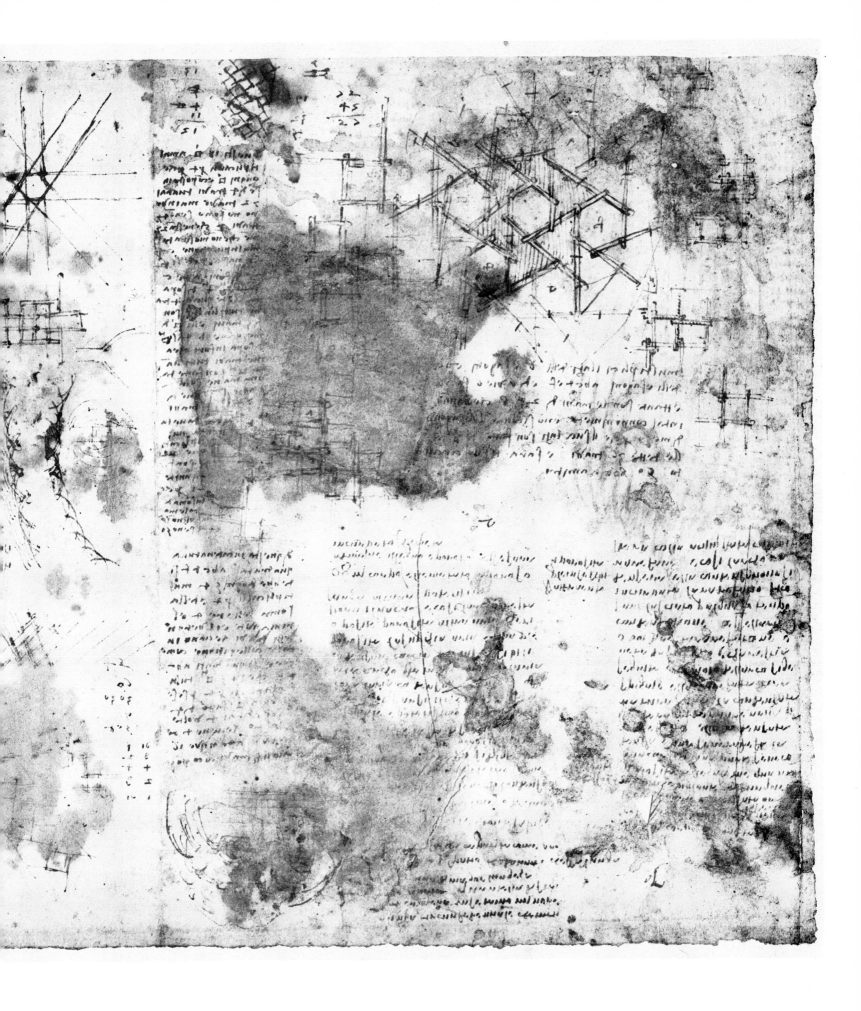

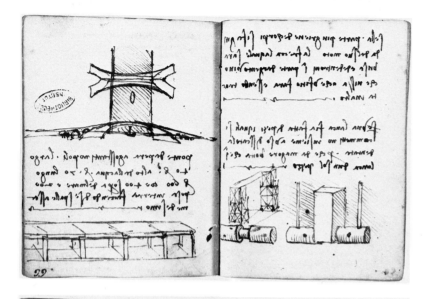

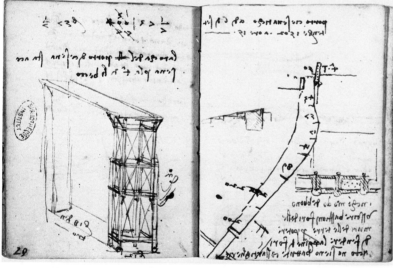

gesticulation, he is the one painter who brings back to life at the end of the fifteenth century, in times of sumptuous elegance, the ideals of the early Renaissance, the *gravitas* of Donatello's and Masaccio's figures, which came from those by Giotto and which recall Dante's lines:

> Now when his feet had put away the haste
> Which robs all actions of their dignity.
> (*Purgatory* III. 10-11. Sayers translation)

Dante's "haste" is the equivalent of Leonardo's "usefulness." The useful man is the one who bends his body to toil, debarring it from the beauty and harmony of an erect position – just as a fortress "bends" itself to follow the line of a rocky peak. The architectural theories of the age of humanism demanded a façade which could be observed from a fixed point so as to evaluate the geometrical organization both of the individual parts and of the whole, a façade onto which the spectator could project an idea of his own measure as in a mirror. In 1490, the same year that Leonardo wrote the enigmatic phrase on beauty and utility not coexisting in fortresses and men, he also produced a work that was to prepare the way for the rise of a new style in architecture: the famous drawing of the man inscribed in a circle and in a square, through which he illustrated the principles of Vitruvian proportions. This drawing alone would be enough to make an architect of him. Not only does he contribute what can be considered the first illustration to an architectural treatise from antiquity, of which only the text had survived, but he interprets the Vitruvian man according to a concept of beauty formed on Albertian modules. He produces an image devoid of volume, delineated with a precise and continuous contour as if it were incised on crystal. The circle and the square within which it is inserted relate directly to the architectural principles of those centrally-planned buildings which constitute the classical ideal of the fifteenth century, from Brunelleschi's Old Sacristy to Sangallo's S. Maria delle Carceri. Yet there is already in this image the germ of that dynamic element which soon would be welcomed in sixteenth-century architecture as a factor of beauty.

The Vitruvian text considers separately the two aspects of the relationship of man within the circle and within the square, and it always appears thus in the illustrated editions of Vitruvius beginning with the first, by Fra Giocondo, in 1511. Leonardo, however, presents the problem pictorially, superimposing the images. The result is a single body with four legs and four arms, like an Indian god, and its inherent dynamism is suggested by the possibility of envisaging the movement from one position to the other.

It was not by chance that this very figure was used by Walt Disney to symbolize the advent of "moving pictures."

There is undoubtedly a conceptual affinity between this drawing and one, equally famous, of twelve years later – the plan of the city of Imola, which is shown within a circle subdivided into eight sectors according to

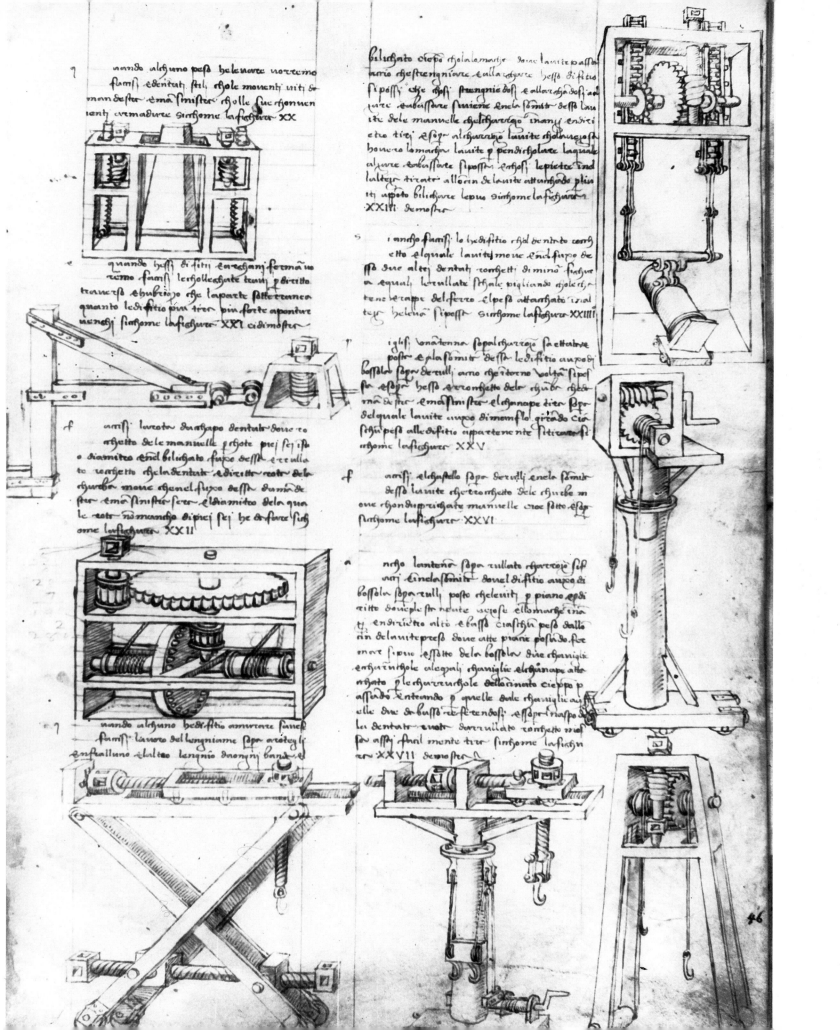

nando alchuno peso helenoue uorremo
fiamsi edenitati stil rhole mouenti uiti d
man dester ema sinister rholle sue rhonnen
renti armadure sirhome lafichura XX

quando hessi difitii torechanj forma uo
rerro faors lorholechate teanj p dirito
tranersi chubrioso che laparte sotterranea
quanto ledifitio piu tren piu sorte apontere
usirehj sirhome lafichura XXI cidimoster

acrissi lareta dunchapo dentala doue ro
rheto dele mamuelle prhote prej serjiso
o diametro enel bilichato suso deff erulla
te torrheto chelendentate adirett roto dela
rhurba moue chenel suso deff damade
ster ema sinister sto e dchamitro dela qua
le roto remancho dipiej serj he unforce sich
ome lafichura XXII

nando alchuno hedifitio amurare fanef
fiamsi lauoro del lengniame sopa artedegli
enstalluno chalto lengnio dnonjni banda el

bilichato etrpo rholalamarche doue lauute passan
morio chestreignioure eullarodgure heff difitio
sipossi etge ghsi strengnia doff eallarchadosi aol
gure eubeissore siniere enela somis deff lau
ite dele mamuelle cheldcharrego manj endiri
eto tiej esogn alchurento lauute rholaurejoso
honero lomarta lauite p pendirhjolare laguale
algure eulassure sipossi erhosi lepietra enal
lultega tirearo alloren delauite attarchado plin
ti appoto bilichoure lepus sirhome lafichura
XXIII demoster

i anrho fianssi lo hredifitio rhil denintro toorh
etto elguale lauutes moue enel sirpo de
ffo due altej dentah rrorhetti di mino sirhure
o equali loreullate sthale pigliando rholeri
tene ierappe delferro elpes attarchato isiol
teja helena sipessa sirhome lafichura XXIIII

iglij enatenna sopalrharrego sa ettabre
posto eplasomis deff ledifitio aupodi
boffola sopa derulli arno chritorno uolta sipes
sa esogn heff errorhfatto dela rhurba rhe
ma dister ema sinister elchanape tier sopa
del guale lauute aupo dimomfio girrdo cio
sirhj pes alledifitio appartenente sitirearesi
arhome lafichura XXV

acrissi alchastello sopa derulli enela somir
deff lauute rhe trrorhetto dele rhueba m
one rhondepringate mamuelle eroe sotto esop
sirhome lafichura XXVI

nerho lanterea sopa erullate erharroje sisi
nerj einelasstenit doued difitio aupodi
boffola sopa erulli posto rhelenitj p piano epdi
ritto doueplestreneate uerosa ellomarte eran
tj endrietro alto elbasso eiasstesti peso dello
rin delauutepress doue atte praare posido stre
onore sopn essatto dela boffola due rhaniglia
erharenrhole alegualj rhaniglie elchanape atta
rhato plecharreurhole dellorinato etrppo p
aisdo erteando p quelle dale rhaniglie ausn
elle due do basso rostrrtendosi essopa rriapso d
la dentato errat doueruilato rorhetto mos
sosu aisj sonal mente tiez sirhome lafichn
era XXVII demoster

46

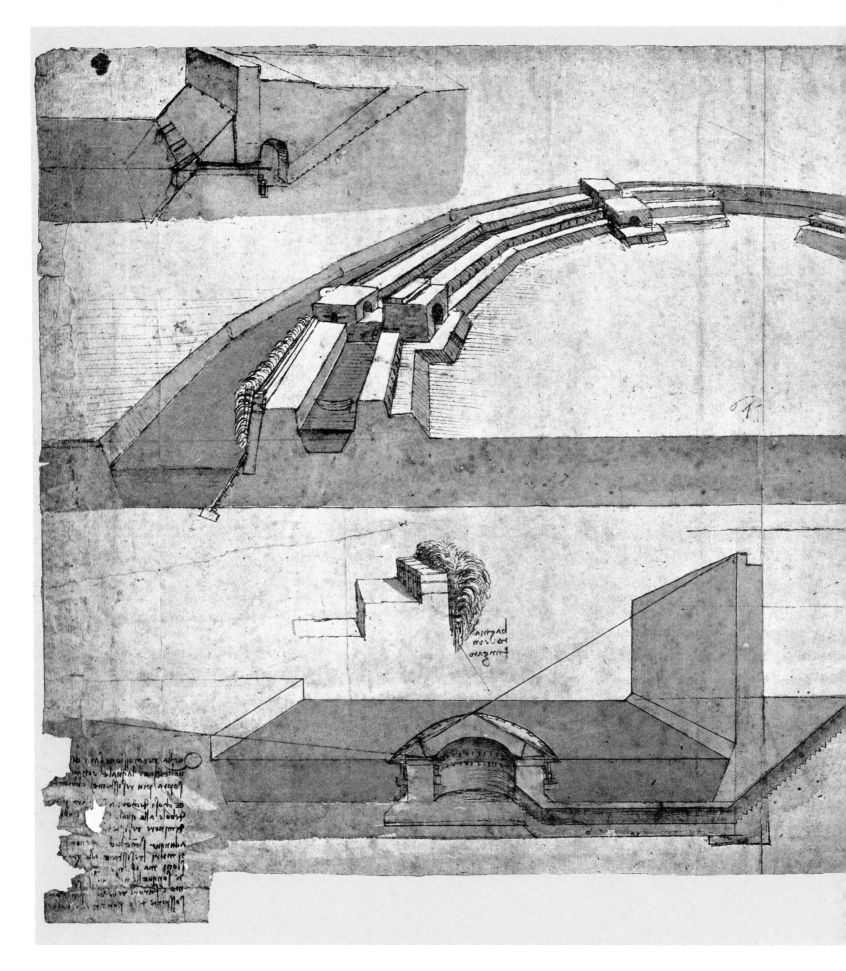

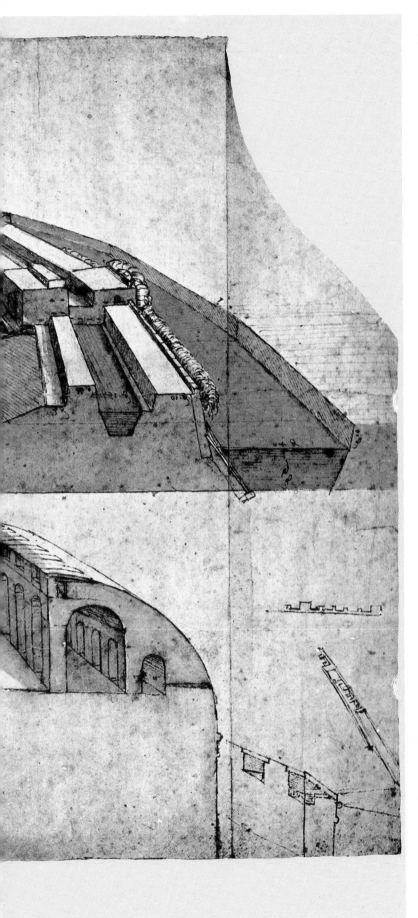

the cardinal points. Both have the same precision of line, the same severity of style expressing the architect's clarity of mind.

In the plan of Imola, however, one can perceive a wider-ranging pictorial vision, as if he had actually seen the city from above through a lens. The vision could not fail to stimulate his imagination. In the same way as he lingers with poetical enchantment over reproducing the effect of water on the pebbly bed of the river, so he senses that the whole urban fabric can assume the character of a living organism and he can therefore allow himself the pictorial license of straining reality by making more sinuous the almost straight course of the Via Emilia, the main road which crosses the city from one end to the other. The dynamic element, which in the drawing of the Vitruvian man was only suggested as a mental game, manifests itself in the plan of Imola with a sense of the majestic flow of forms.

From here it is just a short step to Bramante's Tempietto. This building, deliberately restrained in its dimensions like a programmatic model of sixteenth-century monumentality, puts into effect the principles which had been maturing in the last decade of the fifteenth century in the work of Leonardo and Bramante in Milan. According to the original project handed down to us by Serlio, the Tempietto was to be surrounded by the circular portico of a courtyard based on a square. The result would have been a plastic element contained within a space without any break in continuity, like a nucleus within a vegetable or animal organism. There is no longer a fixed place for the spectator, but an incentive to move around and into the building. This is an architecture, therefore, that appeals more to the senses than to the mind, and that makes use of optical adjustments which Vitruvius himself had mentioned. The lines of vision reach the building from various points, always moving along it in order to give substance to the idea of volume. There is the same sense of plasticity and dynamism that appears in Leonardo's drawings of fortifications after 1500. The military structures seem moulded by the curved paths of the projectiles which cross from all directions like the spectator's lines of vision.

Perhaps I am asserting too much in attributing stylistic characteristics to structures which were conceived with purely practical intentions. But it is impossible to overlook the importance assumed by military architecture in the last decade of the fifteenth century and its subsequent influence on the artistic conceptions of the early sixteenth. This can be traced in Leonardo's writings and drawings. The earlier ones, datable to about 1490, reveal his study of classical and contemporary sources, Vitruvius, Vegetius and Valturio's *De re militari* (1483), from which he derived knowledge of the art of war and the military architecture of antiquity. Subsequent contacts with contemporary architects, Luca Fancelli, Alberti's assistant in Mantua, Francesco di Giorgio, Bramante and later Giuliano da Sangallo, all of whom came to Milan to work on the cathedral at the time that Leonardo was staying there, helped him to draw together a series of ideas and experiences

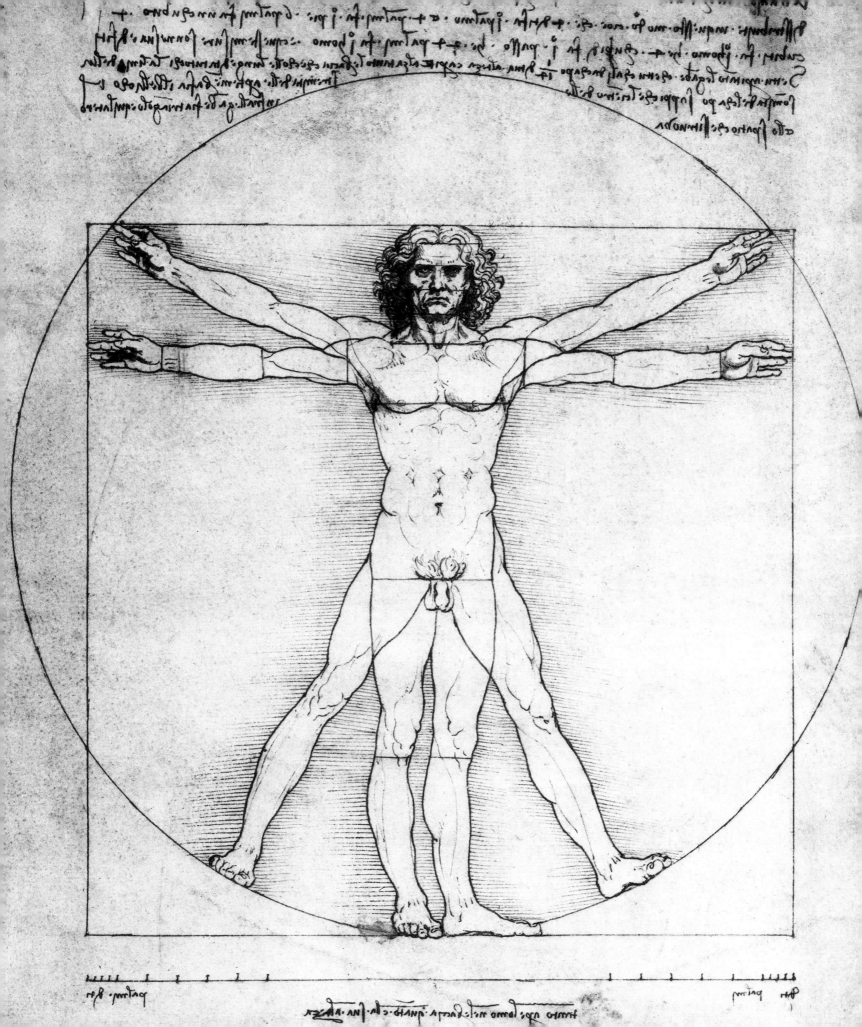

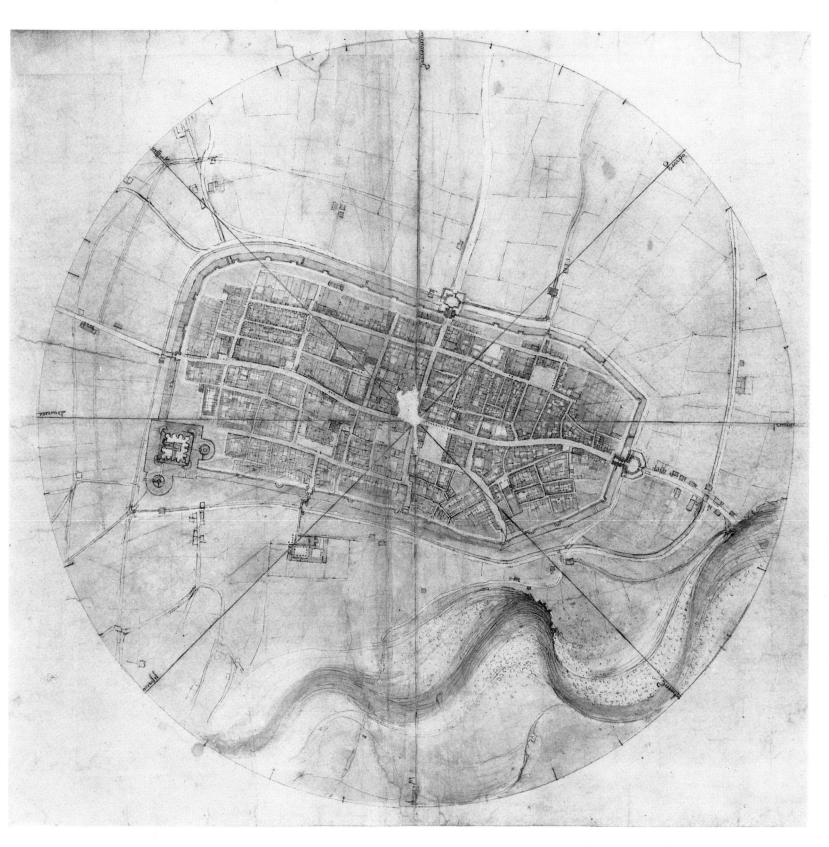

230. *The Vitruvian man*, c. 1490. Venice, Gallerie dell'Accademia.
231. *Plan of the city of Imola*, c. 1502. Windsor, RL 12284.

which were to lead to a new concept of monumentality.

In the meantime, French interference in Italian politics, starting with Charles VIII's campaign in 1494, which culminated in the fall of the Sforza dynasty in 1499, led to an important new development in the art of war. The increased power and efficiency of artillery made it necessary to re-examine traditional systems of defense. Leonardo wrote: "since artillery has acquired three quarters more power than before it is necessary that the walls of the fortresses acquire three quarters more resistance than they usually have." Bastions were introduced to replace the corner towers of castles and fortresses. The curtain walls were lowered, taking on receding profiles so as to better absorb the shocks or deflect the blows from the artillery. Thus the circular form appeared as a prelude to the polygonal and star-shaped forms of the end of the sixteenth century, when a whole city would be built within such defensive walls as at Palmanova. The new principles of defense, both passive and active, formulated in Leonardo's writings around 1500, were to be taken up again and developed by Michelangelo during the defense of Florence in 1527. Moreover, these same principles of dynamics are reflected in Michelangelo's idea for the three-ramp staircase in the entrance hall of the Laurentian library.

A detail of the map of Imola shows the fortress's square plan, with circular towers at the corners and two ravelins. The keep appears to be joined to the south and west curtain walls by means of two communication trenches which mark the limits of a square courtyard with a portico indicated on one side. Comparison with a plan of twenty years later shows that the thickness of the curtain walls was reinforced with a system of large horizontal arches. (I believe that these should be understood not as a summary indication of casemates, but as a suggestion for reinforcement which was eventually carried out by simply thickening the walls.) The fortress and the fortified entries into the city had a strategic importance which Cesare Borgia's military architect could not underrate. This is quite evident in another sheet at Windsor, in which Leonardo had gathered the data he needed to prepare the map of the city. On that sheet, which I made public as long ago as 1955, Leonardo draws the outline of the four sectors of the city and adds details of the two gates and two plans of the fortress. In commenting on the two drawings of the fortress I pointed out that in the top one the two ravelins are shown in the same relationship to the internal structures of the fortress as they are on the map, while in the bottom one the two ravelins, now placed in front of the mid-point of each of the corresponding curtain walls, line up with an internal structure which, in comparison with the one drawn on the map, turns out to have been shifted to the east. I concluded with the hypothesis that in the second drawing Leonardo had adopted a different orientation of the fortress in order to suggest the construction of a new ravelin, to be placed, like the other, outside the city, eliminating the one which had been within it. Nevertheless I did acknowledge the possibility of a project of modification to the internal structures which seemed to take the shape of a porticoed courtyard. That hypothesis, which I could not support with any factual data, was to prove to be exactly the right one, thanks to the restorations carried out by the architect Franco Schettini, Superintendent of Monuments in Emilia, and to his definitive interpretation of those sketches.

The restorations have confirmed that the inner building, the "rocchetta," belongs not to the original mediaeval structures as had been thought, but to Renaissance alterations to which Leonardo must have contributed in 1502. Schettini brought to light the traces of a *quadriporticus*, an arcaded courtyard with arches on each of the four sides, which reflects precisely Leonardo's project for inserting a palatial residence within the fortress. Besides, he has convincingly shown that the two plans of the fortress represent two phases in Leonardo's thought: above is the structure as it existed in Leonardo's time, with an indication of one of the dimensions ("40 feet"), which is exactly the length of the west curtain wall, and in this one Leonardo hints at the proposed modifications, suggesting shifting the south ravelin towards the centre of the corresponding curtain wall. The inner area contained between the keep and the south and east curtain walls begins to thicken with suggestions of rooms which do not yet form the configuration of a courtyard. But in the plan below the ideas are clarified. The south and east ravelins are represented in a central position in relation to the corresponding curtain walls and the inner building has taken shape around an arcaded courtyard placed towards the east. The fortress ceases to be only a utilitarian structure and takes on the character of a noble dwelling-house. Beauty and utility can now coexist.

We do not know how much of the project was ever carried out. At the time of the map of Imola, probably in the autumn of 1502, one side of the portico had already been built and the foundations laid for the other three sides, which have come to light during the recent restoration. The realization of Leonardo's project was not to take into account the suggestion of regularizing the plan, shifting the south ravelin towards the centre – so the arcaded courtyard was built in the south-west section of the fortress, where the entrance was protected by the existing ravelin. Perhaps not even the one portico as it appears today was completely built at the time of Leonardo's stay in Imola, but it is reasonable to believe that it followed the plan which he outlined. Even as it is, a mere germ of Leonardo's intentions, the building is impressive for the significant place it holds within the context of early sixteenth-century architecture. The arcaded courtyard was to have four arches on each side. Leonardo's sketch seems to indicate the use of columns, but the part that was built uses wide piers to support the ample arches of the vaults, in conformity with the Albertian postulate that in antiquity the arch had to rest on piers while columns had to support architraves. A platband that descends from the arch to outline the piers seems to suggest that the structure was to be given vigorous cornices and that slender pilasters were to be attached to the piers. Yet the cornices of the capitals, which break up the continuity of design almost as if to slow

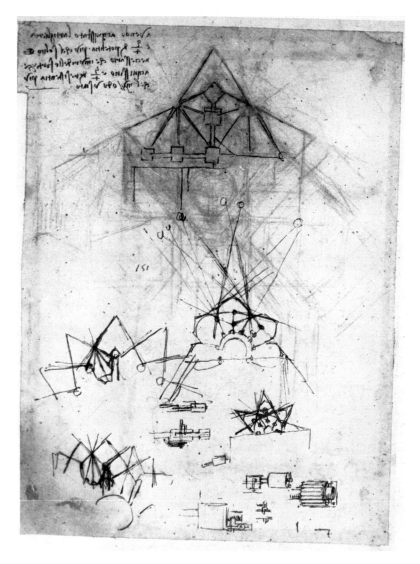

163

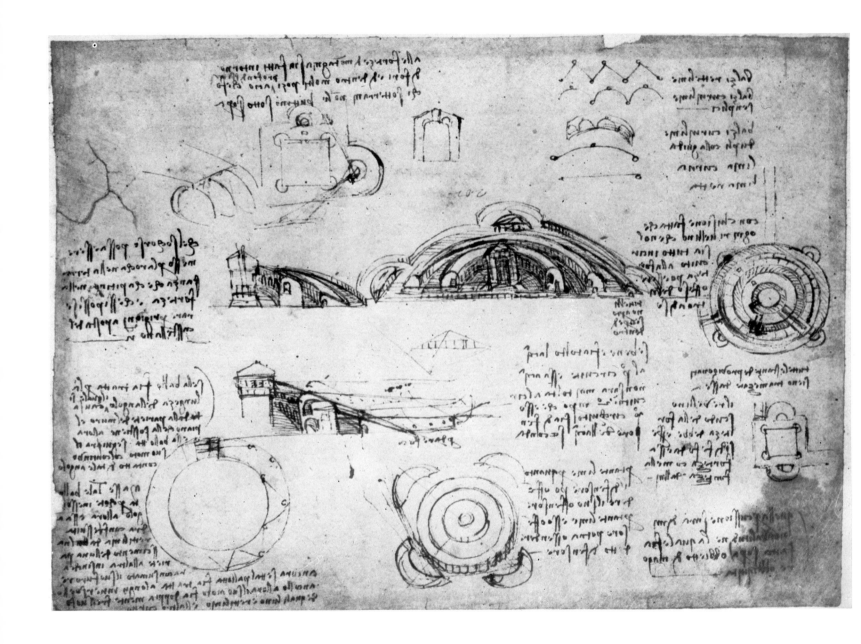

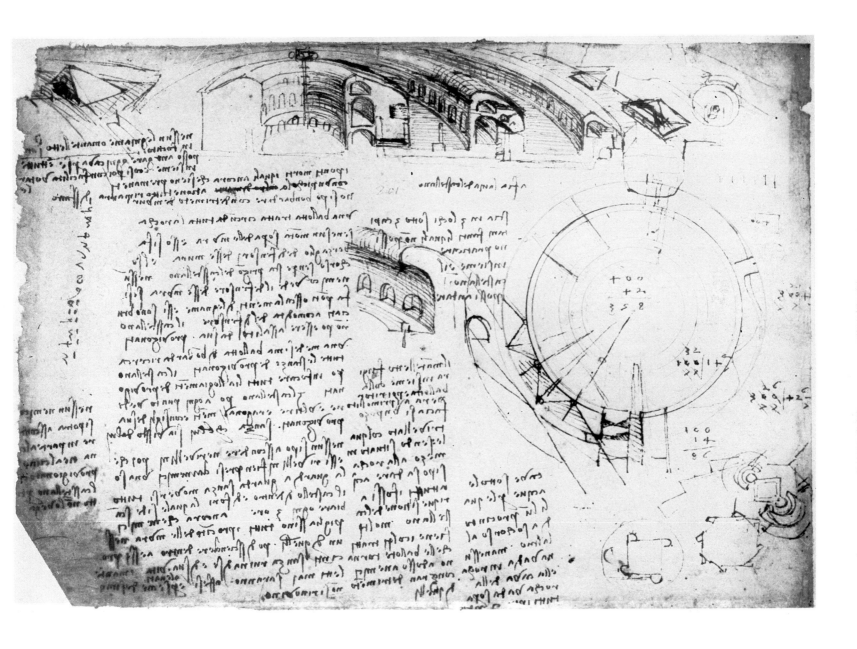

236. Plan of the Rocca of Imola after
restoration.

237. Aerial view of the Rocca of Imola after
restoration.

238. Topographical notes for the plan
of Imola, c. 1502. Windsor, RL 12686.

down the vertical thrust, may indicate a more delicate type of wall
treatment, without the articulation of superimposed elements – a type,
that is, which Leonardo hinted at in some drawings of 1490 and which
he repeated later in the studies for a *villa suburbana* in Milan, around
1497. These drawings feature forms of an almost rural character, such as
appear in the studies for a country villa which have hypothetically been
related to the Villa Tovaglia and in which there is a porticoed courtyard
with surprising affinities to the one at Imola.

The *quadriporticus* would have enclosed a perfectly square space, in
which Leonardo would have applied those principles of interval and
proportional relationships which he represented theoretically in a series
of studies of courtyards on a Windsor drawing of about 1508. A line
starts from the roof at an angle which suggests that angle at which light
must be admitted into the enclosed space if it is to make the most of its
plasticity without violent effects of chiaroscuro; and that line converges
in the centre of the square (which in the drawing is always marked). A
note of serenity, of measure, and therefore of beauty is thus inserted into
a military structure. In the simplicity and solemnity of its lines the
building, made more precious as it would have been by virtue of its
reduced proportions, would have evoked the noble atmosphere of the
courtyard of the Ducal Palace in Urbino and the boldness of the
unadorned arches of ancient public baths. It is dangerous, perhaps, to
attribute to a fragment those stylistic subtleties which often cannot even
be perceived in the finished works. And yet we have sufficient
indications of the way the architect had intended to organize the space,
with a building surrounding an area that had to be partly inserted into
the south curtain wall in order to be perfectly square. That space and
what little was carried out of the building exert a fascination comparable
to that of one of Bramante's first Roman works, the cloister of Santa
Maria della Pace, of 1504.

Leonardo's activity in the service of Cesare Borgia, which culminates
with the cartographic and architectural work in Imola, can be followed
through the notes, many dated, in MS. L, where there are recurring
references to fortifications and where surveys of the fortified wall of
Cesena have been identified. And it was probably in Romagna, after
seeing the daring bridge of Castel del Rio, consisting of only one span of
about 80 metres, built in 1499 by Andrea Furrieri from Imola after an
unsuccessful attempt by Francesco di Giorgio, that Leonardo had the
idea for the immense bridge from Pera to Constantinople (with a span
of 240 metres!) described and drawn in plan and elevation in MS. L, f.
66 r. Franco Schettini has been able to read in Leonardo's sketch an
extraordinary application of mechanical principles going back to the
studies for the tiburio of Milan Cathedral. Pacioli speaks of an ingenious
wooden bridge built in Romagna by "the Duke's noble engineer," a type
of temporary construction which had fascinated Leonardo since the
time he wrote the letter to Lodovico Sforza, although we find no trace of
it in MS. L or anywhere else. That notebook contains, however, a note
for a planned canal-harbour at Cesenatico, and shows that Leonardo

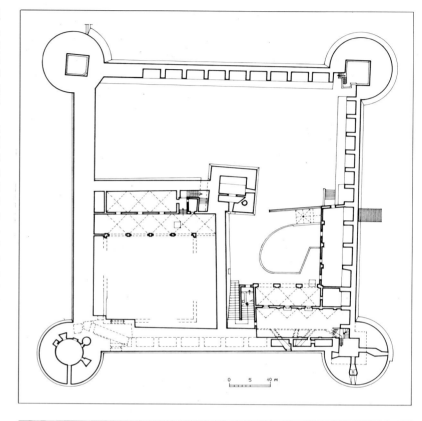

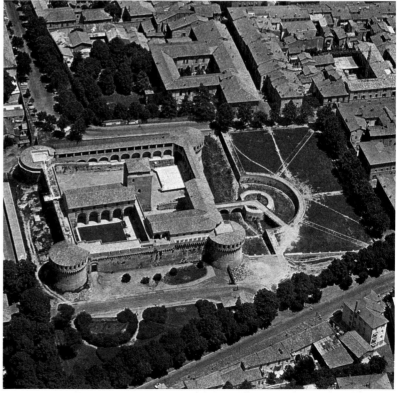

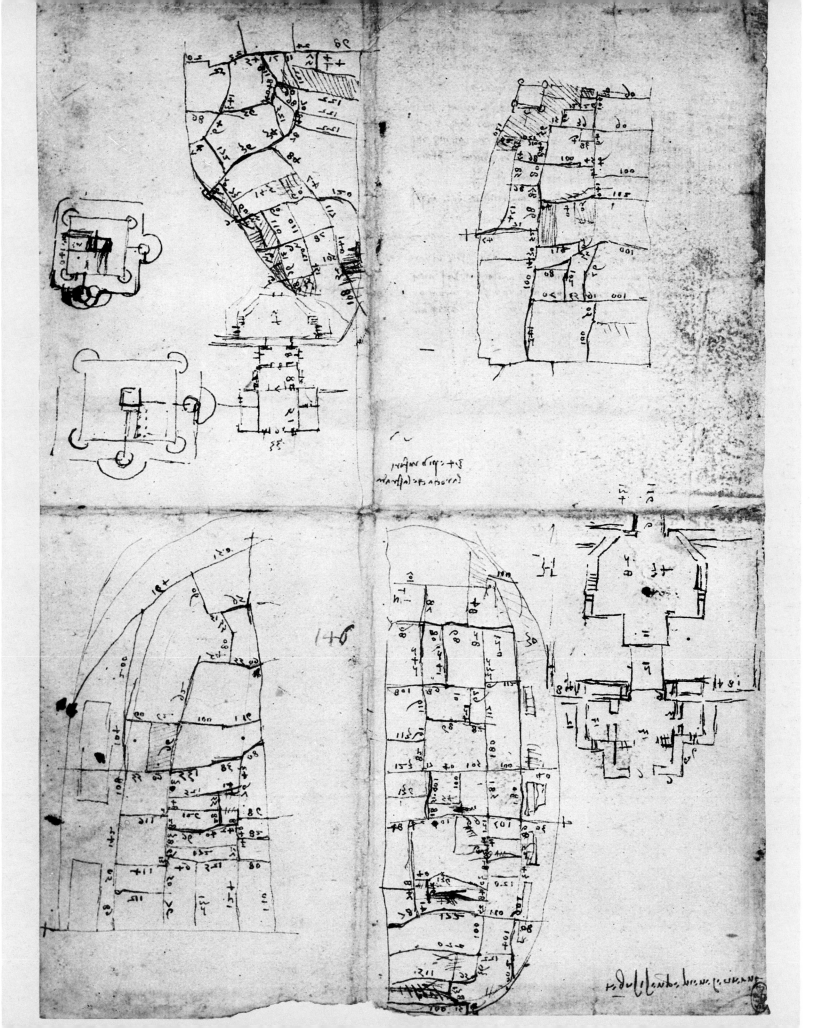

239. Quadriporticus *of the Rocca of Imola.*

240. *Sketch of a portico, detail from f. 220 r-c of the Codex Atlanticus.*

241. *Detail of the arcade of a portico, c. 1505. Codex Atlanticus, f. 202 v-a.*

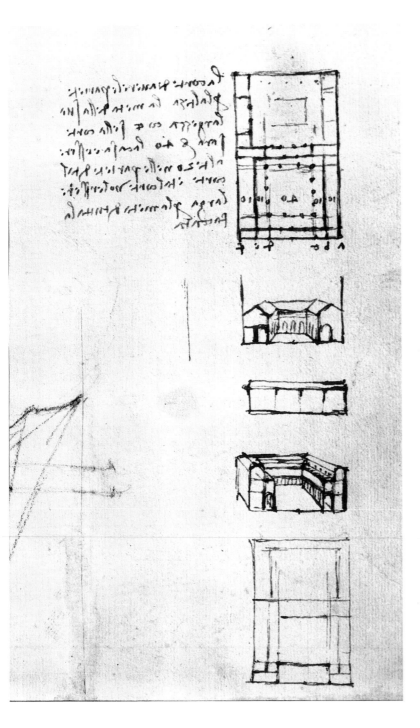

went as far as Urbino, where he surveyed the walls and made a note of a detail of a courtyard with paired corner pilasters, perhaps from the Ducal Palace. He recorded only two characteristic features of that palace: the great monumental staircase by Francesco di Giorgio and the small but equally as monumental Cappella del Perdono, which is attributed to the young Bramante. And Leonardo took note with equal interest of the plan of the menacing fortress of Cardinal Albornoz, facing the Ducal Palace on the opposite slope of the valley.

As we trace the course of Leonardo's architectural career, we realize the effect which his studies of military architecture at the beginning of the sixteenth century must have had on his later ideas: the residence of the French Governor of Milan, of 1508, the refurbishing of Villa Melzi at Vaprio d'Adda of 1513, a new Medici Palace in Florence of 1515, and finally the Royal Palace of Romorantin in France of 1517-18. The fortress is no longer a building which, in order to be useful, cannot be beautiful, but it has been raised to a symbol of regal dignity, order and justice. It is the same idea which Bramante was putting into effect in Rome with the grandiose Palazzo dei Tribunali, a building with a square courtyard and corner rooms which jut out like the towers of a fortress. But Leonardo was never excessive in giving an expression of power even to structures which can assume colossal dimensions. His buildings always have an element of gracefulness and measure which make them pleasant and inviting. Even when the building must assert itself because of its intended purpose as residence of a powerful lord, as in the case of the palace for Lorenzo di Piero de' Medici, Governor of Florence, he finds a way to soften the powerful articulation of its walls with the motif of columns in the form of tree-trunks with branches intertwined to form the archivolts and with a rustication that adds plasticity to the wall surfaces, as if to imply the presence of an organic element which vibrates with energy through columns and arches.

Leonardo's architectural drawings seem to anticipate some of Giulio Romano's mannerist works in Mantua which serve as a frame to a festive pictorial decoration. But above all they must have been admired by Raphael, who had arrived at architecture precisely from painting. Raphael's architecture was formed by Bramante's teachings and carried on the tradition of the architectural programs of Urbino, enriched by a direct study of the antique and by an exposure to Leonardo's ideas. In one of Leonardo's pages from a few years after his stay at Imola various types of hydraulic pumps are indicated, one of which is accompanied by the note: "pump from Imola." He recorded a device which he might have seen used at Imola or which he himself had designed when building work was being done on the fortress. (This calls to mind the note on the sheet of preliminary studies in Windsor: "the cisterns must always be kept full.") Just below this drawing, partly covered by another one, is sketched a detail of a wall of a building which shows the system of paired columns on either side of a large window opening (probably blind) with a triangular tympanum and hefty cornices; all elements that in details and in the whole resemble Raphael's

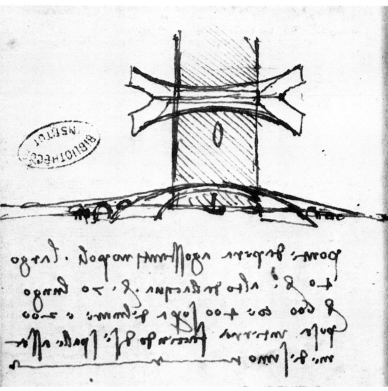

architecture of ten years later, particularly that of the Chigi stables in Rome. In 1515 Raphael was appointed Superintendent of Antiquities with the task of studying the Roman monuments in accordance with a programme of surveys and restorations set out by himself in a long letter to the Pope. In that admirable document Raphael reveals a remarkable sense of history, which he had developed through an assiduous study of Vitruvius. He explains the method which he intends to adopt in surveying the ruins for a planned archaeological map of Rome. His explanation would be difficult to comprehend without the example of Leonardo's map of Imola.

In fact Raphael describes step by step the method Leonardo had adopted, indicating how the circle of two spans in diameter (and that is the exact size of the circle in the map of Imola) when subdivided into thirty-two sectors, serves as a structural basis for the preparation of a map. But in Leonardo's drawing that structural basis is more than a technical element. It rises to the surface like rays of light that blaze out from the centre and transmit vibrations to the whole image.

11. La Verruca

"Leonardo da Vinci came himself with companions and we showed them everything, from which it seemed to us that he liked La Verruca very much, and enjoyed it greatly; and later, he says, he thought of making it impregnable. But this cannot be put into effect at present, because it is necessary to attend to this Librafatta, which is no small deed nor to be little valued; and in the meantime repair it so that it is safe; and then do it with that perfection which that place requires."

Thus wrote the field commissioner, Pier Francesco Tosinghi, to the gonfalonier Pier Soderini on 21 June 1503, while reporting on the progress of the war against Pisa. It is the time of Leonardo's surveys of the course of the Arno near Pisa, when the Republic had commissioned him to work out a plan for diverting the river in order to force the enemy to surrender. We learn this from a letter written by Francesco Guicciardini from the field, dated 24 July 1503, telling how on the previous day he had received a visit from Alessandro degli Albizi, Leonardo da Vinci and others, "and having seen the drawing together with the governor, after many discussions and doubts, I concluded that the work was most opportune, either if the Arno were really to turn here, or to stay there with a canal, at least it would stop the hills from being harmed by the enemy."

The reference here is to the Pisan hills which frame the Arno valley, and which appear in a series of wonderful drawings by Leonardo in the second Madrid manuscript. We have already mentioned the first of those manuscripts in which Leonardo, in the last decade of the fifteenth century and later, put in order his studies on technology and mechanics, presenting them with the neatness of a definitive compilation, and therefore with an almost chilling precision and clarity. The second manuscript, however, which is datable from 1503 to 1505 (or even 1506), the time of Leonardo's frequent travels as engineer and military

*245, 246. Interpretation by the architect
Franco Schettini of Leonardo's project for
the bridge on the Corno d'Oro.*

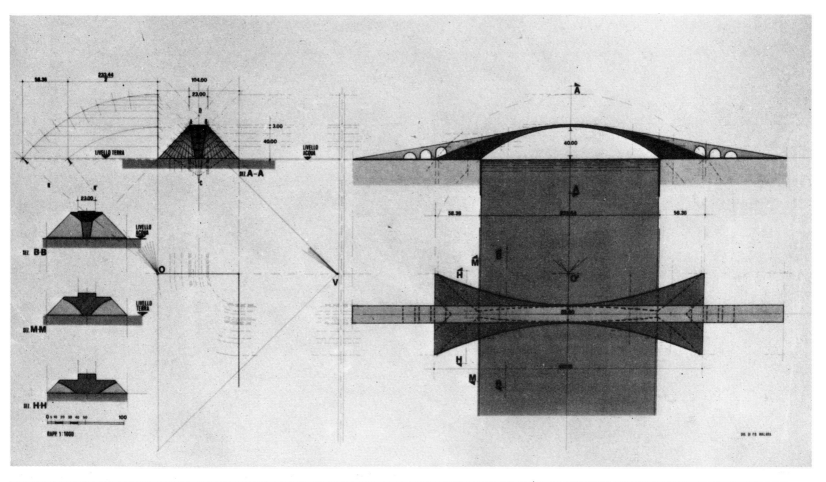

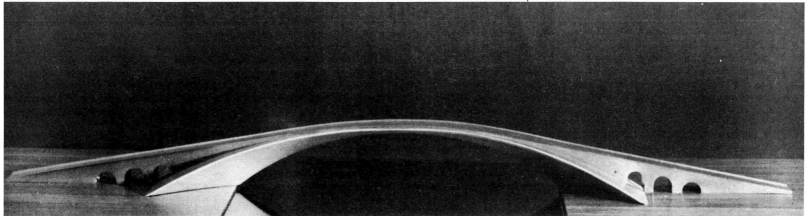

247. *Grand staircase of the ducal palace in Urbino and a bell in Siena, c. 1502. MS. L, ff. 19 v-20 r.*

248. *Details of the Cappella del Perdono in the ducal palace at Urbino, c. 1502. MS. L, ff. 74 r-73 v.*

249. *Urbino, ducal palace, entrance from the Grand staircase to the upper loggias.*

250. *Urbino, ducal palace, Cappella del Perdono.*

251. *Urbino, ducal palace, entrance door to the Cappella del Perdono.*

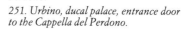

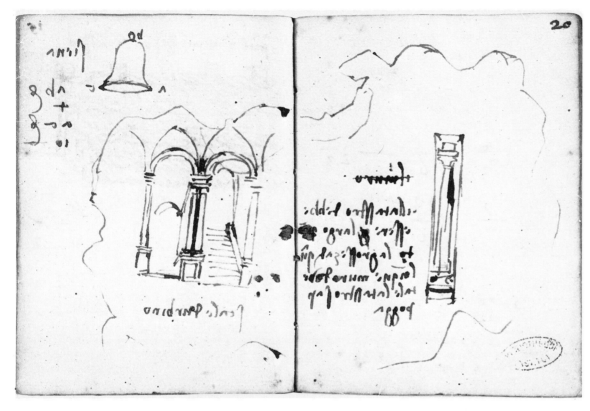

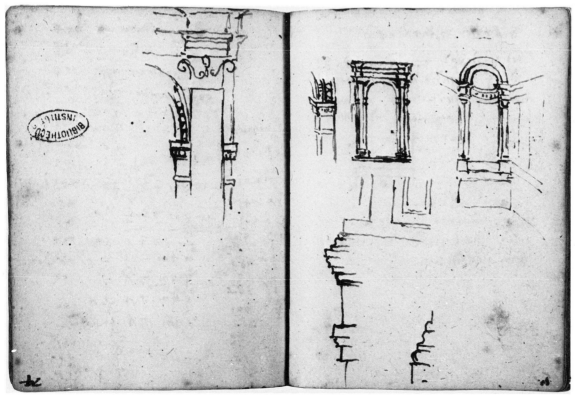

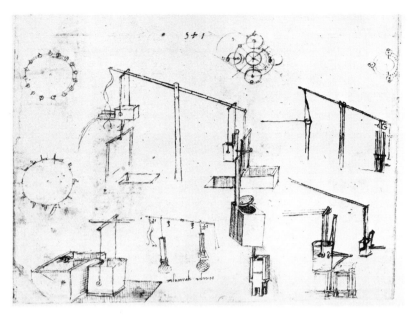

252, 253. Sketch of the wall of a building
with paired columns and window with
triangular tympanum, on a sheet of studies
of hydraulic machines ("pumps from
Imola"), 1506-7. Codex Atlanticus, f. 322
r-b, and detail.
254. Rome, the Chigi stables by Raphael.

architect for the Florentine Republic, presents the more exuberant character of field annotation, enhanced by the use of red chalk. Moreover, the subject matter here is of a type that lends itself to a more impulsive and lively style of writing and drawing, with colouristic touches and always dominated by a dynamic sense of the images: topographic maps where river courses seem to pulsate like veins at the passing of blood; studies of fortifications designed to resist siege artillery and therefore moulded with receding profiles; studies of waters, canals, navigation; studies on the flight of birds, and then notes on painting, with observations on the atmospheric effects of landscape, notes on perspective, colour and human motion, in great part transcribed later in the *Trattato della Pittura*, and finally extensive geometrical studies on the transformation of surfaces and bodies, attempts at squaring the circle and surfaces with curved sides, stereometry – abstract elements, between reality and fantasy, from which emerge the concepts which give shape to the new architectural ideals of the Renaissance from Bramante to Michelangelo.

The second Madrid manuscript contains extensive calculations of excavations, which may relate partly to the Arno project of 1503, and partly to Leonardo's activity as military architect in Piombino in the autumn of the following year. Already for some time he had been concerned with excavation devices, and many of his better-known drawings of excavating machines can be assigned to a period which coincides with that of his town-planning projects in Lombardy, that is around 1493-95. It does seem however that it was only at the beginning of the sixteenth century, or at least at the time of MS. L, where we find numerous notes relating to "scoops" and to problems of excavation, that he succeeded in perfecting the systems in use at the time by proposing a simple but highly ingenious innovation, revolutionizing a method which had remained the same practically since antiquity.

Leonardo had already experimented with a system of excavation in which animal motive power would operate along a spiral-shaped track and he was getting ready to exploit also the mass of falling weights as a source of motive power. Many pages of Madrid MS. I are taken up by theoretical studies on weights – an elaboration of the mediaeval science *de ponderibus*, on which many of Leonardo's practical applications are based. A drawing on f. 96 r of that Codex represents a double-jib crane in a "contextual view," that is in action on the schematically shown bank of a canal. There is no explanatory text, but it is easy to interpret the mechanism as an application of the principle of the *saliscendi*, that is counterweights. It is the same principle that Leonardo applied shortly afterwards in one of his more famous projects for machinery, the canal-excavator that appears on one of the most spectacular sheets of the Codex Atlanticus.

This too is a "contextual view." The machine is placed on rails and is brought forward slowly as the excavation of the canal proceeds. The traditional type of excavator which one can date back to Vitruvius operates sideways, as we can see in another famous drawing from the

Codex Atlanticus. We have many sheets of preliminary studies and also the rough draft of a report which Leonardo intended to submit with the project for the approval of some administrative commission. It probably was a project relating to the canalization of the Arno and therefore datable to the time of the second Madrid Manuscript, around 1503. This would have been a public works project that required a demonstration of efficiency and superiority and of consequent economic advantage. Leonardo's language here becomes succinct and to the point, leaving the conclusive proof to the eloquence of the drawing.

And in fact what could be more telling than a drawing showing the two types of excavating machine working on the same canal? Such was the original drawing and as such I now offer it in reconstruction, putting it back into the "contextual view" conceived by Leonardo. On the left is the traditional machine operated by men or animals walking inside the drum; on the right, already in an advantageous position because of operating frontally, is the machine put forward by Leonardo, which applies the principle of counterweights: the team of workmen is spaced out on three levels and their actions are synchronized so that the containers filled with earth are lifted by the empty containers being sent back down by the weight of the workmen who jump into them! This "contextual view" however does not show these men, who play such an important part in the working of the machine. They are represented only by their tools: spades, pick-axes and barrows.

Much has been written, possibly even too much, on Leonardo's activity as a military engineer, first for Cesare Borgia and then in the service of the Florentine Republic, that is from the beginning of 1502 to the end of 1504. Madrid MS. II contains many pages that reflect the tasks he carried out at Piombino for its ruler, Jacopo IV Appiani, following a program set out by the Florentine Chancery and personally inspired by Machiavelli. In truth Leonardo's work seems to have been limited to the excavation of a ditch, to the construction (or merely the project) of a tower and to the plan for strengthening the city gate, besides some studies concerning the mole. But he made this the pretext for sketching out an extensive treatise on fortifications and ports which some have sought to identify as a compilation based on Francesco di Giorgio's Codex Magliabechianus, whereas the very reverse is true, as Parronchi has proved.

The pieces of information provided by the Madrid manuscript complement those which can be traced in other codexes, including sketches of plans in MS. L and in the Codex Atlanticus, this last sketch identifiable as the work of Antonio da Sangallo the Elder. (The identification is based on comparison with the notes and drawings by Sangallo at the Uffizi. Notes by the same hand in Madrid MS. II, f. 122 r, show that in Piombino Leonardo discussed nautical problems with Sangallo.) And above all, a whole series of studies in the Codex Atlanticus on the subject of the circular citadel and fortresses with receding elevations – studies which even before the discovery of the material in Madrid could be assigned, on the basis of style alone, to a period later than the one

255-257. *Letter from the Commissioner Pier Francesco Tosinghi, from Pisa, to the Republic of Florence, 21 June 1503, with the account of Leonardo's visit to the fortresses of La Verruca and Librafratta. Florence, Biblioteca Nazionale, Carta Ginori Conti 29/108.*

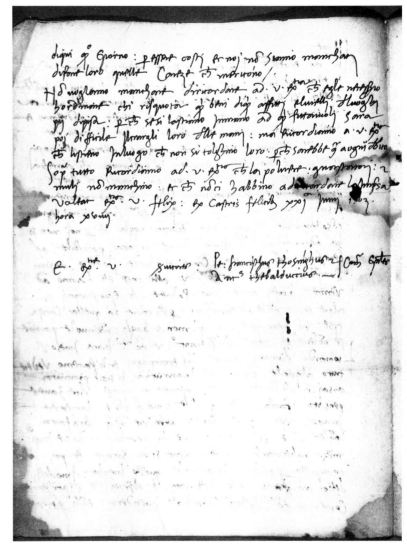

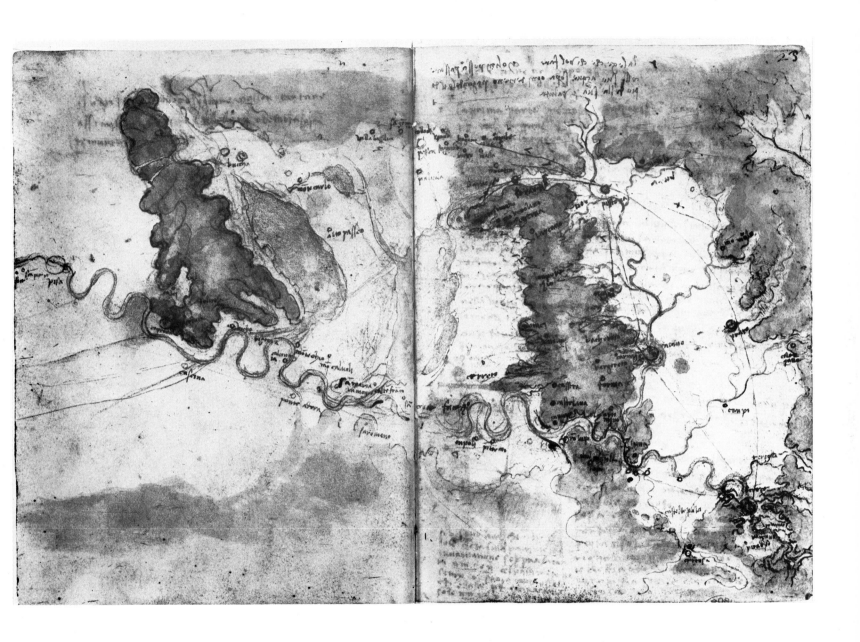

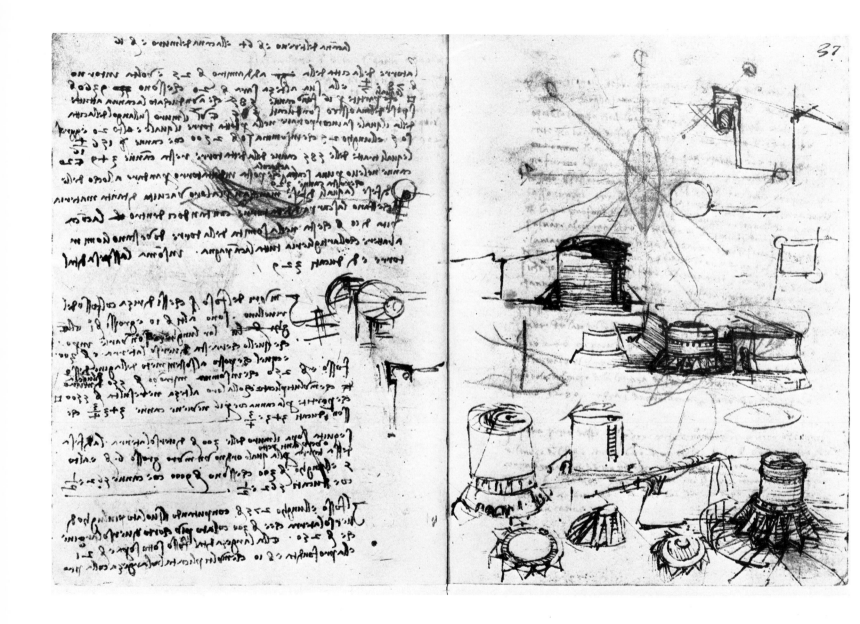

spent in Romagna. And in fact, in presenting them within the context of Leonardo's activity in Piombino, I pointed out in one of the sheets the reference made to the "betrayal" of Fossombrone, which took place on 11 October 1502, as an event already distant in time. This has been taken even further, and it has been suggested that those drawings are only theoretically related to the problems dealt with in Piombino, and therefore belong to a much later period. Style however is a dangerous weapon to use. It is necessary therefore to study f. 120 v-a of the Codex Atlanticus, which contains memoranda datable to the time of Madrid MS. II as well as some sketches of circular citadels not yet recognized as such, but undoubtedly connected with the series of studies on the same subject in the Codex Atlanticus. Nowhere else in the Codex Atlanticus or in any other manuscripts except Madrid MS. II do we find a reference to La Verruca, the fortress which Leonardo inspected on 21 June 1503.

In the by now famous drawings of the Pisan hills in the Madrid manuscript, Leonardo indicates the strategic points, identifying the various places altimetrically. The characteristic protuberance of La Verruca therefore emerges, dominating the whole field of operation. And a quick sketch of the fortress in dramatic close-up, perched on very high rocky peaks – "a cliff which resembles a cluster of towers" as Ammirato would call them – appears in another red chalk drawing on f. 4 r of that manuscript.

From the official papers concerning the course of the Pisan war we can see what strategic importance was attributed to La Verruca, the fortress which Leonardo, according to the document quoted above, had "greatly enjoyed." We can easily believe that it was not just the technical aspect of the fortress set into the monolithic rocks that fascinated him, but also and above all the wild beauty of the place, where his long dreamt-of images of ravines and precipices in the background of a distant vision of waters and mists had formally become real.

We now know that Leonardo's visit to La Verruca made him express the idea of turning it into an impregnable fortress. The mission was therefore assigned to him by the Florentine Republic, even though his name is not found in the official papers. It is a mission that is better explained through the directives sent to the commissioners in the field, by means of which Machiavelli himself, as secretary of the Republic, formulated a plan of attack to take La Verruca by storm. The letter of 14 June 1503 was written – and undoubtedly conceived – personally by Machiavelli: "And since we know how wise these captains are, and equally your diligence, and how you recognize that one makes the best of good fortune by going ahead and using the opportunity well, neither letting the victor's zeal grow cool nor the loser draw breath, we think that you will have already decided to advance and to see rise before your eyes the Verrucola, which has always been a continual annoyance and an obstacle to these places of ours around it, and no little help to the enemy. And we believe the more that you will have arranged to take it by storm, and the more we want you to do so, as in other times such an

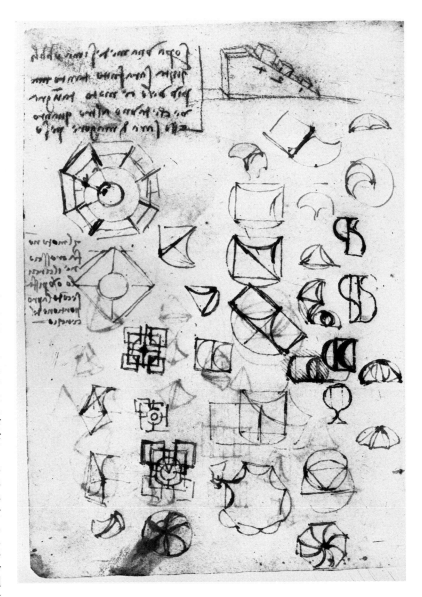

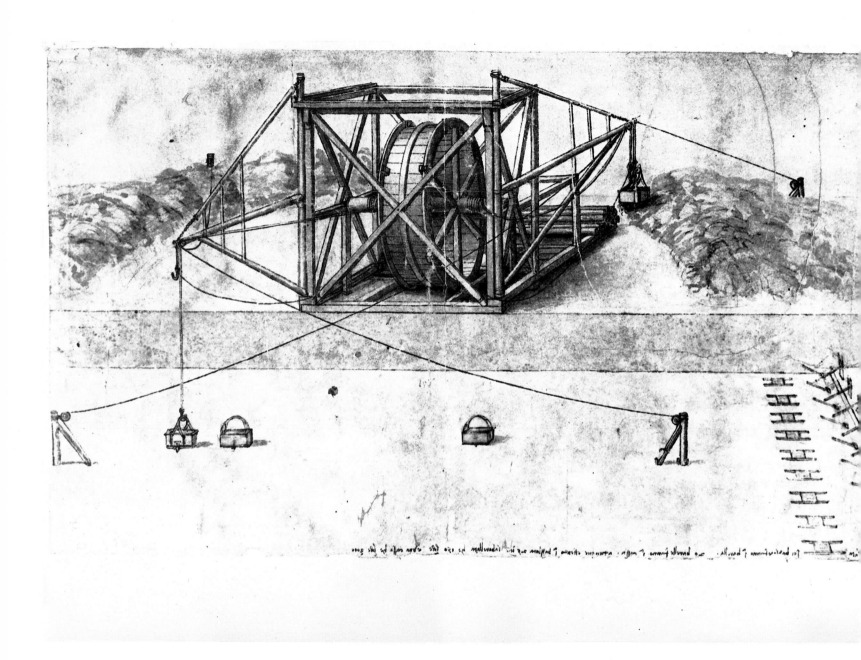

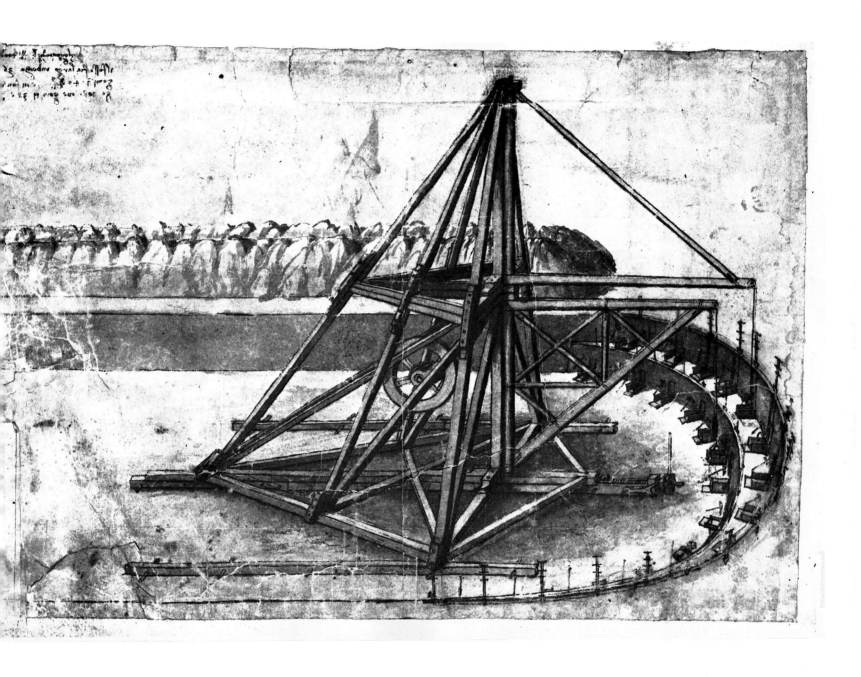

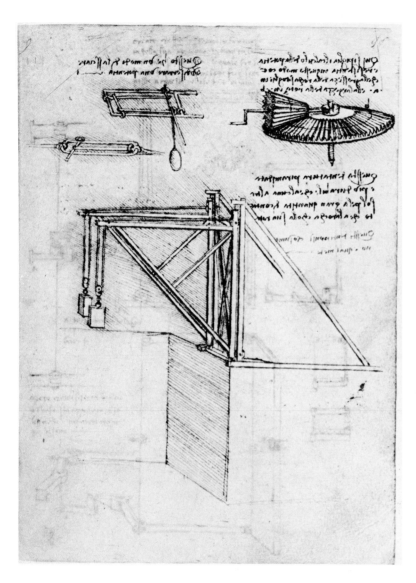

enterprise has been judged not very difficult even by him who is head of these people... and you will advise us should you decide not to undertake the feat, what you should need, as well as what would have to be done later, achieving the feat of the Verruca, and having conquered it." A week later, on 21 June, the fortress was already in Florentine hands and Leonardo was inspecting it so as to recommend the necessary building arrangements. It appears that Giuliano da Sangallo had gone there at the same time. Immediately afterwards, on 26 June, a master-builder, Luca del Caprina, was sent there to carry out the required work. It seems that Leonardo's recommendations, submitted to the Chancery for approval, were accompanied by drawings: "We have seen besides this" we read in the letter which the Florentine Chancery sent to the field on 1 July 1503 "what you write to us regarding La Verruca. We do not wish to omit to tell you that Caprina has not been sent there to give a design for strengthening La Verruca, but so as to help carry out the design that has already been made: because it is our intention that such a design should proceed from those gentlemen, Governors and condottieri in whom, as valiant and most expert men, we wish to place our faith and in no others." It even seems that a model had been prepared (unless by model only a plan was meant). "As regards the Verruca," the Chancery wrote on 5 July 1503, "we remind you that you should hasten to fortify it, on the assumption you have taken the model from these gentlemen condottieri." On 10 October Caprina was replaced by Lorenzo da Monteacuto, the architect of the Villa Tovaglia. Another piece of information that can be gleaned from the correspondence is that on 7 June 1504 Antonio da Sangallo the Elder, chief military architect of the Florentine Republic, on his return from a visit to the fortifications of Librafatta (today's Ripafratta), was requested to go to La Verruca "to check that nothing is lacking," from which we can deduce that at that date the work suggested by Leonardo had been completed or nearly so.

Little or nothing is left of the notes that Leonardo took on that occasion and even less of the projects which are referred to in the official papers. In a detail of the map of Tuscany at Windsor (RL 12683) showing the Arno valley in bird's-eye view looking towards Pisa, the hills roll away one after the other towards the sea, separating the plain of Lucca from that of Pisa; and above, at the beginning of that ridge, the "Verruchola" appears, represented with marked realism as an imposing fortress dominating the whole valley. And beyond the Val di Calci, in the direction of Lucca, we also see "Librafatta," the other fortress mentioned in the document relating to Leonardo's visit to La Verruca.

In modern topographical maps La Verruca is marked only with the symbol used to indicate ruins. Nineteenth-century prints show the imposing fortress framed by the suggestive ruins of the nearby monastery of S. Michele, a place that also appears on Leonardo's map. An accurate study of what is left of La Verruca has allowed us to recognize the modifications carried out in 1503, probably those which Leonardo himself had proposed in order to make it "impregnable." These consist

264, 265. *Studies for the canal excavator,*
c. 1503-4. *Codex Atlanticus, ff. 331 v-a and*
344 *r-a.*

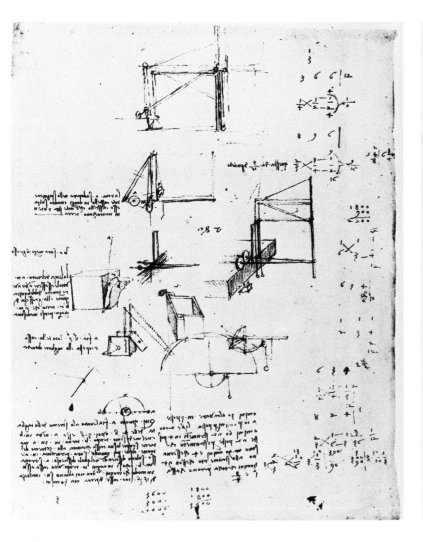

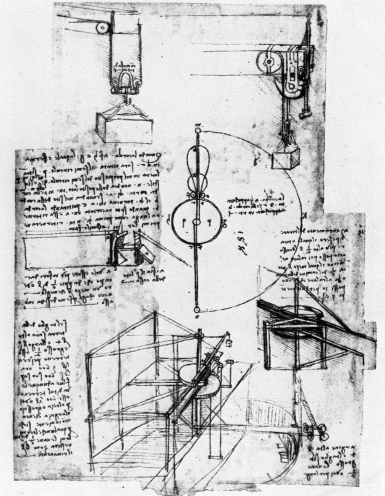

266, 267. Studies on the Piombino
fortifications, c. 1504. Codex Atlanticus,
f. 45 v-b and MS. L, ff. 14 v-15 r.

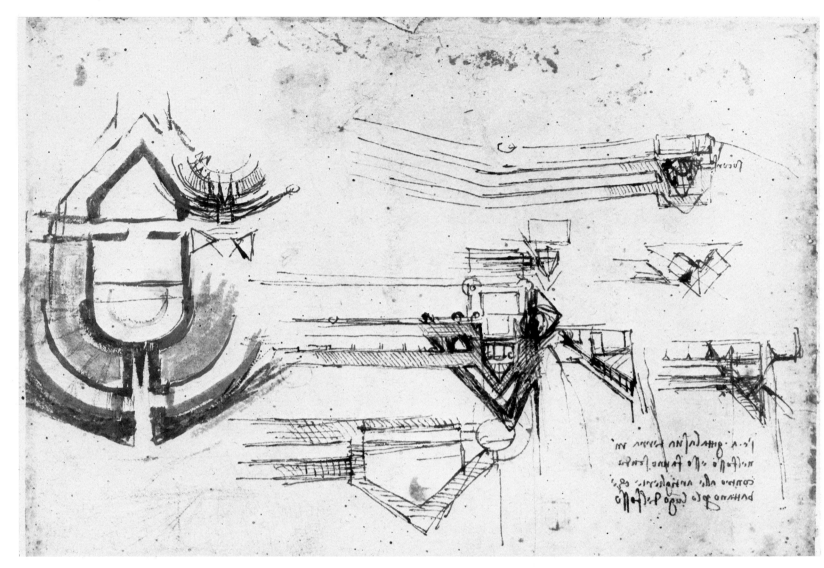

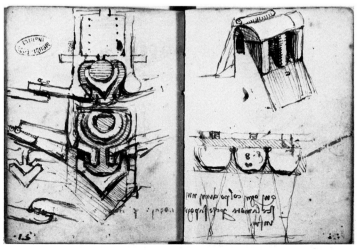

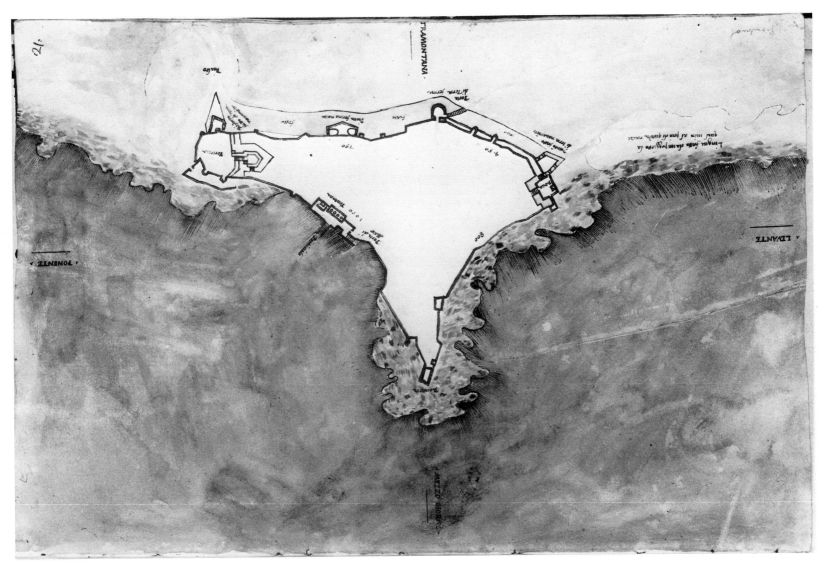

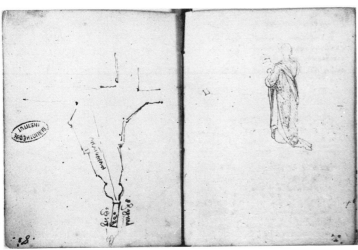

185

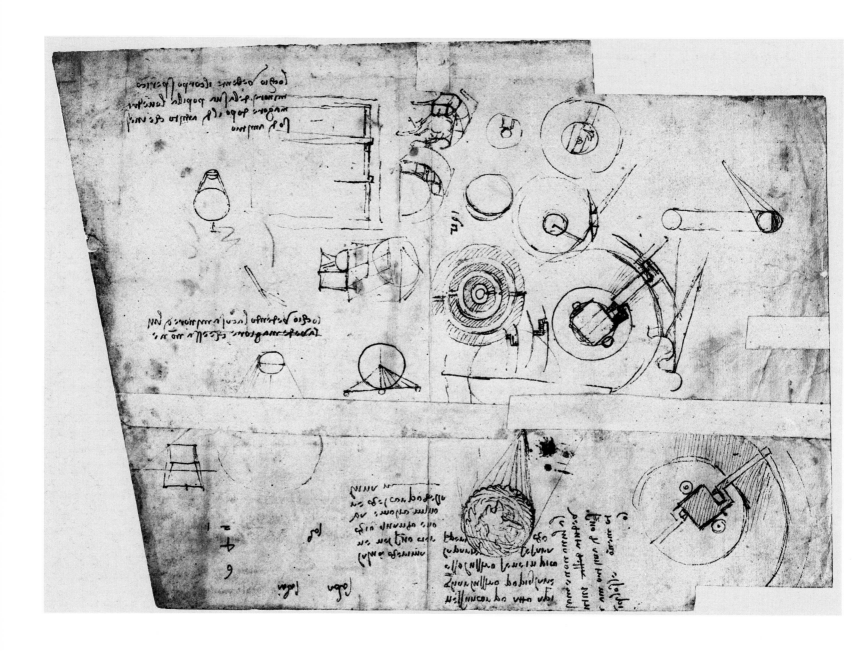

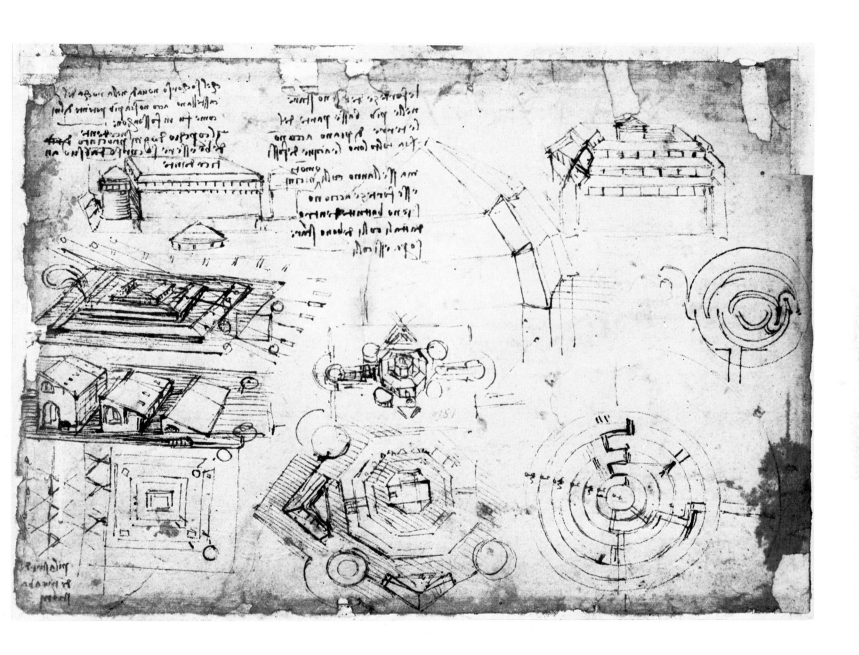

272-274. *La Verruca seen from the path that leads to its only entrance, taken from the same viewpoint as Leonardo's in f. 4 r of Madrid MS. II.*

275. *Aerial view of La Verruca.*

mainly of large circular towers solidly grafted onto the rock, and of a type of gun-embrasure for grazing fire to protect the curtain walls and the only access to the fortress. The same modifications are referred to again on 12 July 1504 in the instructions which the Signoria sent to the new field commissioner, Francesco Guiducci: "... the thing of prime importance regarding this region is the refortification of La Verruca with all promptness; and for this you will find out from Giovanni Antonio da Montelupo and from the commissioner of Cascina, in whose care it is, how near to being finished the work may be; and then you will remind them and order them and write to us what you need there. One thing only we want to remind you of in particular is this: that you should, as soon as you can, have all the materials such as mortar and so forth brought directly to La Verruca so that, should it be necessary to move the camp from where it is, it would not be necessary to stop work on the wall."

La Verruca is already mentioned in the twelfth century, but Dante, who took part in the battle of Campaldino in 1289, only recalls the nearby fortress of Caprona (*Inferno* XXI, 94-5). Having acquired so much strategic importance at the beginning of the sixteenth century, La Verruca was destined to remain merely a name, which Machiavelli himself would take as the excuse for a literary pleasantry in his *Mandragola* (Act I, scene two). For Leonardo it was no longer a name but an image, which could expand and multiply in his landscape drawings and project itself into the backgrounds of his paintings, from the *Saint Anne* to the *Mona Lisa*. It is not surprising therefore that one of the later Deluge drawings at Windsor, RL 12385, in which, as in the others from the same series, the vision is dominated by the majestic and terrifying flow of the waters and by the whirling of the winds, includes in the bottom right-hand corner the characteristic configuration of La Verruca, impervious on its rocky fastness to the fury of the elements which pour down onto the valley in the background and sweep away into a vortex of destruction an entire city – Pisa! So, while we can say that Leonardo's visit to the Pisan hills in 1503 offered him the chance to make observations on ways of representing landscape, we cannot help recalling what Machiavelli writes in the dedicatory letter to *The Prince*: "... in the same way as those who draw landscapes place themselves low on the plain so as to consider the nature of mountains and high places, and to consider that of the lower parts place themselves high over the mountains, similarly, in order to know the nature of peoples, it is necessary to be a prince, and to know well that of princes, it is necessary to be one of the people."

276, 277. *Nineteenth-century views of La Verruca, with the ruins of the monastery of S. Michele in the foreground.*

278. *Stone tablet from La Verruca bearing the date 12 June 1103. Almost exactly four centuries later, in mid-June, 1503 La Verruca was taken by the Florentines, and on the 21st of the same month Leonardo inspected it with a view to making it* inexpugnabile. *Pisa, Museo Comunale.*

279. The only entrance to La Verruca protected by the gun-embrasures in the towers restored in 1503-4.

281. The Val d'Arno from the bastions of La Verruca.

280. The entrance to La Verruca seen from within.

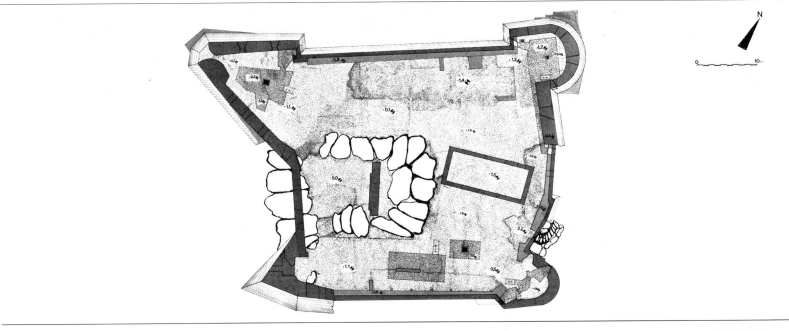

N

0   10

prospetto Cascina

0   10

prospetto Montemagno

0   10

282-287. A comparison of the present situation of La Verruca, with that represented by Leonardo in Madrid MS.II, f. 4 r, helps us to ascertain some important points, such as the place from which the sketch was made, near the road that leads to La Verruca from Vico Pisano two hundred metres before the ruins of the abbey of San Michele on a promontory on the right. We also note that the drawing does not show the corner towers on the side toward Vico with which the present structure is furnished. This makes it certain that Leonardo made the drawing during his inspection tour of 21 June 1503, and these new bastions were probably part of the first phase of the work planned during that visit, when he proposed "... in this way to patch it up so that it may be secure." The work, however, did not need to reach "that perfection which the place requires," since once Pisa was conquered, the fortress would have lost its strategic importance.

From an analysis of the remaining structure, one can identify the changes made after June 1503: they form part of a clear plan of adaptation and reconstruction of the sighting and defense system, designed according to the most advanced dictates of military architecture of the time. Close-range defense on the sides depended on a system of grazing cross-fire with the musketry hidden in low, angled positions, while long-range defense was entrusted to the two towers facing Vico and the one on the north facing Pisa with glacis suitable for holding pieces of artillery of considerable size.

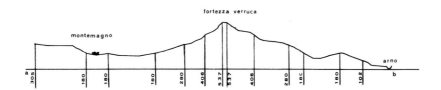

288. Detail of the plan of Tuscany, c. 1503-4. Windsor, RL 12683.

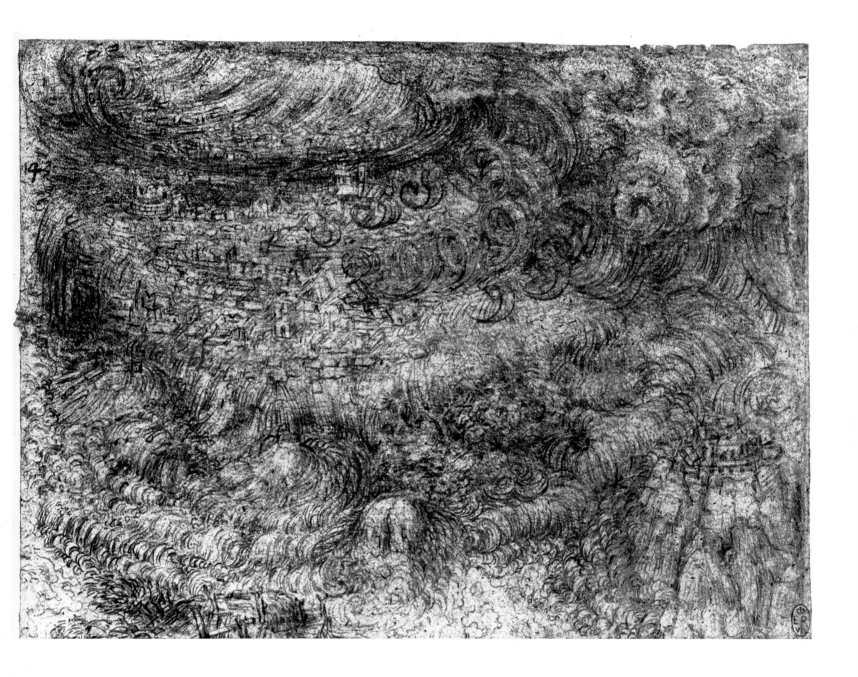

290-296. Francesco di Giorgio, Trattato di Architettura
Civile e Militare. *Codex Laurenziano Ashburnham 361,
ff. 13 v, 15 v, 25 r, 27 v, 32 r, 41 r, 44 v (with annotations
by Leonardo). Florence, Biblioteca Laurenziana.*

The Francesco di Giorgio manuscript in the Laurentian Library (Asburnham, MS. 361), whose pages bearing Leonardo's marginal notes are reproduced here, is most probably the same as the "frāco da siena" records amongst the books owned by Leonardo as listed in Madrid MS. II, f. 2 v and f. 3 r.

Richter published three of the annotations for the first time in 1883, when the manuscript was still in the library of Lord Ashburnham, who had bought it in 1847 from the "Fondo Libri." Acquired in 1885 by the Italian government, the codex was made known by Mancini through a notice published in the same year and through a more detailed study which came out in 1917, in both cases passing over the contents of the annotations. In 1934 Giuseppe Favaro dealt with them in connection with Leonardo's canons of proportion, providing the diplomatic transcription of the still unpublished annotations. To this day there exists no study with a complete and systematic transcription and facsimile reproduction of all these *postille*. In fact only a few have been reproduced in publications on Francesco di Giorgio, for example those by Papini in 1946 and by Arrighi in 1970. In Maltese's critical edition of the Codex Saluzziano, of 1967, they are transcribed as footnotes amongst the complements and variants presented by the Laurentian codex. Above all, what is lacking is a study of the relation of these notes to Leonardo's work, and therefore of their chronology.

It has been suggested that the codex came to Leonardo from Francesco di Giorgio himself when they met in Milan and Pavia in 1490, and that the annotations could be ascribed to that period. But it is more probable that Leonardo acquired (or borrowed) the manuscript after the death of its author (1502). One of his annotations in MS. L (inside of the front cover) indicates a connection with the Sienese architect Pagolo di Vannoccio, who in turn, as Cianchi has pointed out, had been associated with Francesco di Giorgio. There is no doubt however that the annotations must be dated around 1506-8, as I already suggested in 1962, although my proposal was never followed up. This date can be ascertained not only on the basis of handwriting and style, but also on the basis of the subjects dealt with. We can also be sure that they were written more or less at the same time, using the same pen and the same ink. It seems that the content of the annotations reflects not so much a systematic reading of Francesco di Giorgio's codex (which for some reason Leonardo must have kept open in front of him), as the subjects which he was mainly concerned with after 1504, that is geometry, water, anatomy, and mechanics.

The note "practise of geometry," as an expression referring to the geometrical elements, goes back to Fibonacci. It is found on a page which, both for content and layout – texts in two columns – reflects ff. 140-139 (backwards) in Madrid MS. II. And the definitions of the natural and mathematical points, already a preoccupation of fifteenth-century theoreticians from Alberti onwards, can be related to the well-known series of meditations on the "essence of nothingness" in the Codex Arundel. Written in or around 1508, these seem to have originated from the idea of a preface to a "First Book of Water" on which Leonardo was working at the same time as he was drafting a treatise on the subsidence of land and on cracks in arches and walls. Besides the references to the elements of geometry, which could suggest a date not too far into the sixteenth century ("practise of geometry" is the title of some notes in the Codex Atlanticus, f. 334 v-a, which has on the other side a tracing of the map of Tuscany at Windsor, RL 12277) there is a note which points to a date after 1504. This is on a particular aspect of the squaring of surfaces which characterizes a whole series of studies on "falcate" from 1505 to 1509, that is the shifting about of two superimposed equal surfaces to determine an area of excess transferable from one side of a figure to the other without altering its squarable values.

The annotation "on the water in the vase" relates to the illustration and explanation of a "fonte a termine," that is a fountain of Heron, which Alberti had previously described in his *Ludi matematici* and which had fascinated Leonardo at various times in his life. Studies of these fountains in two fragments at Windsor of about 1513 (RL 12691 and RL 12690) are noteworthy for their architectural character, stylistically related to the exactly contemporary studies for the Villa Melzi.

Another chronological clue could be provided by the annotation on the waves of the sea on f. 25 r, a page where Francesco di Giorgio deals with the design of an octagonal "barcho" (park or hunting ground) and with hydraulic engineering works for controlling currents at the mouths of rivers and harbour entrances. It is therefore only indirectly related to Francesco di Giorgio's text. But in the autumn of 1504 Leonardo was studying the Piombino harbour in a series of notes in Madrid MS. II, which are reflected in Francesco di Giorgio's treatment of the subject, and at the same time he was assembling observations on the movement of sea waves. A little later he elaborated on this again in the Codex Hammer, for example on f. 26 v and later still he mentioned it in his notes on the Deluge: "the waves of the sea at Piombino, all of foaming water" (Windsor, RL 12665 r).

It is not surprising therefore that the same type of wave should appear in two illustrations to the annotation, first shown frontally with the crest already turned over and "foaming," and then from the side, reduced almost to a diagram recalling the decorative friezes on Greek vases. The annotations concerning anatomy and mechanics offer more specific clues to chronology. The word "nathomia" (note the identical spelling in late anatomy sheets at Windsor, such as RL 19066 r), which seems to direct attention to the notes on canons of proportion which Francesco di Giorgio draws from Vitruvius, actually is connected with his other note on the preparation of a model – it would seem therefore of a human figure – whose "bust" must be of wax. It is certain that Leonardo used wax models in preparing the studies for the *Battle of Anghiari* (Windsor, RL 12328 r: "make a small wax one of it, the length of a finger") and wax appears in his anatomical investigations, as for example in the process he invented of injecting it into the brain to take an impression of it. But the "model" mentioned here may actually refer to the construction of an anatomical model of a whole human figure, which we know Leonardo had made, or at least planned, around 1506-8, when he was compiling the anatomical MS. B at Windsor. As further evidence for the suggested chronology, the annotations on mechanics concerning "rope and weight" relate to notes drafted on the verso of an anatomical sheet of 1506-8 at Windsor (RL 19141) where we read: "Jl centro dognj gra(*uj*)^ ta^ (*so*) accorda sosspeso (*collassis*)^ e sotto la centrale dessa / corda –," (The centre of every weight suspended on a rope is under the actual centre / of the rope), which expresses with slightly different words the same concept as the annotation of f. 44 v.

The only annotation that can be linked with architectural theories, and that was quoted as such by Richter, is the first one, on f. 13 v. Taken on its own, it would be understood strictly as a note on geometry, but it is written on a page in which Francesco di Giorgio deals with columns so one may infer that Leonardo took to meditating on the geometrical principle inherent in the "strength" of the column, that is in its axis, in accordance with a concept which he expresses, about 1508, within the context of an observation on optics in MS. D, f. 1 r: "Nature did not make the visual faculty uniform in strength, but gave greater strength to this faculty the closer it is to the centre. And she did this so as not to break the law given to all the other powers, which have more value the closer they come to the centre; and this is seen in the act of striking anybody whatsoever and in the supports of the arms of scales, where in coming close to them, the heaviness of the weight decreases; it is seen in columns, walls and pillars; it is seen in heat and in all the other powers in Nature."

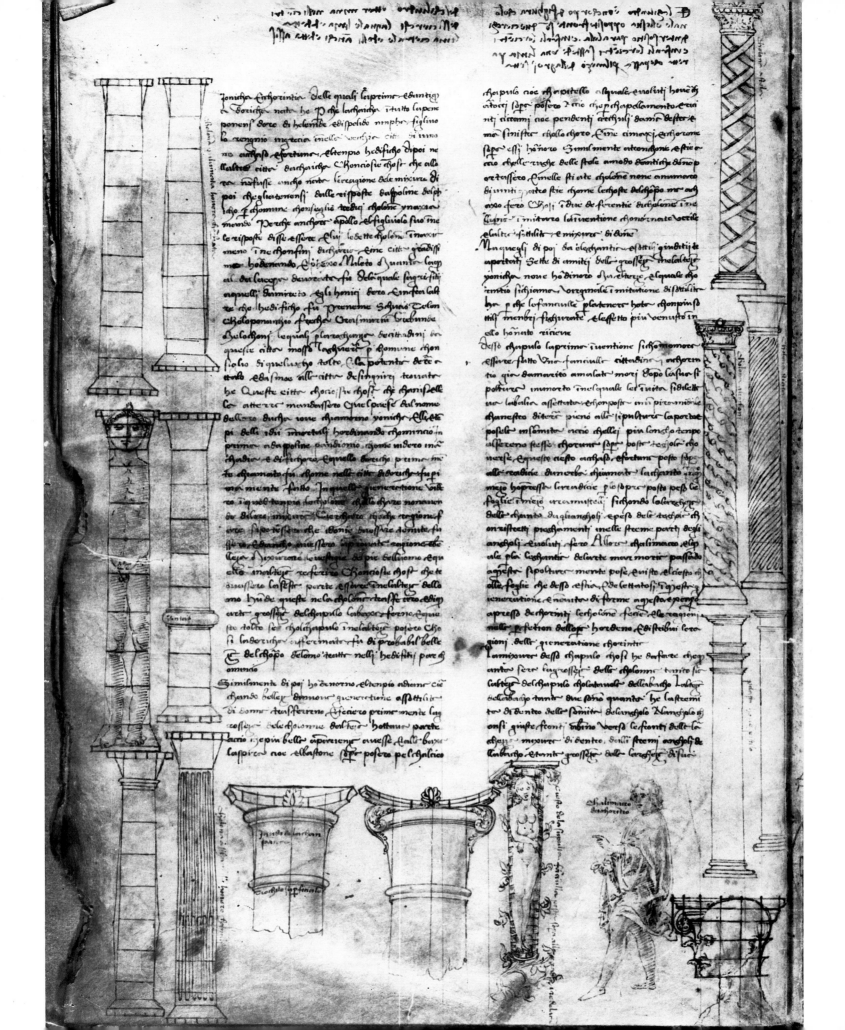

b

et che quanto lechose piu antiche e
vetuste sono tanto piu necessario
pare hesse inovare. Et perche lorigine
dellarchitettura pare lungho tempo hessere cho
minciata. Et che le fatiche loro per dare no
sieno ebandito per dimostrare quanto cho perfe
tione hessa arte achomentiare sia. he da
sapere che magi modo primo mente pon ch
ominciano. Che al prencipio del mondo chegli
huomini a modo di bestie per le champi naschando
el uno cho laltro nosi chonoschano. Dipoi ach
ado e fortuna per lo strepito del vento le palli
dose chaene egli arbori el un cholaltro disfre
ghando el fuocho vnessi datte se. Enonesse
ndo assueti tal chose vedere da quello gi
uon fugiendo. Cacchostorsi i sieme. Evidero
lachongreghatione essere molto utile. Et n
esserlo chonvieni. Et questi chominciaro agli
altri dimostrare lachongreghatione essere
necessaria. Enon sapendo parlare per lo cho
tinovo vso dalchune voci che quelle fa
cieno aintendere lun laltro chominciaro
lequali voci sprememo elchoncietto de
lamente loro. Et questi fermo el nome ale
chose dipoi fugire lemessime qualita
del fredo. E chaldo per le chaverne sottera
ne sasconderono alchuni di tronchoni darbori
coltelli di frasche e chane la sua chasa fa
cie. Dipoi chominciorno a mettervi suso
el loto. Et perche alchuna volta al tempo di ve
rno traevano cholle chalone la pantella
vuono dipoi chi in triangholo e quadra ch
ole la sua chasa facie. Et chi piu bella et chi
piu forte. E chando cheare dimigliore e piu
sottile ingegnio luno che laltro. Et quello
che meglio sapea hordenare maestro in
fra gli altri hera tenuto dipoi per chotinua
mente frequentare piu spesso assottigli
ati in talmodo che perfetta mente larte de
llo hedifichare cho bella gientilezza. Tan
to avere trovata se

ipoi sichome he detto che larte tan
to avere del chorpo omano tratto i f
usse sichome dal mento alle sommita della f

ronte dove le radici de chapelli sono sie la otta
va parte di tutto el chorpo. Similmente la
palma dela mano dal giontura per hensin
lastremita del lungho dito sie el medesimo
dal mento insino ale sommita del chapo la se
ttima parte. Dalle sommita del petto per insino
dove naschono e chapelli la sexta parte. E da
esse sommita del petto al imo del chranco la quarta
parte. E da esso facia ad infime parte del mē
to alle nare del naso e la terza parte dale
nare insino al fine del naso el nascimento
deglj egli simile. E da quel fine alle radi
ci de chapelli e laltra terza parte. El pie
he la sexta parte del chorpo. El bracio el cho
bito la quarta parte. El pie quel medesi
mo. Egli altri membri anchora ano loro pr
oportionate misure lequali glj antichi di
pintori e schultori vsandole grande et in
finite lande ano aquistato. E diligenti e
churiosi architettori ano di ciaschuna chosa
la misura chavato da hedifichare. Cho
me che del chorpo omano el dito palmo
braccio e pie. E questi ano di numero perfe
tto ano distribuiti el quale e greci telon
el chiamano. E gli antichi hordenorno el nu
maro dieci essere perfetto dalle mani el
numero de diti dal palmo el pie trovato
se. Che se dal uno e laltro palmo dalla g
iontura naturalmente dieci sono perfetti. An
chora ap lato pieci quel numero per que
lla chagione essere perfetto perche di ciasch
una chosa laquale monades apresso de
greci si chiama si fa dieci. Perche se dodi
ci he dodici sine aresbono perfetti essere non
possono. Per insino tanto che non venghano
o a laltro dieci. Perche ciaschuna chosa pa
rtichulare desso numero sono. Ma e mate
matici chontra disputando per quella chosa
el numero perfetto dissero essere quello el
quale si chiama sei. Perche hesso numero
a le partitioni per ragione delequali el nu
mero sei hottenghano. Se stante vno
teriens due semisse el quale dimeron
el chiamano quatro il quale texeron el chi
amano quintanum el quale pentemeron
el chiamano cinque ha sei perfetto chon si fa
chose. Et sie assipremendo al quale delle

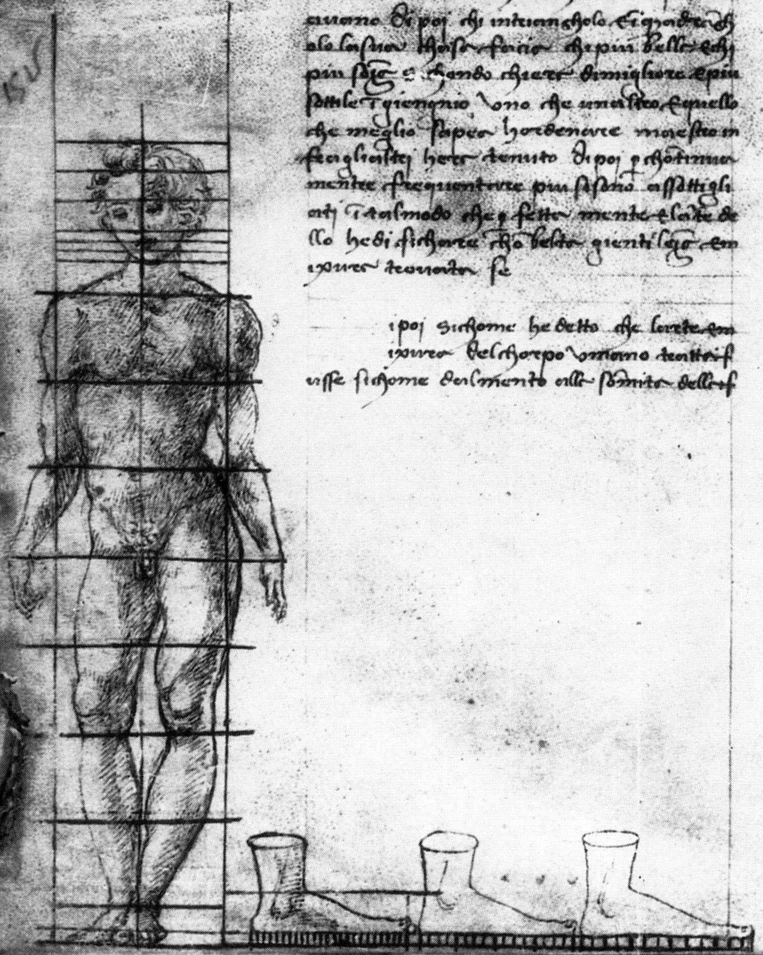

nando elevete della geometria si
n alle architetture necessarie
chonsenso diquello senpre loqu
ale alchuno edifitio terminasi
puo donna dalchune parti della distin
ta mente tratteremo he da sapere chella
praticha digeometria he del misurare secu
ndo i punti tre cioe altimetria planimet
ria steriometria Altimetria he quando mi
sureremo laltitudine elongitudine duna
chosa planimetria he quando lalonghezza
dalchuna chosa misureremo steriomet
ria he quando misureremo lalonghezza, al
larghezza helo profondita secondo chepri
mo modo inestichiamo ledimensioni delle
linie Nessecondo modo ledimensioni sup
ficiali nelterzo modo inistichiamo ledim
ensioni chorperali Chosi i primo diremo
che chosa linia ponto anghollo quadra
chollo cierchullo esimi archulo ronbo ron
boido edmolte altre diuerse fighure le
proportione terminate desse signomegi
formate efighure seremo

Inprimo he da sapere che ponto he quello
parte dello quale he nulla
Linia he lunghezza senza o piaze elisuo
termini son due ponti
Loretta linia he quella chesi distesto ede
ittamente va
Churevo he linia tortuosa
Superfitie he quella chea lunghezza, e anpiez
elisuo termini sono linie
Superfitie piana he quella nela quale tu
te lelinie sono rette
Anghollo he choistumento di due linie no dire
tte menate eguando rette chontenghano
sono chiamato anghollo retto lineo
Inquando lorecta linia stante sopra unre
tta linia fa quelli anghoi essere anghoi
insieme ciaschuno diquelli anghollo retto
Linia soprastante sopello chatetto equella
laquale sotto sta he detta bazzo
Anghollo hottuso he quello che magiore che
diritto
Anghollo archuto he quello chee minore epin
stretto fighure cheretto
Cierchio he fighura piana sotto una linie
detta cierchunferentia

Cientro dicierchio he uponto dalquale tutt
e lelinie menate allo cierchu ferentia u
guali sono
Diamitro dicierchio he una linie men
to plo cientro delcierchio ettermina idu
schun parete delle cerchu ferentia loqu
al linia divide i cierchio i due parti eguu
ali
Sed cierchio he fighura terminato daldia
mitro edaquella cerchu ferentia
Portione dicierchio he fighura terminata
da alchuna retta linia edallo circhu segu
minore homagiore dimezo cierchio
Settione dicierchio he fighura terminata
dalla cerchu ferentia, eda due linie che e
schono dalcientro delcerchio allo cerchu ferentia
fighure trilatere sichotenghano sotto tre lati
fighure quadrelatere se quelle che sichon
tenghano sotto quatro lati
fighure molti latere sechotenghan sotto molti
lati
fighure di cinque lati son chiamati pentachoni
fighure desei lati sichiamano exachoni
fighure di dieci lati sichiaman de schachoni
fighure dimolti lati sichiaman mentanachoni
etrionchoni sono di quatro gieneratione hoto
chonio eproculo yxomiles yxaleon
Chogomiles cioe equilatero e quello chea
due lati eghuali
Hoto chonio he quello cher uno anghollo retto
eldetto retto elmagioi lato i poteniste
Iso proculo cioe equilatero cher tuttte tre
lati uchuali
Ischaleo he quello chee diuersi latero ettu
tette elati disshuali
De quadra choli sono dicinq ragioni cioe
tetrachon equadrati letotri micheses cioe
diuessi latero
Ronbo ronboides trapetios he quello chegli
lati uchali
Ediritti anghoi edinessi latero he quello chea
glilati disshuali
Ronbo he quello chea tutti elati uchali egli
choli noretti
Ronboido he quello chea glilati eglianghoi
chonteavi
Trapetios son quelli che ano ledue lati eguidi
stanti eglialtri due no

circhunferentia [...] fino ellina allalter
perhome p hoffetto fino de eglie votando el
quale intorno brancia vintidue domado qp
to heffere detto elfuo diamitro cioe lali
nir che parte p mezo Nota che volendo tro
vare ladetta mifura ello diamitro deldetto ton
do fopra da partire p la crechunferentia cioe p
tre en settimo cioe p lodiamitro deltondo effe
volessi trovare larirchunferentia p lo diamitro f
nza die moltiplichare lodiamitro p tre en settim
o cioe poniamo che diquesto tondo larirchunfe
rentia fia brancia vintidue finhome hebetto en
eglio trovare lodiamito proveni vintidue p
tre en settimo neuiene sette ettanto he lodia
mitro essendo larirchunferentia vintidue e
p questo modo fitrouar lodiamitro p la crechu
ferentia esse voroi trovare larirchunferentia
p lo diamitro fi montiprichi lodiamitro p tre
en settimo cioe sette vie tre en settimo fa
vintidue ettanto fara larirchunferentia
Hora setti volessi quadrare lodetto tondo mol
tiprichar p la circhunferentia cioe vintidue vie
sette equello cheneviene parti p quatro et
mito fara lanquantita del detto tondo recha
to acquadro che trouerai chenevienne trento
tto emezo ettanto fara diquadro detto todo
havere mente montiprichar lalinir diamittol
fe medesima cioe sette vie sette fa qua
ranta nove equaranta nove pigli undi
ni quattredicresimi chessi trentotto emezo ch
ome prima

b   cio potiamo unaltra tondo chepla fuo dia
mitro he brancia vintinove domando qua
to fara diminuare p ftechiurca lorbine emonti
prichar lodiamitro p tre en settimo edi trenta
inticinque fa settanta cinque e p settimo pi
glia diuinticinq unsettimo che tre equatro
settimi loquale metti fopra offettunta cinque
curai settantotto equatro settimi ettanto fara la
circhunferentia laquale moltiprichar p lafuo di
amitro cioe p vintinove chefara mille hotto
cento hottantanove e due settimi e parti ifp
antro neviene quatro cento settanta due e no
ue vintotrexini ettante brancia fara lofpa
tio del detto tondo

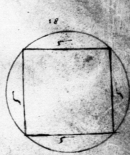

18

p   oniamo fia votondo che lafir circhunferen
tia fia radicie di quanto cento nouanta ta
quarantatre quaranta novexini nelquale todo
vo mettere loquadre magiore chepuoffe p modo ch
ettuttequatro le ftemir deglitriancholi tonchi, lacir
chunferentia effe volessi fape domando quanto
fara p faccia lo quadro chuvole quanto he lo
diamitro p tondo larirchunferentia p tre en setti
mo cverchato viradicie dinove quarantatre
quaranta novexini che neuie cinquanta e
ttanto lo diamitro del todo eradicie dicinquanta
sichse effe radicie dicinquanta he quello med
pimo ediamitro anchora delquadre eghe ho
gni quadrato diamitro fia fotmir dele moltipi
chatione dele due faccie agiongnie fieme poi
partirai radicie dicinquanta tradicie disi
e chenevienne radicie diuinticinq e radicie
diuinticinq fia cinque p numaro e dunq elde
tto quadro fara p faccia cinq sedoni qua
drare detto quadro moltiprichar cino dele faccie
fe medesima cioe cinq vie cinq fa viti
cinq ettanto he quadro

o   o votemo inuintriancholo mettare uno to
do elquale triancholo amodo difichundo
fatto enone aresse lessar faccie vechale luna
ollalter domando quanto giravre detto todo ho
ra poniamo chessir uno trianchole che p uno
faccia fia brancia nove eglialter hotto e laltra
sette e quests ragione tu prima diu chuadra
lotrianchola Diquesto modo ogiongnie tutte lessar
cie fieme che fono vintiquatro pigli lamet

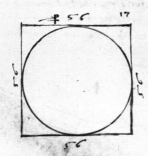
472 9/13   16
25

p   oremo loquadro tanto p luna faccia qua

456   17

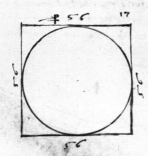

56

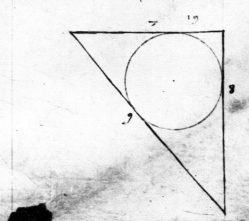
7   19

8

9

32

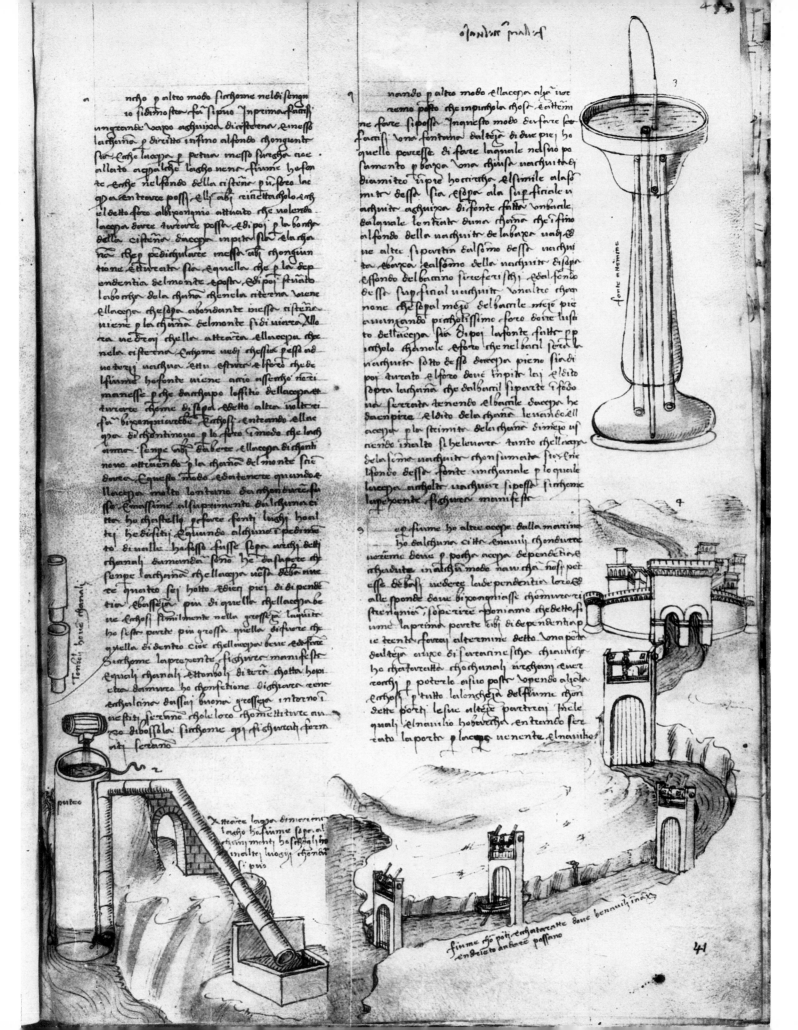

ancho mandate sieno e queste si fichondo altan
do chafferai schianando e diminuendo tō
si possino sinchome lafichura .XXXV. cū
anifesti

   nello si chastello confare chonsue depen
denti uisi enchiasinana uona lomarō
a houe nquesti soue lemannelle p hesse
rieuere mettu sipossino enelli anelli sap
iui deluniti a trauersato palo imezo del
quale la chuppate chatena che ala choue
gia dela chollona fur laquale pesō p pesō
fichondo che sagliè sotto lachelona cha
nuo hesse rapate chatene schianare cō
minui sipossa p che leuti nō piu cheto
uiei p uolte trattano che posono elpeso
esse chala bizongnera enthosi ti parte in
parte fuore sinchome la fichura XXXVI
ci manifesti

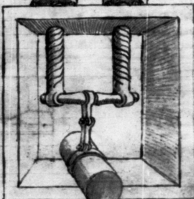

   p che seglia rechara alchuna fermatā
a sō orte parte facirsi el telaio imezo
del quale ō nal ti rota ruoti   chola
uiti che p sianch̄ō sera girando mouere
sotto dessa la chuesa soue eldupprichato de
ano pe gira equali aoue doteli che nel
telaio sono passado ole cha ruchole hon
ure chaluisi sicefacista qui lafichura sī
similmente facirsi el telaio chorulli ele
dentate ruote chole sotto post chuere so
ue el chanape gira cillosto del moto se
lauite che senti delaruote piglia ireulla
to chōsetto edū fare sinchome la fichura dl

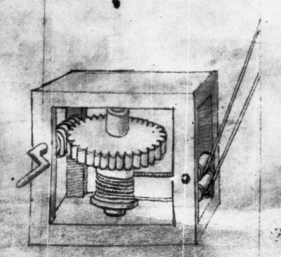

nicho el telaio si furu choruno dototi
roti p diritto elachuene da ogni bōte
soue el chanape giri cimezo dela roti la
bilischato uite lugnale sper telaio chole
mannuelle greaue si possa sinchome lafi
chura .III.

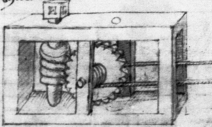

   aniisi el telaio sopa ala rotō dele me
nuelle enel bilischato stile desse erti a
llato chōsetto che nela dentir roti chepsi
ritti nel trauersato stuss dela chuesa uie
ne soue eldupprichato chanape ua chole m
annelle schnidando el chōsetto la bentui
roto moue sinchome la fichura .IIII.

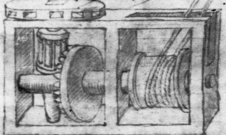

   nello facirsi una armadura di lengnio re
e cholteauresato stuss soue la dentui
ruote disei prei ua chamint da rullato
chōsetto del diritto stile sopal mōo dela ui
te bilischato soue lauesti el timon chuid
ando uia epesto stel disesp delle dentui
ruote u rullato chōsetto i dimmito pie
due   einsti denti dela rot che lachura
schuida chesopa ullostil desse sera i dia
mito dette ruote prei cinqe elachūa
soue sinchome lafichure .V. manifesti
siene edesti denti desserò al simile el fi
sello deruli erulli di forte lengnia facti
equelli derchōsetto sopa lostil deltimone
alquanti piramidali p che pin facilme
te pigliando lasso ҁ

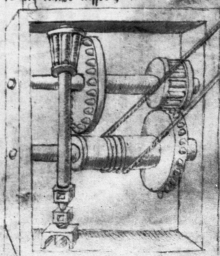

Transcription of the Annotations

Bibliographical References

Arrighi
Francesco di Giorgio Martini, *La praticha di gieometria* from Codex Ashburnham 361 in the Biblioteca Medicea Laurenziana, Florence, edited by Gino Arrighi. Florence 1970.

Favaro
Le proporzioni del corpo umano in un codice anonimo del Quattrocento, postillato da Leonardo. Reale Accademia d'Italia. Memorie della Classe di Scienze Fisiche, Matematiche e Naturali, Vol. V, 1934, pp. 577-96.

Maltese
Francesco di Giorgio Martini, *Trattati di architettura ingegneria e arte militare*, edited by Corrado Maltese. Transcription by Lina Maltese Degrassi. Milan 1967.

Papini
Roberto Papini, *Francesco di Giorgio architetto.* Florence 1946.

Richter
The Literary Works of Leonardo da Vinci... edited by Jean Paul Richter, London 1883 (second edition, enlarged and revised: Oxford 1939).

Saluzzo
Codice Saluzziano in Maltese (see above).

Transcriptions and Comments

1
Folio 13 v (Saluzzo: 14 v). Maltese, I. 56 n. Papini, pl. 284. Richter, § 767.
Upper margin, the first five lines on the right and the last three on the left:
El chilindro e vn chorpo dj fighura cholō/nale elle sua opposite fronte sō due cierchi / djnterpositio paralella . e infrali lor ciētrj / e infrali lor ciētrj (*sic*) sasstēde vna linja pa / retta che passa per il meço dellagrossetta // del chilindro ettermjna nelli ciētri / dessi cierchj la quale linja eddetta / linia cientrale e dalli ātichi e detta assis.
The cylinder is a body of columnar shape, and its opposite ends are two circles enclosed between parallel lines, and between their centres a straight line extends, passing through the middle of the thickness of the cylinder and ending in the centre of these circles; the said line is called the central line, and by the ancients is called axis.
This annotation was probably inspired by Francesco di Giorgio's text on the same page, which deals with the form of columns.

2
Folio 15 v (Saluzzo: 16 v). Favaro, p. 595. Maltese, I. 67 n.
Upper margin, on the right:
Jl modello debbe esser facto cho bussto / dj ciera.
The model must be made with the bust of wax.

On the left:
nathomja.
Anatomy.
Francesco di Giorgio's text on the same page deals with the Vitruvian canon of human proportions. In the corresponding f. 16 v of the Codex Saluzzo (Maltese, I, pl. 28) there is a splendidly executed drawing of a human skeleton in the margin above the illustration to the text relating to the Vitruvian canon. An outline of the same skeleton, in metal-point, can be made out on the page of the Laurentian manuscript as well, and in fact the indication of the upper part of the right femur is quite clear.

3
Folio 25 r (Saluzzo: 25 r-v). Maltese, I. 107 n. Papini, pl. 290 (detail of the lower half). Richter, § 952. See also *Leonardo*, edited by Ladislao Reti, Milan 1974, p. 82.
Upper margin, on the right, with two sketches (the second reproduced upside-down by Richter):
de onda –
Londa (*delle*) del mare senpre ruina / djnantj alla sua basa ecquella par/te del Cholmo si troverra piu bassa che / prima era piu alta sara poj piu bas (...)
On waves.
A wave of the sea always breaks in front of its base, and that portion of the crest will then be lowest which before was highest: it will then be lower...
This annotation was probably inspired by Francesco di Giorgio's text on the same page, which deals with the flow of river waters at their entrance to the sea. A similar note is found in Madrid MS. II, f. 24 r, datable about 1504.

4
Folio 27 v (Saluzzo: 27 v-28 r). Arrighi, pl. I. Favaro, p. 596. Maltese, I. 117 n.
Upper margin, on the right:
Difinjtione dellang della grosse/za delli angholj –
Definition of the size of angles.
On the left:
prati(*g*) cha gieometricha.
Practice of geometry.
Lower margin, on the right, the text edited by Richter, § 44:
Del pu‹n›to naturale
Jlmjnore pūto naturale e magiore dj tuttj / i puntj naturalj matetematicj (*sic*) ecques/sto si pruova perche il punto naturale equan/tjta chontinua eognj continuo edjujsibile inj‹n›/finjto E il punto matematicho he indjvisibile / perche none quantita ec.
On the natural point.
The smallest natural point is larger than all mathematical points, and this is proved because the natural point is a continuous quantity, and everything that is continuous is infinitely divisible. But the mathematical point is indivisible because it is not a quantity, etc.
All the annotations in this sheet relate directly to Francesco di Giorgio's text on the same page, which deals precisely with the "practice of geometry."

5
Folio 32 r (Saluzzo: 32 v). Favaro, p. 596. Maltese, I. 135 n.
Upper margin, on the left:
Ongnj superfitie quadrabile chol sopra/porsi in parte luna allaltra e ancho/ra quadrabile chol torre da v̄ lato he / rēdere dallaltro edetiā chol moto –
Every squarable surface when placed partly on top of another is still squarable by taking from one side and giving to the other, and this even in motion.
This annotation was probably inspired by Francesco di Giorgio's text and illustrations relating to circles inscribed in squares and triangles.

6
Folio 41 r (Saluzzo: 45 r). Favaro, p. 596. Maltese, I. 178 n.
Upper margin, on the right:
dellacqa nel uaso.
Of the water in the vase.
This annotation refers to Francesco di Giorgio's text below, illustrated by a drawing of a "fonte attermine," that is a "fountain of Heron." For Leonardo's studies on this same apparatus see further on, page 311.

Folio 44 v (Saluzzo: 49 v). Favaro, p. 596. Maltese, I. 189 n. Papini, pl. 297.
Upper margin, on the right:
dechorda eppeso.
Of rope and weight.
On the left:
Della resisstētia della chorda.
Of the resistance of the rope.
Left margin:
Jl ce‹n›tro dognj gra/vita sosspesa essoc/to il cientro del / contacto chelluj / a chol suo sossten/tachulo –
The centre of every suspended weight is below the centre of contact that it has with its support.
These notes on mechanics were probably inspired by Francesco di Giorgio's drawings on the same page, which illustrate various ways of lifting weights.

Every book and essay on Leonardo, from the earliest to the most recent, from specialized studies to popular biographies, tends to consider the last fifteen years of his life, from 1504 to 1519, as a period of decline, and therefore to be dealt with more summarily than the years of his youth and maturity.

In all my own writings on Leonardo, and particularly those relating to architecture, I have always given greater importance to the late period, convinced, as ever, of the need to thoroughly till uncultivated ground before moving towards an attempt at an overall view. It is time at last, however, to leave this curious way of working backwards ("Alas! He will never do anything, since he begins by thinking of the end before the beginning of the work," Leo X said of Leonardo), and, glancing at what has been established to modify the general opinion that as Leonardo grew older he went into a decline. In fact, we might speak instead of an apotheosis, a triumph, which, in spite of the failures, the adversities and the hardships of the last fifteen years of Leonardo's life, is shown by the influence of his style and the recognition of his genius.

The development of Leonardo's style along a path that proceeds from delicacy to grandeur of forms, and from subtlety to power of expression, can be better understood when seen against the social and intellectual background of his native city. The factors leading to the grand manner of the High Renaissance are many and complex, but it was undoubtedly Leonardo's return to Florence in 1500 that marked the beginning of a new era in Italian art. That was the moment when he began to express the heroic ideals and sense of civic pride which the city of Florence (with Machiavelli as secretary of the Republic) was renewing through the example of antiquity. In 1505, both Leonardo and Michelangelo had already produced the cartoons for two monumental battle-scenes which were to decorate the new Hall of the Great Council in the Palazzo Vecchio and which, in fact, had been conceived as political and artistic manifestoes. "As long as they remained intact," wrote Benvenuto Cellini, "they were the world's school." And it was certainly that school which drew the young Raphael from his native Urbino and influenced a whole generation of Florentine artists, from Andrea del Sarto to the painters of the School of Fontainebleau. With lapidary brevity Vasari identified the components of Leonardo's style in those aspects of "disegno" that are the essence of his architectural language: "Leonardo da Vinci, beginning the third style which we call the modern, besides the power and boldness of his drawing and the exactitude with which he copied the most minute particulars of nature exactly as they are, displays good rule, improved order, correct proportion, perfect design and divine grace. Abounding in resource, and deeply versed in art, he truly gave his figures movement and breath."

In 1506 Leonardo returned to Milan, staying there in two successive stages until 1513 (from 1507 to 1508 he was again in Florence), this time serving the French governor Charles d'Amboise and even King Louis XII himself. His French patrons immediately recognized his manifold and inexhaustible talents and they valued him not only as an inimitable painter, but also as a skilful architect and engineer. "The outstanding works that your fellow citizen Master Leonardo da Vinci has left in Italy, and particularly in this city, have caused all those who have seen them to feel a singular affection for him, even if they have never met him. And we wish to confess to being amongst those who loved him before we ever knew him in person. But now, since we have employed him here and tested through experience his virtues, we see in truth that his great fame as a painter is obscure compared with the praise he deserves for his other great virtues. We desire to confess that in the work we have asked him to carry out, of design and architecture and other things pertinent to our situation, he has satisfied us to such a degree that we are not only content with him, but have conceived an admiration for him."

Thus wrote Charles d'Amboise on 16 December 1506, as he notified the Signoria of Florence of Leonardo's return. For the first time a patron speaks of him as an architect.

What little we know of Leonardo's work in the service of d'Amboise has come to us from two fragments in the Codex Atlanticus which originally formed a single sheet containing studies and annotations for the project of a villa with a garden to be built in the neighbourhood of Porta Venezia in Milan. The building seems to have been inspired by the Poggio Reale in Naples, which Serlio too had taken as a model. The sketch of rooms arranged around a loggia with classicizing articulation, opening onto the garden, foreshadows Peruzzi's Farnesina, while the chiaroscuro effects on the walls, achieved by the use of pilasters and paired columns, seem to come from a memory of Venetian façades, as in the now celebrated drawing of a villa on the inside back cover of the Codex on the Flight of Birds. The whole project seems to have been conceived to centre around the feasts and entertainments for which the building was destined: the garden is spoken of as a place of delights, with water games, musical instruments and an aviary. It seems that a complex water-clock with an automation to strike the hours was also planned. And there is even mention of a mechanical bird for the "comedia," a detail that can be explained by a series of studies datable to the same time for a staging of Poliziano's *Orfeo*. (These are for an apparatus which applies the principle of counterweights in the same way as for the earlier projects for excavators, by means of which a mountain opens out so as to show Pluto emerging from the Underworld.) Poliziano also inspired the description of a fabulous and imaginary (how imaginary, though?) "Site of Venus" on a sheet of that period in which, next to a study for a fountain with a Neptune in the pose of Michelangelo's *David*, there appears a villa-castle that is a prefiguration of both Chambord and the Palazzo del Te.

Finally, we have notes on the confluence of the canals in the area designated for the building, which in their turn relate back to the extensive studies of the hydraulic system in Lombardy that Leonardo carried out during the whole of his second stay in Milan. It was, in fact, that activity which took him, about 1513, to Vaprio d'Adda as a guest of the Melzi, to whom he proposed a project for enlarging their villa to give

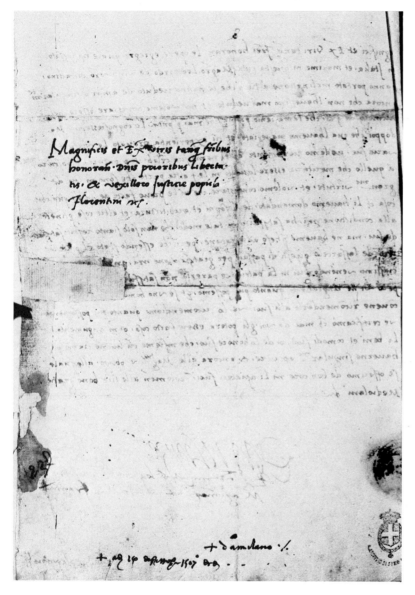

it a scenographic character that seems to anticipate that of Raphael's Villa Madama.

It has also been thought that Leonardo may have participated in the project of the church of S. Maria alla Fontana, which an inscription tells us was founded in 1507 according to the wish of Charles d'Amboise. Some of Leonardo's drawings assignable to that period seem to confirm the hypothesis, but they could reflect a possible relationship of his with those architects in Milan who were carrying on Bramante's teachings, paving the way for Cesariano's already mannerist classicism. Besides, the anonymous author of the *Rovine di Roma*, who might well be Bramantino, drew material from a book on ancient buildings owned by Leonardo. And it was from similar antique examples that Bramantino derived the design for the Trivulzio chapel at S. Nazaro, which was destined to contain the sepulchre planned by Leonardo during those years.

The death of Charles d'Amboise in 1511 marks the end of a brief but splendid period of patronage for Leonardo, who had earned the coveted title of "paintre et ingénieur ordinaire" of the King of France. While he continued to be occupied with canalization and hydraulics (it was at that time that he had a water-metre built to be sent to Bernardo Rucellai in Florence), in October of 1510 he was consulted by the Fabbrica del Duomo about the construction of the choir stalls, together with Amadeo, Fusina and Cristoforo Solari. With the return of the Medici to Florence in 1512 and the election of a Medici pope in 1513, Leonardo's last period of activity in Italy began.

In 1514 Leonardo was already in the Vatican in the service of Giuliano de' Medici, the Pope's brother, but what his exact duties were we do not know. Benedetto Varchi, in his funeral oration for Michelangelo, in 1564, stated that Leonardo "had besides architecture, besides sculpture, painting as his principal art and profession, or shall I say amusement and pastime." He added that Giuliano "an immensely kind and indescribably great gentleman, since he loved him so much, treated him more like a brother than like a friend."

Arriving in Rome in the autumn of 1513, Leonardo was in time to see once again his friend Bramante, who died on 11 April of the following year. He also renewed acquaintance with the still youthful Atalante Migliorotti, a companion from times past and now one of the superintendents of the Vatican workshops. The names of Peruzzi and Sansovino also appear in some of his memoranda from that time.

Staying as a guest in Innocent VIII's Belvedere villa, Leonardo seems to have been principally occupied with the project for an enormous burning glass made up of pieces moulded to a preestablished curvature by an instrument of his own invention – the mysterious "sagoma." With this glass he hoped to utilize solar energy to heat the cauldrons in a dye-works, probably as part of a textile industry development programme in Rome, sponsored by the Medici and the Florentine colony. In a famous drawing of a machine for making ropes, which looks curiously like a fountain with foliate decoration, we can see, in the

Magnifici et Ex viri tanq frés honorandi. le opere egregie quale ha lassato
in Italia et maxime in questa citta Magro Leonardo de vinci vro cittadino
hanno portato inclinatione à tutti che le hanno veduto de amarlo singularmte
ancora che non lhauessino mai veduto. Et noi volemo confessare essere nel
numero de qlli che lamauemo prima che mai p pntia lo cognoscessemo. Ma
doppoi che qua lhauemo manegiato et cu experientia prouato le virtute
varie sue vedemo veramente ch el nome suo celebrato p pictura è obscuro
à quello che meritaria essere laudato in le + altre parte che sono in lui de
gran mte virtute et volemo confessare che in le proue facte de lui de qualche
cosa ch li hauemo domandato de desegni et architectura et altre cose ptinete
alla conditione nra ha satisfacto cu tale modo che non solo siamo restati satisfacti
de lui ma ne hauemo pheso admiratione perilche essendo stato el piacere
vro de lassarcelo questi di passati per gratificatione nra e nő ni ringra
tiassimo venendo lui in la patria cè pareria non satisfare à animo grato et
però vi ne ringratiamo quanto piu possemo. Et se uno homo de tanta virtute
couene ricomendarlo alli suoi ve lo ricomendiamo quanto piu possemo et
ve certificamo ch mai da voi gli potera essere facto cosa o in augmento de
li beni et comadi suoi o de lo honore suo che insieme cu lui nő siamo per
hauerne singularmte apiacere. Et ancora alle Magtie v obligo alleqaule
se offerimo de bon core ni li apiaceri suoi ricomen alle sue bone gratie.
Mediolani die xoy x.bris 1506

[signature] Charles d'Amboise
locumtenens generalis
Magnus magister et maresc allus Francie

[signature] Franciscus

belt-tightening device, the unmistakable Medici symbol of the ring with a pointed diamond, which also appears in a design by Raphael for a Roman villa. This piece of machinery, therefore, bears the Medici trademark and perhaps it might be worthwhile to investigate a possible Medici involvement in the rope-making industry in Rome, in a district that later gave its name to a church, S. Caterina ai Funari; but we need only reflect on the importance that ropes must have assumed at the time of Sixtus V, the Pope of the obelisks.

Leonardo's work and studies in the Vatican are wrapped in mystery. He seems to have been intensely and excitedly active, though only a hint of this reaches us through his complaints against two German workmen who had been assigned to him as assistants. It appears that Giuliano, "who was a great student of philosophical matters, and especially of alchemy" (that is, chemistry), as Vasari says, followed Leonardo's experiments with interest and turned to him for services in architectural matters, such as the project for draining the Pontine marshes, the vast territory which he owned. At the same time, probably before Bramante's death, Leonardo went to Civitavecchia to study its ancient harbour, possibly to take part, as Bruschi suggests, in the papal project inspired by Bramante of recreating there the majestic sea-port city of antiquity. And Leonardo, one can say, had antiquity on his doorstep, if, as it seems, he could see from the windows of his apartment in the Vatican the most famous statues of classical antiquity which first Julius II and then Leo X had assembled in the very courtyard of Innocent VIII's villa, the Belvedere. Thus a sketch on a late sheet of the Codex Atlanticus can be considered as the earliest record of the reclining Ariadne, which shortly before his death Bramante had arranged in a niche-like grotto.

Another person Leonardo would have met in Rome was the venerable Fra Giocondo, Raphael's teacher of architecture. Leonardo himself had mentioned him years earlier for the waterduct which the Veronese architect had built in the garden of the castle of Blois in France. A geometrical diagram on a sheet of the Codex Atlanticus containing studies of loggias and doorways has been taken for a record of the Vitruvian city as found in Fra Giocondo's edition of Vitruvius. But in fact it is one of the many studies of lunulae which Leonardo himself develops in large size in other sheets of the same series, where we also find a record of the measurements of S. Paolo fuori le Mura, dated August 1516. These are all sheets of geometrical studies, in which sketches of centring appear, such as that used in vaulting the new St. Peter's, as well as architectural studies for Florence.

Certainly during his Roman stay Leonardo kept up his connections with Florence. It seems he returned there several times and in September 1514 he went on as far as Parma in the retinue of the papal army, commanded by Giuliano. It was for Lorenzo di Piero de' Medici, nephew of the Pope and Governor of Florence, that Leonardo designed in 1515 an enormous palace on a square plan, with octagonal towers at the corners of the façade, and an octagonal courtyard like the one with the antique statues at the Belvedere. This was to be built across the way from the old Medici palace, on the other side of the street that cuts across the whole of the Medici quarter from the Cathedral to San Marco, on the site where the stables recorded in one of Leonardo's sketches were built between 1515 and 1516.

The design of the new Medici palace shows details of a symbolic decoration on the façade, with columns in the shape of tree trunks, and cut branches, as well as new branches that spring up to form the archivolts. The splendid plant motif has its only precedent in a suggestion by Alberti for the decoration of garden walls (besides the tree trunk-shaped columns recorded by Francesco di Giorgio and used by Bramante on the Canonica of S. Ambrogio). Here the motif has assumed the dignity of a public façade with the heraldic significance of the Medici *broncone* (a sprouting tree stump) which symbolizes the renewed prestige of that family. The building planned for them was designed to take its place as a part of the existing historic and urban fabric. To one side was the old Medici palace, an expression of a mercantile power which had frightened Cosimo himself. The piazza in front of S. Lorenzo was to be opened out like a stage set into an ample space with Michelangelo's new S. Lorenzo façade as its backdrop and with the two Medici palaces, old and new, on one side and the rebuilt church of S. Giovannino on the other. All that remains of Leonardo's grandiose project are a few sketches on a sheet of the Codex Atlanticus and the circumstantial evidence that Michelangelo had been commissioned to close the corner loggia of the old Medici palace.

At about that time, and in Florence, the long-standing antagonism between Leonardo and Michelangelo seems to have exploded into a conflict which had an architectural programme a its root. We have some indication of this in a passage in which Vasari refers to the competition for the façade of S. Lorenzo: "There was enormous dislike between him and Michelangelo Buonarroti, so that Michelangelo left Florence because of the rivalry, with Duke Giuliano excusing him by saying that he was called by the pope about the façade of S. Lorenzo. Leonardo, on hearing this, left and went to France."

This passage offers us the merest glimpse of what must have been a dramatic rush of events, but it certainly also provides us with persuasive evidence that Leonardo did take part in some way in the Medici programmes, of which the project for the S. Lorenzo façade seems to have been only a part. In fact S. Marco was also awaiting a façade. This would explain certain late church designs, such as the one in Venice to which Leonardo gave a strong vertical thrust, pulsating with an almost Baroque classicism. A small and slightly earlier drawing of a basilica on f. 235 v-a of the Codex Atlanticus, *c.* 1510, seems to foreshadow the serene classicism of Peruzzi's Sagra at Carpi of 1515. Moving on from these images we arrive at those enigmatic ones, on French sheets, where the idea of the basilica as a classical temple seems to evoke the Albertian building sketched in the background of his early *St. Jerome*. Among Leonardo's last sheets from his French period, characterized by researches on star-shaped lunulae, we find – next to a perspective view of an ancient arena – that extraordinary volumetric analysis of Bramante's St. Peter's, opened up in an exploded view to illustrate the concept of the interpretation of forms generated by the cube – an idea which can justly be claimed as the symbol of High Renaissance architecture. References to temporary structures on the same sheet as the studies for the new Medici palace may explain the drawings on another sheet of the Codex Atlanticus of that period, which are studies for a festival building, an *arcus quadrifrons*, made of wood, cables and canvas. It may be one of those erected in Florence on the occasion of Leo X's visit on his journey to Bologna, where he was to meet Francis I in December 1515.

It has also been possible to establish that it certainly was the "nazione fiorentina," and therefore its governor Lorenzo di Piero de' Medici, that commissioned from Leonardo the famous mechanical lion – the *marzocco*, symbol of Florence, which on the occasion of the entry of Francis I into Lyons in July 1515 was to walk towards the King and open its breast to show the lilies of France in place of its heart; an ingenious way of expressing the friendship that Florence and the Florentine colony in Lyons wanted to show towards the new monarch.

In Rome, meanwhile, a project similar to the one thought of for Florence was to affect the area between the Pantheon and Piazza Navona, where palaces for the Pope and for Giuliano were to be constructed as well as the French national church. This church as designed by an unknown architect (Leonardo?) in the form of a majestic round temple. Building work on it began in 1515, but it was abandoned when it had reached a height of a little more than ten metres. Later the imposing fragment was demolished to make room for the Church of S. Luigi dei Francesi, on the façade of which were inserted the stone medallions bearing the salamander emblem of Francis I which had been removed from the walls of the demolished temple.

The Medici courts, both in Rome and in Florence, had by then established closer ties with France, Giuliano by marrying Filiberta of Savoy, the aunt of Francis I, and Lorenzo di Piero by marrying the King's niece, Maddalena de la Tour d'Auvergne.

These were Leonardo's last Italian patrons, better known for the tombs that Michelangelo was to build for them in S. Lorenzo. Both died very young, Giuliano in 1516 and Lorenzo in 1519. The meeting of Francis I with Leo X in Bologna in 1515 may have given Leonardo the opportunity of meeting the new monarch, whose Imperial ambitions were to induce Leonardo to join him in France, between 1516 and 1517, to design a large royal residence at Romorantin. The project, abandoned at Leonardo's death in 1519 to be in part taken up again at Chambord, incorporated many of the ideas that were carried out at Versailles a century later.

The enlargement of the old castle of Romorantin was begun in 1512, when Leonardo was still in Milan, but it may be that already then his suggestions were taken into account. It would thus be possible to explain the well-known drawing of a place on a sheet at Windsor which has a study for the Trivulzio Monument on the back. It is certain, however, that as soon as Leonardo arrived in France, in January 1517, he made an on-the-spot inspection of Romorantin together with the King, so as to prepare a detailed project for him. The banks of the river which form the longitudinal axis of the new urban complex are set out in steps along the sides of the palaces which flank it, so as to provide an ample setting for nautical games. The whole city is surrounded and crossed by canals which feed fountains in the piazza and make street cleaning and rubbish disposal more efficient. Finally, another idea that appears is one for an elegant building on an octagonal plan, perhaps a hunting-lodge, which would have stood some distance from the city in the heart of a forest.

But there is more. The King's palace was conceived as the nucleus of a new city organized along the river according to a geometrical model reminiscent of Roman military encampments.

The city is in the centre of France, and therefore at the centre of a projected system of canals planned to create a navigable waterway across the whole nation, from the English Channel to the Mediterranean. It has been rightly said that the concept of the total design, such as is to be realized in the programme of the Tennessee Valley Authority in the United States, began to emerge when Leonardo let himself be carried away by the visionary and enormous possibilities of the plan for Romorantin.

It represents the first proposal for a system of multiply controlled waterways which had to wait until the twentieth century to be brought into being.

299, 300. Detail of the floor-plan of the projected villa for Charles d'Amboise, c. 1506-8. Codex Atlanticus, f. 231 r-b and interpretation to scale.

301. Sheet of studies for Charles d'Amboise's villa, c. 1506-8, reconstructed from two fragments from the Codex Atlanticus, f. 271 v-a and f. 231 r-b.

12. The Villa of Charles d'Amboise

The *villa suburbana* for Charles d'Amboise, French governor of Milan, was designed by Leonardo around 1506-8. All that we know about it comes from some notes and sketches on a sheet reconstructed from two fragments in the Codex Atlanticus: on the left, f. 271 v-a, containing notes on the disposition of the stairs and the organization of the garden; on the right, f. 231 r-b, sketches of plans and elevations. The texts are read from top to bottom and from right to left.

f. 231 r-b
(Plan) "portico hall portico."
(Plan) "*c e b a*; *a* is the Grand Master's courtyard, *b c* are his bedrooms, *e* in his salon; and it can be completely open in front."
(Plan) "Meadow."
"*Fonte Lunga* covered with copper netting, and full of birds."

f. 271 v-a
"The staircase is one and three quarters braccia wide, and it bends back upon itself, and joined all together it is sixteen braccia with thirty-two steps half a braccio wide and a quarter high; and the floor surface of the place where it turns is two braccia wide and four braccia long; and the wall which divides the one staircase from the other is half a braccio, but it will make the said staircase two braccia wide, keeping the room half a braccio wider, which will make the room twenty-one braccia long and ten and a half braccia wide, and it will be fine like that. And we shall make it eight braccia high though by rights it should be as high as it is wide. But such rooms seem gloomy to me as so much height leaves them dark, and the stairs come to be too steep, that is straight.

By means of the mill I shall cause wind to be generated in all summer weathers; we shall raise the spring water, which will pass along through the middle of the separated planks, and which will be like this (diagram); and the channel must be half a braccio wide, keeping the goatskins continuously very cool with their wines, and other water will run through the garden watering the orange trees and the cedars to their need, the said cedars will be permanent because the site will be adapted in a way that they will be easily covered, and the heat which continuously blows during the winter will be the cause of keeping them much better than fire, for two reasons; one is that the heat of the springs is natural and is the same that heats the roots of all the plants, and the second is that fire is accidental warmth for these plants because it is deprived of humidity and is neither uniform nor continuous, as it is hotter at the beginning than it is at the end, and often it is forgotten through the negligence of those who look after it.

The grasses growing in the springs must often be cut down so that the water may be seen to be clear, and only such grasses must be left which are suitable for the feeding of the fish, such as water cress and the like.

The fish must be of such types that do not make the water cloudy, that is neither eels nor tench nor even pike are to be put there, because they destroy other fish.

By means of the mill many water ducts will be made for the house and the fountains in diverse places and paths, where, when people walk along them, the water will shoot upwards from all the ground underneath, so as to serve the purpose of those who want to wet the ladies or others who pass by there, from below.

Above, we shall make a very fine copper netting which will cover the garden and shut in below itself many different kinds of birds, so that you will have continuous music together with the scents of the flowers, the cedars and lemon trees.

By means of the mill I shall make continuous sounds of various instruments, which will play as long as the mill goes on moving."

On the verso of this reconstructed sheet we find: on the right, f. 271 r-e, notes on mechanics and aerodynamics, and below, a plan of the confluence of canals; on the left, f. 231 v-a, a sketch of a mechanical bird ("ocel della commedia"), plans of canals that converge together and fragmentary notes: "Neron da S. Andrea" (name of a watercourse near S. Babila), "fogn... mo. Fa la... as pictured beside here."

These are studies for the layout of the canal adjacent to the property destined for the villa of Charles d'Amboise. In the following illustrations there are other studies of the same problem which reveal, among other things, the intention of building porticoes, covered areas, rustic gates, retractable bridges, and a tower placed at the point where the canals come together.

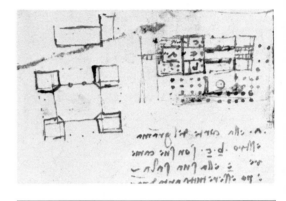

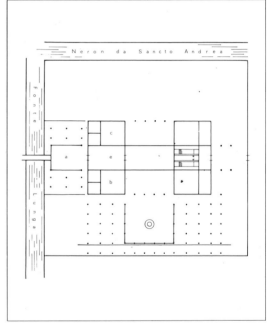

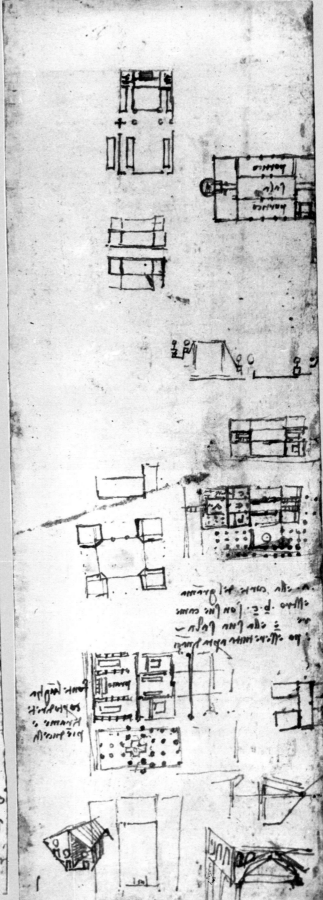

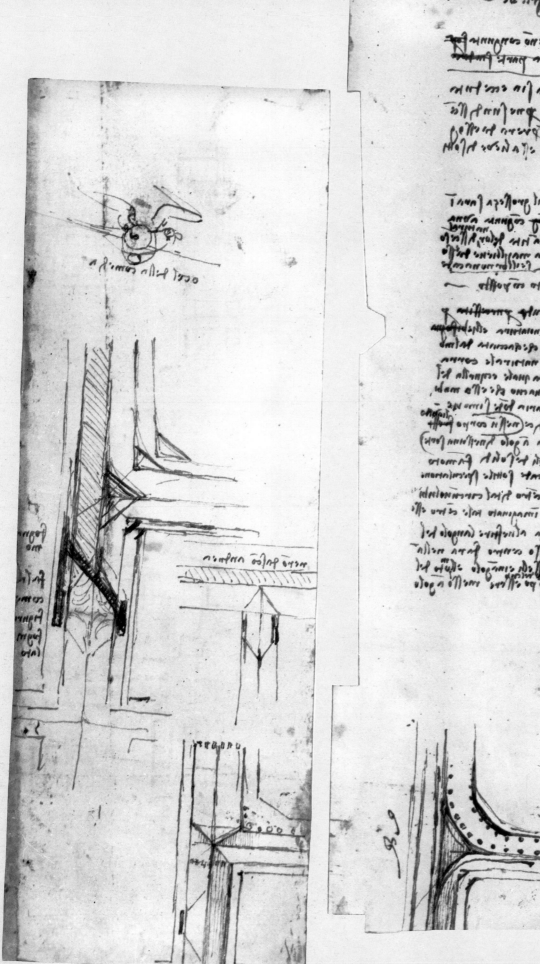

302. *Reverse side of the sheet reproduced on the preceding page. Codex Atlanticus, f. 231 v-a and f. 271 r-e.*

303. *Detail of the topography of the Neron da S. Andrea,* the canal adjacent to the *property of the projected villa for Charles d'Amboise, c. 1506-8. Codex Atlanticus, f. 207 v-a.*

304, 305. *Plan of the confluence of the canals in the area of the projected villa for Charles d'Amboise near the church of S. Babila, c. 1506-8. Codex Atlanticus, f. 305 r-a and v-a.*

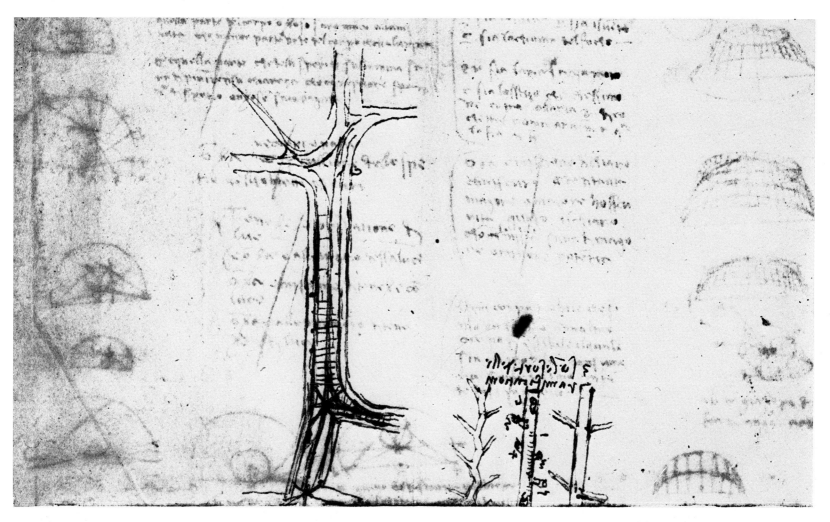

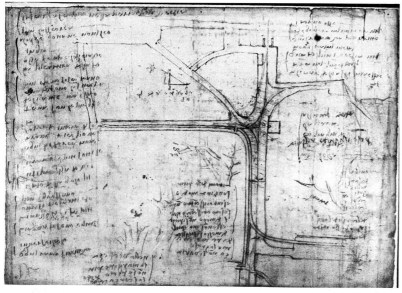

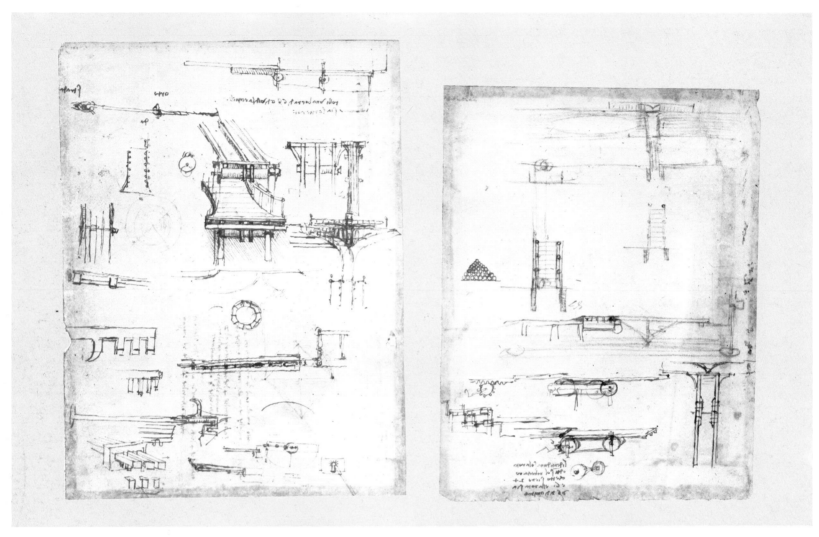

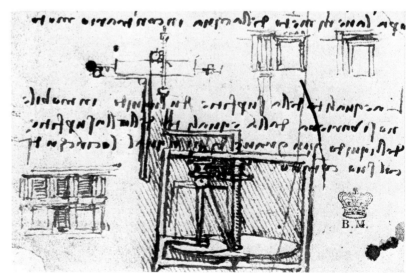

214

309, 310. Architectural studies datable to the time of the projects for the villa for Charles d'Amboise, c. 1508-10: notes on the arrangement of the staircases in a palace, on a sheet of anatomical studies at Windsor (RL 12592 r). In another sheet at Windsor (RL 12591 r) Leonardo considers the idea of giving a country villa a monumental character in a way that anticipates both the Palazzo del Te at Mantua and the château of Chambord in France. The studies of a Neptune with sea-horses seem to draw inspiration from Michelangelo's David and could be related to the project for a fountain for the garden of the château of Bury in France, whose owner, Florimond Robertet, one of Leonardo's French protectors, had commissioned a bronze David from Michelangelo. The texts both on the recto and on the verso refer to an imaginary reconstruction of the mythical Site of Venus in Cyprus. This is an architectural fantasy that places the accent on natural elements in the organization of a garden of delights and is inspired by analogous fifteenth-century interpretations of the Site of Venus, like those of Gherardi da Prato, Poliziano and Francesco Colonna.
On the recto we read:
"For the site of Venus.
I would make the staircase with four sides, by means of which one would reach a meadow made most naturally above a rock, which would be made empty and sustained in front by piers and underneath pierced by a great portico where water may pour into diverse vases of granite, porphyry and serpentine, semi-circular within, and the water spills into these and round about the portico. Towards the north should be a lake with a little island in the middle, on which may be a thick and shady wood. The waters on top of the piers may pour into vases placed at their feet from which little rivulets spread out.
On departing from the shore of Cilicia towards the south, one discovers the beauty of the island of Cyprus, which..."
On the verso, not reproduced:
"From the southern shores of Cilicia one sees further south the beautiful island of Cyprus, which was the kingdom of the goddess Venus, and many, incited by its beauty, have wrecked their ships and shrouds among the rocks encircled by dizzying waves. Here the beauty of the sweet hill invites the wandering sailors to refresh themselves among its flowery verdure, o'er which the winds play gently, filling the island and the surrounding sea with sweet scents. Oh how many ships here already are submerged! Oh how many boats broken on the rocks! Here one could see countless ships: one wrecked and half covered by sand, one showing its poop and another its prow, this its keel and that one its ribs; it's like some great Last Judgement for the resuscitation of dead ships, so many are there covering all the northern shore. Here the north winds, resounding, make various and fearful sounds."

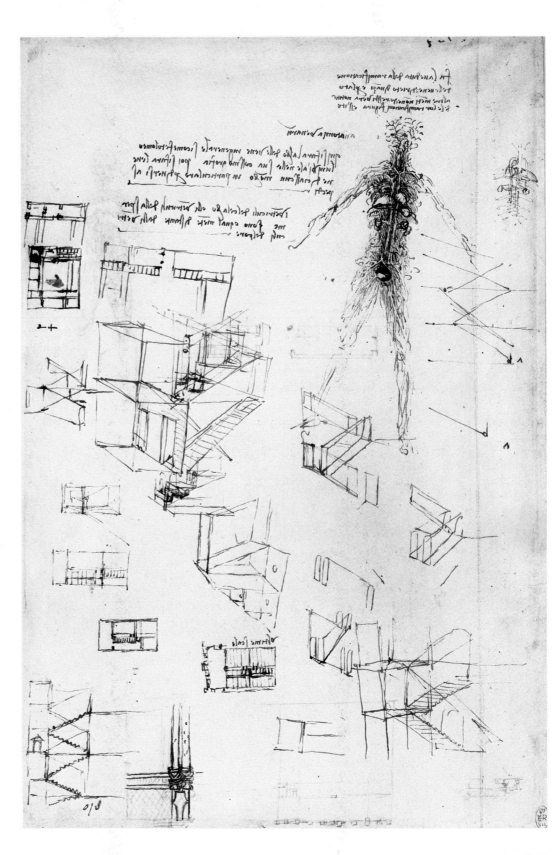

311. *Milan, S. Maria alla Fontana, arcade.*
312. *Stone tablet inscribed with the date of the foundation of the church of S. Maria alla Fontana, 29 September 1507.*
313. *Studies of a church and a fountain, c. 1506-8. Codex Atlanticus, f. 352 r-b, detail.*

314. *Studies on shadows and project for a centrally-planned church, c. 1508. Codex Atlanticus, f. 37 v-a.*

13. S. Maria alla Fontana

The building rose in 1507 on the outskirts of Milan, beyond Porta Comasina, in accordance with the wishes of Charles d'Amboise, French governor and Leonardo's patron. An inscription gives us the exact date – 29 September 1507 – of the foundation of this sanctuary, which d'Amboise wanted built on the site of a miraculous fountain. The work is incomplete, but elements of the porticoes and the apsidal walls show a delicate post-Bramantesque classicism, which relates them to Bramantino's Trivulzio Chapel and Cesariano's S. Celso. In 1507, however, both Bramante and Bramantino were absent from Milan. In search of the architect, therefore, Cristoforo Solari and even the almost anonymous master builders at the Cathedral Workshops have been mentioned, but the complex and imaginative articulation of the general plan easily suggests the mind of Leonardo, who in fact was employed as an architect by d'Amboise at that very time.

The church is built on a slight slope, so that the front part of the nave is at town level while the apse rises higher, above the hall that enclosed the miraculous fountain. This was meant to be flanked by porticoed cloisters, and two bell-towers (only one was erected) were to rise at the corners between apse and transepts, like the ones planned for S. Maria delle Grazie on the model of those at S. Maria dei Miracoli in Venice.

A small sketch in the Codex Atlanticus, f. 352 r-b, which is securely datable to about 1506-8, is vividly suggestive of what the original project for S. Maria alla Fontana might have been like, even to the detail of the cloisters flanking the apse. A little below this drawing is one of a very elegant amphora spurting jets of water on several sides, and next to that a frontal view of the same building, which presents once again the idea of the centrally-planned temple as it was to be actually realized at Todi and Montepulciano. It seems that just about then, around 1508, Leonardo was thinking of a building such as this as a Bramantesque synthesis of architectural forms inspired by Early Christian and Romanesque examples in Lombardy, and Albertian classical elements as at Mantua. The sketches on a page of studies on shadows, Codex Atlanticus, f. 37 v-a, are certainly of the S. Maria alla Fontana period, but the plasticity which Leonardo bestows on these architectural forms lifts them well beyond their likely origins in some late fifteenth-century scheme. As experiments in the vibrant play of light and shadow they presage the Baroque fantasies of Montano.

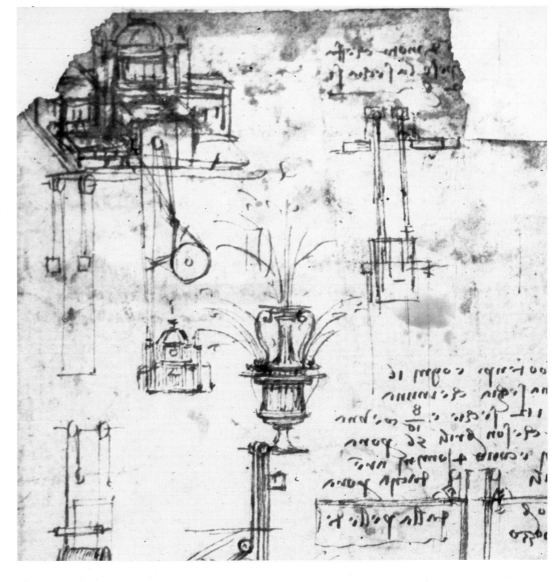

218

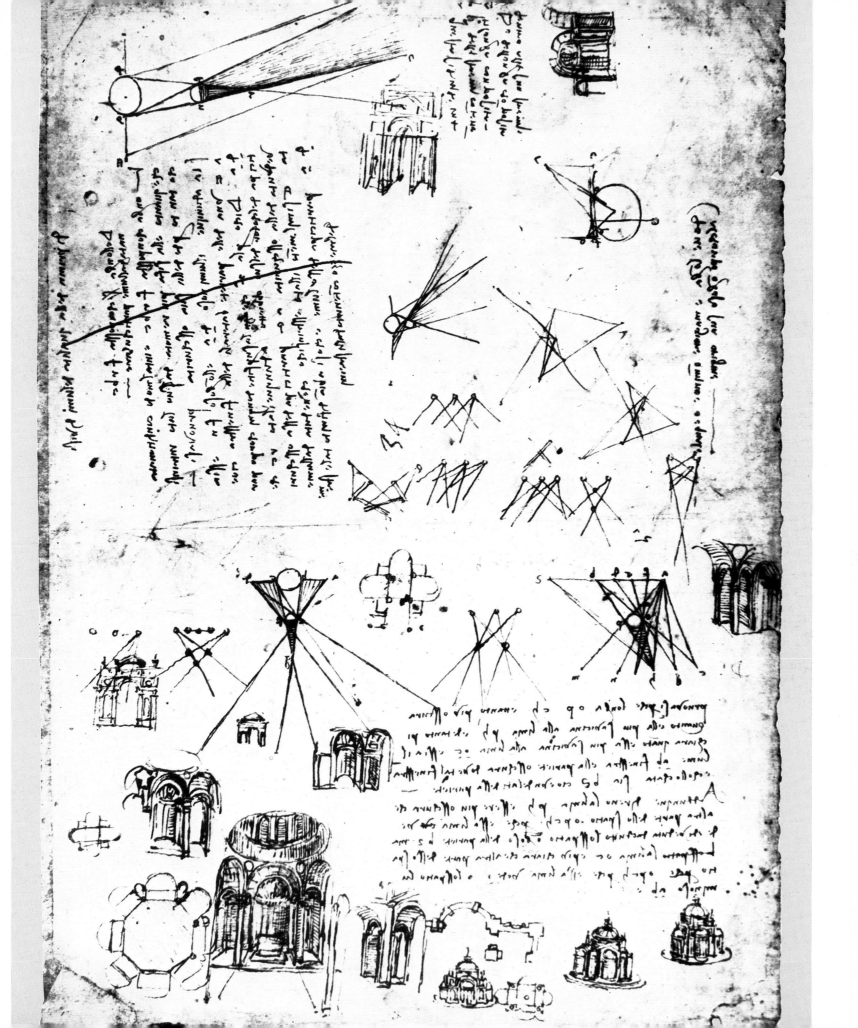

315. *Milan, Trivulzio Chapel at S. Nazaro.*
316. *Transverse section of the Trivulzio Chapel at S. Nazaro (from Rosmini).*
317. *Plan of S. Nazaro and vertical section of the Trivulzio Chapel. Milan, Biblioteca Trivulziana, Raccolta Bianconi.*

14. Il Magno Trivulzio

In his first will, of 1504, the condottiere Gian Giacomo Trivulzio, Marshal of France, made provision for an imposing marble tomb to be erected within the thousand-year-old basilica of S. Nazaro in Milan. Then on 22 February 1507, in a second will, he commissioned the construction not only of a chapel *in ecclesia vel prope ecclesiam* of S. Nazaro, but also *uno sepulcro in ea constituendo*. In his mind the idea of a sepulchral monument had moved on towards the idea of a whole architectural setting, a noble family chapel to serve as crown and showcase for the *sepulcrum*.

Leonardo's projects for Il Magno Trivulzio's funerary monument seem assignable to a period immediately after the date of the second will. An estimate of its costs in the Codex Atlanticus, f. 179 v-b, bears the same ductus as a page of notes on painting and studies of shadows (Codex Atlanticus, f. 199 v-b), datable to about 1508. And a sheet of the same series, but of a later date, f. 277 v-a in the same codex, contains an isolated note which seems to allude to an architectural work whose unfinished state, resulting from a delay in the delivery of the marble, seems to interfere with the terms of the contract: "If the marble were to give trouble for ten years, I do not want to wait for my payment until after all my work is done."

Work on the Trivulzio Chapel was started in 1511 on Bramantino's return from Rome. It is possible that Bramantino's design might have incorporated some suggestions of Leonardo, but there is no proof that the building was conceived especially to hold the equestrian monument he was planning. On the other hand Leonardo's drawings emphasize the importance of the architectural base supporting the equestrian group and show a number of variations on the theme of tombs either placed against a wall (like those by Sansovino in S. Maria del Popolo in Rome) or in the centre of the chapel in a way that seems to reflect some knowledge of Michelangelo's first designs for the tomb of Julius II (and the motif of the captives is undoubtedly owed to Michelangelo).

The estimate of costs gives full information for a scale reconstruction of the pedestal, which in fact has recently been done by G. Castelfranco in a scheme which makes use of the precedents of Verrocchio's Colleoni monument and the Ionic colonnade in an illustration in Fra Giocondo's Vitruvius of 1511.

A fragment removed from the Codex Atlanticus, f. 83 v-b and stuck on the Windsor sheet RL 12353 can be dated about 1508-10 on the basis of the contents of the original sheet, but several drawings of the series seem to be of a still later date. In fact, even those which reflect more closely the cost estimate are on the type of paper used for the Villa Melzi studies of 1513, and even the technique (red chalk and pen) and the style correspond. It is not improbable, therefore, that even around the years 1512-13, not long before leaving Milan to go to Rome, Leonardo was still mulling over the theme of the Trivulzio Monument when Trivulzio himself had perhaps already abandoned the idea.

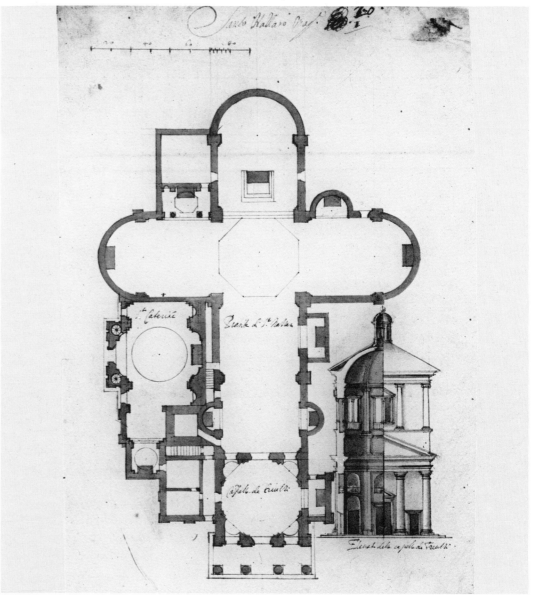

220

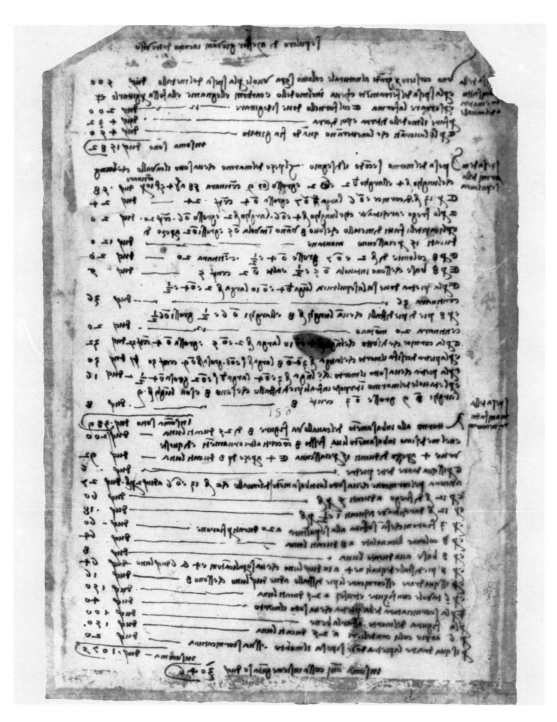

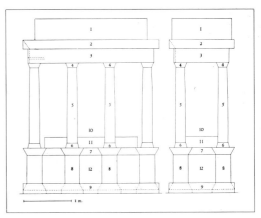

322, 323. *Studies for the Trivulzio Sepulchre, c. 1508-10 (or later). Windsor, RL 12356 v, 12354.*

324. *Study of a prisoner for the Trivulzio*
Sepulchre, c. 1508-10. Windsor, RL 12583.

325-328. *Studies for the Trivulzio*
Sepulchre, c. 1508-10 (or later). Windsor,
RL 12355, 12356, 12360, 12353.

49

·121·

15. *The Villa Melzi*

For a long time during the eighteenth and nineteenth centuries it was thought that Leonardo's first trip from Florence to Milan could be fixed in 1482, on the basis of the foundation date of a building attributed to him exclusively on the basis of style, and therefore without the support of any document or ancient tradition – the Villa Melzi at Vaprio d'Adda. By a singular coincidence it has been possible for us to ascertain that Leonardo actually did go to Milan around 1482, and it is surprising that we can now identify in a series of his architectural studies a project for the enlargement and embellishment of that villa. The project, however, is datable to around 1513, when he was staying as a guest of the family of his favourite pupil, Francesco Melzi, thirty years after the construction of the building. At Windsor there is a series of landscape drawings of the Adda which were done from the very terraces of that villa, looking down towards the swirling waters of the river which shortly after were to be transformed into the terrifying visions of the Deluge.

The Villa Melzi architectural drawings are some of Leonardo's most fascinating, for example those on f. 395 r-b of the Codex Atlanticus. The theme itself – the villa looking down on the river from the top of a high bank that descends in a succession of terraces, ramps and sustaining walls – seems to justify the accentuated pictorial character which he gives to the architectural forms, almost as if they had been viewed at high noon under a light that dissolves the shaded areas so as to show off the vibrant, almost resonant articulation of the walls, punctuated with wide arching windows.

It is obvious that Leonardo was aware of the scenic character demanded by the theme itself. In order to accentuate it he only needed to emphasize the main body of the building by grafting onto it two large square corner towers, raised higher by pyramidal roofs crowned by small lanterns. The towers, in their turn, have smaller structures attached to them, each containing a spiral staircase and each surmounted in the centre by round drums and little domes and on the sides by balconies with balustrades and pinnacles. The façade, once modified in this way, is enlarged even further by the addition of low extensions of five large arches each which, like wings, end with pavilions at each end.

Leonardo is particularly concerned with the linking of the newly-added rooms by means of staircases, passages and exits to the garden. An anatomical sheet at Windsor dated 9 January 1513 (RL 19077 v) contains sketches of plans, identified by Leonardo himself with the note: "room in the tower at Vavèri" (that is at Vaprio), which refer directly to the connecting of the new rooms, as is made clear in an overall plan in f. 61 r-b of the Codex Atlanticus, a sheet of the same type of blue paper as the anatomical series of 1513. Besides the plan, it also contains diagrams of the alternating ramps that connect the various terraces along the river bank at each end. The note written within the plan explains how to get from one point to another by means of the proposed passages: "On the ground floor the passage *a b* will lead into the garden, or rather through passage *c d*; and if you wish to enter the garden by *a b* you

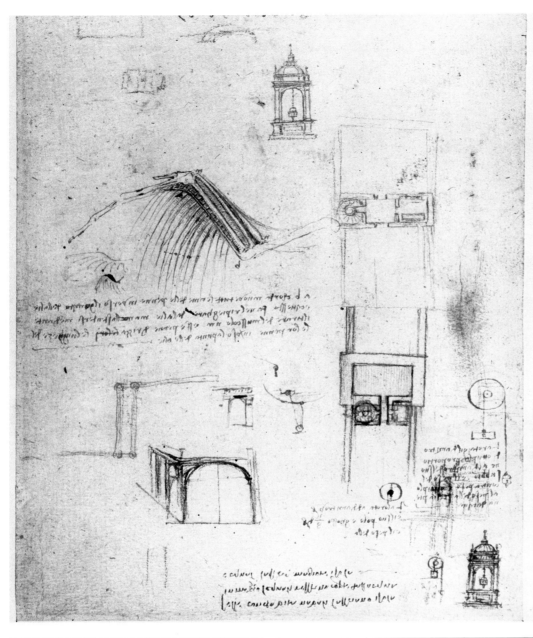

331-333. *Studies for the enlargement of the Villa Melzi,*
c. 1513. Codex Atlanticus, f. 395 r-b; Windsor, RL 19107 v
and detail.

334. *Drawing taken from the preceding illustration.*

can take the cellar staircase below the well of stairs *n m*,
and go down into the cellar by the stairs which are covered
by stairs *n m*, but the door to the garden must be low."
Other sheets and fragments offer the same configurations
of plans and elevations, and show the idea taking shape in
the course of working out the various problems which the
project involved. It seems that something of that project,
about which we know nothing more, was in fact begun,
from what we can see not only in the organization of the
bank into terraces, but also in the main part of the building
itself, which in its extremities shows indications of the
concluding motif of the small pavilions. Even the corner
staircases, in the way they were systematized at the end of
the eighteenth century, seem to take Leonardo's idea into
account.

Had Leonardo's project been carried out in every detail
that he planned, the building would have been seen from
the opposite bank of the river with the theatrical effect of
the arcaded wings open against the light, in a way which
would have stretched far beyond Raphael's concept of the
Villa Madama, thematically identical but tied to classical
models, and even beyond Palladio's visions of buildings
scenographically linked to their settings – stretching in fact
to the aristocratic fantasies of the French eighteenth
century which seem to draw their inspiration from Phi-
libert de l'Orme's festive architectural images, to which
perhaps Leonardo himself was no stranger.

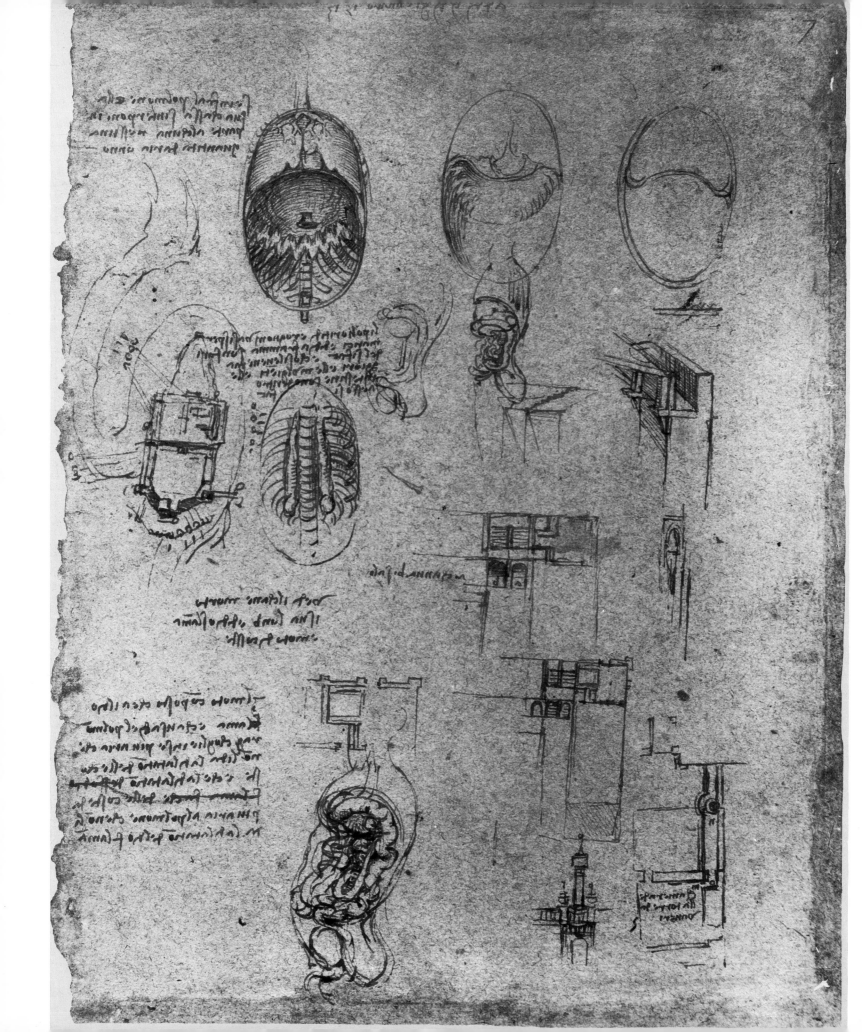

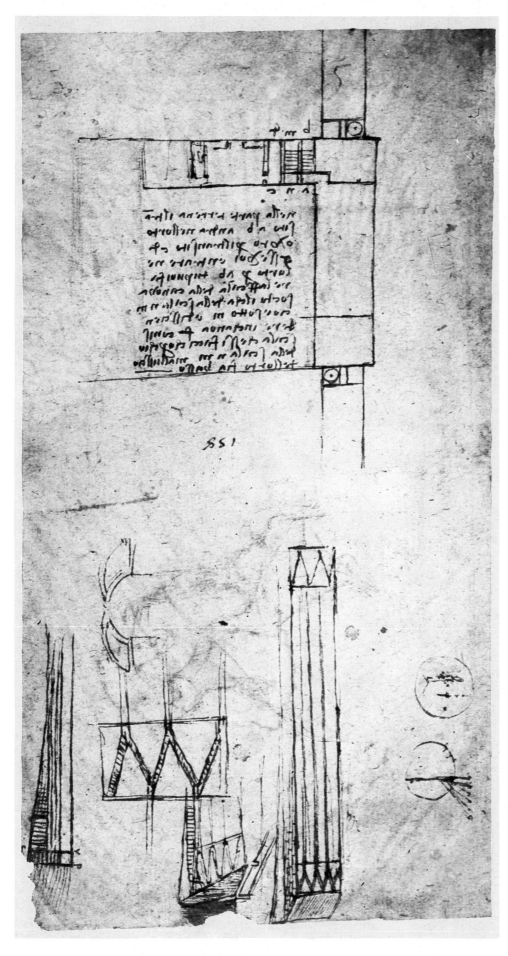

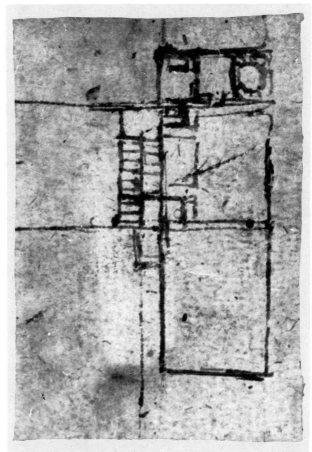

335. *Studies for the enlargement of the Villa Melzi on an anatomical sheet dated 9 January 1513. Upper left is the plan of the castle of Trezzo. Windsor, RL 19077 v.*

336-338. *Fragments of studies related to the projected enlargement of the Villa Melzi,* c. 1513. *Codex Atlanticus, ff. 61 r-b, 153 r-d, 153 r-e.*

Since Mongeri's edition of 1875, with facsimiles of very inferior quality, the Ambrosian Codex, which is often mentioned in studies on Milanese classicism (especially those by Baroni) has not been the subject of thorough and comprehensive study, either from the codicological point of view or from that of the personality of its author and the character of its contents. As far as I know, it has not even been included in any Leonardo bibliography. The page extracted from a book on antiquities owned by Leonardo (here mentioned in the present tense and therefore still extant) can be related, as I suggested in 1968, to the "book of old curiosities" which was one of the books he owned and which he listed in Madrid MS. II. Marinoni, the only person to my knowledge to receive my suggestion favourably, states that the book Leonardo had may have been Bramante's pamphlet *Antiquarie prospetiche romane* (see *Excursus 1*) which, however, has no illustrations except for the woodcut on the title page, let alone the tempietto plan which the anonymous author of the Ambrosian Codex has used.

The codex can be dated earlier than 1503. Before that year Julius II was Cardinal of S. Pietro in Vincoli, and he is mentioned as such on f. 6 in the passage describing the ruins of a hexagonal building discovered in a vineyard he owned outside Rome in the direction of Marino. It is a temple with six independent rooms and a circular base with two steps, built to encase a large column with a statue of Apollo placed on top. This is the same building, therefore, shown on a page without text (f. 11) which originally must have preceded the page with the plan ("as appears earlier" can be read in the text of this last), and in fact includes an indication of the statue in a pose like the Apollo Belvedere. This *terminus ante quem* proves that the author was in contact with Leonardo in Milan before 1500 and that therefore Leonardo by then already owned the book "which had been got in Rome" recorded on f. 57. It is possible that Leonardo got the book from some Lombard friend or colleague. We have seen (*Excursus 1*) that the memorandum in RL 12668 "Gian Giacomo's book" may refer to Dolcebuono. And it seems that he had another book from Amadeo, the one mentioned in Madrid MS. II as "Amadio's book" just next to the "book of old curiosities" and Francesco di Giorgio's book. (Amadeo is called Amadio by the Anonimo Morelliano in his description of Pavia. It is less probable that Leonardo alludes to the popular story *La Bella Camilla*, whose protagonist is an Amadio, especially since the book titles next to it refer to works on architecture and anatomy.)

This collection of drawings of ancient buildings shows that at the beginning of the sixteenth century those manuals of classical forms which, through Montano's famous compilation, were to establish themselves as a most authoritative instrument of inspiration and guide to Baroque architectural invention, were already widely circulated. Bramantino's Trivulzio Chapel itself, conceived as an encasement for the equestrian monument designed by Leonardo, seems to emerge from an analogous climate of lively archaeological interest, which was Bramante's legacy and was to lead to the mannerist classicism of the following generations of

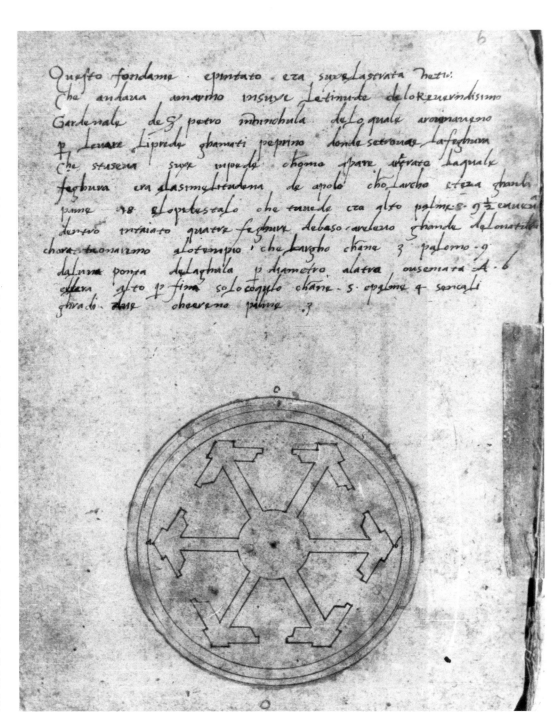

Milanese architects.

The next pages reproduce a few pages from the Ambrosian Codex (the references in the captions are the numbering after restoration), together with transcriptions and interpretations of the texts on f. 6 r and f. 57 r. This last contains the reference to the book on the antiquities of Rome which Leonardo owned.

Transcriptions and Interpretations

The text of the Ambrosian Codex, when one considers it from the point of view of the language, would require a double transcription, diplomatic and critical, to cope with the numerous problems of interpretation posed by its graphic and phonetic peculiarities. In the samples that follow I have adopted a middle way, clarifying the dubious points without altering the character of the original. First we have the text on f. 6 r which refers to the plan of a circular tempietto on the same page and to the elevation drawing of the same building on f. 11 r, which originally must have been next to it. The drawings have been cut out and glued onto the two pages; a statue on the top of the tempietto in the elevation drawing has been indicated in pencil on the paper of the page, not on the drawing.

"Questo fondame (fondamento, pianta), e piantato (dipinto cioè alzato) era suso la strada vechia / che andava a Marino, in suso le tenute de lo reverendissimo / Cardinale di S. Pietro in Vincoli, il quale arovinaveno / per levare le prede chiamate peperino, donde se trovò la fegura / che staseva suso in pede come apare aretrate (cioè nella figura qui dietro). La quale / fegura era a la similitudine de Apolo con l'arco, et era granda / palme 18 e lo pedestalo che tu vede era alto palme 9 ½ e aveva / dentro intagliato quattro fegure de basso rilievo grande de lo naturale; / ch'ora ce ne torneremo a lo tempio, ch'è largo canne 3 e palmi 9 / da l'una punta de l'anguli, per diametro, e l'altra ov'è segnata *a b.* / E l'era alto per fino al suo oculo canne 5 e palmi 4 senza li / gradi due, che erano palmi 3."

("This plan and elevation was above the old road to Marino on the property of the very reverend Cardinal of S. Pietro in Vincoli, which was being dug up in order to quarry the rock called peperino, when the figure was found standing upright as it appears earlier [that is in the illustration before this].

The said figure was like Apollo with his bow and was 18 palme large and the pedestal that you see was 9 ½ palme tall and had four life-size figures engraved on it in low relief; but let us return to the temple, which is 3 canne and 9 palmi wide, taking the diameter from the tip of one angular projection to the other, where it is marked *a b.* And up to its oculus it was 5 canne and 4 palmi tall without the two steps, which were 3 palmi.")

"This may possibly refer to the discovery of the famous 'Apollo Belvedere,' for which see Hans Henrik Brummer, The Statue Court of the Vatican Belvedere, Stockholm,

1970, pp. 44-7 and figures 34 and 35 (an enlarged detail of this indication of the statue). I now reproduce the text of f. 57 r, which describes the plan of a circular tempietto derived from a book owned by Leonardo.

"Questo si è uno tempio lo quale era / in un libro che à M.ro Lionardo che / fu cavato a Roma, e la quale non a-/ veva trovato io, e perché a me pare / trama antica ho voluto fare / la forma, come ell'era, mezza, / con le porte medesimamente / a l'altra banda. Scrivo il mio parere: Io per me dico che non me pare / comodo a nessun bisogno, avendo / tante porte, e non credo che n'avesse / Roma una (cioè una tale forma). e ‹'n›li altr(l) vi è fuserie / in treghe come sta quella ba‹n›da / se‹g›nata a' (alla) lettera A."
("This is a temple which was in a book that Maestro Leonardo had that was got in Rome and which I had not found, and because it seems to me an antique plan I wanted to draw the form as it was, in half, with the doors in the same way on the other side. I write my opinion: For myself I say that it doesn't seem useful for anything; having so many doors, and I don't believe that Roman had one (that is, such a form), and in the others there is fuserie in treghe as on that side shown by the letter A.")

The last sentence was interpreted by Mongeri as follows; "eli altr vie fusene (and the other ways were) intreghe chomo sta quelabada (that side) senata aletera A." The sentence could be interpreted in the sense that on the side indicated by the letter "A" there are continuous mouldings ("fuserie integre"), that is the "fusaroli" mentioned by Pacioli in the Divina Proportione in chapter XVI on cornices. The side referred to is, in fact, without passages of openings, but is made up of a continuous wall with niches. A similar arrangement of niches is seen in the sketches of tempietti of classical descent in the lower part of f. 270 v of the Codex Arundel, reproduced among the studies for the royal palace of Romorantin.

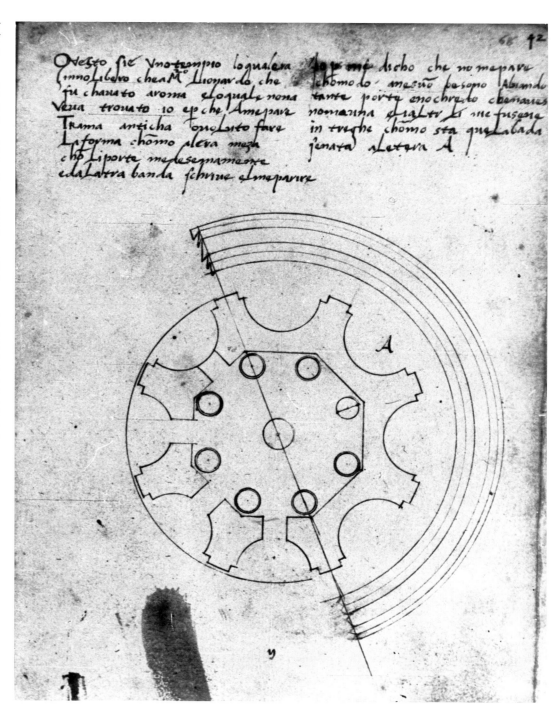

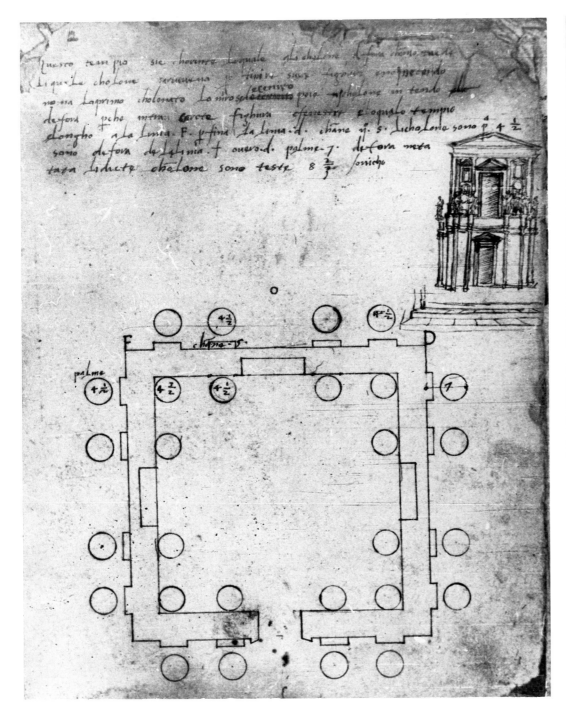

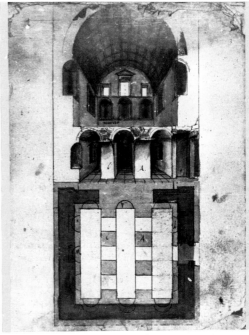

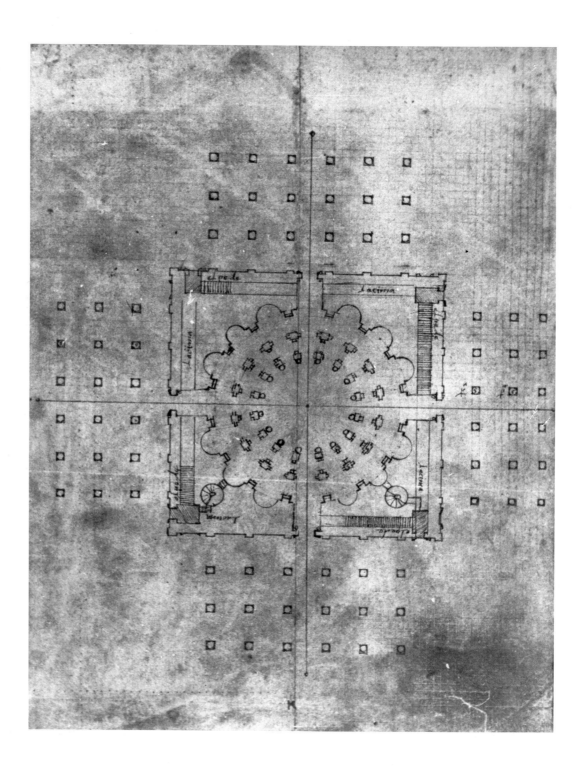

345, 346. Bramantino, *Le Rovine di Roma, ff. 85 r, 84 v.*
Milan, Biblioteca Ambrosiana.

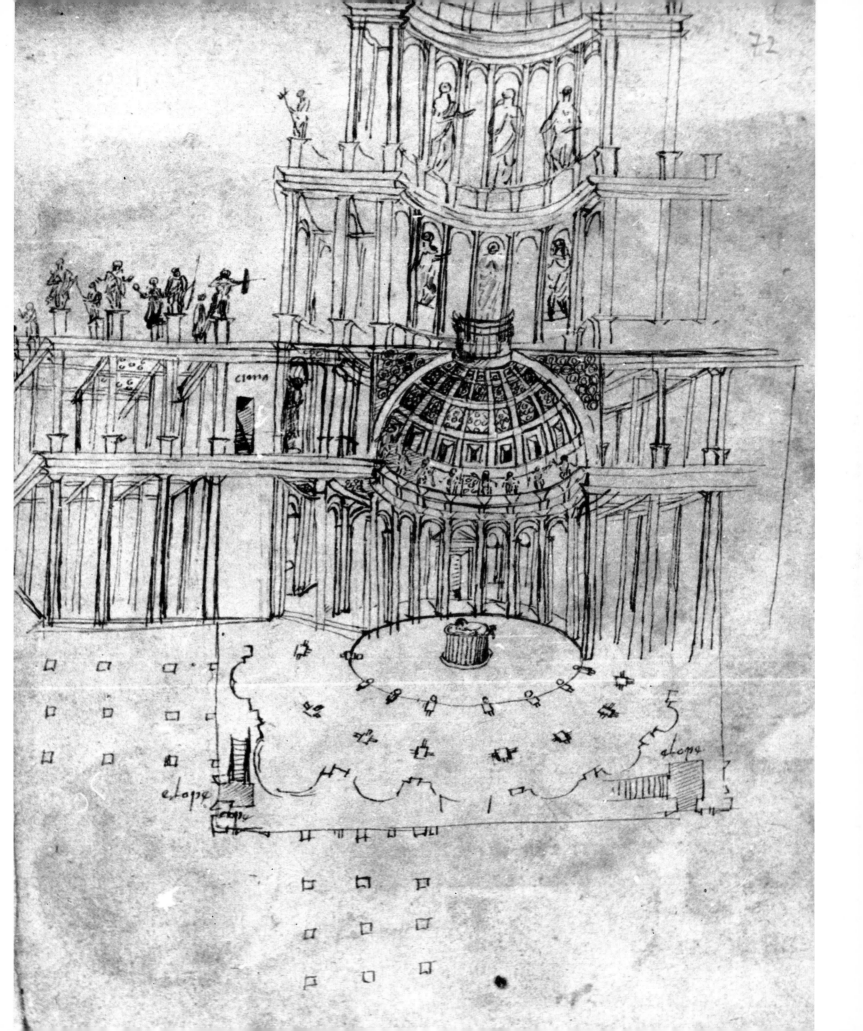

32

V. Rome and Florence, 1513-1516

16. The Vatican

The information we have about Leonardo's stay in the Vatican during the reign of Leo X, from 1513 to about 1516, comes to us from documents and from Leonardo himself, for example in his record of having solved a geometrical problem "on the 7th day of July at the 23rd hour at the Belvedere, in the studio made for me by il Magnifico, 1514."

In October 1513 they were preparing the rooms he was to occupy in the Belvedere, with Giuliano Leno, assistant to both Bramante and Raphael, directing the work. "Things that must be done at the Belvedere in the rooms of Messer Lionardo da Vinci," is the document's title, with a list of expenses involved in repairing ceilings and floors, building wooden partitions for the rooms and the kitchen, altering the windows, and furnishing the apartment and studio with wardrobes, tables, benches, stools, chests and "a bench for grinding colours." Nothing, in fact, that was not functional, and the sobriety that we sense in this makes strong contrast with the splendour of the antiquities in the surrounding spaces, especially in the villa's own courtyard, whose statues included the famous Ariadne, which Leonardo sketched on a sheet of studies of wooden trusses of the sort used in constructing the vault of Bramante's new St. Peter's.

Leonardo's lodgings were in the Villa of Innocent VIII, at the top of the little hill which Bramante had transformed into a stage set of Imperial architecture to be viewed across the vast courtyard linking the villa to the apostolic palaces. A sketch in the Codex Atlanticus, perhaps not by Leonardo, shows the villa in a view from the north-east much as it appears today, notwithstanding successive alterations, above the roofs of the city. Very little is known of Leonardo's activities while he stayed in the Vatican. Without doubt he was mainly expected to produce paintings, but there are references to technological and hydraulic engineering projects for this patron Giuliano de' Medici, the Pope's brother. This would provide an explanation for the appearance of the symbolic diamond ring of the Medici on a design for a rope-making machine; and it may be that Giuliano himself, as owner of the lands of the Pontine Marshes, asked him to undertake a drainage project there.

But it seems that the scheme that most consistently occupied him was that of building a large parabolic mirror of moulded pieces for using solar energy industrially. It is mentioned, in fact, as a source of heat capable of boiling the dyes in all the vats of a dye-works, and it is not improbable that Leonardo was aware of the possibility of using the same device in astronomical observation, directly anticipating Newton's reflecting telescope: "In order to see the nature of the planets, open the roof and show at the base only one planet and the reflecting action of the said base will show the complexion of the chosen planet, but make this base so that it does not show more than one of them at a time," we read in a sheet from that period (Codex Arundel, f. 279 v).

It is in such a context that we find the retrospective record of the parabolic mirror used by Verrocchio to weld the various sections of the copper sphere that was placed atop

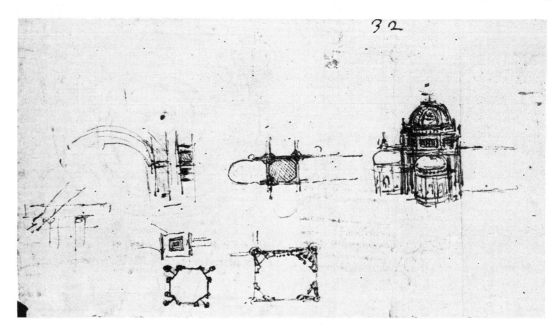

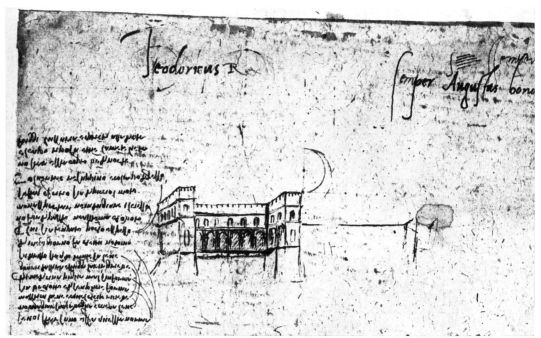

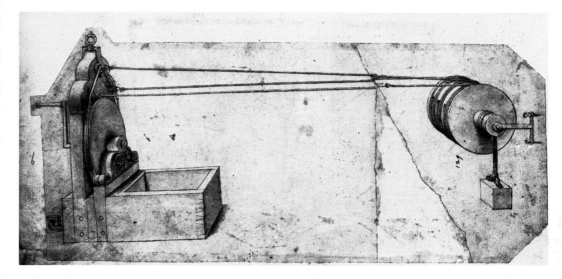

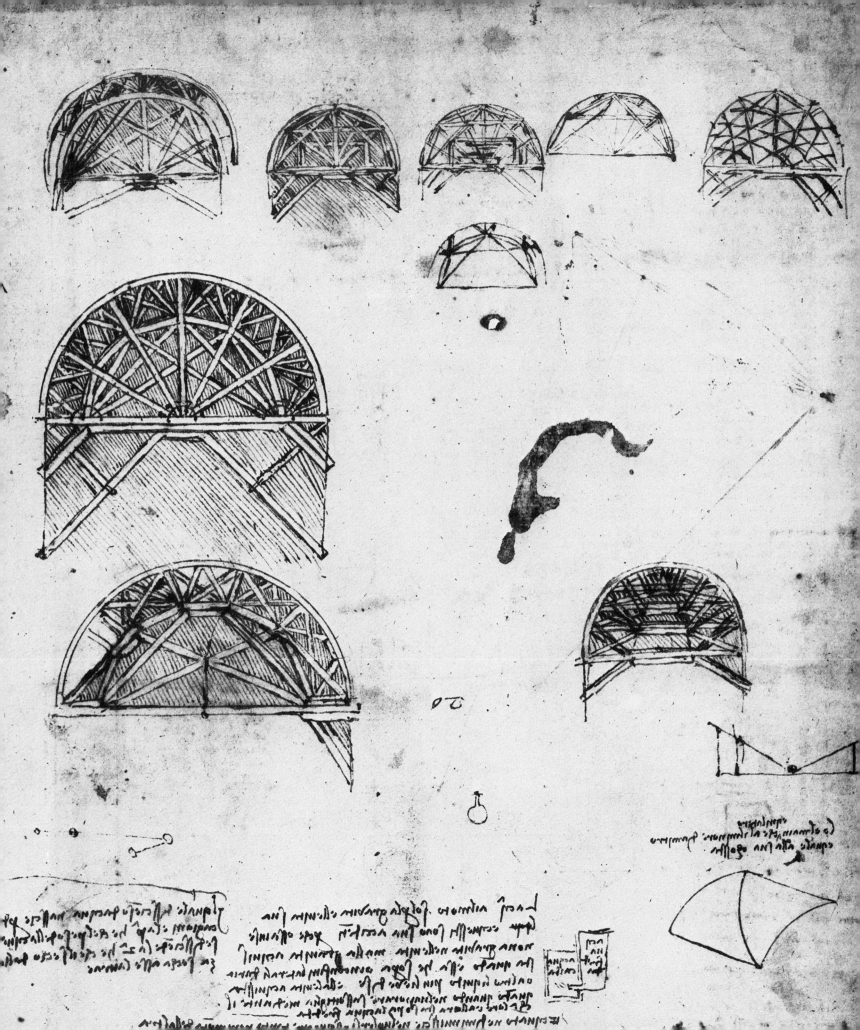

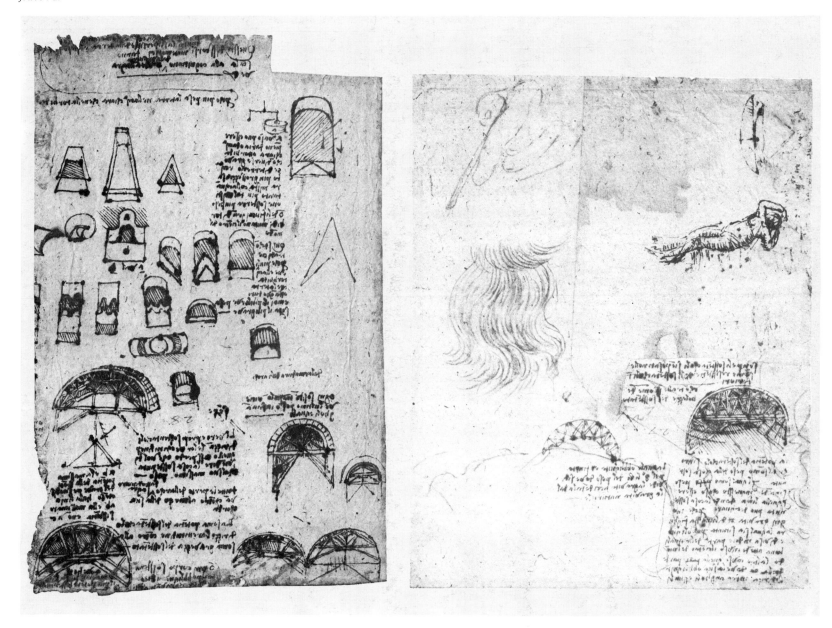

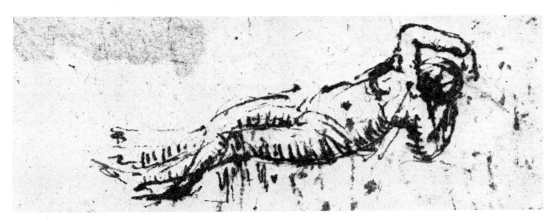

the lantern of Florence Cathedral in 1471. Before long, however, Leonardo came into conflict with two German artisans who were assigned to him as assistants in his mirror-making. One of them even complained about him to the Pope, which led to his exclusion from the Hospital of S. Spirito, where it seems he had taken up anatomical dissection once again. In the autumn of 1514, and for a good part of 1515 until the Pope started on the journey that would end with his meeting the King of France at Bologna in December of that year, Leonardo was absent from Rome. He may have been following his patrons Giuliano and Lorenzo de' Medici, the Pope's brother and nephew, first to Florence and then to Parma and Piacenza. It was probably at the end of 1515 that he met Francis I, from whom he was to receive the invitation to go to France; and there are indications that at that time Leonardo also revisited Milan. It is certain, however, that in August of 1516 he was back in Rome, where he took the measurements of the basilica of S. Paolo fuori le Mura. And he produced at that time, or a little later, the series of meditations on the theme of classical temple façades, possibly related to his projects for the façade of S. Lorenzo in Florence, in which he seems to be reconsidering the architecture of classical antiquity in the monumentality of its structural and geometrical elements.

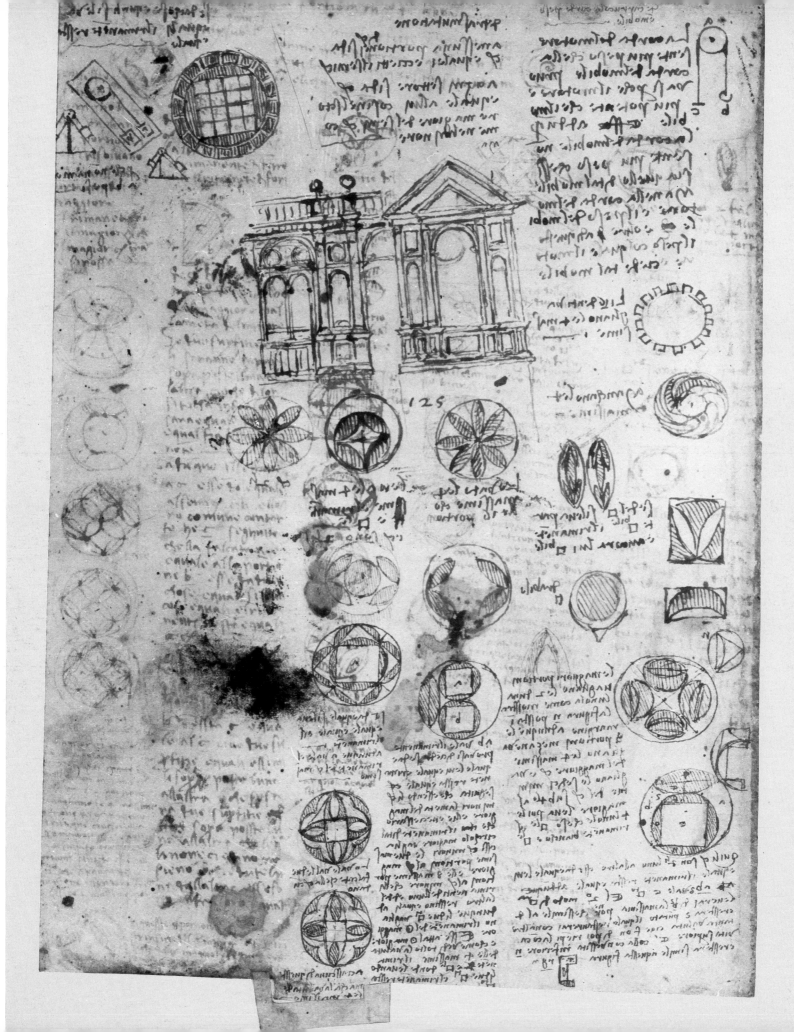

*354-356. Designs for windows and doors
on sheets of geometrical studies of 1515-16.
Codex Atlanticus, ff. 114 r-b, 279 v-a,
281 v-a.*

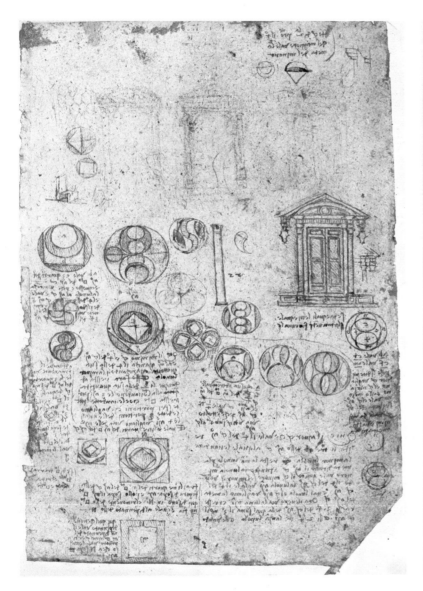

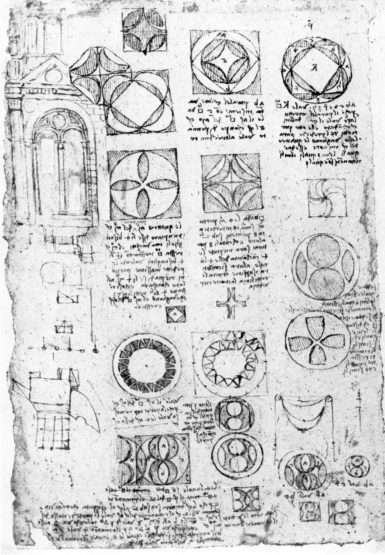

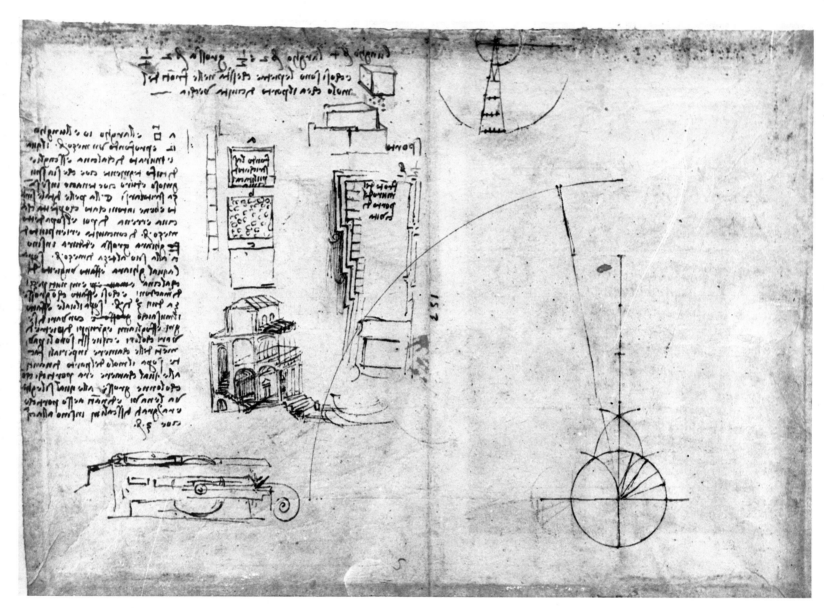

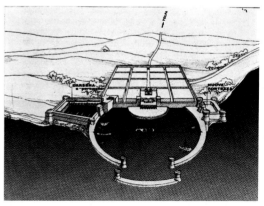

244

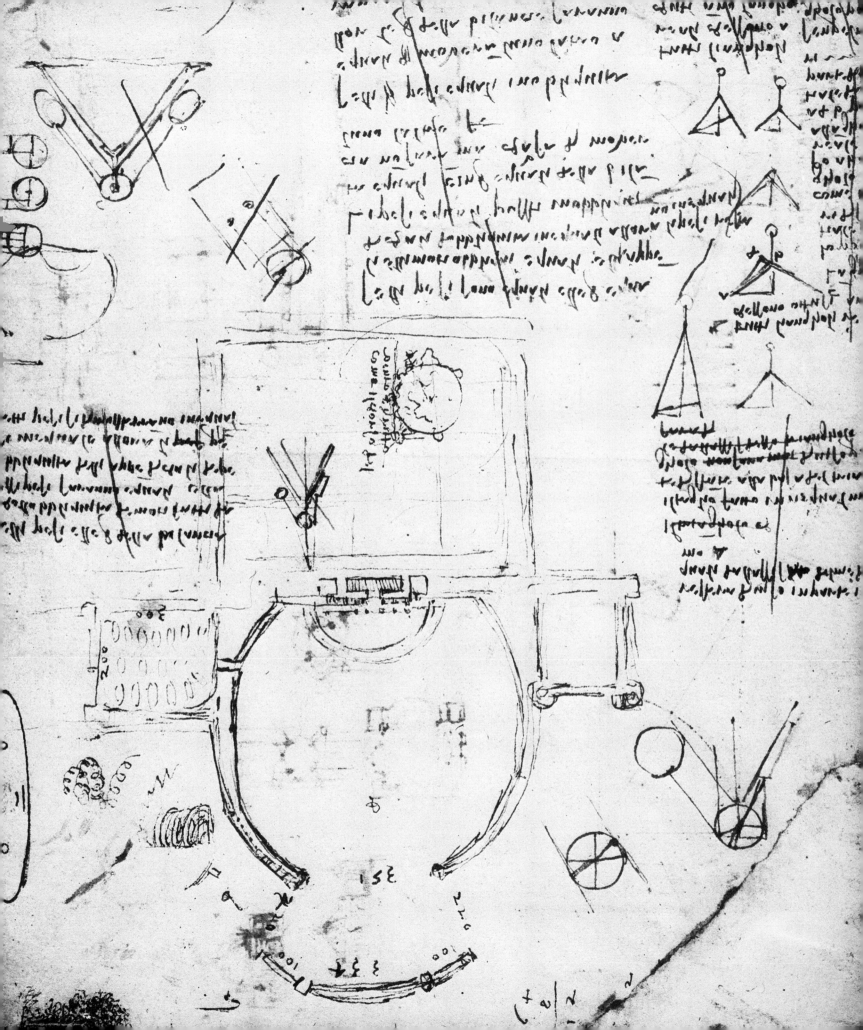

360. Codex Atlanticus, f. 271 v-d.

361. Studies of the part of Civitavecchia, c. 1514. Sheet reconstructed from three fragments in the Codex Atlanticus, ff. 271 r-f, 113 r-b, 12 r-b.

362. Reverse side of the sheet reproduced in the preceding illustration. Codex Atlanticus, ff. 271 v-d, 12 v-b, 113 v-b.

363-365. The spiral-shaped port. Codex Atlanticus, f. 285 r-a, and detail, c. 1515-16. Sketches and notes on harbour engineering, probably relating to the studies for Civitavecchia. At the centre is the sketch of a spiral-shaped port project of the type illustrated later by Teofilo Gallaccini in his treatise Sopra i porti di mare *(Biblioteca Comunale di Siena, MS. L, IV. 3).*

17. Civitavecchia

From 1508 Bramante had been concerned with the harbour works of Civitavecchia, paying particular attention to the defensive system and the dockyard, a project, in fact, in which he was still involved at the time of his death in 1514. It seems that it was precisely between 1513 and 1514 that Leonardo went (or was sent) there, perhaps just to get a clear idea of the work in progress, or perhaps even with a view to the possibility of taking over from Bramante. The plan of the port of Civitavecchia has been recognized in a drawing in the Codex Atlanticus, f. 271 r-f. It includes indications of the urban layout, the docks, fortress and quay, regularized according to an axial plan rather different from their actual layout, and for this reason it has been thought that this drawing was an "archaeological representation" of the port, also because in another sheet of the same time (Codex Atlanticus, f. 63 v-b) the ruins of an Imperial building are suggested. According to a recent proposal by Bruschi this could, however, be the record of an idea of Bramante's to re-create a maritime city of antiquity in conformity with the characteristic configuration preserved on Roman coins, which would have completed a vast building programme begun by Julius II with the new St. Peter's and the Via Giulia.

Leonardo's drawing was originally united with two other small sheets in the Codex Atlanticus so as to form a single sheet folded over several times and containing further references to Civitavecchia. On the same sheet, reconstructed in this way, we find notes on mechanics that were transcribed or elaborated in MS. E in 1513-14, and also studies of ecclesiastical architecture that seem to take as their model the Milanese basilica of S. Lorenzo set in relation to Bramante's project for the new St. Peter's.

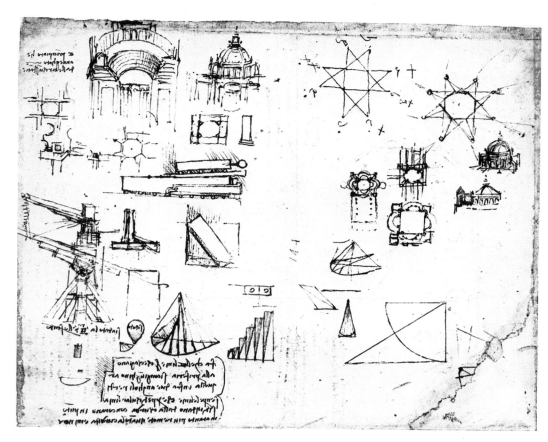

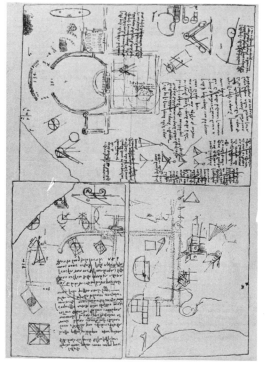

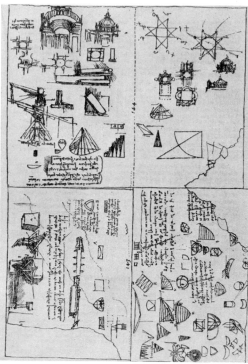

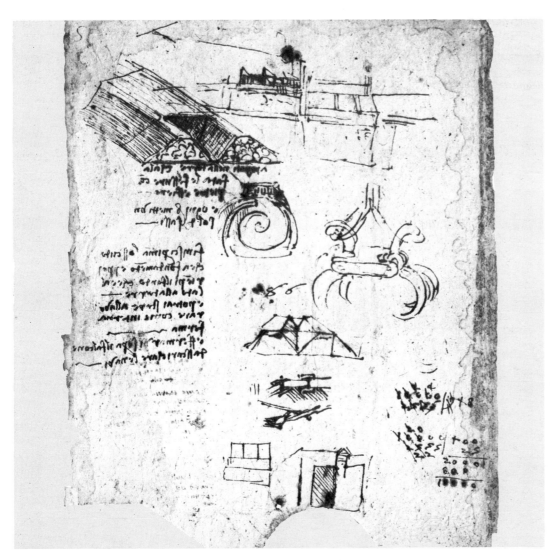

The notes, from top to bottom, are as follows:
"Supported in the tower, stop up the cracks with stones and hay. And every braccio put a layer of pebbles. First finish the shield which has foundations, and then fill the bottom at the side of the tower. And you will be able to stand to work as on terra firma. And fix above there the derrick for unloading the ships."

18: The Pontine Marshes

In 1514 and 1515 Leonardo was working on a project for the drainage of the Pontine Marshes, which is known to us through a famous drawing at Windsor, RL 12684. The date suggested by the style (only the place names were written by Leonardo's pupil Francesco Melzi) is confirmed by the documents which refer to Leo X's proposal to have these swamps drained.

On 9 January 1515 Giuliano de' Medici obtained from his brother, the Pope, the ownership of the lands flooded by noxious waters and gave the master Domenico de Juvenibus the task of working out a plan to drain the waters away, at the same time making sure that the neighbouring landowners would join in the scheme. Four months later, on 19 May 1515, Fra Giovanni da Como was given a regular contract to take charge of the work, and according to a statement by Cesariano (*Vitruvio*, Como 1521), he did actually accomplish the task: "These Pontine Marshes have in our time been cleansed and cleared out by a friar from Como, a thing which the Romans had never been able to do." Here is yet another comparison with antiquity, but no document carries Leonardo's name, even though his Windsor drawing demonstrates the very same plan as that approved by Giuliano, who was then his patron.

In other sheets of the same period there are references to the problem of currents in harbours and coastal regions which it is possible to relate to the studies for the drainage of the Pontine Marshes. In one of these Leonardo makes direct reference to the water system in Antwerp, but it seems certain that the sheet belongs to the Roman period.

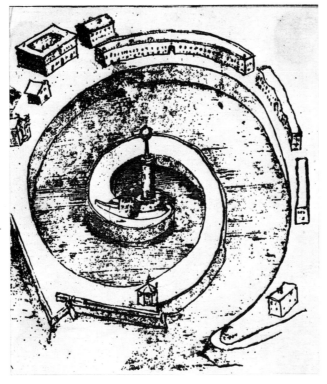

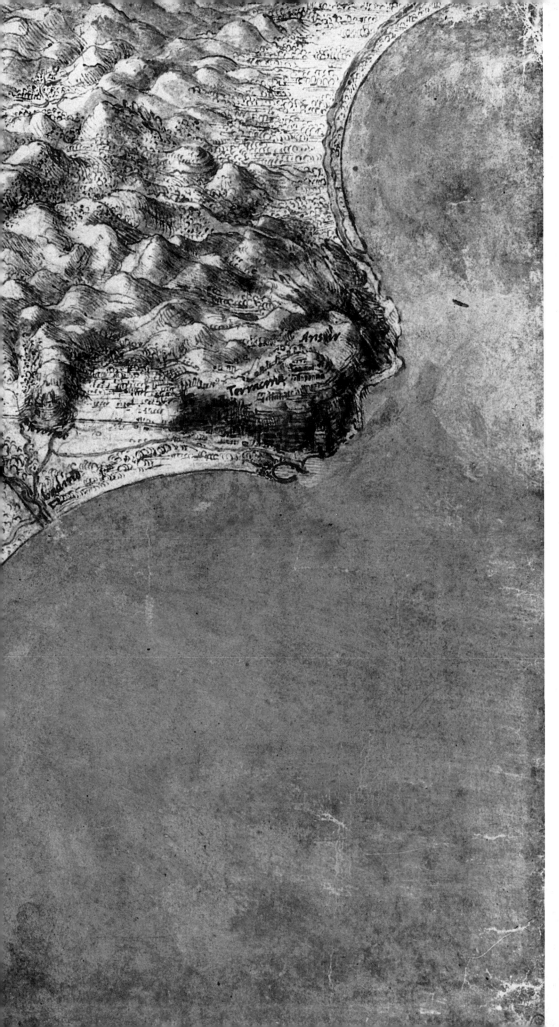

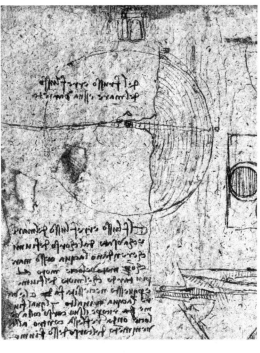

366. *Project for draining the Pontine Marshes, c. 1514.
Windsor, RL 12684.*

367, 368. *Studies on the administration of sea-coasts,
c. 1515. Codex Atlanticus, ff. 167 v-a, 281 r-a.*

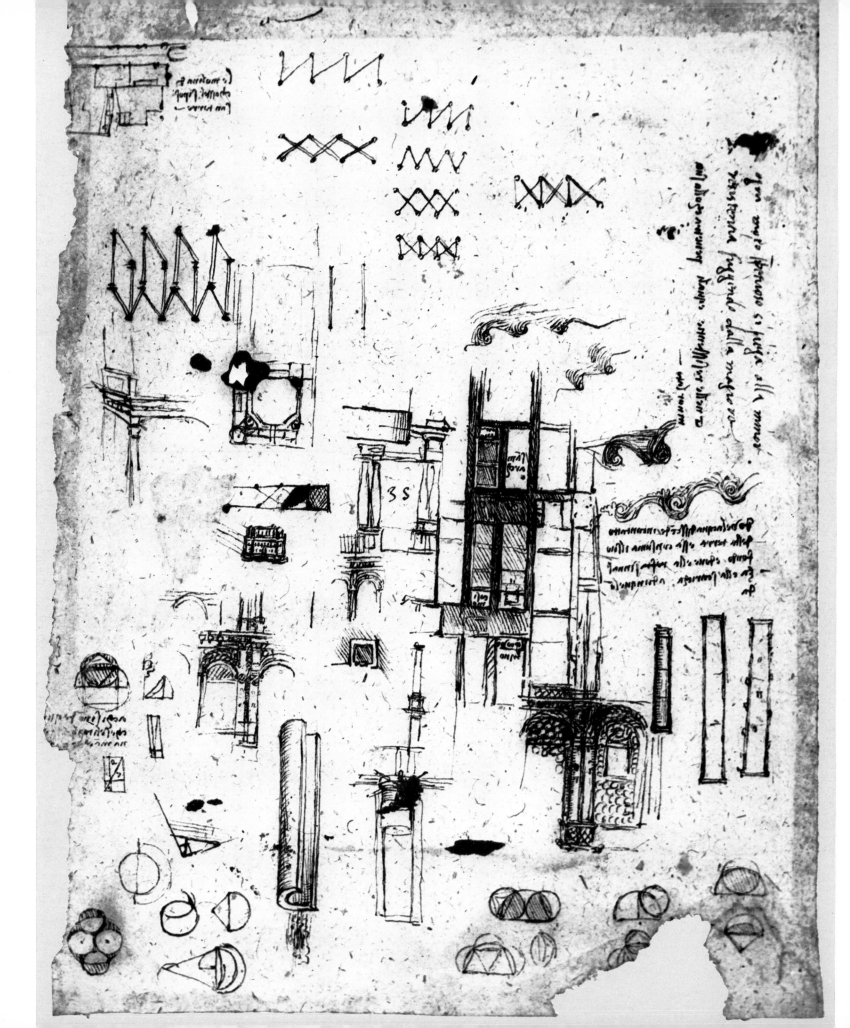

369, 370. Studies for a new Palazzo Medici in Florence, c. 1515. Codex Atlanticus, f. 315 r-b and detail.

371. Scene of the Visitation *in the background of a view of Piazza S. Lorenzo which reflects Leonardo's project of city planning. Libro d'ore of Laodamia de' Medici, British Museum, Yates Thompson MS. 30, f. 20 v.*

372. Layout of the Medici quarter according to Leonardo's project.

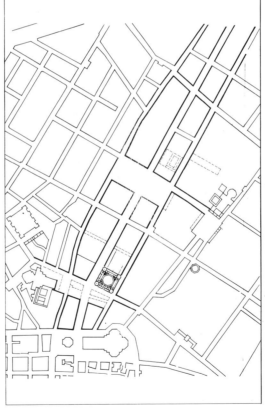

19. The New Medici Palace

On the journey which was to take him to meet Francis I in Bologna in December 1515, Leo X stopped in Florence where, to honour his arrival, sumptuous architectural street decorations were specially built. These were not just done by carpenters and artisans, but major artists like Jacopo Sansovino, Antonio da Sangallo the Elder, Andrea del Sarto and Jacopo da Pontormo also took part. Among the temporary structures they designed were façades for the as yet unfinished cathedral and church of San Lorenzo. It was probably on that occasion that the Medici Pope conceived the idea of holding a competition for the façade of San Lorenzo, but it seems that at the same time he may have considered a plan for the systematization of the whole Medici quarter, which would explain Michelangelo's closing up of the corner loggia of Cosimo's old palace in 1517, placing there his famous windows "supported on knees."

In 1515 Lorenzo di Piero de' Medici, the Pope's nephew, had been elected Governor of Florence. It may be that he himself had planned some urban reorganization centred around a new Medici Palace to be built facing the old one in the Via Larga. We can, in fact, recognize this plan in a series of studies by Leonardo datable around 1515: the piazza in front of San Lorenzo is extended as far as the two Medici palaces, the old one (indicated by Leonardo with the word "Cosimo") and the new one, for which there are details of plans and elevations, with the suggestion of a foliate decoration applied to columns and archivolts alluding to the Medici "broncone" insignia, a tree-stump from which new branches grow to symbolize the renewal of the family's prestige – an emblem which was in fact first used by Lorenzo di Piero de' Medici.

The Medici quarter in Leonardo's sketch includes the area between the cathedral and the monastery of S. Marco, which he indicates with the words "S. Marco." The suggested enlargement of the Piazza S. Lorenzo would have involved the demolition of the church of S. Giovannino, which Leonardo proposed to reconstruct on the side of the new piazza facing the two Medici palaces. The projected new palace is placed in the front part of a separate block, which would probably have provided space for gardens or outbuildings for the servants. On a sheet of the same period Leonardo takes note of the plan of "Il Magnifico's stables," capable of housing one hundred and twenty-eight horses. These were actually built by the side of the monastery of S. Marco between 1515 and 1516, and it may well be therefore that they were part of Leonardo's project. This building complex was later incorporated into the buildings of the *Sapienza*, and Elio Rodio, on the following pages, reconstructs them on the basis of documentary evidence and of what is still visible, suggesting as a result an attribution to Leonardo.

373-375. *Studies of temporary architecture for festivals, with particular reference to the construction of an* arcus quadrifons, *perhaps the one made by Antonio da Sangallo the Elder for Leo X's entry into Florence in 1515. Codex Atlanticus, f. 3 v-b and r-b and interpretative diagram.*

376. *Studies of temporary constructions for festivities, c. 1515-16 (or later). Codex Atlanticus, f. 335 v-e. The building upper left is surmounted by a heraldic lily, perhaps alluding to France. The note relating to a "fireplace in the antique style" is by Francesco Melzi and explains the*

drawing, lower left: "a b are niches where at first men used to sit. In circle a was situated the fire, and these niches were situated in the space of two walls."
Raphael, too, in the last year of his life, was occupied with fireplaces for the Duke of Ferrara.

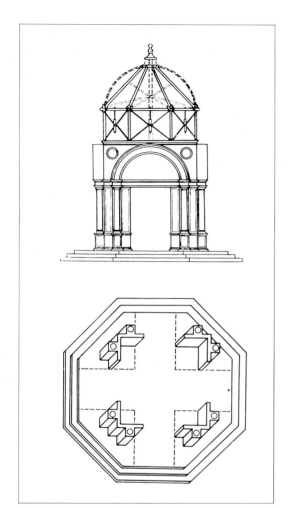

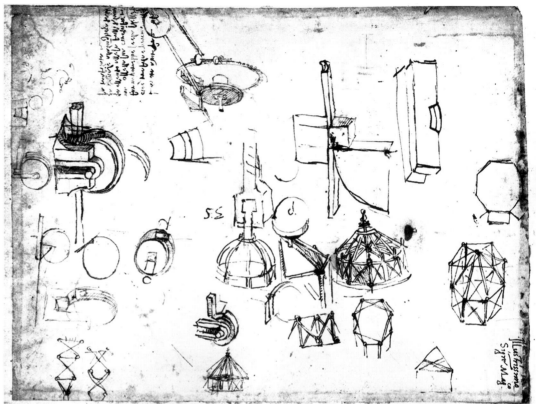

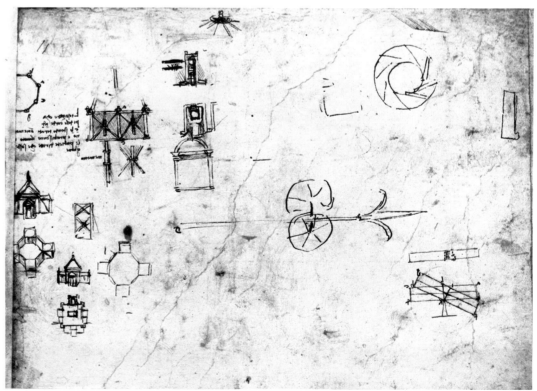

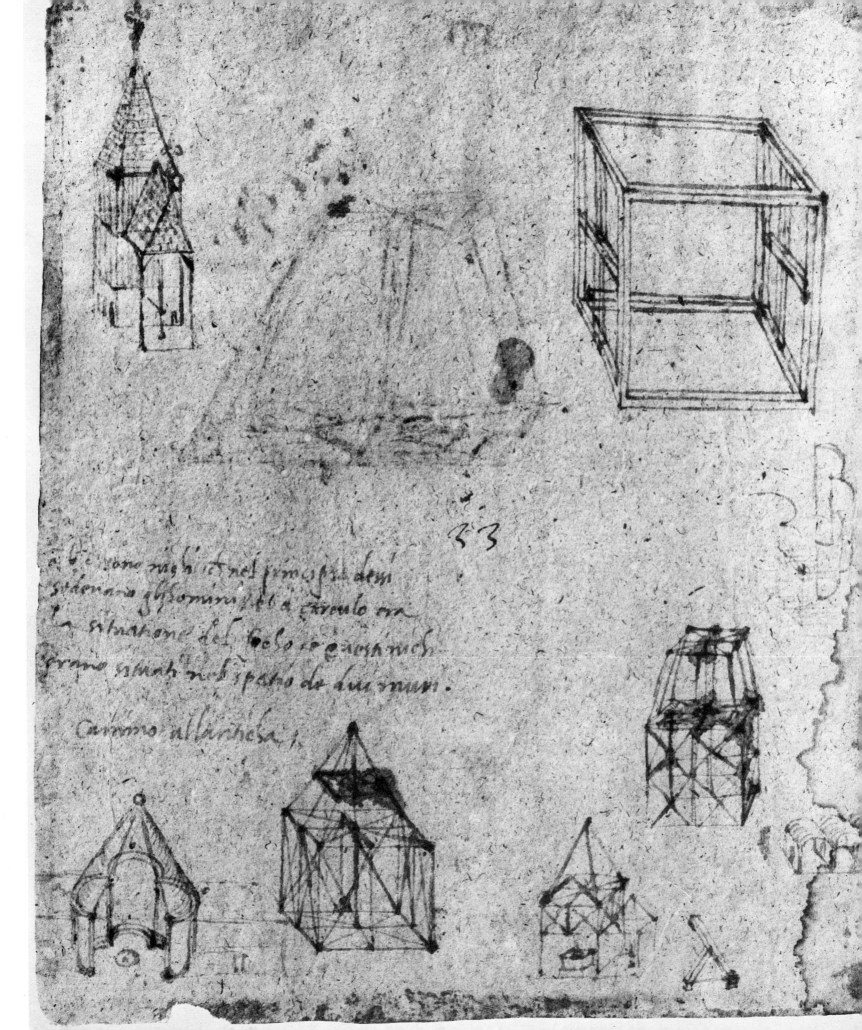

33

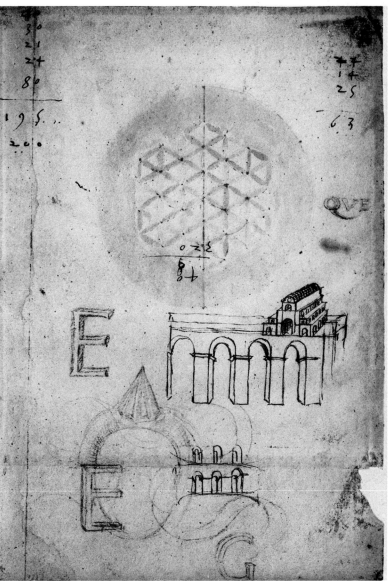

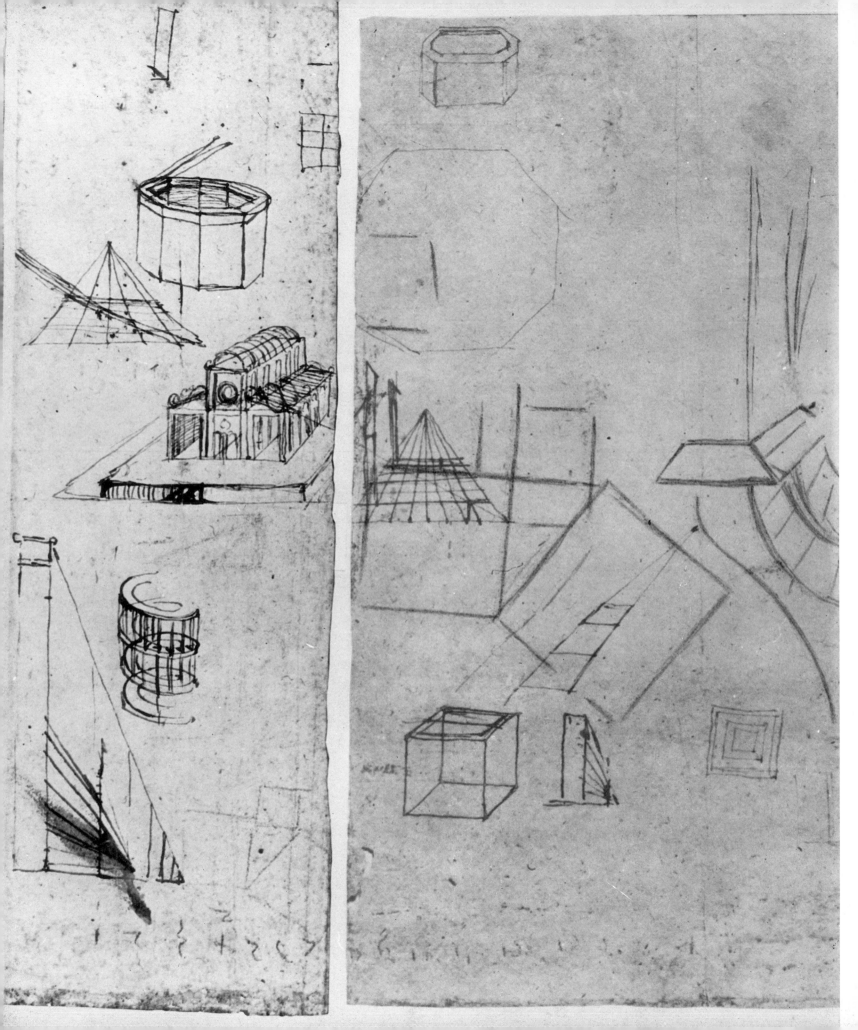

383. *Diagram of the proportional distribution of the spaces in a "model stable," c. 1487-90. Codex Trivulzianus, f. 27 v.*

384. *Perspective view of the "model stable" following the outline shown in the preceding sketch. Codex Trivulzianus, f. 21 v.*

385. *Final elaboration of the project for the "model stable," c. 1487-90. MS. B, ff. 38 v-39 r.*

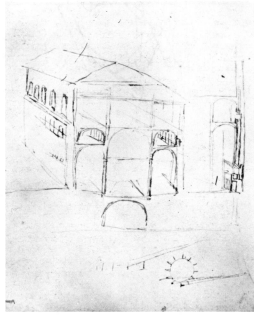

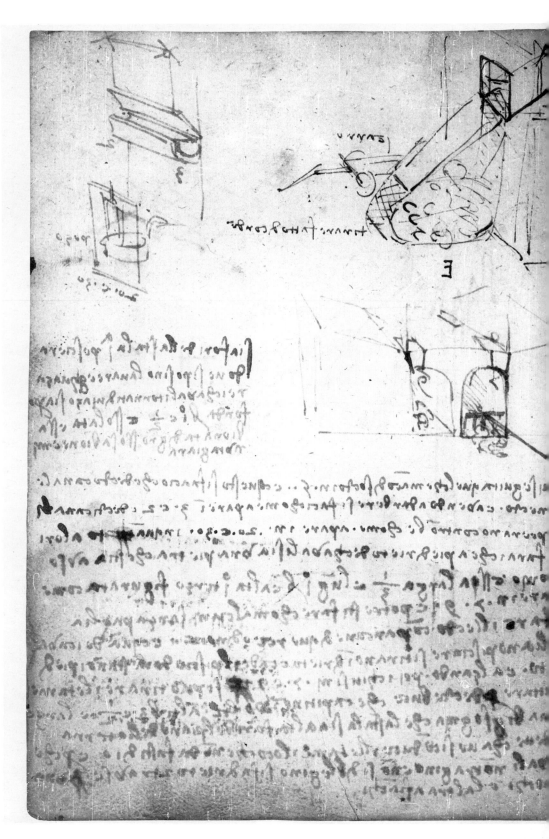

In his projects for stables Leonardo shows yet again how, having focused on a problem, he solves it in the best possible way – in this case with unsurpassed examples of "model stables," which can still be considered avant-garde today. These projects are known to us only through a few sketches and notes, mostly datable to around 1487-90 and probably motivated by a town-planning scheme in Vige-vano or Milan. There is no doubt that these ideas were the source for the project for the Medici stables in Florence of twenty-five years later, referred to in a note in the Codex Atlanticus, f. 96 v-a. In Leonardo's last architectural project, the grandiose royal palace at Romorantin in France, the stables assume the dimensions of a twin palace, but of these we have only indications in plan (e.g. Codex Atlanticus, f. 217 v-c). Sketches and notes in the Trivulzio Codex and in MS. B which date back to the first years of Leonardo's stay in Lombardy, and which are closely related to each other, show the progressive development of the theme and seem to take into account the precedents established by Michelozzo and Francesco di Giorgio.

After a first sketch of the structure in elevation with an indication of the proportional distribution of the rooms (Codex Trivulzio, f. 27 v), Leonardo goes on to a perspectival view of the same stable in transverse section (Codex Trivulzio, f. 21 v), with a few hints on how the interior would be developed and articulated in depth. Here too, as in the preceding sketch, three arches determine the division of the width into three parts. The resulting lateral spaces, both equal in size, are a little more than half as wide and two thirds as high as the central space, the extra height of which is taken up by an arched sectional gallery with three series of small apertures. On the next storey there is a room also divided into three parts and the dividing baffles or piers keep to the partitioning of the arches below. The outside wall has some very clearly drawn arched openings of considerable size, their height being roughly two thirds of the whole wall. There is a pitched roof and the indication of a thick horizontal axis, which seems to allude to the attic floor or to a system of trusses or tie-beams. The pen stroke which connects the two columns supporting the central arch at impost level probably indicates another tie-beam. The ground floor level of the two lateral spaces is inclined towards the level of the central space, under which, as in the preceding sketch, there is an underground passage of the same width but a little less than half as high. In it too the floor is inclined towards the centre line.

The enlarged detail on the right represents an accurate perspectival section of the wall system with the indication, more lightly drawn in, of the side arch which, however, is not in scale, particularly as regards its width, and therefore can only be for the purpose of clarifying the relationship of the wall with the rest of the edifice. The section drawing of the wall shows that, starting from first floor level, it progressively widens towards the ground where it has a double thickness, so that some ducts could be inserted between the two parts of the wall directly connecting the two spaces. One of these ducts is indicated here running from a rectangular hatch on the upper floor, getting gradually larger, until it ends with a hatch on an inclined

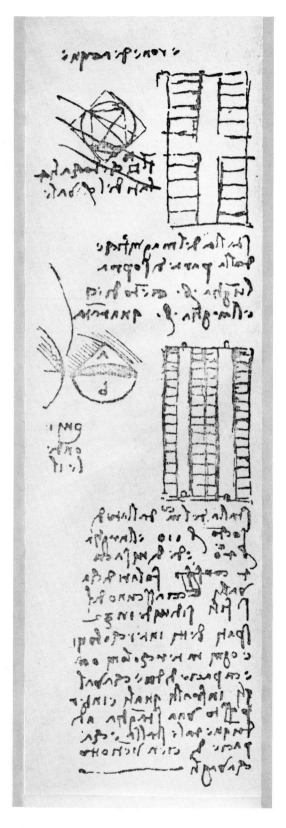

386. Plans and measurements of "Il Magnifico's stables," that is, those of Lorenzo di Piero de' Medici, nephew of the Pope and Governor of Florence, for whom Leonardo had already planned the new palace in Via Larga. The stables were built between July 1515 and January 1516 near the convent of S. Marco. On the second floor are shown wide corridors and compartments, the uses of which are not specified. Codex Atlanticus, f. 96 v-a.

plane leading to the exterior of the building. This plane is completely buried within the double thickness of the wall, while the outer part continues down to the ground, even though an opening (window or oculus) had been envisaged there, as we can see indicated on the outside of the left wall in the drawing of the whole. The thickening of the wall takes place on its inner side, moving it out of true, as can be seen on the right-hand side of the drawing of the whole and in the detail by its side, but Leonardo does consider the alternative of a clearly detached projecting wall. This is shown as an "external tooth" on the left wall, a solution which will be adopted in the subsequent drawing in MS. B. The detail on the right also shows that a quarter of the way up the arch there is a U-shaped channel, one third as wide as the thickness of the wall at that point. Next to it, in parallel, another can be noticed that, like an afterthought, seems to be reinserted in the external part of the external part of the wall. The channel, like the whole opening made in the internal thickness of the wall, is reconnected to the ground and to the main bearing-system by means of baffles which, in line with the columns, seem to carry on, uninterrupted, up to the vault. Leonardo thus considers stabling not as a single entity, but as part of a complete cycle, searching for the most suitable solution for each phase, always correlated to the whole. He therefore chooses to divide the building vertically into three areas corresponding to three separate functions, that is the area destined for stabling, on the ground floor, between the area for the collection and disposal of the sewage immediately below and the area for storing and distributing fodder on the floor above. The three areas are bound together vertically by functional bands, that is by the service shafts in the walls. The hay-loft communicates therefore with the stalls through the fodder rack, while the sloping floor of the stalls communicates through conveniently placed apertures with the underground passage for the collection of sewage below. The whole complex laid out in this way works according to a principle of gravity, while lengthwise three equally functional "bands" are formed: the two side ones, for stabling, with two rows of horses placed back to back, connected by the central one used for access, transit and service. The "bands" for stabling, in their turn, are organized in three lines dictated by the physiological needs involved in caring for the horses, and that is by having the feeding localized on the outer perimeter of the wall, forerunner of the wall with "fitted" or built-in equipment, with the drinking-trough groove below and the crib for the hay above, as a complement to the floor of the stall, which is at a slant so as to eliminate what is superfluous along the margin of the "band."

This kind of mechanized stabling, which facilitates regulated distribution of food and water, would have reduced the duties of the stablemen to a minimum, insuring at the same time the best hygienic conditions.

In MS. B, f. 38 v-39 r, we have a conclusive clarification of the project, with texts and drawings which have been reproduced several times (see for instance Firpo, pp. 90-2, and Pedretti, Richter *Commentary*, II, pp. 37-9). The drawing is no longer as schematic and summary as in the preceding studies, but is worked out with precision and a wealth of detail. From the overall view on f. 39 r, which introduces the codification of the theme of the "polita stalla," Leonardo proceeds backwards as he comments on the various functional phases, which are in fact illustrated on f. 38 v with enlarged details relating to the operations involved in providing the drinking-water, disposing of refuse into the underground passages, and supplying fodder.

Leonardo thus works out in theory the plan of a "model stable" by describing the parts of the modular network and how they are joined, both in structure and in function. It is probable therefore that the Medici stables built near S. Marco in Florence in 1515-16 go back to an idea of Leonardo's. As such they would have been part of his project, datable to exactly the same time, of building a new palace for the Medici next to the one by Michelozzo and therefore on the site which is in line with the convent of S. Marco. The note in the Codex Atlanticus, f. 96 v-a, would therefore be the record of the edifice just built, and in fact the plans and the dimensions indicated by Leonardo correspond to what it has been possible to infer about that building from the structures which were incorporated in later rebuildings and which can be reconstructed through historical and topographical documents. The examination of those structures also allows us to establish a connection with the type of "model stable" propounded by Leonardo about 1490. Next to the first plan (upper floor) we read: "The Magnifico's stables, on the upper part: one hundred and ten braccia long and forty braccia wide."

Next to the second plan (ground floor) we read: "The Magnifico's stables in the lower part: 110 braccia and 40 braccia wide; and it is divided into four rows of horses, and each one of these rows is divided into 32 spaces called intercolumniations and each intercolumniation contains two horses, between which a pole is interposed; therefore such a stable can contain one hundred and twenty-eight horses."

In this last text an error in the calculations has been noticed. Leonardo speaks of two stables next to each other, made up of four rows 110 braccia long and divided in 32 spaces each. He states that each space can contain two horses, so that the total number of horses would be double that indicated by Leonardo, 256 instead of 128. It is obvious on the other hand that Leonardo talks about two spaces in each intercolumniation, and that therefore the intercolumniations are 16 and not 32. In fact one thirty-second of 110 braccia (3.44 braccia, little more than two metres) is merely enough to contain one horse. But aside from this consideration the building itself appears to be composed of 16 intercolumniations, and as such it is structurally identical to the "model," represented in MS. B, where we see a non-bearing column corresponding to the pole which divides each intercolumniation in two.

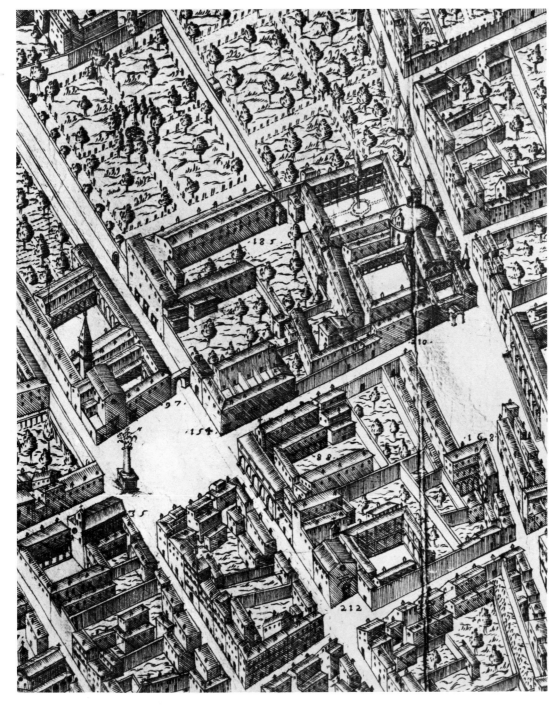

387. *Detail of Bonsignori's 1584 plan of Florence. Visible to the right of the convent of S. Marco is the imposing building of the Medici double stables, the celebrated Grand-ducal* cavallerizza *used as a school of horsemanship and sumptuously decorated by Allori with frescoes representing horses in various poses. It is the only building in Florence that Montaigne, in 1580, records with admiration. A replica of one of the original stables was built a little further away, parallel to Via della Sapienza (today Battisti) and this still exists, while the original building was drastically tampered with in more recent times.*

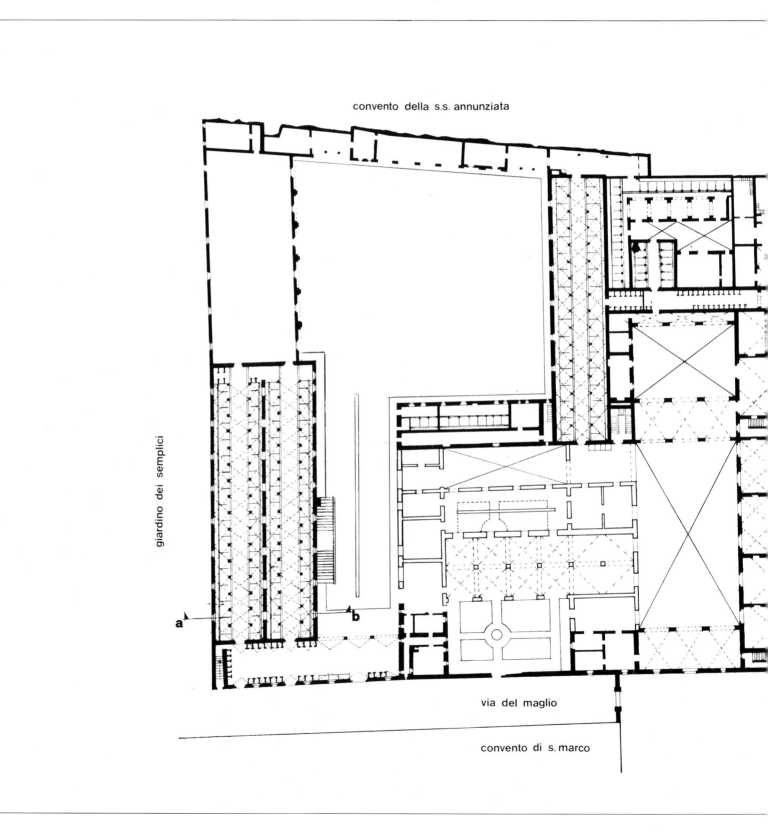

convento della s.s. annunziata

giardino dei semplici

a

b

via del maglio

convento di s. marco

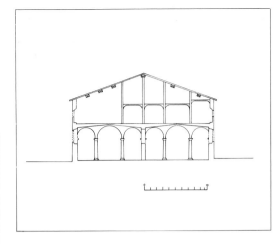

391. View of the interior of the "replica" of the Medici stables, incorporated in the building of the Istituto Geografico Militare. The accuracy of the copy, both in measurements and in details, can be ascertained from documents in the archive.

N

BRACCIA DA PANNO FIORENTINE

100

METRI

58,8

VI. France, 1517-1519

20. Romorantin

Leonardo spent the last three years of his life at Amboise as a guest of the King of France, for whom he planned a new royal residence at Romorantin. The project involved a vast complex of buildings and gardens, crossed by a tributary of the Loire, the Saudre, and would have incorporated the fifteenth-century castle in which Francis I's ancestors had lived. The project reflected the geometrical schemes of Julius Caesar's military camps in Gaul and therefore was most appropriate for the Imperial dreams of the French monarch. "On the eve of St. Anthony I returned from Romorantin to Amboise, and the King departed two days before from Romorantin," we read in the Codex Atlanticus, f. 336 v-b, a sheet of studies of 1517 for the canalization of the Sologne with the indication of the town of Romorantin and its park (lower centre). The project also involved the building of monumental stables, which are in fact indicated in the plan reproduced in plate 393 as part of a whole block. The superintendent of the royal stables was the same Galeazzo Sanseverino who had already been in contact with Leonardo twenty years before in Milan. In 1518 the King made arrangements for the financing of the canal at Romorantin. In the official documents we find no reference to other works, and Leonardo's name never appears. And yet the foundations of the new palace at Romorantin were still visible in the eighteenth century up to a height of about four metres, and the walls of the abandoned building can also be seen in prints and maps of the time. In 1519, when Leonardo was dying, an epidemic at Romorantin forced the King to shift the project to Chambord, which was already beginning to be built in that year further to the north by the river Cousson.

The possibility of Leonardo's participation in the planning of Chambord, the building which officially inaugurates the French Renaissance, has been the subject of lengthy discussion. Yet Italian ideas and concepts were already starting to filter into France at the beginning of the sixteenth century. They are especially noticeable in the castles of Le Verger and Bury, and above all at Gaillon; all constructed for people who had been in more or less direct contact with Leonardo – Marshal de Gié, Florimond Robertet, and Cardinal Georges d'Amboise. It is not surprising therefore that the first ideas for Romorantin may in fact go back to 1512, even before the new buildings of Blois, when Leonardo, in Milan, was engaged in works of architecture and sculpture for his French patrons. This would explain the famous drawing at Windsor of a grand palace by a river which is always assigned to the time of the Romorantin studies, after 1517, but which is actually on one of the sheets of the series of studies for the Trivulzio Monument, datable therefore to about 1510-12.

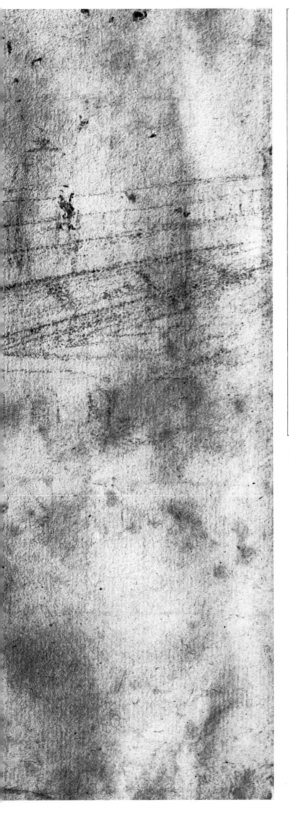

392. *Perspective view of a palace next to a river, c. 1508-10 (or later), on the reverse side of a study for the Trivulzio Monument. Windsor, RL 12292 v.*

393. *Fragment of studies for the royal palace at Romorantin, c. 1517-18. Codex Atlanticus, f. 217 v-c.*

394. *Roman military camp. Illustration by Palladio (1575) to* De Bello Gallico *of Julius Caesar.*

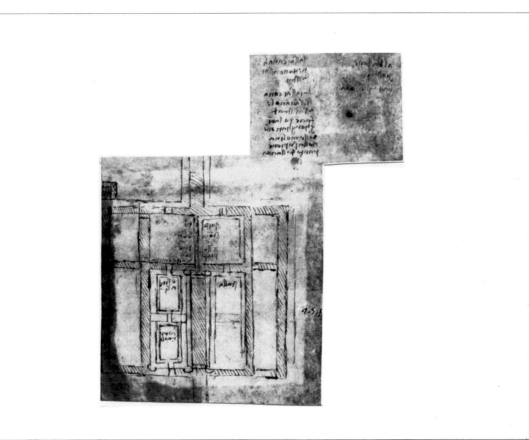

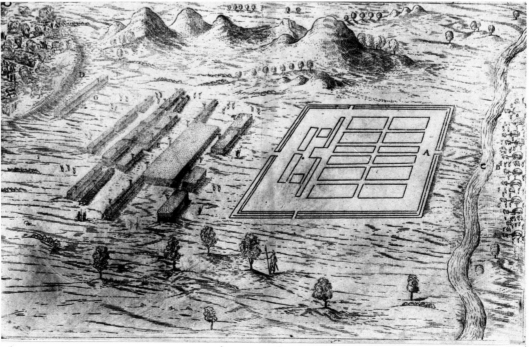

395-398. *Studies for the royal palace at Romorantin,*
c. 1517-18. Codex Atlanticus, ff. 76 v-b, 270 v-b, 217 v-b,
and interpretative diagram of a centrally-planned pavilion.

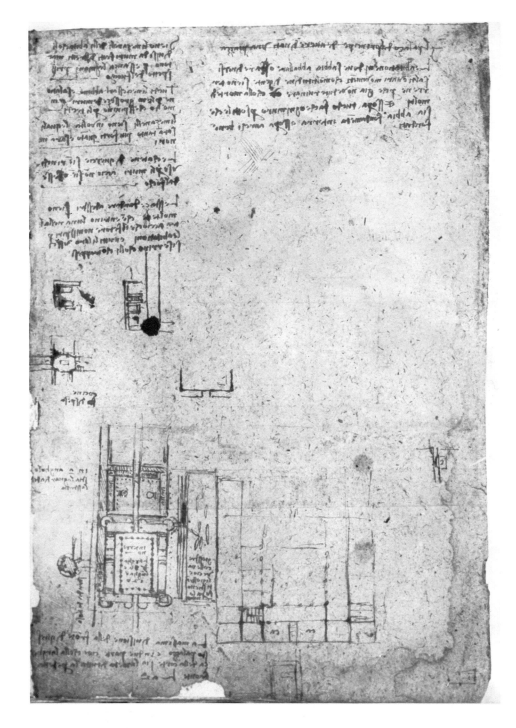

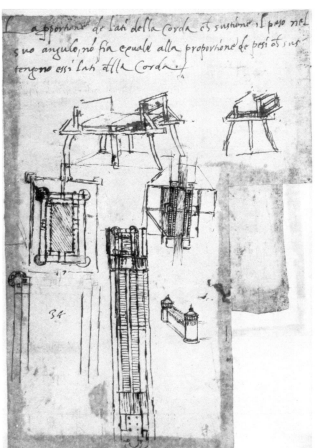

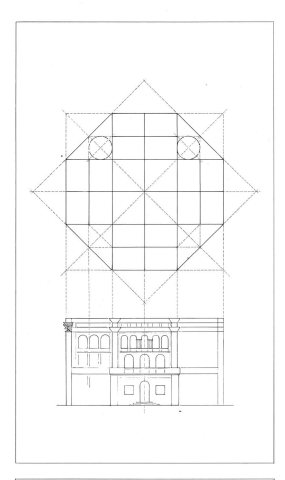

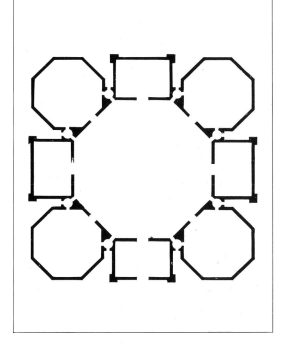

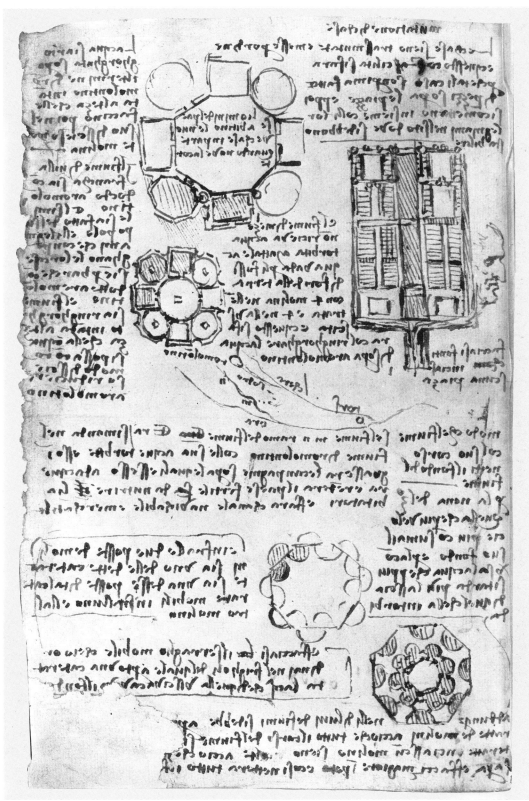

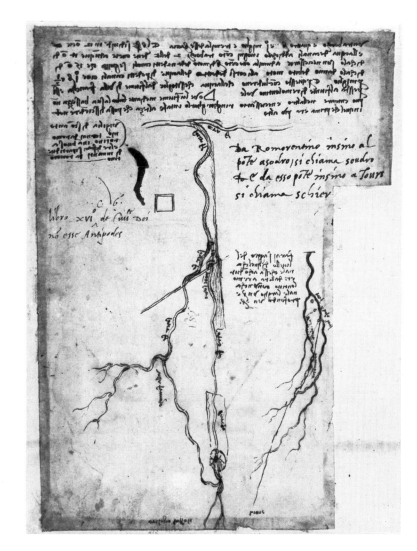

401. Studies on the canalization of the Sologne, with the record of a visit to Romorantin in 1517. Codex Atlanticus, f. 336 v-b.

402. The region of the Sologne on a map of 1682 (Bernier, Histoire de Blois).

SPECIAL PROBLEMS

A/ Fictive Architecture
B/ Theatre Architecture
C/ Ornament and Emblems
D/ Machines
E/ Industrial Design

403. Adoration of the Magi. *Florence, Galleria degli Uffizi.*
404. First proposed interpretation of the Last Supper
architecture as a stage-set fiction (Pedretti 1973).

Pictura autem dicta quasi fictura, wrote Isidore of Seville (*Ethim.* XIX, xvi) and for Leonardo too, as for the perspective painters who preceded him, painting is capable of simulating an architectural space to provide a backdrop for the characters in the *istoria*. In the choir of S. Satiro Bramante applied the pictorial element of that simulation to architecture itself. With indirect lighting and therefore no shadows, the illusion of depth was assured. However, it is by virtue of light and shadow that Piero della Francesca in the background of the Montefeltro Altarpiece reveals the use of an architecture which can be defined as *stiacciata*, as in bas-reliefs or in the theatre. Leonardo uses the same type of architectural representation in the *Last Supper*, but he makes the reading of it deliberately ambiguous by avoiding direct light and false shadows. And in fact the source of the light which defines the architecture of the *Last Supper* corresponds to the vanishing-point of the picture, so that even that contributes to the sense of accelerated perspective depth, which in turn projects forward and expands both physically and spiritually, the figures in the foreground.

Among Leonardo's earliest drawings we frequently find perspective studies that suggest practical applications, the most famous being the one for the background of the *Adoration of the Magi*. Of Donatellian lineage, it constitutes an important element not only in the study of the composition but also of the iconography of the painting. The vanishing-point, moved to the right of the central axis, presupposes in fact a space which continues beyond the right margin of the picture and alludes to an "earlier moment," as in a cinematic panning shot which has left behind the shed of the Nativity. The Virgin and Child have now taken their place at the centre of the Adoration scene, which has as its background the unfolding of the human events preceding the Advent.

In the background of the *Adoration of the Magi* there appear ruins which suggest, in their configuration, a building in the process of being restored, even though just for temporary use. And the Uffizi drawing does show, as it happens, a vast roof cover from the top of the stairs to the ruins on the right which lead to the Nativity scene purposely left out of the field.

Another of Leonardo's youthful paintings, the Uffizi *Annunciation*, whose dating to the time of *Adoration*, around 1478-80, has recently been confirmed (*Burlington Magazine*, June 1977) leads back once more to the format of Donatellian perspective, and thus to the idea of an enlarged predella (and an *Annunciation* for the predella of the *Madonna di Piazza* by Verrocchio in Pistoia, of 1478, is also attributable to Leonardo). This would suggest a more immediate relationship with the architectural framework for which the painting was destined, whether that was an altar whose volumes in frontal view would have been continued with lateral alignment, or a wall such as the one in the chapel of the Cardinal of Portugal in S. Miniato, where a similar *Annunciation* by Baldovinetti seems to continue the idea of the decorative marble panelling of the walls.

Should we in fact be able to establish the setting for which the Uffizi *Annunciation* was destined, it might be possible

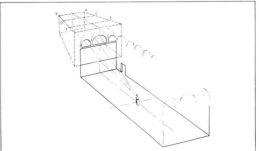

406. *Studies of architecture in perspective, probably for paintings*, c. 1479. *Codex Atlanticus, f. 28 r-b.*

407. *Perspective studies*, c. 1490. Oxford, Ashmolean Museum.

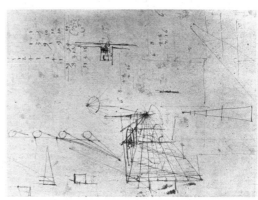

to explain the curious "error" of perspective in the relationship between the Virgin and the highly elaborate lectern. This error perhaps takes into account an optical or iconographical situation. Some sketches on a sheet of the Codex Atlanticus datable to 1479, f. 28 r-b, demonstrate that Leonardo had considered the perspectival view of a portico of the type traditionally associated with the Annunciation scene.

Contemporary with this, or a little later, comes the *Saint Jerome* in the Vatican, in which the architectural element seems to be limited to the small temple in the right background, which could be interpreted either as a recollection of the Albertian façade of S. Maria Novella or as an anticipation of the studies on the Vitruvian basilica begun in Bramante's circle in Milan. On the other hand, the whole composition of the painting, in each and every one of its elements, from the human figure to the lion, and from the rocks in the foreground to those at the back, is articulated architecturally as if it had been conceived in plan.

It is not by chance that the pose of the saint anticipates that of the kneeling man – Bramante himself – on the frontispiece of the *Antiquarie prospetiche romane*.

Leonardo's later paintings can also be explained in this way, from the *Virgin of the Rocks* (especially the second version) to the *Mona Lisa*, the *St. Anne* and even the *Leda*. In all of these the concept of the nucleus in relation to the organic element which surrounds it comes to the fore as in the famous drawing of the foetus in the womb – a concept which is reflected in Bramante's projects for the Tempietto and the new St. Peter's. The generating forces of nature take on tangible form in a perspectival organization of space which makes use of curved lines that suggest a sense of continuous rotation, as of water or wind. Perspective studies on the verso of a sheet from early 1490 in Oxford seem to hint already at the setting of the *Last Supper*. There was probably a more elaborate architectural background in a cartoon now lost which belonged to Pompeo Leoni, and which represented, according to an inventory of 1614, "a life-size female saint, from the waist up, in black pencil with a perspective view of palaces," a description which seems to anticipate portraits by Raphael and Giulio Romano.

The analyses of architectural perspectives in Leonardo's paintings, on the following pages, have been carried out by the architect Giovanni Degl'Innocenti and his collaborators.

Within the general framework of the reinterpretation of fifteenth-century Tuscan and Lombard painting, importance has been increasingly attached to studying the ways in which the various generations and schools of artists succeeded in creating an illusion of space two-dimensionally, either by geometric construction or by suggestion through form and colour. To this end, theoretical studies have been combined with direct, often graphic, analyses of the principal works in question. Interest in this type of research has been further stimulated by the discovery that the architectural backgrounds of certain masterpieces, once transcribed into plan through a system of trial and error, reveal forms, dimensions and spaces very different from those which most observers have supposed. Our ways of seeing have been influenced by modern artistic experiences, we read paintings in a different way and accept different narrative and symbolic conventions so that we cannot correctly interpret space in fifteenth-century painting without a preliminary geometrical analysis.
Accordingly, I have based my research on the principle of retracing the artist's design process, using his own tools: pencils, pens, squares, rulers, compasses and paper of a similar size. Having paper of the right dimensions is, in fact, absolutely essential. Obviously such a method is not intended to verify the objectivity of results, as if nature and space were mechanically transposed in the painting, but rather to arrive at a better understanding of the painter's modes of procedure, the alternatives that he has chosen and even more importantly those that he rejected, the arbitrariness deliberately introduced. It is evident that a geometrical method of analysis can only be applied when the artist himself shows that he has organized his pictorial space through a geometrical method, and when the alternatives can be measured, as variants of the norm or of tradition.
To confine the investigation to Leonardo's works, which will be examined and discussed here as an example of the application of a more accurate method of reconstruction, is justified precisely by this self-limitation. Nonetheless, the method of analysis has been rigorous, in order to provide a stable criterion for comparison or simply for description and comment.

I. *Mistakes and Misunderstandings*

Previous sporadic perspective reconstructions of works by Leonardo da Vinci confirm the limits, but also the possibilities of this method. The reconstruction of the *Adoration of the Magi* by Jean Thiis (*Leonardo da Vinci. I: The Florentine years of Leonardo and Verrocchio*, London 1914, pp. 211-17) reveals aesthetic and interpretative preoccupations which detract from its scientific rigour. The author has not been able to avoid misunderstandings that stem principally from the popularization of nineteenth-century realist principles. In fact, he identifies the illusionistic space with the real one, confusing the coherence of the representation with the mathematical realism of proportions and measurements: he is inclined to correct and simplify. I should mention, apropos of this, Pierre Francastel's still very pertinent remark that reconstructions must enable one "to decipher the *segno*," or "to systematically

explore the volumes organized not by chance but by the will of the artist..." (P. Francastel, *Études de Sociologie de l'art*, Paris 1970). Piero Sanpaolesi's analysis in *Leonardo Saggi e Ricerche* (Rome 1954, pp. 33-9) shows another side of the problem in proposing a partial analysis based on mistaken premises.
In fact, in basing it on the simple convergence of the orthogonals towards a single point, he neglects the complexity of the geometric perspective found in the works of Leonardo and other artists of the fifteenth century, that is to say the foreshortenings of the parallel transversals of the picture, since two or more vanishing-points were often deliberately used in order to modify the too rigid effect springing from a rigorous use of geometric perspective. In this case it is the horizon line which oscillates, while the position of the observer remains fixed.

II. *An "Indeterminate Equation"*

Perspective, whether geometric, chromatic or allusive, is the result of transferring a series of three-dimensional variables into a two-dimensional series. The way of describing those variables pertaining to the drawing by means of straight and curved lines, has already been codified by Desargues, Monge, Hauck and others. According to their formulation the analytical problem is expressed by the following relation:

$$n\ (x,\ y,\ z) \leftrightarrow n\ (x''',\ y''')$$

(*Diagram No. 1*)
or the correspondence between the coordinates of the real or fictitious space and the coordinates describing the two dimensions of the space in the painting; "n" stands for the number of significant points that describe the architecture. The painting furnishes one side of the equation, i.e. the second; and this must of necessity lead us back to the first if the operation carried out by the painter is geometrically correct.
Yet the perspective, even if one does not interpret it as theatrical scenography, is not an autonomous element, but a type of all-embracing environment that involves not only the objects and figures represented, but also the observer, designated by "r" as another term of the equation. This term "r" is in direct relationship with the real or fictitious architecture, but not with the perspective image, which depends solely on the way in which the three-dimensional space is reflected on the plane of projection. As its position in space is well defined, it takes part in the same system of reference as the real space; but it does not belong to the same system of reference as the painting. The most paradoxical case is that of the *Last Supper*, placed high on the back wall of the refectory of S. Maria delle Grazie but designed to be observed at eye-level. A more complete formula now would be:

$$n\ (x''',\ y''') = f\ [n\ (x,\ y,\ z),\ r]$$

In relation to the real or fictitious space, that is the three-dimensional space, the observer "r" can take up an infinite number of positions, defined by the following variables:
(*Diagram No. 2*)
x_0, y_0, z_0: spatial coordinates of the observation point. Furthermore, the relationship between observer and three-

dimensional object is defined by the variables:
β, ϑ: horizontal and vertical angles of collimation of the point of sight, that is the inclinations of the direction of observation in regard to the planes (x, z) and (y, z) of the system of reference.
d: distance of the observer from the picture plane (or plane of projection). If one excludes any effect of anamorphosis, the plane of projection, coinciding with the painting, will always come out orthogonal to the direction of observation.
Analytically stated it emerges, according to the formulation provided by the architect Pier Luigi Bandini, as a generic point, $P_i \equiv (xi, yi, zi)$
$x_i''', y_i''' = f\ [(xi, yi, zi),\ r\ (x_0,\ y_0,\ z_0,\ \beta,\ \vartheta,\ d)]$
or in explicit form:
see Diagram 1.

$$(1)\ \begin{cases} x'i = xi \cos \beta - zi \sin \beta \\ y'i = yi \\ z'i = zi \cos \beta + xi \sin \beta \end{cases} \text{rotation around the axis } y$$

$$(2)\ \begin{cases} x''i = x'i \\ y''i = y'i \cos \vartheta + z'i \sin \vartheta \\ z''i = z'i \cos \vartheta - y'i \sin \vartheta \end{cases} \text{rotation around the axis } x$$

$$(3)\ \begin{cases} x'''i = x''i\ \dfrac{1}{1 + \dfrac{z''i}{d}} \\ y'''i = y''i\ \dfrac{1}{1 + \dfrac{z''i}{d}} \end{cases} \text{perspective reduction}$$

In the process of perspective construction, we begin by knowing the term on the right of the equation and must obtain the term on the left for each significant point. In the process of perspective reconstruction on the other hand, we know the term on the left (measurable on the painting) and must discover the one on the right.
As we have already noted, the observer of the picture does not belong to the system, that is to the frame of reference, of the fictitious three-dimensional space of the painting itself. In changing his position he can create further foreshortenings, for example seeing the painting or fresco from the side as in an anamorphosis and requiring the artist to make continuous modifications so as to introduce the necessary corrections for what we could define as random viewing. This clearly distinguishes the perspective study of a painting from the perspective study of a photograph of an existing architectural setting, since in the latter the connection between the spectator and the camera is provided for in a mechanical and determined way. A chief difference in the possibility of interpreting the painted perspective space is precisely in this condition of viewing, even if considered random and subjective. In stereophotogrammetry for example, the spectator and the

machine must coincide exactly, that is the two photographs must collimate in the optical apparatus (stereocomparator). In fact, only in this way can one decipher the message contained in the image. This already makes the use of photogrammetry incongruous for paintings, whose placement has been in a certain sense free, and perhaps planned with flexibility in mind by the painter, who was interested in formal effects, favoured by an arbitrarily selected distance point, more than in naturalistic results. Moreover, photogrammetry needs two differentiated views of the same object, and therefore it cannot be used when only dealing with a single two-dimensional reduction of the three-dimensional space as is furnished by a painting, even if a camera obscura is used to realize it.

However, it is possible that analogous results can be obtained by mechanical methods based on the preceding considerations, but it is necessary that the painting has an exactly central perspective. This means that the angles β and ϑ correspond to zero degrees so that the direction of observation has no inclination. On the basis of the preceding systems of equations (1), (2) and (3) one obtains:

$$(4) \begin{cases} x'''i = \dfrac{(xi + zi)\ d}{zi + d} \\[2ex] y'''i = \dfrac{yi \cdot d}{zi + d} \end{cases}$$

The system is characterized by four unknowns, $xi,\ yi,\ zi$ and d, in two equations. The presence of four unknowns in two equations makes the system insoluble, but one can determine geometrically the position of d (common to all the points) as the intersection between the horizon line and the diagonal of a regular form in plan, defined by two points P_1 and P_2:

$$d = x_1''' - y_1''' \frac{x_2''' - x_1'''}{y_2''' - y_1'''}$$

(Diagram No. 3)
The system has thus been reduced to three unknowns. The possibility of resolving it and thus measuring the artist's fictitious perspective space are the following:
a/ To find another mathematical formulation of the equations, by writing a third equation which offers us another given quantity, founded on the distance point;
b/ To identify a regular geometric form and on the basis of this to establish one of the unknown coordinates.
This signifies that the possibilities of error derive usually from a mistake in calculating the distance, or from a misunderstanding of the geometrical forms considered regular and chosen as reference for the coordinates. To avoid these errors one must have a very accurate graphic delineation, extracted from the painting, yet some absolutely insoluble problems exist, as the mathematical formulae presented here demonstrate. In fact, the observer by belonging to a system other than that of the painting, is excluded from any possibility of verifying how the space within the picture was organized unless the artist makes

the task easy by giving him: *a* a series of clearly identical architectural forms or *b* precise and unambiguous geometrical forms. However, even in these cases it is always possible that the artist had recourse to certain tricks in order to amplify or reduce the elements in the painting to create illusions as in theatrical scenery. No system of reconstruction, including my own, can avoid these risks. The essential procedure is always the same: the determination of the distance, by drawing a diagonal extended as far as the horizon line, and the calculation of the modular architectural elements which allow the more or less exact establishment, according to the case, of the distances of the architecturally constructed surroundings.

The principal paradox is that the perspective construction, as a reduction of a three-dimensional space to a two-dimensional plane, is unambiguous while the reconstruction *a posteriori* from the two-dimensional plane to three dimensions is not, and allows for numerous variants unless the system is extremely detailed. This means that the picture surface functions essentially as a message which is decoded on the basis of collective, traditional and unconscious visual habits. This is basically the reason why a western perspective construction is not understood by those peoples unaccustomed to these graphic codes, or by animals who may be shown it (notwithstanding the legends told by writers of antiquity). In reality, the only possible verification is that of the historical consistency with other examples and prototypes, to which these perspectives can be compared.

The system is neither analytically nor geometrically soluble. Nevertheless, being a question of a manual process, our knowledge of contemporary architectural projects can help us by comparisons. It is unimaginable, in fact, that painters would have represented a completely different architecture from what was actually being built, or at least designed, in their locality. The public would not have been able to relate to it, just as we, strangers to that time and those traditions, no longer relate to it.

III. *Application of the Reconstructive Process*
The process of reconstruction which we have thus formulated is applied here to five works by Leonardo:

1/ *Annunciation*. Florence, Uffizi, *c.* 1475-78.
2/ *Annunciation*. Paris, Louvre, *c.* 1478.
3/ *St. Jerome*: Detail of temple in background. Rome, Pinacoteca Vaticana, *c.* 1480-81.
4/ *Adoration of the Magi*. Florence, Uffizi, *c.* 1481-82.
5/ *The Last Supper*. Milan, S. Maria delle Grazie (refectory), *c.* 1495-97.

We have made the basic assumption that all the architecture represented in the paintings is regular, that is that the walls or the lines that describe the floors are parallel with each other as these parts of the architecture seem to be made up of square or rectangular elements and not oblique ones or trapezia or rhombi.
In all the works the vanishing-point was easily identified by tracing the orthogonals on the picture plane indicated by the floors, or in the case of the *Last Supper* by the coffered

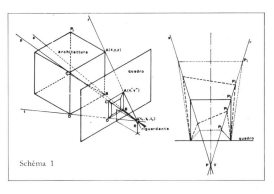

Schéma 1

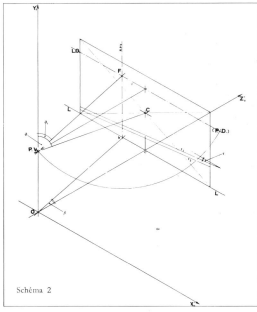

Schéma 2

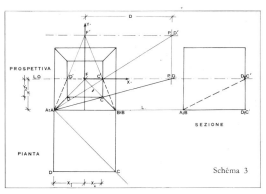

Schéma 3

411. Annunciation. *Florence, Galleria degli Uffizi.*

412. *Diagrammatic analysis of the fundamental elements of the perspective. Reconstruction in plan and lateral perspective.*

413. *Axonometric diagram of the architecture represented in the painting.*

ceiling. Then by drawing the diagonals of the squares formed by the floor or the coffering, without worrying as to whether they were squares or rectangles, we established the distance point of each work. To check the uniform nature of the perspective constructions we drew other diagonals to the same distance-points, with positive results. Once the vanishing- and distance-points were known, the floors (for the *Last Supper* the ceiling) were completed so as to translate onto the picture plane the whole architectonic setting. The height of the observer is considered to correspond to the distance between the horizon line and the line in which the floor intersects the picture plane, that is where it begins to be visible once the architectonic setting has been completed.

On the basis of the following parameters: the vanishing-point, distance, position and height of the observer, and the distance-point, and given the richness of architectural reference introduced by the painter, it was possible to construct a very detailed section of the surroundings. Always supposing that the architecture is regular, we used a similar procedure to reconstruct the plan which, when compared with the section, allowed us to establish the real dimensions of the squares on the floor, or ceiling. The observer in this case functions as an instrument of trigonometric measurement, and possible errors stem only from an erroneous measurement of the distance of the observer and of his height in relation to the plane of the floor. To avoid these errors we repeatedly checked these paradigms. We accompanied the work of graphic reconstruction, whose main stages are shown here with drawings, by the trigonometric calculation of all the intersections. The results are summarized in the perspective schedules accompanying every work. This research on Leonardo's paintings has been notably facilitated by the opportunity of repeatedly examining the originals, and by the availability of unframed photographs realized on plates in a parallel plane and with lenses that give minimal distortion. Checks have shown that the photographs are remarkably faithful to the paintings. Our calculations have deliberately ignored the dimensions of the human figures in the paintings as this would relate purely to religious iconography and the organization of the narrative. Our research was directed only to the architectonic elements.

1/ Annunciation. Florence, Uffizi. Oil on panel, *c.* 1475-78.

Description of the picture plane
Form: rectangular
Height: 104 cm (corresponding to 1.78 *braccio a panno fiorentino* or 21.38 *crazie*).
Width: 217 cm (or 3.72 *braccia a panno fiorentino* or 44.62 *crazie*).
Perimeter: 642 cm (11 *braccia a panno fiorentino* or 132 *crazie*).
Area = 22568 cm² (6.63 *braccia quadre fiorentine* or 2652 *soldi quadri*).

Description of the fundamental elements of the perspective
A. INTERNAL ORIENTATION:
a) *Coordinates of the principal point (vanishing-point)*

$$F \equiv (-0.3; +85.8; +108.35)$$

All the orthogonal lines on the picture plane come together regularly in a single principal or vanishing-point.
b) *Principal distance*

$$D = F. - P.D. = 108.35 \text{ cm}$$

(corresponding to 1.86 *braccia a panno fiorentine* or 22.3 *crazie*).
By extending the sides of the small diminishing squares forming the checkerboard of the floor, we note:
1) The lines running towards the right side of the painting meet in a single point

$$D_1 = F. - P.D._{.1} = 108.8 \text{ cm}$$

2) The lines running towards the left side of the painting converge on the horizon line (L.O.) in an area reducible to a segment whose barycentre has been calculated:

$$D_2 = F. - P.D._{.2} = 107.88 \text{ cm}$$

Note also that the location of the Distance Points (P.D.) is within the area of the picture plane and very near the right and left sides of the painting.

A. 1) FUNDAMENTAL ELEMENTS DERIVED FROM THE PRECEDING:
c) *Horizon Line* (L.O.)
This lies on the surface of the picture plane, passes through F and is parallel to the ground plane α

$$L.O. \equiv (0; +85.8; +108.35)$$

d) *Central Vertical Axis* (R.P.V.)
This lies on the surface of the picture plane, passes through F and is perpendicular to the ground plane α

$$R.P.V. \equiv (-0.3; 0; +108.35)$$

e) *Ground Line* (L.)
Its trace lies in the ground plane and it is perpendicular to the axis Z'_0. It is located 14.3 cm beneath the base of the painting (corresponding to 0.25 *braccio a panno fiorentino* or 2.9 *crazie*).

Graphic determination of L: the painting shows that the foreshortening of the first row of squares on the floor is only partial.
Thanks to the lines produced to the distance-points (P.D.) from the edges of a floor square, one finds by their intersection the location of the first transversal which completely describes, and in a measurable way, the foreshortened lozenges of the floor. By convention we make the transversal thus identified coincide with the ground line L.
B. EXTERNAL ORIENTATION:
a) *Coordinates of the Point of Sight*

$$P.V. \equiv (0; +85.8; 0)$$

b) *Angle of direction or azimuthal angle*

$$\beta = 0° \ 9' \ 31''$$

c) *Zenithal angle*
ϑ_F = angle of elevation or collimation from P.V. on F = 90°
ϑ_C = angle of declination or collimation from P.V. towards C = 100° 22' 6''
d) *Angle of lateral inclination:* τ = nil
C. FIELD OF VISION:
a) *Span of the angle of the cone of vision, by convention* = 60°
b) *Radius of the visual circle on the painting (with centre in F)* = 62.6 cm
c) *Area of the picture plane within the visual circle* 10033.553 cm² (corresponding to 44.46% of the entire area)
d) *Area of the picture plane outside the visual circle* 12534.447 cm² (that is 55.54% of the entire area)
e) *Angle of observation of the entire painting from the Point of Sight* (P.V.)
reads vertically $\sigma = 50° \ 6' \ 3''$
reads horizontally $\gamma = 90° \ 4' \ 45''$
The perspective reconstruction diagrams have been made to a scale 1:6.11 in respect to the original. The axonometric projection has been made to the same scale. The margin of error in appraising the distance is 2.28943 cm in the real scale. The graphic error is about 2 mm.
In his essay "Botticelli, les Pollaiuoli et Verrocchio" (*Rivista d'Arte*, II-III February-March, 1905, p. 37, note 2) Jacques Mesnil had already noted that in the painting "... le

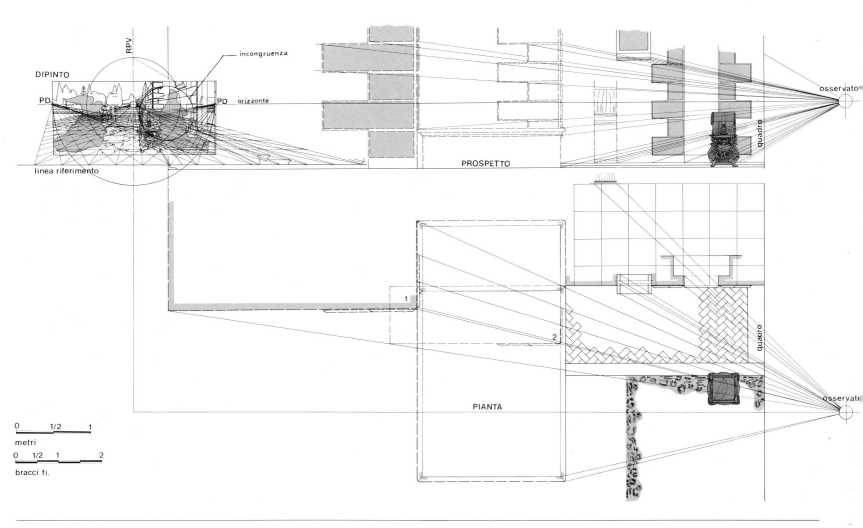

DIPINTO

RPV

incongruenza

PD   PD   orizzonte

linea riferimento

PROSPETTO

osservato

quadro

PIANTA

quadro

osservato

1

2

0   1/2   1

metri

0   1/2   1   2

bracci fi.

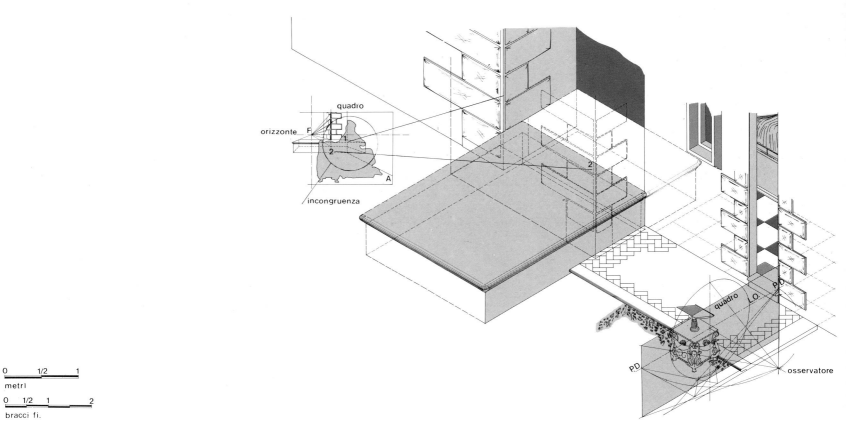

quadro

orizzonte   F

1

2

A

incongruenza

quadro   L.O.   P.D.

P.D.   osservatore

0   1/2   1

metri

0   1/2   1   2

bracci fi.

414. Annunciation. *Paris, Louvre.*

415. *Schematic analysis on the perspective image of its fundamental elements. Reconstruction of the architecture in plan and lateral perspective.*

416. *Axonometric diagram of the architecture represented in the painting.*

bras droit de la Vierge est dans une position absolument irréalisable: la main droite se trouve à gauche du livre posé sur le pupitre, c'est-à-dire tout à fait à l'avant-plan, en avant du bras gauche et même du génou gauche; l'avant-bras droit est à peu près parallèle à la surface du tableau; de cet avant-bras à l'épaule droite, il reste un éspace obliquement de façon à former avec l'avant-bras un angle qui ne serait possible à réaliser que dans le cas d'une rupture complète de l'articulation du coude..." This observation is just and can be implicitly confirmed from the diagram even though in our reconstruction, as we have already said, we have not considered the dimensions and placement of the figures. However, we do not agree with the same author's opinion, which conforms with those of Morelli (1883) and Cavalcaselle (1908), that "Quant à ce... tableau il m'est impossible de l'attribuer... à Léonard." The treatment of religious iconography, the pictorial organization of the narrative, and various elements of style all point to Leonardo as the author of the work, and the most recent studies confirm this.

If on the perspective image we determine by geometrical construction the intersection of the orthogonal that defines the wall of the edifice on the floor with the perpendicular that limits the low wall, we find that the latter is constructed like an enormous stone slab that penetrates the wall itself, and the projecting position of the front edge of the building coincides with the furthest face of the slab. However, the observer has the sensation of extreme regularity and proportional depth in this part, which permits him to interpret it as a low wall or partial diaphragm between the scene and infinity. There is therefore a discrepancy between the observer's interpretation and the geometric construction which at first sight, without the results of the perspective analysis, is concealed by the impression of regularity. Leonardo, who perhaps wanted to suggest a greater depth of the architectural setting in this part of the painting, has masked the discordance by concealing it behind the figure of the Virgin.

2/ *Annunciation.* Paris, Louvre. Tempera on panel, *c.* 1478.

Description of the picture plane
Form: rectangular
Height: 14 cm (corresponding to 0.24 *braccia a panno fiorentino* or to 2.9 *crazie*).
Width: 59 cm (1.01 *braccio a panno fiorentino* or 12.1 *crazie*).
Perimeter: 146 cm (2.5 *braccia a panno fiorentino* or 30 *crazie*).
Area: 826 cm² (corresponding to 0.048 *braccia quadre fiorentine* or 97 *soldi quadri*).

Description of the fundamental elements of the perspective
A. INTERNAL ORIENTATION:
a) *Coordinates of the principal or vanishing-point*
    F ≡ (− 8.26; + 14.6; + 52.9)
All the orthogonals of the picture plane converge regularly in a single vanishing-point.
b) *Principal distance*

D = F − P.D. = 53.57 cm
(corresponding to 0.92 *braccia a panno fiorentino* or 11 *crazie*).
A. 1) FUNDAMENTAL ELEMENTS DERIVED FROM THE PRECEDING:
a) *Horizon Line*
    L.O. ≡ (0; + 14.6; = 52.9)
b) *Central Vertical Axis*
    R.P.V. ≡ (− 8.26; 0; + 52.9)
c) *Ground Line* (L.)
is located 0.83 cm below the base of the painting.
Determination of L. The reconstruction of a checkerboard floor of diminishing squares was made. The construction plane was deduced from the completion of the base of the lectern. The reconstruction having been made, the transversal in the foreground extends out from the base of the painting.
B. EXTERNAL ORIENTATION:
a) *Coordinates of the Point of Sight*
    P.V. ≡ (0; + 14.6; 0)
b) *Angle of direction or azimuthal angle*
    $\beta = 8° 52' 10''$
c) *Zenithal angle*
ϑ_F = angle of elevation or collimation from P.V. on F = 90°
ϑ_C = angle of declination or collimation from P.V. towards C = 97° 17' 43"
d) *Angle of lateral inclination* τ = nil
C. VISUAL FIELD:
a) *Span of the angle of the visual cone, by convention* = 60°
b) *Radius of the visual circle on the painting* = 30.6 cm (corresponding to 0.52 *braccio a panno fiorentino* or 6.3 *crazie*).
c) *The painting is entirely comprehended within the visual circle and its surface is 28.1% of that circle.*
d) *Angle of observation of entire painting from Point of Sight (P.V.)*
    reads vertically σ = 14° 39' 40"
    reads horizontally γ = 58° 15' 50"
The perspective and axonometric reconstruction diagrams have been made to the scale 1:1.54 in respect to the original. The error in the appraisal of the distance in the real scale is about 0.541223 cm. The graphic error is about 2 mm.
The *Annunciation* in the Louvre, although similar in its narrative organization to the *Annunciation* in the Uffizi, offers in contrast to it a regular perspective system.
The vanishing-point is located a little below the upper

edge of the panel and is not central but displaced slightly to the left. The two distance-points fall respectively outside the right and left margins of the painting and their distance from the vanishing-point, measured on the horizon line, is only slightly less than the width of the painting. Some time ago this work was the subject of a graphic analysis by Nielsen (*Leonardo da Vinci og hans Forhold til Perspektiven*, Copenhagen 1897). Our respective surveys differ substantially in their results; in fact in that study the vanishing-point falls outside of the painting. It was this fact that brought Mesnil to state that the work was not by Leonardo and to observe the non-coincidence between the painted horizon, the end of the mountains in the background and the geometric horizon.

3/ *St. Jerome*: detail of the temple in the background. Oil on panel. Rome, Pinacoteca Vaticana, *c.* 1480-81.

Description of the picture plane
Form: rectangular
Height: 103 cm (1.76 *braccio a panno fiorentino* or 21.2 *crazie*)
Width: 75 cm (1.29 *braccio a panno fiorentino* or 15.4 *crazie*)
Perimeter: 356 cm (6 *braccia a panno fiorentino* or 73.2 *crazie*)
Area: 7725 cm² (2.3 *braccia quadre fiorentine* or 907.8 *soldi quadri*)
Note that for this study only the part of the painting where the building is represented has been considered. This part can be inscribed in a rectangle whose sides are distant from the edges of the painting, respectively: from the lower edge 75 cm, from the right edge 6.5 cm.

Description of the fundamental elements of the perspective
A. INTERNAL ORIENTATION:
a) *Coordinates of the Principal (Vanishing) Point*
    P ≡ (0; + 9; + 28.2)
b) *Principal Distance*
    D = P.V. − P = 28.2 cm
(corresponding to 0.48 *braccio a panno fiorentino* or 5.8 *crazie*)
A. 1) FUNDAMENTAL ELEMENTS DERIVED FROM THE PRECEDING:
c) *Horizon Line* (L.O.)
This lies on the surface of the picture plane, passes through P, F_1, F_2 and is parallel to the ground plane α. It is, however, inclined in respect to the base of the painting 4° 40' 39".
d) *Central Vertical Axis* (R.P.V.)
This lies on the surface of the picture plane, passes through

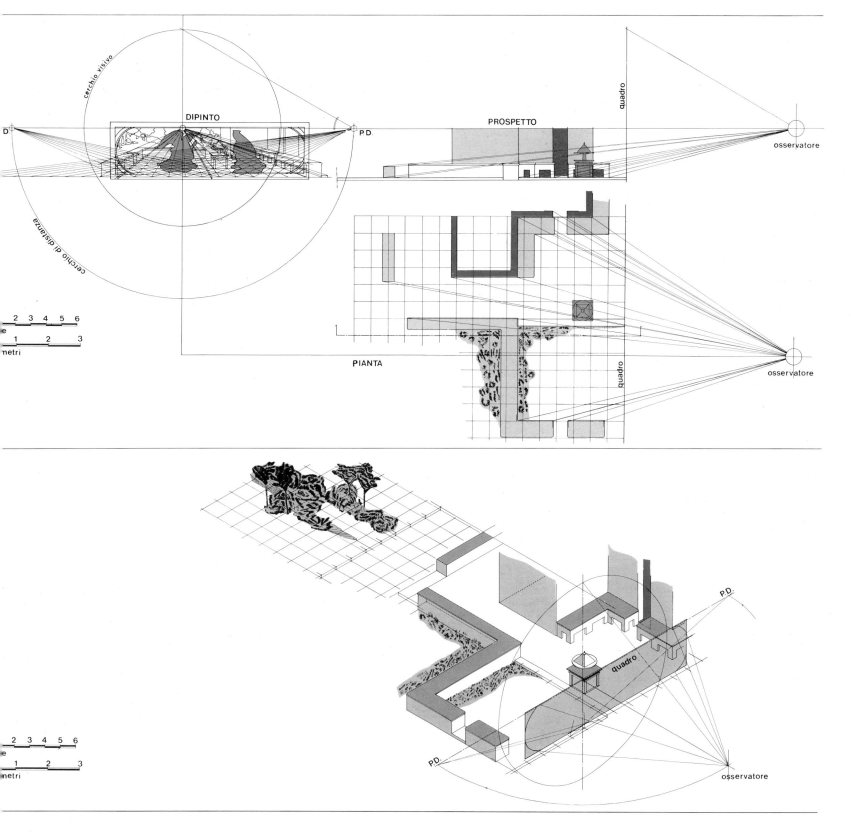

cerchio visivo

DIPINTO

PROSPETTO

quadro

osservatore

D

P.D.

cerchio di distanza

2 3 4 5 6

1 2 3

e

metri

PIANTA

quadro

osservatore

2 3 4 5 6

1 2 3

e

metri

P.D.

quadro

P.D.

osservatore

417. St. Jerome. *Vatican, Pinacoteca.*

418. Detail of the St. Jerome: *the building shown in perspective. Axonometric view of the reconstruction of part of the building, façade and right side.*

419. Detail of the St. Jerome: *the building shown in perspective. Schematic analysis of the fundamental elements of the perspective and reconstruction in plan.*

P and is orthogonal to the ground plane α. It is, however, inclined in respect to the base of the painting 88° 59′ 60″.

e) *Ground Line (L.)*

By convention this is perpendicular to the axis Z'_0, and passes through the corner *A* which is located 6.46 cm from the right edge of the painting and 74.99 cm from its base. The point *A* is the corner of the building that is best distinguished in the perspective and by convention has been assumed as the point united to the projection plane.

B. EXTERNAL ORIENTATION:

a) *Coordinates of the Point of Sight*

$\quad$ P.V. $\equiv$ (0; + 9. 0)

b) *Angle of Direction*

$\quad$ β by convention from the Point of Sight centres directly on *P*, i.e. the angle β is zero.

c) *Zenithal angle*

ϑ_F = angle of elevation or collimation from P.V. on *P* = 90°

d) *Angle of lateral inclination* τ = nil

$\quad$ With respect to the conventional triad of axes X'_0, Y'_0, Z'_0, of the rectangular coordinate system coincident with the rectangle in which only the perspective image of the building is inscribed.

$\quad$ τ = 4° 40′ 39″ with regard to the base of the painting

C. VISUAL FIELD:

a) *Span of the angle of the visual cone, by convention* = 60°

b) *Radius of the visual circle on the painting (with its centre in P)* = 16.28 cm (corresponding to 0.28 *braccia a panno fiorentino* or 3.35 *crazie*)

c) *Area within the visual circle* = 832.8 cm² (corresponding to 0.24 *braccia quadre fiorentine* or 97.9 *soldi quadri*)

The image of the building in perspective is entirely contained within the visual circle.

4/ Adoration of the Magi. Florence, Uffizi, oil on panel, *c.* 1481-82.

4a/ Perspective study for the *Adoration of the Magi,* Florence, Uffizi, Gabinetto delle Stampe e dei Disegni. Silverpoint gone over in pen and bistre, with traces of white lead, *c.* 1481-82.

Description of the picture plane

Form: rectangular

Height: 163 mm (corresponding to 0.28 *braccia a panno fiorentino* or 3.35 *crazie*)

Base: 290 mm (corresponding to 0.50 *braccia a panno fiorentino* or 6 *crazie*)

Perimeter: 906 mm (corresponding to 1.55 *braccia a panno fiorentino* or 18.6 *crazie*)

Area: 47270 m² (corresponding to 0.14 *braccia quadre* or 55.5 *soldi quadri*).

Description of the fundamental elements of the perspective

A. INTERNAL ORIENTATION:

a) *Coordinates of the Vanishing-Point*

$\quad$ F $\equiv$ (+ 3.5; + 8.9; + 83.4)

All the orthogonals of the checkerboard floor converge in a single vanishing-point marked by the artist.

b) *Principal Distance*

$\quad$ D = F − P.D. = 83.45 cm

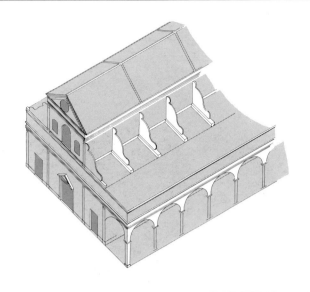

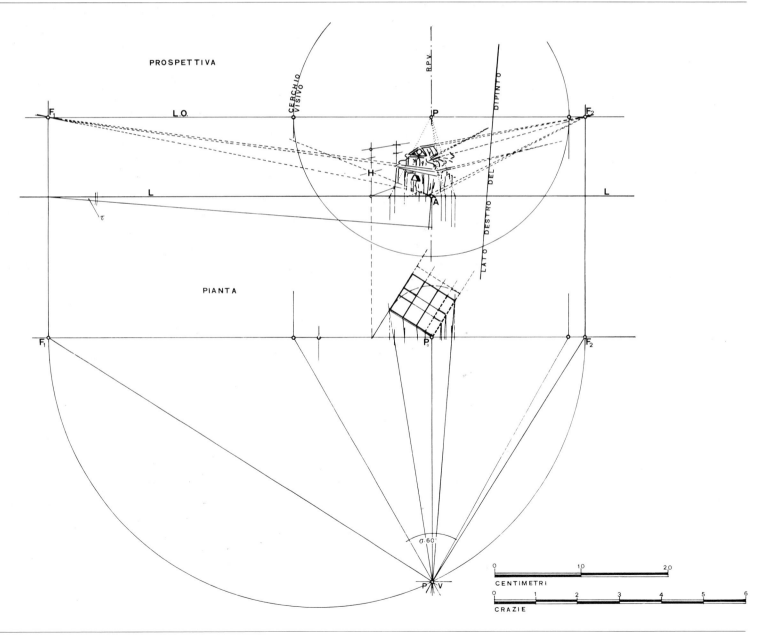

PROSPETTIVA

CERCHIO VISIVO

L.O.

R.P.V.

P

F₁

F₂

DIPINTO

L

L

A

H

τ

LATO DESTRO DEL

PIANTA

F₁

F₂

P₀

σ·60

P·V

CENTIMETRI

0   10   20

CRAZIE

0   1   2   3   4   5   6

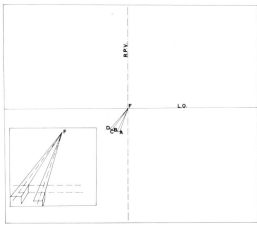

same drawing by Leonardo. The error in the evaluation of the distance is about 4 cm in real scale.

Contrary to other works by Leonardo, the *Adoration of the Magi* allows for an exact analysis of its perspective on the basis of the preliminary drawing of the perspective system. A comparison between the drawing and the painting shows that the orientation of the perspective has radically changed. To show this we need only refer to the diagram (figure 421) in which the two vanishing-points have been made to coincide. One can clearly see the different inclination towards the vanishing-point of the bisecting lines of the two triangles formed by the tread of the first step of the furthest staircase, both in the drawing and in the painting.

The preparatory drawing shows a clearly drawn floor grid and, across this, a diagonal continuing almost as far as the centre of the composition in the direction of the distance point. In the drawing, however, we note a simplification: the difference of level created by the risers of the three steps in the foreground has not in fact been considered, perhaps because this would have complicated the construction as a consequence of inevitable additional projections.

The entire perspective system has been constructed by means of the diagonal (the distance between the observer and the painting in this case is about three times the width of the drawing). Therefore it is impossible to know if Leonardo had also made use of other checks beyond the construction of the foreshortening directly from the plan, and no conclusions can be drawn one way or another from his writings. For his construction he would have been able to make use of an abbreviated version of Alberti's "costruzione legittima," which at this time was very much in use among Florentine artists and which Leonardo himself had investigated. This method consisted of marking on a vertical (in general the vertical side of the drawing) the intervals of diminution of the orthogonals of the picture plane. However, seeing that the drawing does not present a rigorous geometric construction one wonders if Leonardo used an even simpler method, based on the distance-point. According to this method, a point (P.D.) placed on the horizon and separated from the point *F* by an interval equal to the distance between the observer and the painting, when connected to the points that divide the ground line L, determines the points of intersection of the transversals directly on the orthogonales converging in *F*. In the preparatory drawing Leonardo has also indicated the dimensions of the square modular unit which he used to construct the checkerboard grid. By an inverse procedure one can discover the plan and all the other elements that describe the architecture. In this case, the plan is upside-down with regard to the perspective drawing, having been obtained through the diagonal.

The plan, contrary to Thiis's scenographic reconstruction (1914), which did however rightly show the square form, is not regular in the drawing of the transversals and orthogonals which form the grid. This is why the diagonal we have drawn, as a check, becomes a broken line. This, I maintain, is because the perspective is not exact and the intervals on the base line are not equally spaced.

corresponding to 2.5 times the width of the drawing (1.4 *braccia a panno fiorentino* or 17.2 *crazie*)

A. 1) FUNDAMENTAL ELEMENTS DERIVED FROM THE PRECEDING:
a) *Horizon Line*
   L.O. $\equiv (0; + 8.9; + 83.4)$
   This is found on the surface of the picture plane. It passes through *F*, is parallel to the ground plane α and is inclined at an angle of $0° 11' 51''$ to the base of the drawing.
b) *Central Vertical Axis* (R.P.V.)

This lies on the picture surface, passes through *F*, is perpendicular to the ground plane α and is inclined at an angle of $89° 48' 9''$ to the base of the drawing.
c) *Ground Line* (L.)
   Its trace lies on the ground plane α and is the intersection with the projection plane. It is also perpendicular to axis Z'_0. Further, it is located within the drawing at a mean height of 0.93 cm and has an inclination of $0° 11' 51''$ to the base.

B. EXTERNAL ORIENTATION:
a) *Coordinates of the Point of Sight*
   P.V. $\equiv (0; + 8.9; 0)$
b) *Horizontal or azimuthal angle or Angle of Direction*
   $\beta = 2° 26' 13''$
c) *Vertical or zenithal angle*
   ϑ_F = angle of elevation (collimation of P.V. on *F*) = $90°$
   ϑ_C = angle of declination (collimation of P.V. on *C*) = $90° 34' 37''$
d) *Angle of lateral inclination* $\tau = 0° 11' 51''$

C. VISUAL FIELD:
a) *Span of angle of the visual cone, by convention* = $60°$
b) *Radius of the visual circle* = 48.9 (corresponding to 0.83 *braccio* or 9.9 *crazie*)
c) *Area of the visual circle* = 7292.9 cm²
The drawing is contained within the visual circle. The area of the drawing is 6.5% of the entire surface of the visual circle.
d) *Angles of observation of the whole drawing from P.V.:*
   σ = read vertically = $11° 9' 19''$
   γ = read horizontally = $19° 43' 54''$
The scale of the diagrams of perspective reconstruction to the original is 1:2.3; the axonometric 1:2.5 in respect of the

422. *First idea for the* Adoration of the Magi. *Paris, Louvre.*

As far as the architecture is concerned, one can see that the columns which support the terrace on the left are not in alignment but are staggered at regular intervals, thus forming an impossible structure of crossed arches.

For the most part Mesnil's observations about the drawing are mistaken. His intuition seems valid, however, that, in the painting, the background and the human figures in the foreground were conceived separately and without any link with the principal scene.

In the plan, one sees that the checkerboard continues towards the right, probably because Leonardo wanted to suggest that the stable of the Nativity was just "off stage," as it appears in a preliminary drawing at the Louvre.

5/ The Last Supper. Milan, Santa Maria delle Grazie (refectory). Wall painting in oil, *c.* 1495-97.

Description of the picture plane
Form: rectangular
Height: 460 cm (corresponding to 7.9 *braccia a panno fiorentino* or 94.6 *crazie*) (but also to 7.8 *braccia milanesi* or 92.8 *once* or 1.76 *trabucco* or 10.6 *piedi*)
Width: 880 cm (corresponding to 15.1 *braccia a panno fiorentino* or to 180.9 *crazie*) (but also to 14.8 *braccia milanesi* or 177.5 *once* or 3.4 *trabucchi* or 20.2 *piedi*)
Perimeter: 2680 cm
Area: 404800 cm^2

Description of the fundamental elements of the perspective
A. INTERNAL ORIENTATION:
Coordinates of the principal point (or central vanishing-point)
$$F \equiv (-11.08; +250.2; +1007.5)$$
The orthogonals of the ceiling converge in a point 1
$$1 \equiv (-13.31; +259.14; +1007.46)$$
The orthogonals on the picture plane defining the tapestries on the right hand wall meet in point 2
$$2 \equiv (+2.33; +254.67; +1007.46)$$
The two orthogonals of the floor converge in point 3
$$3 \equiv (-22.25; +236.8; +1007.46)$$
The vanishing-point has been defined as being the bary-centre of the triangle delimited by the three points.
Principal Distance
$$F - P.D. = D = 10.075 \text{ m}$$

A. 1) FUNDAMENTAL ELEMENTS DERIVED FROM THE PRECEDING:
a) *Horizon Line* (L.O.)
   This lies on the picture surface, passes through F and is parallel to the ground plane α $\quad \gamma = +250.2$
b) *Central Vertical Axis* (R.P.V.)
   This lies on the picture surface, passes through F and is orthogonal to the ground plane α.
c) *Ground Line* (L.)
   By convention, this is tangential to the base of the fresco.
   The base of the painting is at a height of 2.10 m above the actual floor of the refectory. Z'_0 passes through the intersection between L and the perpendicular dropped from C.
B. EXTERNAL ORIENTATION:
a) *Coordinates of the Point of Sight*

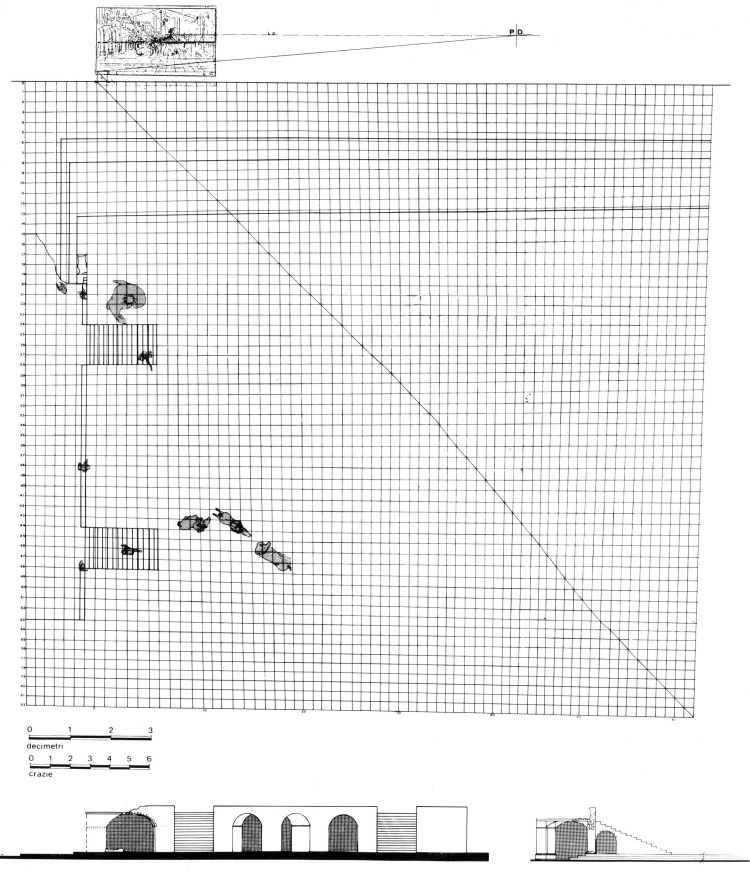

P D

L O

decimetri
0 1 2 3

crazie
0 1 2 3 4 5 6

decimetri
0 1 2 3

crazie
0 1 2 3 4 5 6

PROSPETTI DELL'ARCHITETTURA

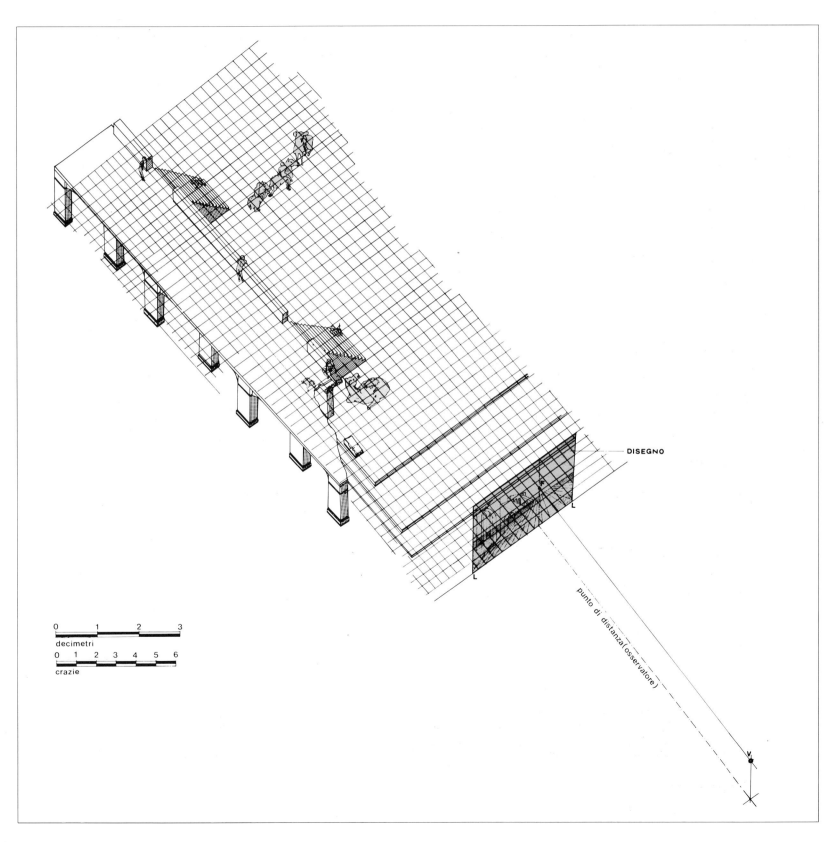

DISEGNO

punto di distanza (osservatore)

decimetri

crazie

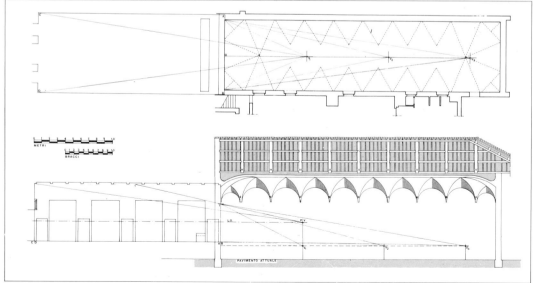

425. The Last Supper. *Milan, Refectory of S. Maria delle Grazie.*

426. *Perspective reconstruction in plan and longitudinal section of* The Last Supper *in relation to its surroundings in the refectory.*

427. *Reconstruction of the perspective calculated as if the main vanishing-point (F) was level with the eye of the average spectator. The analysis has been worked out in relation to the transversal section of the refectory.*

428. *Analysis of the fundamental elements on the perspective image placed in relation to the transversal section of the refectory.*

P.V. ≡ (0; + 250.2; 0)

b) *Azimuthal or Direction Angle*
$\beta = 359°\ 22'\ 12''$

c) *Zenithal Angle*
ϑ_F = angle of elevation (collimation from P.V. to F) = 90°
ϑ_C = angle of declination (collimation from P.V. on C) = 91° 8' 56''

d) *Angle of lateral inclination* τ = nil

C. VISUAL FIELD:

a) *Span of angle of visual cone* σ = 60° by convention

b) *Radius of visual circle on the painting* r = 581.7 cm

c) *Surface of the picture within the visual circle.*
Surface of the visual circle = 1063011 cm².
The painting is contained within the visual circle. The surface of the painting is 38% of the whole visual circle.

d) *Angles of observation from Point of Sight of the entire painting.*
σ = read vertically = 26° 23' 52''
γ = read horizontally = 46° 11' 10''

The calculation in this schedule has been developed from the basis of C having 0.00 coordinates.

The perspective reconstruction has been made to the scale of 1:22.339743 to the original.

The operations of the perspective reconstruction applied to this work by Leonardo have been carried out on a tracing taken from a photograph of the scale of 1:22.4 to the original. The examination of certain architectonic lines and elements has been at times difficult and we have had to repeat various checks to ascertain the regularity of the perspective construction. Recent on the spot examinations have shown the presence of a series of holes corresponding to the major orthogonals on the upper edge of the painting. These holes, precisely because of their location, suggest that Leonardo used them to transfer onto the wall surface the perspective structure previously worked out in reduced scale. Indeed the reconstruction has established that the distance-point is outside the frame of the painting and that the height of the observer in real scale is 4.60 m above the actual floor of the refectory. This is so far up that a person of average height today could only reach it by climbing onto scaffolding or a pulpit. In this case, the extraordinarily elevated eye-height would not only exclude the observer from any realistic rapport with his surroundings, but would also deny him any fixed parameter of spatial evaluation, since he would perceive the architectural perspective quite differently from the way he would if his feet were on the floor. But this accentuates the psychological effect of the narrative. And let us also remember that in Bramante's church of S. Satiro, too, the vanishing-point is raised, allowing the observer, as he moves longitudinally in the real space, always to read the painting, whatever his position. Of course the same thing happens in cinemas and theatres where the various viewing positions, stalls or boxes, are arranged so that the observer will always have a clear view despite the heads of the other spectators sitting in front of him.

In our process of reconstruction we have located the vanishing-point, the distance-point and the other elements that charaterterize this perspective. Furthermore, we have completed both the ceiling and the floor so as to relate

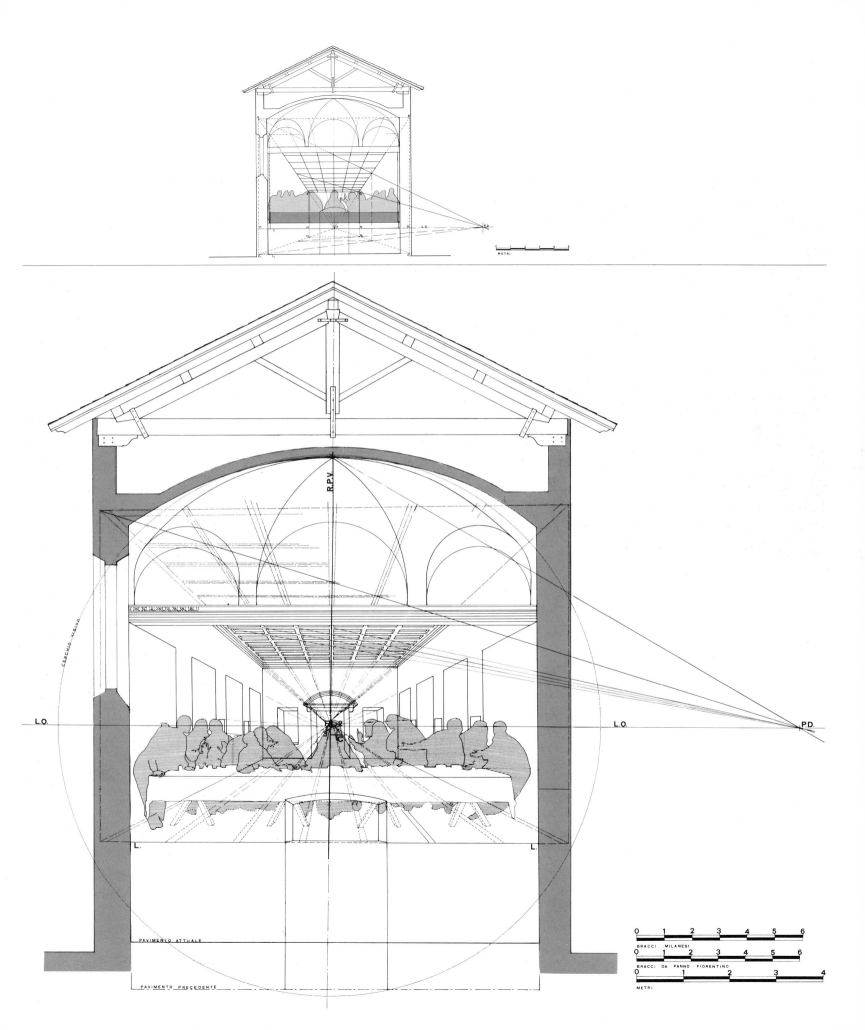

L.O.

P.D.

METRI

R.P.V.

L.O.

L.O.

P.D.

CERCHIO VISIVO

L.

L.

PAVIMENTO ATTUALE

PAVIMENTO PRECEDENTE

0 1 2 3 4 5 6
BRACCI MILANESI

0 1 2 3 4 5 6
BRACCI DA PANNO FIORENTINO

0 1 2 3 4
METRI

them to the projection plane, together with all the painted architectonic surroundings. The coffering of the ceiling meets the foreground above the lunettes and the walls project slightly beyond the right and left sides of the painting. On the basis of these results, we went on to two reconstructions of the fictitious setting:

a/ One which considers the architectural plan to be regular. That is, in this case, the meeting of the walls with the ceiling and the floor forms 90° angles. The plan resulting from this is rectangular and is more than twice as deep as it is wide.

b/ The other considers the architectural structure as a scenographic perspective, similar to that of a theatrical stage-setting. To obtain this reconstruction, we have interposed across the section a backdrop, whose intersection in plan forms a square. Then, by means of graphic processes, the foreshortening of the walls, floor and ceiling were calculated.

Hence the presence of scenographic perspective in the *Last Supper*, already proposed by Carlo Pedretti, can be established on the basis of the findings of the perspective reconstruction.

We gratefully acknowledge the invaluable help of B.A.R. Carter, MA, Professor of Perspective at the Royal Academy Schools, London, in the translation of the above essay.

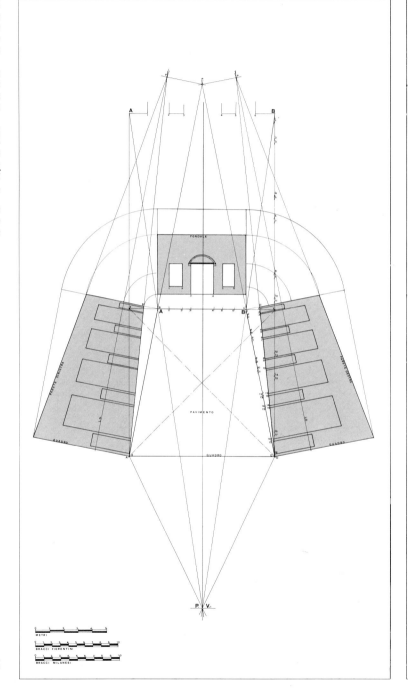

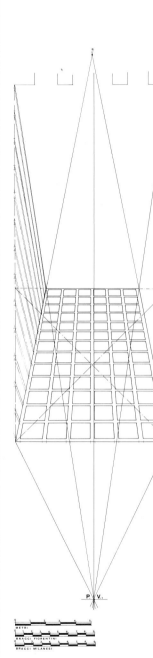

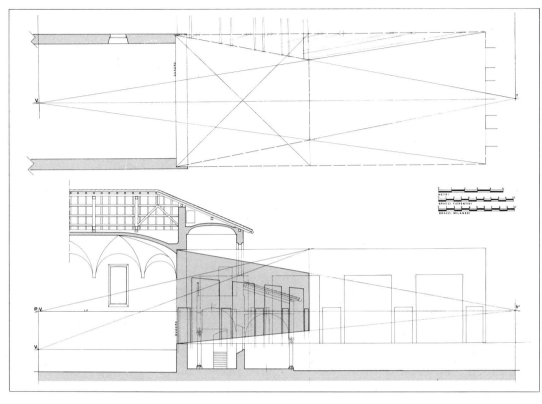

429. *Study of the scenographic perspective: plan of the floor, perspectives of side and back walls.*

430. *Study of the scenographic perspective: plan of the ceiling.*

431. *Study of the scenographic perspective in relation to the architecture of the refectory and to the observer: plan and longitudinal section.*

432. *Axonometric diagram of the refectory setting in relation to the seeming depth of the setting of* The Last Supper *obtained through perspective reconstruction.*

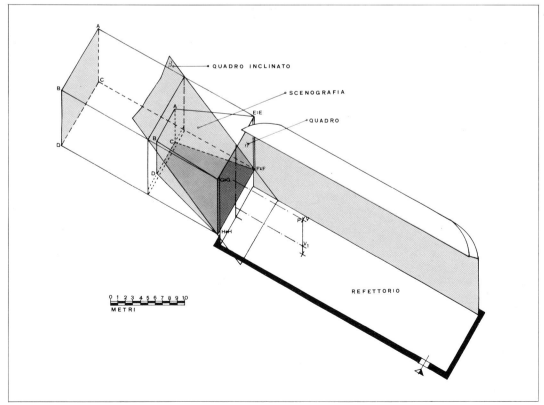

At the age of forty, Leonardo was recorded for the first time in a published work – Bernardo Bellincioni's *Rime*, published posthumously in 1493. Here he is acclaimed not only as another Apelles, but even more as a theatrical producer, the organizer of the *Festa del Paradiso* which was put on at the Castello Sforzesco on 13 January 1490 to celebrate the marriage of Gian Galeazzo Sforza and Isabella of Aragon. Another of Leonardo's contemporaries, his first, accurate and most informative biographer, Paolo Giovio, speaks of him as the "marvellous creator and arbiter of every elegance, and above all of delightful theatrical entertainments." In fact, throughout the whole of the sixteenth century, the memory of Leonardo's work as organizer of festivities was kept alive in the reminiscences of writers who drew on the testimony of his contemporaries to point the way to what would eventually burst forth as the grand spectacle of the Baroque. It is not surprising, therefore, that Leonardo was still remembered in this sense in 1600, at the time of the sumptuous wedding festivities of Marie de' Medici, made famous by the series of paintings by Rubens. On that occasion, after almost a century, Leonardo's mechanical lion reappeared (see further on, page 322).

A theatrical concept is in any case implicit in all Leonardo's pictorial work right from the start of his apprenticeship in Florence. There is no other way to interpret the perspective studies for the *Adorations* of the Shepherds and the Magi between 1478 and 1481. Even the crown of angels revolving above a Nativity scene (an idea taken up again by Botticelli in 1500) can be interpreted as a stage apparatus, reminiscent of those by Brunelleschi, and Michelozzo, too, used it to add an element of animation to the celestial dance crowning Foppa's frescoes in the Portinari Chapel.

According to the theorists of the early fifteenth century, perspective was a measure of space, but towards the end of the century and precisely with Leonardo's *Last Supper*, it began to be used "theatrically" to create a sort of scenic backdrop. Piero della Francesca had already done this in the Montefeltro Altarpiece, and Bramante applied the idea in an even more directly theatrical way in the feigned choir of San Satiro.

The road was thus opened that was to lead to Palladio's Teatro Olimpico. And at the same time, that is in 1496, among Leonardo's sketches there appears that extraordinary image of a classical stage-set, anticipating Peruzzi's and Raphael's "readings" of the Vitruvian text, and providing a further indication of the connection between Leonardo and Bramante in Milan.

It seems quite plain that it was from just such theatrical premises that Leonardo, towards the end of his career as an architect, arrived at those grandiose town-planning projects in Italy and France. It explains the suggested layout of the Medici quarter in Florence of 1515, where, in the vast space in front of San Lorenzo the same scenographic principles can be perceived which Michelangelo later applied to the Campidoglio. It explains, as well, why the royal residence at Romorantin, of 1517-18, was conceived as suitable for nautical spectacles. With these, the Naumachiae of antiquity returned to favour, as Bramante had

already envisaged in that vast stage-setting of Imperial architecture that the Vatican Belvedere was planned to be.

1. Paradiso

Every detail of the entertainment called *Festa del Paradiso* is known to us from the account that an eye-witness prepared for the Duke of Ferrara. Bellincioni himself, author of the libretto, explains that the presentation was called *Paradiso* "because there Paradise was built, with the great ingenuity and art of Maestro Lionardo Vinci from Florence, with all the seven planets which revolved, and the planets were represented by men in the shape and clothes that are described by the poets."

This makes one think of an elaborate piece of stage machinery, perhaps with clockwork movement, but it is probable that the apparatus was much simpler. "The *Paradixo* was made like one half of an egg," reports the Ferrarese envoy, "which, on the inside, was all gilded with a great number of lamps like stars, with some niches where all the seven planets stood according to their grade, high or low. All round the upper edge of the said half sphere were the twelve signs, with certain lights inside glass which made a graceful and pretty sight. In this *Paradixo* there were many very sweet and delightful songs and sounds." It consisted therefore mainly of stage effects achieved by light and sound, while the "turning" of the planets was nothing but the actor's walking, descending one after another from their niches to face the public and recite the praises of the Duchess. In Leonardo's manuscripts which can be related to that time we find no direct reference to Bellincioni's production of the *Paradiso*, besides general notes concerning systems of illumination and decorations made of temporary structures using draperies and greenery which Calvi has already related to the preparations for the wedding festivities of Gian Galeazzo and Isabella. Also missing are the studies for the actors' costumes, which must surely have existed, like the much later ones at Windsor. The only one which, hypothetically, could be assigned to that project is the small drawing of a human figure draped in a classical military manner in Windsor RL 12725, a fragment extracted from f. 18 r-b of the Codex Atlanticus, datable to about 1490. It has been rightly suggested (Brizio) that the decoration of the room itself, with drapery and greenery framing the Sforza and Aragon arms and with compartments "where certain ancient tales and many of the deeds accomplished by the Most Illustrious and Excellent Lord the Duke Francesco were painted" can be seen as a forerunner of programs of wall decoration which a little later Leonardo envisaged for Vigevano and for the Sala delle Asse at the Castello Sforzesco.

2. Danae

On 26 January 1491 Leonardo organized a tournament in the house of Galeazzo da Sanseverino, Captain of the Sforza army and Lodovico il Moro's son-in-law, but the only mention we have of this is in one of the notes where Leonardo gives an account of the misdeeds of his young apprentice Salai. We learn from this that "while certain servants were undressing to try on the clothes of the

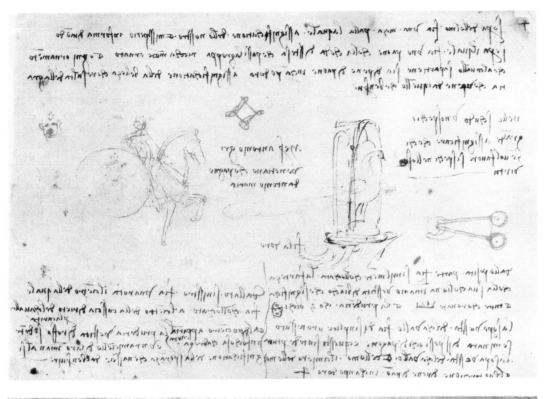

434. Notes for the tournament at the house of Galeazzo da Sanseverino, c. 1491. Codex Arundel, f. 250 r.
435, 436. Sketches for the staging of Danae by Baldassare Taccone, 1496. New York, Metropolitan Museum.
437. Milan, S. Satiro, interior looking towards the apse.

wild-men which were used at the said *festa*, Giacomo drew near the purse of one of them, which was on the bed with other clothes, and he took what money he found in it." It is probable, therefore, that Leonardo was often requested to provide this kind of service, and so the notes and drawings in the Codex Arundel, f. 250 r, could be explained as notes for a tournament. The handwriting and style suggest a date between 1490 and 1495, and in fact the sketch of a horse and rider recall those made for the Sforza Monument. Next to this is the sketch that shows the detail of a helmet on whose hemispherical crown (symbol of "our hemisphere") rises an elegant baldacchino, which acts as a frame for a peacock with spread tail feathers "to signify the beauty caused by the grace that comes from him who serves well." The note "Messer Antonio Gri, Venetian, companion of Antonio Maria" could allude to protagonists of the festival, but it is not sufficient to precisely date the occasion. Leonardo probably alludes to Antonio Maria Sanseverino, Galeazzo's brother – the one to whom Lodovico Sforza had given the Banco dei Medici in 1495 (see above, p. 74). Another indication of Leonardo's relationship with the Sanseverino comes from a sheet in the Metropolitan Museum, New York, which contains notes for a stage setting for *Danae*, a mythological fable told by Baldassare Taccone, Lodovico Sforza's Chancellor. It was in fact in the house of Giovan Francesco Sanseverino, Count of Cajazzo, the older brother of Galeazzo, that on 31 January 1496 that play was presented. Taccone's libretto, which was not published until 1888, and Leonardo's notes, interpreted for the first time by Maria Herzfeld in 1920, give us an idea of the scenic apparatus: to the sound of hidden instruments "a most beautiful heaven" is suddenly disclosed, "with Jove and the other gods lit by an infinite number of lamps like stars." Mercury descends from Olympus and, suspended in mid-air like an angel of the Annunciation, recites Jove's amorous message to the imprisoned Danae. The shower of gold then follows and Danae, having become a star, rises into heaven with so many sounds that it seemed the palace might fall." In the last act the nymphs "seeing an unusual musical star" ask Jove to explain it and at his command the goddess of Immortality appears who, also in "mid-air," explains the mystery, announces the birth of Perseus and rejuvenates the old king, Acrisius, Danae's father, in order to console him. Finally, to please the nymphs, Apollo too descends with his lyre and sings at length, ending by singing the praises of Il Moro. The New York sheet contains a brief list of the dramatis personae and a note preceded by a "4" which is a reference to a text that was on a missing part of that sheet. "4 who marvel at the new star and kneel down, and kneeling and adoring it with music the *festa* comes to an end." The sketches seem to refer to the niche for the announcer and a plan of the stage. In the detail of the niche, with its vault in perspective like Bramante's feigned choir at S. Satiro, a human figure appears seated within a flaming mandorla. A perspective plan of the scenery seems to indicate the position of the niche at the centre of a platform that is made to descend from the ceiling of the room along an inclined plane, probably on rails placed on the side walls. But these sketches are so summary that it

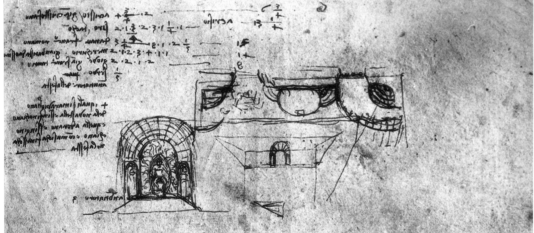

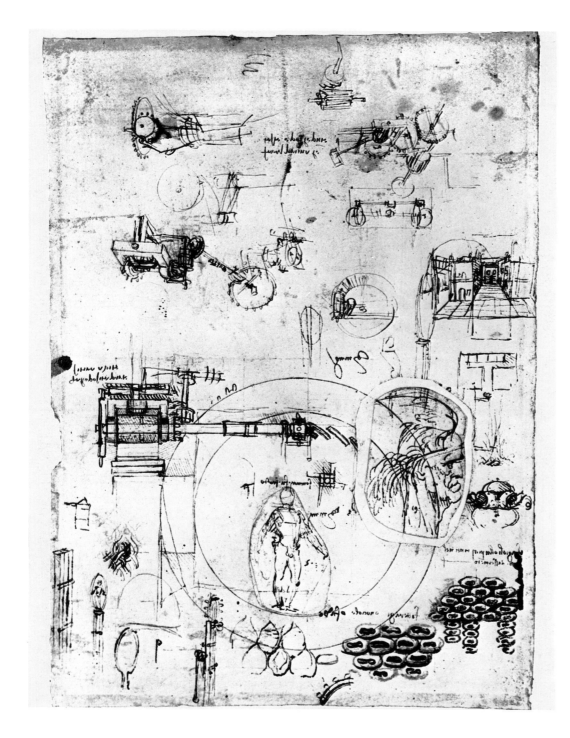

would be impossible to definitely assign them to the fable of Danae if it were not for the notes relating to the actors, with the mention of Acrisius, Sirus, Danae, Mercury, Jove, a servant and the announcer. The part of Acrisius is assigned to one Gian Cristoforo, probably the sculptor Gian Cristoforo Romano; that of Jove to Gian Francesco Tanzio, Bellincioni's friend and editor, while the author himself, Baldassare Taccone, would have played the part of Sirus. The flaming mandorla recalls the one used by Brunelleschi in his apparatus at S. Felice in Piazza, which was recorded in drawings by Buonaccorso Ghiberti. Other notes for the production of *Danae* can be identified in Codex Atlanticus, f. 358 v-b, from which the two fragments at Windsor, RL 12461 and RL 12720, were extracted. These are undoubtedly studies for the actors, possibly Acrisius and Mercury. There is also a little sketch of a town scene here which recalls the Bramantesque engraving which came from Milan around the same year, anticipating the Vitruvian stage-settings of Peruzzi and Serlio. The sheet can be precisely dated to January 1496 because it contains details of a needle-making machine, the design for which appears on Codex Atlanticus, f. 318 v-a, dated by Leonardo himself 2 January 1496. In its turn, this sheet can be related to notes in MS. I, for example on f. 98 v, relating to a stage device in the form of a pillar with a sliding central part that opens to suddenly reveal a standing human figure in a shining mandorla, thus suggesting the effect of a candle flame. It is difficult to say if this was part of the tale of Danae. It is easy, however, to understand how the mechanism worked: the actor was raised through the central channel of the pillar together with the mandorla, which was made of a flexible material and opened like a spring on coming out of the channel. These are just a few indications of the devices Leonardo must have invented for the staging of a mythological fable as richly animated as *Danae*. It is not surprising, therefore, that at the same time, around 1496-97, he should have found such an extraordinarily simple yet ingenious solution to the technological problem posed by a text of Pliny's relating to Curius's mobile theatre (*Nat. Hist.* XXXVI, xxix), a solution which no interpreter before or since was ever able to fathom. Filarete and Francesco di Giorgio knew Pliny's text, but proposed no interpretation of it; and Cardano, in his *De subtilitate* of 1550 went into a lengthy and complex analysis of it without managing to explain how the two parts of the theatre were put back to back. Barbaro, in the famous commentary to Vitruvius published by Marcolini in 1556, limits himself to reproducing Cardano's diagram and confesses to having found himself perplexed until Marcolini himself had the idea that the two parts of the theatre may have been hinged in such a way as to open like a mouth which, however, would have only allowed one to line up beside the other.

Even great archaeologists like Maffei and Canina who later studied the problem did not solve it.

Leonardo formulates the problem geometrically. His explanation is worked out above all with the drawing which takes the place of a demonstration model. The theatre is a cylindrical body divided into two sectors held together by two bands of wood linked like bicycle chains. One of these is on the upper edge and the other on the lower and they run from the farthest point of one half to the opposite farthest point of the other, crossing each other so that when the two halves swing open as on a hinge, they stay connected as they move on past the initial point of contact and remain so even when they come to rest back to back. After this the operation continues and the two halves face each other again, closing the cylinder to form the amphitheatre with arena for the gladiators. An analogous principle is found in the toy being held by a child in a well-known painting by Bernardino Luini – that is, two small tables with three bands for opening alternately a very ancient trick still used in portfolios today.

3. Orfeo

A text in the Codex Arundel, f. 231 v, which Richter made known as early as 1883, refers to the dramatis personae of a theatrical production, probably Poliziano's *Orfeo*: "When Pluto's Paradise is opened, then there may be devils roaring in twelve pots with infernal voices. Here will be Death, the Furies, Cerberus, many naked children weeping; here are fires made of various colours ... they move by dancing."

The sheet is full of notes about a stage machine which are better explained when one considers those on f. 224 r to which it is united. The two sheets are reproduced together here as they were when Leonardo compiled them, and as they still are in the Codex although other sheets have since been inserted between them. It is probable that Leonardo, proceeding as usual from right to left, began with the page on the right, f. 224 r, in which there are two sketches of the stage setting with the mountain that opens and a diagram of the mechanism that goes up and down. The mechanical principle of counterweights, which Leonardo also applied to his excavating machines (see above, p. 180), can be easily interpreted through an explanatory drawing. The style of the drawing, with hatching that curves to follow the form, and the handwriting suggest a date about 1508, the time of the second *Virgin of the Rocks*, of renewed interest in anatomy and above all, of the projects for the villa of Charles d'Amboise at Milan, in particular the notes in the Codex Atlanticus, f. 231 r-b, which has on the verso (f. 231 v-a) the sketch of a mechanical bird with the note: "ocel della comedia." A page from the same time, Codex Atlanticus, f. 131 v-a, contains the sketch of an actual stage structure with schematic indications of the curtain mechanism, which is referred to in the note: "*a b* pull-cord which serves to let the curtain descend to end the play." Just hinted at in the centre of the stage is an outline that can be recognized as the profile of a mountain.

Other possible references to the same construction are found in some sketches and diagrams in red chalk in the Codex Arundel, f. 139 v and f. 140 r (not reproduced), two pages containing notes on flames and heat datable to just this time, 1508-10. Also datable to about the same time is the list of expenses for colours on f. 227 r of the same codex that seems to refer to decoration work of some kind: "in total 120 lire and 18 soldi without the gold; tin to fasten the gold." In conclusion we could consider the famous Windsor drawing, RL 12387, in which there is an

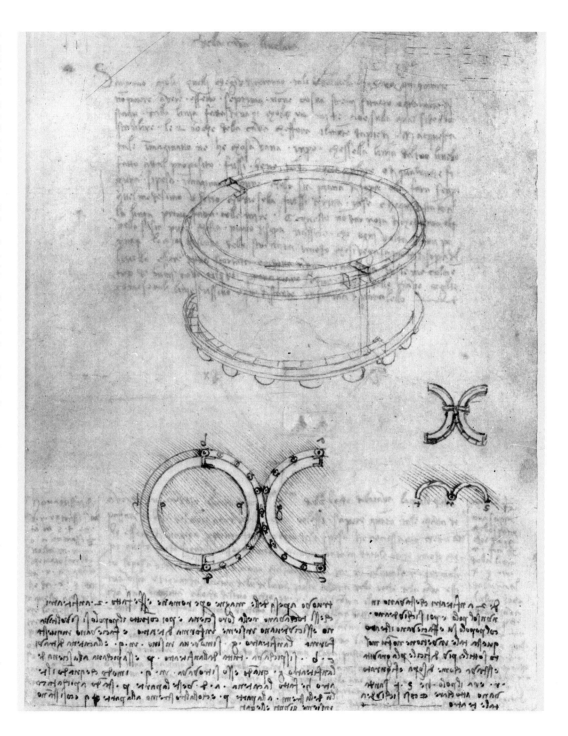

imposing stage set of the same rocky formation as in the sketch of the still closed mountain in the setting for *Orfeo* (note also the little door with steps leading up to it); an explosion, at the bottom, throws stones and smoke all about as if to precede the scenic effect of the apparition of the god of Hell. A copy by a pupil of the same drawing was found during the recent restoration work on the Codex Atlanticus, on the verso of f. 263 v-b, which contains studies for a parabolic compass datable about 1510.

No other documents or testimonies are known that can explain the occasion for these notes, but we known from Giovio and other contemporary sources how much d'Amboise loved the theatrical spectacles with which he entertained his guests. As we have seen, the villa which Leonardo planned for his presented characteristics that can be understood only as having to do with banquets and festivities and that explain the intended purpose of the garden attached to it as a place of delights. In a note relating to the same project he speaks of staircases sufficiently wide to allow the passage of persons wearing elaborate costumes. It has been thought in fact that the costumes he alludes to may be those shown in the famous Windsor drawings, but they are of a later date and should be assigned to some other occasion – perhaps the 1515 festivities at Florence recorded by Landucci, or the even later ones at Amboise in France when in 1518 a *Festa del Paradiso* was staged, recalling the one organized by Leonardo himself in Milan 28 years before.

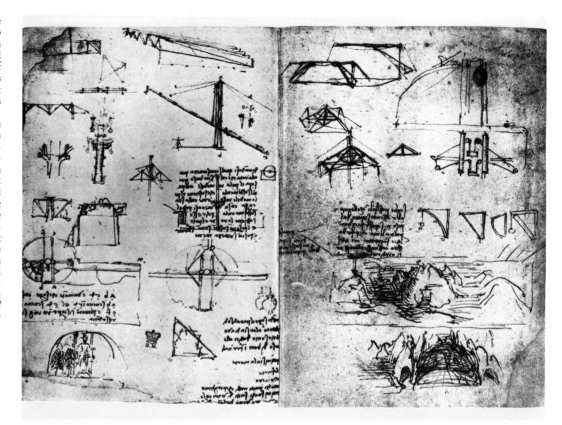

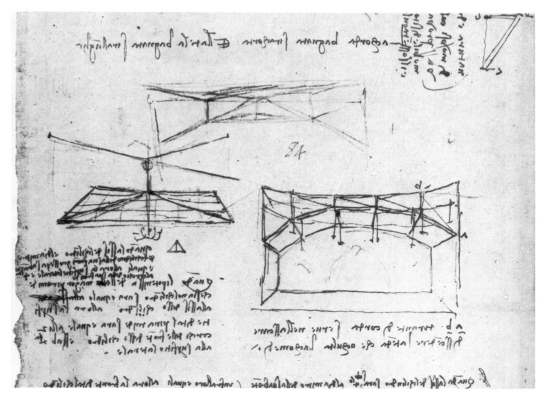

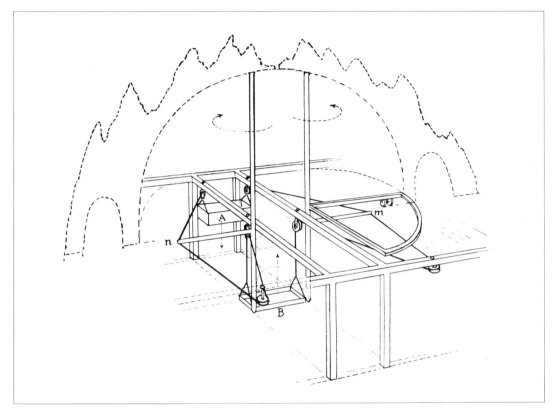

442, 443. *Interpretation of the scenery mechanism for the production of Poliziano's* Orfeo, *and model reconstruction.*

1. The Cartelle *of the Accademia Vinciana*

The complete series of the so-called *cartelle* of the Accademia Vinciana is reproduced here from the copies in the Biblioteca Ambrosiana. They consist of six copperplate engravings that until now have been almost exclusively studied as documents of Renaissance graphic art (especially in relation to the woodcut versions by Dürer) apart from a few isolated attempts to interpret them as esoteric expressions of cosmic concepts, or more simply as products of Leonardo's exuberant *fantasia*, like those which Vasari, speaking of Leonardo's architectural models, had already classified as "caprices." There have been suggestions that they should be interpreted as variations on the theme of the *fantasia dei vinci* (the term which was used in documents of 1492 and 1493 to refer to the embroideries on Beatrice d'Este's dresses) and therefore as hieroglyphics which, alluding to Dante's line "che mi legasse con sì dolci vinci" (that bound me with such sweet ties) (*Paradiso*, XIV, 129) could be understood as an emblem of Leonardo's own name.

The idea that these were the devices of an Academy of Design founded by Leonardo in Milan under the protection of the Sforza has long been abandoned. At a time when the term "Academy" was not yet applied to a school of art of the type introduced in the sixteenth century and described so well by Vasari, Leonardo would have had in mind as an example the first Platonic academy reintroduced in the Medici circle embracing a program of cultural activities from which the mechanical arts, and above all painting, were excluded. The idea of the *vinco* (which could mean a willow branch or tree) would allude therefore not only to Leonardo's own name, but also to the natural, organic environment that the first Platonic academy at Athens had come to be associated with in the sense of a gathering-place surrounded by trees. This leads to the enticing hypothesis that these *nodi vinciani* relate directly to the decoration of the Sala delle Asse at the Castello Sforzesco, since it may have been originally envisaged as a gathering-place for cultural activities. We know from Pacioli of a "praiseworthy scientific duel" organized at the Castello Sforzesco on 19 February 1498, in which churchmen and scholars, theologians, doctors, astrologers and lawyers participated, as did "Leonardo da Vinci, our Florentine compatriot most discerning architect and engineer and tireless inventor of new things, who with sculpture, casting and painting makes his surname come true" – that is *vince*, wins out over every other artist. And besides Leonardo, whose finished works at that time Pacioli enumerated, there was also "his as much as brother, Jacomo Andrea da Ferrara, a most meticulous disciple of the works of Vitruvius."

The *cartelle* of the Accademia Vinciana and Pacioli's statement were perhaps the origin of a fanciful report given by Borsieri in his 1616 supplement to Morigia's *Nobiltà di Milano* of the activities of an Academy for the study of architecture set up by the Visconti about 1380 at the time of the foundation of Milan Cathedral and taken up again by Francesco Sforza (?), first with Bramante and then with Leonardo, "who because of this almost left painting in abeyance," and with Boltraffio. "In this

448, 449. Cartelle *of the Accademia Vinciana. Milan, Biblioteca Ambrosiana.*

450. *Study of interlacing for a* cartella *of the Accademia Vinciana, c. 1493. MS. H, f. 35 r.*

Academy," states Borsieri, "the dainty sort of architecture gave way to the massive, which was taken up again, and whoever in the end knew how to change small bits of flowers into perfect cornices and half-moon windows into square ones prospered there. Thus the plan of Madonna di S. Celso was made in a regulated manner and those of some other churches in Milan which have a certain amount of majesty." This may be Borsieri's only passage which, in the midst of absurd anachronisms, makes sense. But there is another passage which has been curiously ignored and which undoubtedly has documentary value since it speaks of material which Borsieri saw for himself: "I myself once saw in the hands of Guido Mazenta various writings on perspective, on machines and on buildings, written in French characters although in the Italian tongue, which had once come out of this Academy and were attributed in fact to Leonardo himself." Aside from the presumed relationship with a presumed Academy, we have here a reference to exact transcriptions of writings by Leonardo which were done in France. This is not improbable. One can certainly speak of a script in "French characters": the one completely codified by Palatino in his 1545 treatise on calligraphy. And we know that around 1542 Cellini had acquired in France a book on the three arts, Painting, Sculpture and Architecture, "copied by one (of the followers) of the great Lionardo da Vinci." We may ask ourselves how it could be that a copy made when the originals were still in France, remained in France. It is possible that Melzi may have undertaken to publish them while Leonardo was still alive, but it is also likely that the compilation itself was entrusted to a Frenchman with an eye to bringing out a French edition. The transcript was brought to Italy to Cellini, who loaned it to Serlio so that he could publish the part relating to perspective. Cellini, in fact, had wanted to bring out that book of Leonardo's himself but was not able to because it was taken from him. At any rate, we can begin to discern here, even if only through hints, a context within which the Accademia Vinciana *cartelle* may with some likelihood be placed. Their theme is essentially that of inscribing a circle in a square, just as was Leonardo's famous drawing of the Vitruvian man in Venice. The *fantasia dei vinci* introduces an ornamental element that expresses geometrically a concept of the infinite, growing organically through countless variations of interlacing motifs that succeed each other endlessly within the area of a circle. Such conceptual ornamentation can, in fact, be transferred to architectural decoration, as in the case of the Sala delle Asse. The first illustrator of these *nodi vinciani*, Padre Oltrocchi, who around 1785 was collecting material for a study of Leonardo's life and works, probably guessed correctly that they could have served as models for decorative floor patterns.

2. Ceilings, Walls, Doors, Windows, Intarsia Work and Floors
The decorative elements that Leonardo applied to architectural structures, such as friezes, doorways, windows and so forth, can be easily classified according to Tuscan, Umbrian, Lombard and perhaps even Venetian components, all of which contribute to the formation of the

Roman idiom of Bramante, Raphael and Peruzzi. But the interest in interlacing patterns which comes to him from Bramante – the "gruppi (*knots*) of Bramante" – and which he makes intimately his own, seems to survive only in the minor arts, in ceramics, embroideries, engravings and so on. On f. 35 r of MS. H, a notebook he used around 1493 and 1494, we find a study for one of the knots of the Accademia Vinciana, while other sketches of interlacings in the same notebook (f. 32 v-f. 33 r) seem to suggest motifs more adapted to wall decoration. The same can be said of various sketches in the Codex Atlanticus and in other manuscripts reproduced here and datable during the first Milanese period, from 1485 onwards. (See also the discussion earlier in this book on the decoration of Cecilia Gallerani's house). A few look almost metallic, and could relate to studies for dress embroideries, for impressions on leather, or for jewellery or decorations on weapons and armour. One interlacing design within an oval, on the reverse of the famous study for the angel in the *Virgin of the Rocks* in Turin, seems destined for the cover of a book. However, there are also designs for intarsia work, for example cubes in perspective like the geometrical bodies in Pacioli's *Divina Proportione*; and in later drawings datable from 1508 to 1515, naturalistic elements make themselves more insistent, recalling the vegetal decorations of the costumes at Windsor, which in their turn reflect the relief decoration proposed for the external walls of the Medici palace which he designed in 1515. In the Codex Atlanticus there is a large leadpoint drawing (f. 261 r-a) of an interlaced pattern very similar to those in the Accademia Vinciana *cartelle*, but which can be identified as a design for a floor decoration. A detail of the same motif is repeated separately (f. 261 r-b) to show how to subdivide the whole design into many sections to be realized in ceramic tiles. This last design in fact was done life-size, gone over in pen and perforated for transfer onto another sheet or directly onto the tile to be decorated. Among the fragments collected on f. 348 v-b of the Codex Atlanticus is a little sketch which is reminiscent of one of the Accademia Vinciana *cartelle* and can be interpreted as a design for the decoration of the floor of a centrally-planned building (and perhaps it is not just a coincidence that a plan of such a building appears in the fragment beside it). The interlacing leads to, or originates from, the central motif of an eight-pointed star, exactly the same motif which results from the geometrical construction of the plan of a temple in a well-known design in MS. B. (Ash. I, f. 5 v) where Leonardo takes up the theme of Brunelleschi's Angioli rotunda. With this in mind, it is easy to perceive how the floor design would have related the peripheral elements of the chapels and piers to the central area of the temple in such a way that the spectator would have been reminded that he was directing his footsteps across a diagram of the symbolic organization of the space. It is basically the same principle that Michelangelo later applied to the design of the Piazza del Campidoglio, and which may go back to a cosmological diagram by Isidore of Seville. In the proposed architectural context it seems appropriate therefore to attribute a cosmic if not a mystic connotation to these *fantasie dei vinci*.

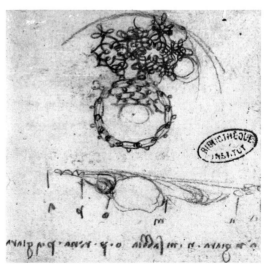

451-453. *Ornamental designs, c. 1493. MS. H, ff. 32 v-33 r, 12 v, 11 v.*

454. *Interlacing design, probably for the cover of a book, c. 1485. Turin, Biblioteca Reale.*
455. *Study for intarsia, c. 1515 (?). Oxford, Christ Church.*

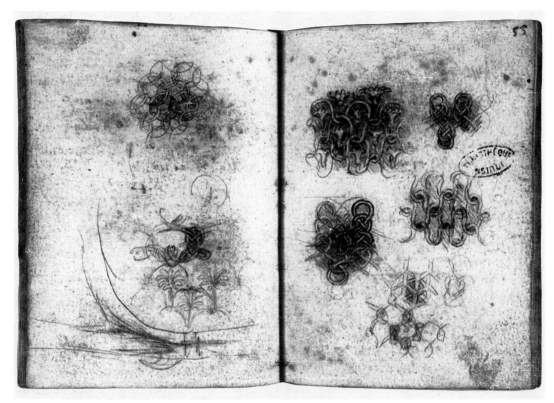

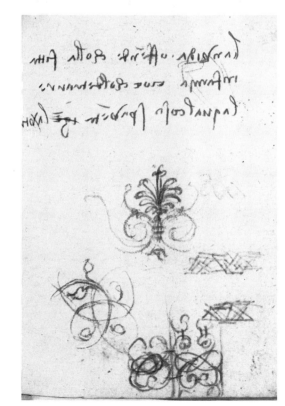

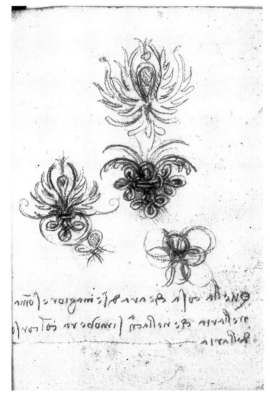

456, 457. Studies of interlacing patterns, and detail of a design for a tile, c. 1495 (or later). Codex Atlanticus, ff. 261 r-a and 261 r-b.

458. Studies of interlacing for
embroidery, c. 1485-87. Codex
Atlanticus, f. 358 v-a-b.

459-461. Studies of architectural
decorations, c. 1490. Bayonne,
Musée Bonnat, detail; Codex
Atlanticus, f. 98 r-b, detail, and
f. 357 v-a.

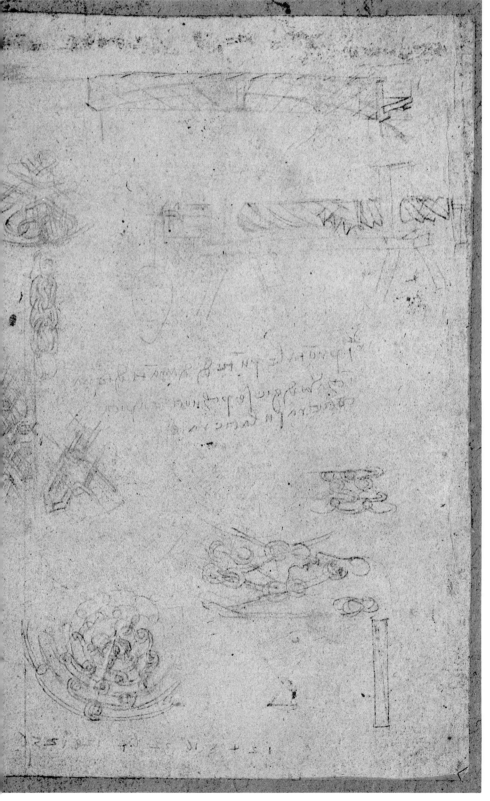

462, 463. Studies of decorative structures, c. 1490-95. Codex Atlanticus, ff. 58 r-b and 342 v-b.

464. Studies for the decoration of a ceiling, c. 1413-14. Codex Atlanticus, f. 375 r, detail.

465, 466. Studies of decorative structures, c. 1510. Codex Atlanticus, ff. 223 r-a and 115 r-b.

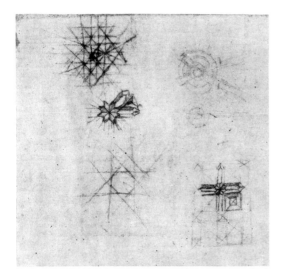

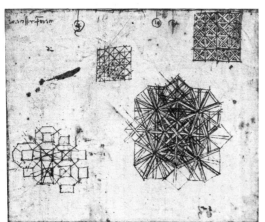

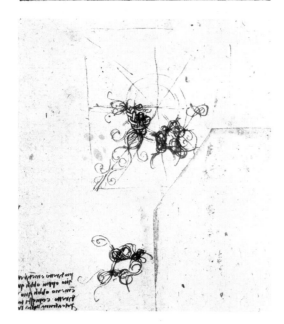

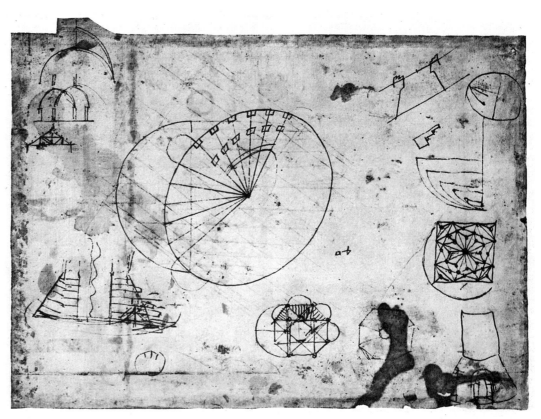

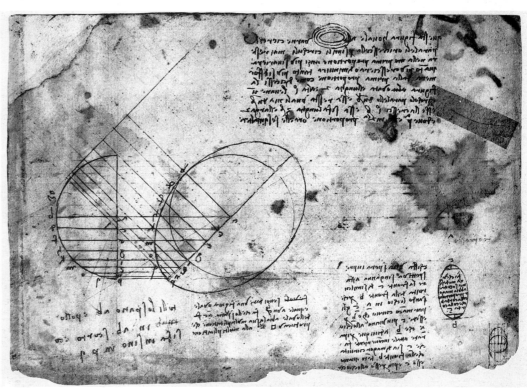

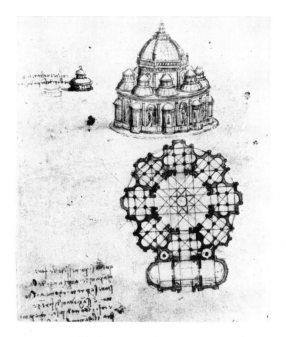

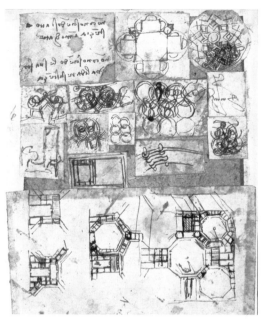

467, 468. *Studies of architecture and decoration*, c. 1490.
MS. Ash. I, f. 5 v, and *Codex Atlanticus, f. 348 v-b-c.*
469. *Rome, Piazza del Campidoglio.*

3. Rebuses, Allegories and Devices

We have seen (*Excursus 2*) that Bramante, like Leonardo, took an interest in the rebus, not so much as a social pastime, but as a hieroglyphic puzzle that could be adapted to inscriptions in place of solemn epigrams in the antique style. One of Leonardo's rebuses at Windsor, RL 12694, seems to indicate the same intention: the letters are capitals, unlike those in all his other rebuses, and they are aligned with the ideograms as in a frieze. It is a fragment of a sentence – "Happy I would be if the love that I bring you..." – which includes the architectural element of a sea-port (*porto* – I bring) – represented by ships passing under an arch flanked by towers, imitating a design that appears on some antique coins.

The same rebus, with lower-case lettering, is sketched out in another Windsor fragment, RL 12699, and gives the complete sentence: "Happy I would be if some of the love that I bring you were returned." with the correction "if some of the love" (*se dell'amore*) carried out through substituting the sketch of a *sedella* (Lombard for bucket) for that of a *sella* (saddle).

The large, well-known sheet of rebuses also at Windsor, RL 12692, in which there is also a scale plan of a palace with a square courtyard (the same, and to the same scale, as one on f. 80 r-a of the Codex Atlanticus), contains some architectural ideograms such as towers, fortresses, chimneys, and one of that characteristic form of a parallelepiped with three holes indicating the *cessi* (lavatories) as in a design going back to antiquity and still in use in the Renaissance. This explains the three little dots in one sector of a room in the plan of the palace. A rare surviving example of a *cesso*, or *necessario*, of the fifteenth century, like those in Leonardo's rebus, is lying in the grass in a corner of the courtyard of the Castello Sforzesco.

Some of Leonardo's allegorical notes contain architectural elements which have not yet received the attention they deserve. An example is his sketch of the traditional allegory of Aristotle and Phyllis, datable about 1485-87, in which the figures still move in the style of Pollaiuolo. Leonardo represents the interior of a Lombard house, with a niche in the wall, a canopied bed, a chest, a bench and a table arranged in a way that is reflected in certain interiors by Bramantino. Through the window, on the sill of which is placed an hour-glass, we can make out a landscape that seems to be of a port or a castle. The niche, which usually had a votive character as in Carpaccio's painting of *St. Jerome*, serves to create a darker area, and throws into relief the emphatic gesture of Phyllis brandishing the whip. But this domestic scene can also be imagined translated into the linearity of a woodcut like those of the *Fior di Virtù* or the *Hypnerotomachia Poliphili*, in which similar interiors appear.

The allegory at Windsor, RL 12497, whose significance is still a puzzle, represents a scene which some have thought to be an illustration of the political allegory outlined in MS. I., f. 138 v, datable about 1497: "Il Moro as representing Good Fortune, with hair, and robes, and his hands in front, and Messer Gualtieri taking his by the robes with a respectful air from below, having come in from the front.

470, 471. Rebus, c. 1487-90. Windsor, RL 12694, 12699.

472, 473. Details of cessi (lavatories) in a sheet of rebuses,
c. 1487-90. Windsor, RL 12692.
474. A cesso in the courtyard of the Castello Sforzesco,
Milan.

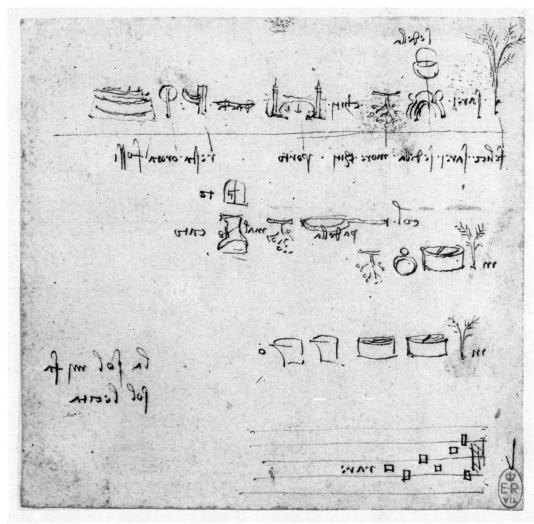

Again, Poverty in a hideous form running behind a youth. Il Moro covers him with the skirt of his robe, and with his gilt sceptre he threatens the monster." And yet, if we study the drawing closely, it does not correspond to the description except in secondary and generic particulars. The description, in fact, does not even hint at the most striking aspect of the allegory, which is that the monster bursts menacingly out of a vast palace, uprooting it from its foundations and carrying it on his back like a pack-animal. This palace seems to anticipate the imposing sixteenth-century forms that immediately recall the Louvre, with the open colannaded *piano nobile* and with a high attic storey which, however, is explained by comparing it with that of the palace represented in MS. B, f. 36 r. An indication of the same type of attic is found on the lower right of f. 231 r-b of the Codex Atlanticus, among the sketches for the villa of Charles d'Amboise. The allegory, its long rectangular form framed with a pen-and-ink borderline, recalls the sketches of theatrical productions in the Codex Arundel, datable to the time of the projects for d'Amboise. The other sketches on the same sheet also seem to indicate some theatrical intention, and in fact could be studies for the representation of a Paradise or an Olympus.

The late drawings of the Deluge, at Windsor, are generally considered as scientific allegories, expressions of terrifying and majestic natural forces that overturn every obstacle in whirlwinds of destruction. And so in RL 12401 we see powerful architectural forms along the ridge of a dike or viaduct which still resist the onrush of the elements: in the foreground rises a structure with pyramidal fortifications evoking the exotic aspect of an Indian temple, and further on, atop the tall arches of the viaduct, buildings with domes and battlements. These are probably imaginary architectural details, but they could allude to Sforza constructions around Bellinzona, where we know that at the time of this drawing, in 1513, there were earthquakes and floods vividly described by Giovio, who tells us among other things that an entire company of Swiss soldiers with their encampment was swept away by the destructive fury. And in fact if one carefully studies Leonardo's drawing one can make out strange floating forms like pennons carried by the wind among whirls of dust and clouds, that may be explained by a drawing in the Codex Atlanticus, f. 317 r-a, where we see field tents uprooted together with their central poles topped by rounded knobs, whose swirling forms assume an almost vegetal character and recall the fluttering banners of the Palio when they are thrown into the air.

The interpretation that can be offered of another late drawing in the Deluge series is more uncertain, however. This is Windsor RL 12388, in which there is the little sketch of a Resurrection scene recalling the one by Signorelli at Orvieto. There are in addition other elements which make one think of the destruction of Sodom and Gomorrah as a Dantesque vision. Dantesque without doubt is the sense of oppression in the drawing of a valley like an abyss with rocky peaks and caverns, shown in section as in an architectural model, and as in the illustrations to Manetti's *Dialogo circa il sito, forma e misura dell'Inferno di Dante* published by Benivieni in 1506.

Above the abyss an enormous explosion produces a thick cloud of smoke and fire from which rains a torrent of flaming arrows. In the sketch above appears a rocky landscape overturned by celestial furies, where one can make out a fortress with battlemented walls and towers. Leonardo's text refers to the effects of light in clouds, smoke and dust and has a detached, analytical tone that seems unaware of any emotional and allegorical aspects in the illustrations to which it alludes.

Among the emblems designed by Leonardo, there are abundant representations of objects of daily use, instruments and tools with which to symbolize the idea of a "device" or to give "body" to a concept. There seem to be no direct references to architecture, but we must at least note the elegant shape of a tempietto with a hemispherical dome and columns given to a lamp in a well-known device in Windsor RL 12701, datable about 1508 and inspired by Alberti's moral fable about the lamp of Plautus. The same idea is expressed in a sketch in MS. M, of about ten years earlier, but with a more realistic representation of the lamp. Besides this we can mention the design of a device or emblem in the Codex Atlanticus, f. 306 r-a, which could be the idea for a book plate or a printer's trade-mark. The object represented there, similar to a well, has never been interpreted. It is, in fact, a travelling ink-well with two small metal tubes placed like a St. Andrew's Cross. The lid is raised along two laces that pass through two holes in its rim and serve to hang the ink-well from a belt, or else from a small wooden box for the tubes, which in its turn gets passed around the belt. The object, complete in this way, appears in the well-known portrait of Luca Pacioli attributed to Iacopo de'Barbari: the wooden box is placed near the edge of the table and the ink-well with tube hangs from it suspended in mid-air. It is an object which must have been very familiar to Leonardo, an indispensable companion in his travels.

The emblem is enclosed in an oval and includes the initials "B.T.," which could stand for the Bartolomeo Tovaglia mentioned in the Codex Atlanticus, f. 367 v-c, or more probably Bartolomeo Turco, Leonardo's friend and correspondent, a traveller and writer with whom Leonardo was friendly about 1508, at the time of this drawing.

480. *Study for the Deluge*, c. 1515. Codex Atlanticus, f. 317 r-a.
481. *Illustration to Dante's Inferno in Gerolamo Benivieni's* Dialogo (1506).

482. *Studies for the Deluge*, c. 1515. Windsor, RL 12388.

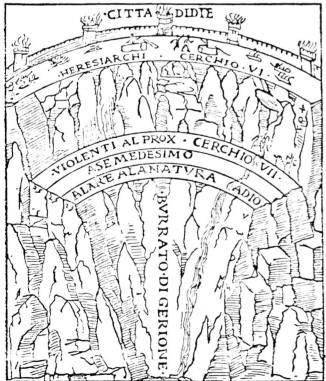

483. Studies of emblems, c. 1508-10. Windsor, RL 12701.
484. Emblem of an ink-well, c. 1500. Codex Atlanticus, f. 306 r-a, detail.
485. Iacopo de' Barbari (?): Portrait of Luca Pacioli. Naples, Museo di Capodimonte.

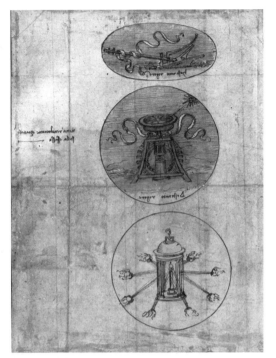

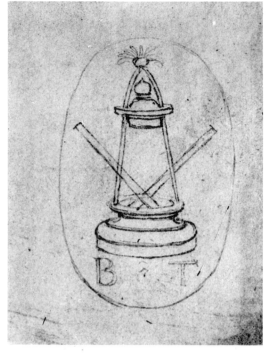

The *ingegno*, in the Renaissance as in antiquity, meant the motor mechanism of a machine and, by extension, the machine itself. (Vitruvius states that the ingenium is a machine which needs only one person to operate it.) From this we get the term *ingegnere*, originally applied to the military and hydraulic architect. The *ingegneri* listed by Leonardo in MS. B, f. 50 v, are in fact architects of antiquity. According to Vitruvius, the construction of war machines, bridges, harbour equipment, ditches and trenches, as well as of canals, aqueducts, pumps and fountains, falls within the competence of the architect. This was equally true in the Renaissance, although military engineering, particularly with Francesco di Giorgio and Leonardo, was already developing into the autonomous discipline which it would become in the seventeenth century. On the other hand, in Italy today the *Genio* (Engineers) is still a military corps that carries out the tasks of the architect of antiquity, just as the English terms "engine" for machine or motor, and hence "engineer" for the driver of a locomotive, conserve a memory of the antique *ingegni* and *ingegneri*.

Both in the Renaissance and in antiquity the term *edificio* could be applied to a machine, whether for war or hydraulics, whose structure or housing could assume the form of a building. (And conversely the term *macchina*, or machine, could be applied to a work of architecture, for example *la gran macchina* of Milan Cathedral, the *macchina* of the dome by Brunelleschi, etc.) Such *edifici* often look like towers or palaces with complex mechanisms arranged inside, as in the case of mills, industrial machines, and above all the so-called *edifici d'acqua*, or hydraulic pumps.

It seems that Leonardo intended to compile a vast repertoire of such machines (Lomazzo speaks of a whole book of mills, now lost), and right from his youth he began a census of them, often showing them in their architectural casings, which reflected the usual forms of fifteenth-century Tuscan architecture. The examples reproduced here are all from the Codex Atlanticus. Even in the simple and functional housing of a pendulum mill, Codex Atlanticus, f. 385 r-b, *c.* 1485-87, we can see a reflection of contemporary architecture in the hint of a two-light window. The categories of *ingegni* most intimately connected to architectural practise are naturally those having to do with hydraulic systems, and therefore such things as pumps, fountains, etc. Clocks, too, whether hydraulic or mechanical that is worked by water or by weights and springs, represent another category of *ingegni* which Vitruvius had already assigned to the architect. Leonardo expended a great deal of time and thought on all this, and an account of this aspect of his technological production could well be misread as presenting yet again an image of Leonardo as an inventor in the modern sense, whereas we ought not to lose sight of the historical, social and economic context in which these products of his inventive capability were seen as the proper work of an architect.

1. Fountains

One of Leonardo's earliest pages, f. 386 r-a of the Codex Atlanticus, datable to about 1480, contains illustrations of

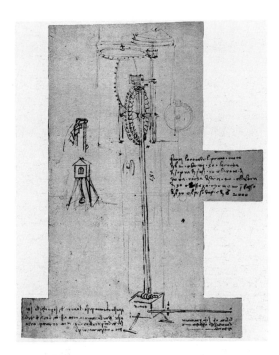

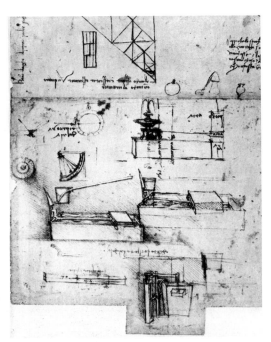

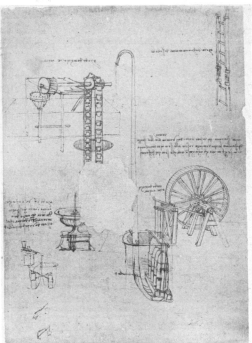

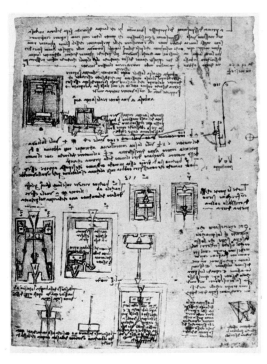

traditional systems for the raising of water. These include a fountain driven by a lead weight which puts the water under pressure (and the sketch, mutilated by a lacuna, gives prominence to the elegant form of a basin), and even a complex hydraulic pumping system which goes on repeating its action thanks to the ancient device of a wheel within which a man or an animal is made to run. Leonardo's note clearly establishes the intimate relationship between *ingegno* and architecture: "This wheel, here below, with a man going round inside it, would have the force to chase the water of a well right up to the top of a bell-tower, by using the *ingegni* and methods which are shown here."

There is another drawing of a fountain, still in youthful style, in the Codex Atlanticus, f. 292 v-b-c, dating from about 1485-87. Once more this is a fountain operated by the pressure of a lead weight. On the same sheet we note details of a device with a float, which can be related to a whole series of studies of *edifici d'acque* on which Leonardo was working at the time of MS. B, about 1487-90. The valve, or *animella* as he called it, is truly the "soul" of a hydraulic *ingegno* and Leonardo pays particular attention to perfecting it according to mechanical principles which later he will recognize again in the functioning of the valves of the heart.

When he was working on his last architectural projects, in France, Leonardo spent a great deal of time working out the mechanism for a fountain. "Amboise has a royal fountain without water" he wrote in the Codex Atlanticus, f. 296 r-a, and on the same sheet, as on numerous others of the same series, appear details of valves and floats whose forms, often schematic or diagrammatic, seem to allude to the same devices which he had already worked on 40 years before.

Sketches and calculations for a *fontana da feste* are found in the Codex Atlanticus, f. 218 r-b and f. 247 v-a, two sheets datable to the last years of the fifteenth century. By association one might recall one of Leonardo's riddles which alludes to fountains as *feste delle piazze*. The fountain's festive character is accentuated in those extraordinary objects designed as decorative centre-pieces for the dining-table: the so-called "fountains of Heron," which fascinated Leonardo so much.

The mechanism and functioning of such a fountain are described by Alberti in his *Ludi matematici*, and we know that Leonardo owned a manuscript copy of that treatise. The same mechanism keeps appearing in his own manuscripts from the earliest to the latest, often beside drawings of the elegant objects which would encase the mechanism. These in themselves reflect the evolution of Leonardo's architectural style. The earliest designs, datable about 1485-87, look like candelabra, with their fifteenth century Tuscan style emphasized by an embroidery of decoration recalling Donatello and Verrocchio. In the later designs, such as those of 1513 at Windsor, the object assumes a more purely architectural form, of sixteenth-century type, with the accent placed on the central element of the column as a support for a human figure, a seated putto or cherub or an almost Dürer-like peasant or slave carrying a basket. We recognize the same classicizing forms of these

491-494. *Studies of fountains of Heron: c. 1487-90. Codex Atlanticus, ff. 293 r-b and 212 r-a, details; c. 1513-14, Codex Atlanticus, f. 384 r-b, and Windsor, RL 12690, 12691; c. 1497-1500, Madrid MS. I, f. 114 v-115 r.*

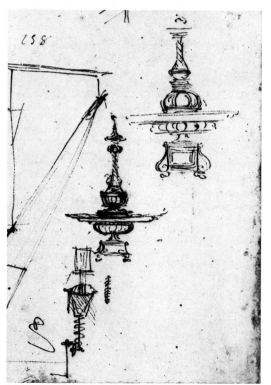

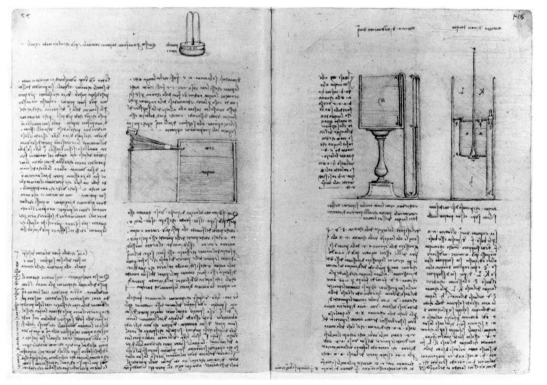

495, 496. Ligny Memorandum. Codex Atlanticus, f. 247 r-a, c. 1497-99. Detail in elevation of a wall with niches, with an apparatus using spirals, probably for manoeuvring curtains or scenery. Sketch in plan of the mechanism with the note: "this may be draped with cloth and then nailed down." Studies of the same contrivance appear on f. 304 r-a. The other notes, added later, consist of a memorandum referring to the time when Leonardo was hastening to leave Milan, in 1499. This is a celebrated text in which he alludes to a projected trip to Rome and Naples with the French Marshal, Count Louis de Ligny. References of architectural interest include "the measurements of the public buildings" and the "Theatre of Verona," probably a book which Leonardo intended to obtain from "Giovan Lombardo." The sheet was originally united to 218 r-b, on which there are calculations and sketches relating to a wine and water fountains for festivals. The same calculations are also found on f. 247 v-a.

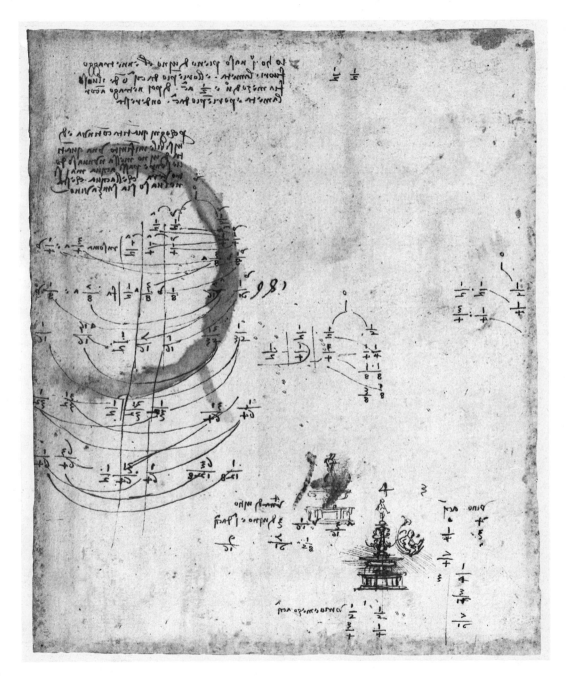

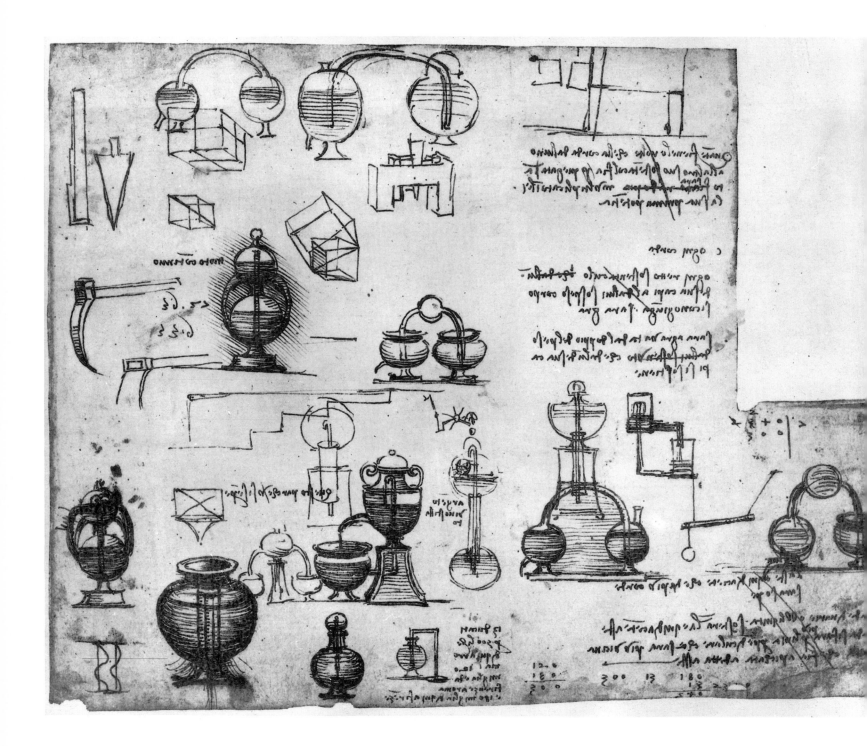

315

late designs in details of hydraulic devices, which must have been inspired by Heron's *Spiritali*, on f. 400 r-b and v-d of the Codex Atlanticus. This sheet also contains an estimate of the cost of a trip from Milan to Florence and Rome and on the basis of style can be exactly assigned to 1513.

2. Clocks and Bells

Among the earliest records of Leonardo's activities is that of June 1481 relating to the painting of the *uriuolo* of the monastery of S. Donato a Scopeto outside Florence. At the same time he had undertaken to furnish an altarpiece for the monastery, which is probably the unfinished *Adoration of the Magi* at the Uffizi. During the siege of Florence, however, in 1527, the monastery was razed to the ground and no-one knows just what this youthful work of Leonardo's, the *uriuolo*, may have been. It could have been a dial, and therefore a "painting" such as the one done by Paolo Uccello on the internal façade of Florence Cathedral, but since he was paid so little for it (firewood to the value of 1 lire and six soldi) it is more likely that it was simply a matter of tracing out a sundial. This would explain certain drawings, including one hinting at a device for incising lines on a wall, on a sheet datable to exactly that time, f. 366 v-c of the Codex Atlanticus. Folio 366 v-b, a sheet of canalization studies belonging to the Romorantin project of forty years later, contains the isolated note "sun clock." Leonardo would certainly have known Vitruvius's pages on sundials and other clocks, no less than those on the same subject in Alberti's *Ludi matematici*, and he would probably have known that Brunelleschi himself, according to his earliest biographer, had worked on clocks "with various and diverse successions of *mole* that he had seen and that had been needed...," the *mole* being wheels and not *molle*, or springs, as one can still read in the Codex Magliabechianus of that biography (II. II. 35, f. 299 v). The suggestion has even been made that a note of Leonardo's in MS. B, f. 50 v, may have illustrated the model of the "kind of springs" which Brunelleschi would have worked on, but the biographer's words are also reinterpreted (in the critical edition by Domenico De Robertis) as regards the allusion to *ingegni* in relation to a principle of clockmaking applied to machines for the practise of architecture: "And having made for his pleasure in the past some clocks and alarm clocks with various different kinds or successions of *mole*, multiplied by many different *ingegni*, all or most of which he had seen, they were a very great help to him in being able to imagine different machines for carrying, lifting and pulling as occasion demanded...."

What Brunelleschi "had seen" in fact were the same monastic alarums that had already inspired Dante (*Paradiso*, XXIV. 13) with the beautiful image of motion gaining speed through a "succession of wheels": "And as wheels in the structure of a clock revolve, so that watching them, the first seems at rest and the last to fly..." (Sinclair)

That multiplication of motion is exactly what Brunelleschi set himself to achieve in his machines for lifting and transporting materials. And we can add that Vasari and Baldinucci in borrowing from Brunelleschi's early bio-

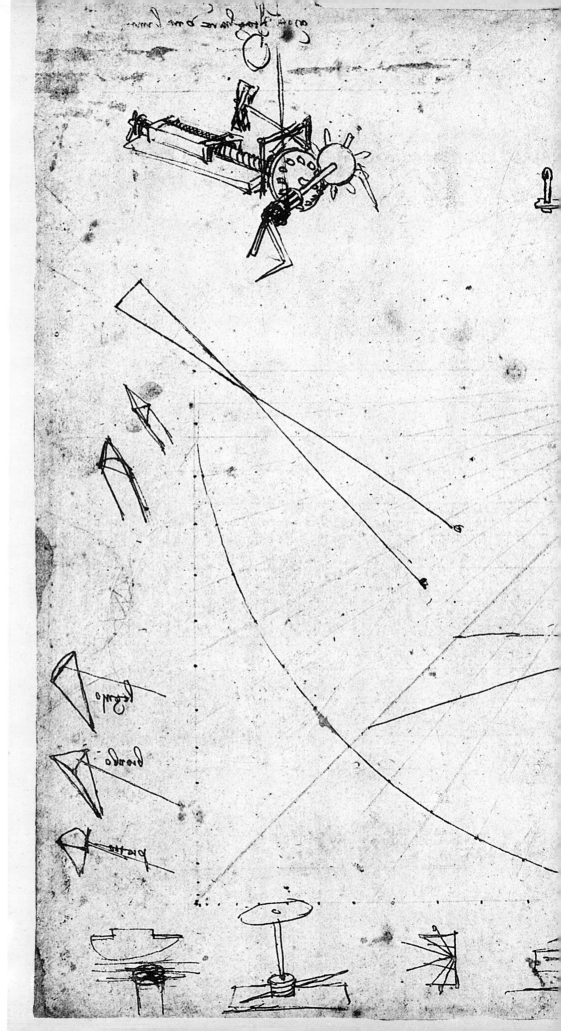

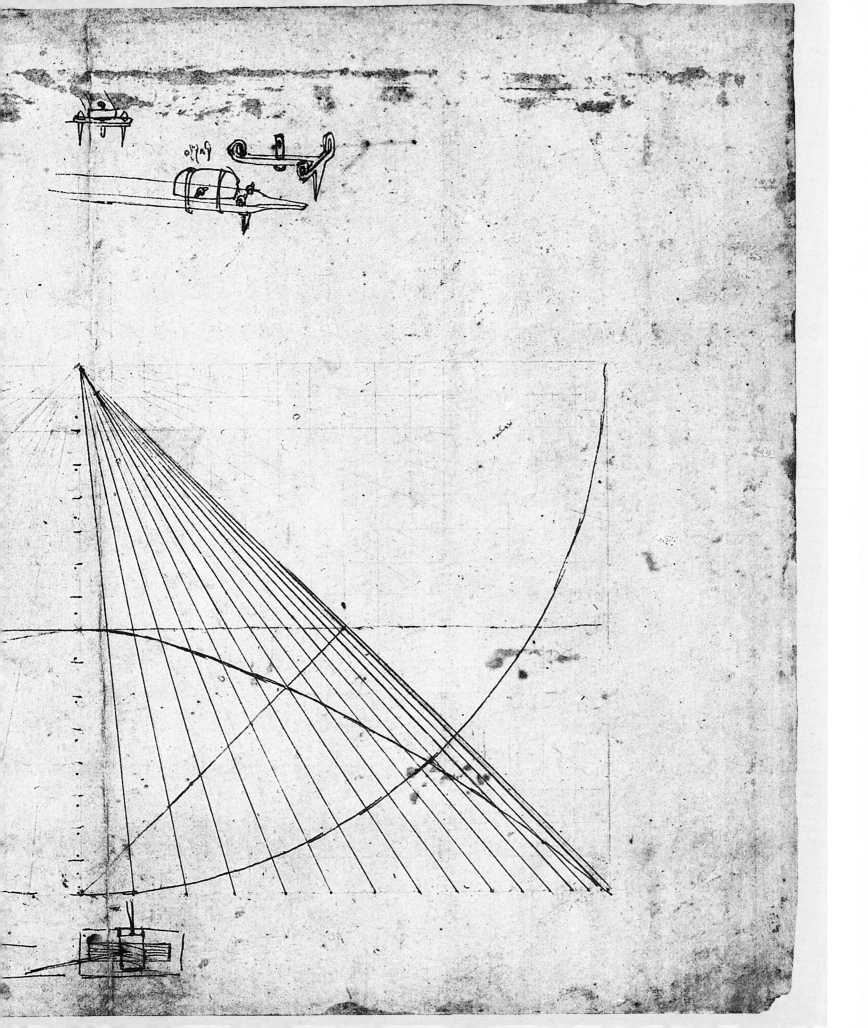

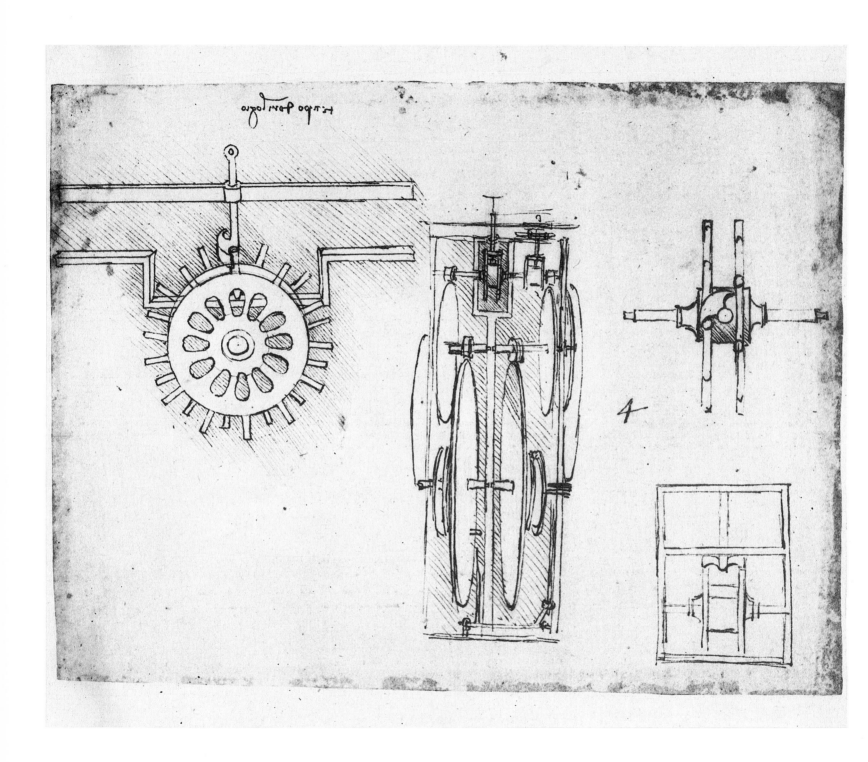

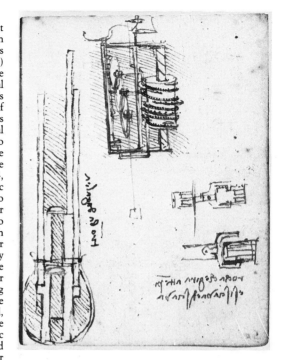

graphy took the information about clocks and the movement of their wheels and do not make mention of springs. Leonardo took a great interest in the mechanism of the clock in the tower of the Abbazia di Chiaravalle, as is shown by the diagram in the Codex Atlanticus, f. 399 v-b, datable about 1495. When he was in Pavia with Francesco di Giorgio in 1490, he would most probably have seen Dondi's celebrated planetarium, which was kept in the library of the castle. It has been suggested that a drawing of epicyclical movement with reference to the Sun and Venus in MS. L, f. 92 v, could be considered as a record of Dondi's planetarium. However, this is a note (like the one on f. 93 v of the same notebook) directly relating to a whole series of studies in the Codex Atlanticus datable about 1497 (f. 27 v-a, f. 366 r-a, v-a), which in their turn are developed further in Madrid MS. I.

One of the earliest sheets in the Codex Atlanticus, f. 347 r-b, from about 1478, contains a summary drawing of machinery with notes that allude to a planetarium ("Mercury, Venus, Earth, Moon, Zodiac...") and we must remember Leonardo's friendship with Lorenzo della Golpaja, who built a planetarium as famous as Dondi's. It would undoubtedly be useful to collect all of Leonardo's references to clock-making (many of which have not yet been interpreted, e.g. MS. L, f. 25 v) and consider them chronologically. This would certainly show that towards the end of the fifteenth century, in Milan, he intensified his study of those mechanisms, which are so splendidly illustrated in Madrid MS. I.

It seems that at the same time he began to work out a system of articulated support for bells which he continued to study until the early years of the sixteenth century. Several of his earliest technological drawings show a device for raising and transporting great weights such as artillery or bells. One of these, in the Codex Atlanticus, f. 40 r-b, partly covered by the profile of a seated man as in certain studies for the *Adoration of the Magi* (and so bearing no relation to the machine), has been erroneously interpreted as a project for an automobile. It is more probably a cart similar to the one studied in MS. B, f. 76 v-f. 77 r; that is, a "cart of easy movement," whose lifting power, which Leonardo defines as *terribile*, is generated by a multiplicity of wheels which interlock with the four touching the ground when the bell is ready to be lifted. Thus when it is towed, the cart lifts the weight that it must transport. Studies on the mechanism of bells are found on f. 70 v of the same manuscript, while on the facing page, f. 71 r, Leonardo shows a system for lifting a bell to the top of a campanile.

In MS. L, datable from the beginning of the sixteenth century, we find allusions to the bell of the Torre del Mangia in Siena (f. 19 v and f. 33 v) as well as a note (on the verso of the front cover) that indicates a relationship with Pagolo di Vannoccio, the architect for the Commune of Siena and an associate of Francesco di Giorgio. Therefore we must keep in mind the context of Leonardo's studies in the field of clock-making in order to ascertain whether their aim, as in Brunelleschi's case, transcends that of technological virtuosity.

3. The Automatons

Within the sphere of architectural projects Leonardo spent some time working out hydraulic devices that fall within the category of automatons. As such, they are reproposals of an aspect of ancient thought (Heron and Vitruvius) which in the late sixteenth century would feed the architects' imagination in planning gardens as special places of delight. We need only think of Pirro Ligorio's hydraulic organ at Tivoli or of the astonishing grottos of Pratolino. In the project for the garden for Charles d'Amboise's villa there is in fact a reference to musical instruments worked by the movement of water, so as to produce "continuous sounds." Leonardo's 1502 reference to the harmony produced by the falls of water in the fountain of Rimini is well known. A little later, about 1504, we find in Madrid MS. II the hint of an idea for a harmonic fountain, a real hydraulic organ for which Leonardo proposed to check Vitruvius with the help of a professor from the Florentine Studio, Marcello Virgili di Adriano Berti: "Ask Messer Marcello about the sound made with water from Vitruvius." Also at the time of the projects for Charles d'Amboise's villa Leonardo worked out a very elaborate hydraulic device, a clock that occupies a whole part of the palace, with tanks for the transfer of the water from one level to another and circular floats that rise along helical axes in order to time the separate moments of the manoeuvre. Two fragments at Windsor, originally united, show the "jacquemart" figure in the act of striking the hour-bell with a hammer, and they include axonometric and schematic views of the agglomerate of cisterns and water pipes for the downflow of the water. Another fragment at Windsor, originally part of a sheet of studies for the hydraulic clock, shows a herculean "jacquemart" figure with a rod for striking the hours. During his visit to Venice in 1500 Leonardo would have observed, probably from quite close by, the clock in the piazza, with similar figures by Rizzo. It is also probable that he knew about the automatons invented by the Paduan physicist and architect Giovanni Fontana who, a half century before, had been interested in self-propelled vehicles, armoured carts, boats operated by a single person, submarines, and even flying machines. "Things like these were made a long time ago," asserts Fontana, "and they can be made again in our time, except perhaps for the flying machine." This may have inspired Leonardo to intensify his studies on flight. And undoubtedly he would have known, at least by fame, the clock with automatons in the cathedral at Strasbourg, which in the first half to the fifteenth century constituted a synthesis of the technological virtuosities north of the Alps. We need only remember that Leonardo had met the architects of that cathedral when working on the projects for the tiburio of Milan Cathedral in about 1487.

Among Leonardo's earliest designs is one of a self-propelled car in the Codex Atlanticus, f. 296 v-a. This is often cited as an anticipation of the automobile, although it is only a vehicle of a kind illustrated by Leonardo's predecessors and contemporaries, from Taccola to Francesco di Giorgio. The stylistic character of the drawing suggests a date of about 1478, and in fact details of the same machine can be recognized in the famous drawing at

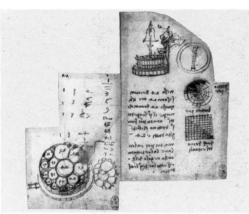

the Uffizi in which Leonardo records having begun "the two Virgin Marys" in December of that year. It can also be compared to f. 320 v-a of the Codex Atlanticus, a page which, like the one at the Uffizi, belongs to the time of the studies for an *Adoration of the Shepherds*, to which the three fragments at Windsor extracted from that sheet refer. The car is propelled by powerful leaf-springs capable of producing the necessary motive force to allow it to complete a relatively short course, such as from one side of a piazza to another. It is therefore probable that we are dealing with a car for festivals, or in fact the motor of an automaton. Thus one of Leonardo's earliest drawings would explain the mechanical principle of a device which he only constructed in the last years of his life – the famous mechanical lion. We know from Lomazzo in 1584, who said his source had been Francesco Melzi, that Leonardo used to make "birds, of certain material which flew through the air," that is automatons, and how "once in front of Francis I, King of France, he caused a lion, constructed with marvellous artifice, to walk from its place in a room and then stop, opening its breast which was full of lilies and different flowers." And again, in enumerating the products of Leonardo's technology, Lomazzo records "the way to make birds fly" and "lions walk by force of wheels." We have seen (p. 209) that Leonardo's automaton was a political allegory of the alliance between Florence and the King of France on the occasion of the latter's triumphal enter into Lyon in 1515. We have been able to ascertain this on the basis of a statement of Michelangelo Buonarroti the Younger in 1600 in his *Descrizione delle Felicissime Nozze della Cristianissima Maestà di Madama Maria Medici*, which is reproduced here (frontispiece and p. 10) from the example in the Biblioteca Riccardiana in Florence. However, nothing more is known of that automaton, and no hint of it is left in Leonardo's manuscripts. But what we do find there are indications of an automaton planned by Leonardo towards the end of the fifteenth century, which was apparently a real robot, of the type of those later constructed by Giannello Torriano for Charles V: a warrior in armour worked by a complex system of cables and pulleys, which articulated his parts, even the jaw, with anatomical accuracy. In f. 366 v-b of the Codex Atlanticus, next to the sketch of a mechanical joint for that automaton, there is a sketch of the corresponding joint in the bones of a human leg. The few indications remaining are found on the few pages of the Codex Atlanticus reproduced here, all datable about 1497. They also include studies of other mechanisms developed in Madrid MS. I, which makes us wonder whether the missing sheets of that codex did not contain detailed and spectacular studies of the robot. The existing sketches do not make clear what the motive force consisted of: perhaps springs, as in the early cart design, or counterweights, as in the clocks. Lomazzo's hint on the way of making "Lions walk by force of wheels" could be understood as a reference to a system that Leonardo had already used in the preceding robot project. In a sheet of sketches for that project, Codex Atlanticus, f. 216 v-b, we read an incomplete sentence with which Leonardo tried out his pen: "Tell me if ever, tell me if ever anything was built in

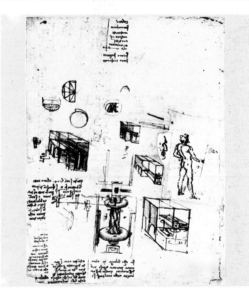

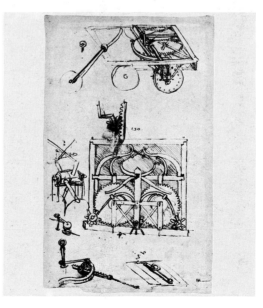

505. *Technological studies and profiles of shepherds for an*
Adoration, c. 1478. Codex Atlanticus, f. 320 v-a, and
Windsor, RL 12438, 12460, 12464.

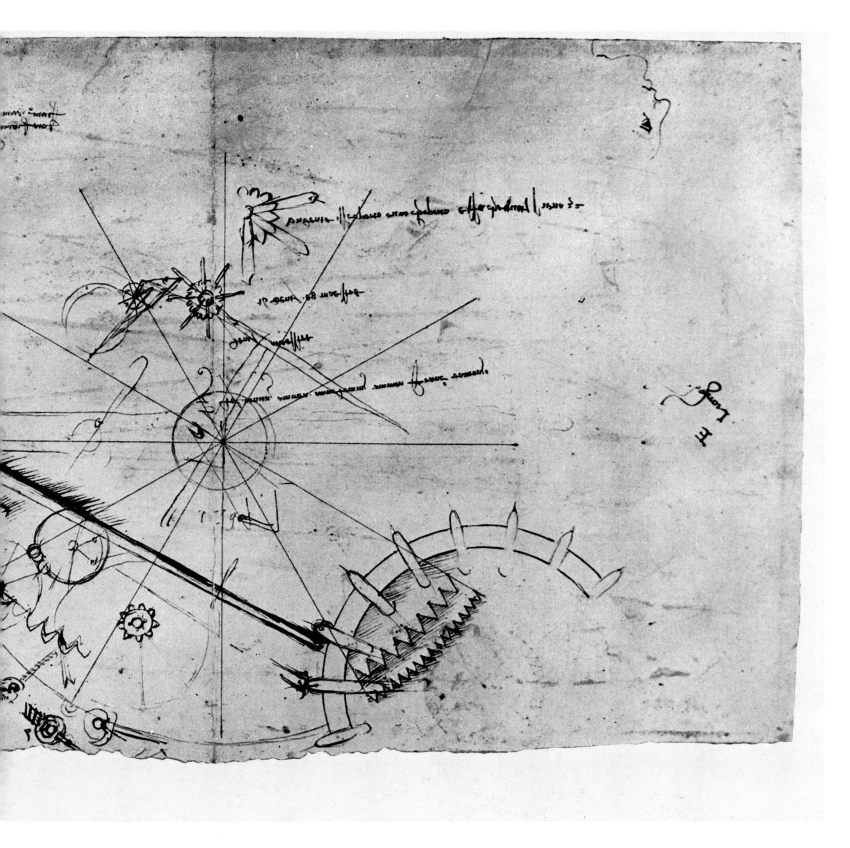

506, 507. *Michelangelo Buonarroti il Giovane,* Descrizione delle felicissime nozze di Maria Medici, *Florence 1600, frontispiece and page 10. Florence, Biblioteca Riccardiana.*

508-510. *Studies of the mechanism for a robot, c. 1497. Codex Atlanticus, ff. 366 v-b, 388 v-a, and 216 v-b.*

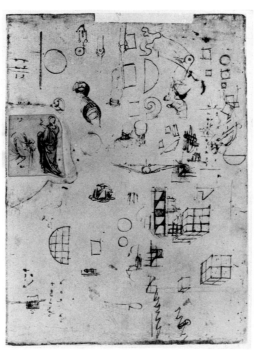

Rome..." Perhaps this is where the idea of the miraculous architecture of a simulated man comes from, a demonstration of *anathomia artificialis* to the contrasted with Brunelleschi's *perspectiva artificialis,* and with which Leonardo, in his subconscious, seems to want to emulate the ancients.

By a curious coincidence, a contemporary of Leonardo's, Benvenuto di Lorenzo della Golpaja, whose writings have preserved a record for us of Leonardo's machines and instruments, wrote the following memorandum at the beginning of one of his codices in Venice: "to remind myself when I go to stay in Rome to make a wooden man who will stand behind a door, and when someone opens the door that wooden man comes to meet him with a stick to hit him on the head, or with a rope to grab him and tie him."

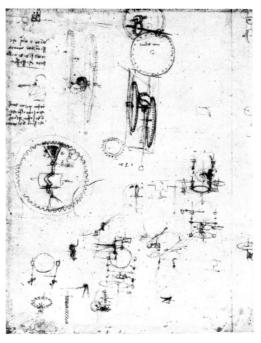

511. Perspective view of a machine for cutting marble, with details in an exploded view, c. 1513. Codex Atlanticus, f. 1 r-c. ▶

Tools/ Utensils/ Everyday Objects

When Walter Gropius established the Bauhaus in 1919 he put forward anew the idea that a building in its totality is the highest aim of all the figurative arts and in postulating a return to "craft" he stated that "to adorn a building was once the most noble function of the arts," and that the "arts," meaning the products of artisans, "were the indispensable components of great architecture."

Gropius' view could be exemplified by the enormous quantity of designs which Leonardo gathered, so to speak, around the edges of architectural projects, and which until recently were assigned to the category of "minor arts": utensils, tools, objects for the house, appliances and gadgets necessary for daily life, in short that complex of technological elements that share in the functions of the building and whose design serves to emphasize their status as a part of "great architecture." This rather neglected aspect of Leonardo's work could fill a whole chapter in the history of "industrial design," and at the same time offer a new contribution to the study of the mutual influence of the arts in the Renaissance, a study brilliantly begun by Ferdinando Bologna.

The argument of the "mechanicalness" of sculpture, which Leonardo used in the famous debate on the hierarchy of the arts, is part of a rhetorical exercise which he sometimes carried to absurd lengths in his desire to have painting recognized as a liberal art. He takes the image of the sculptor's home, "dirty and filled with dust and chips of stone," "with the din of hammering and other noises," and contrasts it with that of the painter, "clean and often accompanied by music." It has been rightly said that this type of debate, which dragged on through the whole of the sixteenth century, had insufficient force to prejudice the allied question of the "major" and "minor" arts. Starting from the time of his apprenticeship in Florentine workshops, Leonardo went on carrying out his own workshop experiments, above all with metallurgy and the working of glass. In f. 32 r-a of the Codex Atlanticus, a page datable to about 1480, we have a synthesis of these early interests, with studies of machines for making burning-glasses, mills and systems of multiple furnaces for metal-casting. He was to make use of these later when planning the casting of the horse for the Sforza Monument, about 1493-95, and in fact one of the notes was added about 1495, or even later. In the last decade of the fifteenth century, in Milan, Leonardo's studio included not only painters, but also technicians, one of whom, Giulio Tedesco, seems to have specialized in making locks. Leonardo would have used them also for preparing models of clock mechanisms of for whatever technical services were necessary. We know that he had worked on devising horse-armour and harnesses and, closely related to these, arms, cuirasses and helmets with an exuberance of new, ingenious and imaginative forms. We find numerous reflections of all this in his drawings, from the earliest to the latest. In fact, he must have learned how to work with the file very early on, and it is not by chance that one of his earliest projects is the well-known machine for making files in Codex Atlanticus, f. 6 r-b. The notes relating to the mechanism for the bath of the Duchess of Milan, dated 1499, indicate that this was

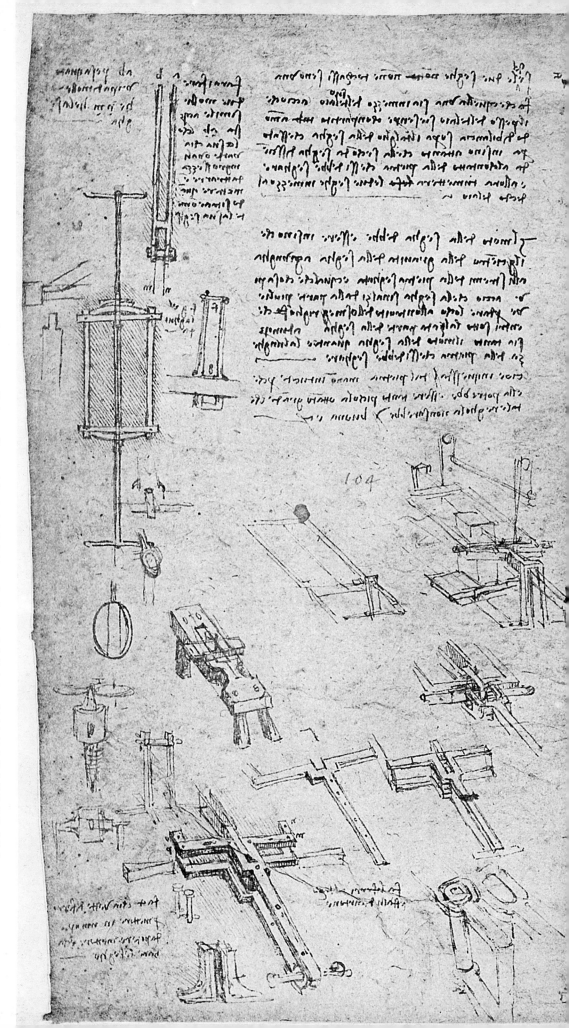

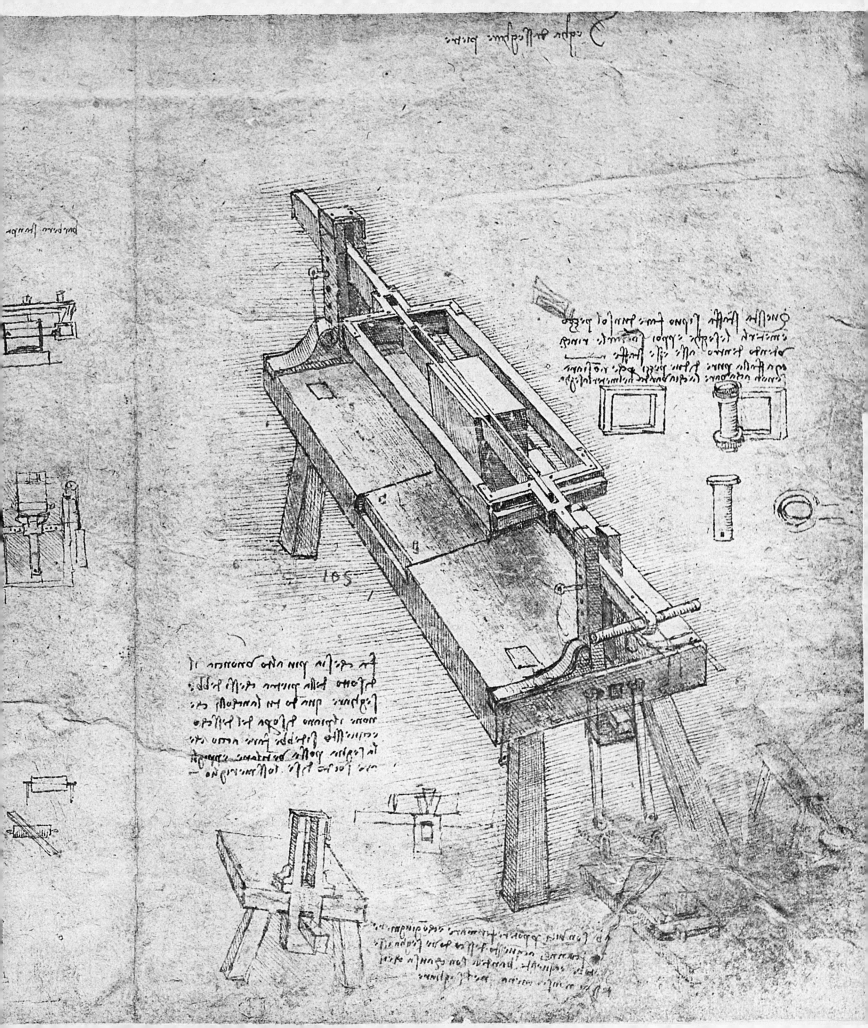

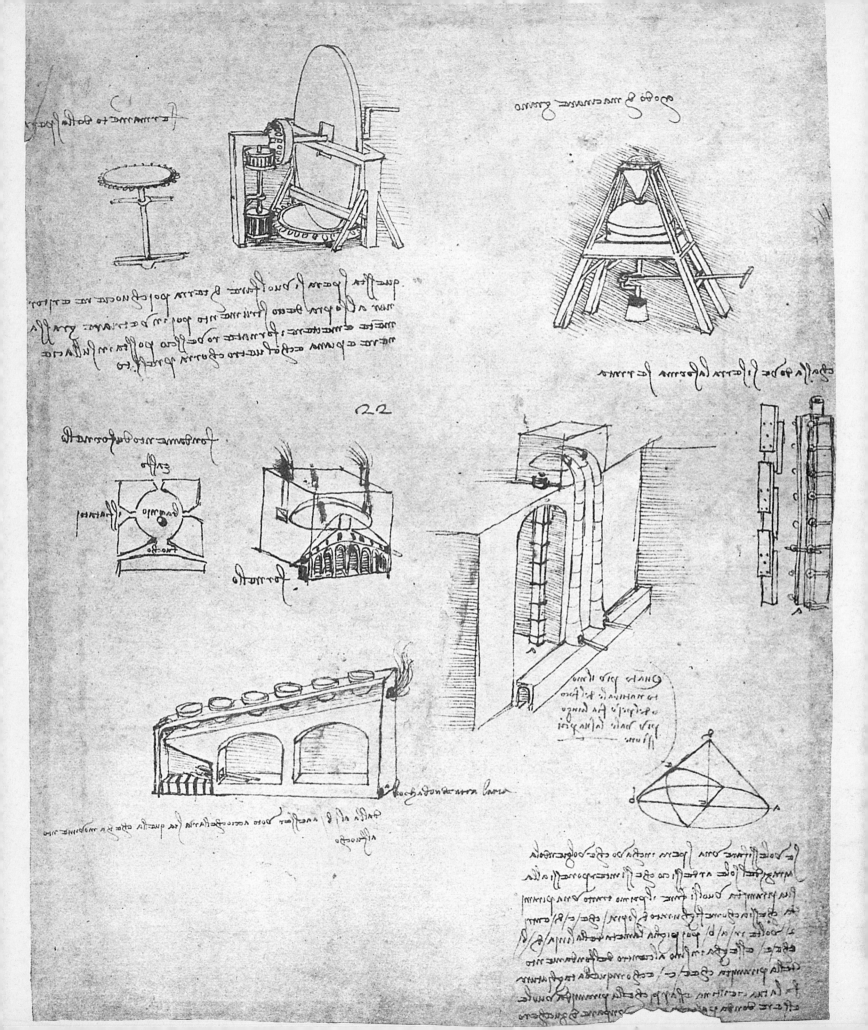

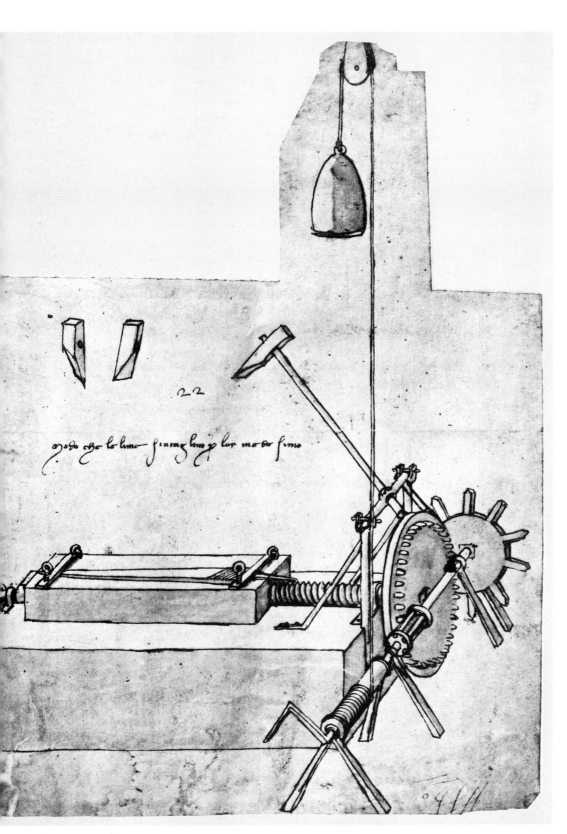

an actual project and show us an image of Leonardo quite different from the one which he himself, in the debate on the hierarchy of the arts, seems to want to present. "The giving of formal commissions was not necessary," wrote Calvi with keen insight "because the Duchess could easily ask her very ingenious neighbour, on some friendly occasion and without ceremony, to devise the mechanism for the bath; and given the artist's natural disposition he may have applied himself to it with more eager interest than to a commission for a large painting."

For a period of a few years, around 1508, Leonardo was deeply involved with developing a pliable material of his own invention (the "membranous glass invented by me," as he himself defined it in a note in RL 12667). This was a material of mainly. organic composition (eggs, glue and vegetable ingredients) processed in some way to imitate the variegated abstract design of *pietre dure* and, could be made into household objects such as vases, carafes, bowls etc. There is reason to believe that the project may have at least been carried through an experimental stage. In fact, in describing the process of the manual smoothing down of the object ("clean off the excess with the hands, they often clean to a knife-edge so that on the surface you see no sign of hand rubbing") he seems to allude to a prototype which he himself had prepared.

The illustrations which follow aim to present an essay on Leonardo as inventor and designer of tools, utensils and general household objects. As for the designs of weapons, those have been chosen which have the greatest affinity with architectural forms. In fact, Leonardo often makes cannon-barrels look like columns, with ornamental detailing derived directly from the designs he intended to apply to buildings. The same can be seen in the drawings of compasses and also some pen quills in the Codex Atlanticus, f. 187 v-b, which could be interpreted as projects for fountain pens. It is not surprising therefore that the very elegant design of a lady's purse in the Codex Atlanticus, f. 372 r-b, evokes the sculptural decoration of the top of a sarcophagus. And the design for a textile machine in Madrid MS. I, f. 68 r, can look like the model of a colonnade. Architectural elements and those of architectural decoration keep appearing in Leonardo's designs of machines and tools, and we have already recalled the machine for making rope, which is made to look like a fountain.

It is most of all within the scope of his profession as painter that Leonardo can tap the resources of his genius for invention and design. We need only recall the interior design project for a "painter's studio" in a manuscript datable about 1492, with movable walls to control the light and a system for raising and lowering the picture to get it out of the way at the end of the days work. Leonardo also designed "night lights," not only with ordinary candleholders, candelabra and lamps more or less elaborately decorated, but also lamps with lenses and above all a table lamp whose intensity could be regulated, with an ample reservoir and a screen. Studies for this lamp in RL 12675 v (and see also Codex Atlanticus, f. 368 v-a, and Codex Arundel, f. 283 v), datable about 1505-7, show the object in the same perspective view that Leonardo used in his

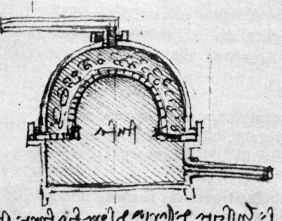

(mirror-script text, illegible)

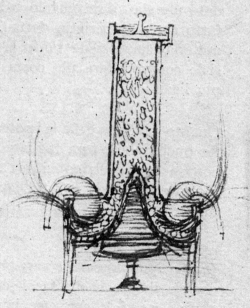

(mirror-script text, illegible)

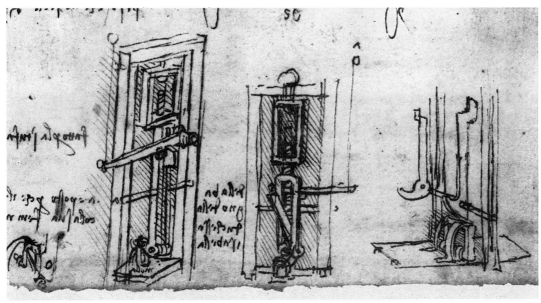

514-520. *The Duchess's Bath, 1499. – 514. Codex Arundel, f. 145 v; 515. Codex Atlanticus, f. 104 r-b, detail; 516-520. MS. I, ff. 28 v, 31 v, 32 v, 37 r, 33 v, 34 r. On a page of mechanical notes in Codex Atlanticus, dated 1 August 1499, Leonardo studies a device "for the stove or bath of the Duchess Isabella." Isabella of Aragon, widow of Gian Galeazzo Sforza, resided in the Corte Vecchia in Milan, where Leonardo, too, was living. Studies for the same device are found in the first part of MS. I and include a note on the regulation of the hot and cold water in the bath. This mechanism is difficult to interpret because the few remaining notes on it deal only with the working of a lever to close a small hatch. It is a subject, therefore, that should arouse the curiosity of those scholars who would like to establish a comparison with similar devices mentioned by Francesco di Giorgio in imitation of Vitruvius. On another sheet of MS. I there is a quick sketch of a "stove" for a bath, which is undoubtedly related to the drawings on a sheet of the Codex Arundel where, in fact, the same "stove," identifiable therefore with the Duchess's bath, is described in its technological components and in its functions. And it is here that, proceeding from practise to theory, Leonardo toys with the idea of a treatise on the "drilling movements of fire that make it powerful for casting," almost a presage of future technological and artistic interests: from the studies on casting for the Trivulzio Monument to those of the Deluge (see illustration 482), in which he speaks "of cloud, smoke and dust, and flames of an oven or red-hot furnace."*

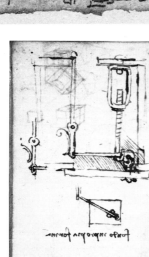

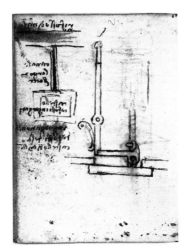

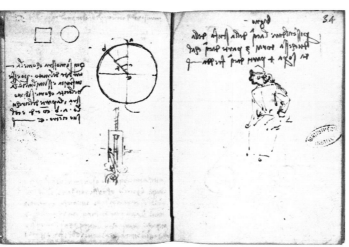

521. Studies of "mixtures," c. 1508. MS. F,
ff. 73 v and 95 v.

522. Helmet for a tournament, c. 1517-18.
Windsor, RL 12329, detail.
523. Sword-hilts, c. 1506-8. *Codex
Atlanticus, f. 133 r-a.*

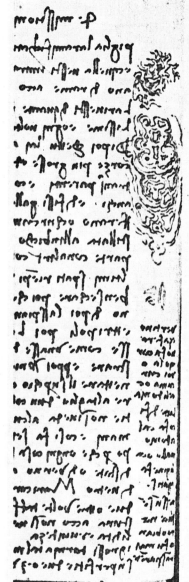
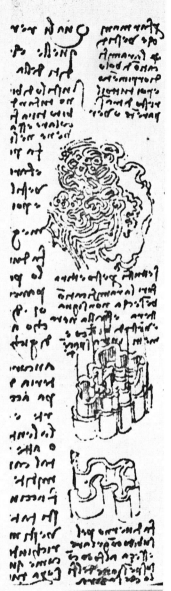

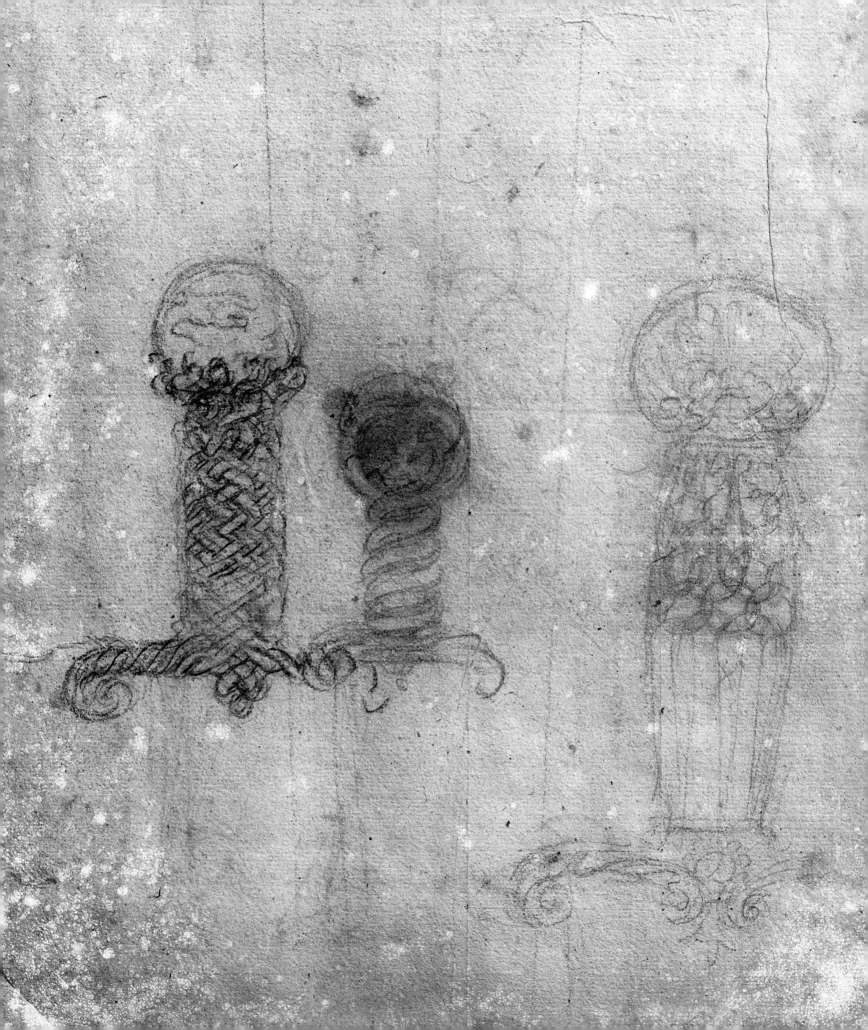

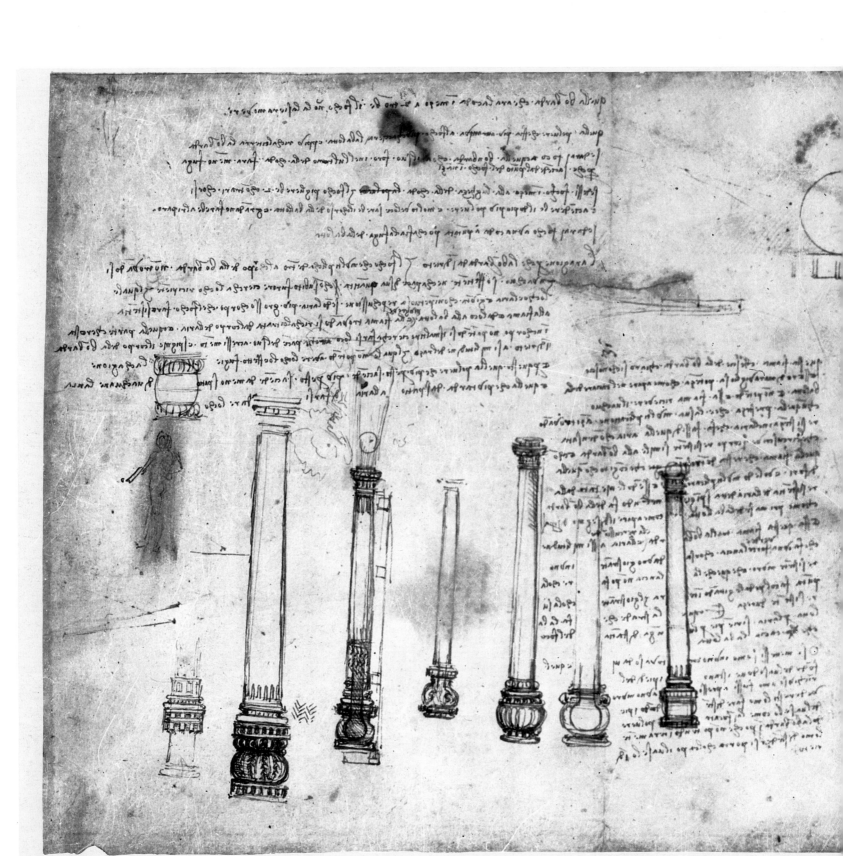

524. *Studies of cannon*, c. 1495-97. *Codex Atlanticus, f. 28 v-a.*

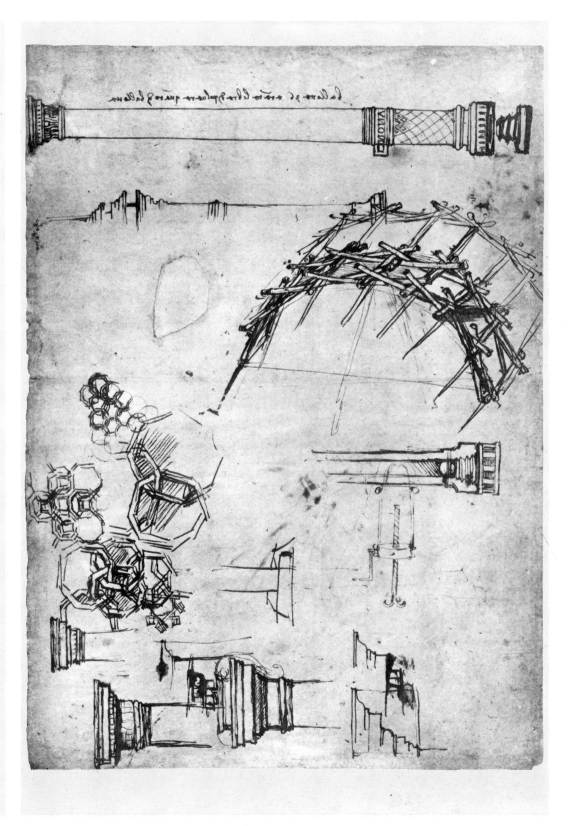

525. *Studies of artillery and a temporary bridge*, c. 1487-90. *Codex Atlanticus, f. 23 v-a.*

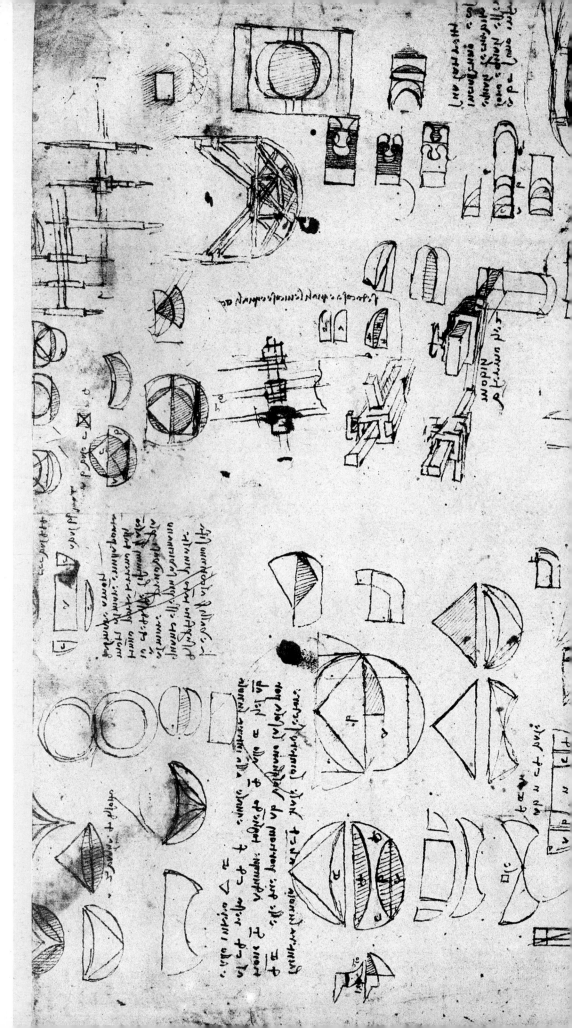

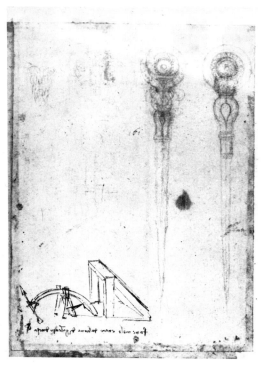

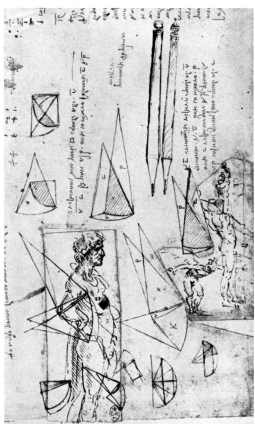

526-528. *Studies of instruments: Codex Atlanticus, f. 177 v-s (compasses, c. 1490); Codex Atlanticus, f. 187 v-b, and Windsor RL 12440 and 12724 (fountain pens, c. 1506-8); Codex Atlanticus, f. 259 r-a (compasses, c. 1515).*

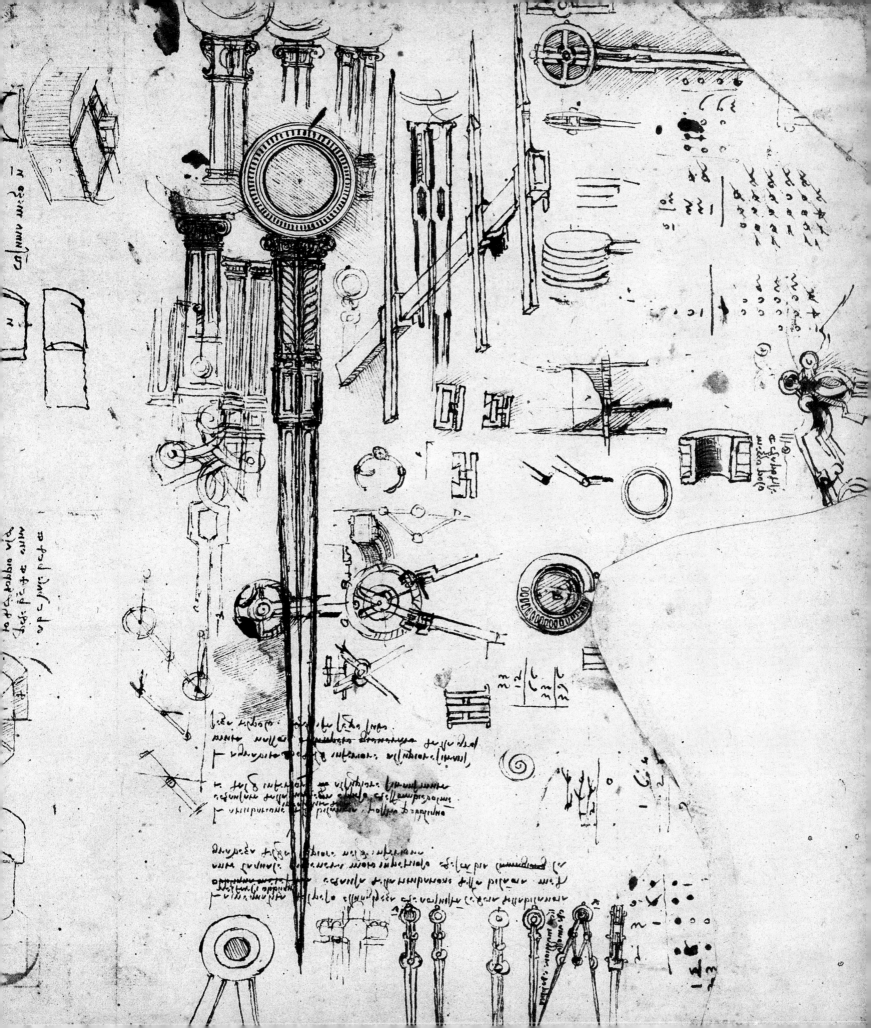

529. *Studies of parabolic compasses, c. 1513-14. Codex Atlanticus, f. 394 v-a.*

530. *Studies of proportional compasses and sketch of a furnace, c. 1513-14. Codex Atlanticus, f. 385 r-a, detail.*

531. *Studies of building tools, c. 1489. Codex Atlanticus, f. 295 v-a.*

532. *Studies of pedometers, c. 1500-5. Codex Atlanticus, f. 1 r-a.*

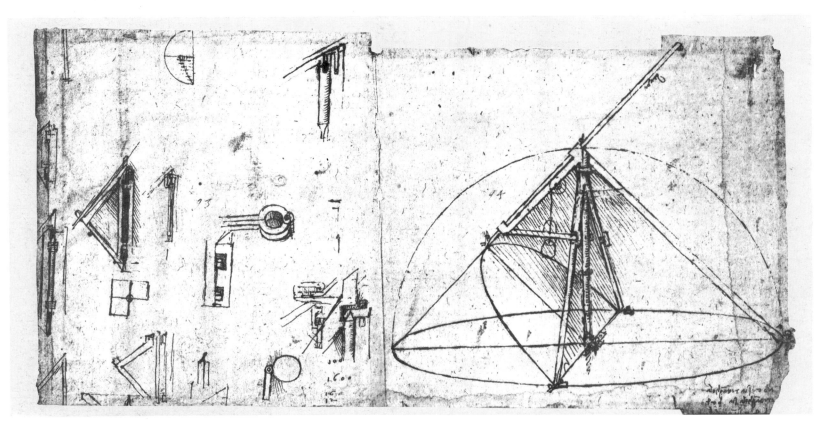

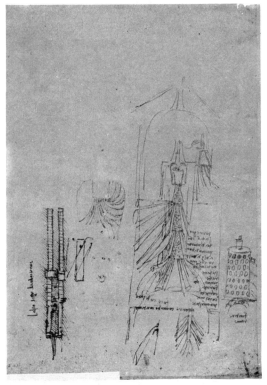

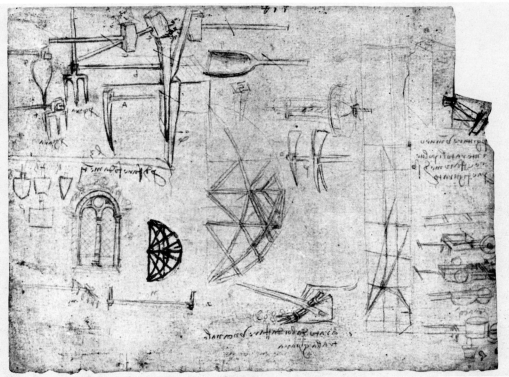

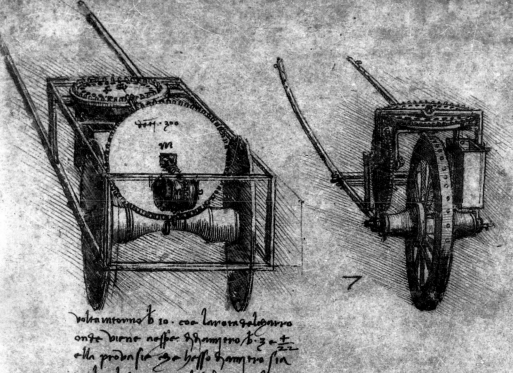
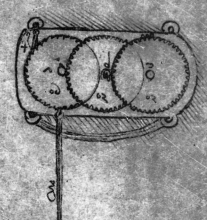

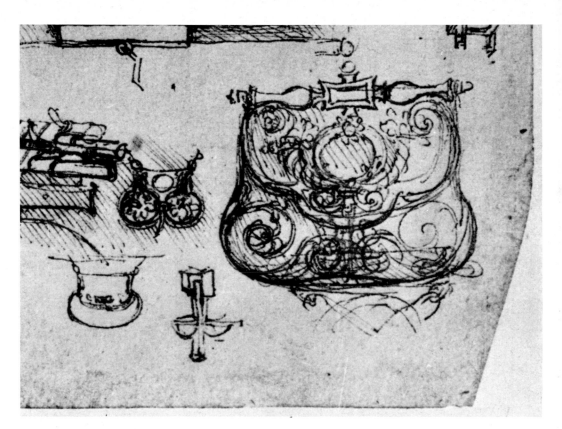

533. *Design for a lady's purse,* c. 1497. *Codex Atlanticus, f. 372 r-b, detail.*
534. *Studies of locks,* c. 1497. *Codex Atlanticus, f. 292 v-a.*
535. *Study of a chain with interlacing links,* c. 1493-95. *Codex Atlanticus, f. 252 v-b, detail.*

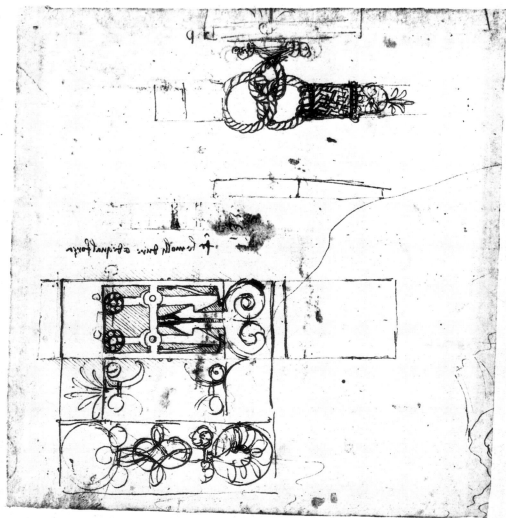

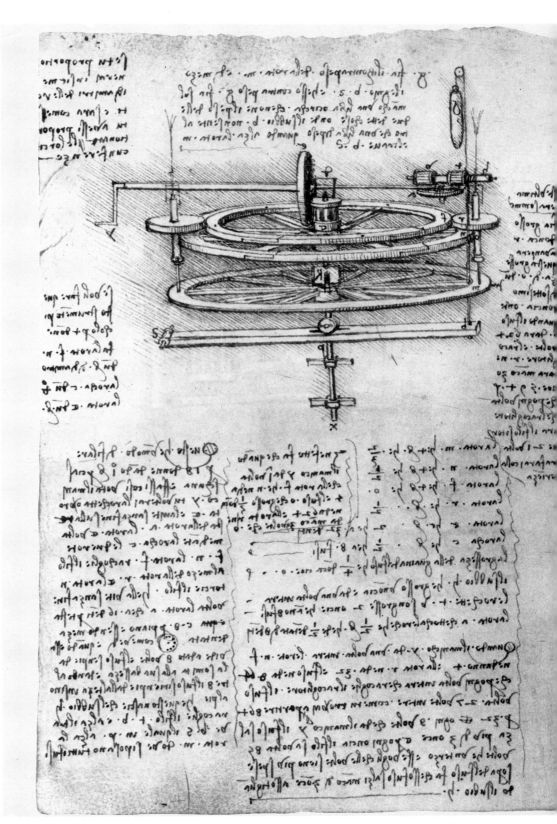

537. Study of a loom and textile machine, c. 1497-1500.
Madrid MS. I, ff. 67 v and 68 r.

538. Study of a physiotherapy chair, c. 1494. Codex
Atlanticus, f. 291 v-a.

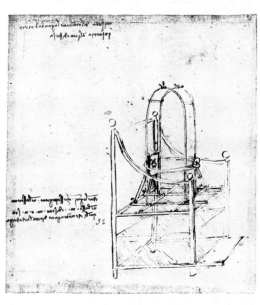

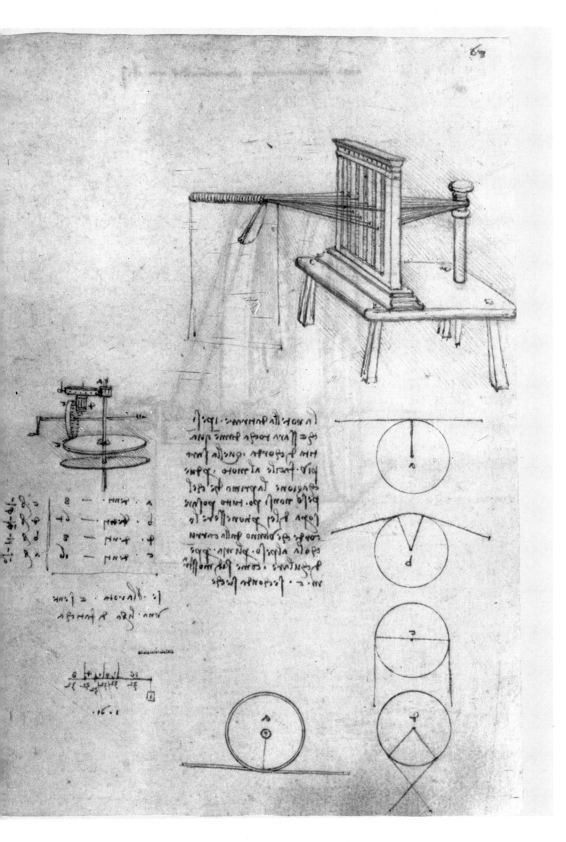

drawings of buildings. The decorative forms of the lamp are only lightly indicated in its turned support, while the functional apparatus is reduced to pure geometrical forms as if it were an illustration for a problem in stereometry. In this Leonardo is still reflecting a fifteenth-century attitude of practical artisanship which never subordinates the functional to the ornamental. These objects, therefore, offer us a less artificial image of the ambience within which Leonardo lived and worked, and with it a more human image of him because even the most commonplace objects could provide the inspiration for a scientific observation: "If the air presses in on itself, as the vessel for pouring rose water in the barber shop shows, it doubles itself."

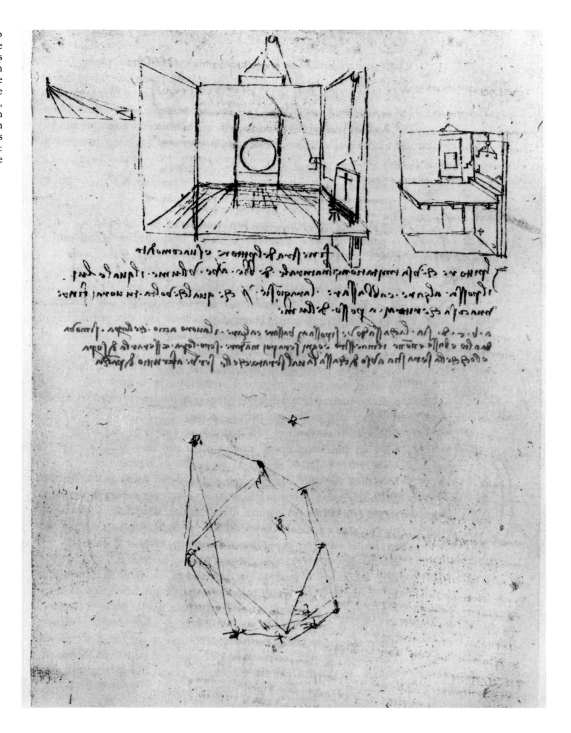

540-542. *Studies for a table lamp, c. 1505-7.*
Windsor, RL 12675 v; Codex Atlanticus, f.
368 v-a; Codex Arundel, f. 283 v.

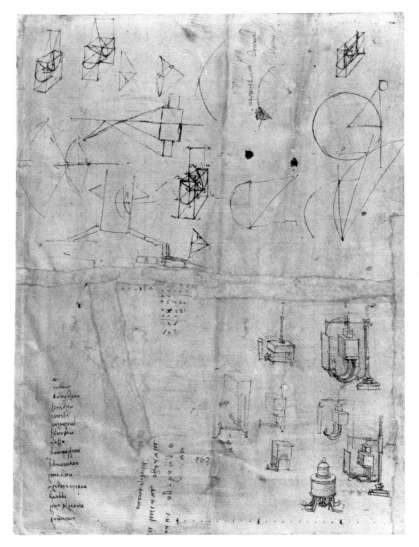

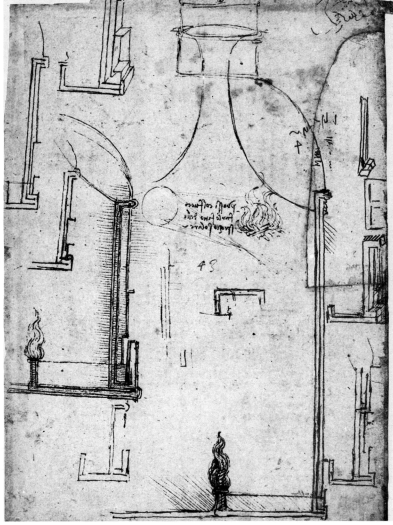

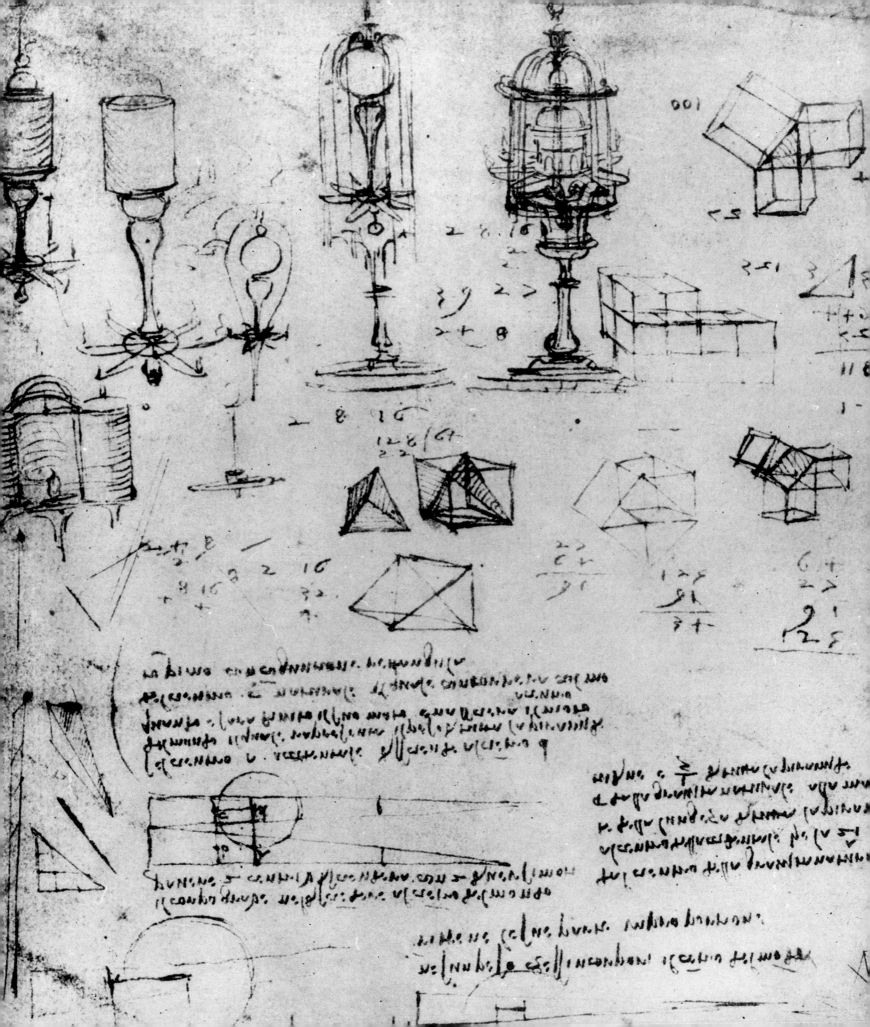

543. Giuseppe Bossi, copy of f. 22 r from the Codex Trivulzianus of Leonardo with comments on the Palazzo dei Sanseverino. Milan, Biblioteca Ambrosiana, MS. S. P. 6/13-D, f. 217 v.
544. Engraving of a drawing of a centrally-planned temple or villa attributed to Leonardo by Carlo Amoretti and now lost. From the 1804 edition of Leonardo's Trattato della Pittura.

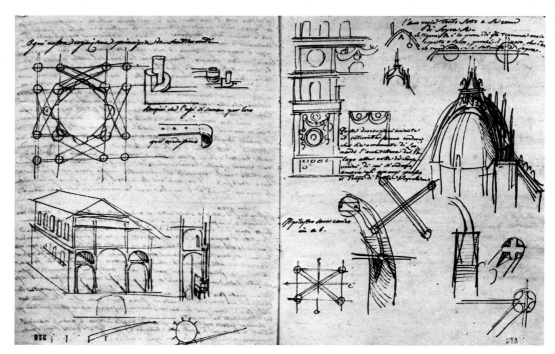

The first studies on Leonardo as an architect go back no further than a century, except for those undertaken by Giuseppe Bossi at the beginning of the nineteenth century with a view to a work on the architecture of the *Last Supper*. This, however was never published. (See *Raccolta Vinciana*, XIX, 1962, pp. 294-95). At that time the Ambrosiana's Leonardo codices, including the Codex Atlanticus, were in Paris, where Napoleon had taken them in 1796. The only codex accessible to Bossi in Milan was the Codex Trivulzianus which, in fact, he transcribed in its entirety, adding a commentary on its texts and drawings, perhaps with the intention of publishing it, following an analytical method which even today has not been applied to the editions of Leonardo's work. Particularly precious is his comment on the drawing of a wall decoration on f. 22 r, as it confirms that at that time the remains of the Palazzo dei Sanseverino outside Porta Vercellina still existed: "These tiny and incomplete decorations make us believe that Leonardo may really have been the architect of the palazzo once belonging to the Sanseverini, whose ruins may still be seen near the Ponte di Porta Vercellina" (Biblioteca Ambrosiana, MS. S.P. 6/13-D, f. 217 v). Oltrocchi's historical studies of 1785, published by Ritter in 1925, were the basis for Amoretti's *Memorie* of 1804, and constitute the first research into the late fifteenth-century Milanese town-planning programmes in which Leonardo participated. It is here that the attribution of the palazzo and the stables of the Sanseverino to Leonardo originated, and Amoretti also published a drawing of a temple of villa attributed to Leonardo. This, however, seems to be of a later date (even Palladian?) and has never again been found in the Ambrosiana collections. Govi also refers to the Palazzo dei Sanseverino in his essay of 1872, which is based mainly on the contents of the Codex Atlanticus. In publishing the anonymous seventeenth-century annotations to the first edition of Vasari's *Vite*, Mongeri showed in 1876 that at that time Bossi's unpublished work was still being consulted. Meanwhile, in Paris, Geymüller's first study of Leonardo's drawings in MS. B appeared, relating them to Bramante's projects for the new St. Peter's. The first systematic study of Leonardo's manuscripts from the point of view of his work as an architect came, in fact, in Geymüller's contribution to Richter's anthology of 1883, with a general catalogue of Leonardo material relating to civil and ecclesiastical architecture, a catalogue which is still a fundamental tool of research today. A new edition of Richter's anthology, with important additions and revisions, appeared in 1939. This takes count, among other things, of the studies on Leonardo's architecture which Heydenreich began to publish in 1929. A later revision came with my *Commentary* on that anthology, published in 1977, which draws above all on Firpo's impeccable synthesis and analysis of Leonardo's architectural studies published in 1963.

Numerous publications on Leonardo as an architect and town planner have appeared in the last 50 years. Most of them thave confirmed the validity and necessity of the method put forward by Calvi in 1925 for considering Leonardo's manuscripts from a chronological, historical and biographical point of view. This method was applied

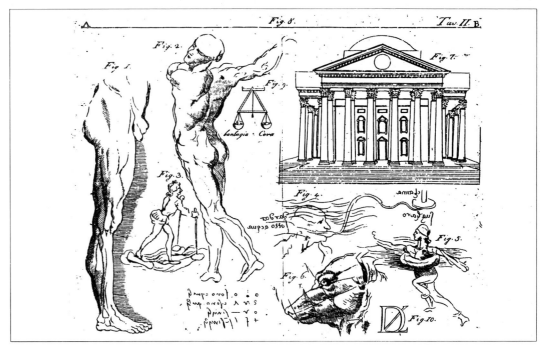

for the first time to a full critical anthology of Leonardo texts, including those on architecture, by Anna Maria Brizio in 1952. This anthology also includes a selection of texts on military architecture; studies on this theme have been intensified in the last years, beginning with those by Ignazio Calvi in 1939 and 1943 right up to the most recent ones by Heydenreich, Reti and Parronchi on the second of the new manuscripts at Madrid.

The bibliography which follows is intended to be complete and up to date. Any omissions – however involuntary – ought not to include contributions of scientific importance. In fact, it has been enlarged intentionally so as to include those publications in which Leonardo is mentioned, even only briefly, for some aspect of particular interest in the context of his architectural projects, and above all in relation to the themes treated in the present book. Ferrari-Brivio's article on the Milan Cathedral tiburio is the unique case of a publication indispensable to the study of Leonardo as an architect even though Leonardo's name is not mentioned in it.

A fundamental work, also from the bibliographical point of view, *Scritti Rinascimentali di Architettura* (Milan 1978), came out when this book had already gone to press and therefore was not able to receive the attention it deserved. It is a philologically impeccable edition of the writings of Luca Pacioli, Francesco Colonna, Leonardo, Bramante, Francesco di Giorgio and Cesariano, as well as the *patente* to Luciano Laurana and the letter to Leo X, edited by Arnaldo Bruschi, Corrado Maltese, Manfredo Tafuri and Renato Bonelli. Besides clarifying Leonardo's contribution to the development of architectural theories from the fifteenth to the sixteenth century, the work presents a complete review of the material relating to the problem of the Milan Cathedral tiburio. Frances D. Fergusson's important work on the tiburio question, which also appeared when the present book was already in process of publication, recognized the close connection between Leonardo's and Francesco di Giorgio's solutions to the problem, which in the present book is taken as an argument for attributing the final model to Leonardo.

Ackerman J.S., *The Architecture of Michelangelo*, London 1961; Italian ed., Turin 1968 (see index).

Ackerman J.S., "Sources of the Renaissance Villa," in *The Renaissance and Mannerism. Studies in Western Art. Acts of the Twentieth International Congress of the History of Art*, Princeton, N.J., 1963, Vol. II, pp. 6-18 (esp. p. 12).

Amoretti C., "Memorie storiche su la vita gli studi e le opere di Lionardo da Vinci" [introduction to the edition of the *Trattato della Pittura* by Leonardo], Milan 1804 (esp. pp. 158-60).

Annoni A., "L'edificio bramantesco di S. Maria della Fontana," in *Rassegna d'Arte*, VIII, 1908, pp. 10-13, 28-32, 70.

Annoni A., "Considerazioni su Leonardo architetto," in *Emporium*, XLIX, 1919, pp. 170-80.

Annoni A., "Tiburi lombardi e cupole leonardesche," in *Atti del I Congresso nazionale di storia dell'architettura*, Florence 1938, pp. 53-6.

Annoni A., "Leonardo decoratore," in *Leonardo da Vinci a cura della Mostra*, Novara 1939, pp. 307-14.

Arata G.U., *Leonardo architetto e urbanista* [Pubblicazioni del Museo Nazionale della Scienza e della Tecnica di Milano nel quinto Centenario della nascita di Leonardo: 11], Milano 1953.

Arkin D., "Le idee di un grande architetto," in *Rassegna sovietica*, III, 1952, pp. 61-6.

Arluno B., *Historiarum ab origine Urbis mediolanensis ad nostra usque tempora Sectiones tres*, Basel 1530 (esp. p. 56).

Arredi F., "Leonardo idraulico," in *Sapere*, IV, 1938, pp. 390-92; reprinted in *Sapere*, special issue, 15 April 1952, pp. 28-30.

Arslan E., "L'architettura milanese nella seconda metà del Quattrocento," in *Storia di Milano*, Vol. VII, Milan 1956, pp. 599-690.

Babinger F., Heydenreich L.H., "Vier Bauvorschläge Lionardo da Vinci's an Sultan Bajezid II (1502-3)," in *Nachrichten von der Akademie der Wissenschaften in Göttingen*, Phil.-hist. Klasse, 1952, pp. 1-20.

Babinger F., "Eine Brücke von Galata nach Stambul-wollte Leonardo in die Dienste des Sultans treten?," in *Die Neue Zeitung*, VIII, 1952, nos. 87-8.

Babinger F., "Un inedito di Leonardo da Vinci. Leonardo e la Corte del Sultano," in *Il Nuovo Corriere*, 23 March 1952, p. 3.

Bach R.F., "Leonardo, an architectural theorist," in *Architectural Record*, XLIII, 1918, pp. 485-86.

Bacchi A., Bacchi G., "Leonardo da Vinci's port-canal Cesenatico," in *Arts and Architecture*, LXXXIII, No. 11, 1966, pp. 26-7.

Baratta M., "La pianta d'Imola di Leonardo da Vinci," in *Bollettino della Società geografica italiana*, XII, 1911, pp. 945-67.

Baratta M., "Sopra le fonti cartografiche di Leonardo da Vinci," in *Atti dell'VIII Congresso Geografico Italiano* (Florence, 29 March - 6 April 1921), Vol. II, *Communicazioni*, Florence 1923, pp. 281-95.

Baratta M., "Leonardo da Vinci e le paludi pontine," in *La Geografia*, Novara 1928, Nos. 1-4.

Baratta M. (ed.), *I disegni geografici di Leonardo da Vinci conservati nel Castello di Windsor...* [Edition of the Commissione Vinciana, *Disegni*, special issue], Rome 1941.

Barni L., "Ricerche intorno all'opera di Leonardo e del Bramante in Vigevano," in *Annuario della R. Scuola Complementare G. Robecchi in Vigevano*, 1926-1928, Vigevano 1928, pp. 46-55.

Barocchi P. (ed.), *Scritti d'arte del Cinquecento, Tomo III...*, Milan-Naples 1977 (esp. pp. 3111-22).

Baroni C., "Una rettifica in tema di biografia vinciana. Leonardo da Vinci fu ingegnere ducale in Milano?," in *Rendiconti del R. Istituto Lombardo di scienze e lettere*, Vol. LXX, issue III, 1937, pp. 1-9.

Baroni C., "Elementi stilistici fiorentini negli studi vinciani

di architettura a cupola," in *Atti del I Congresso nazionale di storia dell'architettura*, Florence 1938, pp. 57-81.

Baroni C., "Leonardo maestro d'architettura," in *Sapere*, IV, 1938, pp. 379-82; reprinted in *Sapere*, special issue, 15 April 1952, pp. 23-6.

Baroni C., "Leonardo, Bramantino e il mausoleo di Gian Giacomo Trivulzio," in *Raccolta Vinciana*, XV-XVI, 1934-39, pp. 201-70.

Baroni C., "Leonardo architetto," in *Leonardo da Vinci a cura della Mostra*, Novara 1939, pp. 239-59.

Baroni C., "Valori ed ombre dell'architettura vinciana," in *Casabella*, XI, 1939, pp. 2-5.

Baroni C., *Documenti per la storia dell'architettura a Milano nel Rinascimento e nel Barocco*, Vol. I, Florence 1940; Vol. II (posthumous), Rome 1968.

Baroni C., *L'architettura lombarda da Bramante al Richini. Questioni di metodo*, Milan 1941.

Baroni C., "Tracce pittoriche leonardesche recuperate al Castello Sforzesco di Milano," in *Rendiconti dell'Istituto lombardo di scienze e lettere*, LXXXVIII, 1955, pp. 1-12.

Bassoli F.S., "L'uriuolo' di Leonardo da Vinci per il Convento di S. Donato a Scopeto," in *Sapere*, special issue, 15 April 1952, pp. 53-6.

Battisti E., *L'antirinascimento*, Milan 1962 (see index and esp. chapter VIII "Per una iconologia degli automi").

Battisti E., "Il metodo progettuale secondo il 'De re aedificatoria' di Leon Battista Alberti," in *Il Sant'Andrea di Mantova e Leon Battista Alberti*, Mantua 1972, pp. 131-56 (esp. note 92).

Battisti E., "Natura Artificiosa to Natura Artificialis," in *The Italian Garden* (First Dumbarton Oaks Colloquium on the History of Landscape Architecture edited by David R. Coffin), Washington, D.C., 1972, pp. 1-36.

Battisti E., *Filippo Brunelleschi*, Milan 1976 (see index).

Beck T., "Die Geometrie Krummliniger Figuren Leonardo da Vincis," in *Zeitschrift für gewerblichen Unterricht*, XVIII, 1904, pp. 108-10, 113-15, 172-74, 177-79.

Beltrami L., *Il Castello di Milano sotto il dominio degli Sforza...*, Milan 1885; definitive edition, Milan 1894.

Beltrami L., "Leonardo da Vinci negli studi per rendere navigabile l'Adda," in *Rendiconti del R. Istituto lombardo di scienze e lettere*, XXXV, 1902, pp. 1-15.

Beltrami L., *La Sala delle Asse nel Castello di Milano decorata da Leonardo da Vinci*, Milan 1902.

Beltrami L., *Leonardo e il porto di Cesenatico*, Milan 1902.

Beltrami L., "Leonardo da Vinci negli studi per il tiburio della cattedrale di Milano," Milan 1903; reprinted in *Luca Beltrami e il Duomo di Milano*, Milan 1964, pp. 357-86.

Beltrami L., *Il decreto per la piazza del Castello di Milano, 22 agosto 1492*, Milan 1904.

Beltrami L., *Leonardo e i disfattisti suoi*, Milan 1919; appendix on *Leonardo architetto*, pp. 179-206.

Beltrami L., *La vigna di Leonardo*, Milan 1920.

Beltrami L., "La ricostruzione del monumento sepolcrale

per il maresciallo Trivulzio in Milano di Leonardo da Vinci," in *La Lettura*, XX, 1920, pp. 84-90.

Beltrami L., *Divagazioni sul monumento funerario di G.G. Trivulzio. Miscellanea Vinciana*, I: I. Milan 1923, pp. 5-21.

Beltrami L., *L'espugnazione di Trezzo nel gennaio 1952 in uno schizzo di Leonardo. Miscellanea Vinciana*, II: I. Milan 1923, pp. 5-13.

Beltrami L., *Un altro contributo di Leonardo da Vinci alla cartografia milanese*, Milan 1923.

Benevolo L., *Storia dell'architettura del Rinascimento*, Bari 1968 (esp. pp. 344-69).

Berghoef V., "Les origines de la place ducale de Vigevano," in *Palladio*, N.S., XIV, 1964, pp. 165-78.

Bertelli S., "When did Machiavelli write Mandragola?," in *Renaissance Quarterly*, XXIV, 1971, pp. 317-26.

Bertini Calosso A., "Caratteri e limiti dell'attività architettonica di Leonardo," in *Atti del IV Convegno nazionale di storia dell'architettura*, Milan 1939, pp. 321-28.

Blunt A., "Guarini and Leonardo" [review of: G. Guarini, *Architettura Civile*, edited by N. Carboneri and B. Tarassi La Greca, Milan 1968], in *Architectural Review*, CXLVII, 1970, pp. 164-66 (with reference to W. 12542 r, which however is a design for a floor; see also Mainstone, R.).

Bolis B., "Leonardo e le strade," in *Le Strade*, XX, 1938, pp. 366-73.

Bologna F., *Dalle arti minori all'industrial design. Storia di una ideologia*, Bari 1972.

Bongioanni F.M., *Leonardo pensatore*, Piacenza 1935 (esp. pp. 197-99).

Borsi F., *Leon Battista Alberti*, Milan 1975 (see index).

Borsieri G., *Il supplemento della Nobiltà di Milano*, Milan 1619 (esp. pp. 57-8).

Bramantino, see Mongeri G.

Brizio A.M. (ed.), Leonardo da Vinci, *Scritti scelti...*, Turin 1952 (esp. pp. 135-46 and 471-85).

Brizio A.M., "Bramante e Leonardo alla corte di Lodovico il Moro," in *Studi Bramanteschi. Atti del Congresso internazionale...*, 1970, Rome 1974, pp. 1-26.

Bruschi A., *Bramante architetto*, Bari 1969 (see index).

Bruschi A., *Bramante*, Bari 1973 (see index).

Bruschi A., "Bramante, Leonardo e Francesco di Giorgio a Civitavecchia," in *Studi Bramanteschi. Atti del Congresso internazionale...*, 1970, Rome 1974, pp. 535-65.

Buerger F., "Vitruv und die Renaissance," in *Repertorium für Kunstwissenschaften*, XXXII, 1909, pp. 199-218.

Bulferetti L., *Leonardo: l'uomo e lo scienziato*, Turin 1966 (esp. pp. 170-82).

Cadei A., "Nota sul Bramante e l'Amadeo architetti del Duomo di Pavia," in *Bollettino della Società pavese di storia patria*, LXXII-LXXIII, 1972-73, pp. 35-60.

Calvi G., *I manoscritti di Leonardo da Vinci dal punto di vista cronologico, storico e biografico*, Bologna 1925.

Calvi I., "Leonardo da Vinci architetto militare," in *Sapere*, IV, 1938, pp. 412-16; reprinted in *Sapere*, special issue, 15 April 1952, pp. 42-6.

Calvi I., "Leonardo studioso d'arte e d'architettura militare," in *Emporium*, XLV, 1939, pp. 291-306.

Calvi I., *L'architettura militare di Leonardo da Vinci*, Milan 1943.

Canestrini G., *L'automobile. Il contributo italiano all'avvento dell'autoveicolo*, Rome 1938 (esp. pp. 287-334).

Canestrini G., *Leonardo costruttore di macchine e veicoli*, Milan 1939.

Cappelli S., "Leonardo architetto," in *Leonardo*. Special number of the Bollettino dell'Istituto tecnico industriale Leonardo da Vinci di Firenze, Florence 1952, pp. 100-2.

Carotti G., *Leonardo da Vinci pittore, scultore, architetto*, Turin 1921.

Carpeggiani P., *Sabbioneta*, Mantua 1972 (reprinted 1977).

Carpiceci A.C., "Rilievi e 'misura' di Leonardo da Vinci a Roma," in *Istruzione Tecnica*, IX, 1973, pp. 257-68.

Carpiceci A.C., "Statistica ed estetica in un progetto di Leonardo minore," in *Istruzione Tecnica*, X, 1974, pp. 33-9.

Carpiceci A.C., *Leonardo architetto. S. Pietro e Roma*, Rome 1974.

Carpiceci A.C., "Armature e macchine di Leonardo," in *Istruzione Tecnica*, XI, 1975, No. 43.

Carpiceci A.C., "Eccezionale incontro tra Leonardo e Michelangelo," in *Civiltà delle Macchine*, XXIII, 1975, pp. 66-80.

Carpiceci A.C., "Cupole di Leonardo e Michelangelo per Roma. Appunti ed ipotesi," in *Almanacco Italiano*, LXXVI, 1976, pp. 146-71.

Carpiceci A.C., *Leonardo architetto. Per una nuova architettura. Per il tempio ideale*, Florence 1977.

Carpi Ceci M., "Analisi delle prospettive di Leonardo," in *Notiziario Leonardiano*, No. 1, 1977.

Cassi Ramelli A., *Dalle caverne ai rifugi blindati. Trenta secoli di storia della architettura militare*, Milan 1964 (esp. pp. 360-79).

Castelfranco G., "Il preventivo di Leonardo per il monumento sepolcrale di G.G. Trivulzio," in *Bollettino d'Arte*, III, 1955, p. 1-8.

Castelfranco G., "Il canale Firenze-mare nei progetti di Leonardo," in *Civiltà delle macchine*, III, 1955, pp. 56-8.

Castelfranco G., "Leonardo a Milano," in *Storia di Milano*, Vol. VII, 1957, pp. 485-531.

Cavallari Murat A., "Significato della componente architettonica padana nella geografia rinascimentale d'Europa," in *Arte Lombarda*, N.S., XLIV-XLV, 1976, pp. 13-28.

Chastel A., "Travaux sur l'architecture italienne de la Renaissance," in *Bibliothèque d'Humanism et Renaissance*, XIX, 1957, pp. 358-75.

Chastel A., *Art et humanism e à Florence au temps de Laurent le Magnifique*, Paris 1959 and 1961; Italian edition, Turin 1964 (see index).

Chastel A., *Studios and Styles of the Italian Renaissance*, Paris and New York 1966 (see index and esp. p. 333).

Chierici G., "Leonardo architetto," in *Palladio*, III, 1939, pp. 193-204.

Chierici G., "L'architettura a cupola," in *Leonardo da Vinci a cura della Mostra*, Novara 1939, pp. 233-38.

Chiodi C., "L'urbanistica vinciana," in *L'Ingegnere*, XIV, 1939, pp. 289-92.

Chiodi C., "Le città ideali di Leonardo," in *Le Vie d'Italia*, LVIII, 1952, pp. 497-503.

Chiodi C., "Le strade urbane di Leonardo da Vinci," in *Le Strade*, XXXII, 1952, pp. 101-3.

Chianchi R., "Figure nuove del mondo vinciano: Paolo e Vannoccio Biringuccio da Siena," in *Raccolta Vinciana*, XX, 1964, pp. 277-97.

Citadella L.N., *Notizie relative a Ferrara*, Ferrara 1864 (p. 341: Leonardo and Iacomo Andrea da Ferrara).

Cook T.A., *Spirals in nature and art. A study of spiral formations based on the manuscripts of Leonardo da Vinci*, New York 1903.

Coomaraswamy A., "Iconography of Dürer's Knots and Leonardo's Concatenations," in *The Art Quarterly*, VII, 1944, pp. 109-28.

Dalai Emiliani M., "Brunelleschi milanese," in *Società Belle Arti. Esposizione permanente* (Milan), No. 3, October-December 1977, pp. 1-2.

Dami L., "Le architetture di Leonardo," in *Il Marzocco*, XXIV, No. 18, 4 May 1919, pp. 5-6.

D'Arrigo A., *Leonardo da Vinci e il regime della spiaggia di Cesenatico*, Rome 1940.

D'Arrigo A., "Leonardo da Vinci, il portocanale e le variazioni della spiaggia di Cesenatico dal 1302 al 1962," in *Rivista di Ingegneria*, No. 5, May 1964, pp. 3-19.

D'Arrigo, see also Migliardi Tasco A.

De Angelis D'Ossat G., "Preludio romano del Bramante," in *Palladio*, N.S., XVI, 1966, pp. 83-102.

De La Croix H., "Military architecture and the radial city plan in sixteenth century Italy," in *The Art Bulletin*, XLII, 1960, pp. 263-90. Reviewed by Corrado Maltese in *Raccolta Vinciana*, XIX, 1962, pp. 325-28.

De Toni N., "Leonardo da Vinci e i rilievi topografici di Cesena (Frammenti Vinciani XVIII)," in *Studi Romagnoli*, VIII, 1957, pp. 413-24.

De Toni N., *I rilievi cartografici di Leonardo per Cesena ed Urbino contenuti nel manoscritto "L" dell'Istituto di Francia. V Lettura Vinciana, 15 aprile 1965*, Florence 1966; reprinted in *Leonardo da Vinci letto e commentato... Letture Vinciane I-XII*, Florence 1974, pp. 131-46.

Dutton R., *Chambord. Ein französisches Schloss mit italienischem Einfluss*, Berlin 1961 (pp. 68-73).

Feldhaus F.M., "Leonardo da Vinci als Städtebauer," in *Zentralblatt für Bauverwaltung*, XXXII, 1912.

Fergusson F.D., "Leonardo da Vinci and the tiburio of Milan Cathedral," in *Architectura*, VII, 1977, pp. 175-92.

Ferrari da Passano C., Brivio E., "Contributo allo studio del tiburio del Duomo di Milano," in *Arte Lombarda*, XII, 1967, pp. 3-36.

Fienga D.D., "Bramante autore dell''Antiquarie prospettive romane,' poemetto dedicato a Leonardo da Vinci," in *Studi Bramanteschi. Atti del Congresso internazionale...* 1970, Rome 1974, pp. 417-26.

Filarete, see Grassi L., Spencer J.R.

Firpo L., "La città ideale del Filarete," in *Studi in memoria di Gioele Solari*, Turin 1954, pp. 11-59.

Firpo L., *Leonardo architetto e urbanista*, Turin 1973.

Fontana V., "'Arte' e 'Isperienza' nei trattati d'architettura veneziani del Cinquecento," in *Architectura*, VIII, 1978, pp. 49-72.

Förster O.H., *Bramante*, Vienna-Münich 1956.

Forster K.W., Tuttle R.J., "The Palazzo del Te," in *Journal of the Society of Architectural Historians*, XXX, 1971, pp. 267-93.

Forster K.W., "Back to the Farm. Vernacular Architecture and the Development of the Renaissance Villa," in *Architecture*, I, 1974, pp. 1-12.

Francesco di Giorgio, see Maltese G.

Fumagalli G., *Leonardo "omo sanza lettere,"* Florence 1939 (esp. pp. 309-14).

Gabrietcevskij A., "Leonardo architektor," in *Sovetskaia Architektura*, No. 3, 1952, pp. 95-104.

Garin E., *La città di Leonardo. XI Lettura Vinciana*, Florence 1972; reprinted in *Leonardo da Vinci letto e commentato... Letture Vinciane I-XII*, Florence 1974, pp. 309-25.

Gattinelli G., "Leonardo scenotecnico," in *Leonardo*. Special number of the *Bollettino dell'Istituto tecnico industriale Leonardo da Vinci di Firenze*, Florence 1952, pp. 103-5.

Gebelin F., *Les châteaux de la Renaissance*, Paris 1927.

Gebelin F., "Châteaux de la Loire," in *Etudes d'Art*, Nos. 8-10, 1953-54, pp. 159-76.

Gebelin F., *Les châteaux de France*, Paris 1962 (esp. pp. 91-9).

Geymüller H., *Les projets primitifs pour la Basilique de Saint-Pierre de Rome*, Paris-Vienna 1875 (esp. pp. 37-8, 48).

Geymüller H., "Leonardo da Vinci as Architect," in *The Literary Works of Leonardo da Vinci*, edited by J.P. Richter, London 1883; second, definitive edition, Oxford 1939, Vol. II.

Gianani F., *Il Duomo di Pavia*, Pavia 1965 (esp. pp. 50-1).

Giglioli O.H., *Leonardo. Iniziazione alla conoscenza di lui e delle questioni vinciane*, Florence 1944 (esp. pp. 46-51).

Gille B., *Les ingénieurs de la Renaissance*, Paris 1964; English edition, *Engineers of the Renaissance*, Cambridge, Mass., 1966; Italian edition, *Leonardo e gli ingegneri del Rinascimento*, Milan 1972 (see index). Reviewed by L. Finelli in *Architettura*, XVIII, 1972, p. 209.

Giovannoni G., "L'architettura del Cinquecento," in *Palladio*, II, 1938, pp. 109-10.

Giovannoni G., "L'urbanistica del Rinascimento," in *L'urbanistica dell'antichità ad oggi*, Florence 1943, pp. 93-115.

Govi G., "Leonardo letterato scienziato," in *Saggio delle opere di Leonardo da Vinci*, Milan 1872, pp. 5-22 (esp. pp. 18-19); reprinted in A. Favaro, *Gilberto Govi ed i suoi scritti intorno a Leonardo da Vinci*, Rome 1923 (esp. pp. 116-17).

Govi G., "Intorno a un opuscolo rarissimo della fine del secolo XV intitolato Antiquarie prospettiche romane composte per Prospettivo Milanese dipintore," in *Atti della R. Accademia dei Lincei*, CCLXXIII, 1875-76, 2nd series, Vol. III, Part III, "Memorie della Classe di Scienze morali, storiche e filosofiche," 1876, pp. 39-66; reprinted in A. Favaro, *Gilberto Govi ed i suoi scritti intorno a Leonardo da Vinci*, Rome 1923, pp. 135-75.

Grassi L. (ed.), Antonio Averlino detto Il Filarete, *Trattato di architettura*. Text edited by Anna Maria Finoli and Liliana Grassi. Introduction and notes by Liliana Grassi, Milan 1972 (see index).

Guillaume J., "Léonard de Vinci, Dominique de Cortone et l'escalier du modèle en bois de Chambord," in *Gazette des Beaux-Arts*, LXXI, 1968, pp. 93-108.

Guillaume J., "Nouvelles recherches sur Léonard et Romantin," in *Bulletin de l'Association Léonard de Vinci*, No. 12, 1973, pp. 19-24.

Guillaume J., "Léonard de Vinci et l'architecture française. I. Le problème de Chambord. II. La Villa de Charles d'Amboise et le château de Romorantin: Reflexion sur un livre de Carlo Pedretti," in *Revue de l'Art*, XXV, 1974, pp. 71-91; reprinted in *Bulletin de l'Association Léonard de Vinci*, No. 14, 1975, pp. 29-47.

Gukovskj M.A., "Ritrovamento dei tre volumi di disegno attribuiti a Fra Giocondo," in *Italia Medioevale e Umanistica*, VI, 1963, pp. 263-69.

Gukovskj M.A., "Leonardo e Galeno," in *Raccolta Vinciana*, XX, 1964, pp. 359-67.

Hale R.J., *Renaissance fortification. Art or Engineering?*, London 1977.

Hersey G.L., *Pythagorean Palaces. Magic and Architecture in the Italian Renaissance*, London 1976 (see index).

Herzfeld M., "La rappresentazione della 'Danae' organizzata da Leonardo," in *Raccolta Vinciana*, XI, 1920-22, pp. 226-28.

Heydenreich L.H., *Die Sakralbau-Studien Leonardo da Vinci's*, Engelsdorf-Leipzig 1929; reprinted, Munich 1971 (with introductory essay of 1969). Reviewed by G. Calvi in *Raccolta Vinciana*, XIV, 1930-34, pp. 39-53.

Heydenreich L.H., "Studi archeologici di Leonardo da Vinci a Civitavecchia," in *Raccolta Vinciana*, XIV, 1930-34, pp. 39-53.

Heydenreich L.H., "Zur Genesis des St. Peter-Plans von Bramante," in *Forschungen und Fortschritte*, 1934, pp. 39-53.

Heydenreich L.H., "Intorno a un disegno di Leonardo da Vinci per l'antico altare maggiore della SS. Annunziata" (summary of information), in *Mitteilungen des Kunsthistorischen Institutes in Florenz*, V, 1937, pp. 436-37.

Heydenreich L.H., "Considerazioni intorno a recenti ricerche su Leonardo da Vinci," in *La Rinascita*, V, 1942, pp. 161-73.

Heydenreich L.H., "Leonardo da Vinci architect of Francis I," in *The Burlington Magazine*, XCIV, 1952, pp. 277-85.

Heydenreich L.H., *Leonardo da Vinci*, Basel 1953; London 1954 (pp. 77-89 and 192: Architecture).

Heydenreich L.H., *Leonardo architetto. II Lettura Vinciana, 15 aprile 1962*, Florence 1963; reprinted in *Leonardo letto e commentato... Letture Vinciane I-XII*, Florence 1974, pp. 29-45.

Heydenreich L.H., "Bemerkungen zu den Entwürfen Leonardos für das Grabmal des Gian Giacomo Trivulzio," in *Studien zur Geschichte der Europäischen Plastik. Festschrift für Theodor Müller*, Munich 1965, pp. 179-94.

Heydenreich L.H., "La villa: genesi e sviluppo fino al Palladio," in *Bollettino del Centro Internazionale di Studi di Architettura Andrea Palladio*, XI, 1969, pp. 11-22.

Heydenreich L.H., "Leonardo and Bramante: Genius in Architecture," in *Leonardo's Legacy*, edited by C.D. O'Malley, Berkeley and Los Angeles 1969, pp. 125-48.

Heydenreich L.H., "L'architettura militare," in *Leonardo*, edited by L. Reti, Milan 1974, pp. 136-65.

Heydenreich L.H., Lotz W., *Architecture in Italy 1400 to 1600*, Harmondsworth, Engl., Baltimore 1974 (chapter on p. 143; see also index).

Heydenreich L.H., "I progetti di Leonardo per fortificare Piombino," in *Almanacco Italiano*, LXXV, 1975, pp. 332-39.

Heydenreich L.H., see Babinger F.

Hoeber F., "Ideale Zentralbauten des späten Quattrocento und der 'Stilo lionardesco,'" in *Zeitschrift für Geschichte der Architektur*, I, 1907-8, pp. 232-535.

Hoffman V., "Leonardos Ausmalung der Sala delle Asse im Castello Sforzesco," in *Mitteilungen des Kunsthistorischen Institutes in Florenz*, XVI, 1972, pp. 51-62.

Horne H.P., "Some Leonardesque questions," in *The Architectural Review*, XII, 1902, pp. 31-8.

Hyman I., "Notes and Speculations on S. Lorenzo, Palazzo Medici, and an urban project by Brunelleschi," in *Journal of the Society of Architectural Historians*, XXXIV, 1975, pp. 98-120 (esp. p. 106).

Kleinbauer W.E., "Some Renaissance Views of Early Christian and Romanesque San Lorenzo in Milan," in *Arte Lombarda*, XII, 1967, pp. 1-10.

Kretzulesco Quaranta E., "L'itinerario archeologico di Polifilo: Leon Battista Alberti come teorico della Magna Porta," in *Atti della Accademia Nazionale dei Lincei*, CCCLXVII, *Rendiconti, Classe di Scienze morali, storiche e filologiche*, vol. XXV, 1970, pp. 175-201 (esp. p. 185).

Lang S., "Leonardo's Architectural Designs and the Sforza Mausoleum," in *Journal of the Warburg and Courtauld Institutes*, XXXI, 1968, pp. 218-33.

Lesueur F.L., "Léonard de Vinci et Chambord," in *Études d'arts*, Nos. 8-10, 1953-54, pp. 225-38.

Lombardini E., "Dell'origine e del progresso della scienza idraulica nel milanese ed in altre parti d'Italia. Osservazioni... concernenti principalmente i lavori di Leonardo da Vinci, di Benedetto Castelli e di Giandomenico Guglielmini," in *Memorie del R. Istituto lombardo di scienze, lettere ed arti*, VIII, 1860, pp. 1-56; second edition, Milan 1872.

Lotz W., "Das Raumbild in der italienischen Architekturzeichnung der Renaissance," in *Mitteilungen des Kunsthistorischen Institutes in Florenz*, VII, 1956, issue III/IV, pp. 193-226. Reviewed by C. Maltese in *Raccolta Vinciana*, XIX, 1962, pp. 339-42.

Lotz W., "Notizen zum kirchlichen Zentralbau der Renaissance," in *Studien zur Toskanischen Kunst. Festschrift für Ludwig H., Heydenreich*, Munich 1964, pp. 157-65.

Lotz W., "La piazza ducale di Vigevano. Un foro principesco del tardo Quattrocento," in *Studi Bramanteschi. Atti del Congresso internazionale...*, 1970, Rome 1974, pp. 205-21.

Lotz W., *Studies in Italian Renaissance Architecture*, Cambridge, Mass. 1977.

Lotz W., see Heydenreich L.H.

Lowry B., "High Renaissance Architecture," in *College Art Journal*, XVII, 1958, pp. 115-28.

Luebke W., "Lionardo da Vinci als Architekt," in *Die Gegenwart*, XXIX, 1886, pp. 307-8 and 331-32; revised and rewritten in *Kunstwerke und Künstler*, Breslau 1888, pp. 217-30.

McCabe J.E., *Leonardo da Vinci's De ludo geometrico*, Los Angeles 1972 (Doctoral thesis, with a study of Leonardo's geometry in relation to architecture; see also by the same author, "Leonardo's 'curvilateral stars,'" in *Gazette des Beaux-Arts*, March 1974, pp. 179-86).

Magenta C., *Il Castello di Pavia al tempo dei Visconti e degli Sforza*, Milan 1883, 2 vols. (see index).

Mainstone R., "Guarini and Leonardo" [letter to the editor, to review by A. Blunt], in *Architectural Review*, CXLVII, 1970, p. 454.

Mainstone R., *Developments in Structural Form*, London 1975 (esp. pp. 283-89).

Malaguzzi-Valeri F., "Leonardo da Vinci e il tiburio del Duomo di Milano," in *Il Marzocco*, 1903, No. 44.

Malaguzzi-Valeri F., *La corte di Ludovico il Moro*, Vol. II: *Bramante e Leonardo da Vinci*, Milan 1915.

Maltese C., "Il pensiero architettonico e urbanistico di Leonardo," in *Leonardo Saggi e Ricerche*, Rome 1954, pp. 333-58.

Maltese C. (ed.) *Francesco di Giorgio Martini, Trattati di architettura, ingegneria e arte militare*. Transcription by L. Maltese Degrassi, Milan 1967, 2 vols. (see index). Review by G. Scaglia in *The Art Bulletin*, LII, 1970, pp. 439-42.

Maltese C., *Gusto e metodo scientifico nel pensiero architettonico di Leonardo. XIII Lettura Vinciana*, 15 April 1973, Florence 1975.

Marchini G., "Il ballatoio della cupola del Duomo di Firenze," in *Antichità viva*, XVI, 1977, pp. 36-48.

Marconi P., "Il problema della forma della città nei teorici di architettura del Rinascimento," in *Palladio*, XXII, 1972, pp. 49-88.

Marconi P., *La città come forma simbolica*, Rome 1973 (see index).

Marinoni A., "Il regno e il sito di Venere," in *Il Poliziano e il suo tempo*, Florence 1957, pp. 273-87 (esp. the appendix).

Marinoni A. (ed.), *Leonardo da Vinci, Scritti Letterari*. Newly revised edition, Milan 1974 (see index and esp. p. 256).

Marinoni A., *I codici di Madrid (8937 e 8936)... XIV Lettura Vinciana*, 15 April 1974, Florence 1975.

Martelli M., "Un disegno attribuito a Leonardo e una scoperta archeologica degli inizi del Cinquecento," in *Prospettiva*, 10, 1977, pp. 58-61.

Meyer A.G., *Oberitalienische Frührenaissance Bauten und Bildwerke der Lombardei*, Berlin 1897-1900, 2 vols.

Migliardi Tasco A., D'Arrigo A., "Leonardo da Vinci e il portocanale di Cesenatico," in *Rassegna dei Lavori Pubblici*, I, 1964, pp. 1-16.

Mongeri G. (ed.), "Postille di un anonimo seicentista alla prima edizione delle Vite dei più eccellenti artefici italiani scritte da Giorgio Vasari pubblicata a Firenze per Lorenzo Torrentino nel 1550...," in *Archivio Storico Lombardo*, II, 1875, III, 1876, pp. 103-8.

Mongeri G. (ed.), *Le Rovine di Roma al principio del secolo XVI. Studi del Bramantino...*, Milan 1875; 2nd edition, 1880.

Morini M., *Atlante di storia dell'urbanistica*, Milan 1963.

Motta E., "Leonardo da Vinci e la cattedrale di Pavia," in *Bollettino storico della Svizzera italiana*, VI, 1884, p. 19.

Muraro, M., "Tiziano pittore ufficiale della Serenissima," in *Tiziano nel quarto centenario della sua morte..., Ateneo Veneto*, Venice 1977, pp. 83-100 (esp. pp. 86-7).

Murray P., "Leonardo and Bramante. Leonardo's approach to anatomy and architecture, and its effect on Bramante," in *Architectural Review*, CXXXIV, 1963, p. 346-51.

Murray P., *The Architecture of the Italian Renaissance*, London 1963; Italian edition, Milan 1971 (see index).

Mušič M., "Po tragovima Leonarda u dolini Soče i Vipave," in *Bulletin Jazu*, XII, 1964, No. 1/2, pp. 9-17.

Mušič M., "Z Leonardom v vipavski in soški dolini," in *Architectura in čas*, Obzorja, Maribor, 1964, pp. 264-69.

Negri G., "Leonardo da Vinci e il Castello di Milano," in *Segni dei tempi*, Milan 1893, pp. 3-42 (2nd edition, 1897).

Nielsen C.V., *Leonardo da Vinci og hans forhold til Perspektiven et afsnit af Perspektivens historie...*, Copenhagen 1897.

Oltrocchi B., see Ritter S.

Ost H., "Santa Margherita in Montefiascone: a Centralized Building Plan of the Roman Quattrocento," in *The Art Bulletin*, LII, 1970, pp. 373-89 (esp. pp. 383, 385, and note 67).

Pacioli L., *Divina proportione...*, Venice 1509; critical edition edited by C. Winterberg, Vienna 1889.

Paladini, G., "Leonardo costruttore e urbanista," in *Leonardo*. Special number of the *Bollettino dell'Istituto tecnico industriale Leonardo da Vinci di Firenze*, Florence 1952, pp. 54-60.

Paladini G., "Leonardo e il piano regolatore di Firenze," in *Bollettino tecnico* (Collegio degli ingegneri di Firenze, monthly review), X, 1952, pp. 84-5.

Panazza G., "Leonardo a Pavia e in Lomellina," in *Leonardo da Vinci e Pavia*, Società Pavese di Storia Patria, Pavia 1952, pp. 63-88.

Papini R., *Francesco di Giorgio architetto*, Milan 1946 (see index).

Parronchi A., "L'allagamento di Lucca," in *La Nazione*, 8 September 1963, p. 3.

Parronchi A., "Distrazioni e sviste di Leonardo copista (o dei suoi commentatori)," in *Rinascimento*, XVI, 1976, pp. 231-40.

Parronchi A., "Ricostruzione della Pala dei Montefeltro," in *Storia dell'Arte*, No. 28, 1976, pp. 235-48 (esp. p. 245).

Parronchi A., *L'enigma della cupola: perché "sanza armadura"* [lecture], Florence 1977 (esp. p. 24).

Parsons W.B., *Engineers and Engineering in the Renaissance*, Baltimore 1939; reprinted, Cambridge, Mass., 1968 (see index).

Pedretti C., *Studi vinciani. Documenti, analisi e inediti leonardeschi*, Geneva 1957.

Pedretti C., "Saggio di una cronologia dei fogli del Codice Arundel di Leonardo da Vinci," in *Bibliothèque d'Humanisme et Renaissance*, XXII, 1960, pp. 172-77.

Pedretti C., "Il 'Neron da Sancto Andrea.' – Ancora del 'Neron da Sancto Andrea,'" in *Raccolta Vinciana*, XVIII, 1960, pp. 65-96; XIX, 1962, pp. 273-75.

Pedretti C., "Leonardo's plans for the enlargement of the city of Milan," in *Raccolta Vinciana*, XIX, 1962, pp. 137-47.

Pedretti C., *A chronology of Leonardo da Vinci's architectural studies after 1500*, Geneva 1962. Reviewed by L.H. Heydenreich in *Raccolta Vinciana*, XX, 1964, pp. 408-12.

Pedretti C., "Leonardo da Vinci e la Villa Melzi a Vaprio," in *L'Arte*, LXII, 1963, pp. 229-40.

Pedretti C., "Dessins d'une scène, exécutés par Léonard da Vinci pour Charles d'Amboise (1506-1507)," in *Le Lieu théâtral à la Renaissance*, edited by Jean Jacquot, Paris 1964, pp. 25-34.

Pedretti C., "La 'Cappella del Perdono,'" in *Raccolta Vinciana*, XX, 1964, pp. 263-75.

Pedretti C., "An 'arcus quadrifrons' for Leo X," in *Raccolta Vinciana*, XX, 1964, pp. 225-61.

Pedretti C., "Leonardo da Vinci: Manuscripts and drawings of the French period, 1517-1518," in *Gazette des Beaux-Arts*, CXII, November 1970, pp. 285-318.

349

Pedretti C., *Leonardo da Vinci. The Royal Palace at Romorantin*, Cambridge, Mass., 1972. Reviewed by C.W. Condit in *Technology and Culture*, XV, 1974, pp. 634-35; C. Gould in *Apollo*, XCIX, 1974, p. 292; J. Wasserman in *The Burlington Magazine*, CXVIII, 1976, pp. 313-15; see also Guillaume J.

Pedretti C., "Leonardo architetto a Imola," in *Architectura*, II, 1972, pp. 92-105.

Pedretti C., "La Verruca," in *Renaissance Quarterly*, XXV, 1972, pp. 417-25.

Pedretti C., "The original project for S. Maria delle Grazie," in *Journal of the Society of Architectural Historians*, XXXII, 1973, pp. 30-42.

Pedretti C., "Newly discovered evidence of Leonardo's association with Bramante," in *Journal of the Society of Architectural Historians*, XXXII, 1973, pp. 223-27.

Pedretti C., *Leonardo. A Study in chronology and style*, London 1973 (esp. pp. 68-77).

Pedretti C., "Il progetto originario per Santa Maria delle Grazie e altri aspetti inediti del rapporto Leonardo-Bramante," in *Studi Bramanteschi. Atti del Congresso internazionale... 1970*, Rome 1974, pp. 197-203.

Pedretti C., "Leonardo da Vinci: 13 marzo 1500," in *Ateneo Veneto*, N.S. XIII, 1975, pp. 121-34.

Pedretti C., "Leonardo da Vinci. Disegno come linguaggio," in *Il Veltro*, XIX, 1975, pp. 27-34.

Pedretti C., *Il primo Leonardo a Firenze. L'Arno, la cupola, il Battistero*, Florence 1976.

Pedretti C., *The Literary Works of Leonardo da Vinci compiled and edited from the original manuscripts by Jean Paul Richter. Commentary*, London 1977, 2 vols. (esp. Vol. II, pp. 23-86).

Pedretti C., "The Sforza Sepulchre," I, in *Gazzette des Beaux-Arts*, CXIX, April 1977, pp. 121-31.

Pedretti C., "Leonardo's studies for the Sforza Sepulchre," II, in *Gazette des Beaux-Arts*, CXX, January 1978, pp. 1-20.

Pedretti C., "Le 'fantasie del vinci,'" in *Almanacco Italiano*, LXXVIII, 1978, pp. 122-31.

Pedretti C., *The Codex Atlanticus of Leonardo da Vinci. A catalogue of its newly restored sheets. Part One. Volumes I-VI*, New York 1978.

Pedretti C., "Tiziano e il Serlio," in *Tiziano e Venezia. Atti del Convegno internazionale... 1976*, Venice 1978.

Pedretti C., "Progetti brunelleschiani a Milano nei ricordi di Leonardo," in *Atti del Convegno internazionale di Studi Brunelleschiani... 1977*, Florence 1978.

Pedretti C., see also Roberts J.

Pica A., "La città di Leonardo," in *Casabella*, No. 93, September 1935, pp. 10-12.

Pica A., "La città di Leonardo," in *L'Ambrosiano*, XVII, No. 73, 26 March 1938, p. 5.

Pica A., "Ancora sulla città di Leonardo," in *L'Ambrosiano*, XVII, No. 85, 9 April 1938, p. 5.

Pica A., "Leonardo da Vinci inventore della città futura," in *Il Popolo d'Italia*, XXV, No. 182, 1 July 1938, p. 3.

Pica A., "L'architettura di Leonardo," in *Il Popolo d'Italia*, XXV, No. 214, 2 August 1938, p. 3.

Pica A., "Architettura di Leonardo," in *L'Ingegnere*, XIV, 1939, pp. 790-96.

Pica A., *L'opera di Leonardo al convento delle Grazie in Milano*, Rome 1939.

Pica A., "Sogno e realtà dell'architettura di Leonardo," in *Annali dei Lavori pubblici*, LXXVIII, 1940, pp. 1-16.

Pica A., "Città di Bramante," in *Studi Bramanteschi. Atti del Congresso internazionale... 1970*, Rome 1974, pp. 117-36.

Pierce J.S., "Architectural drawings and the intent of the architect," in *Art Journal*, XXVII, 1967, pp. 48-9.

Pinto J.A., "Origins and development of the ichnographic city plan," in *Journal of the Society of Architectural Historians*, XXXV, 1976, pp. 35-50.

Popham A.E., *The Drawings of Leonardo da Vinci*, London 1946 (esp. chapter IX "Machinery and Architecture").

Portoghesi P., "Luca Pacioli e la 'Divina Proportione,'" in *Civiltà delle Macchine*, 1957, Nos. 5-6.

Portoghesi P., "Michelangelo fiorentino," in *Quaderni dell'Istituto di Storia dell'Architettura*, Series XI, issue 62-66, 1964, pp. 27-60.

Pozzetto M., "Fabiani architetto del Carso. Il canale di Vipacco," in *Critica d'Arte*, November-December 1976, pp. 3-24.

Prager F.D., "Brunelleschi's Clock?," in *Physis*, X, 1968, pp. 203-16.

Prager F.D., Scaglia G., *Brunelleschi. Studies of his technology and inventions*, Cambridge, Mass., 1970 (see index).

Pozzi L., "Leonardo da Vinci e il disegno del duomo di Pavia" in *Bollettino della Società pavese di storia patria*, III, 1903, pp. 390-411.

Puppi L., "La 'città ideale' nella cultura architettonica del Rinascimento centro-europeo," in *Atti del XXII Congresso Internazionale di Storia dell'arte*, Akadémiai Kiado, Budapest 1972, pp. 649-58.

Puppi L., Olivato L., *Mauro Codussi*, Milan 1977 (see index).

Rackusin B., "The Architectural theory of Luca Pacioli: De Divina Proportione," chapter 54, in *Bibliothèque d'Humanisme et Renaissance*, XXXIX, 1977, pp. 479-502.

Reggiori F., "Il santuario di S. Maria della Fontana di Milano alla luce di recentissime scoperte," in *Arte Lombarda*, II, 1956, pp. 51-64.

Reggiori F., *Palazzo Aliverti a Milano nuova sede del Mediocredito Regionale Lombardo*, Milan 1968.

Reti L., "Leonardo da Vinci and Cesare Borgia," in *Viator*, IV, 1973, pp. 333-68.

Reti L., *Tracce dei progetti perduti di Filippo Brunelleschi nel Codice Atlantico di Leonardo da Vinci. IV Lettura Vinciana, 15 aprile 1964*, Florence 1965; reprinted in *Leonardo da Vinci letto e commentato... Letture Vinciane I-XII*, Florence 1974, pp. 89-122.

Reti L. (ed.), *Leonardo...* [written by S.A. Bedini, A.M. Brizio, M.V. Brugnoli, A. Chastel, B. Dibner, L.H. Heydenreich, A. Marinoni, L. Reti, E. Winternitz, C. Zammattio], Milan 1974.

Reymond M., Charles M., "Léonard de Vinci architecte du château de Chambord," in *Gazette des Beaux-Arts*, IX, 1913, pp. 437-60.

Richter J.P., see Geymüller H., Pedretti C.

Ritter S., *Baldassare Oltrocchi e le sue memorie storiche su la vita di Leonardo da Vinci*, Rome 1925.

Roberts J., Pedretti C., "Drawings by Leonardo da Vinci at Windsor newly revealed by ultra-violet light," in *The Burlington Magazine*, CXIX, 1977, pp. 396-409.

Rosci M. (ed.), *Serlio S., Sesto libro delle habitationi di tutti li gradi degli homini...*, Milan 1966 (see index).

Rosenthal E., "The antecedents of Bramante's Tempietto," in *Journal of the Society of Architecture Historians*, XXIII, 1964, pp. 55-74.

Sanpaolesi P., "I dipinti di Leonardo agli Uffizi," in *Leonardo Saggi e Ricerche*, Rome 1954, pp. 27-46.

Sanpaolesi P., *Brunelleschi*, Milan 1962 (see index).

Sant'Ambrogio D., "La chiesa di S. Maria della Fontana in Milano di presumibile origine leonardesca," in *Il Politecnico*, LV, 1907, pp. 566-79.

Sartoris A., *Léonard architecte*, Paris 1952.

Savorgnan di Brazza F., *Leonardo da Vinci in Friuli ed il suo progetto di fortificazione dell'Isonzo. Lettura tenuta all'Accademia di Udine il 21 dicembre 1933*, Udine 1936.

Scaglia G., "Drawings of Brunelleschi's mechanical inventions for the construction of the Cupola," in *Marsyas*, X, 1961, pp. 45-73.

Scaglia G., "Drawings of machines for architecture from early Quattrocento in Italy," in *Journal of the Society of Architectural Historians*, XXV, 1966, pp. 90-114.

Scaglia G., see also Prager F.D.

Schettini F., "Novità sulla rocca di Imola," in *Rocche e castelli di Romagna*, I, Bologna 1970, pp. 53-86.

Schettini F., "Istanbul/Costantinopoli: un ponte di Leonardo sul Corno d'Oro," in *Parametro*, No. 10, 1972, pp. 68-79. Review in *Architectural Review*, CLII, 1972, p. 188.

Scholfield P.H., *The theory of proportion in architecture*, London 1958.

Serlio S., see Rosci M.

Shearman J., "The Florentine Entrata of Leo X. 1515," in *Journal of the Warburg and Courtauld Institutes*, XXXVIII, 1975, pp. 136-54.

Simoncini G., *Architetti e architettura nella cultura del Rinascimento*, Bologna 1967.

Simoncini G., *Città e società nel Rinascimento*, Turin 1974, 2 vols. (esp. Vol. II, pp. 76-85 and 103-4; see also the index).

Sisi E., *L'urbanistica negli studi di Leonardo da Vinci*, Florence 1953.

Solmi E., "La festa del Paradiso di Leonardo da Vinci e Bernardo Bellincioni (13 gennaio 1490)," in *Archivio Storico Lombardo*, XXXI, 1904, pp. 75-89; reprinted in *Studi Vinciani*, Florence 1924, pp. 1-14.

Solmi E., "Leonardo da Vinci, il duomo, il castello e l'università di Pavia," in *Bollettino della Società pavese di storia patria*, XI, 1911, pp. 141-203; reprinted in *Studi Vinciani*, Florence 1924, pp. 15-74.

Solmi E., "Leonardo da Vinci nel castello e nella Sforzesca di Vigevano," in *Viglevanum*, V, 1911, pp. 48-57 and 138-49; also in *Studi Vinciani*, Florence 1924, pp. 75-95.

Solmi E., "Leonardo da Vinci e i lavori di prosciugamento nelle paludi pontine ai tempi di Leone X (1514-1516)," in *Archivio Storico Lombardo*, XXXVIII, 1911, pp. 65-101; reprinted in *Studi Vinciani*, Florence 1924, pp. 299-336.

Speckel A.M., "Leonardo bonificatore," in *La lettura*, XXXVIII, 1938, pp. 940-42.

Spencer J.R., "Filarete and central-plan architecture," in *Journal of the Society of Architectural Historians*, XVII, 1958, pp. 10-18.

Spencer J.R. (ed.), *Filarete's Treatise on architecture...*, New Haven and London, 1965, 2 vols. (see index).

Spencer J.R., "Il progetto per il cavallo di bronzo per Francesco Sforza," in *Arte Lombarda*, XVIII, 1973, pp. 23-35.

Spinazzola V., "Leonardo architetto," in *Leonardo da Vinci. Conferenze fiorentine*, Milan 1910, pp. 107-36.

Starce F., "Bramanti Opinio super Domicilium seu Templum Magnum: Osservazioni sulla teoria dell'architettura," in *Studi Bramanteschi. Atti del Congresso internazionale...*, 1970, Rome 1974, pp. 137-56.

Statham H.H., "Leonardo da Vinci as architect," in *The Builder*, December 1884.

Steinberg L., "Leonardo's Last Supper," in *The Art Quarterly*, XXXVI, 1973, pp. 297-410.

Steinitz K.T., "A reconstruction of Leonardo da Vinci's revolving stage," in *The Art Quarterly*, XII, 1949, pp. 325-38.

Steinitz K.T., "Les décors de théâtre de Léonard de Vinci," in *Bibliothèque d'Humanisme et Renaissance*, XX, 1958, pp. 257-65.

Steinitz K.T., "The voyage of Isabella d'Argon from Naples to Milan, January 1489," in *Bibliothèque d'Humanisme et Renaissance*, XXIII, 1961, pp. 17-33.

Steinitz K.T., "Le dessin de Léonard de Vinci pour la représentation de la Danae de Baldassare Taccone," in *Le lieu théâtral à la Renaissance*, edited by Jean Jacquot, Paris 1964, pp. 35-40.

Steinitz K.T., *Leonardo architetto teatrale e organizzatore di feste... IX Lettura Vinciana, 15 aprile 1969*, Florence 1970; reprinted in *Leonardo da Vinci letto e commentato... Letture Vinciane I-XII*, Florence 1974, pp. 249-74.

Steinitz K.T., "A Forest in a Castle," in *Terra*, XI, No. 4, 1973, pp. 18-22.

Strack H., *Zentral-und Kuppelkirchen der Renaissance in Italien*, Berlin 1882.

Strzygowski J., "Leonardo, Bramante, Vignola im Rahmen vergleichender Kunstforschung," in *Mitteilungen des Kunsthistorischen Institutes in Florenz*, III, 1919, pp. 1-37.

Studi Bramanteschi. Atti del Congresso internazionale, Milano, Urbino, Roma 1970, a cura del Comitato Nazionale per le Celebrazioni Bramantesche, Rome 1974. For contributions with particular reference to Leonardo see Brizio, Bruschi, Fienga, Lotz.

Pedretti, Pica, Starace, Zänker, for other references, see index.

Suida W., *Bramante pittore e il Bramantino*, Milan 1953 (see index and esp. p. 93 for the *Antiquarie prospetiche romane*).

Tafuri M., *L'architettura del manierismo nel Cinquecento europeo*, Rome 1966 (see index).

Tafuri M., *Iacopo Sansovino e l'architettura del '500 a Venezia*, Padua 1969 (see index).

Thiis J., *Leonardo da Vinci. I: The Florentine Years of Leonardo and Verrocchio...*, London 1914 [translation from the original Swedish edition of 1909], (esp. pp. 211-17).

Thoenes C., "Proportionsstudien an Bramantes Zentralbau-Entwürfen," in *Römisches Jahrbuch für Kunstgeschichte*, XV, 1975, pp. 37-58 (esp. pp. 45-6).

Thyraud J., "Léonard de Vinci et Romorantin," in *Bulletin de l'Association Léonard de Vinci*, No. 12, December 1973, pp. 25-30.

Tomasini C., *Leonardo e il suo piano urbanistico per il quartiere mediceo a nord del Battistero*, Florence 1971.

Tursini L., "Leonardo e l'arte militare" [I-II], in *Rivista di Ingegneria*, No. 10, October 1951; No. 2, February 1952 [I. Navigation, II. Artillery, Architecture].

Tursini L., "Navi e scafandri negli studi di Leonardo," in *Leonardo Saggi e Ricerche*, Rome 1954, pp. 67-84.

Uzielli G., "Ricerche intorno a Leonardo da Vinci. Serie Seconda," Rome 1884; chapter IV (pp. 211-16), *Parere di Leonardo da Vinci e d'altri sopra i movimenti del monte del Re ora detto monte a S. Miniato in Firenze*; see also, pp. 394-95, architecture in the Codex on the Flight of Birds.

Valtieri S., "La Scuola d'Atene. 'Bramante' suggerisce un nuovo metodo per costruire in prospettiva un'architettura armonica," in *Mitteilungen des Kunsthistorischen Institutes in Florenz*, XVI, 1972, pp. 63-72.

Vasari G., *Le vite dei più eccellenti pittori, scultori e architetti*, Florence 1550 and 1568; edition edited by G. Milanese, Florence 1878-85 (definitive edition, 1906); edition of the *Vita di Leonardo*, edited by G. Poggi, Florence 1919.

Venturi A., *Storia dell'arte italiana*, Vol. XI, part I: "Architettura del Cinquecento," Milan 1938, pp. 1-49. Review in *Raccolta Vinciana*, XV-XVI, 1935-39, pp. 414-16.

Verga C., "Un 'rivellino' di Leonardo," in *Castellum*, XVI, 1972, pp. 111-17.

Visconti A., "Leonardo a Milano," in *Leonardo da Vinci a cura della Mostra*, Novara 1939, pp. 109-26.

Vliegenthart-Van der Valk Bouman J.M., "The origins of the imperial staircase," in *Nederlands Kunsthistorische Jaarboek*, XXIII, 1972, pp. 443-54.

Volvboundt P., "Lionardo som arkiteckt," in *Svenska Dagbladet*, 24 November 1952.

Von Stromer W., "Brunelleschis automatischer Kran und die Mechanik der Nürnberger Drahtmühle," in *Architectura*, VII, 1977, pp. 163-74.

Willinski S., "La Serliana," in *Bollettino del Centro Internazionale di Studi di Architettura Andrea Palladio*, XI, 1969, pp. 399-429.

Winternitz E., "Anatomy the teacher: on the impact of Leonardo's anatomical research on his musical and other machines," in *Proceedings of the American Philosophical Society*, Vol. III, No. 4, August 1967, pp. 234-47.

Wittkower R., *Architectural principles in the age of Humanism*, London 1949; Italian edition, Turin 1964 (see index).

Wolf P.M., "Michelangelo's Laurenziana and inconspicuous traditions," in *Marsyas*, XII, 1964-65, pp. 16-21.

Zammattio C., "Acqua e pietre: loro meccanica," in *Leonardo*, edited by L. Reti, Milan 1974, pp. 190-215.

Zänker J., "Il primo progetto per il santuario di Santa Maria della Consolazione a Todi e la sua attribuzione," in *Studi Bramanteschi. Atti del Congresso internazionale...*, 1970, Rome 1974, pp. 603-15.

Zänker J., *Die Wallfahrtskirche Santa Maria della Consolazione in Todi* [dissertation], Bonn 1971 (esp. pp. 77-82).

Zubov V.P., "Léon-Baptiste Alberti et Léonard de Vinci," in *Raccolta Vinciana*, XVIII, 1960, pp. 1-14.

Zubov, *Leonardo da Vinci*. Translated from the Russian by David H. Kraus. Cambridge, Mass., 1968 (esp. pp. 13-5, 25-9, 47-9).

Acknowledgements

This book was written at my home in Los Angeles, California, but it is the fruit of collaboration with Italian friends and colleagues. The publishing house of Electa put the idea to me in the summer of 1976, on the suggestion of Eugenio Battisti, whom I now warmly thank for also having offered me, right from the beginning, the assistance of his students in the faculties of architecture at Florence and Milan. The help they offered me with the greatest competence, enthusiasm and unselfishness constituted a unique experience for me, in twenty years of University teaching abroad. The way in which their drawings and comments fit into the fabric of the work, becoming an integral part of it and simplifying its articulation, shows artistic sensitivity as well as professional skill. These young architects therefore deserve not only my recognition but the gratitude of all those who undoubtedly will profit from their labours and research. They are: Giovanni Degl'Innocenti for the application of the methodology of perspective reconstruction, Pier Luigi Bandini for furnishing and then revising in careful stages the analytical formulation of the procedure, Silvano Salvadori for the administration of the University research seminar and, for help with the graphics, Carlo Bonanni, Claudio Castellini, Mario Consonni, Claudio Degl'Innocenti and Paolo Innocenti.

The research relating to the Villa Tovaglia and to La Verruca was carried out by Elio Rodio together with Massimo Baldi and (for the photographs) Marco Tommasini and Fiorenzo Valbonesi, with the help of Cristina Franzoni, Maria Bondavalli, C. Filice, F. Marascio, M. Vanni and Miranda Ferrara. Other work, equally important, has served only for orientation and thus is not adequately represented in the text, as in the case of the research on the fortifications of Ripafratta and other fortresses near Lucca, which a document shows to have an indirect relation to Leonardo. The research relating to the Medici Stables, which is still in progress as regards the investigation of the masonry, is the work of Elio Rodio and his colleagues.

Advice and assistance has come to me, with cordiality and kindness, from other friends and colleagues, whom I thank here in "topographical" order: Luigi Firpo of the University of Turin and Augusto Cavallari Murat from the Polytechnic in the same city; Maria Luisa Dalai and Aurora Scotti of the University of Milan; Luisa Cogliati Arano of the University of Pavia; Lionello Puppi, Loredana Olivato Puppi, Michelangelo Muraro and Paolo Carpeggiani of the University of Padua; Manfredo Tafuri, Terisio Pignatti, Ennio Concina and Vincenzo Fontana of the University of Venice; Alessandro Parronchi, Franco Borsi, Carla Pietramellara and Piero Sanpaolesi of the University of Florence; Paolo Galluzzi of the University of Florence and Director of the Biblioteca Leonardiana at Vinci; Guglielmo De Angelis d'Ossat, Arnaldo Bruschi, Gaetano Miarelli Mariani and Stefano Ray of the University of Rome. I also thank friends of the "Psicon" group, in particular Marco Dezzi Bardeschi and Marcello Fagiolo.

I would also like to record, with grateful thanks for the facilities granted to me, the institutions and libraries in Milan, Pavia and Florence, and in particular Monsignor Angelo Paredi, Prefect of the Biblioteca Ambrosiana, Dottoressa Mercedes Garberi, Director of the art collections at the Castello Sforzesco, and Dottoressa Giulia Bologna, Director of the Biblioteca Trivulziana; Professor Adriano Peroni, Director, and Dottoressa Donata Vicini, Keeper of the Civici Musei at the Castello Visconteo, Pavia; Dottoressa Antonietta Morandini, Director of the Biblioteca Medicea Laurenziana, and Dottoressa Maria Iole Minicucci, Director of the Biblioteca Riccardiana at Florence. My friends Domenico Barecchia and Teodoro Todeschini of the Soprintendenza ai Beni Ambientali e Architettonici dell'Emilia e Romagna have been lavish with their help as regards the study relating to the fortress of Imola; as has Giuliano Giovannini, Surveyor to the Town of Imola. It is with profound regret and deepfelt gratitude that I record the superintendent architect Franco Schettini, whose restoration work on the fortress of Imola has made an important new contribution to our knowledge of Leonardo's work as an architect; and I therefore thank his widow, Signora Iole Schettini, for having allowed me to consult the historical and artistic material which he had gathered, with youthful enthusiasm, until the end of his days.

The original Leonardo material and other documents are reproduced here with the permission of the institutions where they are preserved.

The drawings by Leonardo at Windsor Castle are reproduced with the special permission of Her Majesty the Queen.

The document in the University of Los Angeles Library relating to the destruction of Leonardo's altar in the Nunziata was kindly drawn to my attention by my student Geraldine R. Bass. The production of the book was carried out in an exemplary way and with a relationship of complete understanding and cordiality between author and publisher. I am grateful to record the faultless organization arranged by Carlo Pirovano, as well as the quick and efficient work of his colleagues, in particular Odilla Marini for the iconographical part, Clelia Ginetti for the coordination of the text and Eliana Gelati and Lucia Vigo for the layout. The graphic designer Diego Birelli, has associated his name with a kind of "typographical architecture" that is unmistakable for taste and style, and it was a real pleasure for me to observe the rapidity and intelligence with which he interpreted my intentions in this volume.

C.P., September 1978

357

**Translation and glossary of abbreviations
and terms for diagrams and drawings
on pages 275-289**

Abbreviations
P.V. (Punto di vista): Point of sight
L.O. (Linea d'orizzonte): Horizon line
R.P.V. (Rètta principale verticale): Central vertical axis
P.D. (Distanza principale): Distance point

Terms

p. 275 (408-410)
Diagram 1
Architettura: Architecture
Quadro: Picture plane
Riguardante: Observer
Schema 1: Diagram 1
Diagram 2
Schema 2: Diagram 2
Diagram 3
Prospettiva: Perspective
Pianta: Plan
Sezione: Section
Schema 3: Diagram 3

p. 277 (412, 413)
Top, 412
Dipinto: Painting
Incongruenza: Incongruity
Orizzonte: Horizon line
Linea riferimento: Ground line
Prospetto: Frontal view
Osservatore: Observer
Pianta: Plan
Quadro: Picture plane
Osservatore: Observer
Metri: Metres
Bottom, 413
Quadro: Picture plane
Orizzonte: Horizon line
Incongruenza: Incongruity
Quadro: Picture plane
Osservatore: Observer
Metri: Metres

p. 279 (415, 416)
Top, 415
Cerchio visivo: Visual circle
Dipinto: Painting
Prospetto: Frontal view
Cerchio di distanza: Distance circle
Quadro: Picture plane
Osservatore: Observer
Pianta: Plan
Quadro: Picture plane
Osservatore: Observer
Decimetri: Decimetres
Bottom, 416
Quadro: Picture plane
Osservatore: Observer
Decimetri: Decimetres

p. 281 (419)
Prospettiva: Perspective
Cerchio visivo: Visual circle
Lato destro del dipinto:
Right side of the painting
Pianta: Plan
Centimetri: Centimetres

p. 284 (423)
Decimetri: Decimetres
Prospetti dell'architettura: Elevations of architecture

p. 285 (424)
Disegno: Drawing
Punto di distanza (osservatore):
Distance point (observer)
Decimetri: Decimetres

p. 286 (426)
Metri: Metres
Pavimento attuale: Present floor level

p. 287 (427, 428)
Top, 427
Metri: Metres
Bottom, 428
Cerchio visivo: Visual circle
Pavimento attuale: Present floor level
Pavimento precedente: Earlier floor level
Metri: Metres

p. 288 (429, 430)
Left, 429
Fondale: Backdrop
Pavimento: Floor
Quadro: Picture plane
Parete sinistra: Left wall
Parete destra: Right wall
Metri: Metres
Right, 430
Metri: Metres

p. 289 (431, 432)
Top, 431
Quadro: Picture plane
Metri: Metres
Bottom, 432
Quadro inclinato: Inclined picture plane
Scenografia: Scenography
Quadro: Picture plane
Refettorio: Refectory
Metri: Metres